John Ciardi

Books by Edward M. Cifelli

John Ciardi: A Biography, 1997
David Humphreys, 1982

Edited Books

The Collected Poems of John Ciardi, 1997
The Selected Letters of John Ciardi, 1991
Index of American Periodical Verse, 1978 (coeditor)
Index of American Periodical Verse, 1977 (coeditor)
Index of American Periodical Verse, 1976 (coeditor)

John Ciardi

A BIOGRAPHY

Edward M. Cifelli

THE UNIVERSITY OF
ARKANSAS PRESS

Fayetteville
1997

02   01   00   99   98   5   4   3   2   1
First paperback printing 1998

Designed by Liz Lester

⊖ The paper used in this publication meets the minimum requirements of
the American National Standard for Permanence of Paper for Printed Library
Materials Z39.48-1984.

Library of Congress Cataloging-in-Publication Data

Cifelli, Edward M.
        John Ciardi : a biography / by Edward M. Cifelli
              p.   cm.
        Includes bibliographical references and index.
        ISBN 1-55728-448-2 (cloth : alk. paper)
        ISBN 1-55728-539-X (paper : alk. paper)
        1. Ciardi, John, 1916–   —Biography.   2. Poets, American—
20th century—Biography.   I. Title.
        PS3505.I27Z63   1997
        811'.52—dc21
        [B]
                                                         97–5394
                                                            CIP

For Warren Stanley Walker
and Kenneth Silverman,

with gratitude

Acknowledgments

When John Ciardi died in 1986, I organized a session in his memory at the next Northeast Modern Language Association meeting, which took place in Boston the following April. By then, I had met most of the Ciardi family and many of his friends—in person or on the telephone or by letters. I was, at the time, working on a much different scholarly project and felt by my Boston program that I had paid suitable respect to this modern American poet whom I had admired over the years—and that I would then return to my previous work. But Miller Williams, John Ciardi's close friend and the literary executor of Ciardi's estate, asked if I would provide an introduction to a slender volume of World War II journal entries, that was to be published in 1988 as *Saipan: The War Diary of John Ciardi*. The next year I was asked to provide a foreword to *Ciardi Himself: Fifteen Essays in the Reading, Writing, and Teaching of Poetry*. This work, plus lending a hand in the cataloguing of Ciardi's papers in the attic office of his Metuchen home, led to my involvement as editor of Ciardi's *Selected Letters*, which came out in 1991. And by then it became clear, to others at first and later to me, that I should put aside my other work permanently and concentrate my energies on a biography of this complex and remarkably talented mid-century American man of letters.

Now, some six years later, that work is done—and I find myself again grateful to many people for providing information on Ciardi's life from his birth in 1916 to his death in 1986. Before her sudden death in 1992, Judith Ciardi provided an endless store of information about her forty years with John. She was open and forthright in all my conversations with her—and there were many more than she could possibly have imagined. Not only that, but she had me working up in John's office for weeks at a time and entrusted me with all the Ciardi papers that I needed for my work. She could not have been more valuable as a resource. I have also been fortunate in that the Ciardi children, all in their thirties when their father died, provided me with as much assistance as I asked for, even when the subject touched on sensitive family issues. For their help, I owe a debt of gratitude to Myra, John L., and Benn. I was also able to interview John's sisters, Ella, Cora, and Edith, who provided both a perspective and a memory bank that was invaluable. Then there were the other hundred and fifty or so people I interviewed for this book. Richard Wilbur, John Stone, Irv Klompus, John Frederick Nims, Paul Cubeta, Dion Johnson, Lew Turco, Harry and Jo Hayford, Elly Welt, X. J. Kennedy, Doris (Holmes) Eyges, Donald Hall, Gil Gallagher, Miller Williams, and many others were able to provide insights that could not have come from any other sources. I am very grateful to all of them—and to Debbie Self and Brian King, my editors at the University of Arkansas Press, who helped me transform my manuscript into a book.

I am honored, too, to thank library staffs all over the country. The largest Ciardi holdings are at the Library of Congress, where Charles J. Kelly and Jeffrey M. Flannery provided cheerful help, and at Wayne State University, where Don Breneau gave up several days to get me acquainted with the collection. And providing me with much-needed help at the University of Missouri-Kansas City (formerly the University of Kansas City) was archivist Marilyn Burlingame. Helping me through the John Holmes material at Tufts was Barbara Tringali. Chautauqua historian Alfreda Irwin supplied records of Ciardi visits there that would not have been possible to get from any other source. Mary Merkosky and Edward Skipworth provided information for Ciardi's Rutgers years. Coordinating my interlibrary loan requests was Maryanne Gray at the County College of Morris, whose other professional librarians were just as unstinting and generous with their time. And the list goes on. Please forgive me for not mentioning all of you by name, but please know that I am nonetheless forever grateful, especially to the research staffs and archivists at Boston University, Dartmouth College, Indiana University, Middlebury College, University of Michigan, Syracuse University, University of Chicago, University of Delaware, University of Massachusetts-Amherst, University of New

Hampshire, University of Texas, and University of Washington. And this is a much-abbreviated list.

I received a great deal of financial backing for this project, too: from the Amelior Foundation, from the National Endowment for the Humanities, from the New Jersey Historical Commission, and from the County College of Morris Foundation. I am thankful also for a CCM sabbatical leave for the time to write a portion of this book. At the Amelior Foundation, my old friend Ray Chambers was there when I needed him. At the NJHC, Dick Waldron helped me through the administrative paperwork. For the sabbatical leave, I am grateful to the faculty committee that recommended me and to Vice President Cliff Wood, who endorsed the recommendation and forwarded it to the president and board of trustees. And the work could not have been completed without the help of Janet Eber, chair of English at CCM, who has encouraged my work in every way she could for as long as I can remember.

Last, my thanks go out again to my friends and family, who continue to suffer my enthusiasms with good grace. Frank Ancona, who provided keen insights into the psychological problems facing John Ciardi, was a constant source of cheerful encouragement. Jim Henderson and Pat Biesty understood that I was off on another project and would emerge only intermittently from my monkish devotions. John Keeler, who can hit a golf ball a pretty fair distance with a baseball grip, enjoyed calling me the "Puritan," providing balance, and keeping me in touch with some parts of the real world. Paul Brezina made sure I knew when the tee time was. My daughters, Lisa Louise and Laura Ann (both with graduate degrees, good jobs, and excellent prospects), are still the joys of my life, as is our newest girl, Elizabeth Louise, Lisa's daughter, born 5 April 1996. My sons-in-law have been excellent additions to the family too, Rick Howe, who recently graduated *summa cum laude* and has begun his own career, and Steven Stibich, who, I hope he doesn't mind my saying, reminds me of myself. My godson, Kyle Poyer, now in graduate school, has also become an important member of the family, as have his parents, my dear friends Carol and Dick. Of course, my most special love and thanks, as always, go to the lovely Roberta Louise, who has been my favorite person for thirty-four years—and my wife for thirty-one. As Mark Van Doren once remarked on his long happy marriage, "A satisfactory life cannot repeat itself too often."

Contents

Preface

One of the aims of this book is to introduce John Ciardi to a generation that may have missed him in its rush to go from beat poetry to confessional poetry to postmodernism. Ciardi belonged to the age just before them, to the poets who were coming of age in the 1940s, the ones he himself had identified in an important anthology called *Mid-Century American Poets* (1950). Thus Ciardi is best remembered and measured against poets like Robert Lowell, Elizabeth Bishop, Richard Wilbur, Randall Jarrell, and Karl Shapiro, among others, and though it may sound surprising at first hearing, Ciardi stands up very well in that company.

However, when American poetry took a left turn during the Allen Ginsberg–led Beat Revolution, John Ciardi kept to his own path. He was not one to be overwhelmed by a new fashion, browbeaten into literary choices that were untrue to his poetic upbringing. Like Robert Frost, whose annual Bread Loaf presence and poetic habit of beginning lightly and ending darkly had influenced him, Ciardi remained wary of free verse (and those who wrote it) all his life. Yet even though he refused to innovate in the same free-verse ways that William Carlos Williams and his followers did, Ciardi's poems were still experimental in the sense that no two are alike; some ideas recurred and some tones came back frequently enough, but Ciardi worked hard to make the form of each new poem match the idea behind it.

He also insisted on using a distinctive twentieth-century diction that came out of his own Boston-Medford-Metuchen-Key West voice box, modified and colored by his platform travels and his English-Italian bilingualism. Ciardi's voice is never poetic in any Victorian or modernist sense of the term, nor are his poems ever genteel, the sort of thing he always called "poesy" to distinguish it from the real thing. Certainly there was nothing genteel about his life. Any such language, still preferred by many contemporary poets, would have been dishonest and pretentious to Ciardi, who always put his own unmistakable, masculine imprint on his poems. Ciardi delighted in being the poet who didn't look or sound like one, in being the anti-aesthete, the opposite of mystical poets of "feelings," like Robert Bly, whom Ciardi regularly scorned as Robert Blah. Real poetry was not the effeminate sort of stuff produced by poetry societies; rather, it was a man's work, sweaty and muscular. And much like Robert Frost, the consummate craftsman, Ciardi never wanted to be caught at his craft, for to be caught at it was the ultimate poetic failure. Readers must therefore look carefully to see that Ciardi only seems to be dancing casually and is, in fact, always waltzing to precise choreography. So one of the reasons Ciardi has been put aside for the past twenty-five years is that, though a skilled poet, he was the anti-aesthete who hid his management of craft behind a deliberately unrefined voice.

But there were other reasons as well. Ciardi saw himself, fellow poets, indeed all men, as a breed motivated by thinly disguised self-interest, an unflattering and unflinchingly honest picture almost designed to draw the wrath of more high-toned readers and poets filled with eighteenth-century notions of the perfectibility of man. Ciardi was certainly not uniformly negative in his poems because he showed again and again that even though men were capable of every imaginable stupidity and cruelty, they were simultaneously capable of the most ennobling qualities, like mercy, love, forgiveness, and the ability to create and preserve. Still, by recognizing and trying to make sense of the world he lived in, Ciardi frequently found himself out of step with other poets, which was off-putting to readers who had become conditioned by the Beats, the confessionals, and the mystics to expect poems to behave in certain ways.

Finally, Ciardi was a man driven to ritual but deprived of the soothing bromides of an inherited religion he could no longer believe in—even of a god he felt man had invented to ease his mortal torments. He would no doubt have liked to believe in God, but it just didn't make sense to him, and to act as though it did would have been the ultimate dishonesty. So Ciardi courageously made what humanistic sense he could of a diminished world and ironically found in poetry what he could not find in religion, the ritual crafting of rhythm, image, diction, and form—an earthly tribute to our *human* possibilities. Free verse did not proceed from the same ritual precisions and therefore did not serve Ciardi's subconscious purposes as well as fixed or semifixed forms. However, his preference for traditional form was not well suited to win popularity contests during the 1970s and 1980s, especially with the radical reformer-idealists of the baby boomer generation, whom Ciardi took to calling, with unfeigned disdain, the "measly generation." Ciardi's attachment to poetic form became an emblem of authoritarianism during an era that believed in starting fresh—or merely disinheriting itself from the past it had grown out of. This was, indeed, the Generation Gap, and so for this sociological reason too, Ciardi has been put on the back shelf.

John Ciardi is properly seen as a writer of consequence at mid-century, a man tormented by personal demons, a man intent on preserving his masculinity, a man dedicated to language and eager to go from one literary engagement to the next—his own poetry, his bench mark translation of Dante, his unique big-man-to-little-child children's verse, and his linguistic forays into word histories, plus his ancillary excursions into television, radio, lecture halls, political campaigns, college classrooms, and more. He was an ever-present and highly visible force in American letters from the mid-1950s to the mid-1970s, an arbiter of taste, a voice of reason, and a spokesman for poetry. He had an encyclopedic mind and memory and was a vivid personality who touched mid-century American society and culture at many points. And, unlike so many poets who withdraw into their own imaginations, only to meet the real world at odd intervals, for most of his life, John Ciardi was a successful man of the world, a poor boy who rode the American dream all the way to millionaire status. From just about every angle, John Ciardi's life is unusual and unusually accomplished.

John Ciardi is singularly independent, not just of the Establishment, but of literary movements and groups and tendencies. This gives his poetry a human, unliterary quality all too rare in his generation.

—Kenneth Rexroth, 1971

I feel uncomfortable, generally, in large gatherings of writers because they always tend to be promoting themselves. We should be a much nobler profession than we turn out to be in practice. Here are the people trying to write the poems of our age, and put fifty of them in a room and they turn out to be fifty self-promoters. And my instinct is to leave.

—John Ciardi, 1983

PART ONE

Footholds

ONE

Little Italy and the Irish Trinity

1916 TO 1936

25 Sheafe Street

On the evening of 18 July 1919, a Friday, Carminantonio Ciardi returned from work angry. He was a successful field agent for the Metropolitan Life Insurance Company in Boston, which meant he collected burial insurance premiums of five and ten cents per week from neighborhood families in the Italian North End. And though he was pleased to have such a good job, he was angry that night because the company had withheld six dollars from his pay envelope to cover expenses for a combination sales meeting and company picnic scheduled for the next day. He was angry about a Saturday morning meeting that would keep him from his family—and angry, too, because he couldn't afford the levy. Antonio, as he was known to friends and family, had a wife and four children to provide for on a tight budget that included, among normal household expenses, a small savings account to complete work on a house in nearby Medford that he and his brother-in-law had put a down payment on. Antonio knew his family was living frugally, perhaps even sparely, but he also knew they faced better times ahead. He had the immigrant's determined singleness of vision and a corresponding faith in the legendary promise of his adopted country. But on the evening of 18 July 1919, Carminantonio Ciardi was angry about the six dollars.

Had the young father worked through his anger that Friday night and paused long enough to assess his life, he would have had good reason to be pleased. Born on 18 August 1882, a few miles east of Naples in a town called San Potito Ultra, Antonio had attended a local school long enough to learn how to read and write before emigrating to the United States in the 1890s. His standard of living in southern Italy had been poor, bare subsistence farming at best, with virtually no hope for improvement, so Antonio followed in the footsteps of other young men of his town and made passage to America—to Dover, New Jersey, where he stayed with a kinsman, Carmine Ciardi, for most of a year. At that point, he made his way to Boston, met a young woman named Concetta Di Benedictis, who happened to have been born only a couple of miles from San Potito Ultra in a town called Monocalzati, and got married in 1906. At first Antonio had been a laborer, but either in Dover or Boston he learned the trade of tailoring. He studied English and bookkeeping at night, however, and gradually became proficient enough at both to become an agent for Metropolitan Life. He had also become, to the proud delight of his adoring wife, president of a North End fraternal group known as the Figli d'Italia, the Sons of Italy. Antonio, according to family stories, "was big and talkative and affable and sometimes fiery and often unorthodox," the last being a reference to his left wing, possibly anarchist, political views, which he expressed often, with firm conviction, and in outspoken terms. At home he read books, sometimes aloud from *The Divine Comedy* or other works of Italian literature, and he sang excerpts from operas that he knew, while his slightly older and almost completely illiterate wife looked on with love and wonder. To her Antonio was a fine figure of a man—handsome, educated, and accomplished.

At age thirty-seven, then, Antonio Ciardi showed all the signs of having worked his way successfully through the beginning stages of his personal life and business career, all in a new country and in a new language, and he was poised for even greater successes during the following decade or so. America was, indeed, the land of opportunity, and Antonio Ciardi stood in 1919 at the entrance into middle-class America, an undreamt chance at social and economic mobility.

In the light of all he had gone through and all that he was looking forward to, the company picnic and sales meeting was little more than a minor unpleasantness, enough to growl about, but not seriously upsetting. Besides, his friends would be there first thing in the morning to pick him up. Early on Saturday morning two coworkers climbed to the fifth floor at 25 Sheafe Street where the Ciardis lived and nudged Antonio along. There was plenty of time to get to the picnic area, somewhere near Dedham, but they were in a boisterous mood and tolerated no dawdling as they rushed Antonio up and out. Undoubtedly his mood had lightened.

Reports of the accident differ. The three men left the Ciardi apartment and joined an unspecified number of others waiting below in two cars. Antonio jumped into the back seat of an open touring car driven by one Cavalcante. The drivers of the two cars pulled away and jockeyed for position on the road, racing along in fits and starts until the accident occurred. By one account the Cavalcante car was sideswiped and Antonio was thrown out, hitting his head on a telephone pole and dying instantly. By another account, Cavalcante hit a girder, which caused Antonio to be thrown out and somehow run over by the car. Two truths returned in the endless reexaminations of the events: Cavalcante had been speeding and no one else in either car suffered anything worse than minor bruises. One unalterable fact remained: Carminantonio Ciardi died a month before his thirty-eighth birthday—not even a month after the third birthday of his only son John. He was buried at St. Michael's Cemetery, in his North End neighborhood, with enough requiem ceremony to fuel a lifelong legend that John Ciardi later described:

> It took four flowerboats to convoy my father's black
> Cadillac cruiser out to St. Mike's and down
> deeper than all salt. It was a very successful
> funeral my mother remembers remembering. *Imagine*
> *what flowers! Even the undertaker was surprised,*
> *he told me! He came with only two flowercars.*
> *He had to send his son all over town like crazy*
> *to find two more, there were so many. Imagine!*
>
> *And when the funeral went to circle the block three*
> *times—those days they did that: it was like the man*
> *coming home again three times for his soul to remember—*
> *we started, and when the first cars came around, the last*

were still blocking the street! Even
the undertaker was surprised! He had to go around two
blocks instead of one to make the circles for the soul!
You were too small to remember, but imagine!

John was not too small, however, to form at that time his only real memory of his father: being picked up to coffin level in the front room of 25 Sheafe Street to kiss his father's icy forehead.

At the time of Antonio's death, there was no thought of legend or an implied elevation of husband into saint. The sudden devastation to Concetta Ciardi and her family was overwhelming and complete. The man who had been at the center of her life and given her both structure and sustenance had been cruelly and inexplicably taken from her. Even with a husband to help, Concetta had more than enough to keep her days and nights fully occupied as she cared for a home, three daughters between ages six and eleven, plus a three-year-old son. With her husband dead, however, she faced an almost impossible task. Neighbors and friends had to wonder how Concetta would cope with her grief and also manage the affairs of the estate—not to mention the day-to-day affairs of her family. Many must have wondered not how she would cope, but if.

However, Concetta Ciardi was made of tougher stuff than any of them might have supposed. She had been born on 8 May 1881 to peasant parents in a town near Vesuvius and was the product of a medieval and ritual society that preserved ancient festivals and a tribal intellect, according to her son, who later claimed this as part of his own background as well. In about 1893, Lorenzo and Marianina Di Benedictis emigrated to the United States, settling in Boston, with their five children, including their oldest daughter Concetta—according to one version of the story. According to another, Concetta remained in Manocalzati when the others left for America, cooking for an aunt who soon afterward tried to marry her off to one of her nephews. Concetta resisted and only then followed her family to Boston. Both versions of the story agree that the trip was harrowing, a nightmare passage in steerage that haunted her all the rest of her days. In "Letter to Mother," Ciardi wrote of her arrival in the New World:

It was good. You found your America. It was worth all
The coming: the fading figures in the never-again doorway,

The rankness of steerage, the landing in fog.
Yes, and the tenement, the reek, and the shouting in the streets
All that night and the terror. It was good, it was all good.
It is important only that you came.

Concetta Di Benedictis no doubt contributed to the family resources through her cooking or as a seamstress, her marketable talents, but little is actually known of Concetta from her arrival in Boston until her marriage in 1906. At that point, however, she moved into 25 Sheafe Street, one of a block-long series of tenement houses, next to her sister Cristina and brother-in-law Alec, an arrangement that would endure at that address and in Medford for at least thirty-five more years. On Sheafe Street, Cristina and Alec had two rooms adjoining Concetta's in the rear on the fifth floor, with the door between the two apartments always open (except on rare feud days), thus creating one large apartment with two families. The "front" door was at the end of a long hallway that ended with steps going up to the roof. The kitchen door was the one everyone used, opening as it did from the stairwell that began on the ground floor next to the Italian bakery shop. (The neighborhood was famous because of its proximity to the Old North Church, with its spire and clock visible from the Ciardi kitchen window; in 1950, the neighborhood would become infamous for the great Brinks robbery.) For some fourteen years, between her marriage and shortly after her husband's death, Concetta Ciardi lived at this address in the North End, Boston's Little Italy, managing her extended household with a gentle authority that was accepted by everyone as second only to Antonio's.

The bride and groom posed stiffly for a photograph on their wedding day in 1906 and thereby gave their son an opportunity many years later to think about his parents as young lovers memorialized by ritual into what he called an "unfinished bridal." And in John Ciardi's eyes, the picture is imbued with sentiment and tenderness:

A ceremonial rose in the lapel,
a horseshoe wreath of pearls in the tie-knot,
a stone-starched collar bolted at the throat,
a tooth on a gold chain across the vest—
this is the man, costumed for solemn taking.

Pompadoured and laced and veiled for giving,
the woman sits her flower-time at his side
badged with his gifts—gold watch on a fleur-de-lis
pin at the heart, gold locket at the throat—
her hand at total rest under his hand.

It was, in fact, a stable, hopeful, even an auspicious beginning to build a family on. Their first child, Ella, was born in 1908; the second, Cora, in 1911; the third, Edith, in 1913. Moreover, all were well provided for. Concetta had become so accomplished as a seamstress that she could supplement Antonio's income by doing odd jobs in the neighborhood, making shirts, baby clothes, little girls' dresses, and so on. And one of her sisters had a grocery store— plus seven children, so Concetta did the sewing for that brood too in exchange for food. The family by all accounts was doing well.

With the birth of their third daughter, however, Concetta and Antonio had begun to feel the pressure to produce a son. And so it was with this added anxiety that Concetta went into labor for the fourth time, this one falling on a sunny Saturday morning, 24 June 1916. Antonio brought the girls up to the roof while Felice, the midwife, and "all the clucking matrons of the tribe" attended to his wife. At 11:30, Aunt Cristina called them down to have their first look at the ten-pound baby, John Anthony Ciardi, a gift from God who immediately assumed the role of royal prince, second only to his father in the family structure, though temporarily under his mother's authority as well. "After three girls," Ella later recalled, "my father was ecstatic."

A short time after the birth, baby John was baptized. The event, like many events in John Ciardi's life, became the stuff of family legend. This one involved the evil eye, which Ciardi described in a note to a poem by the same name as a "still-surviving superstition among Italian peasants." To detect the evil eye at baptism, a family member would pour olive oil into holy water, which then took on shapes that could be read by tribal soothsayers. This, according to Ciardi, is what happened at his baptism. His grandmother mixed the oil and water and discovered the evil eye; an aunt used "bay / Fennel and barley to scourge the devil away"; and Sister Maria Immaculata vowed "nine days' prayer." Nothing worked. The evil eye persisted.

The eye glared through the roosts of all their clucking.
"Jesu," cried Mother, "why is he deviled so?"
"Baptism without delay," said Father Cosmo.
"This one is not for sprinkling but for ducking."

And sure enough, if family legend can be trusted, after the baptism the evil eye dissolved. The story, whether true or not, does identify the rich cultural heritage shared by Boston's Italian immigrants: the Ciardi family, both immediate and extended, was full of colorful characters, tribal mannerisms, and pagan superstitions. And the poem itself reveals the paradoxically self-absorbed and self-effacing thoughts of a one-time royal prince working his way through the mysterious folklore that had surrounded his birth and baptism.

Rejoicing over the birth of a son in 1916 turned into bitter bereavement over the death of a husband and father in 1919. The reversal of fortune was dramatic. Not the least of Concetta Ciardi's concerns was her precarious financial situation. For although Antonio had worked for an insurance company, it is not clear if he had burial insurance for himself, and assuming that he did, that would not have addressed the larger question of supporting a family after the funeral. Concetta, or perhaps someone representing her, made a claim to Metropolitan for a financial settlement because Antonio had died while attending a business function. The claim was denied by the company, which declared that Antonio's death was in no way work related. The company's decision, however, was appealed by the Ciardi family to the Industrial Board of Massachusetts. The board, adjudicating the matter as an arbitrator, decided against the company. They determined that the chief purpose of the picnic Antonio was going to attend was to set sales quotas, and they therefore ordered Metropolitan to pay four thousand dollars to Antonio's widow and children at ten dollars per week, which meant that the family got some financial help through 1926 or 1927.

But a macabre and psychologically disturbing aspect to these payments soon developed. The weekly checks came to represent for Concetta a direct contact from Antonio, not the insurance company. The illiterate woman wove the reality of the check into a myth of survival, and she lovingly forced her sense of Antonio's presence on her son, who from age three to eleven was made to believe that his father had not abandoned him after all, that he was somehow still with him as evidenced by the weekly check. Antonio was not simply a soul to be prayed for in Purgatory (a huge religious obligation Concetta placed on her son to save his father), but he was also a real presence who sent his family ten dollars each and every week, like a dutiful and loving husband and father. "He was 'there,'" Ciardi later recalled, "still watching and still with us, and at night when I managed to squint aside what passed for reality, I sometimes got to the other place where I could talk to him." And in a poem he called "My Father Died Imperfect as a Man," Ciardi remembered again his mother's relationship with her dead husband and the living little boy who was growing every day to look more like his father:

> She made a saint of him. And she made me
>
> kneel to him every night. When I was bad,
> he shadowed me. And always knew my lies.
> I was too young to know him, but my bed
> lay under him and God, and both their eyes
>
> bored through the dark to damn me as I was,
> imperfect as a boy and growing worse.

The emotional confusions created in the young boy by the ambiguous nature of his father's absence protracted his period of mourning and postponed his acceptance of reality.

Whatever psychological groping may be implied by Concetta Ciardi's myth of Antonio's survival, in her day-to-day work she seemed to know exactly what needed to be done. She never showed the least sign of weakness, irresolution, or uncertainty. Various accounts of the next ten years agree that she mobilized her remaining resources, worked furiously at two jobs (by day at Filene's in Boston as a tailor, at night in a candy factory), and refused to consider the humiliation of public assistance. By her children's estimate, Concetta merely played out the rest of her days waiting patiently in mourning (and dressed in widow's black for twenty years) to rejoin her beloved Antonio. But that was at best a stereotyped and romanticized half-truth, for Concetta Ciardi was also a determined single parent who set her jaw to the hard and seemingly endless tasks of daily living at hand.

84 South Street

The first major problem Concetta had to face, apart from Antonio's burial and the tense negotiations with Metropolitan, was the family's long-planned move to Medford. She was fortunate that the burdens of such a physically and emotionally difficult move could be shared with her sister and brother-in-law. Antonio and Alec had purchased the property at 84 South Street (plus the lot next door), facing the Mystic River, together. The property was situated some six miles northwest of Boston and connected by a line of the Metropolitan Transit Authority. When the renovations to the house were completed in 1920, all seven in the families squeezed into the first floor rooms, and rented out the second. As urban as Medford would later become, in the early 1920s it was, in John Ciardi's memory, "a leafy, elmy, sprawly semi-rural town." He remembered swimming in the river and that it "was clean enough to drink from," arriving as it did from an estuary by the Charles and traveling some seven miles to a place called Mystic Lakes. Almost immediately, young John played on a pair of old barges that had been all-but-abandoned across from 84 South Street. All through the 1920s, he watched from their hulls as developers crowded houses next to one another and river pollution became a problem. In his imagination he connected the dying fish in the river to his father's death, a coupling that crept, he said, into many poems written in later years.

The short six-mile move to Medford was full of symbolic significance. Indeed, the Ciardis' North End relatives saw it as a move to the "country," just as sure a sign of upward mobility as it was an escape from the ghetto. Certainly the move accounts for the differences the Ciardi children gradually came to feel between themselves and their North End cousins, explaining in part John Ciardi's later sense of having belonged less to Boston's Little Italy than to the melting pot of its suburbs. In addition, Concetta's successful escape to the country also partly explains why so many admiring North End friends and relatives found their way to Medford in order to consult her about various family matters. She had earned their respect through her gentle yet authoritative manner—and had she not, in her move to Medford despite Antonio's death, lived out his dream? Concetta was therefore treated with deferential admiration by her Boston friends and relatives; she was considered the very model of a decorous and determined widowhood, and she became, despite her self-imposed exile, a respected matriarch of the clan.

Of course, in the early 1920s Concetta traveled frequently to the North End. She went to visit relatives, to shop, and to attend mass at the Italian church, St. Leonard's, where she regularly lit candles for the soul of Antonio. She considered shopping at familiar grocery stores to be necessary, and on those shopping days Concetta usually dragged her son along to show him off and to visit. Of all Concetta's regular visits, one a year became especially important to her, Memorial Day, for on that day, the entire North End joined together at St. Michael's Cemetery to honor its dead. Concetta Ciardi ritualized this civil celebration into religious and mythical significance. Many years later John Ciardi described the annual scene: "She stood me by her beside [Antonio's] stone, once more the man's wife with his son beside her to receive his guests in his last house. It was a meticulous observance climaxed annually by the delegation from *I Figli d'Italia* bearing a large floral wreath whose ribbon read '*Presidente e Fratello* . . . ,'" president and brother. "And she stood by as each man in order shook my hand. I was the sacramental son and she was the man's wife once more keeping house for him. . . ."

By most modern standards, the house on South Street was crowded. But during the family's first two years there, it was comfortable and quiet for young John. Uncle Alec was a barber on Causeway Street in Boston and left for work early in the morning. Aunt Cristina worked at Schrafft's as a candy dipper, so she too left for work in the morning. The girls were all in school. So until John began school, Concetta stayed home, took care of the house, and watched over her boy. Not only was John Ciardi the royal prince prematurely elevated to man of the house, both heady roles for an undeveloped psyche still under the authority of his mother's regency, but he also had his mother all to himself for a good part of every day until September 1922. Young John hardly noticed the crowded conditions.

In Medford Concetta Ciardi's summertime chores included the tending of chickens in the back yard plus a large vegetable garden on the lot next door. Young John helped her. "One of my jobs," he later wrote, "was to go around the streets picking up horse manure to put on the garden. I had a little cart and a shovel and I followed the iceman's horse." At harvest John sold the produce door-to-door from his wagon. Even from his earliest years, he liked to work—especially when he could earn money at it. In fact, as a child John Ciardi had regular dreams about money: "I'd be sitting on a curb and see a penny and then there'd be another and another one, and I would have a whole pot full of pennies." He wrote on another occasion that his "childhood dreams of finding treasure . . . , had always involved heaps of pennies. . . . My recurring dream of great fortune had always found me seated on a curb in the act of discovering hundreds and hundreds of pennies strewn in the gutter, so many that I could hardly grub them out of the dirt and into my pockets and into a heaping cap-full." Money, as a symbol of temporal power, is an aspect of paternal function, so the young Ciardi's recurrent dreams of it may have represented his subconscious grasping at an available substitute for an absent father. Moreover, dreaming this monetary symbol of potency also helped the young man through his other recurrent dream—that of castration.

There were cultural as well as psychological problems for the young John Ciardi to cope with. His parents had been part of the great migration from southern Italy that had taken place after 1880. By 1920, especially after the May arrest of Nicola Sacco and Bartolomeo Vanzetti for two murders in South Braintree, near Boston, a widespread prejudice against the simple Italian-American peasants had set in. Medford, which was about half Irish in 1920, betrayed in Ciardi's recollection "a generalized intolerance for the strange and outlandish," which included his family. His adult reflections on Medford in the early 1920s were somewhat softened by time, but he still recalled being "a little alienated from the society" and feeling "some alienation from my friends," and he recalled fist fights, black eyes, and loosened teeth. The cultural gap between the North End's comforting ethnic homogeneity and Medford's frightening heterogeneity was a wide gulf.

Even within the Roman Catholic community, the southern Italians were a peculiar group, which John Ciardi understood best by looking at his mother, whom he called a "ritual pagan." She and all the Italian peasants, in his analysis, lived according to annual rituals, like those determined by the seasons of planting and harvesting. An overlay of Catholic vocabulary defined their spiritual beliefs, but they had a pagan faith in the strength of their local saint in opposition to the local saints of neighboring towns. "Whatever the case may be from Rome north," Ciardi wrote many years later, "Italians from Naples south are essentially pagans and heretical." That is, they believed in their religion with passionate intensity, but they generally distrusted, and did without (insofar as possible) the Church, which they viewed as natively corrupt. For Concetta, as her son later recorded her voice, "what matters is to live a good life, be good to your family. . . . *Il Signore* [God] knows it isn't easy, what a person has to do. And He certainly did not put his Church on earth for the priests to get fat as pigs off the sweat of the poor people." Her faith in God was clearly purer than her faith in the Church.

Medford's Irish population was fairly well assimilated into the community by 1920, and St. Joseph's Church, which could be seen across the Mystic River from the Ciardi house, was far more mainstream, orthodox Catholic than St. Leonard's in the North End, with its remnants of pagan idolatry. Concetta saw to it that her children went to St. Joseph's for the sacraments and for Sunday school, but she herself rarely attended and had as little as possible to do with what John Ciardi came to call the "Irish Trinity." If she had little faith in the Italian clergy, she had even less faith in the Irish. The problem for Concetta, again as her son later reconstructed it, was language: Medford Catholicism was, unthinkably, spoken in English instead of Italian, which was—and no argument would be tolerated on this point—God's only true language. For Concetta it was a simple matter: "she concluded instantly that Irish priests were frauds." Nonetheless, John took his first communion at St. Joseph's and later was confirmed there. Through most of every year, his sisters walked him across the footbridge for confession on Saturday and mass on Sunday, but in winter they walked across the iced-over river. This picture, as recollected by two of the Ciardi sisters, has the unmistakable glow of nostalgia, but even allowing for some distortion, it is unlikely that St. Joseph's could have been a uniformly unpleasant experience for young John Ciardi in the 1920s. Unpleasantness is, however, what he remembered: "If I have blanked out some instances of priestly kindness, my mind returns to many instances in which the priests of Medford's Irish Trinity seemed to be inflexible, arrogantly self-assured, domineering, and generally suspicious of Italian boys." Moreover, his mother's suspicion of Irish priests had given her son tacit permission for his own distrust, which led him to say in retrospect, "I never met an Irish priest I liked."

Whether Italian or Irish, however, the Catholic Church was at least partly responsible for the "heavy dosage of guilt" John Ciardi felt as a boy. "I found myself in a terrible situation in which thoughts would come into my head, and my indoctrination would say it's a mortal sin to think that thought—but how do you stop thinking a thought?" For the most part, his reflections on guilt were the normal working out of conflicts between parental moralism and childhood life experiences. However, the untimely death of his father created an additional and abnormally difficult layer of guilt for the young boy to work through, for his mother's having him pray nightly for his father's release from Purgatory created the fear in him that he might stop praying too soon, maybe even a single prayer too soon. "At Mother's prompting I had offered up elaborate schedules of prayer to shorten his time in purifying flames, till even the thought of his burning filled me with terror as a continuously present thing." Moreover, the ambiguous nature of his father's life in death, was not just psychologically confusing but infused with guilt as well, for young John worried that his father could ill-afford taking time out from his own Purgatorial woes to be watching out constantly for him—which was the exact state of affairs as Concetta had explained them to her son. John Ciardi later characterized this time of his life as "guilt-twisted."

Making matters worse, John got into a number of scrapes in the 1920s, and he went so far as to call himself "a bit of a roughneck," always ready "to jump up and start a fight." Many years later, Ciardi's tough boyhood behavior prompted his favorite college professor to comment that "until [John] was twelve, he might have taken any of several turnings, for good or for bad, but never for the ordinary." As Ciardi remembered it, up to the age of about twelve, his family obligation was to avenge his father's death by killing Cavalcante: "When I got big I was going to take care of him. Very grand opera." For his mother's sake, however, young John generally kept out of serious trouble, although he did admit to running with a "wild bunch of kids," who, he maintained, were "not evil, but just up to pranks."

Evil or not, punishment from Mother was always waiting when he got home from his "pranks." A cousin who worked in a shoe factory had fashioned a homemade cat-o'-nine-tails that Concetta applied liberally in the hopes of keeping her headstrong young son from going bad. She was no doubt afraid that, without a father to provide discipline, all her children were in danger, so she worked especially hard at this aspect of her duty. Ciardi later wrote that his mother "drove herself by overwork and self-denial to a state near madness. She overfed us, overscrubbed us, and did all but crack our heads open in her fits of discipline, whaling us with whatever came to hand, or throwing it after us if we ran." By the time he was thirteen, however, the young man had already grown taller than his tiny mother—and beyond her discipline. They discovered that they had reached this point on a Sunday evening in March 1929. John had been to Sunday school at St. Joseph's that morning and watched as Father Ryan conducted a St. Patrick's Day "hagiological rally / for the Big Green Team."

> His nose well blown,
> he stood above us, outside the altar rail
> and worked the boys up to three last Green Cheers:
> "Where did St. Patrick come from?"
> "Ireland!" the saved screamed.
> "And where did he bring his blessing?"
> Again: "Ireland!"
> "And where did your fathers come from?"
> Once again
> he got his chorus but he lost my soul.
> I heard a bellowing of lunatic treason:
> "FROM ITALY, BY GOD!"
> And didn't know
> I was the lunatic till he grabbed my ear
> and dragged me to the altar: "PRAY FOR YOUR SOUL!"
> But I'd be damned first.

John ran away from church that day and was too frightened to return to his mother—and the strap. He returned well after dinner and knew what was in store, but he took the whipping without betraying principle. And he did not cry: "I let her work me over till the welts / bled through my shirt and wouldn't make a sound. . . ." At length, realizing the futility of the whipping and the significance of the moment, Concetta collapsed at the kitchen table and cried. John picked up the strap and threw it into the garbage, then he bent over to kiss her forehead. He saw this, and perhaps she did as well, as his official rite of passage into manhood, for after the incident she served him a warmed-up dinner, thereby acknowledging their new and unspoken agreement. By then, however, it was clear to Concetta that, minor incidents aside, her Johnny was, indeed, fairly close to being a good boy and that her worst fears that he would go bad were unfounded.

Few details of the Ciardi family life from the 1920s have survived, but their Sundays were filled with colorful people, Italian warmth, and day-long dinners. Often on early Sunday mornings, Dominic Cataldo ("straw boss of the treetop monkey gang" at Forest Hills Cemetery, which was just across the street from the sparsely treed St. Michael's), came to pick up John and Uncle Alec for pheasant poaching at Forest Hills. Before the hunt, Uncle Alec would drink to the day with a glass of his "mountain breakfast," two beaten eggs in a glass of wine. Alec's obvious attachment to Old World peasantry, however, amounted to little more than small mannerisms compared to that of Dominic Cataldo, whom John later described as

> a long-armed, bow-legged, broken-toothed gorilla
> with a chest of hair that coiled up like black smoke
> from open collar to jawbone, and who was known
> through all the bellowed treetops as Sputasangue,
> which means "Spitblood" . . .

Sputasangue had the keys to the iron gates of the cemetery:

> Sundays at dawn
> a throbbing touring car—a rusty Moon
> that belonged to my Uncle Alec's friend Joe Pipe-dreams—

coughed through the gates. Uncle and Sputasangue
sat in the back, one shotgun left, one right.
Joe Pipe-dreams drove. I rode in front, cocked ready
whenever I got the signal, to jump out
and stuff the haul into a burlap sack.

Back at home his mother and Aunt Cristina harvested dandelions
and mushrooms and started the sauces, and when the pheasants
arrived, they were plucked and cleaned and roasted in the oven:
"Food was the flaming altar of the house."

John's sister Edith recalled the enormous Sunday dinners that
her mother prepared: "Mother would start with soup and end up
with nuts every time. She'd have the soup and then the macaroni and
then the roast and all the vegetables and the potatoes and so forth.
And then she'd have a great big platter of fruit. And then she'd wind
up with dessert after that. It was like Christmas every Sunday."
Edith's reminiscences may have been too rosy, but the truth seems
to be that Concetta was, in fact, a remarkable cook and a welcom-
ing hostess, particularly on holidays. Easter Sunday stood out among
all the others, and Ciardi recorded his childhood memories of that
special meal—of the ritual death and resurrection of the lamb:

A month before Easter
Came the time of the lamb
Staked on my lawn
To frisk and feed and be
My loveliest playmate,
Sweeter for being
Sudden and perilous.

On Thursday before Easter, the lamb would disappear, and young
John "wept a little" for "what business was in the cellar."

But ah came Easter,
My lamb, my sufferer, rose,
Rose from the charnel cellar,
Glowed golden brown
On religious plenty.
How gravely it was broken
Sprigged for a bridal.

Probably in 1928, although it may have been a year or two later, Uncle Alec and Aunt Cristina built a house on the lot next door, where Concetta had formerly kept her garden. They were thus ready to take up separate residence from the Ciardi family for the first time since 1906. By then, with four children rapidly becoming young adults, Concetta Ciardi certainly needed the room, but even such a very short move was attended with some sadness as well, for as Ciardi said of his extended family long afterward, "I felt that I loved the people there, and that's what kept us together."

Uncle Alec, whose "roots were pagan Greek" Ciardi later wrote, was really Alessio di Simone, Alec the Barber, who was said to have fled southern Italy in favor of Boston to avoid conscription. Alec's only faith was in dreams and dream books—plus the daily number he divined and gambled on. Every morning he would analyze his previous night's dream and look it up in the dream book to find a corresponding three-digit number to bet his nickel on. He rarely, if ever, won, but that was always, he said, because he had misinterpreted the dream and looked up the wrong corresponding numbers. He had absolute faith, as one might have in the mysteries of religion, that his system worked. Young John did not consciously perceive Uncle Alec at the time as a father figure and seems instead to have taken him for granted as just another family member to endure. Yet many years later, Ciardi often thought of Alec fondly, as he did in the poem "Alec," where he sorted out some of his feelings and concluded that "I must have loved him, / and did not know it. . . ." John grew to be lovingly nostalgic about pheasant poaching with Alec on Sunday mornings. And on his twelfth birthday, one that stood out in his memory, John received a puppy and a single-shot .22 rifle from his uncle. Moreover, John indirectly but gratefully credited Uncle Alec for his ability to read Italian because Alec kept the Italian language newspaper, Il Messaggero, in the house, which gave John an opportunity to make the transition from speaking fluently to reading fluently.

For the most part, however, John Ciardi was busy being a boy in the 1920s and was happily oblivious to the presence of either his uncle or his aunt during the entire decade. In fact, he was largely oblivious to everyone. In an autobiographical fragment written many years later, Ciardi analyzed his withdrawal from family life as being "partly in self-defense": "There were five women in the family during most of my adolescence—Mother, my three sisters, and an incidental aunt—and every one of them wore her nerves on the outside of the skin. Hysteria was the normal tone of things, all conversations were shouted, all disagreements were screeched, and all sudden action had to be signaled by a scream. . . . Everything happened as if it were part of the finale of *Pagliacci.*" He captured some of it in a poem as well:

> Home was our Asylum. My father died
> but my mother kept talking to him. My sisters screamed.
> My aunt muttered. My uncle got drunk and dreamed
> three numbers a night for a nickel. . . .

And so, Ciardi said, he withdrew: "I grew mental flaps on my ears and began to forget there was a family around me except as something to be wheedled from. I could sit in the kitchen or 'the front room' reading Tom Swift or the Merriwells . . . and not even know that Mother was having another scream in the next room or that my sisters were pulling hair." Books gradually became his conscious escape: "I made a cave of them and crept inside." But being "half-deep in books" while emotional crises went on around him, left him with oddly confused feelings: "I lay / guilty of happiness."

How much guilt intruded on his happiness is not clear. It is clear, however, that he became very self-absorbed, "an insufferable brat," in his own words, although he absolved himself by saying it hadn't been his fault: "I had been trained to be." In fact, John, as the sacramental son, always got what he wanted at his sisters' expense. As he put it, "No one questioned this." Ella, remembering John's childhood, said, "We did not argue as children. He was the baby and we had to be gentle with him." And although they all saw his manipulative tactics clearly, they nonetheless gave him his way as a natural course of action: "I simply acquired with my mother's milk, and from the same source, the standing assumption that I was to get what I wanted because I was a boy, and that they were to defer to me because they were girls. If there was any delay in serving my demands, I could always work-up a tantrum, whereupon Ma would scold them for having upset me." He fully realized as an adult, some fifty years after the fact, how many sacrifices all the women in his family had made on his behalf, particularly when it came time to save money for his college education. "They did without in order that I might have," he said, "and though all of us accepted that arrangement as the natural order of things, I have thought back from this time to that and I know for how much I must ask to be forgiven."

Although John Ciardi later took refuge from the bedlam of his home life through a withdrawal into books, his first contact with public education was inauspicious at best. His formal schooling began in September 1922, when he started first grade at the Craddock School on Summer Street. The day loomed large enough in his memory for him to commemorate it in one of the long auto-biographical poems in *Lives of X*, "A Knothole in Spent Time." His mother took him to school on the first day, a sign of the ritualized importance she attached to her son's education: she was delivering him to a temple. John was not to be ignorant as she was, but liter-ate, a book-reader like her Antonio. Already he was used to his mother's lectures on the "sanctity and omniscience" of teachers and the sacrifices that had to be made in order "that small boys / might 'get an education' and 'get ahead.'" He recalled elm trees and the smell of chalk from that first day, but only one event stayed fresh in his memory, a fistfight. To show that she "meant the day to be ritual," his mother had sewn him a fancy outfit she called a "Buster Brown." To go with his outfit were new shoes and "long white stockings / that buttoned, or tabbed, into my underwear." But when he looked around at the other boys, he saw that he was the only one with stockings, which provoked "a pug-nosed Irish snot" to call him "not only a Dago but a sissy." He knew then that there would be a fight, a not-to-be-forgiven development given his mother's ceremonial behavior toward his first day at school.

But something else happened on that first day that may have been even more deeply troubling in the long run, an emergent iden-tity crisis that suddenly focused when his teacher called on him for the first time as "John Sea-YARD-i":

> Omniscience had changed my name! I was John Sea-YARD-i
> —and not even allowed to argue! What's a teacher
> if she can't say a name right? . . . John Sea-YARD-i . . .
> That was no sound of mine. I was John CHAR-di.

He would be stuck with the public school pronunciation of his name for the next sixteen years, not recapturing the correct pronunciation until 1938, when he began graduate school at the University of Michigan. So, on his first day of school, six-year-old John Ciardi found himself without his name and in the midst of a fistfight which did, indeed, ensue and which cost him the expected bloody jumper, lost button, and grass stains, although they were not as important to him as the strapping he expected and got from his mother:

> Ma would be waiting with that strap. My tail
> would come away from it ridged. Then *she'd* cry,
> and I would have to stop bawling to comfort *her.*
> I've never thought far enough back—not for not trying—
> to understand how we came to that arrangement.
> I know it had something to do with my being ghosted
> into her husband and he into her son.
> Sometimes I think she was beating him for dying,
> and me for not being enough of what she'd lost.

Ciardi seems to have recognized the psychoanalytical truth of the last two lines from an early age. His mother had made him into a substitute for his dead father, what psychologists call a "linking object," to help her endure her loss. Antonio was still "alive" not only in the form of ten-dollar weekly checks, but also in the form of a son who bore a striking resemblance to his father. "Day by day," wrote Ciardi, "I was reputed to look more and more like my father . . . a curiously double state of being myself and being him." Moreover, the son was invested with a scholastic mission to become literate and educated like his father, and thus he became, in a sense, immortal to his mother, who saw her husband kept alive in the form of her son. It is either a testimony to John Ciardi's psychological perceptiveness and intuition or Concetta's transparent mental state that the young man was able to understand the subtleties of the psychology of mourning that were at work. "When I turned out to be an avid and indiscriminate reader," he wrote, "she seemed to rejoice in that as if it were one more proof that her husband had been reborn in me." More darkly, Ciardi said of his mother that she had a "terrible need to make me over into the image of her lost husband." It was, he said, the "first oppression I had to survive."

From 1923 to 1926 John attended the Dame School. He skipped fifth grade and went directly into sixth, in 1926. He boasted of being "pretty good" in school, getting a "double promotion" (mother "felt sure it had been partly my father's doing"), and being in a "special class," although no details of the special class have survived. It is unlikely the double promotion resulted from his first poem, which he recalled writing on the blackboard in the fourth grade:

Rover
Bouncing all over.
HE LIKES TO DO IT.

A more characteristic and defining measure of Ciardi's intelligence occurred in the second grade, as he remembered it in "A Knothole in Spent Time." He was lost in a daydream during class one day when the teacher, thinking to embarrass him into paying attention during class readings, called on him to continue reading from the book at the point where the previous student left off. He was, indeed, caught by surprise, but remembered from "somewhere in a separate haze" the last words he had heard "floating in the elm-tops." The book was open to the wrong page on his desk. He stood up, held the book, and said from memory the next lines and pages, until finally, after what seemed a very long time, the teacher allowed him to sit. He told the story in the poem, he said, because it represented a lost ideal, the reality that, despite his mother's blind faith, schoolteachers were very human and that he could actually fool them. His teacher, whom he called Miss Absolute Void, "was the first chink in the wall / of heavens I had been schooled to as a faith." The real significance of the story, however, is that it describes the moment when he discovered his extraordinary memory, a characteristic of John Ciardi's intelligence that audiences and students and friends and sometimes even casual acquaintances were most forcibly struck by. He regularly and effortlessly summoned up whole poems he hadn't read in many years, or complete scenes from a Shakespearean play, or long sections from *The Divine Comedy*. He seemed always ready to dazzle listeners with extraordinary displays of memory, just as he had done many years earlier when he first fooled Miss Absolute Void.

For grades seven through nine John went to Hobbes Junior High School, where he was not especially bookish, according to his sister Ella's recollection, an appraisal borne out by respectable but undistinguished grades. At home, however, there were some signs of a developing intellectual life as he immersed himself in books: "I had stacks of battered dime novels: Horatio Algers, Tom Swifts, Rover Boys, at least a hundred Frank and Dick Merriwells by Burt Standish." He also read *Gulliver's Travels* and Francis Turner Palgrave's *The Golden Treasury*, a popular nineteenth-century collection of poems that has continued to be reissued through the entire twentieth century. Most important, there was a one-volume encyclopedia his mother had bought for him from a door-to-door salesman, a book she could hardly have afforded. It was known in the family simply as THE BOOK, fifteen hundred pages of text and illustrations on every conceivable topic: "I read it till the binding failed and pages came apart." When it came to early experiments in writing, Ciardi wrote about the temporary hobbies brought to his attention in his search for Boy Scout merit badges—white mice, wild flowers, stones, knots, and so on. The writing was as unimportant as the discarded hobbies, as he measured it later on; but he did say that in the end he remembered being left with the habit of writing.

Ciardi recalled many years later that merit badges and his attachment to his scoutmaster were a "fever" to him in his youth. He was aware that he'd been looking for father figures throughout his childhood and that he had regularly "attached" himself, as he put it, "to any large male figure" who would "tolerate" him. Uncle Alec was apparently gone too much to serve as a father figure and had, at any rate, long since grown accustomed to a different role, one that he seemed to prefer, as a sort of "unacknowledged kin." Jolly Uncle Pat, Concetta's brother, who showed up nearly every Sunday morning with hot Italian bread, might otherwise have qualified, but he lived in another town. And Godfather John Follo, who had promised his dead friend Antonio that he would look after Concetta and her son and who did indeed help them financially at several turns over the years, was also too distant to serve. At age thirteen, however, John Ciardi discovered the Boy Scouts and the scoutmaster who became the young man's acknowledged substitute father, a man whose name has not survived as anything more precise than the abbreviation the boys knew him by, Mr. D.

Knowing that Troop 13 met in the Congregational church on Medford Square, John used to hang around out of curiosity near the entrance. Several of his neighborhood friends and schoolmates were members, and he longed to join as well, even though he was frightened to enter a Congregational church and, in fact, hadn't been invited. Then one night Mr. D. spoke to John outside to ask if he was interested in Scouting, and very shortly afterward John found himself inside a Protestant church—without any observable divine reaction. He joined the Beaver Patrol, was given a free manual that he read at once, and became a Tenderfoot at the next meeting. He continued as a model Scout and moved up the ladder, becoming in quick succession a First Class Scout and then a Patrol Leader. By the time he was sixteen, John had become Junior Assistant Scout Master and was pushing hard to become an Eagle Scout, Scouting's highest honor. However, even though he had accumulated what he called "infinite" merit badges toward his Eagle Scout goal, he lacked the one called Pioneering. He explained later that those who were able to afford Boy Scout camp got this badge more or less automatically but that it was all but impossible for boys like himself who were city bound. The badge called for chopping down saplings sufficient, he said, to "build a little makeshift bridge across a stream." The saplings were already chopped down for the boys going to camp, he woefully recorded, but where was he going to find saplings for such work in Medford?

Although his inability to reach Eagle Scout mattered greatly to John between 1929 and 1932, it was less significant than the crisis of religious faith that he went through because of Mr. D. at about the same time. Mr. D. had not simply taken John into the Scouts, but had taken him into his heart as well for no other reason than that, as Ciardi later put it in an unpublished autobiographical fragment, he "must have sensed how much I needed him." Ciardi felt very open about the love he felt for Mr. D: "I adored him. If God gave me grace, I would make myself as much like him as my faults would permit. He was my perfect man." As a role model, Mr. D. appears to have been very conventional, habitually preaching the values of a good clean life and offering on a regular basis all the homely virtues of Scouting. More important, he gave his time to John, talked to him, and took him into his home. One aspect of their bonding came about because Mr. D. was a carpenter and cabinetmaker and kept a fully equipped workshop in his basement, where he worked with John "patiently and pridefully," as Ciardi later remembered it, allowing the young man to build one lopsided birdhouse after another. But the birdhouses were far less important than the father-son relationship they were also building.

The crisis came at Sunday school. The teacher, probably during the time John was preparing for the sacrament of confirmation, was making the point that salvation was available only through God's true church, which got John to thinking about Mr. D., who happened to be a Protestant. When John raised the question, he was "flatly told" that Mr. D. was destined to damnation, to burn in the fires of Hell. In the same autobiographical fragment, John Ciardi called the Sunday school episode a "comic opera," but while he was living through it, he said, it was all "blood-serious." "I had never doubted the infallibility of the church. The catechism had been drubbed into me from my own pre-dawn and the truth required neither belief nor disbelief; it simply existed as the nature of things. Now suddenly my hero-worship found itself passionately at odds with all that crazy universe." Mr. D. in Hell was, of course, unthinkable, worse even than the condition of his father's soul in Purgatory. And the more he defended Mr. D. to himself against the authority of his Sunday school teacher, the more doubt he felt about the "true church," which of course made him fear for the future of his own soul. He worried about what would happen if he died with the sin of his doubt still upon him—and his father in Purgatory, unable to intercede for him. In the end the young man chose friendship over salvation and later described his crisis of adolescence in the simplest, clearest, and most logical of terms: "If my Perfect Man could not go to Heaven, God was unfair, and I'd sooner go to Hell with the good."

Unfortunately, Ciardi's declaration of religious independence wasn't achieved that easily. His break with the Roman Catholic Church may have begun when he was about sixteen over the question of Mr. D.'s soul, or it may have begun earlier over the question of Irish priests he did not like, but by his own admission it did not end there. "It was at least five years," he later wrote, "before I had wrestled myself to the point where I could speak my denial openly without that sudden shuddering sense of having damned myself forever. And it was at least ten before it had wholly ceased to be an issue." In actual years, the crisis had begun around 1929, when he was thirteen, and was not over until 1939, when he was twenty-three. During those ten years, he struggled with various spiritual life preservers: "The act of ripping out a whole system of nervous belief is a self-assault. And when accomplished it leaves a terrible emptiness. In a fury of trying to fill that emptiness I tried a dozen religions from cynicism, to Baptism, to communism, and all of them ended silly and inhuman, witch dances toward guilt in which the child is accused from birth of his sex, his appetites, and his drive to be himself and human."

Working his way through a spiritual crisis was not, of course, a full-time occupation. High school was. The young man graduated from Medford High School on 14 June 1933, ten days before his seventeenth birthday, then returned for a year of what he termed "post-graduate" studies while he and his family tried to save enough money from their various pay envelopes to send him to college. During the extra year he retook solid geometry, trigonometry, and French. He managed average to high grades while also holding down a fourteen-dollar-a-week evening job as an invoice clerk at a biscuit factory in Boston, a highly coveted depression era position secured for him through the good offices of Godfather John Follo. After he got the job, John's time was fully accounted for. His routine was to sleep four hours after school, get to work at eight o'clock, return somewhere between two and five in the morning, sleep again, then head off to school. He also claimed on a college application that during his postgraduate year he worked for a florist and for Sears Roebuck. Ella recalled that on this twenty-four-hour schedule her exhausted brother sometimes fell asleep at his desk—but the overnight job actually fit in well with Ciardi's natural inclination to work in the quiet dark hours rather than the busier and noisier daytime hours at 84 South Street.

During his teenage years, young John, like thousands of others in the twenties and thirties, rigged up a crystal set—with wire, a Quaker Oats box, and a genuine Brazilian crystal that was so expensive it took him several months to save up for it. But it was worth it when he heard his first quavering radio broadcasts transmitted from nearby Tufts College. He also reported going to movies a little later "to watch Al Jolson and Eddie Cantor perform in black face," admitting that he even "cried when Al sang 'Sonny Boy.'" In 1929, he went to caddy camp (in Bethlehem, New Hampshire, sponsored by the North Bennet Street Industrial School in the North End) and later recalled that he "may have been the worst caddy in the history of the camp." This did not, however, stop him from caddying now and then in the early 1930s at Winchester Country Club, even though, as he said, "I had no eyes for the ball." He usually drew "the grandma duffers," who were easily distracted by a search for "Indian pipes, or lady slippers, or white trillium by the pond." And it was around 1930, too, perhaps in the caddy shack, that Ciardi began smoking cigarettes, a habit that he kept all his life.

As a fifteen-year-old in the summer of 1931, John took a position on board the *King Philip*, a fishing boat out of Boston. He called it in "The Benefits of an Education: Boston, 1931," "not quite a job, / but work, free passage, and a chance to scrounge / nickels and fish. . . ." Those who bought a day's passage got eight hours of fishing, free lines and bait, plus all the fish chowder they could eat between noon and one. In the poem, Ciardi recalled four anecdotes of the fishing boat: helping a drunk to vomit (which he did for five dollars); helping a fisherman haul in the day's largest, pool-winning fish (which earned him two dollars); being kind to an old woman with a nickel looking for "any old fish left over" (which he gave to her for nothing but a blessing); and attending the weekly "girlie show" put on by the VFW and other stag groups (which was profit of still another sort). "If it wasn't an education," Ciardi wrote, "it was lessons / in something I had to know before I could learn / what I was learning."

At age sixteen, John Ciardi was given control of the household at home, for by then the royal prince had grown sufficiently to assume his proper role, at least as far as Concetta was concerned. She ritualized the transfer of power into a formal ceremony, a coronation: on John's sixteenth birthday, 24 June 1932, Concetta presented him with a watch that Antonio had given her, thus passing along to him what she had established in her mind as the family's symbol of authority. "It was my badge of manhood," as he put it, "beautiful and golden, with a quarter moon of diamond chips on the back of the case, and almost inside the prongs of the moon, a single small diamond. . . ." Ella cried when she saw that her mother had given the watch to John instead of to her, but Concetta dismissed her daughter's tears. "'He's the man,' my mother said. 'I didn't promise you nothing.'" The episode demonstrated, as Ciardi later interpreted it, that Concetta needed a man to obey: "Her religion was the man of the house and it was drawn not from the bible and sermon and church, but from the collected memory of the people of the mountain she had been born to." In all, it had taken thirteen years (long ones perhaps for an impatient Concetta) for John Ciardi fully to replace his father in the family structure, but from that time forward, according to Ella, "No decision was ever final until John gave the last word. Mother and I would discuss a problem, come to a decision, but John would have to okay it."

For the next two years, Ciardi's senior and postgraduate years of high school, his mother and sisters combined their efforts to raise money for his college education. "Us girls helped with our paychecks," Edith recalled. "We did what we could. We realized our mother needed the money for him. So I used to bring my pay envelope home unopened, and I would take whatever she would give me for the week. I knew she had to put John through college. I didn't mind at all. Mother was very good to me. I really didn't mind it at all. I didn't begrudge it one bit."

Bates College

Perhaps because of his verbal skills and perhaps because two of his teachers graduated from there, Ciardi applied to the pre-law curriculum at Bates College in Lewiston, Maine. On the information blank, he identified himself as Catholic. His weight was 196, his height six feet and three-quarters inch. He hitchhiked to Lewiston from Boston, according to family legend, wearing patched pants—and returned for the holidays in new clothes bought with money taken from rich students at the local pool halls and poker tables. He moved into 13 John Bertram Hall with Roger Fredland, who remained a lifelong friend, and Solomon D. Chamos, an Argentine Gypsy, according to Ciardi, who disappeared after six weeks. Whether or not Ciardi hustled rich kids at the pool hall, he did begin his college career on a shoestring, with barely enough money to cover tuition and books plus room and board. For pin money he washed dishes in Matthew Frangedakis's Greek restaurant.

Ciardi's record at Bates is incomplete at best, although some details have survived. His transcript shows that he had identical 79 averages in his first and second semesters with courses in biblical studies and Greek as well as English, French, public speaking, and a sprinkling of classes in history and science. He wrote later that he "bored" himself with a year of freshman football at Bates "and gave up athletics forever." He worked on the college literary magazine, the *Garnet*, attended a poetry reading by Maine author Robert P. T. Coffin (finding "his seriousness to be ludicrous"), and heard Louis Untermeyer lecture on the state of poetry in America. A classmate predicted at the time "that within a decade the anthologist [Untermeyer] would be lecturing on one of Professor Berkelman's then-current protégés." It didn't take that long, for in the spring term, 1940, Louis Untermeyer lectured at Bates on "Six Promising Young Poets"—one of whom was John Ciardi.

On 25 May 1935, John wrote home to his family that he was preparing a speech for "hizzoner" Willard W. Whitcomb, "candidate from the Freshman Class for the highly coveted position of Mayor of BATES." He wrote also that he was in the midst of exams that would be over on Saturday afternoon, 9 June: "so if you come up for the 9-10 everything will be hunky-dory and you will have the honor of taking me home." He also instructed them to contact someone named Sonny about a summer job: "Tell Sonny to go ahead with his plans for the store. I'll be there with bells on. Anything that spells money goes. Tell him that as long as there are a couple of bucks in it he doesn't have to ask questions—just tell me what to do and when I can see the green of the dollar I'm off." He asked them, too, if "something might be done about a job at the cemetery? There's a fine chance to make a little dough there."

But work was hard to get for a college boy home for the summer of 1935. Ciardi wrote to a Bates friend, Arnold Kenseth, on 17 August that he couldn't find a job: "I have been doing nothing or next to it all summer. I found no work and I have no hopes of finding any." Five days later, in another letter to Kenseth, he spelled out his uncertainty about returning to school: "The situation concerning my return to Bates is roughly this—meal job? I return; No meal job? I stay home. All I have been able to toss into my well worn sock thus far is $25 worth of filthy lucre. Mother is going to sell an insurance policy which will bring in about $180 more. That sir will be as much as ever I can expect from the family—well if the worse comes to the worse they might be good for another $50 but that is the top. It requires no tremendous amount of cerebral gymnastics to see that if I have to pay for my food I'm not going to stay in Bates long with that amount of the long green. I have written unto and received from Harry W. several reams of torrid supplication—he asking me to return, I asking him to make it possible for me to return by producing the wherewithal to procure victuals for the abdominal cavity that insists on asserting itself from tempis to tempo. As yet, however, the matter remains pendant in atmospheric vacuity." The question was somehow resolved satisfactorily within the next five days, for on 22 August Ciardi wrote to Kenseth to say that he would soon be "hying back to Bates."

Although Ciardi did not say in his last letter to Arnie Kenseth that summer whether or not he had received the aid he had been seeking from Harry W., it was clearly a financial crisis the family was facing, for as eager as John was to work, and as sacrificing as his sisters and his mother were, money had about run out at the end of the 1934–35 academic year. As the level-headed Ella recalled it, Bates had simply drained the family resources, and "at the end of the year mother knew he could not continue there." When John explained how important it was for him to return, however, "mother gave in"—perhaps by cashing in the insurance policy. Everyone understood that the decision to return would cost them all even greater sacrifices than they had already made, but for John they would try one more time, digging deeper than ever into their pay envelopes during the late summer and fall of 1935. In September John returned to Bates for his third semester, this one was even less distinguished than the first two: a 76 average in argumentation, English, fine arts, geology, and classical civilization. He also joined the Heelers' Club and the Spofford Club, the latter a literary group that met in the homes of English professors. He even became assistant editor on the *Garnet* and contributed a poem and a short story to the December 1935 issue.

Twenty years later, Ciardi was quoted as saying that he "cheerfully threw away a freshman year at Bates," but given the enormous family sacrifices undertaken to send him there, his decision to withdraw was anything but cheerful. The chief factor in his decision was financial—tuition was manageable, room and board were not. A lesser factor was that Bates, as Ciardi later put it, was "heavily Baptist" at the time and "relentlessly concerned about my character." Moreover, he cryptically reported, "I ran into various difficulties up there—some to do with emotions, some with cash. . . ." So John Ciardi gave up Bates for Tufts College, which was within easy walking distance of 84 South Street and his mother's home cooking. The decision to attend Tufts was sensible and obvious, but throwing away a three-semester investment was neither easy nor cheerful.

Fifty years after the fact, truly a lifetime later, Ciardi summed up his Bates years and the problems he had faced by saying too nonchalantly, "I didn't find what I was looking for."

TWO

Holmes and Cowden

1936 TO 1940

The Holmes Years

At Tufts College in the spring of 1936, John Ciardi found what he had been looking for, a substitute father and a poetry mentor, both in the person of a young, shy, and charismatic English instructor named John Holmes, who himself had been a Tufts man (class of '29) and had returned as a thirty-year-old instructor on a special appointment arranged by college president James Albert Cousens in 1934.

Even though Holmes had nothing more in the way of credentials than a B.A. in English and two years of teaching experience at Lafayette College, it became indisputably clear at once that he was that rarest of rare things, a great teacher. His success in the classroom was perhaps even more surprising in that he wasn't even an especially good speaker, neither glib nor oratorical, according to Harrison Hayford, who began his studies as a freshman at Tufts in September 1934. Holmes's appeal was far more fundamental than speaking style. "What moved us," as Hayford put it, "was his complete dedication—and the fact that he was in touch with poets we had all read and who sometimes visited Holmes, either in class or at home." And Holmes was widely published in all the major magazines, like *Harper's*, the *New Yorker*, and the *Atlantic Monthly*. In class, Holmes spoke ardently of Robert Frost, Hart Crane, and W. H. Auden, among many others, and in general he had such "an earnest way about him" that he communicated how very seriously he took both his poetry and his students. His students, in Hayford's memory, saw that Holmes was special because he "spent time" with them and showed "a *genuine* interest"—not the superficial sort of thing that insincere teachers frequently act out and that students always see through. His students idolized Holmes as the ideal poet-teacher, and they treated him with heartfelt warmth and respect.

No student, however, connected with Holmes as intensely as John Ciardi. He called Holmes "the master teacher I had always needed but never found." Ciardi recognized the deeper connection as well: "He became the ideal father figure I had been looking for in the wrong places." He followed his mentor everywhere: "I lived on Holmes's shoulder. . . . Since I lived in town, he wasn't even rid of me during the summer. I would bring six, eight, a dozen screaming poems a week, and he would read them, talk about them, tug at them. There were no rules about it. Each poem was its own thing. One would give him a chance to show me something about rhyme, another something about rhythm, another something about imagery, and so on." Moreover, Ciardi did not want gentle treatment: "I was proud of the times when he was rough with me, for he was always gentle with the hopeless, and I knew when he dressed me down that he was taking my scrawls seriously. . . ."

Ciardi later wrote that Holmes, without a Ph.D., was little more than "a tolerated junior member of the department," but that made no difference because Holmes was learned about poetry in ways the other members of the English faculty were not. "It was as if they were all historians of music, while John Holmes was a great piano player. He knew what ten fingers were supposed to do on 88 keys. He had knowledge they didn't even understand. They knew the outsides of a poem, but John Holmes knew the insides." From his first semester with Holmes in the spring 1936, Ciardi knew, "almost at once" as he put it, what he would be doing with the rest of his life: he would somehow manage to earn a living, perhaps after the fashion of Holmes, but he would live, as Holmes did, for poetry.

For his part, Holmes later described the young Ciardi as "a lanky undergraduate, slouching half-diffidently, half-belligerently into [my] office to toss a sheaf of new poems on the desk." He remembered that Ciardi "would bring not one, but five or six poems to the advanced writing class. We did not finish with his, but at the next class he was not interested in those. He had new ones; and better, he said." Holmes reported that Ciardi was not only prolific, an "eruptive" writer, "but one who grew fast, who advanced in skill with every new poem, roving wider and further for new forms, new subjects, new metaphors, new vocabulary." In terms of practical coaching, Holmes taught Ciardi that it was the poet's "great pleasure to make words dance with the exact posture, the same swiftness, the same satisfaction of rhythm that patterned his dance." He taught Ciardi, too, that the poet must "hold to a single ruthlessness of purpose, and that purpose [is] poetry." For the rest of his life, Ciardi remembered fondly and proudly what Holmes had done to help him become a poet: "Time after time, John Holmes nailed down what I had done that was false, weak, dull, random. He didn't have to hammer: his least nudge told me. He fired me up." Ciardi often retold one particular lesson that had scored with him. "I wrote a poem about watching shark fins in Long Island Sound and it was somehow mysterious to see these fins cruising on a swollen silky swell. A glazed surface. I wrote for my teacher: 'A sense of process, a name of the hunting sea / haunts me.' And he wrote in the margin, 'Haunts you hell, when does it haunt me?' Many things turned for me when I read that comment. It hit home to me."

The fact that Ciardi was literally home made more of a difference than he ever admitted. The royal prince was back—to the delight of his mother and sisters, according to Edith, who reported that they were all "tickled silly" by his return. Perhaps it was merely being back at 84 South Street that turned Ciardi around academically, or maybe it was that he preferred the tolerant, non-insistent Unitarianism of Tufts to the moral rectitude of the remaining Free Will Baptists at Bates. Certainly John Holmes was a factor in Ciardi's new-found academic success, but so too were his new friends, especially Harry Hayford and Dick Stephenson, first-floor dormitory roommates in West Hall where Ciardi spent most of his free hours. The three of them spent many an evening deep in heady conversation over literary and philosophical subjects, with Ciardi immovably positioned on the couch, cigarette smoke heavy in the air, pontificating on everything with his customary self-assuredness. Hayford wrote that Ciardi was always at his best "over beer" and that "he allows your sacred convictions no sanctuary, yet he propounds his own dictums with amazing eclat. . . ." Very late on one particular evening, reacting perhaps to the hour as well as to Ciardi's uncompromising and insistent pronouncements, Stephenson sent Ciardi down the hill to his South Street home by saying, "At least *I* pay half the rent here!" Dick Beal was another member of their group, though perhaps a more occasional one, as he had to come down from his second floor room to join the company. Still another was Richard Carpenter, who recalled Ciardi as being "assertive, alert, committed, a formidable controversialist, and a good companion."

Collectively, this is the group John Holmes had in mind when he commented on Ciardi's transition from being a mediocre student at Bates to a good one at Tufts: "He happened to discover that the kind of fierce pleasure he had found in other ways, they found in literature, and in ideas, and in high grades. Loud and long the talk ran on in the rooms in West, and into the early morning. Competition and challenge, in studies, became exciting to him. . . ." Ciardi's first semester GPA was a modest 2.81, but in his second year his cumulative GPA rose to 3.24 and rose again in his last year to 3.36. The competition for grades was intense, and Ciardi went down to the wire in his last semester trying for Phi Beta Kappa. A C in German kept him from achieving the goal by a few tenths of a point, though he did graduate *magna cum laude*. But the loss was particularly galling because Harry, too, had managed only a C in that course yet made Phi Beta Kappa anyway. Holmes recalled the near miss and that John "was not happy that his friends made it." It wasn't until 1952, when the Harvard PBK chapter voted him an honorary membership in return for delivering the official Phi Beta Kappa poem, that John Ciardi began to feel the score had been settled.

To dramatize the story of the college grade competition with Harry Hayford in a poem called "The Highest Place in Town" *(Lives of X)* Ciardi changed the story slightly. He claimed it was *summa* that he had been working toward, not PBK. And the reason he gave for not getting the one grade higher that he needed for *summa* was that he had to work his way through school. He worked for the National Youth Administration (NYA) eking out "as much as $20 a month at 25 cents an hour doing odd jobs around the campus."

I stood in line with other federalists
on crisps of leaves it was dishonor to rake,
though we had to stir them, and watched Harry Hayford
walk his briefcase like a dog on a choke
to the library and one more inch of note cards
for the term paper I meant to beat him in.
"Go, you sweet bastard, go!" I told a ghost
his shadow left on the leaves, and fell to raking
till the crew hissed and I had to scatter my pile
back on the grass like notes I wasn't taking.

He got his *summa*, damn him, and I missed mine
though I outshouted him whole drunken nights
to prove I had a better thesis going,
or a better bellows for what thesis I had.

Either poetic license or a selective memory kept Ciardi from reporting that Harry Hayford, too, had worked for the NYA. But that was
not Ciardi's only job while he was a student at Tufts—he also
worked a jackhammer on the streets of Boston. He told Richard
Carpenter, many years after the fact, that at one point during their
college days, Carpenter, on his way to a rich boy's tennis match,
drove by the construction site where John was hard at work sweating over his jackhammer. These were the real reasons, he said, that
he never made Phi Beta Kappa.

Sweating over jackhammers aside, however, John Ciardi was
drawn every day closer and closer to the old-fashioned notion of a
college-educated gentleman. In fact, Ciardi later recalled that one
of the distinct charms of his undergraduate education at Tufts was
that "the 'gentleman' was still an exalted entity." He pointed out
that "it cost us nothing to address a faculty member as 'sir,'" and
that "we were addressed in turn as 'Mister' or 'Miss.'" And he
praised the high quality of his courses as well. Sophomore biology
(spring 1936) he called a philosophy course "because Professor Neal
was mind enough to make it that." He said he came to a first understanding of time, a frequent subject for his future poems, in
Professor Nichol's introduction to geology (spring 1937). And he
often demonstrated, in lecture jaunts all over the country, that he

had learned enough about serious music in Professor Leo Lewis's class to enable him to draw useful platform comparisons between poetry and music.

The English courses got most of his attention. In 1937-38, Ciardi and Harry Hayford were in Kenneth Myrick's eighteenth-century course and two of Harold Blanchard's courses, the literature of the Middle Ages and seventeenth-century. Ciardi once told Blanchard he was able to understand the medieval mind naturally "because I had been born in the Middle Ages." He put it this way in "A Five Year Step" *(Lives of X):*

> I don't remember what I was arguing
> in H. H. Blanchard's Medieval Lit.
> at Tufts in '37—something to do
> with numerology, and I knew about it
> the way my cousins knew baseball statistics
> by having been raised inside them, but couldn't prove it.
> "It does sound plausible," said H.H.B.,
> "but how do you know if you can't document it?
> Remember, we're not discussing how *we* feel
> but what went on in the mind of the Middle Ages."
>
> "That's just the point," I told him. "I was born there.
> Or else I was born beforehand to where they came."

And Ciardi was as argumentative in class as he was outside. After one of his classroom outbursts, Blanchard, overwhelmed, answered stodgily, "I wish I might have time, Mr. Ciardi, to deal adequately with the stream of words that is flowing from your mouth with such fluency."

At Tufts, too, Ciardi showed an interest in college theatricals by taking six credits of play production plus a course in post–seventeenth-century English drama. He also joined the drama club, known as the "Three P's" (Pen, Paint, and Pretzels) and had a feature role in Maxwell Anderson's *Winterset.* The play was put on in the Jackson Gymnasium, March 2–4, 1938, and "John A. Ciardi" is listed on the playbill as the actor playing Shadow. He summed up the experience: "Shadow was the gangster's henchman. The gangster's name was Trok. Shadow was shot and dumped in the East

River. After taking a shower in my clothes and pouring on some ketchup, I came on stage holding an automatic (with seaweed on it) and I had to die all over the stage, and I was losing my sight as I was looking for Trok to finish him off." Ciardi's experience in *Winterset* caused him to become too self-conscious to continue in the theater and may account for the fact that drama was the only literary form he avoided throughout the rest of his career. "There I was dying all over the stage, and a still, small voice of self-criticism kept saying in my inner ear, 'You know you're making an awful ass of yourself.' I was never able to act again."

Certainly in the audience for John's performance in *Winterset*, probably seated with Harry Hayford, was a young teaching fellow at Tufts that year, Jo Wishart. Josephine Bosworth Wishart, daughter of a Presbyterian minister who was president of the College of Wooster in Ohio, had graduated in 1936 from her father's college and ventured east to Tufts in September 1937 to pursue a master's degree. She was an instant hit. She was lively and vivacious, tall with long brown hair that had a glint of copper. Dick Beal, also a teaching fellow that year (and a man with an eye for feminine charms), met her first and described her to Harry Hayford as "Junoesque." And she was pure rebellion, smoking and taking an occasional drink—and traveling as far as she could from her Presbyterian roots. Once, shortly after arriving at Tufts, she attended a faculty dinner, and afterward, when the old boys on the faculty passed cigars around, she took one and lit up with them. In 1937 Jo Wishart taught freshman English, was "house mother" at Lawrence House on Packard Avenue in West Somerville (an off-campus residence for women), took senior-level undergraduate courses with Hayford and Ciardi, and was a joy to everyone who could admire independence, intelligence, and beauty, especially to John Ciardi.

Jo and John first met in class, but soon began seeing more of each other, going on inexpensive dates, like browsing used bookstores or nursing a Coke at Powderhouse Square. And they became the heart of a small group, with Hayford and Stephenson and an occasional classmate brought in more as a guest than a regular, that met just about every week at Holmes's apartment on Billingham Street. The courtship extended through the fall and early winter of the 1937–38 school year, but it became complicated when Harry Hayford also began showing an interest in the lovely Miss Wishart.

When the first semester ended, Jo moved out of the girls' residence and took a small off-campus apartment of her own. One evening Ciardi stopped by unannounced and found that Jo and Harry were about to go out on a date. He left Jo's apartment, of course, while Jo and Harry went out, but when Harry got back to his West Hall room later that night, John was there, very exercised and banging the walls with his fists, as Harry remembered it. In Harry's view, John was not so much angry with him as with his own bad luck and the circumstances. As Jo recalled it, John insisted that she make a choice right away rather than put an unbearable strain on his friendship with Harry. In March 1938, Jo and Harry announced their engagement, and on 28 May, with Dick Beal along as best man, the couple ran off to Providence to be married. As in the simultaneously occurring Phi Beta Kappa competition, John had lost out to Harry Hayford again.

If there were wounds that needed attention after graduation, John Ciardi left no account of it. He did, however, leave ample records testifying to the close friendship he had with Harry Hayford from January 1936 until graduation in the spring of 1938. They shared courses together, late nights at West Hall, the *Tuftonian*, poetry, and John Holmes. Moreover, the weekly visits to Holmes at his apartment were central to their college careers as well as to their friendship. For Ciardi, however, his developing relationship with Holmes gradually transcended all others, including his friendship with Harry. Years later, Ciardi could recall nostalgically small details of his days and nights at Holmes's house. "His study was always a clutter in surprisingly good order. . . . [H]is lair was lined with books, its walls hung with photos and memorabilia, and its nooks crammed with odds and ends he cherished." Holmes received Ciardi and Hayford and Wishart and Stephenson every week. They read endless poems together, both their own and contemporary favorites, working their way carefully through Eliot's *Waste Land* during one stretch. And they all met fairly regularly at 84 South Street as well, where once Mama Ciardi pulled Holmes aside and asked intently, "My boy, what he do, is good?" She was immediately reassured by Holmes, "Yes, Mrs. Ciardi, what John is doing is very good."

Ciardi was only nineteen in January 1936 when he met Holmes, who almost immediately began introducing his young student to the work of contemporary poets like Randall Jarrell, about whom Ciardi said, "Hey, this guy's good; he sounds like me." Holmes brought Richard Eberhart onto campus (probably in the spring of 1938) and introduced him to Ciardi, who impressed the older poet. Ciardi, Eberhart said, "had great energy, force, and was a brilliant, unforgettable presence." There were others, but for Ciardi the most important and impressive poet Holmes introduced him to was Theodore Roethke. The meeting took place on campus in October 1937. Ciardi described the scene in "The Highest Place in Town":

> It was on the Rez in 1937
> I first met Roethke. He and John Holmes, my teacher,
> father, friend, and host to my blowfly eggs,
> had taught together at Lafayette, and Roethke
> was passing through. I was reading on the grass
> when John called to me and said the hulk beside him
> was Roethke, and told Roethke, stretching a point,
> I was a poet.
>   I think I said hello
> but my throat clicked shut on it. Aside from Holmes
> I'd never been near enough to talk to a poet.
> And couldn't get near enough then, though there he was.
> He asked if I was an athlete. I said No.
> He asked my fraternity. I said NYA,
> and grinned, and hated myself. There must have been more,
> but all I remember from a first of princes
> was "No" and one limp quip and—I guess—"Good-bye";
> though the next night he looked at some of my poems
> and didn't tell me entirely how bad they were.

Ciardi was in awe of Roethke, but he also had an insatiable need to talk about poetry, learn about it from the inside, and discuss it with the people who knew it best. And so it was that Roethke, just passing through and visiting an old friend, found himself at Holmes's apartment the next night reading through a batch of young John Ciardi's poems. One can almost see Holmes grinning over the way his prize student moved in on his old friend to pick his brain and talk intently about the inner dynamics of the poems he was then writing.

Nor did it end there. Within a matter of days Ciardi had a new batch of poems in the mail to Roethke, who had apparently said politely that he'd be happy to see more of Ciardi's poems— sometime. Writing on interoffice memo stationery of the Crystal Tube Manufacturing. Company in what he described as "glaring ink," young John Ciardi wrote an engaging letter filled with a nice mix between maturity and undergraduate enthusiasm. He'd "more than anything else" like Roethke's "slant," his "point of view." He wanted strong criticism, he said. "John Holmes is a swell incentive to me but I'm afraid he's too kind to say 'putrid' once in a while. . . . Do you think you could consult your particular oracle and tell me in so many words what the hell is the matter with the stuff I enclose?"

What "stuff" Ciardi enclosed is unknown, though it may well have been verse that he published in the *Tuftonian* between the November 1936 issue and the Spring 1938 issue, sixteen poems in all. Of the sixteen, seven were "Fragments from a sequence of variations on the sonnet form," collectively titled "To the Man with a Soul." Another, "Humphrey," was a rambling six-page poem about the title character, who asks if he must be cold throughout eternity, "without a woman's body in the night? / And all because I rose to be a God?" This poem, which appeared in the winter 1938 issue, did get Roethke's attention in the summer of 1938, for on 26 August, Ciardi wrote to thank him for his criticisms: "they are wise, tactful, and just what I need." Roethke was harsh enough for Ciardi to conclude, "I suppose the wisest thing for me to do would be to put 'Humphrey' definitely aside," and in typical Ciardi fashion, he ended, "but I can't bring myself to it." He also reassured Roethke that he wasn't taking himself as seriously as the poem might seem to imply. And, of course, he sent a new batch of poems from his notebook, "experimental" poems he said, "mostly variations of line & conversational stress in some cases, maximum compression in others." He added, "I have a fundamental conviction that a poem should dictate its own pattern, which is not a great discovery, but I've been fooling around trying to let each poem make its own form."

All through his two and a half years at Tufts, under the careful encouragement and guidance of John Holmes, Ciardi was doing a great deal more than "fooling around." There is no telling how many poems he wrote in addition to the sixteen that were published in the *Tuftonian*, but the testimony of Holmes and Hayford implies that Ciardi was indeed prolific during those years as he worked constantly to hone his skills and harness his talent. And he did it, at least in part, with his friends at the college office of the *Tuftonian*. Harry Hayford was editor-in-chief in 1937; Dick Stephenson in 1938, and Ciardi was on the editorial staff for three consecutive issues during those years. On the last page of the Fall 1937 *Tuftonian*, Harry Hayford published a picture of Ciardi (hat, topcoat, and ever-present cigarette), and commented, "John Ciardi is a valuable person to have around. Of course he is uncomfortable company at times, especially after dinner when one's stomach feels that all men are brothers, but Ciardi's profound voice insists they are not so." John, he went on, "has his absolute worth. He is a silver mine . . . especially for his endless reserve of poems." And, Hayford concluded, "We contemplate an exclusive Ciardi issue in the near future."

The February 1937 *Tuftonian* contained Ciardi's first published book review, of Robert Frost's *From Snow to Snow*, a special collection of his poems that Frost had selected, in his words, as "most appropriate" for each of the months of the year. Even at age twenty and with an icon like Robert Frost, a favorite of John Holmes, John Ciardi could be sharply critical. He found it "hard to forgive [Frost] for the too-Wordsworthian tone of 'The Tuft of Flowers.' " He liked the lyricism in "To the Thawing Wind," but commented that "there is an echo of Shelley here that makes the voice not quite Frost's own." Finally, he objected to Frost's "tendency to finish with a moral," a characteristic in his view that "mar[red] the pleasure when reading Frost at any length." But Ciardi also acknowledged that Frost's glories were so striking that he could "forgive him anything." Showing through Ciardi's decidedly undergraduate tone were characteristics of his criticism that would serve him well in the future: an engaging honesty, an attractive and self-assured boldness, and the apparently offhanded courage of his convictions. There was also an ease of expression and a sharpness of perception that would become hallmarks of Ciardi's review style, which invariably took the arcane and made it understandable to a general audience.

In early October 1937, at the instigation of John Holmes, Ciardi wrote a letter to Roy Cowden at the University of Michigan asking for information about the Hopwood awards in writing given at that school every year. "My interest," he confessed, "is entirely given to poetry." Applicants were asked to submit manuscripts of their work as evidence of their qualifications, and Ciardi sent twelve poems. After Cowden had read them over three times one evening at home, he called to his wife and read them aloud to her, solemnly announcing afterward: "This year we have a poet coming here to Michigan." In the meantime, Holmes knew some professors at Michigan, and as Ciardi's graduation approached in 1938, he was able to help his young protégé get a scholarship as well as a part-time job to pay for his meals. It may have seemed improbable that John Ciardi would be going off to graduate school in September 1938, considering the family financial situation and his somewhat tentative beginning as a college student in September 1934, but in Ciardi's view it made at least one variety of perfect sense: "Since I had paid attention to practically nothing but English classes at Tufts, I found myself unemployable . . . and had to go to Grad School."

The Hopwood Award

The road to Ann Arbor and the Horace H. Rackham School of Graduate Studies at the University of Michigan was easier for John Ciardi to travel than the road to Bates had been in September 1934. In the first place, he had a tuition scholarship. Second, he had cash, two hundred dollars each from his Godfather John Follo and his sister Ella, money borrowed with the firm and rashly overconfident promise that they would be repaid from the money he fully intended to win with the Hopwood Award. Third, he had the promise of employment, which turned out to be meal money from a succession of NYA student-aide jobs on campus, such as watching rats in a maze in the psychology department, bussing tables at the student cafeteria, and grading papers for a professor in the English department. His prospects in September 1938 were so much better than they had been in 1934 that he took a bus to Ann Arbor instead of hitchhiking. He rented an off-campus room at 423 Benjamin Street and settled in for his graduate-school education.

On 26 October, after little more than a month in Michigan, Ciardi had written to Holmes so often that Holmes in turn sent a reassuring note to Concetta to report how well the royal prince was doing. "I get letters from John often, and he sends me a lot of his new poems. But he doesn't tell me much about himself and what he really does, how long he works, what sort of a room he lives in, or anything. I think that he hasn't found many people he likes to talk to yet, but he likes at least one of his teachers very much. His poetry gets better all the time, and some day he will make a very fine name for himself with it. I think he could publish some of it in good magazines right now. But he wants to keep all of it to submit for the big prizes they offer at the university. I am willing to bet on him to win one of them, too." Of course, Ella or one of the other girls had to read the letter to Concetta, but she must have received the news with more than usual parental pride given the fact that she had invested so much of her psychological makeup in the myth of the learned Antonio's survival in her college-educated son. She had to be especially pleased by Holmes's ending: "He's a fine boy, and the best writer I have had at Tufts College in five years. You should be proud of him." How could she not have been? Physically as well as intellectually, the twenty-two-year-old John Ciardi was impressive. In fact, Professor Roy Cowden was frankly surprised by the broad-shouldered specimen he had hitherto known only through correspondence. "When I first saw him I was startled at the quiet, deliberate bulk of him. He might have come from a year before the mast, or from a business where heavy lifting was the task." He concluded, innocently demonstrating his own stereotyped sense of what the genteel poet should look like: "No one would have guessed him to be a poet."

Ciardi completed his master's degree in English in one full academic year plus the summer of 1939. His program included nine courses (24 credits), plus a volume of original poems, which he elected to write in place of a thesis. He earned seven A's, a B plus, and a B. His most important course in 1938-39 was a six-credit seminar in poetic composition with Cowden. All six of the students in that class were working on book-length manuscripts for the end-of-year Hopwood competition, but Ciardi was head and shoulders above his classmates. As Cowden recalled it afterward, "The other members of the class soon became aware that they had a poet in their midst." In Cowden's judgment, Ciardi was traveling faster and farther than the others: "John was studying poetry as only a poet can study it." Cowden's seminar consisted of one lecture class and one manuscript conference each week. The lectures were difficult to get through, but the conferences were magical. Cowden would read one of John's poems with him, then raise his hand, "hovering over the page in slow figure-eights" until his finger would land just at the place John finally figured out that it would land, thus enabling him to know a split second before it was pointed out where the weakness was. Just how this master mentoring worked was forever a mystery to John Ciardi, but he remained loyally convinced all the rest of his life that "it was great teaching." In the end he called Cowden a "grandfather figure" and wrote without embarrassment, "I loved the man."

Ciardi was learning a great deal more in 1938-39 than what was found in his textbooks and classes. The Spanish civil war, which had begun in July 1936 when Gen. Francisco Franco's right-wing rebels sailed from Morocco and took Cadiz in southern Spain, had emerged as both the galvanizing and polarizing event of the decade. The democratically elected government in Spain was a coalition of communists, anarchists, and all disaffected and disenfranchised people who had managed, legally, to wrest the leadership of the country from the monarchist dictatorship that it had become in the 1920s. In opposition to this elected Loyalist government of Republican Spain were Franco's fascist rebels, supported by wealthy men of property, the Catholic Church, and all those who feared socialist leveling. Internationally, Franco was propped up by Benito Mussolini in Italy and Adolf Hitler in Germany, fascist leaders who were busy just months before the invasion of Cadiz taking Ethiopia and the Rhineland and forming the beginning of a worldwide anti-communist bloc. Americans during the depression years of the 1930s leaned more heavily than ever before or after toward the ideals of socialism and the practice of Russian communism, so it was not surprising that a great deal of public opinion ran against Franco in his attempt to usurp the leftist government that had been fairly elected in Spain. Moreover, public opinion also ran against President Franklin Roosevelt and his Neutrality Act (signed into law on 1 May 1937), which provided him with a convenient reason for not coming to the assistance of the Loyalist government.

For John Ciardi the horror of fascism gradually became dramatically clear. The war had broken out six months after his transfer to Tufts, and it became the occasional subject of late evening conversations at West Hall with Harry Hayford and Dick Stephenson during the 1936-37 school year. By the time school began again in September 1937, however, the communists versus fascists issue had become a continuing debate, occasionally argued by Ciardi and his friends at West Hall, who, though not members of the Communist Party, were sympathetic to it and known, in the language of the time, as "fellow travelers." A year later, when Ciardi arrived at the University of Michigan, the national debate was angrier than ever. The war had become an ever-present reality and Ciardi was swept along by outrage, idealism, and the spirited rhetoric that characterized the debate. Very naturally, even eagerly, he joined his voice to the chorus of worldwide anti-fascist protests against Franco. He said, perhaps with a touch of pride, that some at the university saw him as a "radical": "I supported the Spanish Loyalists and wrote in their support."

Of course, most of Ciardi's Michigan friends also supported the cause. One of his closest friends and allies was poet John Malcolm Brinnin, who was himself a young student at the university and the proprietor of a bookstore, The Book Room, devoted to poetry, occasional poetry readings, and avant-garde literature. In keeping with the anti-fascist spirit of the time, Brinnin also sold copies of the communist *Daily Worker*, but he did so under the table—just to be on the safe side. Then, too, some of their friends at the university had actually been in the war, just recently returned from service in the Lincoln Brigade, which was an American force within the larger International Brigade of foreign volunteer soldiers. It was a dizzying political atmosphere, and Ciardi much later wrote (at a time when he wanted to minimize the idealism of his youth), "I fired off endless poems, signed every zany petition the loonies brought me, and even imagined that I was in some way shooting down Stukas." In 1938, however, Ciardi did not consider himself and his friends in the Michigan literary community as "loonies," because they all believed sincerely that they had "important convictions to utter." As Ciardi explained it to Cowden, "Style and form are only adjuncts to the human problem the poet must face: how to find a semblance of order in a world plundered by the contradictions of its political system."

If Ciardi actually wrote "endless poems" about the war and the political crisis, they have not survived, although two of his early poems at Michigan had a somewhat muted political message under titles that sounded like full-blown propaganda pieces. "To a Young American the Day after the Fall of Barcelona" (which occurred on 26 January 1939) sighs with lost idealism: "Boy with honor in your heart / The world is not the world you dream[.]" He exhorts the young man to use "all resource of infamy / Against the enemy known," or else "leave your world to be undone." In "To One 'Investigated' by the Last Senate Committee, or the Next" the political content is clear even though the biographical analog, if one existed, is not. He asks if the person addressed in the title will "become discreet— / the liar's euphemism—and retreat?" He answers with conviction:

> No, keep your honor clean:
> run to the sea
> and wash your fear in waves:
> be murdered whole
> if courage fails you
> to see honor through.

Don't think, he says, that you can allow "a craven safety / count for honor's part."

Ciardi's most engaging treatment of the Spanish war appeared in a ten-stanza, eighty-line poem called "Reply to S. K." Stanley Kuniholm, the S. K. of the poem, was one of Ciardi's *Tuftonian* friends, although in the 1937–38 undergraduate debate on the appropriateness of Spanish war themes—or any political subject matter—in poetry, they took opposite sides. Ciardi and Hayford were all for it, while Kuniholm and Holmes were against. The poem was a lament over the Loyalist losses at Barcelona and ended with a solemn vision that passed for wisdom:

> You will be safe. But past your shaded light
> The stars are deeper than you know, the sun

More violent than you dreamed, and day and night
Crossed wide with danger where the armed men run.

Ciardi's reply to Kuniholm recognized a disturbing reality, that events of worldwide significance were occurring in one part of the world while his own small world remained tidy and unchanged.

Yes, Barcelona is three thousand miles
From where I write and I have not been there
To count the swollen dead and the jagged aisles
Cut by machine guns in the grain. Here
No motors brawl their anger overhead.
I have not seen the roof split to reveal,
For that one moment when the quick and dead
Are congruent, the bomb's bright cap of steel.

All I remember is the newspaper maps,
Boundaries estimated, casualties estimated, thunder
Of headlines fading away to lower caps—
Print, erroneous and glib. Or from under
The blue-buzzing tube the voice of the announcer,
Modulated, distant, saying: *It is done.*
Careful syllables reciting danger
In a lost land.

              At home there was sun—
Unmenaced bright high noon. The starlings fought
Small skirmishes with sparrows in the oak.
Robins bobbed on the lawn. I caught
A cardinal's whistle and spied him out in the crook
Of the lowest branch, bright red against the green.
The young nephews tumbling on the grass
Came racing out to meet me with a scream
And beg a pick-back ride into the house.

Inside, the world went well: mother had lunch
Spread on the broad white table, in my room
The books were warm bright colors, and a bunch
Of some new-cut and fragrant unknown bloom
From mother's garden-puttering stood in water.

The simple and disarming truth was that devastation in Spain and safety at home simply coexisted. The poem fairly bursts with the heavy-hearted sadness of an idealist who was growing up. What Stanley Kuniholm could not have missed, however, was the timeliness of the content and the high achievement of the poem—their undergraduate debate reargued persuasively in verse.

President Roosevelt could be faulted over his foreign policy decisions, according to Ciardi, especially his lack of vigilance against encroaching European fascism, but his domestic policies were generally beyond reproach. Ciardi later summarized his trust in the New Deal this way: Roosevelt "experimented with government with a bold and convincing sense of improvisation. And he won our imaginations. Thus, my generation came to its first intellectual awareness during a particular sort of social illness. It came to believe that it could locate that illness in conservative government. And it came to believe that it could place its hope only in radical experiments." John Ciardi's left-of-center political views were thus given a simple and succinct theoretical foundation—and an expression—that reflected the sentiments of millions in the 1930s.

Theoretical frameworks, however, did not move Ciardi's blood the way real issues did. He was taken aback by the difference between Massachusetts and Michigan—Boston and Detroit. "In Boston there were only rich people and those who were waiting to be rich," but in Michigan, "a worker was more likely to know he was a worker and to realize his economic stake in the social pattern." He called it a "realistic environment" and claimed that it was "the most valuable thing" he took from his time in Michigan. He remembered for the rest of his life "the bloody battles between the auto workers and Ford's private security force headed by Harry Bennett, Bennett's goons scoring a hideous victory at the Battle of the Overpass, and *Time* featuring bloody photo spreads of union leaders, among them Water Reuther." These scenes Ciardi saw from his nearby observation post at Ann Arbor, and together with his rising anger over the Spanish civil war, they made him into something of a social activist. "All these things and more left intellectuals feeling that there were important things to say. They felt important to me, and the fact that I hardly knew what I was talking about made no difference. My sense of decency was ablaze."

Ciardi also fell in love with a married woman during his time in Michigan, ablaze in a different way. Virginia Johnson was a slender, short-haired woman with a broad, easy smile. A Ph.D. student in psychology at the University of Michigan, she was married to a man who worked for General Motors inspecting buses in Detroit. He returned home only on the weekends. In late January or early February 1939, at the first class meeting of "Special Work in the Psychological Approach to Literary Criticism," taught by Professors Morris and Shepard and assisted by Virginia Johnson, the young poet was apparently smitten. Ciardi invited Virginia for coffee one day after class, she agreed, and they became all but inseparable from that point on, with John visiting her and her sons (Dion, nine, and Ralph, fourteen) at their nearby trailer on a regular basis. As Dion recalled it, their relationship was never clandestine; in fact, it was open and civilized enough for John to get along well with the entire family, including Virginia's husband, Phil. Dick Beal, who visited Ciardi a few times in Ann Arbor, recalled that John "saw a great deal" of an unnamed woman "living in a trailer" and that he thought "he stayed with her a good part of the time." John Malcolm Brinnin recalled that Virginia was a "dignified, older woman," and that she and John were "devoted to each other." Occasionally, he said, the couple would have dinner with him and his mother at their home. He characterized John's feelings for Virginia as "good for John" because "it helped take some of the rough edges off." He added that it was a "positive, ennobling love."

Virginia Johnson, whom Ciardi identified in his poem "Letter to Virginia Johnson" as "doctor, / Scholar and therapist of the wishing nerve," became Ciardi's ideal reader and remained so for many years to come. He wrote to Marion Strobel of *Poetry* on 29 April 1948: "I've had my focus pretty clearly in mind for a long time now. I write to my much admired friend Virginia Johnson, as well stocked, sensitive, and interested a mind as I know, but not a literary specialist. She is an expert psychiatric social worker with a wide awareness of the world and of the arts. I don't think our times are likely to do better, and I like to think that using her as a touchstone I can get a reaction to a poem from a kind of ideal of the non-literary specialist mind."

The spring term had barely begun when the deadline for the Hopwood competition approached. The awards were named after Avery Hopwood, a successful Broadway dramatist in the 1920s, who had left 20 percent of his estate to the University of Michigan as an endowment for annual writing awards to students in drama, poetry, fiction, and nonfiction. The ninth annual awards ceremony was scheduled for Friday, 2 June, with Carl Van Doren giving the Hopwood Lecture on Benjamin Franklin, "The First American Man of Letters." Some nine thousand dollars would be divided among fourteen writers. Ciardi's entry was a volume of verse named "Homeward to America," which he turned in under the pseudonym Thomas Aquinas. The judges in poetry were Horace Gregory, Louise Bogan, and David McCord. Despite his brash overconfidence when he left for Michigan in September 1938, John Ciardi years later remembered being surprised at the announcement that he had, indeed, won the twelve-hundred-dollar prize, the largest in poetry that had ever been awarded to that time. "There I sat, a [soon to be] Master of Arts, holding a check for $1,200 1939 dollars! It was the largest piece of money I had ever held in my hand! Lucky John was rich!" He had arranged with John Holmes that if he won the award, he would send an inexpensive "form" telegram for fifteen cents: "May Easter bless you many years." But in the excitement of the moment and the warm glow of all that money, he sent this instead: "Ring out wild bells twelve hundred bucks." When Ella received a similar wire at home, she was so excited that she forgot to tip the delivery boy. Ella got her two hundred dollars back, as did Godfather John Follo, and some of the money went to Concetta as well. But the bulk of the prize money, including seventy dollars for a "broken-down" 1931 Model-A Ford that trailed "an endless blue fog," went toward a West Coast trip with Virginia Johnson, without her children, stretching from 20 August to 27 September.

Before they could leave for California, however, there was the business of completing three two-credit summer courses for his M.A. Between the end of the spring term and the beginning of the summer term, Ciardi drove his Model-A back East for a brief visit with his family. When he returned to Ann Arbor, he settled into his courses and his summer job as departmental assistant in charge of eleven other graduate students grading papers in Professor Davis's world novel course. In the end, he managed to get through the work, but not without understandable complaints about a hellish schedule. To old friend Arnold Kenseth he wrote that he was waiting "with ill concealed impatience for the god-damn academic grind to come to an end." To Roethke he wrote that "three courses and an assistantship for one summer session keep me pretty close to Ann Arbor." He added that he was writing two papers on "the lower drippings of American Lit.: one on Michael Wigglesworth and one on John Pendleton Kennedy both of whom should have died young." He asked to be forgiven for a messy letter "banged out in frenzy and tumult between a dozen other things." And to his mother and sisters he wrote that he'd "been snowed under a heap of work" since beginning summer school.

Ciardi's short trip home in June had been as much to see John Holmes as it had been to see his family. Holmes, after all, could be counted on to appreciate properly John's Hopwood victory, and Ciardi wanted to be with Holmes, however briefly, to celebrate with his friend, mentor, and surrogate father. And Holmes came through again, this time with news about possibly having John's Hopwood manuscript published by Henry Holt and Company. Holmes knew the trade manager at Holt's, William Sloane, and had proposed to him that a revised version of Ciardi's award-winning manuscript might well be suitable for publication, and would he be interested? Sloane was definitely interested. He wrote to Ciardi on 8 June that he had spoken not only to Holmes, but to Horace Gregory as well: "As a matter of fact, too, Robert Frost has mentioned your name to us in the past, and all these factors combined make us extremely anxious to consider your manuscript for publication." He asked Ciardi to send him the revised work as soon as possible. It was a pleasant prospect—but a harder job that crowded summer than Ciardi let on in letters. He wrote to Roethke on 5 July: "Thanks for congratulations [on the Hopwood Award] . . . , but I'm not at all sure that I've done more than raise a golden splash in a very small puddle. I'm working right now—or have delayed working—on revision & retyping etc. Holt's wants to see the thing & I've promised an ms. by the end of July." Fifteen days later he wrote somewhat matter-of-factly to his family: "I finished the manuscript of the book today and will send it to the publishers tomorrow." One of the poems in that manuscript, "Letter for Those Who Grew Up Together," became Ciardi's first sold poem. It went to *Poetry*, and he acknowledged the acceptance in a letter to editor George Dillon on

27 July. It was not one of the Hopwood poems, he wrote to Roethke on 4 August, but one written "a month or so after the contest closed." On the book manuscript, Ciardi reported to Arnold Kenseth that he was "fairly optimistic about the possibilities of getting it published. Should know sometime in the next month or so, but I won't be reachable until October when I get home [from California] so I won't know until then."

Ciardi's five-week West coast swing with Virginia Johnson included stops in Wyoming, California, and Utah, and, according to schedule, he was back in Ann Arbor by 27 September. After a week or so there, he headed back to Medford alone—and the good news that Holt's had accepted the book. The contracts were signed at once and Ciardi was given a cash advance of one hundred dollars. By 24 October, Ciardi wrote in a letter to John Malcolm Brinnin that he was already reading galley sheets of his book, which was scheduled for publication in January 1940. Advance copies actually arrived well before Christmas, one going to Virginia with an inscription dated 8 December, and one going to John Malcolm, who wrote at once to say how much he liked it. Ciardi was pleased and replied with not-quite restrained excitement: "I'm really almost visibly thrilled with the job Holt's has done on it." That, however, was about as much self-satisfaction as Ciardi allowed himself. In fact, it was only a couple of years later that he not only stopped rejoicing, but actually began downplaying his first modest volume of poems, what he came to call his juvenilia. In June 1942, Ciardi wrote to Alan Swallow, who had inquired about Ciardi's book for an article he was planning, that he'd rather send some new poems along. "The point is I no longer feel I want to be represented by the first book—it's horribly uneven and loose in all but a few poems I still like." Ciardi was ever after hard on that first book of poems (and the Hopwood manuscript it grew out of), although he regularly tempered his self-criticism with a quiet joke or two at his own expense: "That winning manuscript was, alas, a miserable botch, windy, profuse, and founded on verbal indigestion." After some thirty-six years and untold publications, he came to enjoy looking backward at his first book with amused tolerance at his own youthful enthusiasm: "I was actually a published—and even reviewed— poet. . . . I subscribed to a clipping service and treasured the notices from the San Francisco *Bee,* the Boston *Transcript,* and from every Boondock's *Blatt* that cited my golden name."

Homeward to America did, in fact, get reviewed or, at least, noticed in many publications, like the *New York Times,* the *Herald Tribune,* and the *Christian Science Monitor.* Louis Untermeyer gave it a few words in the *Yale Review;* Louise Bogan likewise in the *New Yorker. Poetry* gave it three pages. Ciardi's old Tufts antagonist, Stanley Kuniholm, reviewed it for the *Tuftonian* and someone named Leslie Warren reviewed it in the Bates College literary magazine, the *Garnet.* The review that meant most to Ciardi was written by John Holmes himself in the *Boston Transcript.* The one he never knew about was written by the FBI: "A perusal of the contents of the volume by the reporting Agent did not reveal any verse which would indicate unpatriotic feelings or tendencies but there were many poems which heralded a true love for liberty and the democratic way of life." Ciardi was right in classifying *Homeward* as his juvenilia—but it was promising juvenilia, and that was something he never afterward cared to acknowledge. The reviews were generally good. Bogan called him "gifted" and singled out "Night Freight, Michigan" ("a rare kind of poetic observation") for special praise. Untermeyer said Ciardi's "taste is excellent" and his spirit "is sensitive and yet tough." Ciardi "speaks for his generation," Untermeyer went on, with an "affirmative utterance," but, he added, "Mr. Ciardi is still uncertain of his material, unsure of himself." Frajam Taylor in *Poetry* commented that *Homeward* was a "first volume in which all the fiery eagerness of youth colors and quickens the sober reflections of maturity." The reviewers seemed to agree that there was a lot to like in this new poet, a lot to look forward to—and a lot to improve on. Of course, Holmes was the most comprehensive reviewer and had the most good things to say. "At his best, John Ciardi is notable for rich inventiveness of epithet and image, for a capacity for putting life on the page, and for rhythmic power under control." Holmes said there was "a high percentage of successful and individual poems" in *Homeward* and admired the book's "authentic tone, its reality in achievement." Finally he praised Ciardi's "passionate drive toward self-realization." Holmes may have been too lavish in his praise of *Homeward,* which was dedicated to him, but equally important was that Ciardi himself was too hard on it.

Homeward to America contained thirty-four poems, ran to sixty-two pages, and sold for $1.50. At its best, it is fresh and honest with structured poems that explore personal identity, ethnic and neighborhood backgrounds, and national possibilities. One hears the characteristic Ciardi voice throughout, but though the voice is persistent, it is not consistent. The poems are more than occasionally memorable, as in the first poem, "Letter to Mother," where he tells her that he has to find his own way, his own America, as she did hers. He showed a social consciousness and an easy narrative style in "To Westward," a depression-era poem with "men going nowhere, hands pocketed, heels kicking the wall." The Spanish war poems are also principled statements that work surprisingly well as poems. Some sweetly nostalgic and innocent lines emerge from "Letter for Those Who Grew Up Together" while a more moving moment occurs in his father's "Biography," which traces Antonio's final ride to the cemetery:

> He will go
> Mid-road between the tenements and down
> To the suburban end of time and town
> And through the fields, fade in the final wood,
> And not come back.

For critic Edward Krickle, the major accomplishments of *Homeward* were its theme ("the problems of belief, of definition, of values") and the tone of uncertainty that Ciardi used to pursue that theme. The modern problem that Krickle identified at the heart of *Homeward* is that "certain things from the past can no longer be believed, but what is to replace them?" Perhaps Ciardi had not succeeded well enough or often enough in his first book, according to Krickle, but "the seed of the strongly individual poet that is to come" was evident.

Holmes was certainly right when he noted in his *Transcript* review that some of Ciardi's more recent poems, written after the publication of *Homeward*, were "even better" because "his thinking progresses steadily, widening in scope, deepening in maturity." And he was correct in observing that Ciardi's next book "will be a real event." But he and Ciardi would both have been very surprised could they have known that Ciardi's next book would not be published until 1947, seven long years later.

Ciardi drifted back to Ann Arbor in the first week of January 1940 to see Ginny Johnson, John Malcolm Brinnin, Roy Cowden—and the others of his Ann Arbor family. With his first book in hand, he gave a triumphant reading at Brinnin's bookstore, no doubt thrilled to see the carefully arranged copies of *Homeward* in the window display case. Primarily, however, he was looking for a job, for the Hopwood money by then was nothing more than a memory. When Ginny received John's wire that he would be arriving either on the third or fourth of January, she wrote her parents that she hoped he would "blow in to-night" because "things will sort of fall into place around him." And they did. He stayed with Ginny for the rest of the month, displacing fourteen-year-old Ralph from his bedroom. Midway through the month she wrote again to her parents: "I do love having him." John was never any trouble, she wrote—he was good company and made life easier for her: "Any housework I leave undone he sort of does in passing through a room. He never seems to get at it but you find it done. Pictures get hung and furnaces and things start to work. I wish he would just stay on. . . ." On the twenty-fifth, she wrote again to say that John was still with her and that she would be able to write more often "after John goes—though I hate to have him leave." After he did leave on 1 February, Ginny wrote that he had left "a large hole behind him" and that both boys missed him. Even Ralph, who had lost his bedroom for the month, confessed that there was "something" about having John around: "Aw Hell," he said to his mother, "he can have my room all the time, if he'll come back and stay."

Meanwhile Untermeyer, who had intersected with Ciardi at Bates and been poet-in-residence at the University of Michigan in the spring 1939, had taken a position at the University of Kansas City. When President Clarence R. Decker of UKC asked Untermeyer if he could recommend a young English instructor, he recommended the recent Hopwood Award winner, twenty-four-year-old John Ciardi. Ciardi filled out his application for employment on 12 January 1940. He said he had earned eighteen hundred dollars in 1939 and that he needed twenty-five hundred dollars in salary. He listed Holmes, Cowden, and a full complement of Tufts and Michigan professors as references. He said he weighed 186 pounds and had no church affiliation. He declared himself prepared and willing to teach three courses: modern British and American poetry, versification, and prose composition. Furthermore, he offered to advise "any student literary enterprise—magazine, lecture club, etc." Decker wanted a young poet; Ciardi needed a job; and Louis Untermeyer was there to serve as catalyst: John Ciardi was about to head south and become a college English teacher.

THREE

Teacher,
Gunner, Poet

1940 TO 1945

The UKC and FBI

Clarence R. Decker, former English department chairman and academic vice president, was still new on the job as president of the University of Kansas City in January 1940. The school had merged its professional programs with a new four-year liberal arts curriculum in 1935 and selected its first president, J. Duncan Spaeth, in September 1936. Spaeth retired two years later, however, and was replaced by the popular Decker, who, at age thirty-three, became one of the youngest college presidents in the country. His meteoric rise to the presidency was not surprising considering that he had taken his Ph.D. in 1928 in comparative literature at the University of Chicago when he was only twenty-three and that he had managed in the next six years to teach at four Midwestern colleges and travel widely in Europe and Asia—all before becoming chairman of the UKC English department in 1934 and vice president shortly thereafter. He brought brilliance and a good budget sense to the office of the presidency in 1938. John Ciardi quipped about him that he had "a way with things": "He announced me as Guest Lecturer in Modern Poetry and assigned me to teach five sections of Freshman English, thirty-five to a section." Ciardi added that at $900 a semester, it came to "about $5.15 per student as rounded out to the nearest penny." His salary for that spring term 1940 was actually $800, raised in the fall to $850. It was a squeeze, but he managed: "five dollars would buy me a twenty meal ticket. . . . [and] I was paying four dollars a week for a room." He lived with the Richardson family at 609 East 54th Street, where he was reported to be "a quiet individual who never caused any trouble." "My needs were simple," he said, "a few dollars a month to send to my mother, cigarettes, food, an attic room . . . , and all the girls I could manage to sleep with. Kansas City was a good provider on all points."

With respect to the girls, Ciardi seems to have been especially well provided from January 1940 to January 1942. In three different autobiographical fragments written much later, he spoke of those days with an undisguised, self-satisfied machismo. "In Kansas City in 1941 I developed my spiritual and cultural values at Dorothea Spaeth's modern dance studio, and especially with her dancers, and in particularly intimate tutelage with one of them whose conversation . . . ran to such topics as the vital difference between live foods (most bean sprouts) and dead foods (among which she included aged T-bone rare)." She talked too much, he said, but she had compensating features, "which happened to include buttocks more elegantly and actively convolute in motion than any that had blessed my previous vision of lust." He called her "Glory butt." As glorious as she may have been, however, Ciardi left her during the spring break in 1941, to go to Ann Arbor—at least partly for "a reassessment of a gentle and willowy grammarian named Mag." Virginia Johnson went unmentioned.

Earlier, in 1940, Ciardi had gone with a senior girl and said they had been "in and out of love with one another." But he also described Saturday night faculty parties at that time—without mention of the senior girl he was "in and out of love with": "there was always a bash in which a dozen faculty couples and only one dean got liquored up and swapped wives. At 23 I could use more wives than most." And joking with a straight face about his workload in 1940, he complained to President Decker that there wasn't enough time in the week "to meet classes, grade my themes, have individual conferences, and still fuck all the senior girls. . . ." In another context, Ciardi recalled his women-chasing at the University of Kansas City differently: "I had a number of enthusiastic bachelor researches to undertake. One of them was a girl in Chicago, and one was a girl in Kansas City. I seemed to spend a lot of time on the Streamliners, going back and forth from one to the other. My salary just about kept the Atchison, Topeka, and Santa Fe rolling, as near as I can recall."

When he wasn't crowing over his conquests, Ciardi lorded it over Kansas City's locals. He wrote to John Malcolm Brinnin: "The skyscrapers are nice, but what people. With the exception of the faculty and a few people I've uncovered[,] everyone seems to gush about *art*, and no one seems to know anything about it. I got my picture into the papers when I first got here and so far have received a letter soliciting poems from the S. P. Cruelty to Animals, an invitation to spend the summer on a Kansas estate, forty invitations to dinner—a few with overtones, and a bevy of phone calls. 'Art' & 'poet' are the magic words. Anyhow I've found a few interesting people and I've managed to shake off the rest." He was becoming a minor sort of culture hero, once even featured on a local radio broadcast, speaking on the topic "Men of Arts and Science" and reading some of his own poems as well.

In Kansas City, too, Ciardi took flying lessons. He wrote to Arnold Kenseth in October 1941 that he was attending flight classes given by the Civil Aeronautics Authority. He was hoping to take his private pilot's certificate in November or December and then go on "into the secondary training, then the cross country, then the Instrument Flight training, and finally into Flight Instruction as a way out of Freshman themes." His dream continued much more ambitiously: "In a year or so I can pile up 200-250 hours of solo, get a Commercial Pilot's Certificate with an Instructor rating and pull down a job as flight Instructor at $375 per month. Egad. Or I can go into ferry bombers to Britain at $1000 per ferry, which is no hay. (There's a $5000 bonus if one ferries five over inside of two months—that makes $10,000 in two months—if one lives through it. . . .)" Such rash talk, he added, was to be a strict secret from his family, who would be very upset "if they knew I was spending my spare time jockeying clouds around Kansas City." Ciardi's plans were aborted, however, when his flight instructor gave up on him: "On a clear day I could fly," he later confessed, but "on a hazy horizon I did not know where I was. . . ."

On the literary end of things, Louis Adamic wrote to Ciardi on 4 April 1940 to say that he'd seen John Holmes's *Boston Transcript* review of *Homeward to America* and had become interested in "Letter to Mother." Adamic was about to launch *Common Ground* magazine as the voice of his Common Council for American Unity. The magazine's purpose, as it was stated in its first issue, was "to tell the story of the coming and meeting on this continent of peoples belonging to about 60 different national, racial, and religious backgrounds," which made many of the poems in *Homeward* especially interesting to Adamic. Adamic reprinted "Letter to Mother" in his first issue that fall and then published three new Ciardi poems: "Boston: North End" (spring 1941), "Long Wharf: Boston" (winter 1942), and "The Fourth of July" (summer 1942). On another literary front, poet and anthologist Tom Boggs had written to Ciardi on 16 January 1940, soliciting poems for a book he was then preparing called *Lyric Moderns*. He said he'd seen some of Ciardi's poems the previous summer in Boston and been "greatly impressed." By January, however, Boggs and his wife, Rosemary, had moved to Forsyth, Missouri, only 250 miles from Kansas City, near the Arkansas border, and they courted Ciardi both as a contributor to the forthcoming book and as a kindred spirit who was both good company and relatively nearby. In the end, there were visits and many letters, at least partly to discuss Ciardi's contribution to *Lyric Moderns* (which turned out to be "Night Freight, Michigan" from *Homeward*) as well as other books and magazines that Boggs was editing. Moreover, Ciardi enjoyed both Boggses; he was charmed by the rascally Tom, and he flirted openly with the beautiful Rosemary, who flirted right back.

Ciardi did not immediately head east when school ended in May 1940. He spent June and July in Kansas City, taught in the summer session, and wrote to his family on 29 July that he'd be heading for home with Ginny Johnson, who had clearly not disappeared from his life, at the beginning of August: "She's coming down to pick me up and we're going to stop off at her mother's but she'll come along to Boston soon thereafter, if all goes by schedule." He was on a schedule because he had accepted a fellowship at the Bread Loaf Writers' Conference, held at the mountain campus of Middlebury College in Vermont, beginning that year on 14 August and running to the twenty-eighth. The invitation had come from Ted Morrison, the director of the conference, but behind it was the obvious hand of Bill Sloane, who was watching out for his young author. At the 1939 conference, Sloane had discussed Ciardi with

Louis Untermeyer, just then starting a seven-year tenure on the poetry staff. Untermeyer had already moved Ciardi's career along by recommending him for the position at UKC; this time he sponsored Ciardi for one of six highly coveted fellowships. The Holmes-to-Sloane-to-Untermeyer connection was fortunate because from the outset, John Ciardi and Bread Loaf formed a perfect fit.

Bread Loaf had become the nation's leading writers' conference. Its centerpiece was Robert Frost, whose appearances were legendary, although there were always other fine writers for students to mix with and learn from. And, as an incident featuring Archibald MacLeish, the 1933 Pulitzer Prize–winning poet, had shown only two years earlier, literary egos could occasionally clash. Having opened the 1938 conference with a reading of his own, the politically conservative and professionally jealous Frost was not at all happy when MacLeish, a popular, left-leaning New Dealer, was given an evening later in the week for a reading. On the night of MacLeish's reading, much anticipated by the ever-eager audience of Bread Loafers, Frost sat in the back of the room grumbling out loud over this and that about MacLeish's poetry that displeased him. After creating a number of adolescent, attention-stealing disturbances, Frost somehow managed to set fire to some papers he was holding and then made a scene putting it out. It took several hours, another incident over drinks at Treman Cottage, and the work of intermediaries to settle things between Archie and Robert, though perhaps they were never on quite the same terms afterward as they had been before. The mystique of Bread Loaf, however, included the fact that it was peopled with literary legends, like MacLeish and Frost, and that ego-driven literary fireworks were always possible in the rarefied mountain air.

The clashing of literary personalities was incidental to the real business that went on at Bread Loaf, which was two weeks of the most intense study of writing, from the inside, that was available anywhere. Although sponsored by Middlebury College, the writers' conference was not an academic, credit-issuing, professor-dominated experience. Rather, it was a gathering of apprentices who wanted to learn more about their craft by talking to and studying with accomplished writers and people from the publishing end of the business. It was two weeks of ceaseless attention to craft,

what Wallace Stegner called two weeks of "demonic concentration," interrupted only by meals, cocktail hours, and after-hours
liaisons—if then. It was a heady atmosphere, especially for fellows,
who had all, like Ciardi, published at least one book and were therefore privileged to assist in the teaching; probably just as important,
fellows were also invited to sit with the staff in the dining room and
join the staff-only parties in Treman. The other students were
known as auditors and contributors, none of whom in the hierarchy of Bread Loaf could reach the lofty status that fellows enjoyed.
Moreover, Ciardi was in especially good company in the summer
of 1940, for two of the other fellows were Carson McCullers and
Eudora Welty. Ciardi later called his first Bread Loaf a "wonderful year": "I had just turned twenty-four with a tankful of gas-
fumes, a hot engine, no clutch, and a very tricky steering wheel.
Bread Loaf turned out to be the major over-haul of my life."

Meanwhile, after Bread Loaf, in early September 1940, Ciardi
headed back to Kansas City for another semester of teaching. He
added a course in modern poetry to his freshman English responsibilities, but he reported to Ted Roethke in December that it was
"not very satisfying." That semester was even less satisfying than
Ciardi realized because he was reported to the FBI by a student as
being "very Communistic in his attitude." FBI records suggest that
Ciardi knew of an investigation, although probably not the extent
of it. According to the student, Ciardi had commented in class, "I
regret that some of my friends have been expelled from the
University of Michigan—it was not because of any academic work
nor because of any lack of academic work, nor anything that had
been done around the university—it was wholly and entirely due to
the political views which they hold; they are Leftists. In the United
States we are supposed to have free speech and free press, but that
is no longer true—people cannot express their beliefs and ideals any
longer unless they wish to stand up and take the consequences—
that seems to be the situation at the University of Michigan." The
FBI's file described Ciardi with casual defamation as "a stocky
fellow with Italian violence, so that he could be very stubborn at
times. . . ." He was described as weighing between 160 and 170
pounds with black wavy hair "combed back," "heavy cheek bones,"
and a "stoop-shouldered" posture. He was also reported that same

semester by a married woman in one of his classes as a fascist. In December 1940 or January 1941, this unnamed woman attended a class that Ciardi was teaching, and according to the FBI, she reported that "in one corner of the blackboard was a notice of a Bund meeting to be held, giving the place and date. The notice was not in the handwriting of the Subject and the Subject made no comment regarding the meeting. The Subject did not erase the notice, nor did he act as though he saw the notice." Although the evidence was flimsy on both sides and there was a grim humor in the situation, the fact remained that the FBI was actually investigating John Ciardi as a communist and a fascist at the same time. A great deal besides his modern poetry class was not going very well during the fall semester 1940.

Added to Ciardi's problems was a financial crisis. One can't know if he actually spent as much money as he implied when he spoke of traveling the Atchison, Topeka, and the Santa Fe to see his girlfriends, but he reported himself to his family as being so poor that he had to cancel gift-giving for Christmas 1940: "Just one thing," he wrote on 4 December, "all things considered, it seems none of you can afford to do Xmas in any big way. Nor can I. Let's have it completely understood that we won't send any gifts. I want to send Mother a few dollars, but god knows it will be damn little I can squeeze out of the month when every meal sets me back 50 cents and every day piles up 25 cents or so for laundry etc. . . . So please—it's understood. Let's be intelligent about it. . . . We'll just forget it this year."

Ciardi returned home for the spring term 1941, having been granted a leave of absence "to complete a second volume [of poems]," according to the announcement of President Decker. In an unsuccessful Guggenheim application of 1941, Ciardi wrote that he was planning a second book, *Time in Three Acts*, which he projected as "American portraits and observations." He added that Henry Holt had agreed "to hold a place for it on the 1942 Summer or Fall publication list." The FBI reported in late May that Ciardi moved back to 84 South Street on approximately 1 February 1941, and that he stayed there all spring. Letters testify to a Medford address in March, but Ciardi wrote in a number of places that he traveled widely at about this time. Of his two-year period in Kansas City, Ciardi said "those were travel years—Michigan, Chicago, Kansas City, New York, Baltimore, Philadelphia, Boston." On another occasion, he described his travel slightly differently: "I didn't have any money— I sort of lived like a millionaire. There were places people would let me have cabins, here or there, and I'd read and write. That's all I wanted. Or I'd find some place to shack up, which is more of all I wanted." When he was broke, he said, "I'd find any job I could. I drove a truck for a landscaper one year and did odd jobs another year to get through to September with a few bucks, at which point I'd buy a couple of white shirts and go back to teaching for a semester. And as far as I was concerned, this was a very happy life."

In April 1941, when Ciardi visited Tom Boggs in New York, they might have discussed Boggs's latest anthology, *Compass: A Quarterly Anthology of Modern Poetry*, which featured twenty poets, including Kenneth Fearing, Marianne Moore, Malcolm Cowley, Langston Hughes, and E. E. Cummings. Ciardi was represented by two poems, "Awakening" and "Song for the Face at Your Elbow," plus a prose statement at the end of the anthology called "Credos: What Some of the Poets Believe about Poetry." For "Credos" Ciardi wrote, "The time to worry about style and form, it seems to me, is the time one lives through while writing that first thousand poems for the waste basket." He added sentiments he had earlier made to Roy Cowden that "style and form are only adjuncts to the human problem the poet must face. How to find a semblance of order in a world plundered by the contradictions of its political system. Style and form are simply a way of making the human statement more complete and more true. Otherwise they become mere embroidery. Style and form, I feel, *must always clarify by heightening.*"

During their April 1941 visit, Ciardi and Boggs were surely looking ahead to *New Poets* too, which was due out in six months. Containing the work of seven "young contemporary poets" (Ciardi and Boggs plus Marshall Schact, Robert Claremont, E. L. Mayo, Minna Gellert, and Lucy Kent). Ciardi was represented by thirteen poems in *New Poets*. In July he had written from Medford trying unsuccessfully to get ten of the thirteen placed in *Poetry* before their scheduled late October publication. Two of the poems were being reprinted from *Homeward to America* while a third had already appeared in the *Yale Review*. In addition, the two poems from *Compass* were reprinted, although "Awakening" appeared in its full form as "Elegy: For You, Father" and "Song for the Face at Your Elbow" was retitled "Elegy for the Face at Your Elbow." In the elegy for his father, Ciardi showed that he was already wrestling in his poetry with one of the formative problems of his life, his father's death: "O white enduring skull believe / we loved you well." Poignantly, he confessed that "Now we have need of even dead men's blessings"—and he prayed to his father to come back "Into the light, that even fools may see / The end of heaven and the need of Earth." Another of the poems, "Spring in Statue Square," is a Norman Rockwell urban lyric with a jumble of characters that reflect the American melting pot Ciardi had grown out of:

> Spring is open windows and Molly Picardo
> Laughing across the wash to Mrs. Fink.
> And Margie O'Ryan leaning on the fire-escape
> Vacant and wondering.
>
> Spring is forty-seven kids unrolling
> On a square of concrete and sixteen feet of grass
> Between the statue and the wooden benches
> And the iron fence, alas.
>
> Spring is people loitering on the sidewalk
> Slowed down for something none of them will catch.
> And the girls giggling all the more.
> And the boys needing to stretch.

Although Ciardi continued to publish in the little and big magazines and made tentative plans with Bill Sloane to publish a second book of poems, this small collection would be as close as he would get to it until after the war.

There may have been some travel in the summer of 1941; about the only thing known for certain is that Ciardi was in the Boston area long enough to record his poems for posterity at Harvard. Presumably, when the summer drew to a close, Ciardi bought himself a couple of white shirts and headed back to Kansas City for his last semester of teaching before the war. He left very skimpy information about his life or his work during the fall term of 1941, although there was the unnamed dancer at Dorothea Spaeth's modern dance studio and the flying lessons he undertook in October. In addition, he made some tentative plans to enlist in the Army Air Corps, which became a more pressing issue after 7 December when the Japanese bombed Pearl Harbor and ushered the United States into World War II. Ciardi spent the Christmas holidays with Ginny Johnson and her family in Ann Arbor, arriving on 20 December, as Ginny wrote to her parents, "badly run down." She also said that she and John were "building a joint record collection which is kept here and gave each other records for Christmas." She added: "What we will ever do if we get mad and have to unscramble our possessions, I don't know."

The Kansas City FBI during this period managed to find out a good deal about Ciardi through their various informants, both in and out of the university. One professor reported that Ciardi's record as a teacher was "satisfactory" and that he was "well-liked" both by colleagues and students. The same informant reported that he was "of good character, integrity, discretion and loyalty." However, a female member of the faculty reported that Ciardi "was very conceited and did not have the best judgment." She wasn't sure if he was a communist, she said, but "he was not as strong against Nazism" as she felt he should have been. In her view, "he had a great deal of vanity and as such might betray the country for his own gain." A member of the English department determined that Ciardi was not a communist but was "socialistic minded." The most preposterous of the reports came from an informant who admitted that he had never met Ciardi, nor was he in any way connected with the university, yet because it had been "reliably reported" to him, he passed on the rumor that "the Subject was a Communist." Apparently, neither he nor the FBI worried about accepting such coffee klatch gossip as reliable evidence.

Perhaps the most favorable evaluation of Ciardi at UKC, certainly the only one with a signature attached to it, was from Alexander Cappon, professor of English and editor of the University of Kansas City *Review*, who recalled that Ciardi conducted himself well and that he was "independent, charming, and delightful to be with." Ciardi, though a decidedly junior member of the department, seems to have gotten on well with Cappon, who was a full professor. But even though Ciardi published poems and some prose in the *Review*, he wasn't very pleased with it. Ciardi wrote to Arnold Kenseth in October 1941, that he should, "by all means," submit some poems to Cappon for the *Review,* "though wh[y] the hell you want to publish in it I don't know. I told Cappon its name should be changed to the *Pussyfoot Quarterly.* Anyhow I'm definitely washed up with it and seeking a good virile connection with the *Ladies' Home Comforter.*"

The "virile connection" was clearly a joke, yet behind it were some complicated gender issues that surfaced irregularly throughout John Ciardi's entire life. Normally he addressed them only indirectly, as he did here, but virility, both in and out of poetry, was always important to Ciardi. When he first arrived at UKC, he had been interviewed by the local newspaper and said, "The average American thinks a poet is a sissy, and sometimes he's right. But I think that idea is slowly breaking down. There used to be the same idea about artists, but a few men like [Kansas City native] Thomas Hart Benton changed that." However, he went on, poets like Shelley encouraged readers to think "you have to throw your manhood out the window if you hope to like poetry." One line of Shelley's was enough: "'I swoon, I tremble, I expire.' I closed the book." Twenty-one years later, Ciardi was making the same point, that "American [college] boys worry about being sissies." The key to teaching poetry, he said then, was "to find poems that will not insistently and automatically and inevitably offend the sensibilities of an adolescent American boy." Whether Ciardi's feelings on this issue were the result of his all-female home life or his connection to all-male colleges or some generic chauvinism common to his time, the fact remains that for him poetry was an essentially masculine enterprise—and the UKC *Review* had become sissified into the *Pussyfoot Quarterly.*

Ciardi may have been more obvious than some others of his generation in his male orientation toward poetry, but he was certainly not alone. The early twentieth century had a long-standing sense that masculinity was identified exclusively by action and real-life achievement, while poetry, because it reflected a renunciation of the world, was a powerless feminine affair. Wallace Stevens, telling his future wife about his embarrassment over writing poetry, asked that she keep it "a great secret" because, he said, "my habits are positively lady-like." Robert Frost, writing to Louis Untermeyer in 1930 about an anthology Untermeyer was then assembling, commented that he could "advise" on Poe, Longfellow, Bryant, and

Emerson, but had nothing to say about Michael Wigglesworth, Joel Barlow, Philip Freneau, James Russell Lowell, and John Greenleaf Whittier: "A lot of them were ladies then as a lot are now. I wonder if it wouldn't be found at any given time that most of the contemporary fit to go into an anthology was feminine. The girls keep it up and every now and then a boy whoops it up." Moreover, for the adult Ciardi, as perhaps for Stevens, achieving financial success was a gender-driven masculine obligation—which hardly surprises considering that the only example of paternal function Ciardi ever knew was what his mother saw as his father's weekly ten-dollar contribution to his family's well-being. Money was Ciardi's only available measure for success. But whereas a man like Stevens made his money in the masculine world of business, Ciardi achieved his financial success, improbably enough, in and around the world of poetry, which meant that to Ciardi, his risk of becoming a sissy, "positively lady-like," was ever present. Perhaps to protect himself from this threat, Ciardi developed a subconscious defensive posturing, which may be the most cogent explanation for his lifelong macho behavior and clubby, male-only attitude toward poetry.

Paradoxically, however, given his insistent chauvinism and the fact that poetry became a way for him to express his virility, Ciardi's poems offer an endless procession of mothers, for Ciardi, as one reader put it, "is a very sensitive explorer of the female psyche": "his aunts, his sisters, his grandmother, his mother in particular, are not only seen as the keepers of tradition but as daughters of the Great Mother Earth of whom they know the mysteries." Poetry may have been a masculine business to John Ciardi, but women were at the heart of his world.

The United States Army Air Corps

Rather than be drafted into the service, Ciardi planned to enlist, and so on 5 February 1942, it was announced in the Kansas City newspapers that he had been given a leave of absence from his duties at the university. A couple of weeks later, he wrote to Clarence Decker from Medford asking for a letter of recommendation for what he called "the final round of material I need for this Air Corps business." In the same letter he told Decker he would be leaving for Ann Arbor on 5 March "for two or three weeks" to "pour over the finished manuscript of my would be new book of poems [which by then he was calling *Elegy for the First America*] with Prof. Cowden." The manuscript had already been with a publisher for about six months; in October he had written to Arnold Kenseth that "Duell Sloan & Pearce have been diddling with the ms. of the new book and are being very wonderful and unable to say yes and unwilling to say no (unquote) and will I give them more time?" In Ann Arbor, of course, Ciardi stayed the entire time with Ginny Johnson, assuming as he always did, a man-of-the-house posture, this time, as Ginny put it, "finishing a most beautiful job of doing over my kitchen." He was still there on 31 March when Ginny wrote to her parents that John "will be going shortly, a moment that I dread as he will go home to attend to a few things and then into the air corps." She worried because "his coming back is . . . more problematical than it has ever been before."

On 19 May, armed with the letter of recommendation from Clarence Decker testifying to his "excellent character, unusual intelligence" and the fact that he was "an enthusiastically loyal citizen," Ciardi was back in Boston to enlist in the United States Army Air Corps. He said that at that time he still "had dreams of being a pilot," which is why he signed up as an aviation cadet. Enlistment, however, was not the automatic result of signing all the appropriate papers. He almost didn't make it, as Ginny reported the story to her parents: "The crazy idiot. He was told that 190 pounds was eight pounds too much and to come back when he had lost it. He went home, dieted for a week, drank nothing for twenty-four hours before the examination and just before the examination went to the Red Cross and donated a pint of blood to reduce his weight. . . . [I]mmediately afterward he had lost twelve pounds instead of eight and it is a wonder he did not faint in the colonel's lap." For the next five months Ciardi was on call as he waited for a position to open in the aviation cadet program. During the summer of 1942, Ciardi and Virginia Johnson made plans to move her family to Medford. With her husband in the service and overseas, Ginny and younger son Dion actually moved in with the Ciardis at 84 South Street. Her older son Ralph moved in with John Holmes and his family and attended Medford High School for his junior year, then moved back to Ann Arbor for his senior year. When Ralph moved to Michigan, Dion moved in with the Holmeses. The household at 84 South Street in August 1942 consisted of Mama Ciardi, her daughter Cora (plus Cora's husband and daughter), John, Ginny, and Dion. Aunt Cristina and Uncle Alec had by then moved out, and Ella and Edith were married and living elsewhere.

The relationship between John Ciardi and Virginia Johnson was, from the beginning, a serious and deep commitment. It had weathered the storm of Ciardi's loudly proclaimed Kansas City womanizing and endured from January 1939 through to the summer of 1942, when their feelings for each other apparently became impossible to keep in check. But their worlds were also in turmoil. Virginia's marriage, at least to that point, had just about completely broken down and her commitment to Ciardi seems to have replaced it. But Ciardi was waiting day by day to be called into service, which made everything tentative, unpredictable, and perhaps more romantic. It was simply impossible for them to make permanent plans together—but it isn't at all clear that Ginny ever wanted to. For despite her feelings for Ciardi and the problems in her marriage, she apparently did not seek legal separation in order to gain her freedom. But legal questions, emotional stresses, and the uncertainties of Ciardi's future were all secondary to the one remaining fact, that regardless of how it may have looked to their families and the world at large, at that point in their lives, they needed to be together.

In the meantime, the Kansas City Field Division of the FBI reported on 30 July that they expected Ciardi to be called up "within a few days," and the Detroit Field Division reported that he was living at 1362 Jewett Street (Ginny's house) in Ann Arbor. Agents in Detroit added that if Ciardi did not go into the army, they would make inquiries to see "if he is making un-American statements, or is engaging in activities inimical to the best interests of the United States." On 17 December, they determined that because Ciardi had "an Italian background" and because "there is no indication of Nazi connections, the character of this case is being made to reflect Italian sympathies rather than German."

They did add, however, that Ciardi was "quite anxious to go into the service and do his part in the proper execution of the war."

The call from the army did not come until 28 October, at which point, Ciardi said, he was "delivered by slow freight" to the AAF Classification Center in Nashville, Tennessee, at two in the morning to begin his aviation cadet training. He said that he "slogged through the mud for ten weeks of testing" before the army thought better of making him a pilot and sent him instead to navigation school at Selman Field in Monroe, Louisiana, where Ginny joined him as soon as she could by taking a job with the Red Cross in Biloxi, Mississippi, only about three hundred miles from Monroe. In Nashville from 30 October 1942 until 15 January 1943, Ciardi did well, according to the army: his character was rated "excellent" and his efficiency "satisfactory." For the next two months, until 20 March, he completed the first phase of his training (pre-flight school), where once again his character was rated "excellent" and his efficiency "satisfactory." The second phase of his training in Group IV of Squadron V, lasting through early September, did not go as well, and Ciardi was eliminated from the program on "delinquency charges" on 3 September, the day before his class was to graduate.

Considering that Ciardi had done well in the army through 20 March 1943, the sudden turnabout that led to his dismissal five months later is curious at best, a mystery that existing records do not fully explain. He had given no hint of difficulty in a 31 January 1943 letter to John Malcolm Brinnin, in which he wrote in typical good humor that he was in "darkest Louisiana" and "madly in pursuit of becoming a navigator via the maddest curriculum ever known to man. Embellished with such niceties as wearing gas masks in meteorology class etc." Much later Ciardi made what sense he could of the story and retold it this way for the rest of his life: "I finally qualified as a navigator and received an honorable discharge to accept a commission, but the day before commissioning I was called back and busted to buck private. The Dies Committee of the House [after Martin Dies (D-Texas), chairman of the House Un-American Activities Committee since 1938] in its hunt for un-Americans, had turned up my name on those Ann Arbor petitions [one of which having called for the abolishment of the Dies Committee], and I had been designated a PAF—a Premature Anti-Fascist. PAF was then an official Army designation (it may yet be on my service record). In army thinking, it meant that anyone opposed to fascism before the declaration of war on Germany was probably a communist or a fellow traveler." In one retelling some forty years after the events, Ciardi added these details: "When I finished my navigation training, I received an honorable discharge to accept a commission; that's the way you do it. And you go into town for a couple of days, put up at a local hotel, and go back for the commissioning ceremony. And the day before I was to be commissioned 2nd lieutenant navigator, I was called in by the aviation cadet board [and] busted on obviously phoney charges about having had dust under my bed six weeks before."

According to army and FBI records, including what is known as an official "disaffection investigation," the story went a little differently. Ciardi's flight lieutenant during the summer of 1943, reported that he had ability, but was not an "eager cadet": "Subject was described as being irresponsible and missed many formations. During the last three (3) weeks of the navigation school course, Subject made an earnest effort to improve his military conduct in order that he could graduate with his class. . . ." The FBI checked Ciardi's army and G-2 records and determined that he "was eliminated on character and conduct charges and no loyalty issues arose at that time." As far as the FBI could determine, "the basis for the subject's elimination was that he had accumulated seventy-seven demerits for various rules infractions, such as disrespect for cadet officer, [being] absent from retreat, absent from code class, absent from bed check, and absent from afternoon class formation." Finally, they said, the "G-2 investigation states that other cadets in the subject's squadron and the subject's superior officers considered him to be distant, a poor mixer, and a 'know-it-all' type."

Making the 3 September dismissal hearing more dire for Ciardi was the fact that he had been brought up on charges earlier that summer, on 10 August, when he was cited for "unauthorized absence from post" and was put in "confinement" until graduation, which meant only that he was denied leave for the remaining three weeks of his course. Eight days later, he was cited again, this time for showing "disrespect to Cadet Officer, G. B." Ciardi managed to survive the August citations, but not the hearing on

3 September, which he later dismissed as the unfair ruling of a kangaroo court: "I was disturbed by the image of all that brass lined up at the Faculty Board hearing, all solemn and honorable, and all systematically acting out a lie they knew about, but acting it out in full, straight-faced poopery."

On Friday, 4 September, Ciardi took the matter of his dismissal up with Capt. Charles Coble, the commanding officer, to see if he could do anything to contest his elimination. He told Coble he was afraid the real reason for his dismissal was a "run-in" he'd had at the University of Kansas City with the FBI, although he thought "his trouble with the FBI had been straightened out." He told the story of having been reported in Kansas City by a man he'd never even met and that when he was questioned by the FBI, he "blew his top" and "gave a number of silly answers." Coble denied any knowledge of the FBI investigation, however, and the case was officially closed. Maj. William Fritz prepared the final report for the army and noted vaguely, but for the record, that Ciardi's habits had been "unsatisfactory." On the same day the report was submitted, 6 September, Ciardi poured out his frustrations to a friend at the Hotel Frances in Monroe, but the unnamed "friend" turned out to be another FBI informant who reported to the bureau that Ciardi had been "very troubled and depressed" and "convinced that it was not his military record alone which was responsible for his elimination."

Perhaps Ginny Johnson's arrival in Biloxi in mid-April, or slightly earlier, accounted for Ciardi's unauthorized absences from the base. He had, after all, reinscribed Ginny's copy of *Homeward to America*: "Monroe, April 17, 1943 AWOL." It is possible, even likely, that Ginny traveled up to Monroe often enough for Ciardi to take frequent unauthorized trips into town to see her during the summer of 1943; certainly it would have been much more difficult for him to arrange enough time to visit her in Biloxi. Ginny's presence, Ciardi's accumulated demerits, and the FBI files with reports of his communist leanings (which the army claimed not to know about) combined to explain how Ciardi could have gone from "excellent" ratings to "delinquency" charges all in the space of five months. But there may have been something else as well. An eyewitness reported that in New Orleans, presumably on leave, Ciardi was waiting in line to board a streetcar when he saw a black woman being shoved aside by a white army officer. According to the eye-witness, Ciardi punched the officer in the jaw, which, if true, may well have figured into the tangle of events leading to Ciardi's dismissal from navigation school.

In the end, army intelligence considered the evidence very damaging and concluded its report by going well beyond the parameters of the official demerit investigation, noting that a complete investigation might well prove "that Subject is a Communist and potentially subversive." Ciardi may have been undone merely because some by-the-book army officer decided he was "a poor mixer and a know-it-all type"—or because the FBI had characterized him as "a stocky fellow, with Italian violence" and "Italian sympathies." It seems clear, however, that even though Ciardi had been fully responsible for a great many of his own problems during the summer of 1943, especially his unauthorized absences from post, he was right when he thought the case against him suspicious at best. The army had found reasons to do what it wanted to, and it is doubtful that those reasons ever found their way into official reports.

On the day his classmates graduated from navigation school, Ciardi was there to give them their first salutes as second lieutenants. As the new officers passed by in review, each one handed a one-dollar bill to their classmate who had been busted on the last day of training, one hundred in all. They had formed the plan in order to help Private Ciardi pay for the second lieutenant's uniform that he had already bought but would never use.

No documents have surfaced to suggest how bitter John Ciardi was over his ignominious dismissal from officer training and navigation school in September 1943, but when it came time for reassignment, he later wrote that he "bucked for duty on B-29s on the strength of the rumor that they would be based in liberated Italy for deep penetration into central Europe." By 27 September he was already at Lowry Field in Denver for a twelve-week course in gunner training. (Military intelligence had supplied the brass at Lowry with what was called "Adverse Information": Ciardi was "suspected of being a Communist or an adherent to the Communist Party line" and had actually "been seen with copies of the [Communist Party newspaper] 'Daily Worker.'" They added that he was "well-educated, individualistic, [and] talkative," but that he was also "irresponsible" and had a "superiority complex.") After armament school, Ciardi went to central fire control (CFC) school to become as he put it, "a so-called expert in the remote control gunnery system of the B-29's aborted high technology." The CFC gunner worked twin guns on the upper-rear turret, sometimes called a blister and known as the "barber's chair." There were five other enlisted men on board—the radio and radar operators, plus the left, right, and tail gunners. Ciardi did well at Lowry, being promoted to corporal by late May and to sergeant by late summer. Indications are that he liked his new location and his new work.

The Boeing B-29 Superfortress was a showcase aircraft that had been in development by the Army Air Corps since 1939. At nearly one hundred feet long, twenty-eight feet high at the tail, and some 135,000 pounds, the B-29 was awe inspiring in its dimensions. It had a 141-foot wingspan, could reach a cruising altitude of thirty-eight thousand feet, and carry four tons of bombs for thirty-five hundred miles. It featured four R-3350 engines from Wright Aeronautical Corporation plus two GE B-11 turbosuperchargers. It had six generators (plus an auxiliary power unit) that kept 150 electric motors going. And it cost just over a million dollars. It was the greatest airplane of World War II and the most complex aircraft ever built.

But the Superfortress was also overrun with problems. It was a "challenging" aircraft, according to one pilot, Comdr. Charles Hawkes: "I hated it and I loved it. We had a great admiration for its advanced—and untested—technology, its speed, comfort, defensive weapons. She was extremely rugged, but always unpredictable. Every flight or mission had its problems. Forced landings were common occurrences. Sometimes we wondered whether the battle was with the Japanese or the B-29." Pilots were not the only ones to complain. CFC gunner George Gray noted that "malfunctions were commonplace. Guns would jam, overheated barrels would 'cook-off' rounds, electrical systems would burn out." The most frequently cited and serious design flaw of the B-29 was its propensity to catch fire. The fuel lines would vibrate loose and spill gasoline onto the Wright engines, and fires regularly erupted. Ciardi wrote that in training flights he and his crew put out a fire "at least once in every three or four flights," thus giving an ironic twist to his role as central fire control gunner. The Superfortress (fitted out with what the men called the Wrong engines) may have been a technological wonder, but every flight was an adventure. As one historian of the B-29 put it, "they were nothing but trouble." As John Ciardi put it, "I always thought of it as a stirring sight, even when I expected it to kill me."

In early April 1944, Ciardi was moved to Walker Army Air Base between Victoria and Hayes, Kansas. There the individual members of the combat crews were brought together, hand-picked by the pilots and ready to begin the final phase of their training. They remained at Walker for six months; then, shortly before going overseas, they moved to Kearney, Nebraska, a staging area where crews waited for B-29s to come off the assembly line. It was there too that their twelfth man joined them, the ground-crew chief. Aircraft commander Robert "Mac" Cordray said he "looked at John, as the senior enlisted person on the crew, to keep these guys in line—to make sure they did what they were supposed to do." To Cordray, the twenty-eight-year-old John Ciardi (oldest man on the crew) was confident, friendly, opinionated—and, much to Cordray's dismay as an officer, unimpressed by rank. For his part, even though he did not like everyone on the crew, Ciardi saw it as "the one unit in which I felt mortally enlisted." He said they were all "for one another," that they formed "an intricate pact," and he added that "there was no fraud." As he told Studs Terkel, "You belonged to eleven men. You're trained together, you're bound together."

Probably during the summer of 1944, while he was training with his newly formed crew in Kansas, Ciardi got a letter from his old Bates College roommate, Roger Fredland, who was a naval intelligence officer in Washington, D.C. Fredland reported that every one of the men Ciardi had trained with at navigation school in Monroe, Louisiana, had been reported either missing in action or killed in action. Thus a grim footnote was attached to Ciardi's story of his dismissal: in its wisdom the army had set out to disgrace him but only managed to save his life instead. He suddenly saw himself as Lucky John, and in October, just before shipping out for combat duty, he tempted fate by taking out a three-year renewal to his *Poetry* subscription.

From 5 November 1944 (Kearney, Nebraska) to 10 March 1945 (Saipan), John Ciardi kept a journal, a four-month journey into self-discovery, marked at the outset by soldierly brashness and at the end by an ever-increasing sense of impending doom. The first week of entries begins with Ciardi's description of a thirty-eight-hour leave in Kearney, highlighted by a dinner that Captain Cordray had arranged for the crew. "We had a good steak, all the talk that 12 men on a crew can have in common (whiskey, women and airplanes) and O'Hara, Campbell, Saloz and I had too much to drink." Afterward, he called a woman initialed only as DP, went dancing, and then "settled down for the end of a soldier's evening." He went on: "I wasn't too sure I wanted anything as strenuous as sex, but the uniform seemed to demand it." He did the best he could. "I said 'Goodnight' at least four times at spaced intervals and was called back 'for a while.' It seemed to be a tug of war between glands and inhibitions. The glands finally won, but male physiology, uniform or no uniform, is elastic only to a certain point. My glands having been boiling and cooling off all night[,] I'm afraid she got only what I expected—a fizzle from a frazzle."

On 11 November Ciardi and his crew left Kearney for Mather Field in California (their designated aerial port of embarkation), stopping for a one-night layover at Kingman Army Air Field in Arizona. That night Ciardi watched a large detachment of local air cadets perform their retreat parade, and it stirred feelings. The "white gloves, stiff attention, eyes front" were more than he wanted to be reminded of: "All very pretty," he wrote in his diary, "but my year in the cadets soured me for it. Something about a man standing at rigid attention for an hour—or just standing at rigid attention—riles my whatever it is feeling for whatever it is about human dignity. The retreat parade called it all back." Two days later they arrived at Mather Field where they stayed one day, long enough for Ciardi to win $480 at craps (which he converted into eight cases of whiskey), before shipping out to Saipan.

Saipan, part of the five-hundred-mile-long Mariana Islands in the Northern Pacific, lies some fifteen hundred miles east of the Philippines. Originally Christianized by Jesuit missionaries in 1668, the native islanders were subjected to a series of colonial rulers before the Japanese took over in 1914. Only about fifteen hundred miles from the heart of Japan, well within B-29 striking distance,

Saipan became a prize objective of American war strategists. They acted quickly. Two marine divisions invaded the island on 15 June 1944, followed by the army's 27th Infantry Division, which secured the island by 9 July. The Naval Construction Brigade (NCBs or Seabees for short) had only ninety days to repair the damaged island and convert the small local airport into the huge complex, renamed Isley Field, that was needed for the 73rd Bomb Wing. Miraculously, despite the twenty-three days of tropical rain per month during July, August, and September, the job was very nearly completed when the first B-29s began arriving on 12 October. Wing commander, Brig. Gen. Emmett "Rosie" O'Donnell, arrived a week later to oversee the remaining groundwork and organize the fleet of B-29s into four bomb groups with twelve squadrons each—Ciardi serving in the 500th bomb group and 882nd bomb squadron. In all there would be some two hundred B-29s and approximately twenty-five thousand American servicemen on Saipan by November 1945.

There is a lapse in Ciardi's diary from 15 November, when his crew left for Saipan and 25 November, by which time they had become firmly established on the island. In an autobiographical fragment, however, he described what Saipan looked like when he arrived. The landing fields had been built on a high plateau, he wrote, which became "a forest of B-29s, repair shops, engineer shops, radio shops. There was no end to the shops and the B-29s." Below the plateau, the men lived in tents and Quonsets, so there was a constant stream of men walking up or down roads leading to the plateau. Water was trucked in to a central distribution point where a man from each tent would go to fill one can per day. Ciardi's distribution point was called Rumor Park, site of the post office, water barrels, and benches. He said in his diary that "Rumor Park is as much an institution as a location or a sort of curb market for the rumor grapevine. More or less what the latrine was in training camp."

The first bombing mission over Tokyo was on Friday, 24 November, but Ciardi's crew was not in the attack. Over one hundred planes had gone out; seventeen aborted, and six others could not bomb because of mechanical failures. The targets were aircraft manufacturers, but heavy cloud cover, while ensuring the safety of the planes, also kept the bombers from accurately delivering their payloads. In fact, the "precision bombing" they had practiced back in the States was totally impossible because they were flying into the mysteriously unanticipated Siberian jet stream that blew at about two hundred knots. As Ciardi put it, "bombs blew all over the sky, hitting nothing." Ciardi's diary entry for the day after the first mission, however, was filled with Rumor Park "information" to the effect "(a) that we went in too fast, (b) that things went pretty well snafu, (c) some good hits were made, (d) the next raid will be better." Successful or not, the next day's *New York Daily News* headline read: TOKYO ABLAZE AFTER RAID.

On the twenty-sixth, Ciardi got into a barracks discussion with Ed Levin, who thought of himself as a philosopher. "With my private opinion that philosophy qua philosophy is 50% hoax and 50% a legend unintelligibly stuck together by poets without sensuality or gift of language, the discussion stayed wild." His quarrel, he decided was less with Levin than himself: "I seem to have a grudge against the motivating force of all philosophy—which seems to be to reduce everything to a single explanation." Then, too, he thought, "all the 'philosophy' dished out to me at school was too close a cousin of theology. Neither, it seems to me, do well enough by the people on my block, who are usually very nice people when they aren't busy believing that God the Father is going to keep them in ectoplasm through eternity." Then he paused, almost in embarrassment over his reaction, and concluded: "All my grudges ramble, I see. I think I'm reacting to the increase in local religion before a mission. There's something I just can't swallow about immortality."

Mortality, however, was another matter. Ciardi's crew, still untested in combat, spent another edgy week (including a couple of days on Guam), performing routine work, getting misinformation from Rumor Park, and scurrying for shelter during Japanese attacks. The first attack by Japanese fighter planes came on the twenty-seventh and gave everyone pause, for army intelligence had assured the 73rd Bomb Wing that such attacks would be impossible from any nearby island. They hadn't figured, however, on the Japanese launching their attacks from an island called Pagan, some one hundred miles away. Ciardi described the surprise attack in his diary on five action-filled pages: "The four planes highballed down the landing strip with their guns wide open. Then they peeled off and one buzzed over our area. I woke up when a burst of fifties cut loose about 3 inches over my head—I don't see how it could have been more than three inches. My cot is next to the screen door and the first thing I saw was a hosing of red tracers spurting past the door, and all the ground crew boys from the tents above us panicking past our huts to hide in the coral cliffs." When it was all over, he got a good look at one of the shot-down Japanese pilots, and the image stayed with him: "There were pieces of the pilot everywhere. His torso lay off to one side looking like a smokey roast. His head and both arms and legs were scattered around in the debris."

On December third, Ciardi and his crew were roused before dawn to get ready for their first bombing mission; they were taking part in the third big daylight attack on Japan. The target was the Nakajima aircraft manufacturing plant at Ota, northwest of Tokyo. Of the eighty-six B-29s that took off, six were lost, including the one carrying the 500th's commander, Col. Richard King. The *Heavenly Body*, as the crew had nicknamed their plane, would be in the air for thirteen and a half consecutive hours. The first six hours over the Pacific were boring but anxiety-ridden, and Ciardi joked in his diary that there was "too much water in the Pacific," that it had a sort of "gaudy extravagance": "Oceans are all right as far as they go, but this one goes too far to be reasonable." Once over the target area, however, Ciardi didn't look down at the ocean or land for thirty minutes straight as he and his crew fought off about seventy Japanese fighters: "It was a series of blurs and glimpses. Zekes were barreling all through the formation every way but right side up. All the attacks our ship drew were from the nose—from 10 o'clock round to about 2 o'clock. Our ground speed was about 425 m.p.h. and the Zekes must have been doing as much or more from the opposite direction. That made our relative speeds something over 800 m.p.h. When the Zekes crossed us[,] they went by fast." The crew must have known about the frontal attacks of the Japanese fighters from the crews that had gone on earlier missions, but it was nonetheless difficult to adjust to because they had trained on the assumption that the attacks would come from the rear, after the fashion of the German Luftwaffe. When the attacks came from the front, their own wings were in the gunners' line of fire. "The miracle system required time to set in the attacking plane's wingspan and then to track it for two seconds in order to prime the sealed-off computer, but by then any plane that came into view over the wing was out of range."

After the bombs had been delivered and the Zekes fought off, the crew turned for home. About an hour out of Japan, the number 4 engine began spraying oil and continued to do so for almost an hour before it stopped. Soon after the spraying was under control, number 3 engine began throwing sparks. They anxiously watched for fires as they went along, until they arrived safely at Isley Field. In retrospect, Ciardi wrote in his diary, they had all performed well: "I was cockeyed proud of the crew. Not a rattle in the bunch. The interphone clicked off the attacks easily and accurately. Every man was functioning calmly and well and it was a proud thing to know. This is the pilot's air corps, but it takes eleven men to fly a 29. And eleven men have to lose their fear and be sure of themselves before a crew can function. We functioned."

The next day Ciardi became more sober. He went to see a movie called *A Guy Named Joe*, which he characterized as being about "how to die in an airplane," but, he said, it was "too noble." For one thing there wasn't any music up there, only the various jobs that needed to be checked off: "It's not pretty. I resent the Hollywood touch in it. The Jap our guns shot down a few days ago is the way it ends: a piece of jaw here, an arm there, and a dismembered torso smoking like a charred roast. There aren't enough speeches or parades or posters in the world to make it pretty." Moreover, Ciardi had no faith in Lt. Col. John E. Dougherty as commander of the 500th Bomb Wing, chosen to replace the killed-in-action Colonel King. "What sticks in my craw is that it was Dougherty who ordered five EM [enlisted men] to bail out of a burning ship over Nebraska. He then proceeded to land [the] plane with all the officers intact. Two of the boys who jumped were killed. It's all in the chances of war I suppose, but the big thing is that the men were offered no choice."

The early part of Ciardi's diary had been interlaced with the language of cocky courage and the more sobering language of bodies ripped apart and roasted. Within a matter of weeks, however, his fears had begun to predominate; the mission of 16 December seems to have been the turning point. The diary entry for that day opens with a description of the feelings that had begun to grip him. "Somewhere in the last few days time swallowed and disappeared. It began with one of those sudden chemical anxieties. Chemical because there was no rational part of me in it. We were put up for a mission to Nagoya and suddenly I dreaded it. It made a sleepless night and left me cursing mad in the morning and very glad to get under way. Once I was in the plane and touching the things that had to be done, the anxiety was over. I doubt that it will return."

The mission itself turned out to be a thirteen-hour nightmare. The target was a Mitsubishi engine plant in Nagoya, one of the largest cities in Japan. Soon after takeoff, the gunners test-fired their guns and found that two were out of action. Ciardi set about to do the repairs. He worked on them for four hours, but to no avail. When the formation finally reached land, they were eighty miles off course and began "cruising about Japan for better than an hour looking for the target[,] finally heading into Nagoya straight across the middle of a major airfield we were carefully briefed to avoid." The field had a large number of new, twin-engine Japanese fighter planes, and Ciardi watched them as they took off and climbed to fifteen thousand feet at a seventy degree angle. At that very moment the *Heavenly Body* lost number 4 engine, which meant they lost power and fell behind the formation. When the attackers overtook them, they dropped their bombs on a "target of last resort," fought off their pursuers as well as they could, and headed out to sea. Worsening the trouble was that their instruments showed only four and a half hours of gasoline left. "There wasn't much to do but sweat it out." To lighten the ship they depressurized, put on oxygen masks, and got into the turrets in order to collect ammunition that had to be moved through the cabin and jettisoned through the bomb bays. It was grueling work at twenty thousand feet. The oxygen masks were cumbersome and in the way, and Ciardi finally tossed his aside. Though faint, he continued with the work at hand: "The wind was whistling cold through the open turret but I sweated like a pig while the ammunition belts fell in coils around my feet until I was almost caught in my own trap." Finally, "limp with exhaustion," Ciardi and the others managed to get the belts moved to the bomb bays. The men sat back at last. They continued sending distress signals and crossed their fingers as the "Skipper fondled the throttle settings to get the last bit of good out of the gas." When they landed, they learned they still had some fourteen hundred gallons of gas left—either the instruments or the engineer had screwed up. But the fast and furious action on the mission had, at least temporarily, dissipated the "sudden chemical anxieties" that Ciardi had suffered in the previous night.

The unexpected became routine—and increasingly worrisome. During the mission of 22 December, again to Nagoya, Ciardi was manning the lower forward turret as Japanese single- and twin-engined attack planes came at the *Heavenly Body*. "I set my reticle for 55 feet and caught the [single engine] Irving just as he came around the wing. He came in at about 150 yds. I framed him beautifully, tracked him for a second or so and hit the trigger waiting for the plane to blow up. Nothing happened. The orange balls on his wing glared at me and four guns in his nose went past smoking, and my guns hadn't fired." There were forty to sixty attacks in all, Ciardi reported in his diary, and "I played out the rest of the act with blank cartridges."

The same mission provided two lessons on chance that registered with Ciardi and got him to thinking more heavy-heartedly and persistently about the role of luck in survival. First, a radio report alerted the crew to watch out for a downed B-29, which, as they had been taught, "will float indefinitely after a successful ditching." The problem was that this one was not successful: "the sea was pretty rough, and the plane broke"—and under those circumstances, B-29s "go down like stones." The lesson was clear: "It's another reminder that we live by accidents." The second reminder on that mission came when Doc Grow, the bombardier, attempted to drop "11 500-pounders with instantaneous fuses." His warning lights were telling him the bombs had not dropped, so he called Ciardi to verify. "I couldn't get my head into the blister to look out. The flak helmet wedged in the way. I ripped it off and looked out: no bombs. But cruising along 50 ft. under our open bomb bay doors right down the bomb run was one of [our] boys doing a little sightseeing." Ciardi saw at once that "if one of [the bombs] had hit our little friend down below, both of us and a good piece of the nearest elements of the formation would have been making a badly splashed Christmas in and under Nagoya." In fact, they had all been saved because the *Heavenly Body*'s bomb releases, as Ciardi put it, had "frozen tight," which he recognized as more like a "miracle" than simple good luck. Implied in the story, however, was Ciardi's sense that luck can run bad as well as good; it was just a matter of time until the bad luck caught up with him and his crew.

Ciardi and the crew of the *Heavenly Body* were given a reprieve from 22 December to 14 January, while blister burrs were repaired on the airplane. Ciardi recalled later that although other crews were lost during the time the *Heavenly Body* was grounded, he and his crew were virtually on vacation, "out surfing, playing in the ocean, spear fishing." He estimated a 40 percent chance that he would have been killed at this time if the crew had been taking its normal rotation on bombing missions. Then, in an entry marked "Somewhere in Jan. Probably about the 5th," yet another incident occurred that dramatized for Ciardi the unpredictability of war. Ed Levin, the philosopher, was wounded during a Japanese raid on Isley. No one else had been injured by the "buzz bomb" dropped on the runway, but Levin, as Ciardi described it, was hit in the heel "diving head first into an air raid shelter." The injury was serious enough to keep Levin grounded during his crew's next scheduled mission, which it did not return from. Ciardi wrote in his diary about the laws of probability at work: "It's Levin's luck that tells me something about chance. What I think is that you can and should take all precautions, but no precaution in the world will rule out the overwhelming and forever impact of possibility and impossibility that can happen to you." But it was his own luck he was actually thinking about, not just Levin's. As he explained in a letter to Levin many years later, one Toby Brannick had "volunteered me to fly the next mission in your place." But Ciardi had refused—and therefore lived to tell the story. His luck had held again, but the percentages were against him, and he knew it.

War Poetry and Desk Duty

In the second of two diary entries dated 5 January, Ciardi recorded two small events that had large consequences. He had made friends with an ordinance accountant in the armament office, Tony Purtell, because, Ciardi wrote, he had "a good head" and "an instinct for decency without ever being the moralist." Purtell was also a sketch artist, though he called himself, more modestly, a draftsman. A couple of nights earlier, Purtell had sketched Ciardi from memory, and when Ciardi walked in, Purtell saw at once what needed fixing in his sketch. According to Ciardi, "The portrait was right except gaunt and more esthetic and less beefeater than I am." He analyzed Purtell's talent: "Taken apart his sketches seem to be a whorl of formless scrawling lines. But put together they compose." Ciardi was impressed with Purtell's artistic talent, but the word "compose" suggested another art as well. Earlier that night he had been to the base theater to see the life story of George Gershwin, *Rhapsody in Blue.* He had enjoyed the movie, still another art form, but it was the music that stayed with him. "It was a strong thing to hear Gershwin again. It's too terrific. It fascinated me and suddenly it scared me. I don't want to see it again. I don't know what this sudden flood of hypersensitivity is, but somewhere it flipped a lid and scared me. I listened to the Rhapsody in Blue and thought that I didn't want to die. . . ."

The "flood of hypersensitivity" was art, of course. What he hadn't quite framed as a conclusion to his confused feelings was that he had suddenly become frightened that he would die, and instead of being at the beginning of his own promising career as a poet, he might in fact be at the end. The overconfidence of resubscribing to *Poetry* for three years had given way to a more realistic survey of his chances, and it frightened him. It isn't likely he could have been consoled at that moment, but had he reviewed his poetic output since joining the army, he might have been heartened. Certainly the army *had* made it more difficult for Ciardi to be a poet, a fact that he confessed on a couple of occasions. From Selman Field in Louisiana, he had written to John Malcolm Brinnin on 31 January 1943 to thank him for liking a pair of poems that had appeared in the *Yale Review* the previous month. "But I'm afraid, sadly, that they pre-date the life of action. Trying to write in the army has me badly baffled. I simply grow loud and profane. The job of maintaining poise and perspective at double time develops certain complications. I did manage one, I think, good prose piece, one fairish one, and one poem while home on furlough. And a number of sketchy things Virginia is typing out for me to overhaul." And shortly after the war, Ciardi told a newspaper reporter in Kansas City that though he had written some poems on Saipan, "there was a certain sort of lethargy which left one uninspired to do much of anything except to go and come from raids."

However, all during his service years, despite his "lethargy" and being "badly baffled," John Ciardi wrote, published, received awards, and stored up materials for his second book of poems. It was hardly a fallow period artistically. From the time he joined the air cadets in late 1942 until 1 January 1945, Ciardi had managed to publish twenty-five poems in some of the finest magazines, like *Poetry* (three in October 1942; five in April 1943; three in November 1943; seven in July 1944), *Yale Review* (two in December 1942 and one in December 1944), *Atlantic Monthly* (one in October 1944), and *Common Ground* (one in late 1942). In addition, he sent seven poems to John Holmes for publication in his college magazine, the *Tuftonian* (fall 1944). For the first eight poems that appeared in *Poetry* in 1942 and 1943, Ciardi won the magazine's Oscar Blumenthal Prize, accompanied by a one-hundred-dollar check; he received word of the prize in November 1943, while he was at Lowry Field. Ciardi wrote a note of thanks to editor Peter De Vries: "It's really very exciting to be a small part. And twice so against a background of torn down machine guns and afternoon drill." A year later, when he was on Saipan, Ciardi was selected by *Poetry* as winner of its new award, the Eunice Tietjens Memorial Prize, again accompanied by a one-hundred-dollar check. (Barely two weeks before receiving news of this award, Ciardi had written *Poetry* requesting that author's copies and checks for poems be sent to Virginia Johnson, then at the Riggs Clinic in Pittsfield, Massachusetts: "Mrs. Johnson has a power of attorney from me and will be able to negotiate the check.") In his diary for 7 December, Ciardi wrote that squeezed between three air-raid alerts he received news of having won the prize: "I like being the one to start it." Moreover, the award-winning poems had actually produced fan mail, two lonely letters that arrived the day after Christmas. The first letter writer had seen the poems in *Poetry* and wanted to know if there were more he could read, and the second had written "as an admirer and as an autograph collector." Ciardi called the two letters "an accidental juxtaposition of irrelevancies," but preserved them nonetheless in his diary, no doubt more pleased than he let on.

Meanwhile, amid Christmas Eve celebrations on Saipan, Ciardi experienced one of his most haunting traumas of the war. Carrying a bottle of whiskey, a blanket, a flashlight, and some cigarettes, he was walking alone on the beach near the cliffs where the last of the Japanese had fled six months earlier, pursued by marines with flamethrowers. When the air-raid sirens went off, Ciardi scrambled toward the cliffs for protection.

> I pick a cave,
> bottle in one hand, flashlight in the other
> —and there were all the dead I ever saw
> that dying year, where the flamethrowers had left them
> blown back to the inner wall and toppled over
> on one another, sizzled too dry to rot,
> or so I guessed (and maybe sea-salted).
> Which pocket of Hell was that? Drink to them all.

Ciardi had suddenly entered the *Inferno* of Dante and Hieronymous Bosch, a world of horrifying grotesqueries:

> I sucked the bottle dry,
> beamed in on a gape that had no bottom to it,
> and heard the bottle drop, bounce, and not break,
> sucking the whiskey out of me into dark:
>
> inside the mouth hole of the gaping mummy
> a light-tipped tongue wagged chittering!
>   Then the rat
> leaped out and blurred away across the dark
> faster than I could follow with my light.
>
> A half-hour into Hell and most is known.
> Two other tongues wagged and went skittering
> before the raid thumped out, the All Clear sounded,
> and I went sober Sunday'd to the moon. . . .

Ciardi stored that event twenty-seven years before incorporating it into "The Graph," one of the long poems in his verse autobiography, *Lives of X*.

For someone who claimed that the service had left him "badly baffled" about poetry and suffering from writer's "lethargy," John Ciardi was constantly engaged in his art—writing it, storing away ideas for future poems, accepting awards, even getting fan mail. And when he and his crew mates went to the mess hall every night on Saipan after "lights out," Ciardi, according to Mac Cordray, regularly gave poetry lessons: "Most of our nightly sessions eventually became classrooms with John trying, generally unsuccessfully, to share with us the why of poetry." What John Ciardi could hardly have missed, had he given it some thought that January fifth, when he heard Gershwin again, was the consoling and soul-satisfying realization that even in the army, he had successfully made poetry a part of his reality—his life's work balancing delicately with the life of action. But what he experienced that night instead was fear, less of death probably than of the thought that he would miss out on a life dedicated to poetry. That is what caused his "flood of hypersensitivity."

Meanwhile, the blister problems on the *Heavenly Body* were fixed by 14 January 1945, and for the next two months Ciardi's diary continued, but at longer intervals than before. The entries show a man growing more uneasy by the day. The mission on 14 January was aborted five and a half hours out when a supercharger "went dead." Then, a week later, he wrote dejectedly that "nothing changes until it gets worse. Things stayed dull and static and suddenly the news is that the crew is being split up." It was the worst possible news, and Ciardi's entry sounds tired and whipped: "Cordray is going up to Wing to fly a Super-Dumbo, Mike [O'Hara, navigator] may go to group, and somebody's co-pilot is being shoved off on us as A/C [aircraft commander]. I don't like it. I won't do anything until it becomes definite, but if it goes through as first reports have it, I can't see flying. On the other hand I can't see grounding myself." The crew's last mission together was over Nagoya at twenty-six thousand feet, which, Ciardi wrote in his diary, was "low enough to put everything but piper cubs on our tail."

From a military standpoint, however, a soldier's hypersensitivity was far less important than the disappointing truth that the B-29 bombing raids that had begun in November and continued through January had been ineffective. The precision bombing attacks at thirty-two thousand feet had failed in large part because of the strong Siberian jet stream. Accuracy ratings were so low, in fact, that in mid-January Comdr. Haywood Hansell was replaced by Gen. Curtis LeMay, who soon afterward abandoned the thirty-thousand-foot flights altogether in favor of low-altitude runs and a ten-day March fire blitz, flown at five to seven thousand feet—so accurate that eighty-four thousand people died. Ciardi made three entries in his diary during February, each one expressing his misgivings. "What I discover," he wrote on the first, "is that you have to play tricks with yourself to keep going. It produces all sorts of rationalization, and plain intellectual dishonesty." On the thirteenth, he thought back to his days of training and how he had wondered then what it would be like in combat. "The simple fact is that I couldn't have guessed at all. I don't think I even so much as realized back in the States that there was danger enough anywhere for me to die of." And he continued playing the numbers game, figuring his odds for survival: "Imponderable chance became our life. Irrationally we add our losses per mission, derived percentages, forecast future losses, compute the percentages of our survival. And once we had said 50% or 30% it was as if the sybil [sic] had spoken from a cave. 'Even money' we said. 'Or two to one.' And saying it charmed us back to belief in our physical immortality. It was inconceivable that a man could lose his immortality on an even money chance or even at two to one."

The first diary reference to Curtis LeMay, who had come in "with the reputation of having achieved the best bombing results and the heaviest losses of any commander in the Air Forces," came in the last February entry, dated the sixteenth. By that time, Ciardi had run out of ways to talk himself out of the desperation that had set in. Noting that LeMay's first order had been to lower altitudes from thirty thousand to twenty-five thousand feet, Ciardi stated simply what then seemed clearer than ever to him: "I am not a soldier. If I conceive myself to be anything I am a civilian accepting the risks and restrictions necessary to doing a job that must be done before I can return to my own patterns." And the news continued to worsen as "semi-official rumor" had it that the altitudes would be lowered in five-thousand-foot increments until accuracy improved dramatically. Everyone, according to Ciardi, had the same reaction: "This man I have never seen will very likely be what kills me." When he turned grimly philosophical, he saw himself and all the crews as merely the price that had to be paid to achieve the needed end, "and neither longing nor the will to live mattered in the final balance."

The by-then sporadic diary entries sputtered to a close on the fifth and tenth of March. In the first, Ciardi reported nothing much beyond having been promoted to staff sergeant, but in his last entry, he reported on the first of LeMay's fire raids. "The boys are just back from a razzle-dazzle play over Tokio. They left a general conflagration behind them." A fleet of some three hundred B-29s had flown in at three A.M. at about seven thousand feet, each one carrying forty 350-pound "incendiary clusters." Ciardi had not been part of the attack, having "volunteered to cut high card" with two other crew members to see which one would go. When there was a "flare up," as Ciardi put it, he offered to go, but one of the others beat him to it and "had his stuff aboard in a spite." With that, Ciardi abandoned his diary, although he added a fictionalized footnote to the story of LeMay's fire raids in an unpublished novella called "Able Baker Charlie." At a briefing session, the LeMay character announces his fire-blitz plan to his staff:

> "We," the general said, "are in business. Our job is to drop a bomb where Air Force makes an X on the map. One X in ten isn't good enough." He paused again and went on without any gesture, standing carefully without putting his hands on the chair back. "I know that winds aloft have been consistently beyond anything we could have expected. I know and you know that a bomb cannot be dropped accurately through ten crosswinds starting at 200 to 300 knots at altitude." Without letting his voice rise above the monotone, he summed it up: "We are still in the bomb dropping business, however. If we can't hit the X's from 32,000, we have to go down to where we can hit them. Any suggestions?" One of the colonels hitched in his chair, "You, Tom?"
>
> "Ah'm just wondering what poop we've got on predicted losses. Say we go in at—oh 20,000. Whatta we-all stand to lose?"
>
> Carefully the general sat down and picked up his cigar. "I haven't asked intelligence for estimates on 20,000." He held it without topping off the ash. "Only for the altitude we'll be flying on the next round of strikes."
>
> "What's that, sir?"

"Five thousand," the general said.

He could feel the silence surging around the table, as if each chair had become an electric chair in which every man died to be casual.

Many years later, Ciardi acknowledged LeMay's strategy by saying, "damn his iron pants for having been right at my soul's expense." Somehow, incredibly, LeMay had launched five full-scale attacks in ten days, dropping three times the weight of bombs in that period than had been dropped in all the three and a half months of previous missions. By way of capitalizing on his success, LeMay demanded more air time from his depleted corps of crews: they were to fly eighty hours a month instead of sixty.

Although the odds against survival were getting longer and longer, Ciardi took his turns in the line of fire, silently fighting off the chemical anxieties and leaving no record of his thoughts or feelings. Some six years later, however, he filled in some of the blanks in an untitled autobiographical typescript in which he tried to come to terms with the February and March experience. He wrote at length about his fears, especially of burning to death. "I refuse to tell lies to my fear. I insist upon knowing my fear and the particulars of my death. I will look at the place where my hand will split open in the fire and I will touch the place where my belly will burst." He wrote that every mission brought similar feelings: "This might be the day the fire came, flooding down your throat and sinking in under your armpits, and lashing across your eyes, and sing[e]ing the hair of your crotch." In yet another manuscript, he wrote, "My one pride was to refuse superstition. I wanted not to wheedle." The thought of burning to death, "once I had conquered evasion," he said, was not unbearable: "Three bad minutes in the falling fire. Maybe a bit less with good luck or a bit more with bad luck, but a man can stand plus or minus three minutes of anything once he has to. And then it would have been over and that is what it was to be a man, to be, and to be over."

And then suddenly it *was* over.

Ciardi had written in his diary on 23 January about how his instinct for "self-preservation" was kicking up. "I find myself thinking that it's foolish to stick my neck out over Japan when my real usefulness and capability as a·person and as a unit of society is in writing what needs to be written well." He thought it over and decided that he'd "bow out" if only he "knew how to." Simply quitting any further missions was an option, but he would not even consider disgracing himself in that fashion. "All the same," he went on, "I know I'd grab at any reasonable excuse to save face." The excuse came unexpectedly through the offices of a friend, Nick Brown, who worked in the orderly room on routine personnel matters like payroll and sick leave. It was an unexciting but safe duty. Ciardi had gotten to know Nick by bringing his poker winnings to the orderly room for safekeeping. The money, he told Nick, was to buy him a year off after the war to write—he called it a sabbatical. Nick Brown was impressed by Ciardi's self-confidence and self-assurance, and they talked and argued for hours, once on the merits of "ruthless area bombing," which, according to Brown, Ciardi was for and he was against. They also played endless games of chess that Ciardi nearly always won. And, of course, Ciardi talked about poetry and read from early drafts of poems he had written between missions. Brown became so worked up about poetry that he wrote a few poems himself and sent them off for publication; he felt fortunate to have found a friend like John Ciardi ten thousand miles away from home in the middle of a war.

And so, when Lieutenant Colonel Love, in charge of wing personnel, wandered into the orderly room one day and mentioned to Nick that headquarters was looking for someone good enough with words to write citations and awards, he recommended his friend, the much-published poet John Ciardi. In the most sudden turnabout imaginable, Ciardi went from CFC gunner calculating the odds of survival to a headquarters desk man with a sign that read AWARDS AND DECORATIONS. It was even better than it sounded because the army felt it had to lure Ciardi away from his B-29, so they promoted him to technical sergeant and let him keep his flight pay, too (50 percent above base pay), for occasionally hopping back and forth to Guam with reports to the Twentieth Air Force Board. He had passed through hell and found himself in paradise.

For his last six months on Saipan, April through September 1945, Ciardi wrote not only applications for awards and decorations, but also letters of condolence from Gen. Rosie O'Donnell to the families of the men killed in action. The challenge was to make each letter sound as though the general had personally known each soldier, and Ciardi agonized over the work: "I did the best I could. But it was a bland kind of tinkering with tragedy. It tore me up. Some woman somewhere might treasure that lousy manufactured letter for the rest of her life. . . ." Then, in one of those ironic, not to say grisly, twists of fate that Ciardi was so aware of, his former plane and crew went down over Tokyo Bay on the third mission they flew without him. They took a direct hit in the wing gas tank, "and the plane just blew up, disintegrated in midair." In the incredible chanciness of war, Ciardi had been spared because he had been called upon to write letters of condolence—which he then had to write to the families of his own crew. Once again he was Lucky John.

Letters of condolence aside, Ciardi's new job was very pleasant, especially compared to the sixteen-odd combat missions he had flown from late November through early March. He found himself being courted by everyone on Saipan who wanted a medal—courted and bribed. "Soon even full chicken colonels were stopping by my desk to chat and leave me an extra fifth of the bad whiskey they got for $1.10 a month on officer's ration, and for which GIs of the high-tech army paid $35.00 on the black market." The medals received by the airmen were all well deserved, Ciardi added, but not necessarily the ones worn by the upper echelon officers. He wrote in the *Atlantic Monthly* after the war that "many a Colonel is parading today with medals of my concoction, trophies more of my legalism than of his valor."

During the first nine months of 1945, Ciardi's poems continued to appear. The *Atlantic Monthly* published four (one in February, two in May, and one in September), *Poetry* published five in the May issue, and Oscar Williams, in a twentieth-century British and American anthology called *The War Poets,* used four of Ciardi's poems. The May issue of the *Atlantic Monthly* contained the first publication of one of Ciardi's signature poems, "Elegy Just in Case," which he wrote because he preferred to write his own elegy "just in case" he died and went unelegized. In it he has fun with the official language of letters of condolence and avoids self-pity in favor of a bantering, good-humored flippancy. It begins,

> Here lie Ciardi's pearly bones
> In their ripe organic mess.
> Jungle blown, his chromosomes
> Breed to a new address.

This forty-eight line poem bears the Ciardi hallmark in its cleverness bent to metrical form, in its playful bantering, and in what turns out to be its surprisingly serious end.

On 15 August 1945, the long-awaited V-J Day, victory over Japan, was celebrated, although the official Japanese surrender ending the war in the Pacific did not officially occur until 2 September on board the battleship *Missouri* in Tokyo Bay. By mid-September, having accumulated enough rotation points, as they were known, to go home, Ciardi hitched a ride back to the states. In a jubilant mood, he took his small stake of poker winnings and went on a goodbye-to-Saipan gambling binge, parlaying his money, in one of his versions of the story, into nearly four thousand dollars, which he then doubled on a stop at Oahu before leaving on the final leg of his trip to Sacramento. With terminal leave pay and allowances figured in, he said he became a civilian again with more than eight thousand dollars in his pocket. In an undated autobiographical fragment, however, he said he had "almost $12,000 on discharge"— figuring in his gambling binge on Saipan "and one great night in the transient barracks at John Rogers Field on Oahu, when the dice could do me no wrong."

On 4 October 1945, wearing his Air Medal and Oak Leaf Cluster and clutching several thousand dollars in his uniform pocket, Lucky John was discharged from the army.

FOUR

The Harvard Years

1946 TO 1949

Myra Judith Hostetter

Already by 1946, Ted Morrison was an institution at Harvard as director of the university's English A program, the basic English composition class. Some years earlier, Morrison had begun hiring young but promising creative writers, as yet unable to support themselves as artists, a plan that had the dual benefits of improving English A and giving young authors plenty of time to pursue their own work. The appointments were known as Briggs-Copeland instructorships, and for 1946 Morrison had hired Richard Scowcroft, Delmore Schwartz, and John Ciardi, each one a young but already distinguished author. Morrison, of course, remembered Ciardi well both as author of *Homeward to America* and as a teacher with experience and promise whom he'd seen in action as a twenty-four-year-old Bread Loaf fellow in 1940. Preliminary negotiations for the Briggs-Copeland position may have begun as early as November 1944, when Ciardi wrote in his diary that he had received a letter from Morrison. Details were not firmed up, however, until 20 March 1946, when Morrison wrote that it was time for "putting things definitely down on paper," specifying that the position would be "twice renewable giving a total term of three years [which actually turned out to be seven] at an annual salary of $3000." Ciardi was more than pleased by the money, which he said was more than three times what he had earned at UKC before the war—and then he got good news: "By the time I got there in September," he later wrote, "Harvard had raised it, and then raised it again in October." And all this "for no more than I could get done in two days a week."

But in October 1945, when John Ciardi was discharged from the service in Sacramento, he knew only that Harvard awaited, probably for the fall semester 1946, which left him quite a lot of money and the best part of a full year to spend it: "It took me two months to get home on a coast-to-coast tour of friendly girls I knew." He no doubt stopped off in Denver before heading to Dallas where he gave his silk parachute to one of his old flames. Then he headed to Kansas City to see Clarence Decker and all his old friends, including the dancer who talked about "live food and dead food." He probably stopped off in Chicago to see Marion Strobel and the other staffers at *Poetry* and then headed up to Ann Arbor. Finally, just before getting to Medford, he went to see Ginny Johnson in Pittsfield, Massachusetts, where she was still working at the Riggs Clinic. They had not seen each other in something like two years, and there are no surviving records to suggest the sort of relationship they resumed, but she was still married and he had just returned from a swing through old girlfriends, so their reunion, while surely a happy time for them, was no doubt different from what it had been. They both seemed willing, however, to see what might develop.

Despite his plan to spend the bulk of his "sabbatical" year writing, by late November Ciardi was home and restless. He was running, as he put it, "through a lot of ponderous balancing and counterbalance." He was turning over in his mind a financially attractive invitation—almost an urgent summons from Clarence Decker—to teach permanently at UKC, but the offer from Harvard was home, after all, and near Ginny as well. It seemed too good to pass up. Finally, on 1 December Ciardi wrote to Decker saying he'd decided to take the Harvard offer in the fall 1946, but that he'd be pleased to take a single semester appointment (spring 1946) in Kansas City, "if you can use me." Decker took what he could get, and Ciardi made plans to move back down to Kansas City. He stayed with Ginny as long as he could in Pittsfield, leaving finally on 16 January, and although they could not have known it at the time, their relationship would never be the same again.

The student newspaper at UKC reported on 8 February 1946 that "a great deal of interest has been shown in the courses in English composition, creative writing, and modern literature which are being taught by John Ciardi, American poet, who has returned to the University as an instructor." (The "American poet" already that term had a poem in the January *Poetry* and would have one in the March *Atlantic Monthly*, one in the 2 March *New Yorker*, plus five more in the spring issue of the hometown UKC *Review*—a fair enough record for his UKC family to be proud of.) It was reported, too, about a week later, that UKC's "well-known poet" would be giving a reading of his own poems on Friday, the fifteenth, at the drama workshop. About a month later, Ciardi became the advisor of an undergraduate English department club, the Easy Chair. One of his students that term described him as "a tall, very dark haired young man, very intense, with a very large nose." She added that "he seemed to crackle with vitality and for me, he made those classes come alive. You could tell he loved what he was doing, and he wanted you to love it as well." Clearly John Ciardi had slipped comfortably back into the routines of his old school and his old profession.

The 1946 *Kangaroo*, the UKC yearbook, carried a faculty picture of Ciardi with a thin mustache looking down with deep concentration at a book; a couple of pages away was a picture of a pretty blonde with glasses, Myra J. Hostetter, identified as "Instructor in English." Myra J. was better known by her middle name, Judith; she taught journalism and served as director of university publications. Clarence Decker, perhaps trying to spawn a romance with a local girl and thus lure Ciardi into accepting a permanent position at UKC after all, asked his journalism instructor to interview Ciardi "as a returning hero." Ciardi recalled the interview: "[Decker] told her to watch out for me as a brash young man. Miss Hostetter dutifully watched out for me all through the interview, and that night at dinner, and the next night, and the next, and through the semester. . . ." Judith said, "I guess I just led him on. He said it was the Adele Simpson dress. I had a satin striped dress, and in the cafeteria, you had to go around and get your own food. He followed behind me in that dress, and he said that did it." According to Ciardi, what actually did it was the sight of Miss Hostetter when she "bent down to pick a [cafeteria] tray from the lower shelf of the rack." References to the mysterious Kansas City dancer ended forthwith.

Myra Judith Hostetter had been born on 22 February 1923 in

Hannibal, Missouri. Her German father and English-Scottish mother (the marriage a union of Pennsylvania Dutch and Southern Baptist) owned a farm that was at one time some 640 acres in a place the family called "over-home" in Pike County. Judith was a farmer's daughter, but she was also a straight-A student who left the farm after high school to attend Central College for her first year. She then transferred to the University of Missouri in Columbia where she majored in journalism and continued her straight-A work until she graduated in 1944. She had worked in college on the school newspaper, which she called "a city newspaper published by the university," and with so many men away, she got all the work she could handle, as many as three or four beats throughout the city. After graduation she worked for Harry Truman's hometown newspaper, the *Independence Examiner*, and met the future president in the summer of 1944. By the fall of 1945, however, she had taken a job at UKC. When she returned from her January interview with the "returning hero," she reported to her sister Lu that John "was the most gorgeous thing" she'd ever set eyes on. She had been with a boy named Ted in the UKC newspaper office, she wrote in her diary on 21 January, "then John Ciardi appeared—WOW! He has the genuine 'cultured accent' and is the antithesis of what one expects a poet to look like." A week later she announced to her sister, "I'm going to marry that guy."

That semester Ciardi lived in the Epperson House, a makeshift dormitory on campus, and Judith lived with two widows in western Kansas City. As the semester wore on, they began seeing each other more and more—almost exclusively toward the end. They had lunch together in the cafeteria nearly every day, often went to dinner off campus at the Dragon's Eye, and spent free time together at the "Roost" playing pinball machines. They went to movies, formal and informal poetry readings, and Easy Chair meetings. They also served together as faculty chaperones at several student functions and attended faculty parties together. Sometimes they played checkers, listened to records, or just took long walks together. In June, when the semester ended, Ciardi delivered the "Commencement Ode" and left soon afterward for Denver to see Thomas Hornsby Ferril and others he had known during his B-29 training days. (On the day he left, Judith wrote with suitable restraint in her diary, "I hated to see him go—think he was a bit reluctant himself.") Perhaps he thought the air would clear his head. Perhaps, too, it was then that he summoned up the courage to call Virginia Johnson to tell her of Judith and what he was on the verge of doing—"almost to get her approval," as her younger son saw it. By late June, however, whatever doubts he may have had had disappeared, for he returned to Kansas City and at once proposed. On 7 July, he wrote to Marion Strobel in Chicago, "I shall be in Kansas City for the next three weeks at which time a personal apocalypse descends: I get married and leave immediately for the East."

After the couple had gone to the family farm where Ciardi announced his intentions to Judith's parents, the wedding was hastily arranged for 28 July. (A week before the wedding Virginia Johnson wrote to her parents from Fort Benning, Georgia, where she was preparing to join her husband overseas: "John is being married next Saturday [Sunday actually] and expects to be through Ann Arbor with his wife to see Buddy [Ralph, her older son]. We will miss [him], but perhaps they'll have a cute baby when we get back. I'm awfully glad he's getting married. It is time he did.") The two o'clock ceremony was performed by the Rev. Edward Young at the Country Club Christian Church, which Ciardi pointed out "wasn't truly a golfing date: the Country Club is a district of Kansas City." A reception followed at a small hotel nearby. The newspaper reported that the bride "wore a gown of white jersey fashioned with long sleeves and a draped cowl neckline." The maid of honor was Lulu Hostetter, and there were two bridesmaids; the best man was Dr. Martin Shockley, a fellow faculty member at UKC, who served as proxy for John Holmes, a notoriously infrequent traveler, who couldn't make it from Medford. The newspaper noted that the couple would be leaving for Ann Arbor and Boston after the ceremony and that "for traveling the bride wore a black faille suit with white accessories and a corsage of white gladioli." What the newspaper did not report was that Judith had a lingering case of poison ivy and Ciardi had a terrible cold. "So," as the newly married Mrs. Ciardi later described her wedding night, "I scratched and he snorted."

After their honeymoon week of physical discomfort, the newlyweds, having visited Roy Cowden, Buddy Johnson, and the rest of what remained of Ciardi's extended Ann Arbor family, headed east in early August for Medford, where, because of the postwar housing shortage, they "temporarily" settled into 84 South Street. The arrangement lasted two years. Edith was delighted with her new sister-in-law, "a beautiful girl—a real southern belle," she said. More important, according to Ciardi, "Mother fell in love with her instantly." Cora, however, may have been less enthusiastic, for by August 1946 she was married with three children—ages four, eight, and ten—and looking after her mother as well in the seven room, one bath apartment on the first floor of 84 South Street. When John and his bride moved in, they took the bedroom off the kitchen, forcing the others into the remaining six rooms and bringing the total number in the household to eight, five adults and three children. But as Judith observed, "Cora was a very pulled-together kind of gal, who cooked well and was always organized. She liked me and I helped a little bit, but not a lot."

For his part, Ciardi had no trouble becoming part of an extended family once again. "From the start," he said later, "I . . . was concerned, in a sense, with supporting my mother and helping her. . . . This gave me a kind of purpose. And there is no question that a loving Italian family situation is a steadying influence." Contributing to the extended family's well-being, and being, as he called himself in a letter to John Malcolm Brinnin, "America's Most Married Poet," provided Ciardi with the kind of stability he was ready for. He was happily centered in Medford, happily married, happily home with his mother once again, and happily preparing to launch his career, by bus, to Harvard Square.

Writing and Teaching at Harvard

Richard Wilbur, age twenty-five, met John Ciardi, age thirty, in September 1946 at Harvard. Wilbur was a graduate student at the time, and Ciardi "was already a well-known and much-published poet," as Wilbur later put it. But because, he went on, Ciardi wasn't the sort to "lord it over" people, they became friends immediately, as did their wives. They all socialized together, and

Dick and John began an ongoing anagrams contest that they would continue hotly for forty years. According to Wilbur, Ciardi "was absolutely obsessed with anagrams. He used to assemble them on one side of his breakfast plate in those days." But Wilbur noted early on that Ciardi was more family oriented in Medford than professionally oriented in Cambridge. He said that, although "John was esteemed at Harvard, and had his close associations there . . . , it was never his ambition to blend into the Yard or the Square. He lived his own life over in Medford, where he wrote poems for half or all of every night."

Harvard after the war was, in a sense, getting itself started again. Its mood was distinctly progressive, if not actually left wing, in the view of poet Donald Hall, who was there from 1947 to 1951 and studied with Ciardi. John Reed Study Groups were as available as the *Daily Worker*, which the FBI said, Ciardi then subscribed to at 84 South Street. (Ciardi, in Hall's characterization, was not a Marxist, but "an emotional Leftist.") More important to Hall was the literary atmosphere, including especially the presence of Ciardi and Wilbur and his work with them on the *Advocate*, Harvard's literary magazine. Editing the *Advocate* "was a great deal of fun and *very* literary. We'd turn people down if we didn't think they were smart enough." They also ran about six cocktail parties a year, always to honor a visiting poet like T. S. Eliot or Dylan Thomas, but often for little or no reason. "We always invited Dick Wilbur and John Ciardi. And we would get to meet the young poets on the campus, as well as those living in the area, like Dick Eberhart."

Those were, in fact, years of "poetic ferment" at Harvard, as Richard Wilbur has observed: "There were many poets about, too many to name, and they gathered in small evening groups to read their poems aloud and fish for praise. . . . The poetry reading, a form of concert which had once given pleasure only if the poet were of Robert Frost's magnitude, suddenly became so popular that anyone who had published a book or a few poems in *Accent* or the *Atlantic*, could draw a crowd. And these new crowds wanted not only to hear poetry but also hear *about* it in endless symposia." John Ciardi was one of the brightest young writers at Harvard in the late 1940s, and he took his place at or near the center of this literary excitement. But Ciardi's "difference from the rest of us," Wilbur went on, "was that from any stage, he spoke in a fine strong voice, challenging and amusing his hearers, never referring to notes, thinking on his feet, drawing on his exceptional memory for quotations and instances."

Those same qualities carried over into the classroom. John Holmes wrote that Ciardi's teaching was "forceful, brilliant . . . , a rare combination of scholarliness and earthy humanity." Certainly Ciardi's students had high praise for him and even voted him the most popular English A instructor at Harvard. When he thought back to his classroom career, John Ciardi was modest but pleased with his successes: "I never meant to be a teacher. But once I found myself being a teacher, I was moved to try to be a good one. I even worked myself up to a certain enthusiasm about it. When I got to Harvard after World War II, I was very proud of the fact that year after year the confidential guide which was published by the students would name me as the best of the English instructors—or in the top two or the top three. I worked hard at it and I found rewards in it."

Student testimonials confirm the "confidential guide." George Rinehart, of the publishing Rinehart family, found himself in the fall 1946 with a dozen or so other students in Ciardi's English A class— "quite by accident," as he put it. But after a handful of courses with Ciardi, none of the other English professors would do, he said, "not F. O. Matthiessen, not any of them." For Rinehart, Ciardi was "brilliant and inspiring." He recalled that for every hour in class they regularly spent two hours over coffee. And Donald Hall said that "Ciardi was a superb teacher" and that "he took our writing seriously enough to give us a bad time." On another occasion, Hall said that Ciardi "was a wonderful teacher" and that "one wanted to please him." He took Ciardi's year-long English C (Creative Writing) in 1947-48 with classmates Frank O'Hara and Ted Gorey—plus about eight recently returned veterans and a handful of others. "He'd come in with his thrusting, masculine walk and with his green book bag slung over his shoulder. He'd fling it down and flick his long hair out of his eyes." (And on the hair, Hall elsewhere said, "He was vain and he mocked his vanity; he told us he had insured the black lock with Lloyd's of London.") And of course, they all knew Ciardi's work: "It was very thrilling to be able to go in and take the class from this young poet."

Early in December 1947 Ciardi burst into class with the astonishing news that he had sold what Donald Hall could only recall
as "some unimaginable" number of poems to the *New Yorker* and
that he "had made a downpayment on a new car, his first, and if
he didn't watch out, the next election he would vote Republican."
The car was a 1948 black Mercury bought for twenty-two hundred
dollars, mostly leftover crap-shooting money from his army days,
although the approximately five-hundred-dollar, under-the-table
down payment (new cars were hard to come by in the immediate
post-war period and required a surcharge that did not show up on
the bill of sale) probably did come from *New Yorker* checks. By
February 1947, Ciardi had become one of the *New Yorker's* con-
tracted poets, which meant that for one hundred dollars a year, plus
later cost of living adjustments (the March adjustment came to an
additional $30.95), Ciardi granted them a right of first reading. Five
of his seven *New Yorker* poems brought in $315 more that year alone.
Although Ciardi later exaggerated that he nearly doubled his
Harvard salary with his *New Yorker* money, it is true that poetry was
suddenly providing a significant income boost for Harvard's young
Briggs-Copeland instructor.

As successful as Ciardi was proving to be as a money-making
poet, his primary income in 1946–47 was from Harvard, which paid
him, at least in part, to teach—and which he was obviously doing
exceptionally well. But even though, as teaching fellow David Levin
observed from teaching English A with Ciardi from 1948 on, Ciardi
was "refreshing" and "unpreacherly" in class, many a student found
him difficult. One, thinking back on his weekly six-hundred to eight-
hundred-word essays, said "Ciardi literally tore up my papers with
scathing yet accurate comments regarding my writing style." Ciardi
was pleasant enough in other ways, the student went on, but he was
"ruthless in his criticism of my verbosity." Thinking perhaps of this
young man and others like him, Ciardi later wrote "English A,"
which captures some aspects of his classroom manner, as well as one
of his characteristic voices, that of the scolding teacher:

No paraphrase does
between understanding
and understanding.

You are either
that noun beyond
qualification into

whose round fact
I pass unparsed
and into whose eyes

I speak idioms
beyond construction;
or else get up,

fasten your suffixes
and your hyphenations,
buckle your articles,

spray modifiers
and moods
behind your ears

and take the whole
developed discourse
of your thighs to

any damned grammarian
you whatsoever
wish. Period.

Another later poem, "On Flunking a Nice Boy Out of School,"
has even more bite:

I wish I could teach you how ugly
decency and humility can be when they are not
the election of a contained mind but only
the defenses of an incompetent. Were you taught
meekness as a weapon? Or did you discover,
by chance maybe, that it worked on mother
and was generally a good thing—
at least when all else failed—to get you over
the worst of what was coming. Is that why you bring
these sheepfaces to Tuesday?

They won't do.
It's three months work I want, and I'd sooner have it,
from the brassiest lumpkin in pimpledom, but have it,
than all these martyred repentances from you.

John Ciardi was an attractive teacher with a loyal following, but he was clearly a demanding professor, even a scolding one, who had little use for "martyred repentances" and "ugly / decency and humility." He was uncompromising, impatient, and harsh with all those who would not commit to the hard work at hand. Being a student, like being a poet, was a man's work, not the casual pastime of swooning esthetes of either sex.

In October 1946, the outset of his Harvard years, Ciardi worried that his classroom responsibilities would tilt the balance between writing and teaching toward teaching. He wrote to John Malcolm Brinnin, "I'm teaching English A at Harvard and resenting bitterly the way in which themes and conferences pile up on me stifling my time. I've written nothing worth saving since school started." However, as he had overstated the difficulties of writing poetry in the army, so he overstated the difficulties at Harvard in 1946, which scheduled him for classes only at nine, ten, and eleven o'clock on Mondays and Wednesdays. Obviously he had a great deal of time to write, and he did. His 1947 production, for example, included his second book of poems plus at least twenty-two new magazine publications: seven in the *New Yorker*; one each in *Poetry*, *Saturday Review of Literature*, and *Atlantic Monthly*; four in the UKC *Review*; and the remainder in little magazines. With good reason, Ciardi was looking ahead to a career as a poet, so he was genuinely concerned in October 1946 that students were sidetracking him from his true vocation.

Scarcely two weeks after writing to Brinnin, Ciardi's reputation shot forward again when he won *Poetry* magazine's oldest and most prestigious award, the Salmon O. Levinson Prize (including another one-hundred-dollar check) for a poem that had appeared in its January 1946 issue, "Poem for My 29th Birthday," which he had celebrated on Saipan, 24 June 1945. (He commented on the money: "I don't completely understand the basis on which POETRY makes its awards, and finally I'm reduced to a de facto declaration, knowing no way to quibble with a hale check well met.") It is a strong eleven-stanza poem (in its final form) from a lover to his beloved and is marked by the same life-death tension that marks the best of Ciardi's war poems. Its strong opening has Ciardi's distinctive stamp:

> Once more the pre-dawn throbs on engine sound
> Down coral slope, papaya grove, and pine,
> Into the sea whose pastures girdle round
> The native in his jungle, I in mine,
> And you in yours, O gentle stay at home:
> Your talons, too, have raked the living bone.

And also in October 1946, the same month Ciardi complained to Brinnin about the drain students were on his time, *Poetry* published a new batch of his poems, five in all, including "Poem for My Thirtieth Birthday." (All told, in 1946 he had five poems in the *New Yorker*—"A Christmas Carol" from the 14 December issue brought in seventy-six dollars by itself—one in *Atlantic Monthly*, and twelve in the UKC *Review*.) For a poet who was discovering that he was good enough to publish almost wherever and whenever he wanted, any student incursion on his writing time was apparently keenly felt. The frustrating dilemma was heightened by the fact that Ciardi clearly enjoyed his students and their classroom interaction, at least up to a point.

Perhaps the best indicator of Ciardi's poetic activity in the fall of 1946 was the publication of his second book, *Other Skies*, in October 1947. It came nearly eight years after *Homeward to America* and had a much more difficult birth. The manuscript book, which had gone through a couple of different working titles—and which he had worked hard on before the war, had proven to be in the end a frustrating and disappointing experience. So Ciardi approached his third manuscript book with a greater sense of how difficult book publication could be. He sent the poems to Edward Weeks, poetry editor of *Atlantic Monthly* and editor of the Atlantic Monthly Press (a subsidiary of Little, Brown and Company), sometime early in the spring semester 1946, the primary literary result of his "sabbatical" year spent mostly teaching in Kansas City and courting Judith Hostetter. Weeks had sent the manuscript to Theodore Spencer at Harvard for a recommendation, and Spencer had reported on 12 June 1946 "that it would be advisable to publish it, but with drastic alterations." There was much to like, Spencer wrote, including Ciardi's "sense of metaphor," which he called "fresh and compact." He also liked the "feeling for the rhythm of the individual line," which was "frequently sonorous and moving." He saw "honesty and clarity of observation" in the war poems especially and liked the fact that the poems "vary often and well, which is a good sign." If the war poems were not as good as Karl Shapiro's or Randall Jarrell's, he said, "they are better than most others." And he strongly advised certain alterations, including the omission of a foreword and the elimination of some thirty poems, which he listed by name. Finally he suggested several technical changes and marked them on the poems themselves. Despite his cautionary misgivings, however, Spencer favored publication of the book: "Mr. Ciardi *is* a poet, not a rymester [*sic*], and he ought to be heard."

Weeks did not immediately accept the book after he received Spencer's letter. A month and a half later, on 30 August, Ciardi received word from an editorial assistant that Weeks would contact him in early September with the final word on his manuscript. Ciardi wrote back on 2 September that he would dutifully wait, but "I'll bite my fingernails and hope the boss finally takes the ms." A month later Ciardi was still being strung along: Mr. Weeks, he was told, would be getting back to him within ten days. By 23 October Ciardi was getting decidedly impatient. He wrote to Weeks, "I hope you'll forgive my mother-instinct about that manuscript, but I can't help feeling a bit unhappy about Time's winged chariots careening by me." He worried if it might not be the right time for Weeks to return the manuscript "if your best estimate is unhopeful." Weeks's letter of acceptance has not survived, but must have arrived in early November, on pretty much the terms that Spencer had specified some five months earlier. On 26 November, after reconsidering his poems in light of Spencer's suggestions, Ciardi wrote to Weeks that his revised manuscript "makes sense." He had made it "as tight as possible," and brought the total number down to forty-four poems—and offered to compromise still further by allowing Weeks to delete any five additional poems. In the end forty-two poems remained (six prewar; twelve on training; twelve on Saipan; and twelve postwar)—and the book was scheduled for October 1947 publication.

Other Skies featured several of John Ciardi's *Poetry* award-winning poems and is better than Spencer or Weeks realized. It received many very short notices and a few longer ones that were generally positive, although William Meredith fussed in *Poetry* that the poems tended to be too long and the verse "jingly." Ciardi could take little from such patriotically inspired remarks as Frank Hanlon's in the Philadelphia *Bulletin* (7 December 1947), that he was "a worthy spokesman for the thousands of airmen who whirled about the heavens in sun and cloud warfare," but most of the others were insightful enough, despite the murky language of critics and reviewers, to be encouraging. Gerard Previn Meyer, in the 6 December issue of *Saturday Review of Literature*, praised Ciardi's irony, wit, and high seriousness: "In assimilating both the old poets and the older new poets to his own purposes, [Ciardi] has learned how to tune his instrument so that it can give the clearest of voice to the most disparate experiences." The *Cincinnati Guidepost* said *Other Skies* was "mature and virile"; that Ciardi was "skillful and modern"; and that his verse was "tight and thoughtful." Winfield Townley Scott, in the Providence *Sunday Journal* on 9 November, liked the birthday poems especially, which he called a "personal saga without sentimentality, often with a wry edge; and such sentiment as there is is understated." Donald Hall observed in 1955 that *Other Skies* contained "perhaps the best war poetry so far written by an American who was in combat." Critic Edward Krickel saw the emergence of the Ciardi voice as the most important feature of *Other Skies*, characterizing it as "slangy yet learned, irreverent yet concerned, pious before his own holiness but not beyond self-mockery, in short the American wiseguy with a heart. . . ." Ciardi himself thought it "a wry quirk of history" that enabled him to find "some sort of voice as, of all things, a war poet."

The poems in *Other Skies* all rotate around Ciardi's service experience, and many are first-rate: "Ode for School Convocation," "On Sending Home My Civilian Clothes," "Camptown," "Death of a Bomber," "Port of Aerial Embarkation," "Saipan," "Ritual for Singing Bat," "V-J Day," "Sea Burial," plus of course "Elegy Just in Case" and "Poem for My Twenty-Ninth Birthday." The last poem in the book, "On a Photo of Sgt. Ciardi a Year Later," first published in the *New Yorker* on 18 January 1947, has come to be another of Ciardi's signature poems:

The sgt. stands so fluently in leather,
So poster-holstered and so newsreel-jawed
As death's costumed and fashionable brother,
My civil memory is overawed.

Behind him see the circuses of doom
Dance a finale chorus on the sun.
He leans on gun sights, doesn't give a damn
For dice or stripes, and waits to see the fun.

The cameraman whose ornate public eye
Invented that fine bravura look of calm
At murderous clocks hung ticking in the sky
Palmed the deception off without a qualm.

Even the camera, focused and exact
To a two dimensional conclusion,
Uttered its formula of physical fact
Only to lend data to illusion.

The camera always lies. By a law of perception
The obvious surface is always an optical ruse.
The leather was living tissue in its own dimension,
The holsters held benzedrine tablets, the guns were no use.

The careful slouch and dangling cigarette
Were always superstitious as Amen.
The shadow under the shadow is never caught:
The camera photographs the cameraman.

Safely a civilian for a full year, Ciardi looked back at the photo and
saw deep ironies, for the camera had captured a sergeant who was
constructed by stereotyped expectations of what the fighting man
should look like, "So poster-holstered and so newsreel-jawed." But
though the leather holster suited the cameraman's imagination, the
reality was that handguns were of no use to men on B-29s, and
Ciardi used his holster to hold Benzedrine tablets, more useful to a
man who hoped to stay alert on a thirteen-hour flight than a gun
used in ground combat. Realities were not captured in photographs
like this, only the preconceptions and misconceptions of the person

taking the photograph. As John Frederick Nims put it, the poem demonstrates clearly that Ciardi understood "the difference between the heroic and the heroics." And as John Ciardi put it, "The sergeant does not participate himself in the deception he has been posed for."

The UKC *Review*
and Bread Loaf

During the late 1940s, John Ciardi extended his literary life beyond Harvard's classrooms and his own writing desk by working on the editorial board of the UKC *Review* and teaching at the Bread Loaf Writers' Conference. Even though Ciardi had misgivings about the artistic integrity of the *Review* and had called it the *Pussyfoot Quarterly*, and was otherwise unhappy with it chiefly because it did not pay contributors, the journal nonetheless presented him an opportunity for honing both poetic and critical skills, and Ciardi early on determined to continue his association with it as he began his new career at Harvard.

Ciardi's role was as its unofficial poetry editor, unofficial because the editorial board stubbornly insisted on keeping its collective right to reject submissions—much to Ciardi's frustration and disappointment. When Ciardi left Kansas City for Harvard in late July 1946, he was identified on the masthead as poetry editor; the other editors, however, fully expected him to report back with his recommendations for publication and to allow them collectively to make all final decisions. The arrangement was obviously awkward because poetry submitted directly to Ciardi had to be rerouted to Medford. Sometimes submissions would come directly to Medford, leaving the other editors out of the loop altogether. Ciardi wanted the authority to accept at once poems submitted to him, thus eliminating the delay of mailing his recommendations back to Kansas City, waiting for staff meetings to okay his choices, receiving their decisions by mail, and then contacting the poets. When problems arose in editorial meetings—even over such matters as suggesting word changes or questioning punctuation—their system could limp along interminably.

Therefore, when Ciardi arrived in Medford early in August 1946, he immediately tried to take over the poetry end of the magazine—partly because he wanted the power and partly to streamline their obviously awkward system. He wrote to Decker requesting that he be given more leeway to accept poems on his own: "I know you'll see my point when I say that as long as I'm carried on the mast head as poetry editor, I have to insist on picking out what poetry we print. My name carried as poetry editor tells the reader that I selected the poetry. And I do have a reputation that stands for something; I want to keep that reputation meaning what I want it to mean." Decker replied that he and most of the other editors would just as soon "dump the responsibility" on Ciardi's shoulders but that he was afraid of such "long-distance editing," especially because they didn't have a "full-time secretary to keep our affairs straight." He suggested they change Ciardi's title to "advisory editor," adding that he would have all the "power to act" but that acceptances would be subject to the formality of a consultation with his associates on the editorial board.

Ciardi accepted Decker's authority and, reluctantly, his decision, but he continued to chafe under what he considered the unsatisfactory terms of the status quo—until, that is, his associates balked at rubber stamping a batch of poems by Lindley Williams Hubbell that he had recommended to them. In a letter to Decker dated 11 October, Ciardi accused his "esteemed colleagues" of being "a collection from an academic antique shoppe" and said that they "can't recognize a poem as a poem unless it has Matthew Arnold's a priori endorsement." Then, in a second letter to Decker, written the next day, Ciardi took off the gloves and ripped into his "esteemed colleagues":

> As per my minor acidities of yesterday's note there comes
> the question of Hubbell. Who and what my colleagues are I
> leave Time to forget, but I can't escape the conviction that
> here (as in the case of the WTScott poems—in re which my
> colleagues made the same sort of comments) the judgments
> are pre-conditioned by a kind of academic approach that I
> know quite thoroughly: know it because I can recognize it as
> a stage of my own development and further see it as a stage
> to be gotten through.

In the first place I can't see putting poetry to a vote. Case in point: the votes range all over the place on at least fifty per cent of the [Hubbell] poems.

In the second place the approach is too casual . . . ; a batch of poems appears in the mailbox, is dropped on a desk to be glanced at between the sessions of omnipotence that mark the classroom gesture, and the judgments as likely as not depend on the lecture just delivered on Milton's prosody, or on the oration that just summed up and disposed of Crabbe, or just on what somebody had for breakfast that morning. It's too sterile.

And it tends to lean into that academic mind (as per paragraph one) that wants poems to reassert whatever classic proverbs of criticism one has collected from THE GREAT CRITICS.

I'm obviously being arrogant, but as a rhetorical gesture it will serve. Seriously, I must insist that a poem be judged on its own premises. And seriously, I must insist that it's enough for a poem to be interesting. I can't claim any greatness for this collection [i.e., Hubbell's] but I most emphatically assert that they are interesting. . . .

And while I'm being arrogant let me submit my last offer: a good poet is a better poetry editor than the standard college faculty. Let me run the *Review*'s poetry at my own discretion and on my own authority for a year (meaning kill the backlog and let me start fresh) and see if you don't find visible results. My last arrogance is that you'll never find a better man for the job.

When Decker replied politely on the sixteenth that the editorial board, despite its reservations about Hubbell's verse, had all along agreed to defer to John's judgment, he also pointed out that the "academic mind" was not as bad as Ciardi had made it out to be. Moreover, he said, one man in charge of accepting poetry wasn't necessarily a good idea: "Infallibility we leave to the Kremlin, the Ministerio de la Guerra, or the Vatican." And, he added, "your colleagues have received your stern asseverations with good grace." Decker had addressed Ciardi with the sort of disciplinary tone one might use toward a temperamental teenager—and it worked. On 22 October Ciardi sent his apologies:

Notes from the end of a limb.

Well, it was a good try. I grant, and you probably realize, that my little flare of invective was more a political chicanery than an effort at criticism. I obviously want to get my hands on the *Review*, and Hubbell seemed to provide an opening for plunging in with both feet (in my mouth.)

I regret, from this end of the limb, any distaste my piece of bluster may have left in collective or individual mouths. Especially so since I respect, like and admire at least certain facets of each of "my colleagues." That is seriously and literally so, and I should regret it if my over-the-beers invective appeared too solemn by book and bell in the black and white profundities of Remington #5.

The controversy subsided and Ciardi continued as a valuable contributor to the magazine as well as to the editorial board for the next three years. The *Review* published a dozen of Ciardi's poems in 1946, but his contributions diminished in succeeding years: four in 1947, none in 1948, and six in 1949 (four of which he sent along to accompany a six-and-a-half page review-essay on his books). In the winter 1946 issue, Ciardi launched into something new as he began an irregular series of introductions to the poems of selected contemporary writers. His introductions preceded a poetic credo by the poets themselves plus a sampling of their work. From this series of introductions evolved an idea that would become in 1950 one of the most justly celebrated anthologies of its time, *Mid-Century American Poets*. The first introduction was an inconspicuous and hastily written two-page essay on the work of Winfield Townley Scott. In the spring 1947 issue, Ciardi's second introduction appeared, this one to the poems of Cid Corman, and here Ciardi wrote briefly about Corman's "distinct and moving idiom," then his rhythms and imagery. Ciardi seems here, for the first time, to have recognized the opportunity these introductory essays afforded him—and he began to enjoy the idea of having a pulpit from which to freewheel his passionately believed-in messages about modern poetry.

As if to experiment at greater length with his newly discovered talent, Ciardi also wrote a five-page essay in the same issue as his Corman Introduction—"Bach, Brazil, and Bluejays," subtitled "A Notion of Poetic Style." Here he wrote crisply and confidently about poetry, warming to the enterprise as he went along, capturing his own style as a critic and reviewer, and uncovering a lifetime mission in the process. The essay was an amplification of his two-paragraph *Compass* credo and no doubt also a borrowing of some themes and some attitudes and some tones that he had found useful in his workshop appearances and in his classrooms. But for whatever combination of reasons, "Bach, Brazil, and Bluejays" sounds for the first time like the John Ciardi who would regularly write about poetry for the *Nation* in the early 1950s and for *Saturday Review* beginning in 1956. "To the totally unenlightened all poetry sounds alike," he wrote, "all symphony is one garble of sound." What is this thing called style, he asked, and then answered by saying that the "layman's conception" is that style is a combination of "elegance" and "cleverness," which, Ciardi told his layman, equals "ornamentation," not style. "Style has only one enduring function," he announced, "*to state exactly*. Unless it is a precision tool it is nothing." And how does style affect meaning? He said, meaning "is the product of x and y where x is the compound of whatever happened and y is the compound of the person to whom it happened. And the function of style—of overtone, of metaphor, of cadence, of all the suggestive techniques available to the conscious artist[—] is to state accurately that complex xy: not logically, for logic deletes all the peripheral associations that crowd in upon any experience and moves from abstraction to abstraction, but psychologically with all the richness and separateness of the emotional complex that makes up the writer's reaction to the thing he has felt. Style," Ciardi went on, echoing his *Compass* credo, "is simply a way of making the human statement more complete and therefore more true. It is never justifiable as mere embroidery. *It must clarify by heightening.*" The familiar, informative, and entertaining Ciardi essay, lecture, or sermon—delivered after the fashion of a circuit rider on a makeshift pulpit—was beginning to take form.

In the remaining three *Review* introductions, Ciardi took full advantage of what he by then fully appreciated as a rare platform opportunity to get the message out. He deliberately divided his remarks into two parts: the first being his own general commentary on poetry and the second being his remarks on the poets themselves. In the first, "E. L. Mayo—A Modern Metaphysical" (autumn 1947),

Ciardi wrote about the peculiar connections between modern American poets and the metaphysical poets of the early seventeenth century. They both lived in a period "of vast upheaval in men's minds," he said, and both periods were marked by resulting uncertainties that led inevitably to the death of previous poetic forms. "Metaphysical poetry is metrically involved, torturously passionate-cynical-exhilarated, frankly sensuous, and fiercely intellectualized. Its very nature is complexity, but to simplify rather drastically, its central characteristic is *inclusiveness*." The moderns also had a different umbilical connection, to the nineteenth-century French symbolists: "The structure of the symbolist poem is thematic, as in music. It has nothing to do with oratory or logic. It alludes; it does not argue." And it is altogether beyond paraphrase, which he called "a mockery." "It is the essence of symbolism that the symbol should evoke many simultaneous responses. It should never be thought of as aiming at a single logical prose statement any more than Beethoven's Fifth Symphony should be thought of as saying "Considerations of Fate move me deeply." Ciardi had found his message and his rhythm. President Decker rewarded him with high praise: "The Mayo article, in my judgment, is one of the best pieces of critical writing you have done for us, but all three 'Introductions' are good. When you get enough together, John, I think you will have a swell book of essays. . . ."

Ciardi's fourth introduction to the modern poets was "John Frederick Nims and the Modern Idiom" (winter 1947), and the fifth was "Peter Viereck—The Poet and the Form" (summer 1949), the latter a measured tribute to Viereck's *Terror and Decorum* that would later in 1949 win the Pulitzer Prize. The first part of the Nims essay was about poetic diction, the "modern idiom," which he called "the antithesis of 'poesy.' By poesy," Ciardi went on, "I mean a kind of prefabricated poetry compounded of literary reference . . . , poeticisms, and the vaguely degraded echoes of better poems. In contrast the modern idiom sets itself to define in a photo-vivid focus the immediate data of the poet's experience. It strives to see with its own eyes, rather than with the eyes of preconception. It insists on evaluation rather than easy acceptance. It refuses to accept the limitations of gentility or of 'the beautiful,' and it asserts instead its total right to bring into the poem any range of experience down to the scatological, whereas 'poesy' concerns itself only with the pretty or the sonorous." In the first half of the Viereck essay, Ciardi took on the moralists, the readers who insist "that poetry not only 'mean something,' but that it must deliver a moral exhortation to the good life in about the same terms as the catechism, the sermon, and the political campaign speech." He called this "a nonsense from which few readers recover." And then in what would become another building block of his poetic theory, Ciardi wrote that "the final meaning of any work of art exists not in the subject matter . . . but always *in the writer's devotion to his art form* in which there is forever implicit the faith that art is a valuable way of living. This is the affirmation of every work of art." And he could not resist a side-door slam on his "esteemed colleagues" at the *Review*: "The meteorologist has as little to do with the origin of storms . . . as the critic has to do with the making of poetry."

On the last two days of 1948, Decker wrote twice to Ciardi about the forthcoming Viereck introduction, suggesting again that Ciardi collect all the introductions into a book. On the bottom of the second letter Ciardi jotted down that Viereck's would appear in June, "Wilbur for fall." And then he wrote, "Total plan: Shapiro, Jarrell, Wilbur, Mayo, Nims, Scott, Viereck, Ciardi[.]" The next line had four older names: "Auden, Spender, MacNeice, and Eliot." It isn't altogether clear if Ciardi was thinking of his jottings only as *Review* articles or if they suggest that he had by then begun to think about a book like the one Decker was suggesting—which would make it the conception of *Mid-Century American Poets*.

The other literary arena into which Ciardi extended himself in the late 1940s was the Bread Loaf Writers' Conference, at which he taught for the first time as a poetry staff member in August 1947. He had missed the 1946 conference because he was "distracted by a honeymoon," as he put it, but starting in 1947 he returned to the mountain for the first of twenty-six consecutive years. It became the most ritualized event in John Ciardi's calendar year, an annual pilgrimage made during the last two weeks of every August.

The 1947 conference was Ted Morrison's sixteenth as director. He had begun as a staff member in 1930 and 1931 and taken over the directorship in 1932, by which time he had been thoroughly groomed by the conference's first two directors, John Farrar (1926–29) and Robert M. Gay (1930–31) into the Bread Loaf method, the ironic but essential cornerstone of which was that writing could not be taught. Morrison sometimes fretted over the implications of this tenet, but he embraced it anyway, writing as late as 1976: "Instruction will have little or nothing to offer the great originals," and, in a more sobering tone, "on the downright incapable it will be wasted." From the outset, however, this idea had been a tenet of the Bread Loaf philosophy. John Farrar's 1926 statement of purpose, for example, declared the conference's intention to stress "practical suggestions"; the emphasis would be on "professional criticism that should result in marketable writing." The implication was clearly that the conference was intended neither as a beginner's course nor a summer camp for the untalented. By the time Robert Gay prepared his first Bread Loaf bulletin in 1930, it had become necessary to make a more explicit statement, and he spelled it out in the simplest of terms for the customers who indulged in hopeless fantasies of gaining entry in two weeks to an idyllic literary life: "It is impossible really," he wrote, "to teach anyone to write." Perhaps the hopeless clung to the word "really" as though it qualified the idea in their favor. When it came Morrison's turn to state the idea in his first bulletin, he inadvertently hedged a little too. "It is impossible," he wrote, "to teach anyone to write who is fundamentally without aptitude." Morrison, gentle by nature, perhaps thought he was being too tough on the hopeless, for he softened the blow by adding that "most" people "are more capable than they suspect of learning and profiting by guidance." In his last conference bulletin (twenty-four years later in 1955), Morrison's admonition was wordier but substantially the same. Writers all have to learn their trade, he said, "the question is can any planned course or program advance this learning process?" Well, he began politely, a great deal can be gained by "trying out" one's work and having "intensive shop-talk," but the hard Bread Loaf truth remained: "Certainly no course can provide talent where it is lacking; certainly achievement is not the simple result of any teachable formula; certainly no sure protection can be offered against disappointment."

This exclusionary attitude was designed to discourage those who did not have talent enough for "marketable writing," and it reflected the official position of Middlebury College itself. President Paul Moody had written to Morrison sometime before August 1932 to approve the conference's emphasis on professional writing: "I feel that the further away [the Conference] gets from the strictly academic, the better. . . ." After Morrison's first conference, Moody worried "whether we were not almost on the edge of an academic atmosphere," and still later he told Morrison to recruit "more nonacademic people." From its earliest years, then, Bread Loaf had been designed as a uniquely nonacademic educational experience that would bring together promising writing students with professional writers and representatives from the world of publishing for two weeks of "intensive shop-talk"—not for collegiate, student-oriented courses that might falsely testify to talent or certify the untalented as poets. Surprisingly, perhaps miraculously, the unlikely plan of teaching what could not be taught worked to near perfection for students and staff alike. Within ten years this agreed-upon foundation of instruction at Bread Loaf had become a deeply rooted tradition that produced a special atmosphere and philosophy loosely termed the Bread Loaf method. This is what John Ciardi learned in 1940 when he first experienced the magic on the mountain, learning the Bread Loaf method from Morrison himself and his administrative assistant Richard Brown, plus staff members like Robert Frost, Louis Untermeyer, Wallace Stegner, Fletcher Pratt, and others, including Bernard DeVoto (who was just a "visitor" that year) and special speakers W. H. Auden and Katherine Anne Porter.

In 1947, the only year he attended without Judith, Ciardi joined Morrison, DeVoto, Frost, Pratt, and William Sloane, who had joined the staff himself for the first time in 1945. Ciardi felt from the outset that he was joining yet another family, bonding especially well with DeVoto, Pratt, and Sloane. Moreover, he was honored by the invitation and the open-armed acceptance he was afforded. According to Bread Loaf historian David Bain, Ciardi became "a new locus of energy" at Bread Loaf: he "made himself the conference's anchor in teaching poetry as surely as his deep baritone found a place in the evening singalongs." But it was hard work. Ciardi said that even the veteran staff members "will swear the two weeks is as long as the human nervous system can stand the pace. For the lecturers the pace is the most hectic of all. In fourteen days they must deliver from two to four lectures, lead from two to four workshop clinics, read a pile of manuscripts, and hold individual conferences with the hopeful authors. And they must do all this while living in a cruise atmosphere with something forever going on that one dare not miss, and with the talk and the company forever going on into the small hours." After the 1947 conference, a happy but worn-out Ciardi wrote to Marion Strobel at *Poetry*: "I haven't an appetite left—nothing in fact but a sniffle and a slowly returning sense of reality."

As was the case at Harvard, Morrison came to have the highest regard for Ciardi at Bread Loaf, calling him "one of my steadies" and "one of my best instructors." He added that Ciardi "was very fluent, quick witted, and quick on his feet—quick with his head." Intelligent, opinionated, and voluble, Ciardi always put on a good show, but when Dick Wilbur joined him on the staff in 1950 and 1951, their special friendship, their strikingly different personalities, and their shared sense of poetic purism made for some memorable performances from both men. At Bread Loaf the two friends spoke on alternate days: "We used to exaggerate our inclinations so as to make a contrast," Wilbur wrote. "I would pretend to be pure aesthete and very high-toned, and John would pretend to be sort of a growly proletarian. Actually, we saw eye to eye on just about everything." Ciardi was certainly not the absolute populist he pretended to be in those sessions, but he was, in the late 1940s and early 1950s, uncovering a mission: to train the poetry reading audience so that they might be better able to cope with the so-called "modern poets." The "growly proletarian" was as committed to purism as his elegant friend Dick Wilbur, but Ciardi early on discovered first that he could cajole and coax listeners into appreciating poetry, and later, that audiences would pay handsome fees to have him do so. It was a nearly perfect arrangement.

Presidential Politics— and Controversy

The 1946–47 academic year at Harvard was crowded for John Ciardi as he worked on new poems for the *New Yorker* and taught his classes—improved, he said, in the spring term by "a much better reading schedule: Modern Poetry, *Hamlet*, and [Dos Passos's] *USA*." He was also active in the UKC *Review* and at the same time trying to get Edward Weeks to commit himself to

Other Skies. With all this literary activity going on, it is perhaps surprising that Ciardi chose this time to enter politics. First, he became
executive secretary of the left-leaning Eighth Massachusetts
Congressional District Citizens Political Action Committee, which
shortened to Citizens' PAC. Then, throughout 1947 he was also
drawn into the Massachusetts chapter of the even more liberal
Progressive Citizens of America (PCA), which the next year nominated former vice president Henry Wallace and Sen. Glen Taylor
of Idaho for the presidency and vice presidency of the United
States. On 30 November 1947, in fact, Ciardi made a PCA fund-
raising speech at the Hotel Bradford in Boston and raised three
thousand dollars for the cause.

But Ciardi's involvement in the PCA was just beginning.
On 23 January 1948, he spoke to the Springfield chapter, some 250
people, in the local high school. According to the FBI, "Ciardi was
most militant in his speech," closing with a broad denunciation of
universal military training, the Truman Doctrine, and the Marshall
Plan. Less than a week later he spoke with a dozen others to some
900 people in Dorchester, Massachusetts, delivering the collection
speech—a rally-ending role that had begun to fall on his shoulders
regularly because he had proven to be so good at it. In fact, he was
soon known widely as the campaign's "pitchman," or, as Donald
Hall phrased it, PCA's "golden-tongued boy." On 8 February Ciardi
was elected to the National PCA Executive Board and spoke twice
in the following week, first to the Young Progressive Citizens of
America (Boston University) and then to the New England Students
for Wallace (Cambridge). In Boston his thesis was "Truman has
repudiated every democratic utterance of the New Deal." On
14 March he addressed the monthly forum of the PCA and less than
a week later he spoke at the Lawrence (Massachusetts) Citizens for
Wallace meeting. And so it went in the first half of 1948, leading
the FBI to the obvious conclusion that Ciardi was "actively engaged
in public platform work in connection with [the] Mass. PCA and
[the] Presidential candidacy of Henry Wallace."

As Donald Hall recalled it, Ciardi was hardly alone stumping
for Wallace at Harvard in 1948. The much-beloved American literature professor F. O. Matthiessen, "Mattie," was a well-known
Wallace supporter, and there were legions of others. Hall himself
and some of his friends rang doorbells in South Boston neighbor-

hoods collecting signatures to get Wallace's name on the ballot in Massachusetts. Students everywhere could be seen wearing their blue Wallace buttons, but very few supporters became as recognizable in the party as their "pitchman," John Ciardi. He and Judith "had a great time," as she said later, "charging all around Massachusetts." Ciardi said, "I became a firebrand. I was booked for at least one speech or for a fund raiser every night for months." The Wallace campaign was a social crusade Ciardi could become passionate about. Recalling the summer of 1948, when he traveled frequently with vice-presidential candidate Taylor, Ciardi said he did so well that the party promoted him: "I spouted, money came in, and as a reward . . . I began to travel with the great man himself." From that point on, he traveled with Wallace all through the Northeast and Michigan, but during this extended period of close contact, Ciardi gradually came to know his candidate so well that he realized what a mistake it was to support him. Nagging doubts gradually gave way to serious misgivings, and by about the middle of September Ciardi said he finally became certain that Wallace was a bad choice as his party's standard bearer—and would have been an even worse choice for president.

Election year events, however, swept Ciardi along. Because of what was, in the summer of 1948 at least, his rock solid commitment to Wallace, his ability to raise funds, and his position on the PCA executive board, Ciardi was invited to address the national convention in late July 1948 in the home stadium of the Philadelphia Phillies, Shibe Park. It made sense: this was the party's founding convention, Ciardi was a delegate from the Eighth Massachusetts Congressional District, and he was the party's best pitchman. His work paid off handsomely, for just before Henry Wallace rose to address the convention, Ciardi took the podium to announce the results of his earlier pitch—nearly five thousand dollars in pledges and cash donations, not counting "the hundreds of one dollar bills collected in handfuls by the young women ushers." By the first week in August, when all the nominating conventions had completed their business, the presidential slates were finally in place: the Republicans had nominated Thomas Dewey; the Democrats selected Harry Truman; Norman Thomas represented the Socialist Party, Strom Thurmond was the States' Rights candidate, and Henry Wallace was the choice of the Progressive Citizens of

America. However, barely a week after the Progressives nominated Wallace, the Communist Party Convention chose not to put up a candidate and to support Wallace instead. This was a sobering development for all the Progressives who had taken pains (at least in their own minds) to distance themselves politically from the Communists. But for other Progressives, the ones who knew right along how close their party was to the Communist Party, this political alliance didn't matter at all. After all, as one young, idealistic Wallace supporter from Harvard put it rather casually afterward, "A lot of us were Commies or near-Commies."

Ciardi, however, was not. He recorded his own September drift toward the middle of the political spectrum in a number of places, but nowhere as well as in a 1978 interview. By September 1948, he said, he no longer believed in Wallace:

> I became absolutely convinced he was fuzzy-headed, didn't know what he was doing, didn't realize what a grip the Communist Party had over the Progressive Party. I saw railroading and party maneuvering that were chilling. He seemed to ignore these completely. Suddenly I realized that I was not in favor of this man, but I still had all of September and all of October scheduled. There was no way of cancelling. I had to go through nine weeks of political stumping for a cause I no longer believed because I simply did not know how to cancel out. I could have announced that I was breaking with the party, but that would have been used unfairly as ammunition—it would have seemed a betrayal. I played out the string and when I got into the confessional voting, polling place, pulled the curtain behind me, and voted for Harry Truman. I went home from cause forever.

Right up to election day, Ciardi said, he looked this ethical dilemma squarely in the eye, but went on anyway with what he felt he had to do, although the FBI noted on 19 October that he was showing "a notable decline in public activity." Ciardi wrote later that "not even writing Rosie O'Donnell's graveside PR had I been as miserable as I was during those [nine] weeks." Long after he had fully separated poetry from message, the poet's mission from the politician's, Ciardi called his Wallace work his "idiocy," a "case of malignant decency." And, in a 1983 interview, he cast his 1948 political adventure in even-toned self-deprecation: "I was going to be a do-gooder," he said, "and when I look back at it, it seems to me I used up an enormous amount of energy making an ass of myself." However, he mocked, "if you allow stupidity as a virtue, then the motives were all good." Having put his life on the line for his country during the war, Ciardi had felt an uncomplicated patriotic impulse to work for good government—but it turned out to be much more complicated than he had thought it would be.

Although he made it seem so in later interviews and writings, John Ciardi did not exactly go "home from cause forever" immediately after his Wallace fiasco. It took another full year at least before he may have begun to see his political involvements as a problem. Shortly after the election, on 18 November, the gentle John Holmes, in a four-page letter, took his adopted son to task for his political preoccupations. Years earlier he had tried to discourage Ciardi and Harry Hayford from becoming embroiled in the Spanish civil war; poets all had their principles, of course, but they would be wise, their teacher advised, to avoid the topical in their poems and to keep focused on the true business of a poet. In his letter of 18 November, however, Holmes personalized the point: not only were politics fatally extraneous considerations for poems, but in this case they also posed a serious threat to their personal relationship as well. He noted that "a considerable tension" had grown up between them and willingly took the blame for what he called, in his earnest and honest way, "some pangs of jealousy, for your position at Harvard and for your poetry." But he also had "a most uneasy feeling" that Ciardi's work for Wallace was a "mistake." He called Wallace "a sad figure in contemporary history, almost tragic" and surmised that Wallace had been "used by the Communists completely and cynically." Ciardi could hardly have missed the fatherly pain in Holmes's voice as he went on:

> Well, I'm an innocent politically, or worse, a petit bourgeois dope, but I have an odd feeling that you are, too, and are kidding yourself into a part. But this isn't to call you names that I'm hacking this out. I'm trying to show that what you've been doing politically baffles me, and that I distrust it, and that I have an instinctive feeling you're wrong, in a big influential way.
>
> At any rate, I annoy you, and you annoy me, on political subjects, so we don't talk much about it in company, which is

like pretending it isn't there, a very middle-class and timid way of handling uncomfortable things, at which I am an expert. It would be better all round if we really had this out some day, if we could do it without getting sore, but I should think we could.

Then about the poetry, I suppose I'm having with more pain, and less hysterical wounded ego, what old Hillyer had with me—the hurt of seeing a former student surpass his teacher. Not that I ever really thought I taught you anything you didn't know or wouldn't find out—I mean I truly don't take any credit for your achievements, but I'm proud of you. You might possibly have this happen to *you* sometime! In other words, we're in a very complicated relationship where we're in equal competition, and you're doing far better than I am. I'm a late-grower-up, I'm slow to see things as they are, mostly myself; so all this tortuous analysis is part of a process of growth I suppose.

Holmes's letter identified the tensions between them, almost as if he were a desperate father trying to smooth things over with a headstrong, adolescent son, who, though he did not realize it at the time, would resist parental guidance only to adopt it completely later on. Perhaps Ciardi did experience some part of a revelation about Henry Wallace in September 1948, but his complete, antipolitical, Holmesian transformation would not be completed for a number of years. On 22 September 1962 (significantly three months to the day after Holmes's sudden death) Ciardi turned down an invitation to speak at a meeting of the Emergency Civil Liberties Committee and traced some part of the gradual changes that he had by then undergone: "Some time ago," he wrote, "after a number of years of chasing around after good causes, I came to a decision in which I have by now become confirmed: I am a writer, my work is what I do, and once I have survived the distractions of making a living, my writing gets my energy. My sympathies are with you, but to put it bluntly, they are even more with my workbook. If I can capture a thing there as it should be captured, it will stay captured and said, and that capture and saying, I must insist, is also a public cause." It would have been enough to warm a father's heart.

In April 1949, however, Ciardi was still speaking at Progressive Party rallies. In one, he appeared in Maryland to raise money against still pending state antisubversive legislation that had been sponsored by Frank B. Ober, a Baltimore attorney and Harvard Law School graduate. Miffed at what he saw as a Harvard professor's interference in his efforts to hunt down communists, and citing as well Harvard professor Harlow Shapley's appearance at the Cultural and Scientific Conference for World Peace in New York, Ober complained bitterly and formally in a 26 April letter to Harvard's president James B. Conant. Ciardi, said Ober, had taken part in a "so-called 'Progressive' rally" that

> was not debate, but vilification and falsehood—the usual Communist weapons. They attempted to foment hatred and prejudice in the typical Communist way by stating the proposed laws would send people to jail for activities intended to aid Negroes, Jews, Labor, Catholics, etc., etc. No one reading . . . the law could possibly so construe it with any semblance of honesty. Communists were actually using the Progressive Party and the meeting Ciardi was reported to have attended was addressed by Marcantonio and other fellow travelers in the usual way—so he must have been aware of its nature. His own speech was not reported to any extent and I do not know what he said, nor do I know whether he is a Communist, but I do know the meeting gained some respectability by the statement that a Harvard professor took part in it.

Furthermore, he claimed communism was no longer a "political movement" but had become a "criminal conspiracy," and therefore "the test of a professor's actions ought not to be whether he can be actually proved guilty of any crime. Reasonable grounds to doubt his loyalty to our government should disqualify him" for a position at Harvard.

By admitting that he had learned of Ciardi's attendance only by word of mouth and that he did not know, in any case, what Ciardi said, or if he was a communist, Ober made himself look foolish. President Conant replied on 11 May that he supported both professors and that the principle of allowing professors full freedom to pursue whatever extracurricular activities they chose, regardless of how unpopular they might be, was inviolate and irreversible. He announced that he would have Mr. Grenville Clark, "a senior member of the Corporation and a leader in your profession," write to

Ober with "an account of the history and significance of the traditional Harvard policy." Clark dated his eleven, single-spaced pages of tightly reasoned defense on 27 May, and the matter seemed to be put to rest. However, Ober requested that his letter be published in the *Harvard Alumni Bulletin*, which then seemed to necessitate that Conant's and Clark's letters also be printed. And, because Ciardi had written his own long reply to Ober, that letter too was printed. (He wrote with patriotic forbearance toward the end, "I am opposed to the Ober Bill not because it is against communism but because it is against my belief in democracy. . . .") The issue was dated 25 June, but advance copies came off the press a few days early—and, helped along by news service distribution, the story instantly made headlines across the country.

The story broke on Monday, 20 June, four days before Ciardi's thirty-third birthday. The *Boston Daily Globe* ran a banner front-page headline: HARVARD ANSWERS ATTACK BY LAW SCHOOL ALUMNUS. The *Christian Science Monitor* ran a front-page story, as did the *New York Herald-Tribune*. The *New York World-Telegram* carried it on page twenty while the *New York Times* ran a column and a half on page seventeen. So it went in papers everywhere—and John Ciardi, who clearly had not left cause forever quite yet, found himself in the middle of a national brouhaha. Unfortunately, it wasn't for Progressive Party principles, nor for his work as a poet, that he drew so much attention, but for the constitutional issue of his right to teach at Harvard and have freedom of speech at the same time. Aided by Ober's foolishness and the dignified high road that Harvard had taken as well as the forthright statement in his own defense that he had written to Ober and printed in the *Alumni Bulletin*, Ciardi emerged from this episode as a man of principle, his reputation not only untarnished but actually enhanced—and with wider name recognition that could only boost his value as a platform speaker. It could not have escaped his attention, however, that the Harvard Law School Forum did not invite him to speak with Ludwig Lewisohn, Bernard DeVoto, Harry Levin, and others on 7 October on the subject "What Is New in American Literature?" and that they invited him instead to speak on 30 September, when the topic was "Should Communists Be Allowed to Teach in American Schools?"

FIVE

The Harvard Years

1949 TO 1953

Poetry Editor:
Twayne Publishers

The Harvard Law School Forum's invitation notwithstanding, John Ciardi probably did not worry that he was becoming known for the wrong reasons, for no matter how involved he might have become with party politics or the national debate on freedom of speech, he never lost sight of his most important goals. Before, during, and after the 1948 election and 1949 Ober controversy, for example, he continued to send out poems and had ten published in 1948 (six in the *New Yorker* and one each in *Poetry, Yale Review, Harper's,* and *Atlantic Monthly*) and thirteen more in 1949 (three in the *New Yorker,* six in the UKC *Review,* three in *Poetry,* and one in *Harper's*). And, just as the Ober story was developing, he wrote on 10 May 1949 to Merrill Moore, "Is there any chance of getting past that excellently trained dragon at your gate long enough to talk about that manuscript of poems for Twayne? I've signed on as their poetry editor."

Some months earlier, Ciardi had written an article for the *Chicago Sun Book Week* on "The Future of Poetry Publication." Twayne was just then in its infancy, and cofounders Jacob Steinberg and Wang Chi-chen, having joined forces with a per man seven-thousand-dollar start-up investment, happened to see Ciardi's article. They were impressed with Ciardi's examination of the health of modern American poetry—and even more so with his prescription for its future well being: the need for more reliable publishers and regularly scheduled publications.

The young publishing partners had originally intended their first book to be Wang's translation of a Chinese novel, *Dream of the Red Chamber*, but it wasn't finished in February 1949, so they decided to invest first in Ciardi's ideas on poetry publication. On the eleventh, Steinberg wrote Ciardi, offering to foot the bill for the project, scaled down a bit from its description in the newspaper. As poetry editor, Ciardi would oversee all aspects of the Twayne poetry series, including a first-book contest, and receive a 5 percent royalty for each book of poems he guided from acquisition through publication. Ciardi accepted at once and on the twenty-fourth set down some principles that would guide him. The audience, he said, should be "the reader of general culture," the man "who goes to Symphony, is interested in theatre, keeps posted on art and the ballet, and would like to read and understand good poetry. You see, I mean the civilized man." To introduce his "civilized man" to the poetry of Twayne's authors, Ciardi suggested that each volume contain a preface modeled roughly on his own UKC *Review* introductions. Ciardi conceded that his introductions did not contain "brilliant advances in the art of literary criticism," but they did present "sound critical principles in a jargonless and potentially readable way." This was the chief difference, he said, between his own efforts and that of "the Kenneth Burke's and Delmore Schwartz's of criticism"; they were often "subtle and acute," Ciardi wrote, but they were also "imponderably difficult to read." Furthermore, by aiming the Twayne poetry series toward the reader of general culture, the firm would not be competing with the literary "specialist," who was "already very well served by a number of the little magazines and by James Laughlin's NEW DIRECTIONS. There seems to me little point," Ciardi went on, "in competing with Laughlin's millions or with his particular set of tastes."

Twayne Publishers announced on 29 April that it would be attempting "to promote the writing and appreciation of poetry" and that their efforts would be "administered by John Ciardi, well-known American poet." Their first advertising brochure proclaimed Ciardi's dual aims: "To Serve the Poet and To Serve the Audience for Poetry." With respect to the former point, the brochure said that "there is only one service a publisher can perform for poetry: to publish it regularly and with critical discrimination." As for the latter point, Ciardi wrote, "We think our service to the audience for poetry must go beyond the publication of good poetry. We think the audience can be brought to a richer perception of the poem, and that this, too, is the publisher's responsibility." In the fall, Ciardi wrote several letters that explained the concept, which, he said, "is basically a plan to make book publication available to good poetry . . . by promoting poetry on a subscription basis." He summed it up in a November letter to the influential poet-critic Alfred Kreymborg: "In essence Steinberg would provide the imprint [Wang was a silent partner] and I would provide the manuscript[s] and the general philosophy of the library." Ciardi's "philosophy," it turned out, was built on the safe premise that there would be no best-selling books of poems and that Twayne, which had more profitable books in the works as well, was prepared to absorb marginal losses in the name of "firm good will"—although one of Ciardi's functions as editor was to keep any possible losses to a minimum. Writing about potential cash flow problems to Kreymborg a week later, on 28 November, Ciardi confided that he and Steinberg were "taking their rewards in transit, and none of it in cash. I bless Twayne's generosity in covering our deficit, and I bless all who help keep the deficit manageable."

Editorially, Ciardi had more or less written his own job description. He would receive all manuscripts and make final publication decisions, and he would also supervise a first-book contest and see all books through acquisition, development, and production. Certainly Ciardi enjoyed the power of his new position and the opportunity to exercise his poetic judgment, but he also saw his entry into the world of publishing as a potential career move because he knew his Briggs-Copeland position was temporary. In fact, he energetically and enthusiastically cultivated the publishing field for the next four years with this possibility in mind, which explains unorthodox deductions on his 1949 and 1952 tax returns that claimed he had been "building up a business" and that it had been "all out-go." Yes, he wrote, his 5 percent royalties on books already edited did amount to several thousand dollars, but he hadn't taken any actual cash from the business: "I have judged that our need for expansions of one sort and another should have first claim." But he was looking ahead with high hopes:

"Within a few years . . . I should be drawing quite substantial amounts of money." Ciardi's financial concerns, however, while never far from the center of his attention, did not provide the motivation for his work as the creative mastermind of the Twayne Library of Modern Poetry. The obvious and simple truth was that the position could hardly have been more custom-made for his talents; once again he was the right man in the right place at the right time—a new variation on the old Lucky John theme.

Ciardi's first book for the Twayne Library was a reprinting of John Holmes's 1937 *Address to the Living*, advertised as "a distinguished first book now in its third printing." He explained in a letter that the Holmes volume had been selected just "to get things started while other ms[s]. were in preparation." The first winner of the first-book contest was Marshall Schacht for *Fingerboard*—officially selected by F. O. Matthiessen but with a strong assist from Ciardi—from 250 manuscripts submitted. (In late July, Ciardi playfully reported to Jack Steinberg on the burden of reading so many manuscripts: "I shoulda stood in politics.") The other books in the series for 1949 were *Walk Through Two Landscapes* by Dilys Bennet Laing; *Horn in the Dust* by Selwyn S. Schwartz; *Clinical Sonnets* by Dr. Merrill Moore ("one of America's foremost psychiatrists and its most irrepressible sonneteer"); and *Live Another Day* by John Ciardi. The membership bonus for those who subscribed to at least four of the books would be an anthology of the finest younger poets of the 1940s, *Mid-Century American Poets*, scheduled for December release and edited by John Ciardi. It proved to be the most important book of the lot and one of the most durable anthologies of the century.

After the long wait Edward Weeks had put Ciardi through over the publication of *Other Skies* in 1947, *Live Another Day* must have seemed to balance the scales rather nicely. The manuscript was already completed and Ciardi was in process of preparing it for submission to Macmillan, but, he wrote Steinberg, he'd "be delighted to have it done under the Twayne imprint, though I should have to abdicate the seat of judgment in that case and submit it to your decision." In reality, of course, Ciardi had accepted his own book, argued with no one about what to leave out, and included the preface that Theodore Spencer had urged Weeks to omit from *Other Skies*. *Live Another Day* was published in August 1949, and Marion

Strobel wrote on 21 September, "I *like* your book: it's generous and warm and direct; and lord how I do admire that FOREWORD." And poet James Rorty wrote to Holmes that he admired Ciardi's "mind and muscle": "I shall have my son read Ciardi's book. He had a seminar at Chicago with Tate and needs a corrective."

Live Another Day was reviewed widely in newspapers and magazines all over the country and was praised by critics like Maurice Irvine in the *New York Times* for experiences that were "keenly felt, sharply observed, and expressed with wit." (The *Times* piece was a double review of *Live Another Day* and *Address to the Living*, a pleasing link for Ciardi with Holmes in a review that boded well for the future: "The Twayne Publishers start their Library of Modern Poetry with two excellent offerings.") But the good news came from everywhere. The *Sacramento Bee* praised "a refreshing directness"; the *Long Beach (Calif.) Press-Telegram* liked the "sharp and clear pictures of people"; the *Oklahoma City Oklahoman* called it "strenuous" poetry; the *Youngstown (Ohio) Vindicator* liked the "witty social satire; and the *Newark (N.J.) Evening News* said Ciardi's poetry "is a sometimes strange mixture of lyricism and satire, of bitterness and enthusiasm, of personal probing and social sensitivity, but again and again he writes a poem that deserves to be remembered."

The more self-conscious reviewers, perhaps those with some measure of what they perceived as professional status at stake, were more careful with their praise, but they, too, found much to like. David Daiches in the *New York Herald Tribune Book Review* wrote that "Ciardi is a poet of genuine if unequal gifts, whose best poetry has wit, perception and humanity." He noted crossly what he called Ciardi's "rhythmic monotony" but said, with a certain flair of scholarly loftiness, it was "a fault not uncommon in modern poets," a fault shared "with many distinguished modern[s] . . . , including, in some degree, Eliot himself." Once his scholarly reputation had thus been protected, Daiches conceded that Ciardi's "virtues are more individual and more interesting." Those virtues he identified as "a rich yet controlled extravagance" of imagery ("To Judith"); the capacity to be "witty, humane and grim" ("Three Eggs Up"); and the ability to exhibit "charm and tenderness underlying a tragic irony" ("For My Nephew Going to Bed").

I. L. Salomon, in *Saturday Review of Literature*, took exception to "several egregious expressions," but quickly added, "John Ciardi's skillful projections on a variety of themes in various verse forms and the particularity with which he chooses dissonances, not to shock but to awaken the ear, make him an artist completely absorbed by his craft." Then, ending enigmatically, he wrote that the "experimental extremists" might be critical of Ciardi, but "no intelligent reader ought to pass this book by." In a roundup review of seven books for *Furioso* (Carleton College, Minnesota), James Benziger sounded an almost envious note as he confessed some confusion: "John Ciardi, beloved by the *New Yorker*'s editors and by the awarders of poetry prizes, calls his recent volume *Live Another Day*. I find it hard to know how to take him." It was hard because Benziger had trouble with the breadth of Ciardi's talent, the multisidedness of a mind that encompassed many subjects and treated them in various forms, styles, and voices. Ciardi probably "had a lot of fun," Benziger wrote, "trying out many methods on many subjects," but this "conglomerate style" made Ciardi "something of a virtuoso." And Benziger disapproved of virtuosos.

The most important praise, of course, came from John Holmes, whose approval was still, at this stage of Ciardi's career, almost necessary—and whose appraisal this time once again proved to be both honestly felt and intensely loyal: Ciardi, said Holmes in the *Boston Herald*, "is that rare citizen in modern literature, a man thinking and feeling with equal force and value on domestic, political and philosophical levels. He is lively, and he is thought-provoking. He is tender, and he is scholarly, and mean, and true; he has put it all into this book, justifying the belief his readers have always had in him." Such reassuring praise was psychically critical because of their recent political differences and also because they both realized that Ciardi, by surpassing his beloved mentor, was changing the terms of their relationship. They had already begun, in fact, to change places, with Ciardi helping Holmes's career, yet in 1949, Ciardi still needed the unconditional approval of his sub-stitute father—who held up his end of the bargain by continuing to believe in his substitute son.

Live Another Day, dedicated to Judith, has forty-five poems arranged in seven sections and is the most ambitious of the books Ciardi had thus far published, his announcement in effect that he had completed his apprenticeship and had matured as a poet. Eleven of the poems were originally published in the *New Yorker*, and a great many explore aspects of himself in a sort of unplotted autobiographical journey: "Dead Pigeon on South Street," "Homecoming —Massachusetts," "A Visit to Aunt Francesca," "Christmas Eve," "Letter to a Metaphysical Countryside," "Morning in the Park," and many another. The five-page "Letter to Virginia Johnson" is not a personal reminiscence but a coming to terms with his humanism; that is, it represents his formal rejection of religion for the more explainable possibilities of science: "The skies are silent through every telescope / Of everything but arithmetic and hope[.]" In the end, mankind's "final recognition" will not be of God:

> Our Times, that are an end and a beginning,
> Have closed the age of Faith, and need by need
> Moved out of Heaven through the Ionosphere,
> Believing man is prodigy enough
> To be the measure of his own intent,
> Believing the cavalcade to eternity
> Starts gorgeously, but stumbles at the end
> Into the courtroom of the laboratory,
> Where, measured and confirmed, the question stands
> As it has always stood: Man versus Time,
> But now with Man the judge, by need and reason,
> The Age of Evidence in a natural season.

Ciardi's belief in the Age of Evidence, his earth-bound philosophy that abandons any hope of heaven, is developed at greater length in this poem than in any earlier one. Standard concepts of a personal God had long since ceased to be a possibility for Ciardi, and he had gradually come to believe, with the fundamentalist's fervor, in a substitute religion, the cornerstones of which were the dignity of man and the ritual enactment of everyday language into poetry. "Letter to Virginia Johnson" is bold, as Harvey Curtis Webster in *Poetry* put it, because, "so far as I am aware, no other modern poet has attempted to put into a poem the 'faith' of scientific humanism." In the words of Edward Krickle, Ciardi "carries on here the imagery of man as machine," or "man without immortal soul and without

God," replacing the void with "the values of civilization . . . , the values of a man to live by."

Not linked by a single experience, as the poems in *Other Skies* had been grouped around the war, *Live Another Day* is a richer volume in its wide-ranging points of departure and in its boldly stated "Foreword to the Reader of (Some) General Culture." Written with the same zesty prose that he was using in his UKC *Review* introductions, the foreword contained thirteen principles that constituted a minicourse in how to read (and write) poetry:

1. A poem should be understandable.
2. Poetry should be read aloud.
3. Poetry should be about the lives of people.
4. Poetry should be specific.
5. There is no subject not fit for poetry and no word not fit for poetry.
6. Art from which no personality emerges is dead.
7. In a successful poem the subject must create its own form.
8. Whenever a poem seems to be saying two things at once, it *is* saying two things at once, and should be so understood.
9. There is no such thing as a poem that does not affirm.
10. A line of poetry is a conceived unit, not a typographical fragment.
11. A poem is not a syllogism, and its essential unity and progression are psychological rather than logical.
12. Rhyme (internal as well as line-end) is not an appliquéd ornamentation, but part of the total voice-punctuation of the poem.
13. The norm of English metrics is the iambic pentameter line, but the best poetry is written less out of a strict observance of that line, than out of a sensitively trained memory of it with wide variations in the number of light beats in a foot.

Sometime between 1949 and 1964, Ciardi lost faith in his reader of general culture and determined that "the poet owes him nothing," that a poet had instead to be true to "his own sense of poetry. He may be right or wrong, but he cannot be right except in his selfish concern for his own sense of his form." Later still, in 1986, he said that "poetry—any of the arts—is for those with a willing attention and must not be diluted for those who haven't formed an attention." But in 1949, Ciardi eagerly accepted what he saw as a literary mission to help readers form that attention.

Ciardi wrote in his foreword of the celebrated but obscure expatriate poets like Ezra Pound and T. S. Eliot, damning them both as "baroque," which meant to Ciardi that they composed "inward to other writing, rather than outward to the lives of men." In his view, Eliot and Pound, however good and important they may have been, no longer spoke to men as well as their poetic successors did, those of Ciardi's generation. The problem was, in Ciardi's formulation, that educated and willing general readers of poetry had been bombarded with academically praised but un-understandable "modern" poetry for a generation or more and were out of patience with all poets. Ciardi then reasoned that if poetry could no longer be brought to an audience that felt itself spurned, it would be necessary to bring the audience back to poetry through re-education, which then led to his thirteen principles. It was a simple progression.

Simple or not, however, it was dangerous—and Ciardi knew it. In a letter to Peter Viereck, he defended his decision to publish the foreword, even though it might be construed as "literary suicide" by some of the high and mighty members of the critical establishment:

> I have written honestly what's in my mind, and I refuse to trim it into the vocabulary, the attitudes, and the angles of vision that are popular in the newcritical gloss. Some of the things I have said will be attacked as innocent, by critics who will ignore the fact that I recognize their innocence but had nevertheless to report it as part of what was in my mind. No matter: it stands.
>
> I don't think any writer should refuse his own honesty out of a notion that to say such-and-such will be literary suicide. Everybody is so goddamn restrained. I among them. For Christ sake let's get literature out of the cathedral and have some good sidewalk wrangles about it. . . . The keepers of the castrate Eucharist are going to go into some sort of ritual of excommunication, but fuck 'em I say. You have gusto left, and I hope I have too, and I'm willing to stand by the sense that tells me that gusto is better than the Partisan and the Kenyon.

The letter demonstrates Ciardi's strong sense of purpose and his courage, of course, but it also shows a developing belligerence, a chin-forward challenge to all those who disagreed with him and had nerve enough to take their best shot.

Meanwhile, Ciardi had not forgotten the book-length collection of UKC *Review* introductions Clarence Decker had suggested more than once that he put together. In mid-April 1949, Ciardi began to think seriously again about the project. By then, he had already agreed to terms with Jack Steinberg about the Twayne position and was in the process of reconceiving his set of introductions into an anthology for Twayne, *Mid-Century American Poets*, that would be used as a bonus book for those who subscribed to the Twayne Library of Modern Poetry. He hoped the book—whatever it turned out to be—would also find its own identity as a trade book and fit nicely into college courses as a text on modern poetry as well.

On 15 April 1949, Ciardi brought his new book idea to a select group of friends, who, from about 1948 to 1951, met monthly to discuss and criticize one another's most recent poems. The number of poets in the group swelled occasionally when a visitor like Archibald MacLeish showed up, but for the most part the members were John Holmes, Richard Eberhart, and Ciardi at first, with Richard Wilbur joining soon after, and May Sarton probably joining as a regular some time late in 1949. (Sarton's sensitivity to loudly spoken criticism was a sore point with Ciardi, who felt that for a poet, "slugging is the way to train." He complained to Dudley Fitts in 1955 that it had taken "over a year before the members had stopped being polite. Then May Sarton entered and everybody had to start being polite again. Shit on the trembling reeds.") When the group met on 15 April, before Sarton had joined them, they discussed what Ciardi had come to think of as a 1940s anthology, and on the next day he followed up with letters to Eberhart and Wilbur going over the details once again, just "to put my notions on paper for you." He figured on about ten poems from each poet plus "a statement of working principles" that should be written "free of technical terms of literary criticism." He saw the book as a "round-up of the best poets who emerged in the forties or have done their principle writing in the forties." Most important, like his own foreword in *Live Another Day*, the anthology would be "aimed at the unspecialized but willing reader who might be led to a more alert participation in the poem if he could be given some guidance. . . . I think it can be a good service to poetry and an exciting anthology in general." He was right on both counts.

For the next several months the Ciardi correspondence file is filled with letters to and from the fourteen poets, in addition to himself, who would be appearing in *Mid-Century American Poets*: Holmes, Eberhart, and Wilbur, of course; another group that might easily have been predicted: Theodore Roethke, John Frederick Nims, W. T. Scott, E. L. Mayo, and Peter Viereck; plus a final group Ciardi seems to have had little or no previous contact with: Muriel Rukeyser, Karl Shapiro, Elizabeth Bishop, Delmore Schwartz, Randall Jarrell, and Robert Lowell. In his correspondence with this distinguished gathering of poets, Ciardi again and again returned to the importance of the reader, as here to Karl Shapiro: "My special concern is for the reader of poetry: I cannot escape a feeling that the poets must face the responsibility of providing themselves with a wider audience. That does not mean an all inclusive audience. I mean that with a little less spitting in the reader's eye, and with a little more frank statement of premises, dilemmas, theories, and hopes, a considerable and valuable number of readers could come much closer to understanding and participating in good poetry."

The poets were all pleased to have been selected for the anthology and ready enough to select poems for it, but Ciardi had to cajole several of them, not always successfully, in long letters in order to get some sort of coherent statement of principles that they adhered to. He even prepared fifteen questions to get each poet started, ranging from subject matter, diction, and "spoken quality" to such structural concerns as form, imagery, symbolism, rhythm, and rhyme. He was also interested in knowing how "difficult" the poets were willing to be, what their sense of a line was, and how they treated different levels of meaning. There may have been only fifteen questions, but they were all-inclusive and were intended to help the poets draw out their own working procedures. Ciardi had already written his own statement, which turned out to be a reprint of the forthcoming *Live Another Day* foreword, and so he may therefore have underestimated the difficulties such a proposal would pose for some of the others. And he may also have overestimated the value of such an enterprise. As Richard Wilbur pointed out on the first page of his statement, "Works of art can almost never be truthfully described as applications of principles. They are not coerced into being by rational principles, but spring from imagination, a condition of spontaneous psychic unity." But even with that caveat, Wilbur saw value in the effort and worked out what answers he could in seven full pages.

Shapiro, however, claimed in early July that he couldn't bring himself to do it "without a physical revulsion to the whole business." As late as a month after the September first deadline for submissions, Delmore Schwartz was still writing lamely that he was going through a "new phase" and couldn't do more than say that James Joyce's *Finnegan's Wake* "is the beginning of a new era in the writing of poetry." Elizabeth Bishop managed to say "it all depends" to all but two of the questions. In the end, after much breast beating and many false starts, Shapiro wrote nothing, although he did submit a poem with an earlier draft from which a reader might perhaps deduce some working principles; Lowell begged off entirely because he was feeling "pretty numb," but allowed a Jarrell essay on him to be reprinted; Viereck went on for fifteen pages of self-promotion; and all the rest tried as they could to say something about the way they wrote poems. Remarkably enough, however, when the statements are taken all together, including a new twenty-one-page introduction by Ciardi, they constitute an unprecedented effort by good poets to identify something like the poetics of their generation.

In his introduction to *Mid-Century*, Ciardi appears in his classic pose as intermediary between the modern poets and the educated-but-not-literary readers who need some help. In Richard Wilbur's view, Ciardi's introduction was different from other such introductions because it wasn't for a "highbrow" audience. Instead, "it was recruiting-literature, aimed at intelligent lay persons who needed to be taught how to read poems, how to despise uplift and sentimentality, how to constitute an audience for a new American poetry which, John felt, had at last outgrown the English influence and could treat of realities in a charged version of our native speech."

Ciardi began the general introduction to *Mid-Century* with a teacherly lecture, its breeziness bordering on the peremptory, that surveyed nineteenth-century America's failure to write poetry equal to nineteenth-century England's. In the middle of the twentieth century, he said, "it must be evident to all who care to look that America has achieved an important body of poetry." And it was just as evident, he went on, "that the nineteenth century in America failed to do so." He spoke approvingly of Whitman's "barbaric yawp" as a proper antitdote against the genteel tradition, although it no longer served the same function for modern poets, who had come to the conclusion that the yawp was, "if not an unreal, at least an unrewarding attitude." Moreover, the new poets had captured the "American voice-box." Just as Robert Frost's poems were possible only because he had grown up "with New England in his mouth," so could "the poems of the poets here presented . . . only have been written by men who grew up with American suburb and metropolis and countryside in their speech, *and who had been prepared by their literary ancestors to detect the poetic possibilities of that speech*." Finally, the modern poets had inherited "the ferment of technique" from Ezra Pound, disillusionment's "high priest," whose slogan of "Make it new," had reinvigorated poetry and left midcentury poets "with a stock of techniques richer and more varied than any that had earlier been available to American writers."

The introduction's five-page historical survey was chancy but engaging; it oversimplified and misunderstood some of the significances of nineteenth-century American poetry, but it made up in enthusiasm what it may have lacked in fairness. And that was just the beginning. In part 2 of the introduction, Ciardi took his average reader by the hand and led him through a short course in poetry reading: "I should like to discuss some of the specific ways in which I have observed readers to misbehave towards the poem." And to do so, he began with a nursery rhyme:

> Hickory, dickory, dock,
> The mouse ran up the clock.
> The clock struck one,
> And down he run.
> Hickory, dickory, dock.

Ciardi then demonstrated, neatly and cleverly, that the verse is not as simple as it appears to be, but is rather the product of a long list of decisions: "Why a clock? Why a mouse? Isn't it fairly unusual for mice to run up clocks? What is the point of inventing this esoteric incident?" Eleven more questions followed, plus his own parody written to illustrate his points, and Ciardi was off and running. Five propositions later, Ciardi's triumph came. Attempting to show the reader how to judge good poetry from bad, he established the difference between poetry and poesy (as he had earlier done in his *Review* introduction of Nims), the latter being the sort of versifying admired by "the ladies of the poetry societies." To demonstrate the point, he wrote a sonnet (their favorite form, he said), in poesy:

Threnody

Truth is a golden sunset far away
Above the misty hills. Its burning eye
Lights all the fading world. A bird flies by
Alive and singing on the dying day.
Oh mystic world, what shall the proud heart say
When beauty flies on beauty beautifully
While blue-gold hills look down to watch it die
Into the falling miracle of clay?

Say: "I have seen the wing of sunset lift
Into the golden vision of the hills
And truth come flooding proud through the cloud rift,
And known that souls survive their mortal ills."
Say: "Having seen such beauty in the air
I have seen truth and will no more despair."

Ciardi claimed to have written the entire thing in four minutes and eighteen seconds in answer to a challenge raised by a member of an audience who heard him say that "any reasonably competent craftsman could concoct such a poem . . . in three minutes flat." "Poesy," he proclaimed with the preacher's fire, "is always anti-poetry."

Some of John Ciardi's finest—most memorable—moments as a commentator-teacher are contained in the pages of his introduction to *Mid-Century American Poets*. And even though the self-assuredness of the style may have been somewhat off-putting, the message was so full of the excitement of modern poetry that one tended to forgive its now-and-then authoritarian tone and occasional smugness of manner. Moreover, the book itself was recognized almost immediately as a landmark anthology, with the *Madison (Wisc.) Capital Times*'s review (28 January 1950) reflecting the general tone of admiration throughout the country: it "is an excellent anthology and a different one, sufficiently meritorious to warrant the attention of every serious lover of poetry in the English-speaking world." Such extravagant praise was not uncommon, then or now. X. J. Kennedy wrote in 1986 that *Mid-Century* "remains one of the most revealing anthologies of poetry criticism ever assembled." Judson Jerome called it a "seminal anthology" that he returned to "again and again" and that he recommended "often to others in my books and articles." Philip Booth commented that *Mid-Century* "was, from the start, a high risk/high gain anthology: the risk was in Ciardi's comparatively narrow focus, the gain was in how deeply that focus was illuminated by his choice of poets and poems." The anthology, in Booth's view, became not "a textbook but a catalyst, a source of energy."

Perhaps most gratifying—and useful for book sales—was William Carlos Williams's review in the *New York Times Book Review* (16 April 1950), which said the book was a kind of "treatise on the poem that should be of the greatest interest to the student as well as the curious reader who has begun to wonder what all this pother about modern verse signifies." The book didn't have enough experimental poetry for Williams, but it did contain "some of the ablest work of our day," and, Williams went on, "I salute the discretion and taste of the anthologist John Ciardi." Ciardi was no doubt chagrined to be singled out as an anthologist rather than a poet, but he had to be pleased to have a critically acclaimed book—and to have helped Twayne Publishers take another step toward solvency and artistic respectability. Even in England, the *Times Literary Supplement* (19 January 1951) admitted that although "one begins by feeling distrustful of American poets writing introductions to their anthologized poems, one ends by being interested and impressed."

John Ciardi's reputation as a champion of midcentury American poetry had taken a giant step forward. He was becoming a national presence—an established modern poet seeking to bridge the gap between poets who would not be distracted by an audience and an audience driven to distraction by the poets.

Expanding the Center

Ciardi had been promoted in September 1948 to assistant professor at Harvard, where he had suggested a new course in versification that December, at least in part to reduce his English A responsibility to one course instead of two. "Pleasant as the course work is," he explained to Chairman B. J. Whiting, "it does involve a constant outgo of what I can only call psychic resources. I feel urgently the need to get closer to my own center of interest." But as usual when he made complaints like this, he was doing quite well with his "center of interest." He continued for the next two years to receive checks from the *New Yorker* (which kept him under contract to retain the right of first refusal of his poems), to review Hopwood poetry manuscripts for Roy Cowden, to write new poems, to publish two books, and to start up Twayne's Library of Modern Poetry. He also received an award, the 1948 Golden Rose medal of the New England Poetry Society.

Perhaps the most impressive part of the Ciardi enterprises to Dick and Charlee Wilbur, however, was that he had professionalized his lecture giving by getting an agent, as they learned one evening when they arrived at the Ciardi home for dinner. "[We] found large photographs of the poet," Wilbur reported, "ruggedly handsome in a dignified suit and tie, propped up everywhere on chair-seat, couch, and table-top. These were publicity pictures, and we were to help choose the best one. We learned with astonishment that John had an agent, as nobody else did, that he was going on the road, and that he meant to talk not merely in college auditoriums but in community lecture-halls. . . ." Ciardi had long recognized his own gift as a speaker: his deep, rolling voice plus his broad intelligence, quick wit, ready smile, and missionary zeal had been captivating poetry audiences for years. And, most recently, he had learned that he could also be a powerful political speaker, one who could squeeze cash contributions from Progressive party members better than anyone else. So, capitalizing on his talent by getting himself an agent was the natural next step—and John Ciardi was never one to miss an opportunity. "To begin with," he explained later, "I had been eager to go anywhere for fifty dollars, until Judith insisted I was doing too much. So I doubled my asking fee only to find that I was getting more and

more invitations, whereupon I doubled it again, every increase leading to more invitations." And once he began with an agent, the
speaking engagements multiplied yet again so that soon he was able
to lecture just about as often as his schedule permitted and for fees
far exceeding what other poets were receiving.

As Ciardi's speaking invitations increased, so did his reputation. By 1950 he was well on his way to national fame through his
lectures and speeches (political and poetical), magazine articles,
poems in journals, books of verse, his work for Twayne—and even
through a few controversial newspaper headlines. (With respect to
the headlines, FBI agents on 19 October 1948, concluded rather
abruptly that Ciardi was not in the Communist Party after all and
closed their file; however, they hastily reopened it the following
February when he spoke at a dinner given by the American
Committee for Protection of Foreign Born, an organization on the
attorney general's so-called "designated" list.) Taken in its entirety,
Ciardi's career in the late 1940s was going full throttle, so he must
have concluded that the only thing he could possibly cut back on
was English A—although it was clearly untrue that it was keeping
him, as he wrote to B. J. Whiting, from the long list of things he
called his "center of interest."

Still another center, of course, was 84 South Street. Around
election day 1948, John and Judith had moved up to the third floor,
their first apartment of their own after more than two years with
Cora, her family, and his mother. The five-room attic apartment
had many years earlier been added to the house and rented, but in
the summer 1948, the tenants left so that John and Judith could
redecorate and move in. Ciardi got fully into the domestic spirit,
building a china cabinet, under-sink cupboard, spice rack, numerous shelves, and a magazine rack for the bathroom door. At one
stretch, he recruited some of his favorite students—Frank O'Hara,
Ted Gorey, and George Rinehart—to peel wallpaper while Rossini
overtures played loudly in the background. They were, said Judith,
"the funniest people in the world with tongues like scalpels." They
all drank wine and afterward went down to Cora's for huge bowls
of spaghetti. To the young couple used to cramped quarters, the
attic apartment was palatially large: the living room faced front
toward the river and the kitchen faced the back. In between was the

bedroom; a room for the telephone, radio, and record player; and John's study, which opened in the back onto a porch. The postwar housing shortage had forced many Harvard instructors and their families into one or two rooms or into temporary barracks housing, but John and Judith had been fortunate from the first—and when they moved into their spacious third-floor apartment, they took their first big step toward comfortable living.

Another of John Ciardi's centers was Dante. He had taken a course in medieval literature at Tufts in which *The Divine Comedy* had been assigned, and he had tried then, with limited success, to make sense of Dante's fourteenth-century Italian. They had used the Temple classics, he later said, "with the Italian on one side and some very bad prose-literal translations on the other." None of it made any sense, not the Italian, the English, or the professor. He said he audited another course on Dante (probably at Michigan) with much the same result. He complained in retrospect that "there was something fascinating about this enormous poem that the professors couldn't tell me about," and so he began to collect translations and thought they were all "abysmally bad, one after the other, and I thought if this is the best that can be done, I've got an open field." Part of the problem, as he saw it, was that *The Inferno* hadn't been translated into English by a poet, "except by Rossetti, who was too delicate, and Longfellow who was too genteel. Dante is not genteel. When he dips a sinner in excrement, it ain't 'excrement.'"

In the spring of 1949, as the Ober controversy was about to break and as the Twayne Library of American Poetry began to take shape and as he was preparing *Live Another Day* for publication and as he was formulating his thoughts about *Mid-Century American Poets*, he wrote almost off-handedly to Clarence Decker of a new project. "I'm taking Judith out [to Missouri] late in May and mean to hole up there for a while to work at a long project that has begun to absorb me: I'm translating the *Inferno*. It's fascinating if laborious work." Ironically, the idea seems to have taken shape in English A, which permitted the instructor to choose whatever text he wanted to use in the classroom; Ciardi chose Dante but found that he could improve on existing translations by translating a few passages at a time for classroom use. Ciardi's ensuing twenty-year commitment to translating the entire *Divine Comedy* had thus begun inconspicuously as a classroom exercise that developed very gradually into one of his greatest artistic achievements. Coincidentally, it also represented a publishing opportunity that would yield more than half a million dollars.

To support the early work of his Dante translation, Ciardi applied for a Guggenheim fellowship that he did not in the end receive; however, he did work on the application during the summer and fall of 1949. He wrote to Peter Viereck in July that he was nearly finished translating through canto 8 and that "as soon as I can get those banged up into typescript with a statement of the principles of the translation which will be my project sheet, I'll complete the forms and shoot them in." He had better luck with the Committee on International Exchange of Persons (CIEP) in Washington, D.C. He requested money, according to Gordon Bowles, executive secretary of CIEP, "for research in Italy in the works of Dante, supplementary to a translation of the Inferno with English verse." Clarence Decker recommended Ciardi with glowing confidence: "As a poet, teacher, editor, and all-around human being, John Ciardi is surely an ideal candidate for a Fulbright Fellowship. More specifically, his Italian background, his knowledge of the Italian language, his gifts as a poet, and his enthusiasm for Dante should qualify him as an ideal translator of the 'Inferno.'" Ciardi's talent and Decker's logic were not lost on the committee, which invited Ciardi to lecture in January 1951 at the Salzburg Seminar in American Studies. In addition, Ciardi applied for and received on 17 October a sabbatical leave from Harvard for the fall 1950, which he extended for another half year by taking an unpaid leave for the spring 1951. He had found a way to turn the "long project" that had begun to "absorb" him in the spring 1949 into a paid opportunity to see Europe for the first time, including six important months of self-discovery in Italy.

Before sailing in early October 1950, Ciardi had a great deal to keep him occupied. He accepted Alfred Kreymborg's invitation to appear at the Poetry Society's annual dinner on 2 February, joining Max Eastman, Howard Mumford Jones, and others as a speaker at the society's fortieth-anniversary dinner meeting. It was a staid gathering presided over by aging Harvard poet Robert Hillyer, the outgoing president, who was still furious that Ezra Pound had received the first Bollingen Prize in Poetry in 1949. The thousand-dollar prize for the highest achievement in American poetry had been orchestrated by Archibald MacLeish, former Librarian of Congress, but Pound's *Pisan Cantos* had actually been selected as the best book of poetry published in 1948 by a group known officially as the Fellows in American Letters of the Library of Congress. That group consisted of such mid-century luminaries as Conrad Aiken, W. H. Auden, T. S. Eliot, Louise Bogan, Katherine Anne Porter, Robert Lowell, Karl Shapiro, and Allen Tate. The selection of Pound, however, was violently controversial because of his notorious antisemitism and because he had written the award-winning book in American Army prison camps after his capture for delivering pro-Mussolini propaganda during World War II. Furthermore, Pound was still under indictment for treason, although incarcerated in a mental hospital in Washington until such time (supposedly) as he was well enough to stand trial. Hillyer had led the protest against Pound and MacLeish by writing two long articles in successive June 1949 issues of *Saturday Review of Literature*, one of which had been titled "Treason's Strange Fruit."

Hillyer's position was well known to everyone at the Thursday night dinner of the Poetry Society, but the guests were unprepared for the vicious remarks of Max Eastman, Hillyer's featured speaker, who immediately launched into an attack on Archibald MacLeish for his part in naming the Bollingen Prize judges. "Among those not applauding when Mr. Eastman finished," wrote John K. Hutchens in the *New York Herald Tribune Book Review*, "was John Ciardi, poet and colleague of Mr. MacLeish in the Harvard English Department. 'I am ashamed to have sat at the same table with Mr. Eastman,' said Mr. Ciardi." And according to another account, Ciardi then "stalked out of the room, leaving the assembled poets arguing hotly, while unhappy Chairman Hillyer tried vainly to smooth things over." Ciardi's impulsive act of loyalty prompted numerous letters of support, including one from a New York literary agent in attendance: "Your speech at the end of the Poetry Society dinner last night did a real service to literature. There were a good many of us in the audience who felt a personal gratitude to you for speaking out as you did. You voiced feelings which we lacked the guts and decency to rise and express ourselves. I hope you won't carry away with you the impression that you were associated entirely with fatuous mediocrities, although it is they apparently who are the most vocal in such organizations as the Poetry Society. It is too bad that these people drive away writers like yourself who could make of the Society a stimulating force instead of the kind of well-fed women's club it seems to have become." Ciardi, who was not a great supporter of Pound's poetry, as he had made clear in *Mid-Century American Poets*, had nonetheless stood firm against the sort of dangerous foolishness spouted by Eastman and Hillyer. And in the process, he made the newspapers and gained new admirers, once again.

Ciardi had announced in *Mid-Century* that his own next book would be *The Statistician's Eye* in 1950, which he worked on but did not publish under that title. Holmes read the manuscript in April, "straight through at one sitting," he wrote, and then had "a sort of spontaneous explosion of pleasure and satisfaction and admiration and excitement." The manuscript was put aside, however, probably by Steinberg, because *Live Another Day* had just come out in late 1949. Perhaps, the thinking seems to have gone, it would be wiser to wait a while before coming out with his next book. Ciardi also thought for a while in the late spring and summer about producing a new anthology of modern poetry and wrote to Dudley Fitts that it would be a fresh addition to the existing books. "It won't conflict with NPearson/ WHAuden: they do very little with Mod Pot. They're designed for survey of EngLit. Horsecar [Oscar Williams] has good pocketbook: but in no sense a careful anthology of trends and developments in MODPOT. Only real competitor is Mr. u [Louis Untermeyer's *Modern American Poetry and Modern British Poetry*]. What I want is the book that will put him out of business. The book with everything a man needs to teach a good course in ModPot. And one that will do some teacher-education." Though the book never materialized, it was one of his centers of interest as he waited for October and his trip to Europe.

Also while he was waiting, Ciardi received a renewal contract from Howard Moss, poetry editor at the *New Yorker*, and was pleased by his continued favored-poet status. The renewal began on 11 February and brought the usual one hundred dollars to guarantee the *New Yorker* "first reading" rights to all Ciardi poems, plus a twenty-five percent bonus to the then-current rate of $1.75 per line. The magazine also agreed to pay even more for certain poems that it considered of "exceptional value." Moss was no doubt pleased (though one can never know for sure) to have his judgment and faith in Ciardi confirmed by a reader in mid-June who had liked Ciardi's "Home Revisited: Midnight": "This is wonderful, exclamation point stuff, modern and lovely, with beauty and a beat, tender and terrific."

Of course, Ciardi spent a good deal of time on the Twayne Library of Modern Poetry, too, demonstrating what Steinberg appreciated as "a sure critical touch" and "a good business sense." He worked with poets under contract, tried to develop new book possibilities, and sought to improve the quality of submissions through his network of friends in poetry magazines around the country. He was also busy looking for manuscripts as he rode the circuit: February at the University of Kentucky, March at Ohio State University and the University of Massachusetts; May dates in Pennsylvania and Ohio; ten days in June at the UKC Writers Workshop, then the rest of the month at Yaddo in Saratoga Springs; plus a week in July at the University of Michigan and two more at Bread Loaf in August. As he wrote to Louis Cohn in May about his lecture schedule, "It's the rankest sort of check-chasing but it will pay our passages to and from Europe."

During a brief stopover in early August at 84 South Street, Ciardi had all his favorite students over for dinner. Donald Hall recalled the evening, especially Ciardi's generosity of spirit toward the precocious Frank O'Hara. "Frank was funny—he was short and effeminate, and he was tough. He had a tiny frame, but he was tough! John admired Frank, especially his incredible wit." After dinner, as they sat around the kitchen table finishing off their wine, Hall went on, O'Hara announced to no one in particular that he had no plans for the future: "'I've graduated and don't have anything to do.' So John said, 'Why don't you go out to the University of Michigan and get a Hopwood?' Like that." O'Hara explained that he didn't have any money, so John said he'd get him a scholarship. "So he sat down in front of us at the table, the spaghetti was cleared away, and he wrote a longhand letter to Roy Cowden saying: 'Give this man a scholarship.'" In the letter (which he did type up after his guests had left), Ciardi apologized for the lateness of his recommendation: "Only today I discover that [O'Hara] is just wandering and that he would welcome the idea of graduate school at Michigan and the Hopwood competition." Ciardi wrote that he could speak "enthusiastically" for his former student's talent. "He has taken courses from me for three years and I've had the pleasure of watching him develop in a really remarkable way as a poet. I think too he is just trembling on the edge of real accomplishment: that he has just begun the business of really finding himself and should shoot wonderfully in the next year or two." Ciardi's word went a long way with his own former teacher, whom he still addressed respectfully as Professor Cowden, and O'Hara got both a last-minute admission and a scholarship. Later, he earned the Hopwood Award.

Europe

Busy as John Ciardi was in his various enterprises, which included a late September flurry of letters and meetings with Thomas Hart Benton about a book of collected lithographs for Twayne, Europe loomed large in his imagination. He and Judith got their passports a full four months before their departure, which finally arrived on 4 October when they sailed on the French liner *De Grasse* from New York to Plymouth, England. This was to be their long-delayed honeymoon—and the main reason they had waited so long to begin a family, for Judith wanted to travel in Europe before taking on the full-time responsibilities of mother-hood. They spent what was left of October in London, although Ciardi worked one long weekend writing what turned out to be a controversial essay for Norman Cousins, editor of *Saturday Review of Literature*, who had cabled requesting a summary essay on the career of Edna St. Vincent Millay, who had just died. It seemed odd to Ciardi that Cousins would go across the Atlantic for this essay when so many others could have done the job at home, but Cousins had been so pleased with Ciardi's article "What Does It Take To Enjoy a Poem?" back in December 1949 that he decided to seek Ciardi out, even at such a great distance, for this assignment.

Ciardi's essay, "Edna St. Vincent Millay, A Figure of Passionate Living" (11 November 1950) did more than summarize her career, gently but with perceptive criticism; it also chronicled her beguiling power to move a generation—himself included.

Ciardi's three-thousand-word article reads as a sympathetic tribute to Millay's perfect fit with the generation of the 1920s; moreover, it nostalgically contrasted his own adolescent discovery of her work in 1931, when he was fifteen, to the poetry he had by then become accustomed to: a smattering of Kipling, Markham's "The Man with a Hoe," and Masters's *Spoon River Anthology*. Millay was a revelation and a joy, a liberating poet of youthful spirit and possibility, most suitable perhaps not only to his own but to all adolescent passion and excitabilty. Ciardi's essay captured all those complicated emotional responses and combined them with a critical appraisal of Millay's limitations, a fair and sympathetic reading from start to finish, though one that pointed out that she did not do as well in her later career as she had done in the beginning. "The simple fact seems to be," Ciardi wrote, "that, having outgrown her youth, Edna Millay had outgrown the one subject she could make exciting."

The problem was, as he explained it later, the *SRL* cable had reached him in London "late one Friday afternoon and copy had to be mailed off by airmail on Monday morning. I began to make notes that Friday night but I had few books by me and none of Miss Millay's poetry. My head was still full of her lines, however, and I quoted from memory as I went." He spent Saturday looking unsuccessfully for a copy of Millay, then returned to the essay, still working from memory, typing up the finished essay late Sunday night. "I could scarcely pretend that the passion of my adolescence was still with me as I said the poems over to myself, but I found myself writing with the sort of nostalgia one might feel for a lost love." Early Monday morning he was able to check some of his quotations at the American Embassy Library but had to mail the essay to New York before he could check them all, so he instructed the *SRL* editors to check the remaining three or four.

Unfortunately, the quotations were not double-checked, and the essay appeared with some eight errors, as Norma Millay, the poet's sister and literary executor, pointed out in a long letter to the editor (17 February 1951), which capped off an untold number of angry letters that had been received at the magazine. The letters had objected principally to Ciardi's discussion of himself in the essay and what was seen as his notion that Millay appealed only to the adolescent mind. The tenor of Norma Millay's letter was aggressive, a spirited counterattack that focused on what she saw as Ciardi's postadolescent inability to understand the mature work of Edna St. Vincent Millay. Ciardi had no doubt been right to praise Millay's early work and to point out that her later work was not as good, but more importantly he was giving high praise by suggesting that some part of the poet's work had managed to work its way into the national memory. It was an honest and moving and personal tribute, but it was also candid and seems to have lacked what the audience of *SRL* might have considered to be the proper language of literary obituary. Norma Millay no doubt felt sufficiently vindicated when she pointed out Ciardi's missed quotations, but in the long run it may have been she who missed the point.

The perfect weather the Ciardis enjoyed in London gave way to rainy conditions in Paris during November, when John met the great jazz musician Sidney Bechet, who played nightly at the Vieux Columbier. They "met and talked a number of times in cafes," Ciardi wrote, and Bechet was very interested in knowing that Ciardi was a writer because he was then working on his autobiography. Bechet showed him a manuscript that had been prepared by a woman whom Bechet identified as his secretary, Joan Williams. What excited Ciardi about the document was that whenever Bechet spoke in the narrative, one heard "a powerful and vivid native idiom"; at those times it was clear that one was listening to "a fascinating storyteller." Moreover, Ciardi was acting as a representative of Twayne, which led to a tentative agreement between the two men to publish Bechet's memoir.

Ciardi, however, insisted on editing out all the "vaguely scented purple passages" written by Williams because they jarred so strongly with Bechet's own voice. Ciardi later wrote that Williams "kept injecting her own dreadful prose comments into the manuscript, as for example a passage dictated by Sidney [might be] followed by something like 'As Sidney finished speaking[,] an imponderable silence descended upon the room and his face clenched hard as he thought back to the long years.'" There were further interviews and additional tapings and in the end Ciardi claimed that the first 85 or 90 percent of the published book (some 310 pages of his own typed revisions of the Bechet manuscript) were his writing and editing and revising. Twayne was hoping to publish the book in 1952, but as soon as they announced the title, Joan Williams stepped forward and threatened suit, as Ciardi put it, "to recover what she claimed was her property." At that point it became clear that Williams had not been a secretary at all, but a hopeful ghostwriter, so Steinberg backed out of the deal and eventually sold the rights to Hill and Wang, which finally published the book as *Treat It Gentle* in 1960. "I suppose I could have sued Hill and Wang for stealing my work," wrote Ciardi, "but why bother? The story is told, it is a good one, and I told myself that what work I did was sufficiently rewarded in the doing."

The 1978 Da Capo Press edition of *Treat It Gentle*, reprints the original 1960 foreword by Desmond Flower, who had thanked "Miss Joan Reid" (despite the "Miss," Williams seems to have married in the 1950s and become Joan Reid), "for her successful initiative in bringing Sidney to the recording machine, and for the amount of very hard work she put in." It also contained a new preface by Rudi Blesh, who wrote that "it was fortunate for us all when a history-minded jazz-lover, Miss Joan Reid, got to Sidney in his adopted France." The names of Reid, Flower, and Ciardi appear on the title pages of both editions as being "among those who helped record and edit the tapes on which this book is based." And in the Da Capo edition, Blesh repeated "that we are all deeply indebted to Miss Joan Reid as well as to Mr. Desmond Flower, and Mr. John Ciardi, who transcribed and arranged the taped material."

Who was responsible for exactly what aspect of the transcribing and arranging of tape recordings as well as the refashioning of Bechet's raw material into printable words and paragraphs and then made the story into a book called *Treat It Gentle* remains something of a puzzle that is not likely to be solved without the original tapes and manuscripts, but Ciardi's correspondence with Jack Steinberg shows that he was hard at work editing and retyping the manuscript for Twayne during the first six months of 1952, when he also reinterviewed Bechet in Boston, putting the final touches on the manuscript after "several long sessions with him." Moreover, in a letter to Steinberg of 16 April 1952, Ciardi wrote that Williams's "original ms. contained dictation taken from Sidney's talk plus comments of her own." But, Ciardi continued, "In the finished manuscript *no word of hers appears: not one*. It's all Sidney's talk and talk I have put into his mouth." If this is substantially true, it is hard to avoid the conclusion that Ciardi was the writer who made Bechet's reminiscences into a book—and that Williams did little more than operate the tape recorder. Ciardi's contributions were evident enough for one commentator to remark that "Sidney Bechet's musicianship with words was validated and sustained by his collaboration with Ciardi," adding that "*Treat It Gentle*, though minor to Ciardi's canon, is a major memoir of the popular culture."

During December, January, and early February, John and Judith were in Austria as Ciardi carried out his lecture obligations. He did, however, find time to continue an ongoing correspondence with John Lehmann in England about a proposed book to be called *Mid-Century British Poets*. In a letter dated 16 January, Ciardi reported that negotiations had "hit a snag." Twayne was reorganizing, he wrote, and moving into new offices, and in the midst of this, plus "many long reports across the Atlantic," he had "been forced to concede, though only temporarily I insist, that I would not add any new titles to our poetry list." The reason was, he explained, that sales had fallen off sharply. "NY flatters me with the notion that my absence has had something to do with this, inasmuch as I made the poetry titles and their promotion my personal concern. At any rate, I have had to agree that we should not undertake any new titles for that list until I get back to promote them myself." The decision must have pained Ciardi more than he let on because editing the poetry series had become an important professional and poetical center of his life. But, as he had written to Lehmann, it was only a temporary setback. He would get the series back on its feet when he returned to the States.

For the Christmas and New Year's holidays John and Judith went to Frankfurt, Germany, and stayed with Virginia Johnson and her husband, Col. Phil Johnson. Ciardi left no account of that visit, merely noting, without comment, in one of his undated autobiographical fragments, that he "was in Germany that Christmas visiting a dear friend." Then, in mid-February, John and Judith took a train through the Alps and entered Italy for the first time. In a later undated manuscript called "Italy: The Sense of Rapture," Ciardi wrote that the trip was intended as "sort of a second honeymoon for my wife and me, and if that were not enough, our first Italian city, coming down as we had from Salzburg, was Venice. I was instantly dizzy with it."

The honeymooners stayed in a *pensione* for a few days before settling into the Cavaletto, a hotel on a small canal just behind the Piazzo San Marco. Their balcony looked out on the lagoon that served as an overnight parking lot for gondolas. They would wake, Ciardi wrote, make love before calling for coffee and croissants, and listen to the gondoliers singing beneath their window. When they went downstairs and joined the Italians, however, Ciardi felt an enormous emotional tugging that wasn't always comfortable. "I hardly spoke their language. I walked differently, I wore different clothes, I didn't quite understand how they thought." Yet he felt himself oddly at home: "By blood this was my tribe, these were my people and I liked them, and they were teaching me what I needed to know." And reassuringly, he wrote, "I had no sooner arrived there than I found within myself a sense that I recognized the emotional pattern of the Italian." Venice had made its impression on the thirty-four-year old poet and his twenty-nine-year-old wife: "We were rapturously incoherent with the love of it."

Then, after a brief stopover in Florence, the couple headed for Rome where they spent the next three months. They took an apartment on the Via Montepertica in "a Mussolini high-rise," as Ciardi called it, "that circled the whole block with a large interior courtyard lined with rear balconies." The Ciardis did not behave very much like rich tourists, partly because John felt, as he put it, "the enduring fear" caused by "growing up forever penniless in the Great Goddamned Depression." He said he "had grown up a miser" even when he had money in his pocket and in the bank. "And a miser I remained, despite occasional splurges, especially of over-generous tipping." He might have added that he was also generous to beggars who reached into his heart, as in "Roman Diary: 1951":

A rag woman, half a child,
with a soiled baby, half a bundle of rags,
whined on the Spanish Steps. It takes no words.

I reached into a pocket and found something.
She found words and a tune for them.
Even the flies on the baby rose to drone

Franciscan *deo gratia*. "Hey!" said Coates,
"that was five hundred lira!" Coates had been there
over a month, was an old Roman hand

into everything but his own pocket.
"Don't you know they *rent* the babies?" he said.
"Everything in this crazy town is a racket!"

"We just ate didn't we?" I said—
he might have forgotten: the check
had slipped his mind—"let them eat."

"Ten suckers an hour like you and she'll take home
sixty-seventy bucks American.
That's damned well more than I can spend in a day!"

He was indignant! Why would he travel that far
to walk that tight for fear
the beggars were getting rich? I started to say—

—It wasn't worth it. Not the eighty cents,
not the big boodle in the poverty racket,
not a fool's fear he'd lose what he didn't have.

"If I go broke," I said, "I'll rent a baby."

Whatever "Roman Diary: 1951" may add to the complicated story
of John Ciardi's relationship to money, it also captures one of his
best voices, what Dana Gioia, writing in *Poetry*, called "the unique
tone of Ciardi's best work . . . , the civilized, level voice of a man
talking to his equals." Gioia praised the poem's economy and precision and said it was "refreshing to see a simple narrative handled
so well in verse," noting that "Ciardi's real achievement here is that
he deals so credibly with the complex social and psychological
dimensions of the story."

Even though Judith was in Rome on her second honeymoon,
she had to share Ciardi's attention with Dante: "I drudged night
after night at translating the *Inferno*," he wrote, "calling it a good
night's work if I turned fifteen lines before I slid blissfully into bed
with Judith for [a] 4:00 A.M. 'nooner.'" Progress on the translation,
however, was painfully slow as Ciardi worked through very cold
February conditions, made worse by marble floors that chilled their
Via Montepertica apartment. "I wore two sweaters under a suit
coat and a topcoat and pulled a bridge table next to the miniature
radiator. . . . I shivered and worked at Dante and was happy."

The return home brought John and Judith to Paris in late May, where they enjoyed much better weather, and then to London in June. During the late 1940s, they had often discussed having a family and decided to wait. As Ciardi wrote, "I did want children, more, I think, than Judith did. But at thirty [his age when they married in 1946] there seemed to be no hurry. . . . We decided not to have children until we had had a year in Europe." Judith was less than eager for children and called the decision to wait "the smartest thing in the world." She was once asked in 1951, "What's wrong with you? You've been married five years and no kids." She replied, "Carefully plotted, baby! I don't want any babies!" But there in London, after their year in Europe, Ciardi pressed the point once again, and Judith conceived their first child, Myra Judith, in London at the King's Arms Hotel. Then, with their business in Europe finally finished, they returned home.

Plotting the Future

Ciardi spent the summer of 1951 catching up and getting retracked at Harvard and Twayne; getting ready for the appearance of his next book which he had decided to call *From Time to Time*; and traveling, notably to Bread Loaf and Yaddo. At Bread Loaf, Ciardi and Isaac Asimov met for the first time, and according to Asimov, Ciardi was slim with a "craggy face" and "a magnificent mane of black hair." He also had "an operatic voice that could recite television commercials and hold you enthralled with the poetry of it." That summer Ciardi also published a short story about the war, "The Burial of the Dead," in the UKC *Review*, plus one poem, "Monday Morning Montage—London," in the *Beloit Poetry Journal*.

From Time to Time must have seemed like a pleasant bonus for John Ciardi in the summer of 1951. The manuscript had lain around Steinberg's office for a full year, but in July or early August, it was about ready to come out, updated slightly to include a few poems published in 1950. Ciardi hadn't worked on the book or even thought much about it for over a year. Its appearance was like a welcome-home present, although, perhaps alarmingly, the reviews didn't begin trickling in until early 1952. The new book contained a handful of Ciardi's best poems ("The Lamb," "The Evil Eye," "Monocalzata," "Mystic River," and more), but seems to have crept up unnoticed on the poetry reading public—just as it had crept up on Ciardi himself. A year later he wrote to Theodore Roethke: "For some reason my last just disappeared; mostly it didn't even get reviewed and just stuck itself to the shelves." Milton Crane, however, in the *New York Times Book Review* noticed Ciardi's new book—and liked it. He singled out "the particularity and immediacy" of Ciardi's experiences and said that "the sense of excitement that is communicated stems from the naturalness and effortlessness with which Mr. Ciardi's imagination moves from these experiences to large and complex artistic statements." And Willard Marsh, in the *Antioch Review*, wrote admiringly that Ciardi's language was "as urbane and precise as T. S. Eliot's . . . , but with none of Eliot's chilliness."

The Twayne announcement of *From Time to Time*, with an order form attached, said that Robert Frost had called Ciardi "one of the hopes of American poetry." The announcement also said the poems were "in many ways a new departure," adding that "readers will find his refusal to stay put within a 'type' one of the most exciting characteristics of Ciardi's poetry." The "new departure" was an experimental vein, at times almost elliptical, that struggled under a Wallace Stevens influence; fortunately Ciardi sensed that he was ill-suited to the Stevens' way of doing things and abandoned the experiment as a dead end in his development as a poet. But there was another new direction that produced some of Ciardi's best poetry— not just tribal recollections, but deeply personal self-revelations about his fatherless childhood. In autobiographical poems like "Elegy III" and "Another Comedy," Ciardi looked directly at the demon that had haunted him since his father's death, more than thirty years earlier. In "Elegy III" he wrote of Cavalcante, the man who had been driving the car Antonio Ciardi had been thrown from:

> "It was Cavalcante," my Mother said, "killed you Father.
> My son grow tall and avenge him." (And I was three
> and ready.) "He told him and told him
> not to go fast." But Cavalcante
> was a bad man, and speeding, he killed my Father.

And I who was the only son of that murder
> hunted a name in my dreams and posed for the death
> he begged me to spare him. "Spare you?
> Better," my pose said, "save your breath
for prayer, for I am the only son of that murder,

and my Mother's tears are in me frozen to knives.
> No man is dead who leaves a son in his name.
> Why Didn't You Go Slower!"
> And he begged me to spare him all the same,
but my Mother's tears were in me frozen to knives.

And I was six and seven and twelve and tall.
> I was twenty and grown. I was thirty and remembered
> nothing. And then his name
> came back, and I went to his wake dismembered
into three and six and seven and not at all,

and I stood by the death of the wreck that had been the blood
> and error and evil of all my Mother's tears.
> I stood and I was three
> and there was the dream again. Down all the years
I stood in the wreck of the death that had been my blood.

Ciardi's Hamlet-like failure to avenge his father's death had burst upon him, a sudden recognition of long-repressed feelings that had caused a thirty-year simmering guilt to boil over. This, and all the other feelings associated with his childhood loss, surfaced at the wake of Cavalcante and became objectified in powerfully emotional verse.

"Another Comedy" had been a long time developing. Ciardi had sent the first draft of the first canto to Marion Strobel at *Poetry* in August 1949 and projected eleven more cantos to follow. Although Strobel liked the poem, several questions came up that were partly addressed in a letter Ciardi wrote to her on 1 September defending his technical choices and the tone: "It has to be irascible, irreverent, offensive. I hate to be the unyielding author, but this one I have to stand by as is. For that matter terza rima is like beads on a string— cut it anywhere and the whole thing spills, but even if I could cut it I wouldn't want to." *Poetry* did not publish "Another Comedy," which appeared for the first time as the last poem in *From Time to Time*. In its final version, "Another Comedy" appeared not as a twelve-canto epic but as a seventy-line poem—twenty-three tightly written Dantean tercets complete with the interlocking rhyme pattern of terza rima, plus a trailing last line. The poem puts into imaginative form Ciardi's difficult struggle to cope with the loss of his long-dead father, who emerges here as his son's guide through the underworld. Ciardi dutifully follows his guide and seems to recognize

> his lamp, the spirit
> of that dead passage, a ghost more shadow than light.
> Myself doomed there to follow and to fear it[.]

When they arrive at a "stone cavern," two figures ask his name:

> My guide walked on as if he did not hear
> and left me struggling for a name. But none
> would come. I thought. "I know this nightmare:
>
> I dreamed it seven years running and woke alone
> on spikes of puberty.

His father asks what keeps him, and when he learns it is his name, he asks, "Do you remember me at all?" Confused, the poet asks,

> "What must I do?" And he to me: "Endure
> a change of imagination: I did no wrong."
> The ghosts blew out. I led him back from there.
>
> Goddamn the wood that made his death so long.

This poetic rendering of his many years of emotional suffering had a freeing effect, for his father in this poem gave him permission to let go, end his obsessive mourning, and let his imagination work on something else. With this new-found freedom, the characters switched roles with the son leading his father back. But Ciardi's accumulated pain is nonetheless everywhere evident in this ironically titled interior landscape, the last line of which allows his outright anger to percolate up to the surface.

In early October 1951, however, just when his new book and the Dante project seemed to promise so much for the future, Ciardi was reminded that the time when he would have to leave Harvard was drawing near. In a letter signed by Ted Morrison and B. J. Whiting, written "with all imaginable reluctance," Ciardi was told that "we cannot look forward to your continuing to teach here beyond the expiration of your term as Briggs-Copeland Assistant Professor in June, 1953." Ciardi had known all along that his Briggs-Copeland position was temporary; nonetheless, because of his work at Twayne and his expanded lecture schedule and the ease with which he could arrange these things around a not-too-demanding course load at Harvard, the timing of his termination was difficult. Hoping to enter the publishing world on a full-time basis, Ciardi struck a deal in September 1951 with Jack Steinberg and became executive editor at Twayne. Under terms of his new agreement, Ciardi would earn a 5 percent royalty fee on every book he saw into print and receive a monthly check of one hundred dollars. His new duties included the editing of trade books on every subject, for it was becoming increasingly clear that the Twayne Library of Modern Poets was too costly to continue.

Through the end of 1952, Ciardi was personally responsible for twenty of Twayne's books (on subjects as diverse as art, science fiction, sex, American slang, and Italian cooking), which earned him just over three thousand dollars in all, although he received barely half of it. The next year yielded another twenty-one hundred dollars in royalties, but again, only half was paid to him, which meant that by 1 January 1954, Twayne owed Ciardi more than twenty-five hundred dollars, a significant sum when measured by the fact that it was just about a full year's salary at Harvard. In September 1952, Ciardi wrote an anxious letter to Jack and Joel Steinberg (the latter being the chief financial officer of the company) complaining that they owed him "an uncomfortable amount of money." He had borrowed $1,600 in August, he said, on assurances that he would be receiving a check on the first of every month, but his September check hadn't arrived. "I have had to meet my obligation in the meanwhile and we're damn low at this writing." But as pressing as his debt may have been, the real occasion of the letter was to put the Steinbergs on notice that they would either have to pay up or he would have to consider taking a new teaching job for September 1953. What he unhappily learned in the course of the next year, however, was that, despite his obvious talent in the editorial end of the publishing business and an extraordinary amount of editorial correspondence that led directly to the publication of some thirty-one books, he could not earn a living working for Twayne Publishers. In the meantime, while he was still hoping for the best from Twayne, he took on the daunting task of editing the sonnets of Dr. Merrill Moore, the irrepressible, sonneteering psychiatrist whose books for Twayne sold very well. During the fall of 1951, Moore was working on a sequel to his popular *Clinical Sonnets* (he had also written *Illegitimate Sonnets* and *Case Record from a Sonnetorium*) and asked Ciardi to look them over: "I know I can trust you to be absolutely merciless. . . ." Ciardi did look them over—and returned all but a handful: "One of these days," he wrote with exasperation, "I'm going to buy you a six foot high wastebasket and send it to you as lesson one in English MM: Versification. The wastebasket is a necessary part of your method of writing: an improvisation can hit only now and then. I can't help feeling however that you would hit much more often if a. You'd acquire a set of warning signals to light up when you have committed a cliché. b. You stopped *lunging* from rhyme to rhyme in the course of racing through the poem." Furthermore, Ciardi wrote, "Every idea that goes through your mind and emerges in approximately 14 lines is not an aesthetic achievement." And, he concluded, Moore would need four or five hundred more sonnets to get fifty acceptable ones at his current rate of success. Moore meekly accepted the criticism and remained both agreeable and appreciative, but he was unable to get his new manuscript in much better shape than it was. In the end, he sent Ciardi more than one hundred dollars as "an editor's fee," as he called it, to do the work for him. In a letter of 2 February, he gave Ciardi complete freedom with the poems: "About the rewriting, may I be so bold as to ask you to retouch or rewrite anything you want to[?] I honestly don't care what happens to the individual poems just as long as the book as a whole has 'mass coherence and emphasis'." He said he saw Ciardi as "more than just a friend and editor—you are a kind of literary obstetrician. . . ." Ciardi reported on 21 March that he'd "have the sonnets washed in about 7-10 days," so it appears that he did, indeed, perform an unspecified amount of editing and rewriting on the book that he delivered and Twayne published in 1952 as *More Clinical Sonnets*.

Moore had been an embarrassment dating back at least to 10 December 1949, when Ciardi confessed to Hayden Carruth at *Poetry* about Moore's first book for Twayne, which had been accepted for publication, he said, only because it would sell at least twenty-five hundred copies, enough to cover losses on better books. "But never again," Ciardi announced to Carruth, "I let my arm be twisted on that one." From a business standpoint, however, Moore continued to be money in the bank, and Ciardi had been forced to stay with him—consoled in some measure by the $420 in royalties he received from Twayne for editing the various Moore books plus the more than one-hundred-dollar "editor's fee" sent from Moore directly.

The summer of 1952 went like most of Ciardi's summers: ten June days in Utah, plus dates in Florida, Wyoming, Indiana, Colorado, and, of course, Bread Loaf in late August. Sandwiched in between was a July visit to his in-laws' farm in Missouri, where Judith's parents got their first glimpse of their granddaughter. Myra Judith, named after her mother, had been born on 19 March. On 1 July Ciardi began a one-year unpaid leave of absence from Harvard so that he could accept a Ford Foundation Grant that came through the Fund for the Advancement of Education. The grant was to study the teaching of poetry and creative writing at Harvard, a subject he already knew a lot about, which meant that for his last full year at Harvard, he would be on leave doing work that would not be terribly burdensome. It also meant that there would be a great deal of time to pursue his future plans.

The plans most important to John Ciardi on 5 June 1952 were finding a publisher for his translation of *The Inferno* and finding a full-time job, preferably in the Northeast. He wrote on both subjects to his friend Max Goldberg, a professor at the University of Massachusetts and a founder of the College English Association (CEA), which Ciardi had become active in. "For the next several months," he wrote, "I'm a dead duck. Prentice-Hall sent back enthusiastic reports on the *Inferno* and want to use my version for their forthcoming World Lit Anthol but that means I have to do 11 cantos from the *Purgatorio* and the *Paradiso* by October 1 and meanwhile I've got a summer full of writers' conferences. I don't think I can deliver in time but I'm hoping I can make it close enough to being on time so that they have to play along with me." And then, almost as an afterthought, he asked for "a political favor . . . : I note that John Bruchard will be on your list of [CEA] speakers. I'm angling for a job at MIT as the perfect solution of my problems. He seemed enthusiastic when I saw him several months ago but I've heard nothing from him since. Any discrete plug you can slip in will be repaid you with ichor in heaven and with alcohol when next we meet."

In the fall of 1952, Ciardi was working in several directions at once. He was hoping for the best from Twayne, but hedging his bets by looking around for another teaching job. He was waiting to hear about his translation of Dante from Prentice-Hall, but shopping it to Victor Weybright at the New American Library at the same time. Things were very much up in the air when he wrote to Merrill Moore on 6 November: "And oh brother! This is *top secret*, please. Judith doesn't want it known, although she won't be able to keep it secret for very long, but we slipped up somewhere and we're due for child #2 in May. Personally, I like the idea, but it is a bit rough on her to have two so close together. Thank god she's a healthy beast. But oh the clamps that begin to close on the future."

PART TWO

Eye of the Storm

SIX

The Rutgers Years

1953 TO 1955

From "The Hypnoglyph" to *The Inferno*

On 22 January 1953, midway through his Ford Foundation year, Ciardi wrote to Ted Roethke that he was "homebound": "Judith is mothering again in May and necessity and the psyche both speak for my roostering around the barnyard to protect the nest. Fathering is good stuff." Besides "roostering," Ciardi's chief occupation that year was Twayne, where he was developing science fiction titles from his home office and working on a new concept called Twayne Triplets, which was conceived as a series of books, each one about a "hypothetical (but thoroughly possible) planet different from ours." Once the hypothetical planet had been given its essential characteristics by "a board of highly qualified scientists and consultants," the data was given to three established science fiction writers, each of whom was to write his own story fitting the "facts." The resulting hardcover triplet would therefore be one book with three independently written stories imagined out of the same raw information. By 27 March 1953, Ciardi had eight of these books in various stages of development and production—with twenty-four authors, contracts, and manuscripts to juggle and balance. Ciardi was so encouraged by the enterprise that he tried that winter to form a partnership with Ian Ballantine of Ballantine Books to co-publish a line of triplets in paperback; however, even though he had done all the financial figuring and Ballantine was willing, Ciardi could not come up with more than half of the initial eight thousand dollars he needed, so the deal fell through.

But something else had captured Ciardi's attention. Reading a great deal of science fiction and working with people like Fletcher Pratt, Sprague de Camp, and Isaac Asimov, Ciardi was in the right frame of mind to try out some science fiction of his own. At one of Pratt's regular weekend house parties in New Jersey, in October or November 1952, Ciardi taunted several science fiction writers. "Let's face it," he said half seriously, "you've invented a form in which characterization is irrelevant, motivation is up for grabs, and the narrative may stop at any time for the intrusion of any amount of technical material. . . ." Sure, he said, he had enjoyed some of it, "but don't use the vocabulary in which you would discuss *Moby-Dick* or *War and Peace*, or *The Magic Mountain* for this hoke stuff. Because anybody who picked out the formula could write this stuff, and if he happens to be literate that's an unfair advantage." Playfully needling the sensitive science fiction writers, who had heard all this before from high-toned literary critics, Ciardi was teased right back with a chorus of challenges. If it was so easy, why didn't *he* try it? This was more or less what Ciardi had been thinking about anyway, so he accepted the challenge by spreading a fifty-dollar bet around the room. According to the terms of the bet, Ciardi had a week to come up with the story, which then had to be accepted for publication by one of two or three pre-approved magazines. The story, which one commentator later called "a rich yarn with as many levels as a skyscraper," turned out as a tongue-in-cheek treatment of the scientific concept of tropism, an organism's natural tendency to turn or curve as a response to a certain type of stimulation. He called it "Hypno-Feely" and sent it to the editors of the magazine first on his list, *Fantasy and Science Fiction*. They accepted it at once for July publication, thus winning Ciardi the bet, although they asked for a handful of changes, including the title, which they thought should be "The Hypnoglyph," a word, they said, with "the proper tone of s f double-talk."

Ciardi had every reason to enjoy his foray into science fiction, which for good measure came out quite well with a surprising and satisfying twist at the end, but he was nonetheless uneasy about publishing it under his own name. He requested that it appear under the name John Anthony, which puzzled and disappointed the editors. When they inquired about this in a letter of 21 November, Ciardi answered that "the pseudonym is for hard cause. When my last book of poems came out some of the reviewers had me down as a Philistine for having published in the *New Yorker*. I can imagine what they'd do if they found out I was taking a stab at [science fiction.]" When the editors asked again about the need for a pseudonym in a letter of 6 January 1953, Ciardi was less insistent, possibly embarrassed that he had seemed ashamed of letting his real name be attached to a literary form the editors obviously thought highly of. He wrote them by way of explanation two days later that he had never used the pseudonym John Anthony before, "nor am I especially concerned with hiding from myself. If you want to tell the reader that John Anthony is John Ciardi that's all right with me; I just want the different signature on it to indicate a different category as James Branch Cabell once changed to Branch Cabell to separate one set of books from another." The answer was squirmy and self-conscious, but it nonetheless remained John Anthony.

In later life, Ciardi liked to rehash the details leading up to "The Hypnoglyph" in order to point out how much money he had made on his small bet, for the story continued to be collected in anthologies and translated into numerous foreign languages, until at last he had earned some fifteen hundred dollars from it. But the exercise itself had been enough to satisfy Ciardi's desire to be a writer of science fiction, and once he got it out of his system, he became bored with it. He wrote to Holmes on 30 January 1953: "I am tired of science fiction and wish to find a really good title for the Twayne list."

Just when Ciardi was corresponding with the editors of *Fantasy and Science Fiction* and trying out the pseudonym John Anthony for fear of what the poetry community might do to him if they got wind of what he was up to, he was also submitting poems for inclusion in *New Poems by American Poets*, an anthology being edited by Rolfe Humphries for Ballantine Books. Ian Ballantine himself had wanted Ciardi to be represented in the book and had asked him to send in some poems, but Humphries promptly returned them, scribbling on the bottom of Ciardi's 17 November 1952 cover letter that he could not "warm up to these." He added, "It's possible that I'm a creature of such violent prejudices that your work might get a fairer reading if you cooked up a *nom de plume* and a phony address."

Although he seemed to be twitting Ciardi over "The Hypnoglyph," Humphries was actually striking back for a grudge he'd been nursing since 1949. At that time, Ciardi had rejected a book of poems by a protégé of his, one Constance Carrier, in the Twayne First Book contest—all 250 entrants of which had submitted manuscripts under pseudonyms. Ciardi wrote to Fletcher Pratt on 12 December that Humphries's "real peeve is the rejection of his gal's ms," but understanding the situation made it no less difficult to cope with.

Ciardi, however, should have been prepared for Humphries's insult. The 1949 first-book contest had been won by forty-four-year-old Marshall Schact, and Humphries had criticized Twayne in his *Nation* column of 17 December for "their editorial judgment," which he thought was "less enterprising and ambitious" than it might have been, and because "their young poets seem pretty middle-aged." This prompted Ciardi to defend Twayne, himself, and the contest in a 14 January letter to the editor. In the first draft of that letter, which Ciardi did not send, he had written, "If Mr. Humphries knows of any good manuscripts available from any of the sweet young things at his academy I can promise them an eager and sympathetic reading." If that attack was too personal to use, Ciardi was no doubt reasonably pleased with the language he did use: "I can't pretend to understand Mr. Humphries' peculiar insistence on youth, but let me explain to him that Twayne is not opposed to youth as such. It may be, however, that since we are considerably closer to it than is Mr. Humphries, we are less nostalgic for it. Whatever the case, we do not plan to require a birth certificate with each manuscript." Clearly Humphries hadn't forgotten that Ciardi had had the last word in that public exchange.

Later, when *New Poems by American Poets* appeared, with some of Humphries' poems in it, Ciardi wrote a review that attacked what he called "the wispier talents here presented," including Humphries and his "clerkly tick-tock verses." Ciardi also quoted the *"nom de plume"* insult, especially Humphries's claim to be a man of "violent prejudices," in order to say that Humphries was too "pale," not man enough, to "work up a really satisfactory violence." Maybe it was sweet for Ciardi to say, a satisfying venting of bitterness over having been omitted, but it seemed to signal worse things to come. The two men shared many friends, Holmes in particular, who were genuinely disappointed at the ongoing feud, but they nonetheless remained sworn enemies through the rest of their lives, with Humphries at one point going so far as to back out of a speaking date when he learned that Ciardi would also be present.

Ciardi was doing much more than toying with science fiction and feuding with Rolfe Humphries during his year off from teaching. There was also Dante. In the first week of January 1953, Ciardi's long labor of translation began to pay off when the UKC *Review* published five cantos of *The Inferno*. He wrote at once to Clarence Decker to say he was "delighted by its appearance": "I may honestly say that I have really labored at it, and I think I may claim it's the first translation into idiomatic English." But seeing it for the first time in print, Ciardi worried about some of his decisions in translating. On 23 January, he sent a copy of the *Review* to Richard Wilbur expressing some concern over the fact that he had "worked many lines so that they won't come out metrically unless they're read with meaningful emphasis," a Frost borrowing that he was afraid would "stumble some readers." And he worried too about the rhyme pattern he adopted (a three-line variation on the heroic couplet, with the middle line unrhyming) in place of the interlocking stanzas of terza rima that strained the limits of English rhyme. The number of near-rhymes also troubled him. As he explained to Dudley Fitts in April: "My starting premise is simple here: it can be made to rhyme precisely. But every version that does rhyme it, rhymes at the expense of idiomatic diction. On careful reading you can see the line being beaten into place to produce a rhyme word. I simply decided to rhyme exactly where diction permitted and to rhyme any which way where it was a choice between rhyme and diction. That may be a poor premise but I'm afraid I'm stuck with it now."

But while Ciardi was simultaneously pleased with and worried about his translation, he was also working hard to revise it for book publication. The New American Library of World Literature, paperback publishers of Signet Books and Mentor Books (with a slogan at the bottom of their letterhead that read, "Good Reading for the Millions") had been interested in Ciardi's *Inferno* since October or November, but through the first week in February, no word had arrived on their decision. Ciardi wrote on 9 February to hurry them along, citing his second-choice publication possibility of Twayne doing a textbook edition that he would have to start on soon if it were to be available to students in September. He would need word from the paperback house as soon as possible. On 3 March final word arrived that NAL would be going ahead with his translation for the Mentor line, which was followed shortly by contracts and a five-hundred-dollar advance, plus assurances that they were all "very enthusiastic about this project." At the same time, the NAL editors were actively, but unsuccessfully, searching for another commercial house to handle the hardcover trade edition that Ciardi was eager to publish in advance of the paperback edition.

Between March and May most of the details of the publication of *The Inferno* were worked out, including the historical introduction by Archibald MacAllister of Princeton, who had been a reader of the translation for NAL and recommended publication. When Ciardi wrote to thank MacAllister for the suggestions he had made in his report to NAL, MacAllister wrote back: "The excellence of your translation and the depth of your interpretation filled me at the time of reading with so much enthusiasm that it was only with considerable difficulty that I kept myself from writing you directly." He wrote later in the *Yale Review* that when he first read the translation, he had been "struck at once by the sense of an unusually vigorous personality at work." However, he went on, "my indignation was aroused by what seemed to me unfair poetic practice, e.g., words that seem to rhyme but actually do not. Reading on, I lost my irritation as I realized that these tercets, with the first and third lines rhyming, often imperfectly, were carrying the narrative along in much the same manner of *terza rima* and with the same relative unobtrusiveness of rhyme as in the Italian. The style, moreover, was plain as much of the 'Inferno' is plain, dramatic where Dante is dramatic, with touches of vulgarity and grim humor to match those of the original which are normally glossed over or unrecognized." He admired Ciardi's scholarship (despite what he termed Ciardi's "modest disclaimers" to the contrary), which demonstrated "profound understanding of the poem on all its levels."

As Ciardi was seeing to the business of producing his translation of *The Inferno*, Judith was busy producing their second child, John Lyle Pritchett Ciardi, who arrived on 2 May. Ciardi announced the news to Vernon Shea, one of his Twayne authors: "Wife Judith is flourishing. For some girls maternity is a beauty treatment, and, blessedly, she is some girl." Moreover, the timing could not have been better because barely two weeks earlier Ciardi had finally gotten a job for the fall.

Rutgers

Leaving Harvard was made somewhat more difficult for Ciardi by Archie MacLeish's effort to have him rehired. The Briggs-Copeland assistant professorship was definitely over, but a retirement had opened up a slot on the permanent faculty and there was a chance that Ciardi might be asked to fill it. According to Ciardi, MacLeish took him aside one day and said, "You know, we've been discussing [you], a lot of us. We'd like to keep you here. You don't have a Ph.D.; you're not in the academic tradition. Would you consider a tenure instructorship?" It is uncertain how serious the offer was, if indeed it was an offer, or if MacLeish had any authority to make it. "Bless you, Archie," Ciardi recalled his answer, "that's beautiful of you . . . and I like this funny little club they have here at Harvard. But I am in danger of becoming a citizen of Cambridge, and it seems a limitation to me, not an achievement. I'm going to have to shoot out into the world and see what's going on there. I think I'll try my hand at the publishing business." In Judith's more bluntly stated recollection, "John didn't want any of that Old Boy's Club—and he didn't want to be an instructor."

In December 1952, Ciardi was thinking of taking at least a one-semester appointment at UKC, for the fall 1953, teaching courses on Dante, modern poets, and how to read poetry. But late in January he received a cautiously written letter from J. Milton French, chairman of the English department at Rutgers College, the oldest and most distinguished of the Rutgers University branches. They were thinking of expanding their offerings in creative writing, he said, and were making inquiries about young writers for positions on their staff. Ted Morrison had recommended Ciardi and so French was writing to see if he might be interested. He was. Not only did the position suit him, Ciardi replied, but New Brunswick would be much easier than Medford for those two to three dozen annual commutes into Twayne's New York offices. He gave the names of Archibald MacLeish, Bernard DeVoto, and Thomas Hart Benton as additional references. And, "if you wish more," he said, try Howard Mumford Jones and Norman Holmes Pearson. If that list didn't get its message across, French wasn't paying attention. Ciardi clearly wanted the job—and in a burst of premature overconfidence, he wrote almost immediately to Holmes: "Have a job offer from Rutgers. May go there. But details pend."

Some of those details were supplied by Horace Hamilton, a Twayne author who happened to be a professor in the Rutgers College English department. Ciardi asked in a letter about salaries and real estate prices—and hoped perhaps for more information about the job. The real attraction, he wrote to Hamilton, was the nearness to New York: "Eventually, I hope to work out a part-time teaching schedule for the love of it, and to concentrate on publishing." But Hamilton had little information beside some general salary guidelines and an idea or two about what fifteen thousand dollars might buy in neighboring Bound Brook. About the job, he knew very little: he presumed it was "a new sort of 'resident-writer' post," but "never were we very clear as to the exact scope of the incumbent's activities—save that he conduct a seminar for writers, probably three times a week." Less than a week later, Hamilton wrote again to say that the idea for the new creative writing position had come from the president of the university, Lewis Webster Jones, and filtered down to the department through channels. Hamilton added that French had seemed to bury the idea in a December committee meeting, which was why Hamilton had had no wind of it prior to Ciardi's letter of inquiry. He was "agreeably surprised" to hear that the position for a creative writing specialist was being discussed again.

In February, French invited Ciardi to New Brunswick for a "visit," which was made on 7 March, and five days later Ciardi wrote with bad news. Now that he understood the position as "a writer-in-residence who will devote himself to creating an active writing group at Rutgers," he didn't see how he could do the job with a four-course load, three of which being writing courses that, he said, would be twice as burdensome as other courses. Plus he was insulted by the one-year offer, hardly fitting for a man like himself, who had "achieved a certain reputation and known-qualification as a writer and as a teacher of writing." No, he would need at least a three-year commitment at the rank of associate professor, plus "a free hand as a department irregular" teaching two courses at first, though allowing for a third course in versification "should there be a need." Surprisingly, after discussing the matter with his dean, Harry Owen, French wrote back on 20 March, more or less agreeing to Ciardi's terms. He would have no more than forty students and only three sections that would meet fewer than nine times per week with student conferences figured in. They were ready to ante up sixty-five hundred dollars, with the last five hundred added for moving expenses. And they had themselves a deal.

A couple of weeks later, Harry Owen wrote to Ciardi, introducing himself as a former dean of the Bread Loaf School of English, which met every summer before the writers' conference began. In that position, Owen had known of Ciardi's work for many years, though he had never actually met him. He had, however, followed Ciardi's career and was the one who "suggested" him to the English department. Ciardi had known from the start that Morrison had had a hand in his being considered for the Rutgers job; now he realized that another Bread Loaf connection had also been involved. Good fortune continued to follow from the 1940 fellowship he had received at Bread Loaf after the appearance of *Homeward to America*. Perhaps he thought of himself as Lucky John once again.

Owen had played a more dramatic role in Ciardi's hiring than John ever knew. According to Remigio Pane, who was chairman of the Italian department at Rutgers College at the time, there was stiff opposition to Ciardi's appointment among the old guard at the English department. French, himself, was opposed, ostensibly because Ciardi did not have a Ph.D., though more likely, in Pane's view, out of jealousy over John's national reputation that neither French nor any of his people could match. During January, February, and March, Owen and Pane met frequently over lunch to discuss ways of overcoming English department opposition, and according to Pane, Owen was prepared to bring Ciardi in as a Dante man if need be. The important thing was to sign him up for Rutgers, one way or another. In the end, however, the Dante sidestep wasn't necessary because Owen had control over some scholarship money that was coveted by French for the English department, and French seems suddenly to have reconsidered his opposition and come to the conclusion that John Ciardi was, after all, the best man for the job. Moreover, he also agreed that though Ciardi would be brought in as a lecturer for the first year, he would be promoted to associate professor in September 1954, with the understanding that a tenured full professorship would follow in 1956.

All this special treatment, as recalled by Fred Main, who joined the Rutgers English faculty from Harvard at the same time as Ciardi, made Ciardi stand apart from his colleagues—protected by a sympathetic administration but resented by the English department academics as an exception to the rules that the rest of them had to live under. Moreover, according to Main, in social situations John would humorously mimic French's academic mannerisms and language, thus in a sense putting himself in open contempt, not only of the man himself, but of the narrowness of the academic mind as well—much as he had once maligned the academics on the editorial board of the UKC *Review*. Ciardi did not see himself so much as an exception to the rules as simply above them, someone who came to the position with genius and accomplishment rather than the arid endorsement of some graduate school that distributed Ph.D.'s as if they were union cards. But for those at Rutgers to whom a professorship was the pinnacle of a professional career, Ciardi's hiring must have seemed at best a mixed blessing: he was undoubtedly good for the department's national reputation, but he was also an irritating outsider.

In the spring of 1953 Ciardi knew nothing about the opposition to his hiring. All he knew was that he needed a job and Rutgers was perfect, near enough to New York for him to explore the publishing business, and not so demanding that it would interfere with the lecture money that was increasingly available to him. It was, indeed, a good fit, and the announcement of Ciardi's appointment was made by the university in early July and reported in the *New York Times* on the sixteenth.

As usual with Ciardi there was a great deal to do and little time to do it in. He had to wait for the formal decision and announcement from Rutgers before he could move his family to New Jersey, and in the meantime he was working hard on the "final final" draft of *The Inferno* for NAL, which he delivered on 1 June. (There is no record anywhere of any sort of report to the Ford

Foundation or to Harvard, but Ciardi may well have had some sort of written obligation to conclude for them at about the same time.) And then, too, he was entering on the "check chasing" time of year, with June stops in Superior, Wisconsin; Minneapolis, Minnesota; Bowling Green, Kentucky; Nashville, Tennessee; then to his in-law's farm in Missouri where he would pick up his family and drive back to Medford. After the Fourth of July, he scheduled a trip to New Jersey to do some house hunting, which according to John's sisters, just about broke his mother's heart.

The house hunting had been prepared for earlier in his letters to and from Horace Hamilton. "My notion," he had written Hamilton on 22 April, "is not to buy the house we should ideally like, but one that is easily re-saleable in the efficiency bungalow motif which I consider something of an abomination but which seems to unload easily." Hamilton scouted out some new development homes in a place called Thomae Park in Bound Brook and reported in a long letter of 6 May that these seemed "slightly superior" to any of the others he and his wife had seen primarily because there was a beautiful view of the Watchung Hills—what Hamilton professorially described as "umbrageous surroundings." Letters passed between Ciardi and the real estate agent handling Thomae Park, and early in July he went to see the model—a six room, one-and-a-half bath, three bedroom split-level at 243 Frank Street. He signed an agreement on 24 July, putting seventeen hundred dollars down and promising to pay fifteen thousand more at the closing, scheduled for 10 September, which gave him little more than ten days to pack and conclude leftover business in Medford, after coming back from Bread Loaf late in August.

For about the next five years, Rutgers and John Ciardi were a good match. His first office mate was Raymond Beirne, who was a Ph.D. candidate, teaching English composition. Beirne remembered how "novel" it was, and "controversial," to hire a writer, someone without a Ph.D., at that time. And he remembered, too, how popular Ciardi was with the students—in classes, in conferences, and in the offices of the *Anthologist*, Rutgers' literary magazine that Ciardi served as faculty advisor. Mark Musa, one of Ciardi's best students who went on to translate Dante himself, called Ciardi, "the best—wonderful." Another student, Walter Joyce, later wrote in tribute of Ciardi: "During my four years at Rutgers, he was the only teacher who ever suggested to me that there might be such a thing as education and that it might be fun." And, he said, Ciardi "managed to show those of us lucky enough to work under him that he did care very much about human beings." On occasion, too, he invited classes to his home, as he did in the fall of 1958, according to John Bauer, a student in Ciardi's poetry writing workshop, who also invited his teacher to speak to his fraternity brothers about poetry. (Ciardi was very impressive in his talk to the brothers, Bauer said, with his six-foot physical presence, full operatic voice, and practiced platform manner winning over even this unlikely poetry audience.) All told, Ciardi's impact at Rutgers was obvious from the very beginning. The Rutgers *Targum*, the school newspaper, editorialized in 1953 that it was "amazing" to see such "a marked increase—perhaps it could even be termed a rebirth—in serious, creative writing by University students. Professor Ciardi is certainly serving as a stimulating influence for the Rutgers man with literary ability."

But Ciardi was also a challenging, even a daunting, figure for undergraduates who wanted to be writers. He explained it this way in 1961: "Although one has to do it carefully, I spend a great deal of time discouraging students. I do that for a very simple reason: I've seen too many people gamble too much on too little. Being over-encouraged by sympathetic teachers, they committed too much of themselves to a rather precarious business." And it must have been discouraging, indeed, to find a firm blue line drawn across one's paper, put there "at that point at which I should have stopped reading had I been reading as an editor." The blue line, according to Ciardi, made a statement: "From here on, the paper gets read, but you haven't earned it; you're subsidized by the state of New Jersey."

Dan Jaffe, who became a poet and college professor himself, was a student of Ciardi's at Rutgers between 1953 and 1955, and wrote about how "terribly discouraging" it often was trying to please his teacher. Students "complained bitterly," according to Jaffe, as their best poems failed under Ciardi's unyielding examination. Moreover, it was infuriating to inflated student egos when their teacher could, and did, dismiss their commonplace verses to a single line said better by a master poet. One wounded student struck back weakly, saying that Ciardi "had been seduced by his initials into thinking he was a deity." However, even though they sometimes felt "intimidated, angry, humbled, frustrated, [and] uneasy," wrote Jaffe, students understood from the outset that Ciardi would not patronize them and that "he had not come to Rutgers to feed slop to our egos." They were never in danger of being "coddled" because they were "sensitive, talented, neurotic or personable." The lesson Ciardi was teaching, as Jaffe finally and gratefully came to understand it, had to do with a certain kind of professionalism that Ciardi was insisting upon: he made his students see they were "learning a trade," in Jaffe's terms, not simply making themselves "available for admiration." As the individual semesters inched along, Ciardi would win over many wounded student egos, which gradually began to take pride in the higher standards demanded of them. "We valued his tough-minded estimation of our work more than any appreciative sighings," Jaffe said, adding that "by the end of the semester we shuddered at our earliest efforts. We had come to realize that by professional standards Ciardi had treated us gently." And they gradually came to understand the truth behind one of Ciardi's favorite classroom epigrams: "Until passion is technical, kisses are blubber."

There was another side to John Ciardi, too, for he also enjoyed tipsy evenings with student friends like Ed Kessler and Alan Cheuse, when he would drink too much and brag that he had put himself through college by writing other students' term papers—and boasted for the first time on record (though certainly not the last) in the late 1950s that he was the "richest poet in America." This turn on the idea of rich poet versus poor professor was one that Ciardi loved to make, usually as a snide formulation designed to twit genteel academic sensibilities that were often offended by any talk of money at all. In fact, high-mindedness and vulgarity had always coexisted in John Ciardi, making him at once an artist of finely tuned perceptions as well as an earthy man, occasionally coarse, who was fond of bourbon, boasting, and good companionship. At times the high and low could be seen side by side, as in his supportive 8 April 1953 letter to good friend Richard Wilbur, over what Ciardi considered an unfair review by one Thomas Cole of Wilbur's *Ceremony*: "The current POETRY is in with the review of *Ceremony* which is largely full of shit; all these juiceless and joyless sons of bitches kneeling before poetry and praying for significance, God, and renunciation instead of enjoying it. I get more furious at that particular tone than at any other. Fuck the significance friend; let's dance. This to

say against the thin shadow of Thomas Cole that I like your dancing and that it's a damn sight more filling than Cole's aesthetic-reli-
gio crapicus."

Meanwhile, in 1952–53, fifteen of his poems appeared in
magazines as popular as *Harper's*, *Atlantic*, and the *New Yorker*, plus
the more literary publications like *Poetry* and *Kenyon Review*. And on
24 July, *Yale Review* accepted "Three Views of a Mother" for its
December issue. Concetta Ciardi was about seventy-two in 1953,
one of her last years of health before slipping into a gradual senility that reduced her to a nursing home several years before her
death in 1966. When "Three Views of a Mother" was written, however, enough of her was left, physically and mentally, for her son to
be charmed by as she picked up her infant granddaughter. The old
woman and the baby girl, one born in about 1881 and one in 1952
would span nearly two centuries and two worlds, and both were
connected by Ciardi, who wanted to capture his shifting relationship to them in a poem. "Three Views of a Mother" turned out to
be a three-part poem of eighty-two lines—and one of Ciardi's finest
works. Maxine Kumin, for example, has said it is "surely a classic"
and Diane Wakoski that it is Ciardi "at his most brilliant." The first
section has the mother and infant intermingling in space and time:
"Good soul, my mother holds my daughter, / the onion-skin
bleached hand under the peach-head." Section two follows
Concetta in the garden through the year:

> When the jonquils open she makes a life of them.
> Before the radishes come she is off to the fields,
> scarved and bent like a gleaner, for dandelions.
> When the beans are ready she heaps them in a bowl.

Winter is hardest on her:

> She is not easy to be with
> here by the buried garden. Winter mornings
> she wakes like shrouded wax, already weary
>
> of the iron day. *Ti-ti*, she says to the child,
> *la-la*. A piece of her life. But her mind divides:
> she knows there is seed enough for every forest,
> but can she be sure there is time for one more garden?

Section three is longer than the first two, beginning with Concetta on a mushroom hunt the first sunny day after three rainy ones. She returns with a "sack bulging full":

> I see her eyes
> hunting for praise as she fishes up a handful
> and holds them to the light, then rips one open
> for me to smell the earth in the white stem.

And as they sit at the kitchen table cleaning the mountain of mushrooms that rise between them, Concetta recalls a story of her childhood, her voice gaily lifting as her heart lightens in memory:

> "Once when I was a girl I found a fungus
> that weighed twenty-eight kilos. It was delicious.
> I was going to Benevento for the fair.
> I cut across the mountain to save time,
> and there it was—like an angel in a tree.

> "You don't see things like that. Not over here.
> My father ran from the barn when I came home.
> 'Didn't you go to the fair?' he said. But I laughed:
> 'I brought it home with me.' He wouldn't believe
> I'd carried it all the way across the mountain,
> and the path so steep. I made a sack of my skirt.
> He thought some fellow—I don't know what he thought!"

> *Ti-ti. La-la.* The memory works her fingers.
> "Oh, we were happy then. You could go in the winter
> and dig the roses and cabbages from the snow.
> The land had a blessing. In the fall in the vineyards
> we sang from dawn to sunset, and at night
> we washed our feet and danced like goats in the grape vats.
> The wine came up like blood between our toes."

The story, as joyous in the telling as in the hearing, was clearly but a single bond between mother and son, one of the threads that connect the generations, but this one was lovingly poignant as well because both understood the limits of time that were pressing them, and Ciardi observed near the end of the poem with perfect equanimity and age-old wisdom, "I think perhaps this woman is my child."

Although John Ciardi had been distracted in the 1952–53 school year by business concerns, his growing family, the uncertainty of a teaching position in the fall, science fiction, a Ford Foundation grant—and even a minor feud, he was still writing well. In fact, as in the case of "Three Views of a Mother," he was never better—and he was on the brink of even more impressive achievements as a reviewer, translator, and poet.

The Nation and *The Inferno*

In September and October 1953, three unsigned book reviews by John Ciardi appeared in the *Nation*, tryouts perhaps. They were followed on 14 November by a signed review called "Poets of the Inner Landscape," an ambitiously succinct essay on Conrad Aiken's *Collected Poems*, Theodore Roethke's *The Waking Poems 1933–1953* (which would win the Pulitzer Prize that year), and Karl Shapiro's *Poems 1940–1953*. Ciardi was introduced to the readers of the *Nation* as the author of several books and a lecturer at Rutgers, who would be "regularly" reviewing poetry from that point on. Ciardi's first signed review for the *Nation* was, not surprisingly, an engaging essay with rapid summations, perceptive judgments, and a special fondness for Roethke, who remained one of Ciardi's poetic heroes: "His style seems most nearly founded on Christopher Smart, Blake, the Elizabethan rant, and the backwoods brag, all scattering free, but always with a sense of breaking through a tremendous formal control. Roethke's strength is that he never talks about his subject matter but enters and performs it." From this beginning, John Ciardi continued to write for the *Nation*—at least thirty reviews (signed and unsigned) over the next thirty months—not stopping until early 1956, when he agreed to become poetry editor of *Saturday Review*.

During his *Nation* days, John Ciardi produced many a trenchant comment on America's poets. Of Wallace Stevens' *Collected Poems*, Ciardi wrote on 16 October 1954: "if Stevens doesn't win the Pulitzer for '54 [which he did] the committee might as well turn the prize into a blue ribbon and award it at the National Horse Show, for any relevance it will have to poetry." He wrote of Stephen Spender and W. H. Auden on 23 April 1955 that "Auden has been the schoolmaster of the spirit, Spender more nearly its chaplain," a distinction made to emphasize that Auden would "do anything but permit himself to be clumsy" while Spender was always "willing to trample the poem in order to declare the age." E. E. Cummings, said Ciardi on 12 February 1955, was "both silly and profound," a man who had "set out to perfect the sophomorism of the race." And of Kenneth Burke's *Book of Moments*, Ciardi wrote on 8 October 1955, that although there was "a sometimes happily haunted sense of the voices of poetry" in it, Burke had "wasted no significant amount of time in revision" and might well have improved his poems "by the application" of his own "critical guides." Ciardi also praised Archibald MacLeish's poetic drama, "This Music Crept by Me upon the Waters" (2 January 1954), stressing its technically accurate reproduction of American speech, and William Carlos Williams's "immense inventiveness" in the making of "free cadences [that] are haunted by the richest memory of meter" (24 April 1954).

On balance, Ciardi's reviews were entertaining, incisive, and disarmingly honest, neither obsequious nor abusive, and, partly because they were written in the first person, the reviews found a general audience, not just the handful of literary specialists who might otherwise have happened to read them. Ciardi managed to make the poetry being reviewed, indeed poetry itself, seem accessible, an aspect of John Ciardi's genius that would become very important to magazine readers by the end of the decade.

For reasons having to do, perhaps, with his privileged position as a boy child in an all-female household or perhaps owing to an embarrassed sensitivity that he was engaged in what was generally considered a sissified profession by masculine standards, John Ciardi had a tendency in his reviews to be harshest with women poets. In his review of *Poems* by Leonie Adams, *Collected Poems* by Louise Bogan, and *Mine the Harvest* by Edna St. Vincent Millay (22 May 1954), Ciardi took them all to task. "Miss Adams's poetry," he wrote, "is a difficult labor." He praised her "carriage, passion, and passionate management" but quoted a poem that he said could have been written "at any time between 1575 and 1625. Is it fair to ask how many centuries the poet can afford to put by? In diction?

In movement? In awareness?" And isn't it, Ciardi went on, "reasonable to think that it is easier, or at least less relevant, to rewrite even Shakespeare than it is to find the form of what lives? . . ." Then he dismissed Louise Bogan by saying that she and Adams "were sisters in the same aesthetic convent," wondering "why that sisterhood insisted on wearing its chastity belts on the outside." (Still, he said, perhaps remembering that Bogan had been a judge who helped him win the Hopwood in 1939, he could become "immediately engaged" by some of her poems: "Miss Bogan began in beauty, but she has aged to magnificence.") Of Millay, whom Ciardi had already written off at her death, he said she was "self-dramatizing," someone who had written "bad poetry to the high causes of World War II." He quoted some of what he called her "dreary lines" and said that "when she aspires to the high serious, she is least successful," reaching the merely "elocutionary" because "her poetic gift was no vehicle for the intellectual."

Ciardi seems to have taken special pleasure in blasting May Sarton's *The Land of Silence and Other Poems* on 27 February 1954 when he added up her adjectives: "I count 'deep' thirteen times, 'intense' nine, and 'pure' eleven." The adjectives fell into "an emotional area," according to Ciardi, that represented "an aesthetic position to which I must register myself as absolutely, fiercely, implacably, violently opposed. None of Miss Sarton's recurring adjectives has a specific sensory content. None of them identifies a quality in the observed object. All of them assert, as distinct from 'objectify,' an emotion in the poet." These were surely the same terms Ciardi had used to criticize Sarton at the monthly poetry meetings in and around Cambridge with Holmes, Wilbur, and Eberhart, the meetings after which, she said, she often cried herself to sleep. But Ciardi had convinced himself that his remarks were the sort of harsh workshop language that forged good poetry—and that real poets had to be toughened to such language in order to see their own weaknesses. His review of Sarton had taken the same tone.

But Ciardi saved his strongest critical language for Frances Frost's *This Rowdy Heart*, which he reviewed on 4 December 1954, a prelude to his controversial, headline-making review of Anne Morrow Lindbergh two years later in *Saturday Review*. He opened by lamenting the flabby and forgiving state of poetry reviewing in general: "I begin to think reviewers have entered some sort of age of tenderness, the founding faith of which seems to be that respect for the human feelings of the writer is reason enough for not calling a bad book bad in so many words. I say nonsense." And so, the tone having been set, he got down to business: "I think Miss Frost has written a bad book, I think it is bad in ways that can reasonably be identified. . . ." He admitted that he might be wrong, but he looked carefully at what he thought was her bad writing, for instance her "stagy" New England characters, who spoke in a language that was "dull, coy, and thrice-told." Then he quoted a particularly bad poem in full, "Cradle Song," in order to examine its badness: it was "silly-coy," and Miss Frost had not thought the poem through "its own metaphoric levels." And then there were all those "confusions in the simple literal saying of the idea," which led to the comment that "Miss Frost misreports the fact of what she is talking about." And then, in conclusion, Ciardi blasted her for being what he thought of as too feminine, that is, without enough of the masculine virtues of true poets: "Poetry requires more than sensitivity and decency—which Miss Frost clearly has; it requires also a talent and the hard insistence of an aesthetic discipline, neither of which I am able to find in her poetry." Sensitivity and decency were feminine virtues (even when found in men)—aesthetic discipline was masculine.

Frances Frost's book had been one of the first in a poetry publishing venture, not too unlike what Ciardi himself had under-taken at Twayne, sponsored by George Abbe, who wrote to com-plain of Ciardi's "rather sweepingly harsh" review. It was hard for him to believe that Frances Frost could be "that totally bad," Abbe said, and, anyway, most of the reviewers had been kind in order to support his worthy but still struggling poetry book club, which, he said, "is new and needs encouragement." Ciardi replied:

> You publish a book, a reviewer or poet [writes] the review, you are more or less either a bastard or a good guy not on your reasoning but on whether you were "cooperative" or not, or "favorable" or not. I began a May Sarton review with "I must file a dissenting report on May Sarton's new poems." The rest of the review was reasons and analyses as specific as I could make them of my reasons for the dissent. I know damn well that this was received not as a process of poetic discussion but as a stab in the back. That's wrong. I think *This Rowdy Heart*, as stated, is a bad book. I think the reasons for

and sources of that badness may be reasonably demonstrated. And, as stated, I may be wrong. But any disagreement with my reasoning or analysis must be in terms of the specific evidence presented. . . .

Ciardi then went on at some length to show how he had experienced the same difficulties Abbe was facing when he was running Twayne's Library of Modern Poetry—which had produced a sixteen-thousand-dollar deficit, he said. The same was in store for Abbe's new poetry book club, Ciardi predicted, and it was all traceable to too much kindness toward poets: "Much as I like you, I suspect you're probably a damn lousy judge of poetry anyhow, being much too kind, and much too much a man of honorable conviction and commitment to an intellectual ideal. More poems, I shall insist, die of decency than of any other single aesthetic cause. I honor your decency, George; [however,] I cannot count it as a reliable aesthetic criterion." Frances Frost had unwittingly become the occasion of a John Ciardi position paper on the state of poetry and poetry reviewing.

In June and July 1954, Ciardi wrote reviews for the *Nation* of three translations: Dudley Fitts's *The Lysistrata of Aristophanes*, Marianne Moore's *The Fables of La Fontaine*, and Louis MacNeice's *Goethe's Faust*. MacNeice was "always adequate, sometimes brilliant, and intelligently faithful throughout." Fitts had proceeded on sound principle by going for "faithfulness rather than strictness" and had produced "a powerful experience in English." Marianne Moore, however, had followed "Pound's practice as a translator, attempting to reproduce every rhythm and every rhyme while maintaining natural word order, the active voice, natural sentence structure and idiom." He called this "superb theory," but "impossible":

> What, one must ask is a translation? And for whom? The Poundian theory implies a display of virtuosity which is observable only by those who can read the original. What does it matter that Pound has "reproduced" Cavalcanti's "exact" rhythm and rhyme scheme unless one reads the translation with the original before him? And in that case why not read the original? If, on the other hand, one is reading in English in the hope of finding a self-sustaining English poem that attempts to convey the force of the original, this sort of "exactness" is irrelevant.

Ciardi admired Moore's "witty pedantry, dry precision, and passionate sense of form," but even so, "one is too often conscious of what a hard time Miss Moore is having with her details, which, like her language, are constantly being buffeted about by the overbearing demands of the rhyme. Hardly a poem is free of rhyme-forced breaks in word order and idiom, or of rhyme-forced paddings and tautologies."

The subject of translation, of course, was one that Ciardi by then knew well. In the middle of June, at the same time he was reviewing Moore, Ciardi's version of *The Inferno* was published almost simultaneously from the same plates by Rutgers University Press and the New American Library (Mentor Books), and shortly thereafter, on 18 July, he had an essay (taken from his "Translator's Note" to the book) on translation in the *New York Times Book Review*. He wrote there that "Translation is the wrong word, especially when applied to poetry. The idea of 'transposition' is much more fruitful":

> When the violin repeats what the piano has just played, it cannot make the same sounds, it cannot form identical notes, and it can only approximate the same chords. It can, however, produce recognizably the same air, the same "music." But it can do so only when the musician is as faithful to the self-logic of the violin as he is to what the piano has just played. A violin played as if it were a piano is simply no music. Language, too, is an instrument and it follows a logic (or illogic) of its own which is called idiom. To offend that natural idiom for the sake of dictionary equivalence is to mistake four strings for eighty-eight keys. It is the music one must go for, not the notes.

In his own effort to arrive at an English equivalent to Dante's music, Ciardi had been careful to avoid what he called the "falsely genteel language" that other translators regularly used, which caused them to miss the real diction of Dante, whose poetry "is best conceived as the perfection of the spoken language." This common error, Ciardi went on, "is neither Italian nor English but simply Translatorese, a jargon not in the voice box of either language, but simply adrift in the vacuum between two dictionaries." If Ciardi had been severe in his criticism of Marianne Moore's work as a translator, he was at least speaking from the vantage point of one well-versed in the subject.

In the spring of 1953, when NAL committed itself to the paperback edition of *The Inferno*, its editors had agreed to help Ciardi find a suitable house to produce a hardcover version, which he very much wanted to have published in advance of the paperback. In April, Atlantic Monthly-Little Brown was suggested, then in May, Houghton-Mifflin. But neither one worked out. In September, Ciardi sent the manuscript to Indiana University Press, but in October, though "the decision was a close one," they, too, decided against proceeding because *The Inferno* was "too risky." But sometime between November and January, after he had begun teaching at Rutgers, Ciardi reached agreement with Roger Shugg, director of the Rutgers University Press, to publish *The Inferno*. Ciardi gave the editors at Mentor credit for placing his translation and called it "an odd coincidence" that both he and his book wound up at Rutgers: "One department accepted the book, another department accepted me. . . ." Shugg left RUP in April 1954 and was replaced, in yet another coincidence, by Ciardi's old friend Bill Sloane, who therefore did not accept *The Inferno* for Rutgers, but saw it through production and into print.

The Rutgers edition came out slightly before the paperback, in time for Ciardi's thirty-eighth birthday, and the translation won wide critical acclaim at once. In the *New York Times Book Review* for Sunday, July fourth ("Translated into American"), Dudley Fitts wrote that he had been acquainted with the work-in-progress from the earliest going and had quarreled with Ciardi "in the unlovable role of devil's advocate" about rhyme, meter, and diction. "Nevertheless, I feel now what I have felt from the beginning: that here is our Dante, Dante for the first time translated into virile, tense American verse; a work of enormous erudition which (like its original) never forgets to be poetry; a shining event in a bad age." Richmond Lattimore wrote in the *Nation* on 28 August ("The 'Inferno' as an English Poem") that Ciardi wrote in "plain, simple English," that the rhyme was "unobtrusive" but helpful, and that the poem "swings along at a good pace." Ciardi's version did not become "stiff and tortuous," according to Lattimore, as the then still-in-use and widely-praised Laurence Binyon version occasionally did. Lawrence Grant White, in the 18 September *Saturday Review* ("Dante for Americans") called the Ciardi work "excellent," citing the modified terza rima in particular, "which reads easily and flows smoothly." Randall Jarrell wrote in the *Yale Review* that Ciardi's "translation of the *Inferno* has more narrative power, strength of action, than any other I know." Even John Crowe Ransom was quoted as saying: "John Ciardi commands a diction which is fresh and sharp, and I think this version of Dante will be in many respects the best we have seen."

Some, however, were less enthusiastic, like Hugh Kenner in *Poetry* and Howard Nemerov in *Sewanee Review*. Kenner preferred Binyon and wondered why another translation was needed at all when Binyon's was still in print—an obviously tenuous critical stance. Nemerov was confused by Ciardi's claim that he was trying to arrive at an English equivalent to Dante's idiomatic language. He wondered what idiom Ciardi was reaching for and found fault with certain diction decisions as well as some aspects of the rhyme and rhythm. In the end, Nemerov railed at large against an age that encouraged poets "who do not write free verse but a 'loosened' iambic pentameter." That which most readers and reviewers had praised in Ciardi's rendering of *The Inferno* into idiomatic American English, Nemerov chose to condemn.

But from nearly every other quarter, appreciative reviews, written with respectful admiration—even awe in many cases, came pouring in. None, however, would mean as much to John Ciardi as the later tribute of Archibald MacLeish. When the one-volume hardcover, Norton edition of Ciardi's complete *Divine Comedy* came out in 1977, Ciardi dedicated it to MacLeish and quoted a tercet from the first canto of *The Purgatorio*:

> I saw, nearby, an ancient man, alone.
>> His bearing filled me with such reverence,
>> no father has had more from any son.

The "ancient man" in the poem was Cato, praised by Virgil as "a symbol of perfect devotion to liberty"—a fair description of MacLeish as well, who had become an outspoken champion of liberal principles during the 1930s and 1940s and who had long since become another of Ciardi's father figures. When Archie received his copy on 21 December 1977, he wrote at once, "So, at last it is here, filling the house like the presence of a warming fire in the hearth." MacLeish had been brought up on Dante's *Inferno*, his mother having read it to him before he was ten, and so he had developed a special feeling for it throughout his life. He could not, therefore, have been more moved than by having Ciardi's monumental translation, its position already well-established by 1977, dedicated to him. He wrote in gratitude to his young friend: "I have been reading slowly in my room at night—silent room—your great translation of the great poem. Never more than a few lines at a time so that the images have time to grow and fix themselves. But always enough so that I can hear and afterward recall the two rhythms—yours and his—the two tongues speaking—the deep space of time between them—not voice and echo but voice and voice. You have given me many things . . . , but never so great a gift as this. I think it will last as long as there are voices on this earth of ours. I send you, my dear friend, my admiration and my love."

If MacLeish's was a tribute from the older generation, Richard Wilbur's was from Ciardi's. As a close brother poet, Wilbur had seen portions of the *Comedy* as it was being translated and had commented on passages and praised Ciardi's work from the beginning. After Ciardi's death, Wilbur wrote down his admirations: "John's translation simplified the rhyme-structure of the poem, for the sake of greater fidelities, and it is the glory of his version that it matches Dante's whole range of voices, being beautifully harsh where Dante is harsh and, what is most difficult of all, simple where Dante is simple. I think there is no doubt that John Ciardi gave the English language its best *Commedia*."

Perhaps so. At the end of the twentieth century, the Ciardi translation continues to be popular at colleges throughout the country. One of the primary reasons for its enormous, half-century success was the paperback edition, which made Dante so widely available—"Good Reading for the Millions." Priced at fifty cents, *The Inferno* sold nearly 60,000 copies in its first six months on the stands, and earned Ciardi twelve hundred dollars at two cents a copy. By 1957, Ciardi was earning three cents per copy on the 27,000 sold that year, which brought the total number up to 215,000. In 1977, Ciardi reported to Eric Swenson of W. W. Norton, before his translation of the complete *Commedia* was published in hardcover, that NAL was selling about 200,000 copies of *The Inferno* each year, and had sold almost two million copies since 1954. By March 1991, Judith Ciardi estimated that the book had sold between three and four million copies and earned the Ciardi family more than half a million dollars. More Americans in the second half of the twentieth century experienced Dante through Ciardi's translations than from any other.

In the summer of 1954, however, long before the enormous success of his translation could even have been imagined, the words that John Ciardi returned to again and again in unspoken hope were those of Dudley Fitts: "Here is our Dante, Dante for the first time translated into virile, tense American verse. . . ." Ciardi was doubly pleased because Fitts had praised him both as a translator and a poet, for it was as a poet that Ciardi wished to be known. And as usual, even while the rave *Inferno* reviews were coming in and he was preparing for his second year at Rutgers, Ciardi was fully engaged in a new verse project, his most ambitious book to date, a volume of new and selected poems.

As If

From Time to Time had come out in 1951, but had not sold well, so some poetry readers may have remembered Ciardi primarily from *Other Skies* and *Live Another Day*—as well, perhaps, as his high-profile magazine publications. By 1954, Ciardi had a new book of poems in mind, more or less built on the premise that the poet's self-examination, if it probed deeply enough and found the right language equivalent, could serve as everyman's self-examination. In an undated autobiographical fragment, Ciardi wrote, "I ask questions of my past as well as of my present, because both lie at my center. . . . If I can ask the questions of my shadows deeply enough, they will be the questions that lie in every sane man's shadows." In 1954, with this idea in mind, Ciardi intended to call his new book *A Specimen Ego*. On 17 January 1955, he wrote to John Holmes about the already completed manuscript as well as the title: "I feel very strongly, or, rather not strongly but natively, that if a writer gets deep enough into himself he reaches everyone. Somewhere at some point, maybe at what Jung thought of as the Unconscious, everybody has been with everybody else. . . . Every ego, truly found, is, therefore, a specimen ego. I'd like to find enough of who I am to make the scratching really a specimen. So the title."

Holmes, however, had misgivings about the title. "It feels too strained," he wrote, "and I guess what is really bothering me is that I think it would make you vulnerable to a lot of mean cracks from reviewers, and I guess that that is what worries me, because I like you so much I don't want anyone to do that to you." Then he thought some more and added, "God knows you have a forceful individuality, but I don't think you're a big ego, conceited, self-centered. And Specimen seems to me to have overtones of Average, of Typical. As if you called it Just Another Guy. I wish you'd think some more about a title." Five days later Holmes reiterated his fear of the word "ego" in the title and reminded Ciardi of "the other possible gambit, that the reviewer would say, Hell, this ain't no 'specimen,' this is a very unusual guy, an extraordinary fellow, lookit all he's done! What's average about him or ordinary? . . . You may have been specimen at birth, but look what happened? How many specimen egos translate the Inferno?" On 22 January Ciardi dutifully deferred to Holmes: "And you're right about the title. I have finally turned back to one I've had in mind for some time and which is much in my mind as a poetic key-idea, and a life-idea: *As If.* All poetry is AS IF, and the sum of all AS IF's is IS (or maybe). Anyhow, that's the one I'm sticking to and damn all."

As If: Poems New and Selected came out in September 1955, the first of nine books of Ciardi's poetry to be published by Rutgers University Press. It had seventy-three poems in all (143 pages), including forty-five new poems and twenty-eight reprints, broken up into eight titled sections. It was called a "generous collection" by Maurice Irvine in the *New York Times Book Review* (20 November 1955), who wrote, "When you have read the book, you have been for a while in remarkably good company." I. A. Salomon in *Saturday Review* (11 January 1956) praised Ciardi's "brilliantly executed" poems memorializing his father, and said in admiration: "Such is the mastery of Mr. Ciardi's craftsmanship, [that] each of the eight sections is written in its own key." Judson Jerome in the spring 1956 issue of the *Antioch Review* wrote that Ciardi was "a poet with more flexibility, more range, more depth, more solid achievement than any I know of who has emerged in the last ten or fifteen years." And Ernest Sandeen in *Poetry* (July 1956) liked what he called "the sweat of the engagement"—identifying Ciardi's "greatest talent" as "his ability to create images which stir the mind in wide deep whirlpools of associations."

There were dissenting opinions, of course, like Bernard Brodsky's in *Chicago Review*, that said *As If* was "spoiled by a slavish cleverness." And Randall Jarrell was put off by what he called in the *Yale Review* Ciardi's "crude power." Unconsciously, perhaps, holding on to the association of poetry with feminine sensibilities, Jarrell could do little more than complain about Ciardi's masculine virtues, which he took by definition to be antipoetic: "The hesitations, reticences, and inabilities of the poetic nature . . . are unknown to natures of such ready force, natures more akin to those of born executives, men ripe for running things." More recent commentary, however, has been less troubled by Ciardi's strength. Edward Krickel wrote that in *As If* it is Ciardi himself who "holds everything together, not Ciardi as poet but Ciardi as subject for the poet." And the Ciardi who emerges in *As If* "is a happy husband, a survivor of a war, an Italian-American who has made a passionate pilgrimage to his parents' old home." Alice Smith Haynes in the *Dictionary of Literary Biography* (1980) wrote that "with the publication of *As If* . . . , Ciardi succeeds in organizing his various pieces so that critics who wondered earlier now see clearly a mosaic of considerable breadth emerging."

Some of that breadth is suggested by the number of new poems that would become cornerstones of the Ciardi canon: "Men marry what they need. I marry you"; "Elegy" ["My father was born with a spade in his hand"]; "Three Views of a Mother"; "Poem for My Thirty-Ninth Birthday"; "Flowering Quince"; "Two Egrets"; and the first of a group of eight poems collectively titled "Fragments from Italy": "Nona Domenica Garnaro sits in the sun / on the step of her house in Calabria." Of "Flowering Quince," a poem in which he wrestles with his impulse to believe in God every spring when flowers bloom, Ciardi wrote in a letter to E. L. Mayo his attitude toward art, God, and nature:

> As for the neutrality of nature, however, I must insist that right or wrong I believe in it. I guess fundamentally you're a religious man and I'm not. At least not in terms of God. In the illusion of writing I sometimes feel the great taskmaster's eye but for me it is a tenet of my own belief in the continuity of a tradition in whose presence I feel richer than I do in its absence. I know what the religious argument could answer to that but it doesn't concern me. "Isn't that the same as a religious

belief?" I'll say, OK if you want it that way, but I still stand by my belief in the neutral mindlessness of the universe and what I had in mind was not religious but a sense of wishing to identify with the long human tradition of art because I think it is the richest thing I can observe in the universe.

One of the more remarkable things Ciardi learned about the universe he located in a book by John Crompton, *The Life of the Spider*, which he then folded into a poem called "Thoughts on Looking into a Thicket." A particular type of spider, *phrynarachne d.*, had evolved a unique protection over the eons of geological time—it had learned "the art of mimicking a bird turd":

> "It is on a leaf," writes Crompton, "that she weaves
> an irregular round blotch, and at the bottom,
> a separate blob in faithful imitation
> of the more liquid portion. She then squats
> herself in the center, and (being unevenly marked
> in black and white), supplies with her own body
> the missing last perfection, *i.e.*, the darker
> more solid central portion of the excreta."

Once again, the "neutrality of nature" had impressed itself on Ciardi's consciousness—and once again he delighted, "Have angels / more art than this?" The question runs to the heart of Ciardi's poem because he had stumbled on a way to celebrate the "miracle" of life in purely earthly terms. "Thoughts on Looking into a Thicket" became, in a sense, Ciardi's humanistic answer to Robert Lowell's religiosity in "Mr. Edwards and the Spider." Ciardi's poem was his creed: "I believe the world to praise it." He was respectfully genuflecting before the dignity and beauty of nature and pausing in wonderment at the persistence and insistence of all life forms on the planet. The application of this sermon from nature comes at the end of the poem:

> [M]y body eats me
> under the nose of God and Father and Mother.
> I speak from thickets and from nebulae:
> till their damnation feed them, all men starve.

John Holmes had written Ciardi on 25 January 1955, eight months before *As If* was released, "You're up in the Pulitzer running or will be with this book. . . ." He repeated his prediction in a letter on Christmas Day, nearly a year later. And at least one other reviewer, I. A. Salomon of *Saturday Review*, seconded Holmes's high opinion: "I have reread AS IF with pleasure several times in the three weeks I have lived with it. Among other awards, it ought to have the Pulitzer, and I hope that my review just completed for the SR will bring you a host of readers." The timing would never be better for a Pulitzer Prize for Ciardi, and perhaps sensing that, he allowed himself to think a little about it—although when he replied to Holmes's Christmas letter, he made it seem as though he was more interested in the money than the honor: "[There is] nothing I'd like better," Ciardi wrote. "The prize itself isn't worth much . . . these days, but it could be made to pay off in large chunks of lecture-platform, and on that point I am one of the true and faithful." But such cynicism coexisted with other feelings, such as the ones on *As If* that he expressed in a letter to Holmes on 26 October: "Too many of the poems in [my] other books have been a kind of fooling around I enjoy, but they tend to obscure the poems that scratch real itches. I tried to isolate those as nearly as I could. There is also the fact that I have tried on a lot of different bathing suits in my various plunges. I think these go in bare ass, and better that way. I mean to become a crotchety old bastard whose function is to tell Mrs. Featherhump that God wants me to ignore her and go to bed with her daughter. No, not that. That was a while back. What I really want is to know what I'm dying of. That's crotchety, but it's a praise too, and it begins with a refusal, which is the rock on which acceptance has to stand."

Ciardi was not among the finalists for the Pulitzer in 1955, which was awarded to Elizabeth Bishop.

SEVEN

The Rutgers Years

1955 TO 1957

Director of the Bread Loaf Writers' Conference and Poetry Editor of *Saturday Review*

By August 1954, after twenty-two years of directing the Bread Loaf Writers' Conference, Ted Morrison had had enough. He had begun to feel "stale" in the position, according to Bread Loaf historian David Haward Bain, and he worried that his personal weariness might be robbing the conference of its vitality. He had already done yeoman service just by keeping the conference together during the Great Depression and World War II, so it is hard to attribute Bread Loaf's postwar malaise to Morrison. But the problem, according to Bain, was Morrison's failure to keep a core of returning staff members in the late 1940s and early 1950s, which meant he had a hard time reestablishing the prewar traditions and maintaining the continuity of the conference. In addition to Robert Frost, who was on the mountain every year, Morrison *had* attracted many good people after the war for late-August appearances: Karl Shapiro, A. B. Guthrie Jr., Mark Van Doren, Arthur Schlesinger Jr., Ian Ballantine, and Saul Bellow, among others, but as Bain recorded it, "connections to the conference, inheritance and bequest of tradition, and acknowledgment of the ghosts who had begun to populate the verandas, the classrooms, and the lecture hall could not be forged to a faculty cottage full of passersby, no matter how distinguished. Continuity was simply missing." Then, too, Morrison's decision to step down was hastened by a personal tragedy: in the winter of 1954, an automobile accident near the Bread Loaf campus claimed the life of his only son. So for a combination of good reasons, when the writers' conference rolled around in August, Morrison announced that 1955 would be his last year as director.

At the time of his announcement, Morrison said he felt no sense of urgency about the fate of the conference, although some of his staff, as he put it, were "much more apprehensive." He began to share some of their anxiety when one of the trustees at Middlebury College "proposed a nephew who was assistant professor somewhere." That, Morrison said, "sounded ominous to me, so I decided I had to come through with a nomination. I began to think that no one at Middlebury College really had any grasp of what the place was like or what it should be—or how to run it." His first choice was Wallace Stegner, who had been a semiregular on the mountain since 1938, but Stegner wasn't available. "And it just suddenly dawned on me one time, why, here's John Ciardi right here, and he's the man."

When first approached in mid-July 1955, "the man" was reluctant to accept. Ciardi wrote on 2 August to Morrison: "When I say I really believe I am the wrong man for it and that I must do my best to persuade you to that effect, I am mostly counting the weight of my present crazy commitments. I add Rutgers, Twayne, a heavy and quite lucrative year-round lecture schedule, a commitment to get to work on the Purgatorio, a far behind schedule ms. for Houghton Mifflin, my own writing, and a number of family considerations." In addition, he said, he had "very little temperamental inclination to administrative detail." These were serious objections, and Morrison and Middlebury College administrators were actually becoming fearful for the future of Bread Loaf when no amount of cajoling seemed to move Ciardi during the first week of the conference in August—but he finally came around. "For six weeks," he wrote to Dudley Fitts on 2 September, "I had been saying no, I can't, lack time, can't afford it. Then after three days of long soul-talks I seen my duty and couldna shirk it, so am now officialwise Director of the Bread Loaf Writers['] Conf. A loveslabor mostly." He echoed the sentiment in a letter to Read Bain on the same date: "One more chain at the ankles. But this one for love."

The formal announcement came from Samuel Stratton,

president of Middlebury College, on 30 August and seemed to become official the next day when the *New York Times* ran a story with a picture of the thirty-nine-year old poet-professor from Rutgers, who had signed on for eight hundred dollars per year. In his letter of acceptance, Ciardi launched his regime by addressing two relatively minor issues. First, he made it clear that Judith would not be serving as unofficial conference secretary, which Kay Morrison had done "so gracefully and well through the years." Second, he said something would have to be done to upgrade meals: "My comment on the Inn food is very simply filed: I refuse to eat it. The quantities strike me as niggardly and the preparation as simply insolent." Ciardi was making a point: he had limited time to dedicate to Bread Loaf, but if he was going to be its director, he intended to oversee even the minor details. And just in case Samuel Stratton and Stephen Freeman, vice president in charge of the language schools—which included the writers' conference—hadn't figured out the sort of director Ciardi would be, he was putting them both on alert.

The "soul-talks" that led to Ciardi's decision had to have been with Morrison, plus Fletcher Pratt and Bill Sloane—and maybe as well with Benny DeVoto, who had been an important advisor and friend of the conference since 1932 and was a special speaker in 1955. Perhaps even Robert Frost, whose first conference had been in 1927 and who had missed only one since 1935, had urged the younger poet to accept the position. But Ciardi knew instinctively that if he took the job it would be an uphill struggle, for in addition to his own busy schedule and distaste for "administrative detail," he would be doing without not only Morrison but also his able on-site assistant, Richard Brown of the Middlebury College English department, who had served in that capacity since 1932. A new director and a new assistant would have a lot of work to do just to keep up existing standards without the additional burden of having to reenergize the conference. Ciardi was understandably wary, but no sooner had he decided to step in than matters got worse: within a few months DeVoto and Pratt were both dead, and Ciardi's challenge loomed as even more of a "backbreaker," as he called it in a 1 September 1955 note to Dan Jaffe, than it had at first appeared to be.

Surviving letters, many to new assistant, Paul Cubeta, a recent

Yale Ph.D. and a Shakespeare scholar teaching at Middlebury, show that between September 1955 and August 1956, a great deal of Ciardi's time went into preparing for the 1956 conference. And a lot of that time went into the search for staff members. For that year and every year thereafter, Ciardi looked for good writers with reputations, who could speak effectively about writing, and in addition, as Judith put it, "they had to be marvelous at the staff [social hours] in Treman [Cottage]." But finding such people was never easy, for faculty got little pay, no travel allowance, and had to give up two whole weeks. There were compensating enticements, of course, but staffing was an annual problem right from the start. Ciardi's correspondence that first year included many faculty recruitment letters—plus a steady stream of letters and memos about the proposed new snack bar, the new budget, policy questions, fellowship inquiries, the schedule of events for the 1956 conference, and more. But Ciardi threw himself into his new responsibility and was, as Morrison later said, "immensely successful," despite the long list of other matters that crowded his life.

And it was crowded. For one thing, in the summer of 1954 Ciardi had begun buying real estate—a house in Metuchen on "pure spec," as he called it in a letter to Dudley Fitts. It was the first of about twenty-five that he and Judith bought and sold over the next thirty years. Three months later they bought another, this one a local two-family house. However, their biggest real estate deal to that time came shortly after they returned from Bread Loaf in September 1955, when they sold 243 Frank Street, Bound Brook, and bought a huge home at 31 Graham Avenue in Metuchen for twenty thousand dollars—plus another three thousand dollars in improvements. (Any fleeting thought Ciardi may have had about doing some of the work himself went by the board when, after about a month in the new house, he came down with what he called a "wrenched sacroiliac," which sidelined him completely for two weeks in October, caused him to cancel a lecture trip to the West Coast, put him on very limited duty until Christmas, and cautioned him against overdoing it in the future.) Thirty-one Graham Avenue was a large, white, eighty-year-old house with high columns that made it look stately and plantation-like. Inside there were ten rooms and five and a half baths—plus a two-car garage. Perhaps the

Ciardis felt they needed more room because Judith had given birth to their third child, Benn Anthony, on Christmas Day 1954. Certainly their "new" suburban mansion was plenty big enough for a one-year-old, a two-year-old, and a three-year-old to ramble around and grow up in. But upgrading homes kept Ciardi thinking about his financial obligations—and ways of meeting them. Making a dollar was more important than ever.

Moreover, Ciardi's professional life was filled up with even more duties than those he had listed in his letter to Ted Morrison in the summer of 1955. For one thing, he was in charge of the poetry section of the next edition, number 9, of *New World Writing*, which kept him corresponding with poets all over the country—Conrad Aiken, John Frederick Nims, James Wright, Henry Rago, David Wagoner, May Swenson, Ted Weiss, Stanley Kunitz, Richard Wilbur, and many others. He received the Harriet Monroe Memorial Prize from *Poetry* (including one hundred dollars) for three poems that had appeared in the May 1955 issue: "Thoughts on Looking into a Thicket," "On Looking East to the Sea with a Sunset behind Me," and "Elegy" ["My father was born with a spade in his hand"]. He also served on the Shelley Memorial Award jury; continued reviewing books for the *Nation*; considered a job switch in November to teach creative writing at Brooklyn College; appeared on a CBS radio broadcast on Wallace Stevens in December; and became a director of the national College English Association at its end-of-the-year meeting. And most important of all, sometime in December Norman Cousins asked Ciardi if he would be interested in becoming the poetry editor of *Saturday Review*.

When Cousins first broached the subject, Ciardi replied that he was "uneasy" about it: "I had, I told him frankly, thought the poetry was mushy, and its poetry commentaries (Robert Hillyer's stupid—and ignorant—series of attacks on Ezra Pound, for instance) [were so annoying] that for years I had refused to submit anything to *SR*." In fact, only one of Ciardi's poems had ever appeared in the old *Saturday Review of Literature*, "Summer Night" (9 August 1947), plus three essays, including the one on Edna St. Vincent Millay (11 November 1950) in which he had quoted some poems from memory and gotten a few lines wrong. Despite some angry reader mail on that occasion, Norman Cousins wanted the not-yet-forty-year-old poet to be his next poetry editor. Being a poetry editor had always interested Ciardi, as far back as his association with student literary magazines in college, at the University of Kansas City *Review* (which was still carrying his name on its masthead as late as the summer issue 1956), and at Twayne. So despite being "uneasy" about *SR* because it was what he called "relentlessly middle brow" and always "in danger of having the obvious thing to say on the widest range of subjects," it seemed an almost foregone conclusion that Ciardi would accept. But as was his habit, especially where poetry was concerned, he was driving a hard bargain.

On 29 December Ciardi wrote a long letter to Cousins outlining the conditions under which he would accept the position. His first priority was returning the 213 poems that the late Amy Loveman had accepted, about a two-year supply: "I see nothing to do but bounce it all back." Each poem would be returned with a long form letter explaining his action. (In part, it said he regretted "any disappointment that may follow," but he could not "honorably, apologize for what I do in conscience.") Any poems Cousins felt compelled to publish of the backlog had to appear before Ciardi could be announced as the new poetry editor. With the same tone he had taken with Clarence Decker when he wanted total control of the poetry end of the UKC *Review*, Ciardi wrote to Cousins: "I take a personal pride in the fact that I stand for something, and I cannot permit that reputation to be blurred. Once announced as po ed, therefore, I must insist that I be consulted on all matters relevant to poetry. All in good faith, all in good reason, but if I am mastheaded as poetry editor it must follow that anything to do with poetry will be my doing." And he wanted more than the one hundred dollars per month that had been offered, which Cousins was willing to discuss.

If Ciardi had presented his points to Cousins as conditions, in his own mind it was already settled, for on the very same day, he wrote to John Holmes: "This in haste, but I want you to know what is not yet formally announced but what I would very much like to be spread about quietly among good people, that I have signed on as po ed of the *Sat Review*." Then, poet to poet, Ciardi offered a brief manifesto on future poetry policy at *SR*:

1. Poems alive are better than poems dead.
   sub 1: adjectives don't take the place of things.
2. Damn well more venturesomeness applicable. I'll be
   bucking some pretty fat attitudes and can't full throttle
   at once, but any similarity between future *SR* poetry
   and RPT Coffin will be just as dead as each other.
3. Prompt bounce if bounced and acceptance as prompt
   as can be. . . .

Many years after the fact, Ciardi wrote gently about his predecessor
and her backlog of poems: "Amy Loveman had been a sweet and
kindly person but a sentimental rather than a disciplined reader of
poetry. Through her long friendship with the Poetry Society of
America she had allowed *SR* to become almost a house organ of PSA,
and PSA, whatever its social graces, was not exactly the heartland of
authentic American poetry." But back on 30 December 1955, in a
letter to Dudley Fitts, he'd been more impatient and less gentle: "Am
ass deep in the remains of Amy Loveman. What a load of crap."

Ciardi would prove to be a great asset to *SR*, but in some ways
his selection as poetry editor was a surprise. William Rose Benét,
one of the founding editors of the magazine and its only poetry
editor, had overseen *SR*'s poetry and poetry reviews in a gentle-
manly, even genteel, sort of way until his death in 1950. As Norman
Cousins put it, "Bill Benét sometimes allowed his personal qualities of kindness and supportiveness to affect the choice of poetry
in the magazine." Amy Loveman was another of the founding editors, "one of the noblest and kindest humans on this earth," according to Cousins, and she picked up the chores of "acting poetry
editor" in 1950, although to Ciardi she had a marked preference for
"poesy"—what he called "little mediocrities, sonnets that sounded
as if they were written not by human beings, but by The Official
Voice of the Sonnet."

Meanwhile, looking for a permanent replacement for Benét
in the early 1950s, Cousins had begun following Ciardi's contributions to the *Nation* and thought that the young poet-professor-
translator-reviewer might do well as *SR*'s new poetry editor,
although he knew full well that Ciardi represented an altogether
new energy level and that poetry in the magazine would be treated

very differently under a Ciardi administration. But he liked Ciardi's reviews, which he called "crisp, articulate, provocative," and he recalled "that Bill Benét had thought highly of him." And long afterward (after periods when he might have had reason to question his own judgment), Cousins was more certain than ever that he had made the right decision because Ciardi proved to be "unambiguous, unequivocal, uncompromising": he was "the stern sentry at the gate, permitting no one, however needy, poignant, or appealing to cross the threshold to the pages of *SR* who didn't meet his standards." Ciardi's sure sense of who he was as a modern poet and what he was after, plus his determination to present the best new poets of the age, all represented a clear break with the magazine's not-very-bold past—and to his credit, Cousins shrewdly saw Ciardi's appointment as not merely good for poetry, but good for business as well. Moreover, he liked the masculine style of this former B-29 gunner, whom he characterized as a "combination of a Hemingway big-game hunter and a charging fullback."

Cousins may have thought he was taking a gamble, considering the type of readers he had, but he seemed to sense from the outset that Ciardi would add an exciting new element to the *Saturday Review* mix—and that he would challenge the stereotype of poets as effete and bloodless. Sparks were almost guaranteed. The official press release of Ciardi's appointment was dated 29 March 1956.

Then, with his first Bread Loaf conference still four months away and the announcement of his new job as poetry editor at *Saturday Review* barely in print, Ciardi wrote to Paul Cubeta: "The American Academy of Arts & Letters has offered me a fellowship [its *Prix de Rome*] to the American Academy in Rome from Sept. to Sept. of next year and I shall leave with the family soon after BL returning in time for BL '57. The year in Europe will compound some problems, but I am sure they will remain manageable." Ciardi would be working on his translation of the *Purgatorio* during the period of his fellowship in Rome, according to the announcements put out by Archibald MacLeish, president of the American Academy. It was clearly a wonderful opportunity, and opportunities seemed to be tumbling over themselves to reach Lucky John in 1955 and 1956.

Ciardi may have been too quick and nonchalant in his assurances to Cubeta that all the problems at Bread Loaf would "remain manageable," but he did have a plan. Bill Sloane would take care of most of the important decisions for the 1957 conference as a sort of unpaid associate director, and Paul Cubeta would take care of the daily matters that called for immediate attention. (As it turned out, however, Cubeta, too, had to perform his duties long distance as he spent the 1956–57 school year on a grant at Harvard.) Meanwhile, Ciardi in Rome planned to coordinate Bread Loaf business "via airmail." The plan wasn't as naive as it seemed on the surface because he would not be leaving until after the 1956 conference, which meant he would have one full year's experience behind him—and he had learned a great deal already, including a management style and a sense of what needed to be done. He had, in fact, displayed an immediate knack for the job, probably owing to his deep affection for the institution, its people, and its traditions. His time was almost all spoken for, so he worked quickly and effectively when he turned his attention to Bread Loaf, making sure that one way or another everything got taken care of, and ending more than one letter, as he did on 5 January 1956 to Stephen Freeman, with a plea for forgiveness: "I obviously have too many jobs for decent letter writing." But even Ciardi's letters were nearly always better than he let on—interesting and personal, clear and economical—and the jobs relating to Bread Loaf did get done. Paul Cubeta wrote to Mary Moore Maloney on 30 July 1956: "Captain John runs an efficient ship, and I've never worked so hard for anyone in my life. But the conference looks terrific so what the heck." With what he had learned and accomplished in 1955–56, Ciardi felt no doubt that he would be able to keep things together well enough from Rome for the 1957 conference to take place, and then, as he said, perhaps with more hope than certainty, forever after he would give Bread Loaf all the time it needed, each and every year.

The 1957 conference was a year and a half away on 9 February 1956 when Ciardi wrote to Robert Frost that he was looking forward to seeing him that August, although Ciardi made it clear he was not being so presumptuous as to extend an actual invitation: "I can't insult you by *inviting* you to Bread Loaf; that would be too much like inviting a man into his own house." But he did invite Frost to submit a poem to *Saturday Review*. Frost wrote back on 3 March:

> Dear John:
> Listen to the name reverberating through the mountains.
> You read my poems. I read yours. You ask in yours if God

loves you. By all the signs he is playing you for one of his favorite boys, professor, publisher, editor, lecturer, director, and accepted poet. We all love to watch you go it. Glad to do any little thing I can to add to your happiness. Count on me of course for the Conference and perhaps a poem before too long for your department on Norman Cousin's [*sic*] magazine.

The real occasion of the letter, as Ciardi later said, was that Frost signed it "Robert." They weren't equals, of course, but they were to be on a first-name basis. The Frost letter was like a papal blessing. There were rituals and traditions to be observed at Bread Loaf, and the old man who reigned supreme was putting himself at the disposal of the young man. Ciardi was sensitive to all such symbols and preserved them with a strong sense of being true to the people and the ideals of the conference he had inherited.

Despite his commitment to conference traditions, Ciardi instituted a number of changes during his first year. For one thing, he invited some new people, like Merle Miller and Leonie Adams, to join the staff and quietly dropped May Sarton—which added to her grievances against him. He also arranged for two new fellowships provided by publishers, one from Holt in Frost's name, and the other from Houghton Mifflin in DeVoto's. In addition, scholarship aid was expanded, and a couple of social customs were modified. For example, even though they had done so on a regular basis for at least the previous five years, fellows would from then on be expected to take turns as bartenders, mixing up midday Bloody Marys and afternoon martinis at Treman. And the director's luncheon table, where Morrison and selected staff members had made themselves available every day to eat with the conferees, was discontinued in favor of a series of informal coffee hours. The new luncheon arrangements, which would include in future years the placement of the staff dining table onto a dais, were needed, in Ciardi's view, to protect the staff from being overwhelmed by what he called "arm-grabbers," that is, students who always seemed to expect more in return for their tuition money than could reasonably be given—one of the Bread Loaf traditions Ciardi, like the other directors before him, wanted to minimize, if not eliminate. Ciardi was also in total agreement with previous directors when he stated in his first *Bulletin* in 1956, "Writing, of course, cannot be taught. It can, however, be learned, and Bread Loaf assists the learning process by contagious enthusiasm and by the orderly exploration of principles in lectures, workshops, and individual criticism." But, he cautioned in sharply unambiguous terms, "No one should come to Bread Loaf in the expectation of having his mediocrity flattered."

Ciardi's *Bulletin* comment had made its point: those who signed up should not expect to be mollycoddled for two weeks in August. But though it had been firmly stated, it was meant to give pause, not offense—and 1956 egos were not, in any case, as easily bruised as they would be a decade later. Moreover, Ciardi was right to be honest with potential customers *before* they actually paid their money and showed up on the mountain.

Either way, however, Ciardi was too busy as a poet-professor in 1956–57 to second-guess himself about minor Bread Loaf changes. In February, Folkways Records put out an album of Ciardi reading from *As If;* in March he published an article in *Think*, the IBM house organ, called, "Why Read Modern Poetry?"; he lectured in Virginia and Oklahoma, among other stops; and on 20 June, he was approached by Henry Thoma of Houghton Mifflin to see if he might be interested in preparing the poetry section of a literature textbook—an idea that caught Ciardi's imagination and became *How Does a Poem Mean?* four years later. In early August he submitted a pair of poems to M. L. Rosenthal, then poetry editor of the *Nation*, thus beginning an association that Ciardi valued highly. Although they met only at large social functions and never became friends, Ciardi liked the way Rosenthal picked at his poems by mail, helping him to sharpen them and bring them into better focus. He followed Rosenthal's suggestions for improving both poems that August, and one of them, "Memory of Paris," was published in the *Nation* on 15 September 1956.

On 14 April 1956, Ciardi published his own poem, "For Bernard DeVoto," in *Saturday Review*, the first of many of his that would appear there in the next fifteen years or so. Three weeks later his first essay appeared, "Everyone Writes (Bad) Poetry," in which, as the headnote stated, the new poetry editor "outlines the principles that will guide him in selecting verse for this magazine." He admitted in the article to being "human, partial, and imperfect," but he would nonetheless "separate the poetry from the self-expression."

This was necessary, he wrote, because poetry was "a life-summoning force on the order of a religion." Slovenliness would not be tolerated, especially when it came to "a heavily adjectival style," all forms of "verbal clichés," and "moral messages": "Poetry is neither moral nor immoral. . . . More poems die of platitudinous decency than of any other cause." And why was it, he wondered, that so many "sweet, sincere, and dull people . . . are almost invariably sonnet-addicts"? No matter: "Write sonnets if you must but—barring the miracle— do not expect to find them in the pages of this magazine." Thus the new standards were set, and the confrontational—and inevitably controversial—Ciardi era at *Saturday Review* had begun, accompanied by twenty-three poems of the new order by such poets as May Swenson, Louis Simpson, Stanley Kunitz, James Wright, Howard Moss, Walker Gibson, and Philip Booth.

After one more article of his own, "Poverty on Parnassus: The Economics of Poetry" (28 July), in which he examined the pluses and minuses of poets being increasingly associated with universities, Ciardi went to Bread Loaf and at the same time prepared himself and his family for their trip to Italy. Then, on 7 September, the Ciardis left the port of New York on the steamship *Roma* bound for Naples. By the beginning of October, they were settled in at Viale Giuseppe Mazzini 112, in Rome, about two miles from the academy, which was not able to accommodate a family of five. The $3,000 stipend covered his own travel expenses, the family's living expenses, $150 for books and supplies, $300 for European travel— and $700 that had to go back to the academy to cover its expenses. His monthly check from the academy came to about $150, which was supplemented by some grant money from Rutgers plus about one hundred dollars a month each from *Saturday Review* and Bread Loaf. Ciardi operated on a careful budget in Rome, but he had enough money to hire a live-in maid and take a train to Switzerland to buy a Volkswagen for $1,200, which the family used in Italy and then shipped back to the United States in July 1957. The fall months went by quickly as Ciardi worked on *The Purgatorio*, played pool with the artist Zubel Kachadoorian at the academy's billiard room, and saw as much of the surrounding area as he could.

The *Saturday Review* work seemed to fall into place as early as 10 October, when Ciardi wrote to Cousins that he had received "a couple of well-selected batches of poems" and that some contributors were sending submissions directly to him through the academy's address in Rome. But a month later Ciardi received a handful of poems written by friends of Norman Cousins and sent along by Cousins himself. Ciardi wrote a short rebuke to Cousins, saying that some of the poems had "sincerity" but no "pleasure," and that they all had too much message. Of one of the authors, Ciardi wrote, "She writes the way I sculp[t]: very solid, but the ears are always wrong. I conclude that everyone has passion, but there has to be that other passion, too—the passion for heroes with real ears. This sermon you may file under the 11th Commandment: Thou shalt not ears-drop." Cousins felt the sting, but ignored it.

Then on 21 November, Ciardi received a list of poems accepted but waiting for publication, which included seven clerihews by Clifton Fadiman that Ciardi had explicitly ruled out for the magazine. He wrote a memo to Cousins reminding him that the poems were not to be used as anything other than "captions to cartoons." Or maybe, he said, the poems could be "quietly eliminated." Either way, Ciardi announced to his boss, "these botches must not run as straight *SR* poetry. In Shakespeare's name." Perhaps, Cousins may have thought to himself, he had underestimated the headstrong independence of his new poetry editor.

In the midst of this thrust and parry between Cousins and Ciardi, Ciardi went on the offensive. On 15 December, in *Saturday Review*'s poetry issue, Ciardi set the stage in a long teacherly article called, "What Every Writer Must Learn," in which he stressed that "art is artifice": "The writer must learn beyond any flicker of doubt within himself that art is not life itself but a made representation of life." The article was a reworking of Ciardi's opening talk at Bread Loaf in August, which underscores the fact that he was treating *SR* readers—and especially the editor-in-chief—as students who needed a fundamental lesson or two on poetry. And so it was with his long-standing zeal to teach Americans how to read modern poetry, set against the troubling interference of Norman Cousins in the poetry pages of *Saturday Review*, that Ciardi decided to use the first opportunity that came to hand for a controversial review, "clearing some of the national air," as he put it. It would be, in Ciardi's judgment, the sort of review that one rarely ever read—a harsh appraisal based on the expertise of a qualified reviewer. It would put into practice for the student-writer (as well as the student of writing) some of the tough-mindedness implied in "Everyone Writes (Bad) Poetry." Ciardi sensed that the time was right to explode the genteel fantasy-world of bad poets who were regularly aided and abetted by inept or overkind reviewers.

In an *SR* end-of-year roundup of the best poetry books published in 1956, Ciardi saw an opportunity. The column, titled "Verse to Remember" and appearing on 22 December, began by mentioning the year's most forgettable book that was nonetheless being bought up in great numbers. Ciardi wrote: "If there must be special honors for the worst 1956 book by a known-name poet let them be granted to Anne Morrow Lindbergh for *The Unicorn and Other Poems.*"

Anne Morrow Lindbergh

On 12 January 1957, Ciardi's full-scale review/ attack on Anne Morrow Lindbergh was published in the *Saturday Review* as "A Close Look at the Unicorn," a title supplied by someone at *SR* in place of the one Ciardi had chosen, "The Slovenly Unicorn." It was aimed not only at Lindbergh's poetry, but at the legions of so-called critics and reviewers who had abdicated their responsibility when they chose not to show just how bad Mrs. Lindbergh's book was. Ciardi meant his review to be yet another of his lessons on how to read (and write) modern American verse; only this time he had the entire *Saturday Review* readership for his audience—plus one man in particular, Norman Cousins, who clearly needed a few more lessons, Ciardi thought, not only in evaluating poems but also in leaving his poetry editor to take care of business as he saw fit. If no other reviewer was prepared to say honestly what was wrong with Mrs. Lindbergh's poetry, presumably out of sympathetic deference to her as a symbol of ladylike gentility, John Ciardi would step up and do the job—for poetry's sake.

Mrs. Lindbergh was a woman of "great personal distinction," Ciardi acknowledged, a woman whose name and six earlier books ensured a wide sale, at $2.95 per copy, of her first book of poems, for which, he said, "I have, in duty, nothing but contempt to offer." *The Unicorn and Other Poems* was "an offensively bad book—inept, jingling, slovenly, illiterate even, and puffed up with the foolish afflatus of a stereotyped high-seriousness, that species of esthetic and human failure that will accept any shriek as a true high-C." Ciardi allowed this to stand as his thesis, and with an evangelist's fervor he undertook the proof of it by going on to specify "the particular badness of this sort of stuff." He didn't have to look far. His third, fourth and fifth paragraphs addressed the book's first poem, "The Man and the Child." The man, he said, was "exquisitely foolish"—and the poem had a "clash of cliché," a "tortured and rhyme-forced inversion," and an overall "dull nothingness." Poem two was just as dreadful, but with the added burden of bad grammar. By the third poem, Ciardi had become "accustomed to mindlessness" and began to skip pages. The next poem he looked at, on page eighteen, was so bad that he reminded Mrs. Lindbergh "that freshman English students are required to take remedial courses when they persist in such illiteracies." What becomes clearer and clearer, Ciardi said, "is the fact that [Mrs. Lindbergh] is constantly in trouble with the simplest of rhymes . . . and that, lacking first a sound grammatical sense and second anything like a poet's sense of words and their shades of meaning, she is defenseless against her rhyme-schemes and will commit any absurdity while entangled in her own harness." The whole book came to "low-grade poetry and low-grade humanity," something that in the end, Ciardi wrote, is "an assault on one of the most enduring sanctions of the total human experience"—that is, poetry itself. To Ciardi, Mrs. Lindbergh had committed sacrilege: "For a person of poetic pretensions to misuse language itself in so slovenly a way is certainly akin to Original Sin, and in the absence of the proper angel I must believe that it is the duty of anyone who cares for the garden to slam the gate in the face of the sinful and abusive." Finally, by way of conclusion, Ciardi addressed a poem that was "as pedestrian, tone-deaf, and silly a proposition in intellect as ever befuddled a high-school valediction." One quatrain was particularly offensive as well as physiologically impossible:

> Down at my feet
>> A weed has pressed
> Its scarlet knife
>> Against my breast.

This was, indeed, he wrote, "miserable stuff."

Ciardi's Lindbergh review led Norman Cousins to say later of his brash poetry editor that he was "the least temporizing man I ever met," with "no talent for ambiguity, either in his opinions or his relationships." Certainly there was no temporizing in his now well-known review of Mrs. Lindbergh's poems. He had been harsh in his straightforward comments, irreverent some people seemed to feel, yet his review had been written with reverence toward poetry, which to Ciardi was the ultimate and most unassailable of all moral high grounds. And in this Ciardi was like Edgar Allan Poe a century earlier, whose critical message, delivered in blunt language, was that there was too much undiscriminating praise being paid to the most mediocre of poets.

According to Dorothy Herrmann, Mrs. Lindbergh's biographer, "Anne was deeply wounded by Ciardi's scathing comments," which, she added, were "needlessly venomous"—although Herrmann conceded that Ciardi's review was "in the main correct," for Lindbergh "was not a very good poet" and was indeed guilty of the high-seriousness that Ciardi accused her of, and which Herrmann herself described as "cloying." Regardless of how right Ciardi was, however, as soon as the review began appearing in subscribers' mailboxes, a steady stream of letters to the editor began to build into a river of protest. All those readers who had grown up with William Rose Benét and Amy Loveman, plus standards set by the Poetry Society of America, were lying in wait. They were angry with Ciardi for returning all those "accepted" poems and setting a new tone—one that could be condescending as well as autocratically abrasive—for the poetry pages of *Saturday Review*. Ciardi's treatment of Mrs. Lindbergh was simply more than many readers would tolerate. No accurate count of the number of letters has survived, but Cousins called it "thousands" and said that "nothing in the previous history of the magazine had gotten under the skin of more readers." One reader wondered why Ciardi took "a baseball bat to club a butterfly?" Another reminded Ciardi that "one may chide a lady but no gentleman slaps her in the face." And a third, with perhaps more insight than the writer imagined, wrote, "I suggest you let some other reviewer take over women poets, especially if they are successful."

The debate escalated into something like a minor national scandal, with Ciardi critics and supporters showing up everywhere.

The *San Francisco Call* (9 March) came out for Ciardi, "who is no angel but a sound judge of poetry." The *Cleveland Plain Dealer* (24 February) thought that Ciardi "might have expressed himself more gently— and just as effectively." The *Nashville Tennessean* (10 March) offered that Ciardi was "on the side of the best critics now writing." The *Catholic Messenger* of Davenport, Iowa (17 March), reported that "Ciardi's language was strong, but the evidence to support his indictment was abundant." And the news item was carried in similar fashion in newspapers and magazines throughout the country—the *Omaha World Herald*, the *Chicago Tribune*, the *Buffalo Evening News*, the *San Diego Union* (which reprinted the entire review), the *Boston Globe*, the *Raleigh Observer*, and so on through all the large and small markets of America. It was even covered by *Time* magazine's issue of 18 February as "Critic Under Fire." The *Saturday Review* was being treated to more print space than Norman Cousins could have bought with a major and very expensive advertising campaign.

After the first wave of protests had been printed in *SR*, a "counter-wave," as Cousins termed it, came in, defending the beleaguered poetry editor. The entire uproar was astounding, and Cousins was suitably appreciative. He cabled Ciardi in Rome on 7 February, "Please telephone me collect immediately. Hellzapoppin and I couldn't be happier but we have to check signals." Soon, however, as Cousins later remembered it, he became uneasy about the tone of the debate, frightened perhaps that the controversy might have an overall detrimental effect on the magazine. He wrote that since "a fairly substantial number of readers" wanted him to step in and settle matters, he thought it might be a good idea for him to do so. His primary reason for getting into the fray at all, however, was that he had been captured by the impassioned rhetoric of the debate: "I had been drawn into the affair emotionally, as had everyone else." He said he thought that, at the very least, he could serve as a referee and "lower the temperature of the controversy." He was wrong.

In the 16 February issue Cousins published an editorial, "John Ciardi and the Readers," which tried lamely to straddle the controversy but came out instead as a rebuke to his poetry editor. He said that Ciardi had the same authority over his department as other editors in the magazine had over theirs, and it was precisely because Ciardi had this authority that his review had to be published as written—even though Cousins apparently ran it "with the greatest personal pain." He was the editor-in-chief, he said, but sometimes there was very little he could do to keep an article from being published, and this, he implied, was just such a case: "We find ourselves in total disagreement, but we bite our critical lip and send the copy to the printers." Occasionally, however, Cousins went on, "our restraint breaks down and we indulge ourselves to the extent of a dissenting opinion." And with all that as a preface, Cousins then took his poetry editor to task. He began by saying Ciardi had been wrong when he charged in self-defense that "few of his [letter-writing] critics knew anything about poetry"—but then, with more poetic justice than Ciardi could have hoped for, Cousins poured out his ignorance:

> Our main argument with Mr. Ciardi . . . involves the basis of his criticism. It seems to us that his critical yardstick for Mrs. Lindbergh's book was better adapted to the measurement of prose than poetry. By applying a rigorous test of meaning to each phrase, by insisting on precision in punctuation, by X-raying the intent of the author throughout, he has given literalness far more sovereignty than it needs or enjoys in verse. The important questions about a poem are not limited to its word-by-word or line-by-line content or structure.

The real issue, as the readers of the magazine had already made clear in their letters to Cousins, was that Ciardi had not been a gentleman; it was an issue Cousins tried to finesse in his editorial: "[Ciardi] also dismisses too lightly, it seems to us, the protests involving the question of taste in the manner of his attack. We don't see anything inconsistent between good criticism and good taste." Cousins thought he was being the very model of conciliatory moderation. Certainly, he concluded, what he had just written was "not intended to chastise Mr. Ciardi," who had added since joining the staff at *SR* "real salt to our stew." Ciardi, however, understood at once that he had been cut off at the knees and that the only salt in question was being rubbed into his wound.

For the same 16 February issue, bolstered by the announcement two weeks earlier that he'd been elected to the prestigious National Institute of Arts and Letters—and unaware as yet of Cousins's editorial rebuke, Ciardi wrote an apologia of sorts, "The

Reviewer's Duty to Damn / A Letter to an Avalanche." Stationed as he was in Rome, and therefore out of touch with breaking developments at the magazine, Ciardi was blithely pressing on in much the same tone that he had adopted in his original review. Of the hundreds of letters that had been received, Ciardi said in his "Letter to an Avalanche," only two had been favorable. But that, he thought, was clearly irrelevant: "I am not yet persuaded . . . that the avalanches of indignation are an intellectual measure I can respect. If the excellence of poetry were determinable by a national election, I have no doubt that Edgar Guest would be elected the greatest poet in the English Language—by a landslide. I doubt that he is, and I doubt the pertinence of the present avalanche." Furthermore, he said, the ad hominem attacks on him were equally irrelevant: "The avalanche may be right about me. But my character has nothing to do with the proposition I have put forth, and with the principles I have attempted to introduce as measures of Mrs. Lindbergh's poetry." And, he went on, Mrs. Lindbergh and her poetry were not, in the final analysis, the real issue: "I am trying to establish as a policy of this magazine that poetry is a serious, dignified, and disciplined human activity which is not to be debased in the name of a counterfeit sentimentality that will not bother to learn the fundamentals of its own art." Again, Ciardi stood firmly on the high ground—but Cousins's editorial had given irate readers the sweet satisfaction that they had been heard and that the upstart poetry editor had been brought down a peg or two by his boss.

Ciardi received the 16 February issue in Rome on the thirteenth and was predictably furious. He fired off a special delivery letter to Cousins, saying that because of the editorial, there was now "serious question as to my ability to continue as Poetry Editor of *SR*." Worse was that because of Cousins's comments, it was also "more or less embarrassing to both of us for me to resign now." And anyway, he didn't want to resign, although he would "unless we can work out a clear and firm understanding." Ciardi sent along a statement about Cousins's editorial that he wanted Cousins to publish "reasonably soon." In it Ciardi said he had "to reject this article [i.e., Cousins's editorial] and to disassociate myself from its principles, assumptions, and conclusions." He would continue as poetry editor only if he could be assured of complete "autonomy on all matters pertaining to poetry." Cousins was to understand that Ciardi would be holding true to all the principles that had hitherto been guiding him—and if Cousins could not accept that either now or sometime in the future, he was under obligation "to accept the resignation I offer . . . herewith."

The next day, the fourteenth, Ciardi wrote Cousins again, this time to say that the public statement he had demanded could be attached to his forthcoming article, "The Morality of Poetry," which had been pushed up from a May publication date to 30 March on the schedule. That article, he reasoned, was a detailed reply to Cousins's editorial and was therefore the proper place for his statement. But two days later, still unable to contain himself, Ciardi typed up a three-page, single-spaced letter to Cousins in which he spelled out "why I am so powerfully distressed." The most important problem was that Cousins had printed the editorial instead of taking the matter up with Ciardi privately as an internal matter that could be straightened out for the future. Since Ciardi had been publicly embarrassed, he felt he needed "some public acknowledgment of the fact that I reject your views." It was not true, he said, that he had "violated good manners," for he had never attacked Mrs. Lindbergh "as a person," and "I see no need to apologize to Mrs. L as a writer who has offered shoddy goods for sale." The crux of the matter, however, was that Cousins, "with the peculiar authority of your editorship's last word, [said] that I am unqualified as a literary critic by a kind of literalism that makes me blind to the total significance of the poem."

Cousins was clearly out of his depth here, and Ciardi simply would not tolerate this particular brand of high-handed editorial grandstanding by his boss. "Is it so impossible to see," Ciardi asked, "that my intention in total policy is to provide *SR* readers and even the nation's book reviewers with critical principles that can serve viably to measure poetic performance? *SR* has a terrific educational possibility and responsibility. If I am allowed to do my work, I can not only make *SR* a real center of poetry discussion, but I can [also] raise the whole level of poetry discussion in the U.S. I certainly cannot do so if the editor himself walks in spouting such random and irresponsible assertions."

Cousins replied on the twenty-first that he still took exception to the "manner" of Ciardi's Lindbergh review and was "shocked" that the "ambush" had been prepared "even before a book came along on which you could snap the trap," which was his interpretation of Ciardi's admission in a 7 February letter that he had "personally hatched this controversy." (On 25 February Ciardi clarified this point for Cousins by pointing out that he had meant merely that "I was going to say by chapter and text exactly what I thought was wrong with the next really bad book that came along by a known-name author.") Regardless, however, Cousins went on, he had wanted Ciardi to become poetry editor after William Rose Benét's death in 1950: "I sought you [then] as his successor, but you had other commitments at the time." And, Cousins concluded, nothing had changed: "I most emphatically want you to stay as poetry editor." The olive branch had been extended, and four days later Ciardi accepted it, although he couldn't resist picking at the scabs one last time in three more single-spaced pages, at the end of which he wrote: "Well, peace. I promise you in open faith to do the best I can for both *SR* and for what I believe to be a living view of poetry."

On 30 March Ciardi's "The Morality of Poetry" (subtitled "Devotion and Discipline vs. the Pushbutton") brought down the curtain on the Anne Morrow Lindbergh affair—almost. This feature article got top billing on the magazine's cover that week and ran for about eleven columns. It began with an across-the-board damnation of poetry societies, newspaper verse, and the school system—all of which conspired to create a situation in which it is possible for "the well-intentioned person who is 'interested in poetry' to be offered any number of socially endorsed counterfeits without ever experiencing a real poem." The poet's morality is different from the everyday standard ("a cliché is not only a sinful slovenliness; it is an enemy of mind and hope"), and it is discipline and devotion that raise language to art (defined as "the mentality of human passion"). "Without mind enough," Ciardi continued, "which is to say without gift enough and discipline enough, passion is mush."

"The Morality of Poetry" was a long delivery of familiar lecture notes, another lesson on poetry to the uninitiated, and it would have done nicely as Ciardi's final salvo on the Lindbergh affair, his pitch for devotion and discipline, had it not been for one unfortunate reference at the very beginning:

> My acquaintance with the poetry features of our news-
> papers is far from total, but I have looked about me, and I
> have yet to find a single regular columnist or feature writer
> on any of our large-city newspapers who is competent to dis-
> cuss more than the spelling of poetry. . . . Occasional reviews
> by guest specialists in the Sunday *New York Times* and *Tribune*
> begin to discuss poetry in viable terms. Yet after some years
> of sampling the editorial-page poems of the daily *Times* and
> *Tribune* I have not yet been able to find a poem that rises above
> a heavy-footed mediocrity. In fact, by a kind of Gresham's
> Law, the bad poetry drives out the good. Real poets refuse to
> submit their work to those pages.

Ciardi's blunder here was not merely that many real poets did occasionally publish in the *New York Times*, but that by placing such a
broad indictment, he incurred the wrath of two influential men,
J. Donald Adams, former editor of the *New York Times Book Review*,
and Thomas Lask, the *Times* poetry editor.

To Lask's long list of good poets the *Times* had published,
Ciardi stood corrected (more or less graciously) in the 11 May issue
of *SR*. But to Adams's sharp attack a week earlier, Ciardi remarked
condescendingly in his published reply that he would overlook it as
"the kind of mistake a man may fall into in white heat and then live
to regret." The "white heat" was clearly visible, but the regret never
followed. Adams was beside himself with a consuming rage that he
had kept repressed after Ciardi's Lindbergh review, but which came
bubbling up when he read "The Morality of Poetry," which, he
blurted, "stirred up my adrenal glands." For Adams, Ciardi's great
sin was an "obtuseness typical of the academic mind." Ciardi's
words were "marred by his constitutionally academic approach."
And again:

> I am fed to the teeth with the presumptuous, half-baked,
> wet-behind-the-ears, and holier-than-thou attitudes of so
> many of our academic critics. They need to get about more
> and breathe, now and again, a less rarefied air than that
> which customarily surrounds them. They are mentally
> ingrown, intolerant towards anything which does not square
> with their dogmatic obsessions as to what they think poetry
> should be and do.

That he should have been accused of being "academic" must have been shocking to Ciardi, who always prided himself on being a maverick in the academic establishment. Yet he also knew that he was partly guilty as charged, for he did use his professorship as a badge of authority whenever he spoke out in lectures and in the pages of the *Nation* or *Saturday Review*. When he presumed to instruct the general public on modern poetry, he did so as a teacher, but he never saw that educational function of his life's work as being "academic," a word he used over and over again with the same contempt as J. Donald Adams. But Adams's judgments on modern poetry had long been suspect; he was a man whose "successive attacks on modern poetry" had first been brought to Ciardi's attention by Alfred Kreymborg in a letter dated seven years earlier, 29 March 1950. He wasn't a man to be taken especially seriously, and so to Norman Cousins, Ciardi breezily dismissed Adams in an 8 April letter: "Let me add, *entre nous* that I do happen to think the man is incompetent—chatty, vague, and imperceptive." But he was not so dull as to miss Ciardi's condescension, nor so forgiving that he could get over Ciardi's treatment of Mrs. Lindbergh. Worse for Ciardi, he was in a position to exact revenge.

And so the Anne Morrow Lindbergh splash, as well as its succeeding ripples, gradually gave way to a calm sea at *Saturday Review*—which could only mean that another storm was brewing. It came in the form of a poem, "Victor Emanuel Monument (Rome)," by Harold Norse, and it resulted in Ciardi's expulsion from Italy.

"whispered assignations"

In some ways the Lindbergh affair had been exacerbated by Ciardi's long-distance editorship, but ironically that same distance from *Saturday Review* provided a sort of buffer zone that protected Ciardi while he toiled away, by day at the academy and by night in his apartment, which was so cold that he called it his "marble tomb." And his translation of *The Purgatorio* went fairly well, well enough in about early March for Ciardi to remark offhandedly in a postscript to a letter to Cousins, "I've made the halfway mark of *Purgatorio*. Semi-Eureka!" But quite apart from the explosive Lindbergh controversy and Ciardi's demanding work schedule, the Ciardis as a family were enjoying their Roman holiday enormously. They loved Rome, but at the same time they strutted their differentness. As Ciardi put it, "Instead of doing the children up as little Lords Fauntleroy and Little Lady Whatever as the Romans do, we let them roll around in play clothes, ragged and happy as you please. So here come three ragamuffins hand in hand with a tall blonde foreigner (Judith) and a shaggy slouchy male (me) in chinos and an obviously expensive sports jacket. We were traffic stoppers. Every female and most of the males we passed stopped dead in their tracks and turned around to do a head to toe inventory." Being the center of attention, in more ways than one, may well explain the happy contentedness of Ciardi in Rome, for he was a man who was never known to shrink from a spotlight.

In addition to the trip to the Swiss border to pick up their Volkswagen, John and Judith also visited Florence and Venice, where they stayed once again at the Cavaletto, the hotel they had been to in 1951. On 4 March they left Rome for two weeks in Greece, a trip Ciardi managed to have paid for by the United States Information Service in return for some lecturing. When they were not traveling, the Ciardis seemed to be entertaining, either with other fellows and their wives (the painter Zubel Kachadoorian, for instance, or the novelist Ralph Ellison, or the sculptor Milton Hebald) or with Americans passing through Rome. In the spring of 1957, Archie and Ada MacLeish spent several weeks in Rome, and Harry and Jo Hayford arrived in the late spring when John drove them all around Rome, "pointing out every fountain and driving like a madman," according to Harry's recollection. David Levin, who had been a colleague at Harvard, visited and, as Levin recalled it, although Ciardi had "always been generous of spirit," he was on this occasion "generous of pocketbook too," lending Levin one hundred dollars. Irv Klompus, Ciardi's friend and physician from Metuchen, and his wife, Ruth, visited the Ciardis, probably in late March and early April, and all four piled uncomfortably into the Volkswagen for long jaunts to Florence and Venice, where Irv had to attend a few Rotary meetings. And also in the spring of 1957,

Ciardi met Gertrude Kasle and her husband, Leonard, who were modern art patrons visiting the Kachadoorians, thus beginning a warm friendship that lasted for the rest of their lives, with Ciardi scheduling brief holidays with them in Detroit whenever his lecture schedule could be routed in their direction, some sixty stopovers and miniretreats through the years.

Probably during April or May, after the visit of the Klompuses, the academy secretary, Margarita Rospigliosi, arranged an audience for academy fellows and their families with Pope Pious XII. Knowing of the upcoming audience, Dr. Klompus had made a special request for his patients back home: would John get some rosaries blessed by the Pontiff himself? (They were to be thought of as "placebos of good will" or perhaps as "medical talismans.") At the appointed hour, the ladies were to wear black dresses and the men white shirts, and there were other detailed instructions "for assembly, transportation, and etiquette," as Ciardi recalled it. In Ciardi's version of the story, Irv provided a shopping bag full of rosaries, but there was a problem: each one had to be visible at the blessing ceremony. "I had to stand with both arms outspread while Judith draped rosaries from them from wrist to shoulder. I had never been spread wider to holiness, nor had I ever been closer to looking like a street Arab turned vendor." Irma and Zubel Kachadoorian recalled that the academy fellows were all gathered in the Vatican waiting room when John remembered that he hadn't brought the rosaries. John then "dashed out and returned with armloads of religious beads and St. Christopher medals, one of which dropped to the floor and was lost forever in the plush oriental carpet. But he was ready for the papal blessing when it finally happened."

Of course, Ciardi was also writing and publishing during his time in Italy. There were poems in the *Nation*, *Harper's*, *Poetry*, *Atlantic*, and *Saturday Review*, and on 17 February he wrote to M. L. Rosenthal asking if he would edit for a fee of one hundred dollars a collection of poems, which turned out to be *I Marry You* in 1958. He wouldn't be able to get a manuscript in shape for a couple of months yet, he said, but he wanted Rosenthal's sharp eye on the poems. So Ciardi was typically overextended in the spring 1957, when Harold Norse's fifteen-line poem appeared in the 13 April issue of *Saturday Review*.

In "Victor Emanuel Monument (Rome)" Norse described the monument as a "marble typewriter," guarded by Italian riflemen, "the hand- /picked of all Italy." The soldiers were dressed in "scarlet fez and blue / pom-pom," and they displayed "all the brilliance of the male panache." Having established the beauty of the young soldiers in their colorful uniforms, Norse concluded that the soldiers, on any given night, could be seen "in whispered assignations / picking up extra cash from man and boy." The homosexuality in the poem was clear—too clear for 1957—and was scandalously offensive to the Italian government. A week after it appeared, Cousins wrote to Ciardi that he'd "been catching merry hell about it—and from good friends too. Yesterday the Ambassador from Italy sent a representative to convey the formal objections of his government over what he termed an item of international libel." On 26 April Ciardi declared that he had no idea how "this horrible Norse blooper" could have occurred, although his official explanation was that the Norse poem had inadvertently been placed in the "accepted" envelope rather than the "rejected" envelope and then mailed to *SR*'s offices in New York. However, he thanked Cousins for backing him up and said he would take full responsibility and offer apologies to all offended parties. One such party was Count Luigi Ferraris, vice consul of Italy, in Newark, New Jersey, who wrote a letter of complaint and protest to Ciardi, who again accepted full blame: "I can only speculate that in the mechanical business of folding sheets of paper into an envelope, I forwarded the wrong poem." On 8 May, Ciardi wrote to Cousins saying it seemed "that the mistake on the Norse poem has pretty much slipped by without ruckus," but that week, just as Ciardi was about to leave for Sicily, he was called into the foreign office by the Roman police and asked to leave Italy by 16 June. The next day he sent off another of his three-page, single-spaced letters of protest, this one to Count Ferraris, and then on 30 May, perhaps on his return from Sicily, he sent a "CONFIDENTIAL: NC ONLY" letter to Cousins, which contained a two-page "Information Summary." He had already booked passage home on the *Constitution* for 23 July; his apartment in Rome was leased until 1 August; and his home in New Jersey was sublet until the same date. It was just not possible, he explained, for him to leave Italy on 16 June. He sent one last letter on 5 June to Fernando Tambroni, the *Ministero dell'Interno*, and explained once again how sorry he was about the whole affair and why he could not leave Italy on the sixteenth.

Although he was under threat of imprisonment, Ciardi defiantly stayed put and kept to his original plans, uncertain if the police would actually show up and arrest him. In the meantime, he received a letter from Cousins, who reminded Ciardi of how things actually stood: In reality, he wrote, "what was involved was something more than a mistake in submittal. I doubt that we would have published the poem if you had not written a notice on it approving it and suggesting that we run it in connection with some special issue on Italy." The truth seems to have been that Ciardi had liked the poem and either missed its offensiveness or dismissed it as irrelevant.

Between Anne Morrow Lindbergh and Harold Norse, Ciardi had kept Norman Cousins scrambling for six months. "Later in the year," Cousins wrote Ciardi on 15 June, "when you come back to New York—on your own terms of course—we'll get together and swap notes and yarns on what to me is a quaint fact; namely, that far more volatile than puny issues such as radioactive fallout or NATO is poetry. You somehow have managed to find the magic formula for rescuing it from an oppressive tranquility."

EIGHT

The Rutgers Years

1957 TO 1961

A Changed Literary Landscape

When the Ciardis arrived in New York on 1 August, after an Atlantic passage that had left John slightly woozy from seasickness, Irv and Ruth Klompus met them with two station wagons. (According to Ciardi four months later, the good doctor had forged a letter from the head of New York customs instructing his men to extend every courtesy to the returning Ciardis, which meant, as John put it, that they were immediately paged, given deferential treatment, and "were out of there in no time.") By six o'clock in the early evening, the family was settled back into 31 Graham Avenue, where neighbors had stocked the refrigerator, spread flowers all around, and set up a buffet supper. The homecoming was great fun for Ciardi as he told and retold the story of his deportation until the small hours of the evening. The comforts of home were temporary, however, for in twelve days the family squeezed into the Volkswagen (which had made its own Atlantic crossing) and headed up to Bread Loaf, which Judith described in a letter to the Kachadoorians as yet another kind of homecoming: "This lovely spot in the Green Mountains, surrounded by rounded low mountain tops, with the greenest grass in the world stays the same. It has never been more beautiful and every view is a painting with marvelous green-gold light and sparkling air." And, as an added touch of home, Ciardi took Irv and Ruth Klompus along, the first of more than ten years of service for Dr. Irv as the Bread Loaf staff physician.

Ciardi was fortunate that Bill Sloane and Paul Cubeta had performed their Bread Loaf duties well, for he had not done as much airmail directing as he thought he would. From Rome on 25 May he extended his personal thanks to Cubeta and hoped that some special and official recognition would follow from Middlebury. As to Sloane, on whose shoulders the bulk of the work fell, a personal tragedy kept him from attending the conference he had put together. Judith reported in a letter to the Kachadoorians on 18 August that the night before Sloane was to leave for Bread Loaf, his wife was "attacked by a local character" and "stabbed with a pen knife several times." She would be all right, according to Judith, but they would all miss Bill at the conference because "no one insults Ciardi as skillfully as Sloane does." Hectic last minute adjustments had to be made to the schedule of lectures, conferences, and readings, but everything fell neatly into place and the conference went on pretty much as planned and without any apparent hitches.

Ironically, considering the lingering Lindbergh resentments and the fact that Ciardi had very little to do with the actual staging of the 1957 conference, enrollment was actually up—and college officials were crediting Ciardi for a job well done. Even more ironically, they may have been right to do so because his undeniable, though certainly controversial, national prominence probably did account for the increase—or at least some part of it. Regardless, the 173 paid customers for the 1957 conference went a long way toward soothing any anxiety Ciardi might have otherwise felt as he drove up to Vermont on 12 August. Moreover, Ciardi had to be pleased, and relieved as well, by the staff that Sloane had put together. Bud Guthrie, Kay Boyle, Mildred Walker, and Nancy Hale would handle the fiction, while joining Ciardi at the poetry end were Leonie Adams and David McCord—with a huge assist from Robert Frost and a special appearance by Richard Wilbur, whose *Things of This World* was about to win the 1957 Pulitzer.

As to fellows, the conference boasted May Swenson and Dan Wakefield, among others, and in Wakefield, Sloane had found just the right man to serve as bartender at Treman Cottage. (Wakefield happily recalled his 1957 "initiation" to Bread Loaf as "one of the best times I'd had since my Boy Scout days at Camp Chank-tun-ungi in Indiana.") Finding a suitable bartender was an important consideration for Sloane, who had written in light-hearted complaint to Ciardi almost two years earlier, that the fellows they'd been getting in recent years were "deficient," which "necessitate[d] a great deal of barkeeping and dish washing from your humble servant." What they needed were fellows with "a strong instinct for hospitality and housekeeping," and "such people," Sloane continued in high spirits, were "often found in juvenile ranks." Droll as Sloane may have been, he was reflecting the sort of hierarchical social structure that seemed to him time-honored; that is, he fully expected every freshman class to join the fraternity by undergoing some friendly pledging. Not every fellow, of course, was as eager as Wakefield. Paxton Davis, a fellow in 1956, was one who bristled at the social stratifications: "The focus of everything for faculty and fellows was Treman. Customers were banned and often cruelly pilloried behind their backs. Fellows were invariably told they had no duties to perform except to make the martinis before lunch and dinner." But despite all that, Davis said Ciardi "ruled the roost amiably and firmly," and the conference "had been exciting in its way"—and "valuable."

Trudy Drucker, a contributor in light verse in 1957, was unaware of any social tensions at the conference and remembered instead that she and those whom she knew on the mountain that summer "worshipped the ground Ciardi walked on." She never forgot Ciardi's opening talk, during which he told them that "writing is not taught here; it is inhaled." And Edward Kessler recalled the 1957 conference as the one which marked a turning point in his life. He had quit his job and gone to Bread Loaf, and one afternoon Ciardi, who had taken an interest in the young man, asked what Kessler's plans were. When Kessler replied he had none, but that he was hoping perhaps to study poetry someday in graduate school, Ciardi picked up the phone and spoke to the director of graduate studies at Rutgers, who accepted Kessler on the spot. That sort of spontaneous sponsorship of talented writers was in the best tradition of Bread Loaf, in Ciardi's judgment. Hadn't his own career been pushed along by Ted Morrison after the 1940 conference and by other Bread Loaf associations ever since? In future trips to the mountain, Kessler saw Ciardi help many others as well: "His generosity to me was equalled by the help he gave to many aspiring writers: in guidance, in support and recommendations, and often financially."

Early evidence of uneasiness over the Bread Loaf social order had been barely detectable in the remarks of Paxton Davis—and it was simply unthinkable that Ciardi, who was just coming into his own as one of the country's brightest literary figures and as a crusading national spokesman for poetry in 1957, at age forty-one, might be on the verge of becoming a member of the older generation. However, despite the many Trudy Druckers and Edward Kesslers of Bread Loaf, there were also some Paxton Davises, and those with the greatest gift for prophecy might have begun feeling slightly anxious about the future.

The winds of change, however, were less obvious at Bread Loaf in August 1957, than they were on the national literary landscape. When thirty-year-old Allen Ginsberg published the antiauthoritarian *Howl and Other Poems* in 1956, a dramatic new poetic direction was being taken, although the more conservative contemporary observers hoped they were witnessing nothing more than a poetic aberration instead of a book with lasting influence. Ginsberg's long rhapsody, a centennial tribute of sorts to Whitman's "Song of Myself," was a passionately written cry against a repressive society. That Ginsberg saw himself as a revolutionary social commentator is clear from the poem's famous opening: "I saw the best minds of my generation destroyed by / madness, starving hysterical naked[.]" Quite apart from any literary reasons, however, *Howl* was immediately given a niche in American literary history when its publisher, Lawrence Ferlinghetti of City Lights Books, was arrested in March 1957 for publishing what the police called an "obscene" book. Ferlinghetti was acquitted on 3 October by San Francisco municipal judge Clayton Horn, who wrote a thirty-nine page opinion that said in part that "Howl" did not seem to him to be without redeeming social value: "The first part of 'Howl' presents a picture of a nightmare world," the judge wrote, and "the second part [is] an indictment of those elements in modern society destructive of the best qualities of human nature."

With so much national publicity, ten thousand copies of *Howl* were in circulation by November 1957; it was becoming a best-seller, with new button-down readers to go along with the hip nonconformists with goatees who went to coffeehouses like Six Gallery in San Francisco where Ginsberg had introduced his poem at a 1955 reading. (The country had to wait until 1958, however, before Herb Caen tagged the entire bohemian crowd as "beatniks.") The Beat poets, as they soon came to be known, were a new branch of experimentalists, who quickly pitted themselves against older, more traditional, modern poets. In 1959, the almost-always-kind John Holmes (who was then conducting a poetry workshop at the Boston Center for Adult Education with Anne Sexton, Maxine Kumin, and George Starbuck among his students) commented that there weren't too many Beat poets "who are as competent—this is just a technical matter—at their trade as the other kind are that they despise so." And then, warming to his subject, he went on: "Many of these 'Beat' poets are ignorant, and they want to be. They want to start things instead of building on anything that has been done. I'm afraid that their skill is lacking; some clumsiness shows as artists, if you want to put it that way."

Ciardi's response to Ginsberg and the Beats was curiously divided. On the one hand, judging from Ferlinghetti's letter in reply, Ciardi seems to have written a sympathetic letter of congratulations to him in November 1957 and to have had something in mind for a possible *Saturday Review* article. Ferlinghetti wrote, "Thanks for the nice letter. Hope these clippings will serve your purpose." It isn't clear what Ciardi's purpose was because no article on the *Howl* affair appeared in *SR*, and Ciardi's only article on the Beats as a group appeared on 6 February 1960, "Epitaph for the Dead Beats." But that premature burial notwithstanding, Judson Jerome, in a poem called "A Decade of American Poetry: 1957–1967," said that although he (Jerome) thought *Howl* was unreadable, "Ciardi did not sneer. / He quoted, 'in the total animal soup of time,' / and there pronounced, 'If Whitman is poetry, / then that is poetry.'" Furthermore, Ciardi said in an interview that *Howl* contained "an impressive catalogue in terms of pace, sustainment, freshness of the elements, integrity, and coherence of the parts." And Ciardi also testified in court on behalf of William Burroughs, one of the authors to whom *Howl* was dedicated, supporting the 1959 publication of *Naked Lunch*. Ciardi was not, however, fond of Jack Kerouac, arguably the best known and most important of Ginsberg's dedicatees. When asked in 1960 what he thought of Kerouac, a fed-up Ciardi answered, "Well, I'm not his psychiatrist, and I'm not interested in his precious psyche. When I read a piece of fiction, I expect art, discipline. Mr. Kerouac is just plain dull." And when he was asked what he thought of the "Beatniks," he replied, "The whole beat generation is not a literary movement; it's a fad. I'm already tired of talking about them—and in five years nobody will be."

In his "Epitaph for the Dead Beats," Ciardi sharply summed them up:

> It wasn't much fun as rebellions go. Heaven knows the young need their rebellions. And let it be said of the Beats that there was a time when they might almost have been taken as an intellectual uprising. By now, however, it seems clear enough that the rebellion has gone for kicks, that what offered itself as intellectual refreshment has turned out to be little more than unwashed eccentricity. . . .

Ciardi blasted the Beats' "insistence on the holiness of the impromptu" and dismissed Kerouac especially as "a high school athlete who went from Lowell, Massachusetts, to Skid Row, losing his eraser en route." He continued to praise "Howl" as "a compelling piece of writing" and refused to accept Ginsberg's pronouncement that it had been written without revision. And Burroughs, according to Ciardi, was "his own kind of madman," one who "has admitted revision as part of his craft" and who "would have written exactly as he does write had there never been a Beat Generation." In his conclusion, Ciardi delivered some middle-aged advice to the younger generation: "I hope the next time the young go out for an intellectual rebellion, they will think to try the library. It's still the most subversive building in town, and it's still human headquarters." Ciardi was right, but he missed the developing generational malaise that was suggested by what he called a "joint" in Denver that billed itself as a "Beat dive" and every night had a "fifty-foot line of high school and college kids waiting to get in."

Perhaps the Beat poets did not amount to much more than frustrated attention getters during the first television decade of American history, self-absorbed writers who insisted on spilling out the shocking elements of their own overwrought emotional lives. Perhaps their greatest interest lies in the fact that they came along during a sterile period of national history when President Dwight Eisenhower watched over the country as it transformed itself into and then out of what was popularly known as the "military-industrial establishment." But though they may seem quaintly archaic, like the furniture of a bygone era, the Beats did have a more lasting impact than Ciardi guessed they would. He had written in his 1950 introduction to *Mid-Century American Poets* that Whitman's self-proclaimed "barbaric yawp" had spent itself out in the work of such twentieth-century "yawpers" as Edgar Lee Masters, Vachel Lindsay, and Carl Sandburg. He went on: "I know of no good poet writing today who feels compelled to this sort of catalogue of the melting pot, or of the sweat-soaked glories of barbaric America." Just seven years before *Howl*, Ciardi had predicted that poets would nevermore explore American themes "in the hortatory and over-simple manner that characterizes the 'yawp.'" But when it reappeared in *Howl*, ushering in what Robert Lowell hailed as a "West Coast Renaissance," it made the sort of poetry that Ciardi wrote and championed suddenly appear "to have gone stale," in the words of Judson Jerome. What followed, wrote Jerome, was a "poetry explosion," and it was to last much longer than the five years Ciardi predicted for it. The Beats had, in fact, given sensitive souls everywhere permission to abandon traditional, disciplined poetic craft in favor of what Ciardi considered little more than overindulged self-expression.

"dedicated to the profit motive"

When the Ciardis moved back to 31 Graham Avenue in September 1957, some back-to-earth realities burst in on John and Judith. They hadn't lived there, except for twelve days, since late August 1956, and a great deal of work that had been postponed for a year had to be tackled. The centerpiece was the new kitchen, which took most of the fall and winter—plus untold amounts of cash—to complete. When it was finished the following spring, it had birch cabinets and paneling, Sicilian cart parts collected in Italy on the walls, and, as Judith wrote to Irma and Zubel Kachadoorian on 29 April 1958: "I have an acre of counter space and a super deluxe two-oven electric GE range!" But back in January, however, still in the midst of the work, Ciardi was decidedly tired of the carpenters who, he wrote to Milton Hebald on the fifth, had "descended" on them like locusts in October and were "still eating us bare." Apart from the overall uproar and displacement caused by the contractors, however, the Ciardis spent a quiet winter. They got their first television that Christmas and developed into homebodies, as Judith somewhat guiltily acknowledged to the Kachadoorians: "I've done more looking and less reading than I'd like to admit this winter." But staying at home, without many guests, seemed to suit Ciardi just fine: "When John returns from a trek and lectures and receptions," Judith wrote, "the last thing he wants to do is go to another party. That means no company have crossed the doorstep, and I think that's too bad."

Too bad, perhaps, but Ciardi was very busy "setting his table," as he liked to call a man's responsibility to his family. He was teaching at Rutgers, although it was increasingly clear to him that he was losing money by being tied down to a teaching schedule—plus he lectured, wrote essays and poems, selected *SR*'s poetry, translated *The Purgatorio*, invested in real estate, and accepted free-lance work whenever it came along. He was doing very well, well enough to make a somewhat awkward but obviously sincere offer to help the financially strapped Kachadoorians. Ciardi playfully referred to himself in a June letter to them as "Old Daddy Warbucks" and said he was printing money "almost as fast" as his wife and the carpenters went through it. He wanted to send them money: "Do you need any and how much? Seriously, I'm loaded. I've been hitting the lecture circuit from here to there like a schizophrenic centipede and making them pay till anybody but me would be ashamed. . . . My only regret is that I seem to have reached the summit: at this point the next step up is sky. If it weren't for Judith I'd have resigned from Rutgers this past year. Why teach school when two lectures come to over a month's pay[?]" Three weeks later Ciardi wrote again, this time offering to buy some of their work: "The carpenters have redescended upon us and next the house painters and we ain't rich any more on account of I have just invested in a piece of real estate which is supposed to turn into somebody's college tuition in time, so we are down to less than 12 figures, but the offer [to buy a painting] still goes and if you run short just say the word. There's always an odd thousand or two in the other pants pocket." Ciardi's references to money and financial success are frequent in his correspondence of this period. In early May 1958, he wrote to Glenn Bishop that he was "dedicated to the profit motive" and that he sought "to honor it at every chance": "By an act of poetic justice I make the people interested in poetry pay through the nose. . . ." In September he wrote to his stockbroker that he might someday get tired of real estate and "start dumping some houses, but right now I'm averaging about 18% return on the blessed things, plus some real tax breaks." And in October, Ciardi wrote to Karl Shapiro and asked if he was doing any lecturing: "I'm doing too damn much but I just can't resist getting filthy rich."

On 13 November 1957, the *Newark Star-Ledger* reported that Ciardi and three other men from New Jersey were accused by the House Un-American Activities Committee (HUAC) as being "among the leaders of an organization accused . . . of a nationwide campaign to discredit the FBI and cripple the nation's antisubversive programs." The organization was the Emergency Civil Liberties Committee (ECLC), which Ciardi supported but which he virtually resigned from five years later when he wrote to Corliss Lamont of ECLC that he was no longer available to speak at meetings because he had to conserve his energies for his work: "My sympathies are with you," he wrote, "but to put it bluntly, they are even more with my workbook." Of course, the HUAC charges caused a flurry of activity among local FBI agents in Newark, who determined that Ciardi should remain on their A List, the section of their index reserved for the most subversive "un-Americans." But the only observable negative impact the HUAC listing had on Ciardi was that the Hanover College (Indiana) faculty decided against giving him an honorary doctorate, according to a letter from Leland Miles (who resigned from Hanover's English department in protest) to Ciardi on 12 February 1960. That possibly disheartening news was softened, however, four days later when President Nils Wessell of Tufts invited Ciardi to receive an honorary doctor of literature degree at their commencement exercises on 12 June. The privilege of receiving an honorary doctorate from his home town alma mater was made sweeter still when it was announced that John Holmes would be his faculty escort. It would be a father-son affair and a proud moment for all—including wife, children, sisters, and mother.

All through the late 1950s, Ciardi's schedule was hectic to frantic. In the fall of 1957, for example, he made twenty-four day trips to New York, mostly to the *Saturday Review*, but also to Twayne and the CBS television studios. In October he made quick trips to Maryland and Pennsylvania. In November he was in San Marcos, Texas. That month he wrote to Milton Hebald: "My last three days in NY have been spent in busy sessions of saying no: Three publishers have been buying me drinks and suggesting a book on my *Saturday Review* articles but all of them want the articles rewritten to a different slant and I ain't rewriting nothing. . . . Then three long sessions went into saying no to a guy who wanted me to do an Educational TV series for the good of the world but without enough inducement to my idealistic sense of cash." By January 1958, however, Ciardi had agreed to do a series of fifteen shows called "The Open Mind" for the Metropolitan Educational Television Association (META) for three hundred dollars per episode. But in June when the first program was filmed, Ciardi vehemently objected to the amount of time required of him and offered his resignation: "Time means everything to me. I am frankly doing too many things, and . . . TV is the least relevant of them." He spent three days a week at Rutgers, he said, and one at *SR*, plus there were the "constant rush jobs" for Bread Loaf and the "everlasting" pressure of setting up his next lecture series. Plus he hated the format of hosting a program where he had to line up guests and then nurse them through the production. He offered to do all the talking himself. One way or another, however, by the middle of July he had somehow completed the first three episodes, when the program was unexpectedly canceled—much to Ciardi's relief.

In late April 1958, as Judith had written to the Kachadoorians, Ciardi was "dashing like a migratory bird all over the East": Maine, New York, North Carolina, and South Carolina, and then further inland to Milwaukee, Kalamazoo, and Pittsburgh. He was scheduled for Ann Arbor on 22 May, she reported, where he would be the Hopwood Lecturer on the subject of "The Silences of the Poem." In July he would be in Pennsylvania and Wisconsin. And so the time between September 1957 and September 1961 flew by as quickly as the mile markers on the highways Ciardi traveled. And wherever he went, the reports on his visit were more or less like this one by Guy Owen about Ciardi's 1960 stop at Florida's Stetson University: "Ciardi literally took our campus by storm. Delivering lectures, reading from his latest book of poems . . . , talking endlessly with students and faculty, visiting as many as five classes a day, he seemed to have the energy of a whirlwind."

Meanwhile, if he wasn't otherwise engaged in "check chasing," as he usually called it, Ciardi went to the New York offices of *Saturday Review* on Thursdays. He found the poetry rejection end of his work "onerous," as Judith once characterized it, but, she added mischievously, "I think he . . . rather likes 'crusading' a bit in the cause of poetry." Just as important, perhaps, was that he earned an extra twenty-five hundred dollars there in 1957 and thirty-five hundred in 1958, which came to nearly half his yearly salary at Rutgers. He would never again cause a national uproar on the scale of the Anne Morrow Lindbergh affair, but he never let up in his *SR* articles either: "The Shock Reaction to Poetry" (20 July 1957); "The Poet's Duty to Poetry" (Ciardi's half of a low-grade debate with Lord Dunsany, 19 October 1957); "The Birth of a Classic" (on Archibald MacLeish's *J.B.*, 8 March 1958); and "A Poem Talks to Itself" (24 January 1959). Some of his articles, in fact, became minor classics of outreach to the poetry-reading public he had been working for so many years to instruct: "Robert Frost: The Way to the Poem" (12 April 1958); "Dialogue with an Audience" (22 November 1958); and "The Environment of Poetry" (19 September 1959). Perhaps the best of these appeared in the *Saturday Evening Post* (1960), "The Act of Language," where he made the point that subjects provide "no indication whatever" about what a poem truly is:

> But if the meaning is not in the subject, what then does a poem mean? It means always and above all else the poet's deep involvement in the four basic elements of his trade [i.e., rhythm, image, diction, and form]. It means not the subject but the way the poetic involvement transfigures the subject. It means, that is to say—the very act of language by which it comes into existence. The poem may purport to be about anything from pussy willows to battleships, but the meaning of any good poem is its act of language.

And Ciardi found just the right way in "Dialogue with an Audience" to explain why great art is never as popular as commercial art: it is, he wrote, the difference between the "vertical" audience and the "horizontal" audience. "The horizontal audience consists of everybody who is alive at this moment. The vertical audience consists of everyone, vertically through time, who will ever read a given poem. . . . All good poets write for the vertical audience. The vertical audience for Dante, for example, is now six centuries old. And it is growing. If the human race has any luck at all, part of Dante's audience is still thousands of years short of being born."

> The point is that the horizontal audience always outnumbers the vertical at any one moment, but that the vertical audience for good poetry always outnumbers the horizontal in time-enough. And not only for the greatest poets. Andrew Marvell is certainly a minor poet, but given time enough, more people certainly will have read "To His Coy Mistress" than will ever have subscribed to *Time, Life*, and *Fortune*.

Ciardi's notion of the audience for great art proved to be one of his most popular and durable formulations and earned a place in the national vocabulary.

The Frost essay was a tribute, an admiring explication of "Stopping by Woods on a Snowy Evening," prepared, as usual, for *SR*'s regular readership, which meant, therefore, that Ciardi made it into something like a classroom exercise. It was also typical Ciardi in that it seemed to be written with an off-handed brilliance, as though it were the result of a sudden thought that hadn't needed to be wrestled into shape. The essay turned out to be both an engaging discussion of the dramatic scenes in the poem as well as a sharp analysis of its internal logic. But, in describing the poem's weary speaker and his sudden impulse to surrender and be covered over with snow, Ciardi used the term "death wish," which, he later said, "is a phrase I should never have used." He realized too late that the term "sounds Freudian. And . . . any Freudian terminology would get [Frost's] back up. . . . For two, two and a half, three years thereafter, Frost went around lecturing saying, 'Ciardi says I've got a death wish. No such thing. That's not what the poem was about.'" Ciardi was right, of course, despite Frost's denials and his oft-stated platform reproaches, and for those who needed more than the text to see it, John Evangelist Walsh has shown that the origin of the poem dated back to a 1905 incident when Frost, just before Christmas, stopped his sleigh in a driving snow storm near his farmhouse in Derry, New Hampshire, where he wept because he was unable to buy gifts for his children. Frost's overwrought emotional state triggered a momentary desire to surrender and be covered up by the snow, a death wish of the commonest sort, the same type of thing that most people experience in their lives without considering themselves suicidal. Frost, however, chose to use Ciardi's reading as a platform gambit that put him in league with those who were outraged at any suggestion that their favorite poet might be either a careful technician or a deep and dark thinker. The gambit worked so well that Frost decided to keep it as a semipermanent part of his act, much to Ciardi's chagrin.

Although the contretemps may have come to very little in the end, it was nonetheless unfortunate, for as Richard Wilbur remarked, "It mattered a great deal to John that Frost had a real respect for him. Frost did read John's poetry and did see virtues in it, did speak well of him." Anything that might have threatened that respect would have troubled Ciardi a great deal, and so he must have been relieved at Bread Loaf, where there is no evidence to suggest their cordial relationship had cooled. Moreover, Ciardi would have been very pleased if he had known of the conversation Stanley Burnshaw had with Frost on 27 March 1959, the day after Frost's eighty-fifth birthday celebration in New York. Frost, according to Burnshaw, "was full of ideas about Ciardi, more than his most assiduous hearer could hope to remember. John was not only clever, charming but sharply perceptive. Maybe at times a bit blunt, though *his* frankness was healthy. Maybe at times too sure of his judgment or seeming to be, forgetting the danger of getting things wrong. And a poet, a good one, too. A good companion. Also a bold one."

At Bread Loaf Frost remained a fixture, though a rapidly aging one between 1958 and 1962, which was his last conference before his death on 29 January 1963. His one annual evening lecture was advertised every year and continued to be the conference's highlight, so much so that in 1960, outsiders poured into the theater and effectively kept many of the paid-up Bread Loafers (and some staff as well) from attending—a situation that Ciardi controlled the next year by issuing tickets. Frost's presence helped Ciardi make Bread Loaf an artistic success for the customers from 1958 to 1961, but recruiting a "name" faculty to back him up was another matter. In 1958 alone, Ciardi was turned down by John Steinbeck, Wallace Stegner, Edwin O'Connor, Frank O'Connor, John Cheever, and

Philip Roth. Ralph Ellison was persuaded to attend in 1959 and Allen Drury in 1960, but Drury and Ray Bradbury both made last-minute excuses on the eve of the 1961 conference. In poetry, Ciardi was able to recruit John Frederick Nims in 1958 (who would be on the faculty for all but three conferences over the next fourteen years); William Meredith in 1959; and Howard Nemerov in 1961. But the bulk of the work fell on tried and tested Bread Loafers like William Raney, Nancy Hale, and Bill Sloane, plus trustworthy others who knew either Ciardi or the conference: Catherine Drinker Bowen, Leonie Adams, Eunice Blake, David McCord, and Dudley Fitts. Richard Wilbur was a special speaker on poetry in 1959, and Ciardi even brought back Ted Morrison in 1958 for a one-night appearance that was successful enough to be repeated for the next seven years. The fellows during those years included Dan Jaffe (1958), Anne Sexton (1959), X. J. Kennedy (1960), and Lewis Turco and Miller Williams (1961). Others of note included Alan Cheuse, a waiter in 1959, and "scholars" (a new category at Bread Loaf beginning in 1959) Gloria Oden and Edward Wallant (1960) and A. R. Ammons (1961). Scholars were actually scholarship winners who were supported by a new fund that Ciardi created to bring younger writers to the mountain—a fund to which he donated his own annual staff stipend, three hundred dollars in 1959.

Ciardi arrived at the 1959 conference in his first Cadillac, a used 1956 model that he had picked up at an estate settlement. He joked to the Kachadoorians that the car came not only with "push-button windows," but with "self-dispensing prophylactics in the back seat" as well. It was another measure of his success and stood in stark contrast to the Volkswagen he had driven to Bread Loaf in 1957 and 1958. By every standard, Ciardi's lot in life was improving, and he reveled in his material wealth as well as in his prominence in the world of poetry. He had earned his position by dedicating himself to his craft and following one achievement after another until he stood among the country's literary elite. He was understandably proud of all he had accomplished and the money he had earned by age forty-three, and he enjoyed flaunting it—out loud and often. Psychologically, this may have been nothing more to him than a way of expressing what he deemed his success as a father. It may have been a satisfying I-told-you-so to the fates that had given him poverty as a child. But for whatever combination of reasons, Ciardi happily ran the risk, at Bread Loaf and elsewhere, of alienating himself—by his talk of money, real estate, and material possessions—from the generation of younger poets, who, because they had not known him in his years of struggle, had begun to see him, despite his obvious good qualities, as a well-to-do, somewhat out-of-date, middle-aged spokesman for the poetry of the GI generation. Ciardi seemed oblivious to any criticism of him that may have surfaced at late-1950s Bread Loaf conferences and saw himself at the start of the 1959 conference as a success story, a role model whom younger poets could look up to. Hadn't he looked up to Holmes, Cowden, Roethke, Frost, and others? He no doubt thought, rather innocently, that it was time for the younger poets to look up to him.

Alan Cheuse, who had been invited by Bill Sloane to attend the 1959 conference as a waiter, provides a good example of the distance that was beginning to separate Ciardi from some of the younger people at Bread Loaf. Cheuse was a Rutgers undergraduate and had wanted to take a course with Ciardi in the spring 1959, but settled for a different course with Sloane when Ciardi took the semester off on an unpaid leave in order to travel the lucrative lecture circuit. David Bain described Cheuse as "a vaguely Bohemian kid" with a finely tuned social conscience. That summer, at a Bread Loaf party held in Middlebury College's nearby ski lodge, Cheuse became wild when, during a sing-along, the partygoers began singing "Old Black Joe" in the presence of Ralph Ellison. There is no record of Ellison's reaction, but Cheuse wrote of himself that he "became incensed" and "leaped up and knocked over the huge trash bin full of beer cans, effectively ending the party." David Bain wrote that Cheuse

> was at the edge of a group that invaded Bread Loaf that year, many of them on waiters' scholarships but also others among the regular clientele. Mirroring the times, and to the bemusement and even chagrin of many, they derided authority, smoked marijuana, held impromptu meetings, and boldly became fixtures at the restricted, nightly faculty parties. They caused quite a stir: beatniks at Bread Loaf!

According to Bain, the noisy crowd at Treman got so out of hand in 1959 that Ciardi would now and then call out with the frustration of a host whose party had been crashed by undesirables, "Who the hell *are* all these people[?]" Of course, he knew who they were and was really saying, "How the hell did all these uninvited guests get in?" He meant Treman to be a sanctuary for the staff, not a place where they could be hounded by the paying customers, who had plenty of time during the long business days to press their points. To oversee an orderly social code for the conference, especially for Treman Cottage, Avis DeVoto, Benny's widow, was brought in as something like an etiquette supervisor in 1960, a position she kept for about ten years.

X. J. Kennedy was a fellow in 1960. He had to read a few manuscripts and "hobnob" with the paying customers, he recalled, which meant that he was to sit at their tables during meals, thus sparing faculty, who sat off to one side. Kennedy remembered this aspect of Bread Loaf dining room etiquette as a great source of irritation to some people. He also recalled Avis DeVoto's instructions that year:

> We were told that nobody was to come into Treman Cottage except the staff and the fellows. Once in a while an invited guest was all right, but we should make sure we didn't invite a guest very often—if at all. Our task as fellows (we lived in rooms upstairs) was every morning to go around the cottage and collect the drinking glasses from the night before and wash them before noon, when the drinking would start again with Bloody Marys. This may sound like a trivial task, but there was a hell of a lot of glasses in that cottage that we would find every morning.

When Kennedy went up to Ciardi in Treman to introduce himself on the first day, Ciardi took the occasion to bring the young man down a peg or two. He had too often seen inflated egos among young writers, who needed a dose of reality rather than more bouquets: "Oh, yes, I've looked at your stuff—I've seen a lot better." The remark was sufficiently harsh to deflate Kennedy at the time, although he came to realize that Ciardi was "simply making an observation of fact. He had read many young poets in his time." Still, Kennedy could not help thinking Bread Loaf was, on balance, "an uncomfortable situation." He remembered in particular how Ciardi defended the policy of protecting the faculty from the paying customers: "I don't want a lot of bozos wearing down my staff.

These people came here out of the goodness of their hearts because we hardly pay them anything, so I want them to at least have a good time."

Ciardi argued as he could (and as often as he could) to improve the salaries of the staff, and of his assistant Paul Cubeta especially. He wrote on 31 July 1959, for example, to Middlebury vice president Steve Freeman that Cubeta took care of "endless details," carried on a "staggering correspondence," did an "extraordinary job," and so on for nearly two pages before asking that additional money be tacked on to Cubeta's stipend: "It would be an act of intelligent administration," Ciardi reasoned, "to offer Paul an additional token." And the same was true of the staff, whose low salaries were not only an embarrassment to Ciardi, but also a thorny issue in his annual recruitment work. In a letter to Cubeta of 7 July 1958, Ciardi worried about how he could attract good people "to carry the burden of the continuity of the Conference" at the low rates Middlebury was willing to pay. "We must remember," Ciardi wrote, "that for years BL traded on the long standing loyalties of Wm Sloane, Fletcher Pratt, Bernard DeVoto, Theodore Morrison, and Robert Frost. All of whom donated their services, in effect. That situation has changed and I see no likelihood of developing such a core of patrons. I have to do my best to reward those who do their best for us, especially those I lean on during the year as well as during the conference." And so Ciardi argued every year for more money for staff members as one sort of reward, with other inducements being less tangible—the unique literary excitement on the mountain, plus the clubby, boozy, literate fun of Treman Cottage, a place where staff could enjoy an after-hours, members-only time away from the paying customers.

But if Ciardi could at times be overly protective of the staff and brusque to the young poets, he was also mindful of Bread Loaf's tradition of helping all those whose manuscripts were clearly superior. His generosity had never been questioned and was on display once again when he invited Miller Williams to become a Bread Loaf fellow on 18 May 1961:

> I think it would be a powerful thing for you as a person and a damned useful thing to you professionally, to have the experience of the conference under your belt. There will be all sorts of editors and publishers around, as well as a tremendous list

of good American writers to bang heads with. This year's poets, for example, are Dudley Fitts, Howard Nemerov, and John Frederick Nims, with a couple of appearances by Frost and a couple by me when I can stop counting directorial paper clips long enough.

I hope you will give it some serious thought. I am urging it as something that could possibly be very valuable to you for a long time to come.

Ciardi never lost sight of the Bread Loaf ideal that had been handed down to him and been so important to his own career. And very quietly, when he found out Williams and his wife didn't have enough money left to get home after the 1961 conference, Ciardi gave them two hundred dollars of his own money. He explained that back in 1940, an unnamed staff member had given him a similar gift with the only stipulation being that someday he help some other needy poet. Sloane later told Williams that he knew of three other struggling poets who had received two hundred dollars and the same story—and that there were probably others as well. Ciardi may have talked too much about his money, but untold examples show how generous he was with it.

Books upon Books

Amid the frenzy of John Ciardi's professional life in the late 1950s, he published *I Marry You* in 1958, *39 Poems* and *How Does a Poem Mean?* in 1959, plus two books for children, *The Reason for the Pelican* in 1959 and *Scrappy the Pup* in 1960. And even more astounding, he was also working on four other manuscripts that would be published in 1961. In addition to *Saturday Review*, which published four of his poems between 1957 and 1959, his poems appeared in *Atlantic Monthly*, *Nation*, *American Scholar*, *New Yorker*, *Ladies Home Journal*, *Poetry*, *Antioch Review*, and *Yale Literary Magazine*. The first canto of his translation of Dante's *Purgatorio* appeared in the first two numbers of *Venture* in 1959. Somehow, through the dizzying whirl of personal and professional activity, John Ciardi continued to be characteristically prolific.

I Marry You, subtitled *A Sheaf of Love Poems*, was a bold effort that put Ciardi in double jeopardy among critics, who would measure not only his poetry, but his manner of loving as well. Yet, even though he knew as a gambler that a book of love poems in an antiromantic age faced long odds, Ciardi pressed on, determined to make this small tribute to married love part of his poetic canon. And he kept his fingers crossed. The poems had, after all, been carefully crafted, so he had some reason to hope for the best from reviewers—and because they were love poems, he could also hope for a wide popular readership as well. Predictably, reviewers tended either to love it or hate it—and everyone had a published opinion, even Ciardi, who wrote what he called a "statement of intent" (rather than an actual self-review) for *SR* on 21 June 1958. *I Marry You*, he said, was "a poetry diary of a happy marriage: not an Important Poem in the batch, but only poems for my wife's and my children's and my remembrance as the world changes out from under us." His aim was "to find the private center" of his marriage in the expectation that the poems "will touch some part of everyone's truest privacy." As to the noticeable amount of death in the poems, Ciardi replied that "love and death are forever entwined," for "love would be unthinkable were we immortal: where would the urgency of love come from?"

Edward Krickel, however, thought *I Marry You* was "a relative failure," although he conceded that for a modern poet, the subject of love was difficult to encompass in the nonsentimental and non-religious terms that the modern age seemed to demand. "Ciardi's efforts," Krickle wrote, might actually be "the more heroic, the more certain to fail because of the secular assumptions with which he had to work." The unnamed reviewer in the *Times Literary Supplement* liked "Two Egrets" particularly and found ten poems "truly original," but he objected to the "heavy, unfunctional imagery and needless violence of expression." Radcliffe Squires, in *Michigan Alumnus Quarterly Review*, said that Ciardi was here "at his worst," for, as he wrote, the love poems were "vulgar and tasteless." Thom Gunn, in *Yale Review*, wrote that the "particularity of [Ciardi's] images do not often lead up in any connected manner to the final statements." And John Thompson in *Hudson Review* wrote a parody of Ciardi, a dialogue between an ADMIRER and a NON-ADMIRER, at the end of which

Thompson advised Ciardi "to tone it down, to play it straight, to stop loading . . . lines with lumps of 'imagery.'"

Love poems are especially easy targets, as the critics demonstrated, but the reviewers were sharply divided in their opinions of *I Marry You*. Charles Poore, in the *New York Times*'s "Books of the Times," said the book showed Ciardi's "mastery of convoluted clarity," and he admired Ciardi's "striking images of observation." Kenneth Rexroth, in the *New York Times Book Review*, called Ciardi's love poetry "truly refreshing . . . , singularly free from the vices that beset most American poets nowadays with their provincial imitations of English Baroque verse and their trivial ambiguities." And he praised Ciardi's courage: "It is a great thing to write sharply personal poems about the intimacies of marriage and parenthood in a time when most of one's colleagues dread and eschew the slightest hint of the personal." Paul Engle in the *Chicago Tribune*, characterized *I Marry You* as "the sort of poetry for which many people have been clamoring: direct emotion glittering clear on the page." James Wright in *Poetry* was "struck by that special combination of tenderness and roughness which characterizes this poet when he is in his form," adding that *I Marry You* was "beautiful and alive," and "easily the best single book of Mr. Ciardi's" that he had ever read. From around the country, praise for *I Marry You* poured in: the *Denver Post* (14 September 1958) said it belonged "in the great tradition of love poems"; the *San Francisco Chronicle* (17 August) said the poems do, as Ciardi wrote, "touch some part of everyone's truest privacy"; and the *Newark (N. J.) Evening News* (27 July) called the poems "technically brilliant and essentially modern." On 30 November 1958, the *New York Times* named *I Marry You* one of the 250 outstanding books of the year, and Ciardi was happy to hear that sales were good on the $2.75 book: 550 copies in the first two weeks of December alone, and 2,790 since its May publication. (It would sell more than 5,000 over the next two years.)

Originally, Ciardi had intended to add his love poems as another section of *As If*, but Bill Sloane, as director of the Rutgers University Press, decided they would make *As If* too long, so Ciardi settled on a five-poem sequence called "To Judith" instead. Over the next two years, Ciardi wrote and rewrote the poems, arranged and rearranged them. In February 1957, he hired M. L. Rosenthal to make detailed comments, which led to several more revisions—

even to previously published poems, like "Men Marry What They Need," which had appeared in *As If* in a slightly different form than it was to take in *I Marry You*. The slender, twenty-eight-poem new volume contained eight reprints in all, seven of which had appeared in *As If*. Its first section dealt with romantic love, the second addressed parental love, and the third faced death.

"Most Like an Arch This Marriage" is one of the two or three finest poems in the new book and another of the ones Ciardi is best known for. It is held together by the extended metaphysical conceit expressed in the title.

> Most like an arch—an entrance which upholds
> and shores the stone-crush up the air like lace.
> Mass made idea, and idea held in place.
> A lock in time. Inside half-heaven unfolds.
>
> Most like an arch—two weaknesses that lean
> into a strength. Two fallings become firm.
> Two joined abeyances become a term
> naming the fact that teaches fact to mean.
>
> Not quite that? Not much less. World as it is,
> what's strong and separate falters. All I do
> at piling stone on stone apart from you
> is roofless around nothing. Till we kiss
>
> I am no more than upright and unset.
> It is by falling in and in we make
> the all-bearing point, for one another's sake,
> in faultless failing, raised by our own weight.

M. L. Rosenthal especially liked the "two joined abeyances" in stanza two but wondered on the worksheet Ciardi sent him if the entire stanza did not "foreshadow the final one too fully." To which Ciardi replied:

> I ponder this objection but I can't find it. Lines 3 & 4 seem as right as I can imagine them—a sort of scholastic proposi- tion of the case, it[s] fullest abstraction. So full in fact, that I have to doubt it in stanza three. I can't imagine how you take them to foreshadow stanza 4 which is full of sexual action—

about as far as the poem could go from the "philosophical dispassion" of stanza 2. Am I smoke-screening something in all this? (And certainly that's a perfect definition of an arch in stanza 2—so perfect that I stole it from an architect without a blush. No borrowing. A clean theft.)

Years later, Ciardi commented in a letter to John Frederick Nims on the third and fourth lines of stanza two: "Two joined abeyances become a term / naming the fact that teaches fact to mean."

> The shimmering word in those two lines is *term* with all its consonant ambiguities: fixed point (come to terms); duration (spring term); completion (terminus); an expression (a language term); and more. As for the second line: facts do not mean anything per se . . . , then one fact completes the series in which the sum of the parts is more than all the parts. Crudely: the key fact brings all the other facts into relation in such a series.

Here was a poem that "rode easy in harness," the Frost ideal that Ciardi used so often in his lectures; moreover, it was wonderfully simple in its central image, yet odd enough to satisfy Ciardi's taste for the metaphysical. And although one gets at first reading the sense of the sturdiness and beauty of Ciardi's arch and marriage, it is with subsequent readings that the poem itself emerges as equally sturdy and beautiful, with its easy handling of the iambic pentameter line, its unifying rhymes, and its intricate pattern of opposites that come together in a delicate kiss to form the strength of an "all-bearing point." Yes, he said, his marriage was "Most like an arch—two weaknesses that lean / into a strength." Emotionally, intellectually, and structurally, this was one of Ciardi's best performances.

On the dust jacket of *39 Poems* (which Ciardi had intended to call *In the Year of the Longest Cadillac* until Sloane vetoed the title as too long), were comments from MacLeish and Fitts, plus quotes from the *New York Times* and the *Virginia Quarterly Review*. MacLeish emphasized Ciardi's "unique voice," and Fitts identified the "central quality of Ciardi's style" as "tremendous violence joined to tremendous control." Josephine Jacobsen in *Poetry* said the new book was "nourished by three outstanding qualities: a marriage of passion and intelligence, a brilliantly assimilated technique, and a refusal to play safe." She saw a few "poetic dangers" that "dog" Ciardi, but she did not want to see them scrubbed out entirely, she said, because they also account for the "quintessence of his flavor." Jacobsen identified the "poetic dangers" as first, a "zeal bursting its poetic bounds"; second, "oversimplification"; and third, "the conviction that the smell of sweat is the opposite of the smell of ink— a not wholly unwelcome tenet."

Once again, the new book was looked over by M. L. Rosenthal for a one hundred dollar fee. Ciardi sent the poems and fifty dollars on 14 March 1959, with a request that Rosenthal "pull no punches." "I truly want to know what you think," Ciardi wrote, "in whatever detail you are able to manage, but if you can't detail your reasons, write STINKS in the margin and I'll buy that." A little more than three months later, on 22 June, Ciardi sent the manuscript of *39 Poems* to the Rutgers University Press and wrote Rosenthal with thanks—plus the remaining fifty dollars still due. Rosenthal's worksheets have not survived, but Ciardi gave some indication in his letter about his indebtedness:

> I have had to hold out for my own eccentricities in a number of places, and the result may disappoint you in some instances, but I hope you will forgive me that pigheadedness that strives to be a faith, however mangled. Your comments have led to a number of precious cuts and revisions. At least the cuts are precious. Of the revisions, God knows. But I did weed out a couple of "meats" [and] cut the Wallace Stevens poem ["A Praise of Good Poets in a Bad Age"] as you suggested (a special thanks for that) and several others.
>
> I think the points at which I balked most were the points at which you seemed to be hearing echoes I could not hear in my own ear. I could only guess I hadn't made my own movement clear and made some punctuation changes in several instances. I hope the changes will emphasize my intended reading.

And with that, Ciardi let *39 Poems* go to press. On 23 September, with the book in production, Ciardi wrote Holmes, "I am reasonably pleased with this collection. Who can get pleased? But there are some poems I feel very right about in the total. And they are MY poems. No fooling about that. My poems in my own way. . . ."

And once again Ciardi reviewed his own book in *Saturday Review* (2 April 1960), but this time he did so with a mischievous grin at the one hundred disapproving readers who had written to the magazine taking him to task for having reviewed *I Marry You*. The headnote to Ciardi's review of *39 Poems* carried this disclaimer written by someone else at the magazine: "It is perhaps worth noting that *Saturday Review*'s other editors customarily permit their books to be assigned to dispassionate outside critics." But Ciardi wrote back with a gleam in his eye:

> Gentle (and not-so-gentle) readers, I do happily confess that it is fun to stir up the beast in you, but tell me—what am I to do? Shall I get a pal of mine to say it is the greatest thing since Homer? Shall I dig up some student I flunked out of school and give him a chance to get even? As poetry editor, I must pass on all poetry reviews. That makes it an inside job no matter how handled. Let it, therefore, be declaredly an inside job.

"Art," Ciardi wrote more seriously, "is a certainty men can live by." And at their best, the poems in his new book, like the best of his poems in the older books, are physical representations of order and discipline and controlled passion. They are, in this sense, the embodiment of the values Ciardi espoused—the certainties he tried to live by.

Perhaps it was just as well that Ciardi promoted his book in *Saturday Review* because it received relatively little critical attention, as Judith remarked in a letter to the Kachadoorians, "He has gotten some small favorable reviews but the *Times* either doesn't recognize it or has lost it!" Reviewed or not, *39 Poems* has a great many poems that show Ciardi to excellent advantage, including "Abundance," "A Dream," "After Sunday Dinner We Uncles Snooze," "To Lucasta, About That War," and "A Thousandth Poem for Dylan Thomas" among others. It also contains three more of Ciardi's best-known signature poems—an impatient scolding of the meek in "In Place of a Curse"; a loving meditation on his parents in "Bridal Photo, 1906"; and "The Gift," a quietly life-affirming poem about a Jewish survivor of a German concentration camp:

> In 1945, when the keepers cried *kaput,*
> Josef Stein, poet, came out of Dachau

like half a resurrection, his other
eighty pounds still in their invisible grave.

Slowly then the mouth opened and first
a broth, and then a medication, and then
a diet, and all in time and the knitting mercies,
the showing bones were buried back in flesh,

and the miracle was finished. Josef Stein,
man and poet, rose, walked, and could even
beget, and did, and died later of other causes
only partly traceable to his first death.

He noted—with some surprise at first—
that strangers could not tell he had died once.
He returned to his post in the library, drank his beer,
published three poems in a French magazine,

and was very kind to the son who at last was his.
In the spent of one night he wrote three propositions:
That Hell is the denial of the ordinary. That nothing lasts.
That clean white paper waiting under a pen

is the gift beyond history and hurt and heaven.

Josef Stein, Ciardi later wrote, was "a sort of German-Jewish equivalent for 'John Smith' for the poem was meant as an elegy for all the
Jews who suffered the Nazi atrocity." This particular survivor was
nursed back to health, a "miracle" that Ciardi plays nicely against
the word "resurrection"; however, the poem is more than an empa-
thetic evocation of suffering because Stein was a poet, which in the
end provides the redemption that made his life worth resuming. The
irony lies in the fact that despite resurrection and miracle, the language of religion, Josef Stein's salvation is achieved through poetry,
which is a life-giving force of *this* world—"the gift beyond history
and hurt and heaven."

The manuscript of Ciardi's textbook, *How Does a Poem Mean?*,
was delivered to Houghton Mifflin on 1 June 1958, and copies of
the book were delivered to him on 14 March 1959. It was issued as
a separate paperback for two dollars (followed by a four-dollar hardcover) and as part three of *An Introduction to Literature* with coauthors

Herbert Barrows, Hubert Heffner, and Wallace Douglas. Through 1996, the second edition (coedited by Miller Williams) was still in print, a financial and critical success from the outset, and a touchstone poetry textbook that has taught more than one generation about poetry's inner dynamics. "In it," Peter Gorner once wrote, "Ciardi poleaxes the paraphrasers and teaches children to *experience* meaning, urging them to champion the inventive and joyous and stop worrying about the sheerly literal." Its endurance is the result of its clarity and organizational common sense, the pairing of poems to make points, plus helpful concepts like the "sympathetic contract" between reader and poet, and the idea of motion and countermotion to discuss the musical dance of poetry. And the book made money, doing "better than well" in its first two years, as Ciardi wrote to Holmes in 1961—and then selling some 300,000 copies through 1972. As late as the early 1990s, it was still selling about 3,000 copies a year.

Less than two months after the March publication of *How Does a Poem Mean?*, Ciardi went to Detroit for three days of a two-week exhibition of Ciardiana, engineered by businessman Charles Feinberg, who had persuaded Ciardi to donate worksheets, books, letters, and manuscripts to the Wayne State University Library. Ciardi lectured at the Detroit Public Library on 5 May for five hundred dollars, visited Gertrude and Leonard Kasle, and reported on the event to the Kachadoorians in a letter of 8 May—which he ended with a postscript: "Wayne State University Press has just published (already!) *John Ciardi: A Bibliography*. Wanna touch me?" The sixty-five-page bibliography was carefully and professionally prepared by William White in an edition of 550 copies. Moreover, the work is all but indispensable, given Ciardi's nearly nonexistent, catch-as-catch-can filing "system." Even in 1959, Ciardi's records were in a mess, as he explained to White: "I'm not a very systematic person. I do have some pack-rat instincts, but they are slovenly too." Being a person who was "poor at keeping files and records," Ciardi was pleased that the bibliography would be a way for him to jog his own memory of items long since written and forgotten.

In September 1959, J. B. Lippincott published Ciardi's first book of children's verse, *The Reason for the Pelican*, which was named by the *New York Times* as one of the ten best children's books that year. Eunice Blake was then children's book editor at Lippincott, the "juvenile" editor, as Ciardi liked to quip—which thus made all the other editors "senile." Here, too, was another Bread Loaf connection, for Blake was on the staff for the first time in 1957, probably recruited by Sloane in Ciardi's absence, and immediately became a fixture for the next ten years. At the 1958 conference Blake had urged Ciardi to try his hand at some children's poems and then reminded him again in a note of 4 September. He said at the conference that he already had some, written years earlier when he was teaching at Harvard and living at 84 South Street with his sister Cora and her family. Those poems were stuck away in a file somewhere, he said, but he would search for them. When he located them and sent them along, he received a contract in the return mail, with a check for $500 as an advance, "which," he said, "I'd never gotten for a book of poems before." The truth was that the book had actually been ready for publication since November 1951, as Ciardi had written at that time to Theodore Roethke: "I've got a book of children's poems due late next year. Now being illustrated. To be called THE REASON FOR THE PELICAN." And on the reverse side of his letter, Ciardi included the title poem. That earlier book, of which there is no record other than Ciardi's one-time reference to it, had obviously been abandoned, but now, seven years later, Eunice Blake saw to its handsomely paid-for revival. And with the encouragement of a five-hundred-dollar-check in hand, Ciardi sent a few of his *Pelican* poems to the *Ladies' Home Journal*, which bought "Rain Sizes" and "There Once Was an Owl" for three hundred dollars more. So, Ciardi said, "this yellowed folder that had been in my files for about ten years turned out to be worth eight hundred bucks right off. . . ." And just as gratifying, as Judith reported in a letter to the Kachadoorians, "Myra is dancing around on air these days since advanced copies of John's book of children's poems arrived—'The Reason for the Pelican' is dedicated to her. . . ."

Leaving the Academic Life

John Ciardi began at Rutgers in September 1953 and resigned at the end of June 1961, after what looks like eight years of teaching. However, he was a full-time teacher in only three of those years, 1953–54, 1954–55, and 1957–58. He spent 1956–57 in Italy and taught only the fall term in 1958–59. He took an unpaid leave of absence in spring 1959 and all of 1959–60. In 1960–61, he taught one six-credit course a week on Saturday mornings, technically half-time for purposes of salary. Of course, he lived in Metuchen, very near his Rutgers office and the classrooms of students who held him in high regard, but it is nonetheless difficult to identify Ciardi very strongly with Rutgers. He worked hard to make his stay there a success, but after he was launched into something like celebrity status at *Saturday Review*, which opened up more-lucrative-than-ever-lecture opportunities, it was only a matter of time until he resigned from the university to earn his living doing the things he had previously considered supplementary to his salary. It was a bold move he was contemplating—and a fateful one.

From the outset, Ciardi had taken an active role at Rutgers, not only in the creative writing program (working up new courses, sponsoring speakers, advising the editors of the literary magazine, etc.), but also in university matters, serving, for example, as convocation speaker kicking off the 1954–55 school year to some twenty-four hundred students. His talk was titled "Another School Year—Why?" in which he forcefully explained the students' need for a liberal arts education. He recalled for his audience a young pharmacy student at the University of Kansas City who had complained about having to read Shakespeare. Shakespeare, Ciardi told the young man, was a part of his education because he had enrolled in a college, not a "drugstore-mechanics school." Furthermore, that young man would be getting a B.S. degree, not one that said he would be a "Qualified Pill-Grinding Technician." Rising to the mood, Ciardi rolled on: "I am here to tell you that the business of the college is not only to train you, but to put you in touch with what the best human minds have thought. If you have no time for Shakespeare, for a basic look at philosophy, for the continuity of the fine arts, for that lesson of man's development we call history—then you have no business being in college." It was Ciardi at his best, speaking not for himself but for all educated men before him—all of western civilization in fact. He didn't blush at all in the pronouncement of his judgment.

But there was much more. Ciardi appeared on radio and television in 1954 and 1955 with Remigio Pane of the Italian department, talking about Dante. He spoke down the road at Princeton on the anti-intellectualism that draped itself in "yelping patriotism and muscular arrogance." He considered himself then, and would in the future, as an independent-minded intellectual who was capable of free thought: "The special obligation of the intellectual," he said, "is to resist the New Orthodoxy. He has no duty to survive it. Only to resist it by every means short of abandoning what he is: a free mind bent on reaching his own conclusion." He appeared in late 1954 on several radio programs called the "Rutgers Report on World Affairs," discussing the McCarthy committee and its communist witch hunts. On 1 June 1955 he sent a two-page letter to Rutgers president Lewis Jones about several "notions that have been forming in my mind." Specifically, he wanted a magazine to reach out to the New Jersey high schools from all branches of Rutgers. He thought a Ford Foundation pilot grant might be possible and saw that it would create a full-time job for someone, not he himself, "though I'd be willing to give a year to setting it up." He also proposed the purchase of art prints and musical recordings with areas for students to look and listen: "My thought, of course, on all counts is to see more ideas-in-transit at Rutgers." And on 14 June 1955, Ciardi sent a sixteen-page, single-spaced study to President Jones, "The Rutgers Plan for Mass Education in the Humanities," another Ford Foundation idea. Ciardi was, in short, a vital member of the Rutgers community.

Ciardi took the spring 1959 semester on unpaid leave in order to finish *The Purgatorio*. As he wrote to the Kachadoorians on 6 February, however, finishing "would be a lot easier to do if I could just get started (the last ¼ of it remains to do), but day by day goes by and other things keep coming up." He never did get to Dante that term. In a 16 June letter to the Kachadoorians, Judith put it in plainer language: John had taken his leave "to polish off the *Purgatorio*," but "when a fat check was waved, off he went, until [he] got far behind on doing anything but catching planes." At this point Ciardi had to make up his mind about Rutgers, and he did so in a letter of 10 June to Milton French, who was still head of the English department. He had a "true devotion invested in Rutgers," Ciardi wrote, but he did not see how he could continue as a full-time professor "for the next four or five years." After that, he would have enough money "to permit a semi-retirement," and at that point, he said, he would "very much like to take on more teaching and more faithful attendance to the botherations of general management." For the moment, however, his problem was all too clear: "My lecture schedule around the country is such that any given day of the week can represent three or four thousand dollars worth of lectures." He couldn't remain at Rutgers at such extreme economic penalty, although he did not want to sever ties altogether, which struck him, he said, "as an act of disloyalty."

Privately, Ciardi was less loyal. He prepared an essay in about 1958 called "Democratic Education" in which he worried that education could become so democratic that "standards are trampled underfoot." As he warmed to the topic, he wrote that we are "flooding" our campuses "with the oafish products of an oafish school system." And to illustrate his point, Ciardi used his own classes in English composition as an example. He was always given the students who scored highest on a placement test, but "with rare exceptions those best 25 freshmen at Rutgers were hopeless. After three times around I simply refused to take on any more of them. I did not join a college faculty to teach junior high school English." Six years later, long after he had left Rutgers, Ciardi was still angry about the state of higher education. He wrote in a *Saturday Review* essay, "I was once employed as a teacher-critic of student writing, but gave up my professorship and my cozy tenure because I could no longer bear to apply splints to those compound fractures of the emotions that students think of as writing." And Ciardi wrote to Read Bain on 7 August 1959 to explain why he had already taken half a year off on unpaid leave and was about to begin a full year on the same status.

> Reasons: first, that students are beginning to bore the hell out of me; second: that colleagues are beginning to be more boring than the students; third: avarice, in that I can get most or all of a month's pay for a single free-lance lecture; fourth: for the fun of it, in that I like tooting around the country on airplanes; fifth: avarice again—how many rich poets do you know? Having just completed a quick survey, I discover that E. Guest, A. MacLeish, and I are the only poets in America who drive Cadillacs.

And turning the same idea over in his mind in an *SR* essay three years later, Ciardi wrote that "most academics begin by making a central decision about money and the competitive life. I myself made such a decision until I found that planned poverty among sheep bored me."

By September 1959, Milton French was already planning for personnel needs in 1960-61, so he wrote to Ciardi asking for a commitment. No correspondence between Ciardi and French exists for this period, although they may well have met to discuss the questions at hand; however, on 4 November Ciardi had lunch with Rutgers' new president, Mason Gross, to hammer out some new relationship he might have with the university. His first thought was to become poet in residence, a position and title that did not then exist at Rutgers. He hoped he could keep up his connection with the university, including salary and benefits, without being tied down to anything more restricting than one class meeting per week. Maintaining his previous teaching schedule would be impossible for him—and not sensible either given "the number and quality of writing students of late." His other thought was to create a graduate course "for teachers on the teaching of poetry" that he could teach once a week. There seems to have been little interest in Ciardi's becoming poet in residence, but the graduate seminar was seen by Gross as a good way for the university to keep its star performer. The six-credit course, to meet on Saturday mornings, was developed in November to be The Method of Poetry, which Ciardi envisioned as a classroom implementation of *How Does a Poem Mean?*, published only eight months earlier. It would cover in four, seven-week sections "the four poetic elements"—rhythm, image, diction, and form. On the eve of his first class, Ciardi wrote to Dan Jaffe that his new course "camouflages in catalogue as Poetic Method. Is in fact How Does a Poem Mean for Teachers."

Six months later Ciardi turned in his resignation to Rudolf Kirk, the new English department chairman. He said he did so "regretfully" and that only his need to free his time for writing would have been compelling enough as a reason for him to take such a step. He wrote in an autobiographical fragment a summary of all that led up to his decision: "I hesitated, I discussed possibilities with Judith at great length, always understanding my obligation to keep the family solvent. I even went on half-time for a year teaching a seminar in Poetic Method in the School of Education—a long Saturday morning stint that left me a roving week. In the end my salary for the year came to about two or three lecture fees on the circuit, and to that mathematics Judith conceded."

Money seems to have been Ciardi's primary reason for resigning from Rutgers, but being a nationally known literary figure no doubt made full-time school teaching seem a quaint and parochial business at best. Moreover, he had never gotten on well with academic types and spurned run-of-the-mill scholarship as a boring enterprise that fed neither the mind nor the spirit. Academic types, perhaps at the University of Kansas City and Harvard, but certainly at Rutgers, liked him no better, for he had but an M.A. and was seemingly outside the regular university rules, a literary "star"—and therefore a source of irritation and tension. Moreover, Ciardi had little patience for fools, whether in his classrooms or in the faculty lounges. One doesn't have to dig far below the surface, then, to see the root cause of Ciardi's desire to resign, nor the good things that came out of it for him. But he also paid a price, not just because he left his reputation in the hands of the very English professors whom he irritated, but because his sudden separation from the academic world put him out of touch with the inner dynamics of student thought and behavior, which turned into open rebellion in the 1960s. Had he remained in teaching, Ciardi might not have been so ill-prepared to cope with the Bread Loaf crisis that had already begun to build.

Concetta Ciardi
and John, ca. 1918.

Antonio Ciardi, ca. 1918.

John Holmes,
ca. 1938.
COURTESY OF
THE CIARDI
COLLECTION

Roy Cowden

John Ciardi,
ca. 1939, University
of Michigan.

Virginia Johnson, ca. 1940.

Bread Loaf fellows, 1940: *front row, left to right,* Marian Sims, Ted Morrison (director), Carson McCullers; *standing, left to right,* Eudora Welty, John Ciardi, Brainard Cheney, Edna Frederickson, and Louis Untermeyer.

John Ciardi, ca. 1944, U.S. Army Air Corps.

Ciardi, ca. 1947, at Harvard, with students and holding a copy of *Other Skies*.

John Ciardi, August 1949, at Bread Loaf. On the back of the photograph is this inscription: "To John Ciardi from one of the students at the conference who found your lectures the major event." It was signed Beatrice Roslin.

Judith Ciardi, ca. 1951.
COURTESY OF THE
CIARDI COLLECTION

John Ciardi at
Bread Loaf, 1954.
COURTESY OF
TRUDY DRUCKER

Ciardi takes over the Bread Loaf directorship from Ted Morrison,
August 1955.

John and Judith Ciardi at Bread Loaf, August 1955.

Passport photo, 1956, before leaving for the American Academy in Rome. *Clockwise,* Judith, Myra, John, John L., and Benn.

John with Myra, ca. 1958.

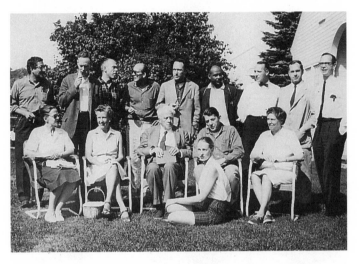

Bread Loaf staff, 1959: *front row, left to right,* unknown, Nancy Hale, Robert Frost, John Ciardi, unknown; Judith is sitting on the grass in front of John; *standing, left to right,* Richard Gehmann, William Sloane, Hollis Summers, William Raney, unknown, Ralph Ellison, unknown, William Meredith, Paul Cubeta.

Ciardi on location in Dallas for the CBS program *Accent*, December 1961.

PHOTO BY JOE LAIRD

John and Judith in front of their home at 31 Graham Avenue, ca. 1965.

Ciardi and Archie MacLeish at Bread Loaf, August 1967.

Ciardi and family at ceremonies in Monocalzati, summer 1969, making Ciardi an honorary citizen of his mother's hometown and unveiling a bronzed translation of a Ciardi poem about the town. Photograph taken at town hall, after a long parade. Ciardi, *center left;* Judith (the only blonde), *one row below;* Myra, *foreground looking down;* Benn, partially blocked next to Myra; and Jonnel, *far right.*

Ciardi, beleaguered Bread Loaf director, April 1971.
PHOTO BY LAVERNE CLARK

Ciardi, recording a segment of "A Word in Your Ear," which was broadcast on National Public Radio's *Morning Edition* from 1977 to 1986.

Myra and Benn,
1977.
COURTESY
MYRA CIARDI

John and Judith at
John L.'s graduation
from law school,
1981.
COURTESY
MYRA CIARDI

John L.,
Christmas
1982.

Myra,
Christmas
1982.

Benn,
Christmas
1982.

Ciardi, spring 1984, as first Distinguished Visiting Professor
for the Caroyln Benton Cockefair Chair in Continuing
Education, University of Missouri-Kansas City.

PHOTO BY MICHAEL MARDIKES,
UNIVERSITY OF MISSOURI-KANSAS CITY

Ciardi in Key West, working on the *Browser's Dictionary*, ca. 1984.
PHOTOGRAPH BY JIMM ROBERTS

Ciardi reading to
children, ca. 1985.
COURTESY OF THE
CIARDI COLLECTION

In one of his last speaking engagements, Ciardi at the
International Poetry Forum in Pittsburgh, March 1986.

NINE

"The Capitalist of Po Biz"

1961 TO 1968

Scrambling for Dollars

Back in 1958, Detroit millionaire Charles Feinberg had written to ask what Ciardi did with his worksheets and manuscripts because, he said, they would be valuable to collectors like himself. Ciardi wrote back with mock astonishment, "You're kidding about worksheets and manuscripts. Yes, I more or less stash them away though I only began a while ago, having always thrown them out to keep from drowning in paper, but I think you're just asking with a thought to subsidize the penniless poets and egad here I am practically The Capitalist of Po Biz, milking the lecture platform of $1 million a syllable." Feinberg had asked the sort of ego-gratifying question that at its heart acknowledged Ciardi's position among contemporary poets—and he got back a self-conscious exaggeration in response. Three years later an interviewer asked Ciardi, "How does being famous affect you? What happens to a man who rises from anonymity to the point of becoming an established institution?" Once again caught off guard, Ciardi this time answered perhaps too seriously: "Well, I don't know that I'm an established institution. . . . Every once in a while it bothers me to find that I'm not anonymous." In fact, John Ciardi did make a transition between 1958 and 1961 from a man of modest reputation to a national figure whose name and voice and features were identifiable to millions of people, and during the decade of the 1960s, he would become a bona fide celebrity, capitalizing on his fame and cashing in on every opportunity that came his way. Moreover, once the short leash Rutgers had kept him on was removed, opportunities came even more rapidly. At one point, in about 1965 or 1966, Ciardi confided to Miller Williams during a long distance telephone call that he'd just learned from his accountant that with all his assets tallied, he was actually a millionaire—but just barely. It was a good feeling. Where else but America could a poor boy from Boston's Little Italy parlay a career in poetry (of all things) into a million dollars?

Ciardi's first opportunity in the 1960s was a column in *Saturday Review* to be called "Manner of Speaking." The magazine, with its twenty-three thousand subscribers, had been bought in 1941 by Everette L. DeGolyer, who transferred majority ownership to Norman Cousins, his long-time editor, in 1956. In February 1961, *SR* was sold to the McCall Corporation, owned principally by Hunt Foods and Industries, which was owned in turn by Norton Simon. Cousins agreed to the deal only because the new owners insisted that he remain as editor-in-chief and agreed that *SR* would be maintained "as an autonomous and editorially independent publishing entity." Shortly after the sale, Ciardi agreed to expand his responsibilities at *Saturday Review* from poetry editor to columnist and was one of the factors contributing to the soon-to-be-realized 63 percent increase in subscriptions, which rose to 400,000 in 1964—and then to 510,000 in 1967, with advertising revenues also increasing sharply.

Ciardi's first column appeared on 15 April 1961 without a title (although it was called "Letter Writers" for a collection of his columns published eleven years later as *Manner of Speaking*). He announced that to the extent that he could be tempted to answer his *SR* mail at all, he would do so publicly, in his column; certainly, he had no intention of answering mail personally. The "Herculean letter writers" of *SR* would be disappointed by the lack of any personal response, he wrote, but it couldn't be helped. The letters would go unanswered because "to answer them would not be a chore but a career." Plus, he had his real work to do. And there were plenty of other good reasons for ignoring his mail, like those pesky schoolboys who regularly wrote for help on term papers. At first he had written helpful letters to them, but he had decided to stop: "I am persuaded we have reared an unmannerly generation unto ourselves," he confided to his readers. "Not one of the young whelps I wrote to took the trouble to say thanks." From the very beginning, then, if the tone of his first column is any indication, Ciardi enjoyed his new role immensely. And why not? He'd been on the receiving end from readers many times—and he liked dishing it back out, twitting *SR*'s readership with gentle scolding, and playing the role of Lord Protector of Inherited Values.

For the first year, "Manner of Speaking" appeared every two or three weeks on subjects as far-ranging as his spring lecture trip; a woman who had tried to pass off a Richard Wilbur poem as her own submission to *SR*; the public library in East Orange, New Jersey, which had fifteen people arrested for overdue books; his hatred of government meddling in the lives of the people through unnecessary licenses and permits; and racial prejudice, about which he had this to say: "Our survival, I suggest, depends on how well we do in breaking down the divisions of mankind in order to let the total race emerge as one union." Of course several columns were given over to poetry—on rhyme, metaphor, luck, and the suggestion of five different students at five different lectures that his translation of Dante was as "creatively demanding" as composing the original, which Ciardi brusquely put aside as "a species of oversimplifying stupidity." The range of subjects was proof that Cousins had lived up to his end of their bargain, which Ciardi characterized as an "understanding that it was my page and that I could fill it as I pleased."

In general, Ciardi thought *Saturday Review* was a dull magazine—which may be why he stirred things up so often—but he nonetheless spoke and wrote regularly about how much he enjoyed his role as columnist. Late in his *SR* career, he wrote, "I confess I am not sure why I find pleasure in writing it. I once asked a Vermont farmer why his horse chewed the tops of the fence posts. 'Well,' he said, 'that's the goldurned animal of it.' Over the years I have taken to writing this column as that horse took to chewing fence posts and for no better reason [than] my farmer could give. It is probably a foolish thing to do it, but that's the animal of it, and I am happy to be given my regular supply of fence posts."

During the 1960s, Ciardi made a lot of friends in his columns —and just as many enemies. He had a knack for infuriating readers, as for example, John H. Steinemann of San Diego, who wrote to *SR* (1 July 1961), "There is nothing so depressingly exasperating as the puerile, self-centered outpouring of trivia and unmitigated hogwash purveyed by your poetry editor, John Ciardi. It seems that, like some horrible plague, he spreads over more and more of *SR*'s otherwise splendid pages. Please reassure me that we may hope to find less and less of this noxious sophist in the future." But in the same issue came a letter from M. L. Warden of Miami, who wrote, "I have observed with pleasure the increasing number of articles written by the gifted John Ciardi. Here's hoping we'll see still more of his work in *SR*." A letter from Richard O'Donnell (15 December 1962) in New York suggested a new organization, OHIHJC—"Oh, How I Hate John Ciardi." It would be a national support group with local chapters: "Just get together the people in your neighborhood who jump up and down in rage whenever they read Mr. Ciardi's column in *SR*. I find that when I jump in unison with others it's much easier to discharge my wrath." But, the letter ended, "Do not ever, ever, ever, let Ciardi go. He is the nation's No. 1 cure for boredom." It seemed that for every negative letter like the one from Virgil J. Vogel in Chicago (2 May 1964), which said that Ciardi was "the most intolerably egocentric smart aleck since Shaw," there was one like Lola Albright Chadney's (Sherman Oaks, California, 23 April 1966): "I love John Ciardi so much *almost* every week that I can't stand it! When his column does not appear in an issue, I am disconsolate." Norman Cousins had been right about Ciardi from the beginning: any writer who could generate that much mail was excellent for the intellectual health of his magazine—and invaluable to his subscription department.

Ciardi understood his own value to *Saturday Review*, and in November 1962 he renegotiated his deal with Norman Cousins. Yes, he wrote on the twenty-eighth, he liked working at *SR* because he liked the people he worked with and because he felt a "rapport" with the readers. But could he continue turning down "excellent offers" at twice the money? And surely, he wrote, even better offers would be coming along in the future: "We both know they will." He called *SR* his "proper home," but "it's my allowance I am unhappy about, Daddy. That, and my sense that you are a very slow man with a buck." He had been receiving $250 a month for the previous six years as poetry editor, plus double normal rates for his own poetry published in the magazine. He nowhere mentioned in surviving correspondence the exact figure he was earning per month from the column, though he did write to Cousins that "the pay was not enough." He added, half in admiration, that Cousins was "the toughest turnip to get blood out of I have met in my adult life." He did get some raises over the next several years, but he wrote in the end that his pay "was never very much" and that he was "several times on the point of quitting over its meagerness." He summed it up as "a hobby job," one that earned him at most $4,000 a year—a figure that he deliberately understated. Yet the regularity of a monthly check, even a small one, once he had left Rutgers, must have been especially welcome. And by 1967, he was actually earning $6,000 a year as poetry editor, plus additional fees for lead articles and his column. He wasn't earning a fortune at *Saturday Review*, but his part-time salary was no doubt more than the $9,500 he had earned in his last year at Rutgers as a full-time professor.

Stretching from October 1961 to September 1962, Ciardi was drawing yet another paycheck, this one from the CBS television network to host a weekly cultural magazine show called *Accent*. He earned five hundred dollars per week for most of the programs, although he was paid twelve hundred for the one-hour special that aired on 4 January 1962, *Accent on 1961: A Public Memoir*. In a note to Paul Cubeta (so hastily written that he neglected to date it, although September 1961 seems likely), Ciardi apologetically handed off some unidentified Bread Loaf director's work that he should have done himself but couldn't fit into his schedule:

> I won't try to explain the insanities in which I am living these days. Returned from a long tour to West Coast and back, got off plane at 3:05 A.M. into bed at 4:00 (that was Wed. A.M.) up at 8:30 and to NYork for a lash of conferences, rehearsals, dress reherasals [*sic*], and finally taping of this TV Show I'm starting (ACCENT CBS Sat 1:30), home exhausted to a month's mail still unanswered and with a stack of stuff to get read and studied before leaving tomorrow for Boston where, on Monday, we tape another show. Stop for a lecture at Yale on way back, shoot down to Penna for a show on the Amish, lecture for two days at Juniata College, Penna, return to Yale Nov. 3 for a show on [Eero] Saarinen—and so it goes.
>
> Please understand as you read inclosed rough-rough-rough out. Can you blend it with last year's letter? Will it

stand as is? I see the urgency but I'm nailed to the rafters. Must get a staff lined up in December if at all possible— expect to be in Europe for four or five shows in January. The show itself is fun. What bitches it is that I was already committed to a pretty full lecture schedule. Can't cancel now. Must, therefore, jump from one to the other.

Please forgive. I'll make it up someway.

Fortunately, Cubeta kept things together very well, and it isn't known how or if Ciardi ever made it up. He did, at least, acknowledge his debt.

Accent had been on the CBS network every week from 26 February 1961 to 14 October before Ciardi's first appearance. Beginning with the program on 21 October ("The Rebellious Mind Behind the Iron Curtain"), Ciardi became the permanent host, succeeding James Fleming, Alexander Kendrick, and Winston Burdett —all of whom had taken turns at the job. Ciardi's programs, except for two repeats in early February, ran every week through 31 March 1962, when the taping of new programs ended. For the next week, and running through 3 June, *Accent* reruns were plugged into the time slot, with Ciardi learning on 13 April that the show had, in fact, been permanently canceled from the lineup. He reported that day to Leonard Kasle that he had received the news "with slightly mixed emotions but with what is in general a sense of relief." The half-hour cultural programs had treated a wide variety of subjects—like John Adams, Eero Saarinan, Sinclair Lewis, D. H. Lawrence, Ethan Allen, and two shows on the Elizabethans. There were programs called "Brecht and Theatre in the 60s," "Theatre in Dallas," "The Children and the Poet" (which featured poetry written and recited by a third-grade class in Farmingdale, New York), and much more.

When the program was taken off the air, Ciardi actually had very little time to redirect himself toward his own long-deferred projects because a month later, *Accent* was revived as a summer replacement show. This time it came back as a travelogue, *Accent on an American Summer*, and CBS broadcast it in prime time, 7:30 Thursday nights, from 7 June through 6 September. Programs were shot on location at Oahu, Hawaii; San Francisco, California; Reno, Nevada; Aspen, Colorado; and Yellowstone National Park, Wyoming— among other places. There were programs on Thomas Jefferson from Monticello, Thomas Hart Benton from Kansas City, and Shakespeare from the American Shakespeare Festival in Stratford, Connecticut. On 28 June, John Ireland, Colleen Dewhurst, and Ossie Davis starred in Archibald MacLeish's verse drama "The Fall of the City." The last program, "Pearl Harbor: Unforgotten," was a moving re-creation of the day that signaled America's entrance into World War II, 7 December 1941.

In mid-May, as Ciardi was gearing up for that long summer of traveling, rehearsing, and shooting, he had to ask Paul Cubeta once again for help with his Bread Loaf obligations. He wrote that he and the film crew would soon be heading off, "crazy and all over the country." Ciardi was clearly unhappy about asking Cubeta once again to do more work than he was normally responsible for, but he saw no alternative. And after all, he reasoned, his schedule without *Accent* would presumably open up in September 1962, which meant he'd be able to get back to a normal work-year and resume doing his Bread Loaf work the way he wanted to.

By 1961, however, *Saturday Review* and *Accent* notwithstanding, John Ciardi was earning most of his living on the lecture circuit. As Walter Bezanson observed in November 1966, "Not since the days of the old Methodist preachers has there been a more ardent circuit rider." Richard Wilbur called Ciardi a "deservedly popular figure" on the lecture circuit and described his method: "As notions occurred to him, or recurred to him, he would come up with entire poems pretty flawlessly delivered or illustrative lines well-remembered. And it would turn out to be a very good associative tissue of material which he wasn't thinking of for the first time, but which he was lacing together once again in a way he had never quite done before." All through the 1960s, Ciardi worked hard at making money on the lecture trail, booking, through his lecture agent, up to six weeks on the road every fall and up to six more every spring, primarily on college campuses. Lucien Stryk called Ciardi's lectures "electrifying, delivered in a measured, yet powerful manner," with "his frequent potshots . . . well-aimed—always at the stupid, cruel, dangerous." George Garrett characterized the bold Ciardi manner as "basic pontification." And X. J. Kennedy said admiringly that he was a "real pro": "He was like a journeyman, a very skilled and experienced one, doing time in his trade, no matter who the customers were."

Ciardi thought, spoke, and wrote often about earning a living on the lecture circuit. He liked to turn it over in his mind, not so much to second-guess his decision to leave teaching, but to wonder at his own good fortune. Instead of teaching for nine months in order to have three months free to write, he could lecture for three much more lucrative months to gain nine months to write. Yes, lecturing was tiring, especially when it became the principal source of his income and not just the dollars he earned to sweeten his standard of living, but it was worth it. When he once tabulated the amount of time he spent lecturing, he said it came "to a quarter of my life spent chasing after cash. Nor will I apologize for that. A man owes no apology for what he does to feed, and even spoil, his family. Nor is three months out of the year a bad balance." And Ciardi lectured for all the traffic would bear. He wrote to Theodore Roethke on 7 September 1961, "I stopped being expensive some time ago in order to become exorbitant. . . ." In an interview with the *Tuftonian* in 1961, he underscored the importance of money: "There's no other reason for getting on a platform. Nobody's ever found out who he was while giving a lecture. Nobody's ever discovered anything about himself of any real consequence on a platform. The only reason for getting up on a platform is cash. And since you're doing it for cash, it may as well be a lot of cash." He added a characteristic brag and quip that he would repeat often over the next twenty-five years: "I'm not sure but that the lecture platform is the best racket since bank robbery was declared illegal."

Ciardi was perfectly at ease with such talk because confessing that he was motivated by money—and made lots of it— seemed human and honest to him. It seemed never to have occurred to him that talking about his fees, his real estate, and his stock portfolio might offend some people and that his financial success was one subject he might profitably leave unspoken. And even if the idea had occurred to him, he would have been powerless to suppress it, for his financial successes had long since become important psychological expressions of his masculinity, not just in his conversation and columns, but in poems too, like "Back through the Looking Glass to This Side":

Yesterday, in a big market, I made seven thousand dollars
while I was flying to Dallas to speak to some lunch group

and back for a nightcap with my wife. A man from Dallas
sat by me both ways, the first from Campbell's Soup,
the other from some labeled can of his own, mostly water,
and Goldwater at that. Capt. J. J. Slaughter

of Untied Airlines kept us all in smooth air and well
and insistently informed of our progress. Miss G. Klaus
brought us bourbon on ice, and snacks. At the hotel
the lunch grouped and the group lunched. I was,
if I may say so, perceptive, eloquent, sincere.
Then back to the airport with seventeen minutes to spare.

Capt. T. V. Ringo took over with Miss P. Simbus
and that Goldwater oaf. We made it to Newark at nine
plus a few minutes lost in skirting cumulo-nimbus
in our descent at the Maryland-Delaware line.
"Ticker runs late," said the horoscope page. "New highs
posted on a broad front."—So the good guys

had won again! Fat, complacent, a check
for more than my father's estate in my inside pocket,
with the launched group's thanks for a good day's work,
I found my car in the lot and poked it
into the lunatic aisles of U.S. 1,
a good guy coming home, the long day done.

Home Life

John Ciardi's period of full-time teaching had ended
in December 1958, when Myra was six, Jonnel five, and Benn four.
None of them had a very firm recollection of their father with a
regular job, like other kids' fathers, but they were old enough in
1961 and 1962 to know that their dad was on television, a celebrity,
although, according to Jonnel, they never talked about it. Ciardi's
well-paid traveling for television shoots, plus his lucrative lecture-
circuit touring, however, proved to be a mixed family blessing.
"Come spring and come fall," Ciardi wrote, "my wife becomes a

widow, my children have no father, and my soul belongs to Harry [Walker, Ciardi's agent]. . . ." Ciardi was setting his table very well, but in his absence the children became increasingly difficult for Judith to manage, for she was a single parent for at least three months every year and was not cut out to be a disciplinarian. As Jonnel recalled it, she just couldn't keep up: "We were *very* devious and quickly outpaced her." As early as 1959, in fact, Judith had written to the Kachadoorians about problems with her older son: "Jonnel is huge and handsome and impossible; he and I fight all the time and there's no telling what kind of psycho bills I'm starting, but maybe we'll grow out of it." In 1960, she made mention in another letter to the Kachadoorians of "the eternal discipline problem with the offspring. I am sure I'll never have an ulcer—I yell too much." Yelling at and to one another was established early on as a characteristic of the Ciardi household.

Yet Jonnel was able to recall but a single time throughout his childhood that he had been spanked by his father, whom he called "fairly mild-mannered." Ciardi, who never had a father at home during his own childhood to model himself after, measured success as a parent largely in dollars and cents terms, although he was also a physical presence—loving, sarcastic, and demanding. He was strictly old-world to Jonnel, who complained during his adolescence in the 1960s that his father's "temper and Italian *padrone* syndrome were always there." Jonnel, fueled by his generation's rejection of the older generation's "illegal" and "immoral" war in Vietnam, resisted at home and elsewhere the concept of automatic respect for one's parents and elders. He could not understand that, as he put it, his father "had this idea that deference was owed him simply because of his feudal rights." As a young baby boomer, Jonnel was simply displaying the standard rejection of GI values that was emerging in the 1960s. The GI's, regardless of their personal sacrifices during World War II and the postwar role they played in establishing the United States as the greatest superpower in the world, had not earned the deference they demanded—not, that is, according to their disaffected and alienated children.

In a lighter and more mischievous vein, it was the irrepressible Jonnel who convinced his younger brother that their father, who went on so many business trips and came back rich, was actually a mob hit man. The truth won out in time, but, as Ciardi wrote in an autobiographical fragment, "I came out of it substantially diminished in Benn's eyes," for Benn "liked the idea of being the only kid at school whose father was a genuine hit man. He even had some sort of secret dream that I would teach him the trade so that he might grow up to travel all over the place and return well-paid, and stay in bed until noon."

As the 1960s wore on, Jonnel turned out to be his father's chief antagonist at home, the one who had the biggest and loudest fights with his father. (Benn recalled that while he and his brother both sassed Ciardi, Jonnel never knew when to quit—"fuckin' pighead," he said, "just like dad.") Later Jonnel characterized the Ciardi family life as "fairly contentious," recalling dinner table scenes at which his father "would declare something—not just say it, but *declare* it—and that was it. He would sit there at the dinner table and observe his unworthy children, then he would make piercing comments." Perhaps comments like these accounted for the high-pitched exchanges that Ciardi wrote about in a 1964 "Manner of Speaking" column: "Loud is only the rustle of beginning at my house, and a roar punctuated by a shriek here and a thud there is only the warmup. In a few minutes you can't hear the lynxes for the hyenas and you can't hear either for the elephant stampede. Then, by the time you get all that on tape along with a sound track from the Battle of Leyte Gulf, all you have to do is send in a squadron of banshees for fighter cover, play it all inside a sealed boiler, and that's home sweet home."

In the summer of 1964, Ciardi packed the family into "Eunice," a white Cadillac named after Eunice Blake, J. B. Lippincott's editor, who had sent a fat check just when their previous car stopped running. The royalty check turned into a car-deposit check, and the Ciardis were off on a long, cross-country car tour: "I wanted our monsters to grow up with a long memory of the sweep of their continent and I wanted them to know how high its spine goes." They made stops in Missouri, the Tetons, Yellowstone, Denver, and back by way of Mount Rushmore and the Black Hills of South Dakota. Along the way there were lecture stops at East Lansing, Michigan; Bozeman, Montana; and Pocatello, Idaho: Ciardi had told his lecture agent that he needed just enough money "to ship the freight on and show a small profit." "The world, I am happy to say, has spoiled me to the point at which I flatly refuse to travel unless I am paid for it."

None of the children were baptized, but all had unofficial godparents and attended Sunday school at the First Presbyterian Church in Metuchen. According to Myra, her parents "thought we should have religious instruction even though they weren't particularly interested." Myra's interest in music, and in singing in particular, was evidenced early as she sang in the church choir, and on days when she had a solo, Judith would actually attend services, sitting as inconspicuously as possible in a back pew. In September 1962, Ciardi wrote without enthusiasm in "Manner of Speaking" of his children's church-going: "Our local Presbyterian Church has a good choir, my daughter likes to sing, and my wife happens to feel more comfortable when she can edge the kids to Sunday School. The kids seem to enjoy Sunday School there, and there they go." Ciardi had not, however, swayed from his own atheism. In 1963, for his Tufts reunion booklet, he described his religious convictions as "None." But he couldn't leave it at that: "It is possible," he went on, "to feel religious about the universe, but the universe shows no signs of insisting upon it. I have, in fact, a step further to go. Having seen so many of our intellectuals raise a question in something like its full complexity only to withdraw into religious answers that are simpler than the question as asked, I have come to think of religious conviction as a refuge from intellectual effort. And I prefer the effort to the refuge."

By her own account, Myra's experience at Metuchen High School, beginning in 1966, was pleasant, unrebellious (though she had a boyfriend at Columbia University during the antiwar riots), even old fashioned. She had lots of friends, got into no trouble, didn't take drugs, sat on the student council, and participated in school plays and community theater. In the same year, Jonnel, who was bright enough to skip the fourth grade, was sent to a private prep school for his secondary education. The Pingry School in Elizabeth, New Jersey, had accepted Jonnel in April 1966, "dependent on his maintaining satisfactory grades, attitude and citizenship." Ciardi sent a special delivery $225 deposit on 17 May, three days before the deadline. But Jonnel was unhappy there through 1969, when he was expelled and forced to finish up at Metuchen

High School. He didn't like what he called the "goody-goody boys" of Pingry. He realized the school had been selected for him by virtue of its academic reputation and in the hopes that it would provide him with some advantages, but he had difficulty getting through a troubled present in order to arrive at some indistinct better future. "I didn't like the idea of the school," he said later; "it was ultra-ultra conservative—and I was very rebellious. I wore my hair long just to aggravate people." His behavior in this period of his youth was consistent with the pattern of chronic underachieving his parents had seen all along, behavior that was accompanied by a loud, quarrelsome, and stubborn attitude.

Young Benn was his father's favorite, and for him Ciardi had the greatest patience and worrisome fears. He wrote in his column of 11 May 1962 of his seven-and-a-half-year-old son: "I happen to have one happy slowpoke at home, the sweet oaf of my litter, and my fear for him is exactly that he is too disgustingly close to his mindless peer group." It was a fear that was eerily prophetic as Benn would succumb to the lures of alcohol and drugs in high school, developing a habit that he carried through to the mid-1980s. He lived by the self-destructive slogan of the sixties: sex, drugs, and rock n' roll—and he found, or made, trouble wherever he went. In a follow-up column on 26 May, perhaps still thinking of his relationship to Benn especially, Ciardi mused further on the problems of parenting: "For myself, I am moved to hope that I shall never ask of my children more than the right to be seen through their own mistakes. I shall hope for love, wistfully if need be, but the day love runs aground on respect, I shall know I have been a stuffed shirt."

Beginning with the advent of the Beat Generation (which was transformed by the long-haired baby boomers in their hippy phase into the age of movements—civil rights, anti-war, and counter culture), Ciardi had begun to lose his identity as a spokesman for America's younger poets. "To the Reader of (Some) General Culture" was quaint next to the poetics suggested by "Howl." Ciardi's opposition to the baroque qualities in Pound and Eliot was mild in its criticism when compared to the wholesale changes in attitude toward poetry that were beginning to emerge. Instead of being the young poet speaking for a new, post-Eliot view of poetry, he became an older poet defending traditional poetic values. He spoke for form and tradition to a generation that felt suffocated by them and that needed to break loose from such restrictions in the name of greater honesty and freedom to express truths in a way unencumbered by poetic "irrelevancies" like rhyme, meter, stanza—or anything else that reeked of history. Their motto was "don't trust anyone over thirty." Ciardi fought them at every turn. As early as September 1962, he railed against America as a "youth-centered" country and condemned the new crop of young people as a "dreary, pampered, overinflated, and underpowered generation":

> They have no values but their silly group. They were born and live in a mental uniform. They live in a patois far to one side of the mother tongue of mankind. The word "sir" has all but disappeared from the vocabulary of citizens under ninety. To ask of these young clods the discipline of study is to insult their arrogance. . . .

> We have gone so far in our permissiveness that the idea of accepting the guidance of their elders seems an affront to these young. Several times after lectures I have run into college students who were flatly indignant at faculty regulations. "What right," one such oaf asked me last year at Duke, "has the college to make me take a language course?" He actually suggested picketing the administration building.

> I told him he was a sick and puny product of progressive education, permissive parents, and his own coddled ignorance, and that the university would probably do well to kick him out. It simply had never occurred to him that in applying for admission he had submitted himself to the standards set by the faculty and that it was not his job to make those standards but to meet them as set. What I see as symptomatic in him was his assured assumption that his own ignorance was sufficient to define the educational standards of a great university. Nowhere in him could I find any recognition that his elders might know more than he or that they might be worth taking half-seriously, if only in sufferance.

> The back of my hand to him—and the front of my doubt to his measly generation.

But in 1962, Ciardi's battle with the "measly generation"—including battles with his own children—were just beginning.

The troubling direction of the younger generation was underscored for John Ciardi by the passing of the older, for on 22 June

1962, John Holmes died very suddenly at age fifty-eight. The previous July, Holmes had written to Ciardi that he was "in discomfort these days—for three months—with muscle-strain or lameness all through chest, shoulders, and upper back," but the symptoms were attributed to anxiety, and tranquilizers were prescribed. "It never goes away to stay, and it somewhat cuts down my drive to do as much as I want to do; a damn nuisance." In the winter he had a lingering respiratory ailment accompanied by pains in his hip and legs, but though he'd been hospitalized briefly for bursitis, no one caught the underlying problem at that time. In April Holmes was admitted to the Peter Bent Brigham Hospital, and before he was diagnosed with cancer of the esophagus, generally thought to have been the result of his constant pipe smoking, he wrote to Ciardi that he'd been admitted to the hospital "for new strategy and examinations for my 10-month-old bursitis. . . . I'll be here only two more days, so a reply sent to home is best." The extent of the problem was not fully known when the long-in-coming diagnosis was finally made, and April turned into May before doctors explained to Holmes and his second wife Doris that the cancer had already metastasized into his spine, thus accounting for his leg pains. Holmes would never leave the hospital. To eliminate the pain, doctors performed an irreversible surgical procedure, done only when there is no chance of recovery, blocking off the nerves to his legs.

Holmes had been hospitalized for about two months before he died. Perhaps his burden was eased slightly when he recalled that his beloved Tufts had promoted him to full professor in 1960 (a long twenty-six years after his 1934 hiring, however) and had awarded him an honorary doctorate just weeks before his death. Moreover, he had been deeply touched and pleased by Ciardi's tributes to him in the "Manner of Speaking" column called "A Praise of Good Teachers" (8 July 1961). He had written his thanks to Ciardi a week later: "Your warmth is a quality I've always pointed out to people, well knowing it myself. Warmth plus a generosity plus knowing that your praise in the piece you wrote will do all teachers good. Hot as I clutch it to my own breast, I am certain that it also makes other teachers glow." Also just before his death, and further testifying to a life well spent, Holmes was elected a Fellow of the American Academy of Arts and Sciences. Moreover, his 1961 *The Fortune Teller* had been nominated for a National Book

Award, cause for celebration at first, though it gave way to a deeply felt disappointment later when he lost to Alan Dugan's *Poems*. Ciardi reported in "Manner of Speaking" (11 August) that shortly before his death, Holmes had felt the sting of neglect, because "he wanted consumingly to be recognized as a poet." It wasn't that Holmes had wanted to be considered the "Great American Poet," Ciardi wrote, because Holmes "had no such pretensions": "But he knew the good of his poems was there and he complained that it had not been received." By way of eulogy, Ciardi wrote this of Holmes (perhaps in terms he would have liked for himself some years later):

> He stood outside the main current of literary fashion because the voice and the character upon which he insisted were to one side of the most popular literary taste. John Holmes was not an intellectual, nor a yea sayer, nor a defender or castigator of the age, nor a purveyor of messages. He never wrote and never tried to write an Important Poem. What he wrote might better be called Small True Poems. His poetry is local, personal, and, if anything, intellectually timid. What he felt at home in was not the great forensic crossroads of the age, but the side streets of his own life and the house and furniture of its days.

Meanwhile, Concetta Ciardi's decline into senility seems to have begun about 1960, when, after several other incidents, according to family members, she was discovered taking her daughter Ella's electric stove apart. She was visiting with Ella for a week in Brookline to give Cora a short break, for Cora was having a hard time coping at 84 South Street after her husband, Tom, had died the year before of a heart attack. According to Cora, the decision to put her mother into a Somerville nursing home was very painful, so they put it off as long as possible. There is some disagreement as to the year Concetta was admitted, but a pair of letters from Ciardi in early February 1964, one to his mother and one to Ella, suggest that 1964 was the probable year. Cora took the physical and emotional brunt of the painful years between 1960 and 1964, with a major assist from Ella and financial support from John. On 5 February 1964, Ciardi wrote to Ella, with whom Concetta was then staying, to ask how things were working out—and how they might be better. "Would it help if you had a woman in a couple of days a week? Can you get one? Judith and I were thinking it might take a load off your back if you could find such a woman—God knows you have enough to do and Mother isn't easy to get along with at all times. We should of course want to pay for the woman. See if you can work out something that makes it a bit easier for you." And in his letter to his mother of the same date, John wrote as though she would understand what he was saying: Was she comfortable at Ella's? Was there anything she needed? He would send money for anything at all. The children were all taking music lessons. Judith just got a new set of "porcelain crowns": "If she bites I am lost!" He closed by telling her to take care, sending all their love, and asking her "to try to be a little cheerful about things." She may have been in noticeable decline, but John was behaving as though she had enough of her wits left to follow a pleasant sequence of thoughts from a son to his mother.

Soon, however, the nursing home became their only choice as Concetta became less lucid and more of a threat to herself and others. Cora went to see her on a regular basis, getting to know the staff, who always had a tray of food sent up so that Cora could eat with her mother. But it wasn't long before Concetta could not recognize any of her children, although she clutched to her breast a little doll that slept next to her at night and that she called Johnny. According to Cora, John got up as often as he could to see his mother and took care of all the nursing home bills: "She couldn't have wanted a better son." On 21 April 1966, Concetta Ciardi died with her children around her. It was a scene her son never forgot. "She rambled to her witless end in the nursing home," he wrote nearly twenty years later, "but I was out of tears. I had spent them all in the years of watching her lie in that bed like an unburied corpse." Her death had been a "mercy," he wrote: "What a sad frayed end of a heroic woman!" Soon Concetta was reunited with Antonio in a grim parody of their marriage, which Ciardi captured in "Epithalamium at St. Michael's Cemetery," finished in time for inclusion in his 1966 collection, *This Strangest Everything*. The bitterness Ciardi felt over his mother's decline and the suddenly remembered and reexperienced pain of his father's early death mixed together:

My father lay fifty years in St. Michael's bed
till we laid back the covers and bundled in
the hag end of his lost bride, her wits shed
some years before her light. O, bones, begin
with one gold-banded bone. The bride is dressed
in tissue, ten claws folded on no breast.

Sometime afterward, too late for *This Strangest Everything* but in time
for his next collection of poems in 1974, *The Little That Is All*, which
is dedicated to Concetta, "in loving memory," Ciardi wrote a ten-
derer poem called "Addio":

The corpse my mother made
panted all one afternoon
till her father called down, "Oh, stop that!"

I saw her hear and obey
and almost smile
to lie down good again.

Then that blinked gone.
She gaped, her face
a run wax she ran from.

I kissed her forehead and thought,
"It will never be warm again."
Oh daughter, if *I* could call!

The fact that he could not provide the link between his
mother's generation and his children's caused Ciardi great personal
pain. He later said on a radio broadcast, "My mother remained a
peasant woman to the end; the earth was important to her. I wish
I could teach that to my children. I have put a suburb between them
and Adam and Eve. They are the children of tomorrow; they have
no past. Even though their grandparents on one side are Missouri
farm folk and their grandparents on the other were Italian mountain farm folk, they know nothing about it. They have no way of
realizing what this life was when you sweat your bread out of the
soil. Something is lost if we lose that connection entirely."

Principles, Positions, and Personality; Honors, Hobbies, and Health

Despite the steadily increasing tensions between Ciardi and the "measly generation" and the draining experiences of burying his mother and surrogate father, John Ciardi had a remarkably good decade in the 1960s. His books were being published at an incredible speed, academic and publishing honors piled up, real estate transactions and stock purchases added to his fortune—and he even had his celebrity status confirmed by two appearances on Johnny Carson's late night television talk show. When the rest of his activities are figured in—like lecturing, Bread Loaf, *Accent*, "Manner of Speaking," and the continuing Dante translation—it made for a productive and lucrative decade that swept by like a summer storm.

A minor controversy in 1961 arose from Ciardi's outrage over racism in the South, which was the subject of a pre–"Manner of Speaking" essay on 4 February called "Jim Crow Is Treason." "The South," Ciardi wrote, "cannot be left to handle the issue at its own pleasure because it has no solution within itself, but only temporizations and evasions." He asked, "How are we to win the dark-skinned peoples of the world to our cause of freedom and survival so long as a dark skin remains the uniform of peonage at home?" The article was instantly opposed by the Tarrant City White Citizens Council in Alabama, which brought pressure on the Alabama Education Association to cancel Ciardi's scheduled spring appearance, for five hundred dollars, to speak about poetry. The AEA did, indeed, cancel Ciardi's lecture, claiming a schedule problem, but when the real reason came out, Ciardi withdrew his original gracious acceptance of their explanation and sent a registered letter saying, "You now owe me $500. Bigotry must be paid for." (When artist Raphael Soyer in New York heard the story, he wrote to Ciardi, saying, "I hope you collect the 500 bucks. Let them learn how expensive bigotry can be.") In the end, Ciardi was invited by the Rev. Alfred W. Hobart, pastor of the Unitarian church in Birmingham, to deliver his talk on poetry on 17 April, which he did (reportedly for nothing) to the church's first desegregated audience and with the lights of many police cars flashing through the church windows. Thus Ciardi anticipated by a month the famous Freedom Riders who arrived on buses in Montgomery, testing segregation laws and touching off riots that would persist through the decade.

In a related note, for his twenty-fifth reunion at Tufts College in 1963, Ciardi was asked to deliver the Alumni Day speech to some five hundred people, which he published as a "Manner of Speaking" column on 22 June. He delivered an old-fashioned liberal sermon on the side of reason and racial harmony. "I wonder how many [of us] are returning now ignorant of the fact that we are living during a revolution," he asked. "The American face of this revolution is the face of the American Negro. . . . These Americans are declaring that we cannot survive as a nation in which nine-tenths of our citizens are automatically superior to the other tenth because of skin color and racial features." And in a column two weeks later, he asked, "How much can the peace marchers take in the course of passive resistance before their rage and disgust rise in them like vomit and they turn from a Martin Luther King to the violent exhortations of the Black Muslims?" Ciardi was clearly in tune with the social and civil rights issues facing the nation in the 1960s—and prophetic as well.

Ciardi spent a month in the early summer of 1963 teaching modern poetry at the University of Wisconsin-Milwaukee. He got back to New Jersey long enough to load the family into his car and drive up to Chautauqua where he lectured, his first appearance there, on 22–24 July in the open-air amphitheater that seats some fifty-six hundred culture seekers. For Ciardi this was another tying of psychological loose ends, for he was, in a sense, replacing John Holmes, who had been Chautauqua's poet-in-residence. It was another good fit for Ciardi. In his column of 12 October, he joked that the average age of the Chautauquan was "107¾," but that collectively they formed an excellent audience, "no matter how many hearing aids were in residence." Moreover, he enjoyed several events during the three days he was there: an all-Schubert program, *Figaro*, a children's concert, and *Much Ado About Nothing*. He especially enjoyed sitting with Benn in the choir stalls three feet behind the trombones at the children's concert. "To be sure, we couldn't hear what the other side of the orchestra was playing, not more than half the time, but we got the brass in full blare, and Benn liked it that way; so did I." Unfortunately, the accommodations were very poor. The family had been put up in the annex of the Athenaeum Hotel, which, according to long-time Chautauquan opera singer Gil Gallagher, was "near the early morning laundry sounds and garbage trucks." Making matters worse was that the hotel had put up cots in the room for the children, so the entire family was cramped and uncomfortable. When Ciardi was invited back for the first week in August 1964, for a series of lectures called "Poetry Is For People," Gil Gallagher interceded on his behalf, and the Ciardis were put up in the guest room reserved for special visitors. Thereafter, Ciardi was upgraded again to the Nina Wensley Guest House, right across the street from the amphitheater, where he and Judith stayed on their many subsequent visits.

As another measure of the popularity he enjoyed and the respect he was held in, Ciardi received three honorary doctorates in quick succession during the 1963–64 school year. The first came in December 1963, when Wayne State University in Detroit gave him an honorary Doctor of Humanities degree because, as the commencement program said, he was "an outspoken foe of the meretricious and the slovenly." The second was from Ursinus College in Pennsylvania on 8 June 1964, when the dean presented Ciardi to the faculty with these words: "Mr. Ciardi's is a voice that expresses the humanist's hope, in our proudly be-gadgeted age, that having achieved a technology, mankind may yet go on to achieve a civilization." Six days later, at Kalamazoo College in Michigan, Ciardi delivered the commencement address and picked up his third degree in six months—plus a check for five hundred dollars and expenses. No part of Ciardi's ego was invested in academic honors, but he could not help being pleased by the recognition. And when the honor was accompanied by a fat check, the pleasure was doubly sweetened.

During the 1964–65 school year, Ciardi was the John Holmes Visiting Professor of English and Poet in Residence at Tufts, according to the contract letter mailed on 27 August 1964. His salary was set at three thousand dollars, "payable [for tax purposes] March 31, 1965." Ciardi called himself "a very part-time visiting professor," spending two or three days on campus in the fall and spring semesters. X. J. Kennedy had replaced John Holmes as the creative writing man at Tufts and was in charge of setting up Ciardi's schedule. Kennedy saw a curious dynamic at work during that year. Ciardi had many old friends at Tufts, according to Kennedy, people who "loved and idolized" the now famous 1938 graduate. In fact, Kennedy recalled, Ciardi was even offered a chair on the board of trustees, which he declined. Those, however, were honors based on age and deference as well as past accomplishments—not as persuasively relevant to the current crop of students as they had been to their elders. When some members of Kennedy's Poetry Writing Workshop went to see Ciardi, "some of them, I guess, thought that Ciardi was sort of over the hill," Kennedy reported. "It was the '60s, and they were beginning to think that the older generation had nothing they could profit from." Kennedy's perception was ominously seconded a year later in a letter to the editor at *Saturday Review*, from one Martha Mendenhall of Alexandria, Virginia, who commented that there were "rumblings" in Washington-area colleges "that Ciardi is not camp": "Couldn't he have a small advisory committee of a few younger men of this world, at least as a sounding board, before he tosses out old-hat ideas? . . ."

Tufts students may have begun thinking of Ciardi as over the hill, but they did, however, profit from his work on what the university called the "Ciardi Report" (and he called "The Tufts Plan"), which was actually the Committee on Student Publications that was grappling with how much authority the faculty and administration should have over student publications. The answer as phrased in the "Ciardi Report" was none. This liberal, anticensorship policy circulated on campus in January and was implemented for the spring term, 1965. Sometimes, according to the "Ciardi Report," the student writer is "the young madman who has plunged into the wild sea of language and experience in the hope of floundering toward some vision of life." But even then there can be no censorship: "Unless we are prepared to defend him at those times when his compulsion toward the honesty of his vision, no matter how mismanaged, brings him into conflict with the more sedate views of the community, we cannot wish him well in his seeking, nor can we fulfill our purposes as a University." For Ciardi, the principles at stake were self-evident, as was the underlying assumption that young writers, even "the young madman," had to be given the freedom to pursue ideas and artistic forms—and that they needed to be protected from timid professors and community-minded administrators who worried more about endowments than freedom of expression. No matter how unpromising Ciardi thought the younger generation was, he stood arm in arm with them against the censorship that the university threatened to impose.

In addition to everything else that was happening throughout the decade, Ciardi was on the road every fall and spring, and his correspondence for the 1960s is characteristically redundant with itineraries. On the fall 1962 tour, for instance, he delivered thirty-five lectures, traveling on forty-one airplanes from Boston to Los Angeles. During one West Coast week in late April 1963, he spoke at seven colleges (from Stanford to Barstow Junior College) plus a teachers' convention in Newport Beach before heading off to Tucson and then points east. He wrote of his spring 1964 tour that he was going "from here to Oahu, as it now looks, with looping swings to everywhere in between." One of those stops "in between" was at Purdue University, where Felix Stefanile delivered a two-thousand-dollar check and a warm introduction to Ciardi, who gave, according to Stefanile, a "rousing, two-hour speech, in which he thrilled a packed house at our enormous Loeb Theatre." In addition to his 1965 tours, Ciardi was invited by Gen. Carlos P. Romulo to lecture for a week in late July at the University of the Philippines, which turned into a twenty-four-day excursion that also included a three-day visit to Bangkok and nine days in Rome, where he stayed with Milton and Cecille Hebald. In February 1967 he was "cruise poet" (with Judith) in the Virgin Islands and Puerto Rico. Then in May, Scandinavian Airlines invited Ciardi to help them inaugurate new direct service from Copenhagen to Leningrad; that turned out to be just before his scheduled spring lecture tour, which meant that part of his flight schedule went from Leningrad to Moscow to Stockholm to New York to Philadelphia to Chicago to Kansas City to St. Louis to Los Angeles to San Francisco and back to Los Angeles again. Then in August, just before Bread Loaf, Ciardi packed the family for another visit to Chautauqua. For all the world, John Ciardi seemed like a human illustration of Newton's first law: once set in motion, he remained in motion.

Ciardi was at rest and at home, however, when, on Tuesday, 16 March 1965, at 8:00 P.M., the Educational Broadcasting Corporation aired a special thirty-minute program on Ciardi as the first of its new *Creative Person* series. Filmed at Ciardi's home in

Metuchen, the program was billed as "a portrait of the poet, his life, and his work." There was a scene of the family having breakfast together, and another of the poet in his attic office, which they called his "studio," where he talked about being a poet. The camera followed Ciardi to his office at *Saturday Review*, then to Metuchen High School, where thirteen-year-old Myra would be heading the following September. There was even a breakfast scene shot at four in the afternoon with Judith ("in such lounging duds and in such a hairdo as no morning of this world has known") fixing pancakes for exceptionally well-behaved children. In the end, miles of film were edited down to a half hour that Ciardi characterized "as a fair enough look at whatever was being looked at."

The sequence shot at *Saturday Review* contained another dramatically contrived moment, that of the poetry editor rejecting poems at an astonishing speed and tossing them into wire wastebaskets as he explained, "I read just the first line—it tells me all I want to know." The "hold" basket got some of the poems, and these were the ones that got a careful reading later. (The system was defensible, he would afterward write, because "the badness of bad poetry is immediately obvious.") The made-up scene of Ciardi tossing poems into wire baskets was true enough to the editorial principle he worked by, but it was also misleading in its central image and negative in its implied insensitivity. Ciardi had described his method in fairer terms a year earlier to an interviewer: "Physically, what I do is to come in on the average of one day a week. I have a secretary who sorts things for me, and it takes a certain amount of time to run through the submitted poems. There are usually a pile of them that have come in during the week, but they're rather low-grade, so it doesn't take long to reduce a three-foot stack to a two-inch stack. But the two-inch stack takes a lot of reading. Usually I slip it into my briefcase and take it home with me." Even his 2 January 1965 "Manner of Speaking" column ("The Editors Regret") was better than the misleading television message:

> In any case, let me assure [the "plaintive matron"], and any other reader who may care, that I do personally see all poems submitted to *SR*. There is no preliminary screening process. I look at them all. But let me note a difference between "looking" and "reading." "Reading" means all the way through and then, probably, over again. "Looking"

means reading until the eye has come on a reason for rejecting the poem. The first cliché is generally reason enough. In most cases, moreover, the first cliché is likely to be the first thing in the poem. It usually has to be because the second thing in the poem is the second cliché, and the third thing the third cliché, and so on. The only thing that can follow is one of those awkward rejection slips that no one has ever been able to phrase in a satisfactory way—or a personal note to the hundreds of submitters each and every week.

Ciardi actually wrote many such personal notes, many more than he let on, but invariably rejected poets carried around resentments that the television program only reinforced.

In September 1966, John and Judith decided "on a crazy impulse" to move across town to 359 Middlesex Avenue, where they would spend the rest of their lives. Built around 1890, the house was set back on two acres with a detached building out back that served various purposes over the years, from garage to recording studio. The house had a full basement and three floors towering above it. There were fourteen rooms in all, including seven bedrooms. But as Ciardi reported to Milton Hebald, "what it most of all comes to is the fact that I can now look forward to having a really decent study [twenty by twenty and soundproofed] after years of crapping around in these slanting attic walls." The decision had been made so quickly that they weren't able to sell the Graham Avenue house before moving, although they hadn't needed to: Ciardi paid cash for the new property and had no mortgage on the old one, having tired of carrying a mortgage and paying it off in 1963, only eight years after purchase. The family spent November and December packing things into boxes and finally moved on 16 December, two weeks after the last member of their family arrived—a black and tan German Shepherd that would soon be over a hundred pounds and was called Dippy, a nickname for Serendip. It was an ironically unmenacing name, for as Ciardi reported, "He earns his living as a watchdog and his growl is worth believing when you come to the door or go near the car when he's in it. Off his territory and out of the car, however, he has nothing to protect and is ready to like everyone."

Politically, Ciardi identified himself as "a reluctant Democrat" during the 1960s, and his advice was to "hold your nose and vote the straight Democratic ticket." He voted for Lyndon Johnson in 1964, and during the 1968 presidential election, he registered both a political preference and his view on the war in a letter to Norman Cousins. He preferred, he wrote, that Hubert Humphrey would win and "take the position that we negotiate [with North Vietnam] hopefully but that we can not give away our commitment to the self determination of South Vietnam. We were supposed to be in there to assure [a] free election, and we still have a duty to provide that assurance." With respect to Civil Rights, Ciardi hoped Humphrey would say:

> Let every bigot in the land hear me declare that racial prejudice is a treasonable breach of the American faith and that it will not be tolerated. Let every man with a heart for the good of our possible America pledge with me to root out of our lives both the malice of the white supremacist and the convulsion of the black power extremist. And let every man of good conscience stand with me to confess the guilt of our crimes against the Negro in America.

Ciardi claimed in a 1964 self-description that he didn't get involved with hobbies or organizations because he was too lazy. "I used to have character and purpose and even civic pride," he wrote, "but my electric tools are rusting away in the cellar, my golf clubs haven't been used in ten years, the chess set must have grown into the woodwork of the cabinet by now, and I am unknown to the PTA, and grateful for it." (By way of organizations, be it noted that the FBI wrote with untiring doggedness in 1963 that Ciardi was "listed as sponsor [of the] National Committee to Abolish the House Un-American Activities Committee," which they identified as a communist front group.) In 1967, however, Ciardi identified his hobbies, apparently rediscovered, as golf and gardening—although it is clear that his real hobbies were poker, gin rummy, and the stock market. (His competitive nature was apparent every day, whether at anagrams, cards, checkers, Scrabble, cribbage, Trivial Pursuit, or the *New York Times* crossword puzzle, which he solved daily with dazzling speed and a ball-point pen.) Every month or so the poker game was held at the homes of the regulars: Ciardi, Irv Klompus, Norm Abrams (a lawyer), Ben Rabin (a dentist), and the Miller brothers (of unrecalled profession). The stakes were high enough for a man to lose more than a thousand dollars in an evening, and sometimes went as high as five hundred dollars a bet in five-card stud, although it was rare for anyone to lose as much as five hundred dollars for the night. They played a dollar ante, pot limit, and played five-card stud or regular draw poker with nothing wild—a purist's game. Doc Klompus said that Ciardi "played cards like an enlisted man, as if his life depended on every card." They now and then referred to themselves good-humoredly as the Bagel and Lox Society or the Central New Jersey Bagel and Loan Association. The high stakes gin rummy games took place at the Metuchen Country Club (with a group familiarly known as "the animals"), either after a round of golf or in place of it. As much as three or four thousand dollars would often change hands, according to Judith. But according to Klompus, who acted often as Ciardi's financial adviser, Ciardi's gambling at cards paled next to his stock-market chances: "He played the stock market like a crap game—he took appalling risks. He was *very* impatient." But he was either well advised or lucky because among the skimpy financial records still available for this period, Ciardi's brokerage reports show that he had only about $6,500 invested in twenty-five companies on 23 February 1962, but that three years later he was doing so well that he could shift $16,500 from his own portfolio into a starter account for Judith.

In most ways, Ciardi's health was fine during the 1960s, notwithstanding a lifelong preference for T-bone steaks and high cholesterol foods, like duck and Kentucky Fried Chicken. He was generally overweight, 220 pounds in 1967, for example. He also liked crab meat but was allergic to it, so he deliberately, in the view of Doc Klompus, took a great health risk by taking an antihistamine first and then eating as much crab meat as he wanted. He drank black coffee, smoked as many as four to five packs of Lark cigarettes a day (later shifting to the lower tar and nicotine Vantage brand) and often drank a bottle a day of J. W. Dant, one hundred proof Kentucky sour mash. He had a traveling bottle, too, that he took with him for airplane trips and hotel rooms on the lecture circuit. He sometimes drank late into the night because of recurring insomnia, which he refused to treat with sleeping pills. In short, though he enjoyed good health through the 1960s, he had enough bad habits to die of.

With hindsight it is possible to conclude that as early as the mid-1960s Ciardi first referred indirectly to the impotence that he suffered during the last years of his life, a condition partly induced by years of heavy drinking and then by diabetes. In later years, he would make more frequent notice of his condition, always in self-deprecating jest ("Doctuh! I need to have my sex drive lowered, from here [pointing to his head] to here [pointing to his genitals]"), but in his 16 April 1966 column, he wrote with something like subtlety, "I hereby announce that I never even think of assaulting girls until they are at least eighteen (and preferably at least thirty-eight) and that these days any such notion of my notion is purely conceptual." Three months later he wrote in another column, "As with all men in their time, I used to think of myself as a lover. Now, alas, I calculate myself as an estate." He was only fifty at the time. Two years later he wrote in a letter to John Nims, "Grant me at least that next to lust—anent which I grow, alas, more noumenal [i.e., perceived through the intellect rather than the senses] these days—avarice is the most attractive sin."

"Daddy was charming . . . and Mom was First Lady."

Every August in the 1960s, John Ciardi loaded the family into one or another of his Cadillacs and joined his colleagues at Bread Loaf. Perhaps because of the insane pace of his life, Ciardi came to look forward to tradition-laden Bread Loaf as a blessed refuge and retreat where he could renew friendships and be in touch with the spirit of the place and the ghosts of ,cherished friends who had died. When it came to Bread Loaf, the entire Ciardi family was in uncharacteristic agreement. As Jonnel put it, "The real pleasant memories were Bread Loaf. That was magical for everyone in the family—we all had our own reasons for loving it." For Ciardi, it was the connection with the past, the endless talk, and the good fellowship at Treman that mattered most. He saw himself, set apart with his family in the ample and comfortable director's cottage, as the host of a two-week party attended by a couple of hundred apprentice writers, a dozen master writers, plus another fifty or so attendant staff members—all gathered out of the world for the express purpose of talking about literature. It was, as he liked to say, a "land-locked shipboard cruise." For Ciardi, Bread Loaf was an exhausting and exhilarating mix of work and play that helped charge him up each and every year. For Myra, who went from nine to sixteen during these years, Bread Loaf was an experience touched with family pride: "Daddy was charming and held forth over the conference, and Mom was First Lady."

The turbulent 1960s, however, were about to disrupt family harmony, as rising adult baby boomers were preparing to face-off with mid-life GI's, creating a generation gap like none other that had preceded it. Still, in 1961 Ciardi felt blessed, both at home and at Bread Loaf. "Basically," he wrote, "I think I'm one of the luckiest people in existence. It's all pretty much gone easy for me." But important changes were even then taking place, symbolized perhaps by Richard Rovere's 1962 use of a new term, "The Establishment," to identify the self-satisfied status of the mid-life GI generation that would reach the pinnacle of its political power in the landslide victory of Lyndon Johnson in 1964. Certainly by then, Ciardi's future problems had not yet shown themselves in a way that could claim his undivided attention. He wrote that year with good humor that he dutifully obeyed his wife and children, plus his lecture agent, his secretary at *Saturday Review*, and Paul Cubeta, "who really runs the show."

It was not, however, always easy. Ciardi often, for example, worked up a genuine anger over "the school system" and the "measly generation" it had created—if for no other reason than that these were the young people he was seeing more and more of at Bread Loaf. He wrote in 1962, identifying early on what many see as a flaw in late-twentieth-century educational theory, "Among the diehards, I am forced to believe that our School System is in fact turning out some sort of intellectual rabble in the name of democratic education." Two years later, he said in an interview that "not long ago a man who was ignorant knew it. Now we have a school system that doesn't educate people, but does succeed in camouflaging their ignorance." The current generation "may be good salesmen," he said, "but they know nothing of their own language or its achievements. . . . They're ignorant about music, about the arts in general, yet they feel free to have opinions about them." Ciardi wondered "what the presence of these democratic slobs does to the standards of the college," a worry and an anger that produced "Who Writes the Contract?", a "Manner of Speaking" column that appeared on 23 October 1965:

> College, as some students are sure to argue year after year, is an important social experience for which they are paying. They aren't of course, or they are paying no more than a sliver of the whole budgetary pie, but the college budget is not likely to mean anything to an undergraduate. He has it in his head that his (or Dad's) money is running the place, and why, therefore, should he not be free to decide what he gets for his cash? His is the simple and simple-minded argument that the customer is always right (and what right has the faculty to decide what courses a man should take, or to make all those rules about how he shall behave even outside the classroom?).
>
> Before the students get around to deciding for themselves what will constitute their education, let them be reminded that on entering college they submit themselves as candidates for a degree the requirements of which are at the discretion of the faculty, and the grant of which is faculty certification that the student has met not his but its requirements. Even if the liberal arts college cannot define all of its own purposes (primarily because it has too many), it still has as firm a duty as has the school of medicine or of engineering to establish the terms of the contract under which its degrees will be granted.
>
> The terms of that contract are set forth in the college catalogue. In it, every incoming student is free to read them for himself. If he does not like the contract as offered (denominational colleges, for example, have a right to impose doctrinal and moral restrictions that might be intolerable in a public institution), he is not required to sign. He is free to contract with another school if he can, or to go on about his own business. He is not free, however, to violate a contract to which he has committed himself.
>
> That, gentlemen of the entering class, is the nature of the contract, and let there be no nonsense about whose opinion is as good as anyone else's in a free country. The freedom of the classroom is the freedom to grow within the measure of sound intellectual standards. Take those standards into your

head before you try taking the curriculum into your hands. Or get out of school and be as free as you like—and as ignorant. If only until the draftboard catches up with you and submits you to another set of notions.

Ciardi's ideas about a college education may have seemed doctrinaire to some in 1965, but they were little more than common sense to a generation that had been educated in the 1930s (or earlier) and fought in World War II. The GI generation felt betrayed by the coming-of-age baby boomers, who, in turn, held their GI elders in contempt for creating a material culture that was seen as spiritually barren. Moreover, those who lived by the slogan, "if it feels good, do it," were becoming so self-absorbed that they became temperamentally unable to tolerate any restrictions imposed by the older generation, whom they saw as "fat cats" who were mishandling social and political issues of the 1960s, not World War II defenders of the free world. They were most especially unwilling to tolerate any such authoritarian pronouncements as John Ciardi was dispensing.

And when they began drifting into Bread Loaf with their restless rebelliousness, anti-authoritarian mindset, and a preference for undisciplined free verse, the collision with Ciardi was inevitable. He would have them defer their free-verse experiments until after they had studied poetic forms; they insisted on rejecting the past and rushing headlong into the future. Ciardi's anger with the Bread Loaf boomers—no doubt fueled at home by the challenge to his authority by his own children—was not something he cared to overlook. At Bread Loaf Ciardi chose to make a stand: to the extent that it was a school at all, Bread Loaf would not be compromised. He could do nothing about what was going wrong at American colleges (although he did try to bring attention to the problems of higher education in his columns and lectures), but at Bread Loaf he was the director and could bring reason and firm principle back into the curriculum. The battle lines were drawn.

Ciardi went on the offensive time and again in a variety of formats. About poetry, he often spoke of the "disciplined containment of the medium" and illustrated his point by saying that no amount of sitting at a piano will come to anything "unless there are some educated fingers between the passion and the instrument." He often used the Frost gambit about "the pleasure of taking pains." On other occasions, he talked about how "we demand difficulty even in our games," pointing out that the fun is in the "arbitrary imposition of difficulty." When someone refuses to play by the rules, he chooses an easier way out: "It is easier to win at chess if you are free, at your pleasure, to change the wholly arbitrary rules, but the fun is in winning within the rules. No difficulty, no fun." To a violin-playing young poet, Ciardi wrote on 17 September 1963, "A poem's reader doesn't give a damn how the poet feels (& shouldn't) but only how the poem (a managed illusion—like your fiddle) makes him (the reader) feel. Sure you feel important about your emotion. Why not[?] But you have to feel important about your techniques too. Passion plays no fiddle until the fiddler's hands have gone to school."

But none of this was new to Ciardi in the 1960s. They were the same messages about poetry he'd been preaching since 1940, at the University of Kansas City. On 16 February of that year the school newspaper ran a story about their new "modern poet," saying that traditional poetic forms were "important" to Ciardi, who advocated "mastery" of existing forms "before a young writer begins to experiment seriously." That was an article of faith to Ciardi, who believed it as fervently in the 1960s as he had in the 1940s. The student poets of the 1960s and later, as Ciardi never tired of saying, believed "that the only prerequisite for poetry is the excitation of one's own ignorance"—and then he typically added, "I can't stand the stuff they spill on the pages." If the would-be poets "get excited enough about something, it's a poem. They don't think they need to hear the echoes of the poets of the past." Or he put it this way: "Students, as I watch them, all seem undisciplined. They're all screechers of their feelings rather than shapers of the language." And on yet another occasion he wrote with equal measures of perception and bitterness, "With their generation [he was speaking of his own children's] they were secure in a full set of intellectual values—all the way from 'I think/I feel' to 'in my experience' and on to 'everyone is entitled to his own opinion'—which is at least an assertion to the basic right to equality in ignorance."

Despite the high principles of Ciardi's pronouncements on poetry and his undisputed talent at delivering the message, Bread Loaf executives gradually soured on their director, and for reasons that at first had nothing to do with the paying customers. Paul Cubeta, who had served as conference assistant director from 1956 to 1964, believed that Ciardi had slipped during those years. Cubeta was frequently overburdened either because Ciardi was in Italy or was traveling with the *Accent* program or was on the lecture circuit. As Cubeta saw it, Ciardi had lost interest in the details of the conference by 1964 and had noticeably curtailed his participation in conference activities. In his view, Ciardi had become more involved with staff socializing at Treman Cottage, including the "care and nurturing" of Robert Frost, than in students, manuscripts, and workshops. He said that Ciardi slept too late in the mornings, played too much cribbage and gin rummy, and "showed a carefree attitude toward the proceedings by casually asking who was coming this year, as though he didn't know the faculty he was responsible for inviting." Vice President Stephen Freeman claimed that he "enjoyed and admired" Ciardi and that he "never had a quarrel with John Ciardi," but according to David Bain in his history of Bread Loaf, Freeman, a teetotaler, did have a serious quarrel with Ciardi over the alcoholic consumption at the conference. Ciardi, whose own capacity to hold one hundred proof J. W. Dant bourbon was legendary, claimed quite reasonably that he was unable to control the drinking habits of 250 adults.

Meanwhile, unaware of the growing discontent of management toward his work as director, Ciardi went about his Bread Loaf business with love, even though he sometimes became characteristically short-tempered and impatient. He sometimes seemed to ignore the conference and take it for granted. He sometimes made a little fun of the customers and the staff. And he probably did spend too much time at Treman. Yet Ciardi also capitalized on his national reputation and fund-raising prowess to collect some twelve thousand dollars in endowments by 1963, which he intended for three standing scholarships. In June 1965, Ciardi got Richard RePass, director of the Weekly Reader Children's Book Club, to donate four thousand dollars for the endowment of a fellowship in children's literature, with Xerox, the parent company, pledging ten thousand dollars more to endow a lectureship in juvenile literature. And Ciardi himself put three thousand dollars into the juvenile literature fund, "as an item of personal faith in Bread Loaf." He also maintained high enrollments at the conference; quietly dipped into his own wallet to help students and faculty with money problems; turned back his four hundred dollar fee as poetry lecturer; helped pay for a new porch on the Annex; urged the administration constantly to raise staff salaries, especially Cubeta's; and worked hard every year to recruit the best faculty possible. Perhaps most important, he spread the Bread Loaf gospel from coast to coast on the lecture circuit and praised it in his column many times—though never more completely than he did on 19 October 1963. There was the scenery to love, he wrote, and the memories, but most of all, the talk: "I know of no place on this earth that can offer two weeks' worth of such talk," the kind made special by the "quality of the talkers" and the fact that it was all delivered "from *inside* the writing."

With respect to Ciardi's visibility and his participation at each Bread Loaf conference, and the customers' attitudes toward him, there were mixed reactions. And if a few staff members were unhappy either with Bread Loaf or Ciardi, others were very pleased. The turning point seems to have been the 1965 conference, when Edward Martin, known by the nickname "Sandy," took over as assistant director. To Ciardi, who had every reason to think in September 1964 that Martin would be a good replacement for Cubeta, the new man nevertheless represented yet another break with the past. Change was of course inevitable, but Bread Loaf thrived on continuity, links with the past. With the passing of Benny DeVoto, Fletcher Pratt, Robert Frost, and right after the 1964 conference ended, William Raney, plus the loss of Paul Cubeta to a Middlebury promotion (to say nothing of the deaths of non-Bread Loafers Holmes and Theodore Roethke, who died in August 1963), Ciardi took sole responsibility for preserving Bread Loaf's distinguished past. Only Bill Sloane was left from the 1940s to help him continue the Bread Loaf tradition.

Moreover, social changes in the real world caused corresponding changes on the mountain every August during the 1960s. Tradition-laden Bread Loaf, led by a GI generation authority figure like Ciardi, was an easy target for the young idealists who, like Ciardi, believed they were taking the high road. Increasingly during the decade of the 1960s, students "demanded" that high school and college administrators yield control of their institutions and curricula. (Wasn't the older generation proving its own incompetence every single day by its mismanagement of the Vietnam War?) It was an egalitarian movement, and even merit-based privileges were forbidden in the name of democracy and anti-elitism. The idea of an earned hierarchy, that deference was due to those who were older, wiser, and more distinguished, was absolutely foreign. At Bread Loaf some participants took special exception to the outer trappings of such a hierarchy, like the staff-only policy at Treman cocktail hours or the long, raised table at the dining hall. Perhaps matters were reduced to the absurd when one person in 1966 even challenged the Bread Loaf custom of calling a manuscript discussion between faculty and contributor a "clinic," because it suggested that student work was "a disease which had to be diagnosed."

But even in the face of this sort of activism in the 1960s, Ciardi refused to be steam-rollered into submission. His attitude toward the Bread Loaf students may have been expressed best in a "Manner of Speaking" column (22 July 1967) on demonstrators and demonstrations: "The only thing that counts in the ritualized psyche of the demonstrator is emotional charge. It is the faith of this ritual that any absurdity, half-truth, or flat lie, when it is ardently and persistently proclaimed, will attract other emotionally charged persons to the demonstrators' cause, thereby establishing a mathematics of irrationality. . . ." Nonetheless, matters deteriorated at Bread Loaf, and in 1968, during a presentation by Lew Turco and Miller Williams, Ciardi interjected a rather long comment from his first-row seat and was interrupted by an impatient young man with a demonstrator's sense of cause, who yelled out, "Mr. Turco, could you ask Mr. Ciardi to shut up because we came to hear you and Miller Williams this afternoon." For John Ciardi, the talk at Bread Loaf had suddenly turned ugly. Making matters worse, Sandy Martin was eager to fall in line with student demands. He suggested many compromises of conference policy that Ciardi disregarded, and when Ciardi suggested that the average age of the conference members be raised to avoid the confrontational youngsters, Martin disregarded the instruction and complained to Steve Freeman about the impasse that had developed between himself and Ciardi. When a woman named Bea Levin wrote an angry piece in the *St. Louis Post Dispatch* (3 March 1968) about her 1964 experience at Bread Loaf, disburdening herself of long-simmering complaints about intolerance, hostility, elitism, and bad manners, Freeman called on Ciardi to explain himself. Her complaint was not new to the conference,

Ciardi said, but even though he'd thought about various changes, he saw no "good reason" to do so. Having a reserved dining table for staff members, for example, was merely sensible because they tended to arrive late from cocktails at Treman. Yes, he would continue to urge the staff to spend an hour in the evening at the barn for mingling—and most of them did—but, he said, "I think that is all we can do." All the rest of her complaints came to nothing, Ciardi went on—Levin was merely like every other Bread Loaf customer who had come to the conference to be "discovered" and gone home undiscovered and unhappy. Moreover, there is no record that Freeman even saw the much fairer appraisal by David Rabe in 1969 in the *New Haven Register*. It may be that by then Freeman's antagonism toward Ciardi had taken root, but one thing was certain: the tenor of Bread Loaf talk had taken yet another turn for the worse. Ciardi had to realize by then that the Bread Loaf administration was watching him guardedly, if not disapprovingly.

TEN

Binge Worker

BOOKS OF THE SIXTIES

Children's Verse

An interviewer in 1973 counted up the books Ciardi had published after leaving full-time teaching, twenty-two in fifteen years, and asked in admiration how he'd been able to keep to such a strict work schedule. Ciardi's surprising reply was that he did not keep to any schedule at all, that he was, as he put it, "no good at strict disciplines." He confessed he was "a binge worker," by which he meant that he would regularly "putter and neglect and put off" and then suddenly become "absolutely irresponsible to appointments [and] promises" when he fell into a "working streak." His three months of furious travel each year yielded him nine months to work at his desk, plenty of time to wait for the binges, which, considering his more than book-a-year productivity, came more regularly than he had perhaps implied.

For John Ciardi the years between 1958 and 1966 were one long binge of children's verse, ten books in all: *The Reason for the Pelican* and *Scrappy the Pup* came out in 1959 and 1960; in 1961 two more appeared, *The Man Who Sang the Sillies* and *I Met a Man*; then three more in 1962, *The Wish Tree* (prose), *You Read to Me, I'll Read to You*, and *John J. Plenty and Fiddler Dan*; then one a year from 1964 to 1966, *You Know Who*, *The King Who Saved Himself from Being Saved*, and *The Monster Den*. After that spurt, Ciardi seemed to lose some interest, perhaps because his children were entering puberty—ages twelve, thirteen, and fourteen—and "began to be in a hurry to grow up," as he put it. The books of children's verse began appearing at greater intervals, *Someone Could Win a Polar Bear* (1970), *Fast and Slow* (1975), and *Doodle Soup* (1985). (Three more children's books were published posthumously, a collection of forty-four poems, *Blubberhead, Bobble-Bud & Spade* [1988], *The Hopeful Trout and Other Limericks* [1989], and *Mummy Took Cooking Lessons and Other Poems* [1990].) Six of the first eleven books were illustrated by Ciardi's old Harvard student, the incomparable Edward Gorey, whose droll, deadpan sense of humor was a perfect match for Ciardi's sharp wit. Their collaboration seemed to underscore an agreed-upon principle of loving strictness. As Ciardi put it, "I love to scold children, but if you do it in the right way, they know you're having fun with them."

Binge work or not, Ciardi's children's verse was very successful. William Jay Smith wrote that although the twentieth century "has made few additions to the lasting body of children's poetry . . . , many of those that are worthy are the work of John Ciardi." X. J. Kennedy lavished even higher praise: "Practically singlehandedly, he changed the whole character of American poetry for children." There were other tributes as well, like the 1962 Junior Book Award from the Boys' Clubs of America for *The Man Who Sang the Sillies* and the 1966 Rutgers Award for making "a distinguished contribution to literature for children and young people." Moreover, the 1962 poem, "Mummy Slept Late and Daddy Fixed Breakfast," was immediately popular among youngsters, who even ten years later selected it as their favorite poem in a national survey of fourth-to-sixth-graders conducted by the National Council of Teachers of English. This particular honor, more perhaps than his many other awards and prizes for adult verse, especially delighted Ciardi because, as he was fond of saying, "the children are a jury that can't be rigged." And ten years after that, in 1982, when the NCTE chose him as winner of its Award for Excellence in Poetry for Children ("in recognition of a poet's aggregate body of work for children ages 3 to 13"), Ciardi once again felt the sweet satisfaction of having written well for an audience he truly loved.

Yet controversy hounded Ciardi all through his career as a children's poet, too. His poems were too violent said one group of protective parent-critics who were upset at Ciardi's playful rendering of the violence displayed by their children every day. It was as though the parents could make the violence go away by making believe it did not exist—and here came Ciardi to remind them that it did. Irritating his critics even more, Ciardi refused to give an inch. He pointed out that when he was a child (and wasn't his childhood like theirs?), he recalled "intensities and losses" that contributed to a time of "madness" and "disproportion"—and not a time for "sugar-coated moralities." And in one of his better-known characterizations, Ciardi brushed aside most contemporary children's poetry because it seemed to be "written by a sponge dipped in warm milk and sprinkled with sugar." Moreover, he went on, "it's written for angels, perfect little celestial beings. We never had those in my family. We had savages. . . ." His critics, he was saying, were in a state of denial, for it didn't take anything like a university-supported study of child psychology to discover what every parent and every child observes first-hand of family life: children are naturally violent. "One of the best things children's poetry can do," Ciardi answered his critics in reasonable self-defense, "is to catch up that violence in the measure and play of rhyme, rhythm, and form— and so make a pleasant, if momentary, assurance of it."

On another occasion, when he was questioned about the wisdom of referring to his own children as monsters in *The Monster Den*, Ciardi patiently but persistently explained once again, keeping to his belief that his poems were good for children, who would instantly recognize themselves and enjoy seeing their playful violence contained in measured forms:

> Children are savages: I think they need fairly strong stuff. As I recall it and as I observe it, childhood is a time of enormous violence. It's emotional violence; everything is out of proportion. If you have six buttons and your brother steals one button or loses it, this is a great federal charge and requires a war and a great flashing of tempers. Or another time a huge thing can go by unnoticed. The imagination of a child is high-pitched; he has extravagantly bad dreams; his language and natural metaphors are violent. My feeling is that if we can take this sort of violence and convert it into play within formality—make a little dance and rhythm of it—I don't know what else that could be except therapeutic.

A number of the parent-critics, however, remained unpersuaded that Ciardi's poems were therapeutic. He liked to tell two stories to show just what he was up against in this world of adults who did not understand children or what made them giggle and laugh. The first story he recorded in "Manner of Speaking" on 14 July 1962, under the title "Let the Healthy Be Tended, Too": At Bread Loaf in 1961, two women, whom he called Militant Virtues, strode uninvited into a quiet coffee break to object very indignantly to a pair of his poems, one called "Halloween" in *The Reason for the Pelican* and one called "The Happy Family" in *The Man Who Sang the Sillies*. "Does it give you any real pleasure," they wanted to know, "to disturb children?" It turned out the Militant Virtues taught disturbed children somewhere in New York, and some of the children in their classes had been frightened by the poems, one or two even to nightmares, according to the ladies. Ciardi understood at once. He had written the poems "in the happy conviction that children were small savages with a glad flair for violence" and had therefore "violated the rules of therapy to which [the] Militant Virtues were dedicated." "Halloween," he explained, had merely "played at being spooky," while "The Happy Family," and here he could not resist the sarcasm, had been written "in such horrendous detail that the poem barely made the pages of a radical magazine called the *Ladies' Home Journal*." "The Happy Family" has a father's playful silliness at its heart. It is built on the proposition that children generally behave as though they have a screw loose, and so it follows that good parents must make certain the screws are all tightened before the kiddies go to sleep at night. It is a matter of the utmost importance to keep all heads on all shoulders all night.

> Children's heads are very loose.
>> Mother, Father, screw them tight.
> If you feel uncertain use
>> A monkey wrench, but do it right.
>
> If a head should come unscrewed
>> You will know that you have failed.
> Doubtful cases should be glued.
>> Stubborn cases should be nailed.

It seemed incredible to Ciardi that he needed to explain what would have been patently obvious to every earlier generation—that this was all in good fun and that healthy children, like his own, for example, knew the difference between a "story thing" and a "for-real thing." Marie Ponsot, reviewing *The Man Who Sang the Sillies* for *Poetry*, might well have taken the Militant Virtues to task had she known about them: "John Ciardi's verse for children is so good," she wrote, "that self-conscious adults can read it aloud without pain. . . . Ciardi is relaxed, in control, not faking; there is no hint of winnie-the-poohery. He is a grown man addressing his juniors, willing to entertain them. He is comical in a way that makes children grin and quickly appropriate his nonsensical jugglery."

Ciardi was surely moved by the plight of any disturbed children who could not tell the difference between the real and the make-believe, but it was important, he said, to stand up for the rights of the overwhelming majority of children who could:

> What man can fail to weep for a child born helpless into a world that terrifies and that offers no real love a child can bring his terror to for comfort, and from which he can saunter off feeling soothed, laughing, and cocky again?
>
> But is every Militant Virtue right? Whether the poems were good or bad, they were meant for fun. They were meant for the dance and joy of healthy children. Much of my own pleasure in writing children's poems has been in having my pleasure shared by children, individually, in groups, and many times in classrooms. Is one to destroy the pleasure of the healthy because the sick are not equal to it?

He knew he would not persuade the Militant Virtues, but he hoped the schools, libraries, and social agencies would be more reasonable: "In mercy's name let the sick be tended from the heart. But let the healthy be tended too."

The second story concerned *I Met a Man*, published in 1961, when Myra turned nine, but written, as Ciardi noted in the book's preface, in time "for a special pleasure: I wanted to write the first book my daughter read herself." (Adding to her delight, she went along with her father to read a poem from the book on NBC's *Today Show* with Dave Garroway.) The book had been based, Ciardi explained in his preface to parents and teachers, on the four-hundred-word vocabulary list used in the first grade, although the poems got a little more challenging as he introduced additional words toward the end of the book. He was hoping to improve on first-grade readers that always relied on something like "Look! Dick. Look!" It was a good starting principle, but *I Met a Man* was objected to by an unknown number of professional educators, which prompted Houghton Mifflin, hoping for greater sales, to set up an interview between Ciardi and one especially indignant grade school curriculum expert, who smugly offered to point out just what errors should be corrected for the second edition. One poem was "I Met a Man That Was Trying to Whittle":

> I met a man that was trying to whittle
> A ship from a stick, but little by little
> The ship he whittled grew littler and littler.
> Said he with a sigh, "I'm a very bad whittler!
> I've whittled my ship till it's small as a boat.
> So he threw it away and cut his throat.

"This one," said the curriculum expert with all the educationese he could summon up, "did not encompass optimum archetypal behavioral patterns." Ciardi listened in something like stunned admiration to this display of graduate-school-of-education language, when he suddenly had an idea for a new concluding couplet:

> And when he saw his head was gone,
> He whittled another and put that on.

This, he thought, was a "happy ending," and he included it in all subsequent editions of *I Met a Man*, but he never saw anything in the poem, or the book, that might "damage a little psyche." It was no worse than Mother Goose herself:

> There was a man in our town
> And he was wondrous wise,
> He jumped into the bramble bush
> And scratched out both his eyes.
> And when he saw his eyes were out
> With all his might and main,
> He jumped into another bush,
> And scratched them in again.

"I love that little poem," Ciardi wrote: "I think it's one of the best of those of Mother Goose. There is violence in it, but what difference does it make? It is not violent violence. It is play violence, dance violence. . . ." Another poem, "The Cat Heard the Cat Bird," which Ciardi called "a pure exercise in matching sounds," described in delicious mischief how the thin cat got to be a fat cat by eating the cat bird. The school administrator said it was "definitely inconducive to the ideal classroom function atmosphere-wise." And of a double limerick that began "I said to a bug in the sink, / "Are you taking a swim or a drink?" the school man could only murmur disapprovingly, "It certainly does make the American home sound unsanitary." Ciardi saw the overzealous, bureaucratic, jargonistic education major as a problem of modern society, but, he typically added, "in mercy, let me say that I don't really think of him as representing the school system, but rather as a private disaster that had gotten itself publicly affiliated."

If reviews across the country can be used as a measure of the book's approval rating, Ciardi ought not to have been too disturbed by the overly solicitous school administrator. The *Kansas City Star* (27 May 1961) called *I Met a Man* "original, gay and imaginative"; *Books for Young Readers* (spring 1961), said it was "a true delight"; the *Rockland (Mass.) Standard* (17 August) said it was "definitely a superior book for little children"; the *Minneapolis Sunday Tribune* (25 June)called it "a refreshing departure"; the *Austin (Tex.) American Statesman* (30 April) said it was "charming"; and the *Denver Sunday Post* (30 April) called it an "inviting treat." Professionals also liked the book. *Library Journal* (15 June) predicted it would be "a favorite for all ages" and said it was "Highly recommended"; *Publisher's Weekly* (22 May) called it "a delightful collection of nonsense poems"; the *Book Reviews* of the Association of Children's Librarians of Northern California (no date) reported that it was "an entertaining book of imaginative, humorous verses which will be enjoyed by the child reading to himself or by classes or families reading aloud together"; *Grade Teacher* (Fall 1961) said it was "a real gift to all beginning readers"; and *Horn Book* (April 1961) reported that though the poems were "not always easy, nor always obvious," *I Met a Man* was "an honest and original attempt to make both poetry and learning fun." Finally, Walker Gibson, reviewing the book for the *New York Times Book Review* (16 July) also liked it, saying that the minimal vocabulary had made the book into a "tour de force for a professional poet." He wrote that the poems were "on the whole sharp, amusing, and unsentimental," adding that they were "not only readable but also entertaining for a bright first-grader." He ended perceptively by noting that the new book "lacks the sophisticated zaniness of the author's earlier *The Reason for the Pelican*, and may therefore be a little less attractive to parents. But that may be just the point: here is a witty book for the beginning reader that he is actually expected to read for himself, with a minimum of assistance from the old folks."

The uncontested truth—notwithstanding the crankiness of "militant virtues" and indignant curriculum "experts"—was that Ciardi loved children, and his poems show it. The humor, the silliness, the playfulness are everywhere evident, as is his delight in words and images and rhythms. He shifts tones and forms and becomes conspiratorial with the kids in one poem and very parental in the next. In his use of strange creatures and made-up names, Ciardi is often compared to Edward Lear and Lewis Carroll—even Mother Goose. Moreover, Ciardi never talked down to children and maintained an easy-to-spot honesty that children respected. As one third-grader reported, "He made me feel like jumping into the poem. . . ." And there was something else, the reassuring presence of a daddy, as one seventh-grader put it, who "double-checked to make sure nothing was wrong." For children, at least, fatherly authority figures were good to have around.

Walter Bezanson prepared a program note for the 1966 Rutgers Award which sketched out Ciardi's accomplishments in children's verse. He liked that "the smoke of battle still hovers over [some poems], the odor of parental harassment mingling with the fragrance of affection." He was especially pleased that Ciardi could and did scold and spank misbehaving children in his poems: "One of your innovations, among many, is that you have returned the spanking to children's literature, no mean achievement in a saccharinely permissive society." Then, after a pause and a second thought, he added, "Or if it is a *mean* one, you balance it off with plenty of love and kisses." And in a nice distinction, Bezanson said that Ciardi didn't write "children's poetry so much as poems and songs for kids—small fry who hoot and holler; get bumps and wet feet; like to get even with each other; scrape their knees and cry when they do it; revel in being silly; and above all—hate going to bed."

> Perhaps what you celebrate most, Mr. Ciardi, is the sheer
> exuberance of healthy children, hungry to know about the
> big world, eager to knock it about and be knocked by it, if
> need be. You win their trust. You do not patronize. You do

not talk to them in pretty bows and ribbons, as if you were their mother. Nor do you pretend that you, too, are a child. You write as a man to a child, as a big scary man even, one who explodes one minute, turns beguilingly gentle the next, and then, to their infinite delight, joins them in dancing the sillies.

Moreover, even though such formidable poets as Theodore Roethke and Randall Jarrell would be publishing books of children's verse soon after Ciardi, it was then considered a risky business for any serious poet who valued his reputation. When Ciardi helped break this new ground, he was courageously working a field that X. J. Kennedy said was, at the time, "slightly disreputable, something that a really good poet wouldn't do." That perception would be altered in a matter of a decade or so, but Kennedy maintained that Ciardi "was responsible to a large extent for this change in climate." For Kennedy the Ciardi influence was powerful and enduring with its emphasis on children as real people "with feelings and resentments," people who might even "occasionally punch one another in the snoot." Kennedy said that Ciardi gave us "real kids and actual, fallible families," that he "let in a blast of fresh air" with his contemporary subjects and diction: "He altered the way we look at poetry for children, helping us see it as a fun-filled romp instead of a saccharine pill or a dose of propriety. He addressed himself to actual twentieth-century American kids with all their faults, kids who . . . sometimes prattle on at a great rate about nothing much, or taunt younger siblings with their own superiority." If this could be called "binge work," it is hard to imagine how it could have been more successful—or influential.

Dante "by itch and twitch"

Ciardi was not merely on a decade-long tear of writing children's poetry, however. In 1961, his translation of *The Purgatorio* appeared, followed by nine more years of intermittent but painstaking translation until *The Paradiso* appeared in 1970. It was February of 1960 when Ciardi finally sent all but the last two cantos of *The Purgatorio* to his editor, Arabel Porter, at the New

American Library. The delays had been unfortunate but unavoidable, after all, and Ciardi was neither chagrined nor apologetic when he mailed the manuscript: "Having been this slow, I see no merit in trying to rush too fast at the end. It has to be done right." In fact, *The Inferno* had come out in 1954, only six years earlier. And even though Ciardi had spent a year in Rome from September 1956 to September 1957 at the American Academy, in theory working on *The Purgatorio* full time, that year had been eventful to say the least as he had had to deal with the Anne Morrow Lindbergh firestorm, the Harold Norse poem over which he had nearly been deported, and a steady stream of visitors. To have completed the translation in six very busy years that also included teaching at Rutgers and lecturing all over the country was actually quite remarkable.

Within two weeks of its receipt at NAL, the manuscript was read and returned by Giorgio de Santillana at MIT. He reported back to Porter on 26 February that he was "very much pleased" with the translation, notwithstanding some "verses that cannot and will not scan." But more important than occasional failures, said Santillana offering the highest praise, were Ciardi's successes in rhyme and metric: "There are points—in fact a few points—where he actually improved on the original, which is a pleasant thought." And Santillana was pleased by Ciardi's effort "to bring in some American verse techniques to affect a bridge between two very different feelings of musicality," even though he noticed occasional breakdowns that he hoped would be revised into better shape before publication. He had worked extra diligently on his reading of the text, he wrote, "because [the translation] was very good, and minor faults should not be allowed to mar such an accomplishment." Archibald MacAllister, who was once again asked to write an historical introduction, agreed with Santillana, saying that the translation was "sensitive and perceptive" and that readers would find Dante's *Purgatorio* "more accessible than has hitherto been possible without a good command of the original Italian."

It took nearly two years for *The Purgatorio* to be published, with final proofs getting to Ciardi in mid-September 1961 and publication scheduled for November. The title page announced that this was "a verse translation for the modern reader," but in a six-page "Translator's Note," dated 12 May 1961 (and printed with minor changes as "Translation: The Art of Failure" on 7 October in *Saturday Review*), Ciardi admitted at once that any translator's effort to explain his methods was bound to become "an apology for failure." The best anyone can hope for, he wrote, "is no more than the best possible failure." Still, he tried. He demonstrated part of his meaning in a brief discussion of connotations and word histories, just the sorts of things that are impossible to capture from one language into another. Then he reported once again that he had begun translating Dante years earlier because none of the translations then being used in classrooms had "satisfied" his "sense of the original." And he also explained again that the heavy burden of rhyme in terza rima could be made to work in English only at the expense of meaning, which was why he settled for two rhymes per stanza and gave up the interlocking quality of Dante's tercets. Finally, to illustrate the exact nature of his "failure," he traced one of his three-line translations from Dante's original Italian through five drafts, thus hoping to explain both the problems he had faced and the decisions he had made. These were clearly the sorts of problems facing all translators, and Ciardi earned both respect and admiration, first by being so refreshingly clear and disarmingly honest, and second by sharing his misgivings about the compromises he had made.

In the end, Ciardi wrote, translation came down to a matter of "*feel*," for "what has any poet to trust more than the *feel* of the thing?" And then, in another of his quirky but apt prose captures, Ciardi said that the translator should concern himself with the theories of translation "only until he picks up his pen," at which time "he has to write by itch and twitch, though certainly his itch and twitch are intimately conditioned by all his past itching and twitching, and by all his past theorizing about them."

Then, at the end of his translation of the thirty-three cantos of *The Purgatorio*, Ciardi tacked on still another *Saturday Review* article, this one called "How to Read Dante," which had run in the issue of 3 June 1961. In this twelve-page essay, Ciardi appeared as the teacher once again, this time helping the uninitiated to appreciate the great master. "All one really needs," he wrote, "is some first instruction in what to look for," and Ciardi then delivered a minicourse on *The Divine Comedy*, including Dante's midlife determination to find God, the obstacles thrown in his way, and the guides provided to help him toward the light. He explained why there could be no short cuts between salvation and total understanding, and he explored Dante's sin of acedia, "the failure to be sufficiently active in the pursuit of the recognized Good." He described the five levels of meaning in *The Divine Comedy* as well as the moral universe that Dante had understood full well as part of the world he lived in, but which he nonetheless had to imagine into existence. Ciardi marveled at the architectonics of the poem and the mind which could construct it, and he drew attention to Dante's method of "back-illumination" by which the master systematically clarified earlier questions in later cantos. Ciardi's "students" appreciated the lesson. As Frances Carter from Santa Monica, California, observed in a letter to the editor of *SR* on 17 June: "Though repeatedly exposed to 'The Divine Comedy' through higher education, I have never before been given a footing secure enough to launch me on its journey."

In 1963 Ciardi gave permission for selected passages of his translation of *The Inferno* to be used as the subject of drawings by Rico Lebrun. It was a collaboration he was especially proud of because Lebrun was, to Ciardi's way of thinking, the perfect illustrator of Dante, much better than Gustave Doré, whose nineteenth-century illustrations of Dante had long since become standard. The trouble with Doré, wrote Ciardi in a brief introduction to the book, was that he did not understand Dante. It had been left to the modern age and to Lebrun, an artist who was not bound to "literal surfaces," as Ciardi put it, to create "a series of interpretations that clearly declare their authority as graphic conceptions while faithfully rendering a sense of Dante." A limited, two thousand–copy portfolio edition of the Ciardi-Lebrun collaboration was published in November 1963 by Abe Lublin, a print wholesaler who ran Kanthos Press. One hundred of the copies were numbered and signed and sold for $350.

Ciardi also observed in his comments on the Lebrun illustrations that every soul in Dante's Hell "suffers endlessly and to no end," which led him to the enduring relevance of *The Inferno*: "Is there any need to list," he asked, "how many good artists have seen that state of pointless suffering as the human condition of our times?" And then by way of answer he added, "The agony of meaningless and endless distortion is a theme that suggests itself persistently to modern man." This question of the relevance of Dante was no doubt on Ciardi's mind five months later when Roy P. Basler, director of the reference department at the Library of Congress, invited Ciardi to be the featured speaker at a program of lectures the library was sponsoring in May 1965, in honor of the seven hundredth anniversary of Dante's birth. As a poet, Ciardi was asked to share (for a one-thousand-dollar honorarium) "his personal reading and assessment of Dante." The event was sponsored by the Gertrude Clarke Whittall Poetry Fund and would take place at the Library's Coolidge Auditorium and be broadcast over the radio. Pamphlet publication of the three lectures would follow. In a series of letters to Basler through 15 January 1965, Ciardi kept fiddling with his paper, changing the title from "The Longest Walk in the Universe" to "Dante's *Inferno*: The Concept and the Vehicle" to "Hell and the Twentieth Century" to "The Relevance of the *Inferno*"—the title he finally settled on on 19 February. On 20 April the Ciardis attended a White House dinner-reception with President and Mrs. Lyndon Johnson, and finally the event itself was held on Saturday, 1 May. J. Chesley Mathews and Francis Fergusson spoke at the afternoon session, and at 8:30 that night, Ciardi delivered the evening talk, introduced by L. Quincy Mumford, Librarian of Congress, with a special greeting from Sergio Fenoaltea, Ambassador of Italy.

"The Relevance of the *Inferno*" (also published as "The Relevance of Dante" on 15 and 22 May 1965 in *SR*) is Ciardi's fullest and deepest commentary on *The Divine Comedy*. Quite apart from any religious, antiquarian, historical, or philological interest one might have in the work, Ciardi wrote, one is left with the "power of [Dante's] personal genius," his power to speak in particulars and reach to universals. For Ciardi, Dante's relevance was in his ability to imagine an artistic structure large enough for his task—and then to find language sufficient for the enormity of that task: "It is the magnificence of the metaphoric invention that thrills the reader." For Ciardi, of course, Dante's relevance is found in his intellect, not in the religious codes he dramatized; it was the superstructure as well as the delicate detail work that thrilled Ciardi's mind, not the theological principles nor the hope of salvation. Most of all, Ciardi was moved by the accuracy of Dante's insights into the human psyche: "The figures we meet at every point in Dante are the populations of our own nervous systems. Dante will remain relevant to mankind for exactly as long as those values we call the humanities are relevant to it."

The 1965 celebrations at the Library of Congress were in one sense a cause of sadness for John Ciardi, according to his "Manner of Speaking" column on 19 February 1966. It turns out that he had been hoping all along that *The Paradiso* could have been completed by then. He knew that "one more translation could hardly have added anything to the mountain of Dante's merit," yet, he said, "it would have pleased me to have been able to lay my sheaf on the centennial mountain." The binges of translation, however, had not come often enough. His desk had been constantly covered with things that seemed necessary to do before getting around to Dante: "Before I was entirely aware of it, eighteen months had gone by with hardly a lick of work on the *Paradiso*." That, he vowed in his column, was about to change. In a remarkable display of single-mindedness amid the details of an extraordinarily busy period that included moving to a new home among many other things, Ciardi set about to complete *The Paradiso*, and thus bring to a close his work on *The Divine Comedy*. On 30 October 1967, twenty months after taking his vow, he wrote to Milton Hebald: "*Paradiso* moves along slowly but I am at last grinding to the top of Heaven." In November, he wrote to Miller Williams that he still had one more week of lectures to complete, "then nothing till I finish the *Paradiso*—not reason, not responsibility, not social commitment—nothing till I get the Hell out of heaven." On 30 January 1968, he wrote to his Chautauqua friend Gil Gallagher that the job was done: "I want you to know that I did the last line of the first draft of the *Paradiso* and have only the sandpapering left. . . ." Eight months later, in September 1968, Ciardi wrote to Williams that he was still "sweating at the final typescript," but on the twenty-third he wrote to Dan Jaffe that typing, revising, and sandpapering were all finally finished: "Toward celebrations, I finally delivered the typescript of *Paradiso*—good riddance to Heaven."

"the poet's necessary love
for the living language"

Filling out the publication frenzy that followed Ciardi's resignation from Rutgers were four books of his own poetry: *In the Stoneworks* (1961), *In Fact* (1962), *Person to Person* (1964), and *This Strangest Everything* (1966), plus two more folio-sized limited editions in 1967, *An Alphabestiary* (which was also issued by Lippincott as a slip-cased trade book) and *A Genesis*. Both limited edition books were collaborations with artists, like the 1963 Dante collaboration with Rico Lebrun, and like that book, both were produced by Abe Lublin, though this time under the imprint of Touchstone Publishers. For *Alphabestiary*, Ciardi worked with his old friend Milton Hebald, who provided original lithographs to match Ciardi's poems, which, as the antiwar "B is for BOMBERS" suggests, were clearly intended for adults, not children:

> B is for BOMBERS, our national pride.
> And also for BOYS who like Bombers to ride.
> And also for BLESS in "God Bless Our Side."
>
> B is for BAD (the Enemy) whom
> we Bless our Boys' Bombers Bravely to Bomb.
> And for BELLS we ring out when we welcome them home.
>
> B is for BANNER, which proudly we hail.
> For BLAST and for BRASS and for BURIAL-DETAIL.
> And for BILLY and BUCK, who are studying BRAILLE.

The poems had originally appeared in five consecutive issues of *Saturday Review* during July 1965, and by October, agreement had already been reached with Lublin and J. B. Lippincott for the publication of the deluxe ($350) and trade ($5.95) editions. By May 1966, Lublin had also lined up Gabor Peterdi to do fifteen etchings to accompany fifteen previously published Ciardi poems—all but two of which taken from 1960s books: *In the Stoneworks*, *Person to Person*, and *This Strangest Everything*. *Genesis* is arguably the most visually arresting and artistically satisfying of Ciardi's portfolio collaborations, thanks mainly to Peterdi's haunted forms and rich colors. This book, with three options, was priced at $2,000, $1,500, and $750.

Rutgers University Press quoted a pair of reviews for the dust jacket of the third printing of *In the Stoneworks*. Richard Eberhart's praise in the *New York Sunday Herald Tribune* focused on Ciardi's "conceptions" that he said were "massive and rich, occasionally satirical, sometimes playful, always honest and usually straightforward rather than devious or too contrived." The *Library Journal* thought the poems were "robust, witty, virile" and then spoke in admiration of Ciardi's "independence of thought and tone, or rich brash language, occasionally of form." And an unnamed reviewer in the *Chicago Sun Times* (quoted on the dust jacket of the third printing of *This Strangest Everything*) seemed to like Ciardi's "semisneer" and the fact that "his gusto and loud charity are masculine." M. L. Rosenthal reviewed *In the Stoneworks* for the *Reporter* and called Ciardi "a splendid Master of Fireworks," which was a sometimes "irritating" characteristic that coexisted with "a quieter sensitivity" that Rosenthal wished would emerge more often. He noted Ciardi's television work and what he identified as the "public or cultural 'significance'" of Ciardi's poems. Other poets, according to Rosenthal, were "ruthlessly at odds with the whole prevailing order of our society," but not so John Ciardi, who was very much "at home" in it—though he was no Philistine. Rosenthal wrote that Ciardi's "most serious work" had a "rather bitter 'set,'" although he also saw in Ciardi an "ebullient" poet who wrote with "much joy and wit," a man with "the poet's necessary love for the living language. . . ." He seemed to enjoy Ciardi as "a banger-together of arguments," a man who liked "to make loud noises," even though this seemed to stand in the way of what he called "sufficient expression" of the "inwardness" he felt to be present but undeveloped in many poems. Edward Krickel, however, saw in the new book no advance of Ciardi's art from *39 Poems*, although he did concede one point: "No matter how simply it begins, any Ciardi poem is apt to turn into a complex of ironic interrelationships that probe deep into human experience."

In the Stoneworks contained many poems for Ciardi to be pleased with, like "Bedlam Revisited," a sardonic commentary on his childhood recalled in about 1960 from the safety of his upper-middle-class lifestyle in suburban New Jersey:

Nobody told me anything much, and that
so wrong it cost me nothing—not even love—

to lose it. All but the Boss, the Cop and the Ghost of
the Irish Trinity. Those I sweated at
so hard I came up hating. But still grew fat
in a happy reek of garlic, bay, and clove.
I was crazy, of course, but always at one remove.
I tried on faces as if I were buying a hat.

Home was our Asylum. My father died
but my mother kept talking to him. My sisters screamed.
My aunt muttered. My uncle got drunk and dreamed
three numbers a night for a nickel with cock-eyed
Charlie Pipe-Dreams who moseyed along half-fried
every morning at seven. The old boy schemed
for twenty years that I knew of before he was reamed
by Family Morticians. But I'll say this—he tried.

There were other tribal poems, like "Aunt Mary," who "died of eating twelve red peppers / after a hard day's work." It is a poem in
which Ciardi wears his sense of humor as protective armor until he
suddenly realizes how much his aunt had meant to him, and then
he tenderly comes to terms with his loss. It was in this book too,
that Ciardi retold the story he'd heard so often from his mother
about his father's funeral: "It took four flowerboats to convoy my
father's black / Cadillac cruiser out to St. Mike's and down /
deeper than all salt."

 In the Stoneworks also contained several poems on subjects that
were already favorites: straight autobiographical reminiscenses, like
"A Dialogue in the Shade" (between his two selves, the "Damaged
Angel" and the "Improved Ape") and "Faces" (a bitter observation
on the depths of inhumanity he had once faced while hitchhiking
from Ann Arbor to Boston in the late 1930s). Then there were the
observations of nature that produced such poems as "An Island
Galaxy," a belated Saipan memory about "a flooded tire rut" that
had been transformed into "a galaxy / of pollywogs." The sight
led Ciardi to wonder what he could learn from this spontaneous
eruption of life, but he concluded that it, like our larger galaxy, is
utterly without meaning: "Universes happen." In "The Bird in
Whatever Name," Ciardi wrote about a variety of bird that tends
symbiotically to the African rhinoceros by living off its grubs and

lice. This was another in an intermittent series of poems, like "Thoughts on Looking into a Thicket," which celebrate nature's odder affirmations of a life-asserting principle:

A bird with a name it does not itself
recognize, and I cannot recall—
if ever I knew it, and no matter—
lives off the great gross Rhinoceros of Africa.

The slathering hide of the great gross Rhinoceros,
slabbed like a river in a stiff wind,
is rancid at the bent seams, and clogged
with lice and fly-grubs at the pores and pittings.

The Rhino-bird, whatever its unknown name,
attends its warty barge through the jungle,
the feast of its own need picking the tickle
of many small corruptions from behemoth,

who, impervious to all roarers, is yet defenseless, alone,
against the whine of the fly in his ear, and stricken
to helpless furies by the squirm of the uncoiling grub
tucked into the soft creases of the impenetrable.

My bird—and oh it is my bird and yours!—crawls
him as kissingly as saints their god, springs
circling over him to foretell all coming,
descends in the calm lapses to ride a-perch on his horn

or snout. Even into the mouth and nares of the beast
he goes—so some have reported—to pick infection
from power. And can the beast not love
the bird that comes to him with songs and mercies?

—Oh jungle, jungle, in whose ferns life dreamed itself
and woke, saw itself and was, looked back
and found in every bird and beast its feature,
told of itself, whatever name is given.

Ciardi said of *In Fact*, which was published barely a year after *In the Stoneworks*, that it was "an experiment in writing the poem quickly, easily, spontaneously. Most of those poems came very rapidly, very quickly. But it is not an economical way of writing poems at all. You have to write a hundred before you can keep one. But somehow, when they work on a quick run, improvised—that air of improvisation is nice. But it is an experimental book." Perhaps it was an experiment that failed, for the new book was filled with too many slight poems that, although frequently clever and competent, did not add up to much, either individually or collectively. Judson Jerome commented in a full-page review called "The Wedding of Mercy and Self" in *Saturday Review* (23 March 1963) that "no one (least of all John Ciardi) would call *In Fact*, his ninth collection of poetry, a great book or even a particularly important one," although, he said, it was "damned enjoyable reading." Richard Howard wrote admiringly in *Poetry* of Ciardi's eye and ear, but he said something was missing, "some note of stay, a conviction beyond the podium chuckle." And Edward Krickle harshly summed the book up as "trivial, the weakest in the Ciardi canon": "The perception is there, but no great substance. He is not really involved—perhaps that is what we miss, Ciardi himself."

And yet Ciardi scored with more than a few of the poems in his new book. For example, in what seems to be an autobiographical poem, "Miss Olivia Branton," he told the story of having fallen in love with his dim-witted high school English teacher: "I mean, my God, there comes a time when / you have to love the helpless just because they / are helpless, than which no one more uniquely was." Another successful poem was "A Fable of Survival," about suburban Metuchen, a field Ciardi often worked, with mixed success, during the 1960s. In this case, the poem worked well with its narrative structure, characters, and dialogue, plus a nice turn at the end that recalled Frost. Ciardi imagined that one of his neighbors had been digging an air-raid shelter on weekends and had stopped for winter. He imagined having the couple over for drinks and playing devil's advocate with the husband, asking "How deep *was* deep enough?" But the neighbor "had religion": "He had the Truth. He had, by God, the Truth." The neighbor's wife took Ciardi aside and scolded him, but he defended himself by pointing out "that mind's the only shelter left—whatever / shelter there is in that. . . ." But the neighbor's wife had the last word: "But *look* at him! He's twenty pounds younger. / Tough as nails. And brother, he's got *fervor!*" And that was something Ciardi understood, passion—no matter what it was for. He ended the poem with a line set apart: "That's when I understood about survival."

In Fact had humorous poems, love poems, autobiographical poems, nature poems, suburban–New Jersey poems, and poems about poems. There were also bird poems like "In Some Doubt but Willingly," "One Jay at a Time," "As I Would Wish You Birds," and "Bird Watching." In the last of these, Ciardi focused his attention on feeding his backyard birds and attracting now and then "the one impossible bright bird" that shouldn't be there—a "miracle" he called it, the same word he used so often to describe the minimum requirement for the writing of a poem. Ciardi became so engrossed with the metaphorical connections between birds and poems that he carried the idea over into his next book two years later, *Person to Person*. The first poem in the new book was "The Size of Song," which begins with what seems an offhanded observation, that in the world of birds, the small ones do the singing. Then in the second stanza, Ciardi observed that big birds also lose the ability to fly, and suddenly, as though he hadn't thought of it before, he ended the poem with the metaphor he'd been developing all along, that poets are just like birds: once you have given up the skies, he says, you are left with your own weight— "And your last ties to anything that sings."

"The Size of Song" was one of four that had appeared in *Saturday Review* (2 May 1964) as "A Garland of Birds," the others being "Birds, Like Thoughts," "Gulls Land and Cease to Be" (which misprinted "Chase" for "Cease"), and "Yet Not to Listen to That Sung Nothing." They served almost as an announcement of his sub-urbanite's fascination with backyard birds, which he acknowledged, though without discernible enthusiasm, in an interview twenty years later: "I like to watch birds. I do not miss looking at a bird if I can help it. We sometimes have quite an active bird life in our hemlock thicket outside the breakfast room window." He invested plenty of enthusiasm, however, in his poems about birds, and they represent some of his best work—animated, carefully observed and written, and filled with wonder. In "As I Would Wish You Birds" *(In Fact)*, for example, Ciardi catalogued and characterized half a dozen birds before settling his attention on the gull, "ultimate bird / everywhere everything pure wing and wind / are. . . ." And in "Gulls Land and

Cease to Be," Ciardi captured in a delicately yet tightly written poem the visual image of a gull landing, complete with the symbolic reality that once landed, like poets, they've lost their magic:

> Spread back across the air, wings wide,
>   legs out, the wind delicately
> dumped in balance, the gulls ride
>   down, down, hang, and exactly
> touch, folding not quite at once
>   into their gangling weight, but
> taking one step, two, wings still askance,
>   reluctantly, at last, shut,
>   twitch one look around
>   and are aground.

Ciardi's endless fascination with birds, his never-ending pleasure at watching and listening to them, and his sense that they were both poetry in motion and symbols of the poet—all reveal themselves in an untold number of poems, like "Two Egrets" *(I Marry You)*, which were "like two white hands / washing one another / in the prime of light." In the last two lines, the egrets and the hands are joined into "a prayer / and the idea of prayer." Where birds and poetry were concerned, John Ciardi could almost turn mystical.

But *Person to Person*, despite beginning with a string of seventeen very fine poems followed by at least seventeen more of high quality, ran afoul of one of Ciardi's greatest friends and supporters, Dudley Fitts. Ciardi had sent the manuscript of his new book to Fitts for comment and criticism during the Christmas season 1963, but he could not have been prepared for Fitts's reply. The qualities he most admired in Ciardi's work were still there: "this damn straightness, or honesty, or integrity; the harshness of image and cadence; the technical control." But he disapproved of what he called "a factitious celebration of grime and sweat; too much talk about yourself and family . . . ; [and] a tendency to shout-down instead of speaking up."

> What am I trying to say? . . . CALM DOWN! By this time
> you no longer need to prove that you have balls, fought a war,
> are a good friend, love your family, and like moola. You never
> had to prove these things anyway. I would say that if you

prune away the rhetoric of this kind—a matter of six or seven complete pieces and some internal tinkering with certain of the rest—, you will have a meanwhile book: one that will not enhance, or be seen as an advance, but at its best more of the very fine same. I imagine you are neglecting poetry for verse—children's verse, occasional verse . . . , and minor orphicisms in a manner of speaking. I'd rather have you devote yourself to Dante and criticism than to these three types of exercise. Try to get back to that *rauco stil nuovo* [hoarse new style] of ten years gone.

Ciardi was stunned by Fitts's criticisms, shaken by the very idea that such an old friend could find so much to dislike about him and his poems. He understood that Fitts was suggesting such fundamental changes that he would literally have to re-invent his character. Still, he managed a letter of sincere thanks on 21 January. "For better or worse," he replied, "I must live in what worl[d] my emotions find and what emotions my world finds. If the tone of it offends and yet seems true to my nerve-thickets, I have to risk the offense. But think of that, please, as my confusi[o]n only and not yet so confused as to be marred by ingratitude."

Four days later Ciardi wrote to Miller Williams to say that he had sent the manuscript of *Person to Person* to Rutgers University Press. He reported that Fitts had "generally raised Hell with it and ended up giving me something like C-/D- on it, with which grade I walked the floor for two days, reading and re-reading, and finally decide[d] it was no go and that I would let it stand exactly as submitted to Rutgers. It takes some sort of madman to veto D[.] Fitts on every point, but it was either that or try to turn into someone else and by now it's too late for me to try."

Following his instincts proved to be a good idea, however. Another old friend, John Malcolm Brinnin, wrote his approval of *Person to Person*: "God, how I admire and envy your energy and range and, need I say it? the high incidence of excellence." And the critics responded favorably. One called it Ciardi's "best and most significant volume of [the] decade"; another admired Ciardi's "cheerful scepticism" and "easy, offhand way with the reader." And a third liked the personal poems especially because "they seem to achieve a kind of generality in which readers can find their own meanings as well as his." And although no one would ever mistake the voices of

John Ciardi and Robert Frost, more than one critic recognized an intangible Frost-like quality that they liked very much in *Person to Person*. Moreover, the book also sold four thousand copies in its first year, selling out four printings—another measure of success that Ciardi valued. And, in fact, the book did contain some excellent poems that add a great deal to the Ciardi canon. There are at least eight very fine nature poems, like "Bees and Morning Glories," "Sea Marshes in Winter," and "An Aspect of the Air"; about as many fine autobiographical and tribal poems, like "Tree Trimming," "My Father Died Imperfect as a Man," and "Elegy" (for Uncle Alec); plus some miscellaneous pieces that might be called occasional, like "On Flunking a Nice Boy Out of School," "Reality and Willie Yeats," "What *Was* Her Name?" and "One Morning." The last of these is about Benn, somewhere between his fifth and ninth birthdays:

> I remember my littlest one in a field
> running so hard at the morning in him
> he kicked the heads off daisies. Oh, wild
> and windy and spilling over the brim
> of his sun-up juices he ran
> in the dew of himself. My son.
>
> And the white flower heads
> shot like sparks where his knees
> pumped, and his hot-shod
> feet took off from time, as who knows
> when ever again a running morning will be
> so light-struck, flower-sparked-full between him and me.

Ciardi managed to capture just the right balance between the enjoyment of a sweet morning with his hard-running son and the bittersweet realization that such moments are as brief as they are rare.

But among the many achievements in *Person to Person*, it is "Tenzone" that tells most about Ciardi as a poet and a man. The poetic form called "tenzone" (Italian for "poetic contest") dates back to twelfth-century Provence troubadours who invented it and carried it to Italy where it flourished through Dante's time and the poets of the *dolce stil nuovo* (sweet new style). It contained an argument or verbal exchange, as for example in Ciardi's version between

Body and Soul, and it appeared originally, as it does in Ciardi's poem, with a strong dose of personal invective. There was no set pattern for the "tenzone," but the poems were always written in formal verse. One critic observed that Ciardi's management of the form was "rendered unique by its compelling tension, the vigorous antagonism of the speakers, the intense rhetoric, and the prevalent ad hominem type of argument." The debate between Body and Soul takes place in sixty lines divided exactly in half. The Soul speaks first in five six-line stanzas rhymed ababcc, then the Body replies stanza by stanza and point by point in a dazzling poetic performance in which Ciardi created a set of strict restrictions for himself, and then managed to achieve perfect freedom within his self-imposed boundaries.

The Soul accuses Ciardi of everything it considers vile. He is the "well-paid" and "well-known" poet, the "middle-high / aesthete of the circuit. . . ." He is a "waster of talent," and some even "snicker at the thought of talent in him." He's a "greedy pig" who wants it all: "He's a belly, a wallet, a suit, a no-score / of the soul." Poetry, the Soul says,

> is what he gabs at, then dabbles in when he finds
> hobby time for it between serious pitches
> for cash, free-loading, and the more expensive bitches.

He's "A con man. A half truth. A swindler in the clear. / Look at him guzzle. He actually likes it here!"

The Body, however, is not reduced to quivering nerve-endings under the Soul's assault. Ciardi isn't even defensive. Instead, he attacks right back. He calls his Soul (and by extension his louder-than-ever critics who leveled the very same charges) an "aspirant" who was a "bang-kneed / eternalist of boneyards," a "monk of dark-celled rays," and a "heretic, ignorant, Jesuit." And more: his Soul is a "scratcher of scabs" and an "ectoplasmic jitter." It was he, not his Soul, says the Body, who "spent / those twenty years and more in the polyglot / of nightmares talking to Pa[.]" And it was he who had the courage "to revise you by light": "You're a glowworm. A spook. A half-strung zither / with a warped sounding box."

> Yes, I like it here. Make it twenty times worse
> and I'd still do it over again, even with you

like a monkey on my back. You dried-out wet-nurse,

       think you're the poet, do you? You're the wind that blew
on ashes that wouldn't catch. You were gone

       the instant I learned the poem is belly and bone.

The relentless introspectiveness of "Tenzone" is one of Ciardi's characteristic tones, a rough and tumble, even truculent, attitude he liked to adopt. In this particular manner of speaking, Ciardi was able to re-examine and reassert himself—and the process was completed here with an unflinching, uncompromising, and sometimes even uncomfortable honesty.

Ciardi's fourth and last book of poems in the 1960s was *This Strangest Everything* (December 1967), which was as poor as *Person to Person* was good. Uncharacteristically, Ciardi seems to have been drawn to lyrical statements that were self-consciously poetic—either grand (and often obscure) observations on the human condition or poetic rambles that were almost too laconic to work. And yet, the book had merit, too, because salted among its forty-seven poems were some excellent ones that have to be put high on Ciardi's lifetime list of achievements: "Small Elegy," "The Catalpa," and "Tommy's Pond," all stoical observations of nature; "Daemons," "Boy," and "Talking Myself to Sleep at One More Hilton," all autobiographical or tribal poems; or his tribute to Theodore Roethke, who had died in 1963, "Was a Man," which is a rollicking song, without a false note in any of the fifty-four lines that capture the personality and largeness of that "roaring" man who could "outyell" all Michigan. Toward the end of that poem, Ciardi suddenly lowered his voice and bowed in admiration:

But once he sat still and began

       to listen for the lifting word,

       it hovered round him like a bird.

       And oh, sweet Christ, the things he heard

       in Saginaw, in Michigan.

But notwithstanding a few notable achievements in *This Strangest Everything*, the book was a disappointment, and one wonders how much of that might have been the result of Ciardi's new attitude toward the reader. In 1949 he had written in *Live Another Day* that he wrote poetry for the reader of some general culture, someone like Virginia Johnson, whom he had in mind but didn't name. By April 1967, however, he had completed his change of mind and heart, and announced his revised view in a "Manner of Speaking" column: "[Poets] are, I submit, just about all the first audience a good poem is likely to find. Let a poem be written to satisfy today's poets and it will probably satisfy some of tomorrow's general public, but let it be written for today's general public and tomorrow it will not exist."

Perhaps the school system, a permissive society, and the "measly generation" had persuaded Ciardi that the reader of some general culture no longer existed as he or she had in earlier decades. But one also hears in this change Ciardi's resistance to the protest poetry that was flourishing in the 1960s, what he continued to think of as a fatal sacrificing of the poem—a betrayal of it—for a potful of message. On 6 January 1968, Ciardi wrote "On Poetry and Sloganeering" in "Manner of Speaking" in response to letter writers who were accusing him of "selling out" because he did not write antiwar poems. He told them of his own long engagement with poems of moral outrage and principled self-righteousness during the Spanish civil war (remembering but not saying that John Holmes had tried in vain to dissuade him from that course). He advised the young "to put their aesthetic faith in language and form itself. . . . The poet, away from his desk may be the activist of all causes. Once at his desk and into his poem, however, he must be a poet or nothing. Let him bring every living issue to the writing. But then let him write to the writing itself, toward the joy of sensing the language take form."

Poetry of message, whether written by established poets or Bread Loaf students—and no matter how nobly motivated—was a type of propaganda that passed for poetry only if one didn't examine it too closely. But this was hardly a point the social activists cared to hear, especially from a former B-29 gunner who had turned fifty in 1966. And to make matters worse, Ciardi further separated himself from the young people of the 1960s by continuing to insist that poetry students at Bread Loaf be expected to master technical disciplines before being allowed the earned freedom of free verse. This, of course, merely fed the mutual distrust that was already well advanced between Ciardi and the younger poets. Still, had Ciardi been less prominent on the national scene or weaker as a principled spokesman for poetry—or just less courageous, the collision between himself and the baby boomers might have been avoided. Unfortunately, neither he nor they would budge from what they all saw as the moral high ground.

ELEVEN

"The goddamn world closing in"

1969 TO 1972

Riding High

By 1969, John Ciardi was almost an institution in American letters: his enormous popularity with audiences continued across the country; his name recognition was high because of his television program eight years earlier and his long-running "Manner of Speaking" column in *Saturday Review;* his poetry was as good, and sometimes better, as any he had ever written; he had branched out very successfully into the world of children's literature, and his translation of Dante's *Paradiso,* the last part of a twenty-some-year project, was nearing completion. And even though there were a few nagging problems associated with his summer retreat at Bread Loaf, he seemed secure there too, another acknowledgment of his reputation and position. Certainly Ciardi could be excused, under the circumstances, for not sensing the erosion of his reputation as a mid-century American poet and man of letters: by every available standard, John Ciardi was at the top of his profession.

In 1969, for example, Ciardi served as a judge in the children's literature section of the National Book Awards, although his influence and popularity in that field were felt that year at the local level, too, as witness the fact that the Cuyahoga County Public Library system opened the John Ciardi Children's Room in its Garfield Heights branch in Cleveland. In 1970, Ciardi received an honorary doctorate from Bates College, an especially sweet recognition from the school he had fled in 1936. In 1971, there were more honorary doctorates—from Washington University (St. Louis), Ohio Wesleyan College, and the University of Delaware. In January, February, and March 1972, he was poet in residence at the University of Florida. On 27 March, he read his poetry for a one-thousand-dollar honorarium at the Library of Congress, and six months later he agreed to write an article for the Boy Scout magazine, *Boy's Life*, for another thousand. That summer, too, Ciardi asked Miller Williams to coedit with him a new edition of *How Does a Poem Mean?*, which had sold some 300,000 copies and earned over one hundred thousand dollars in its first ten years. And in September 1972, Ciardi made another of his routinely memorable college appearances, this time at the University of Mississippi. Evans Harrington of the English department there wrote afterward to say that John had been "charming and dynamic" and that he had been tempted to photocopy some "letters of adulation" but didn't because John had no doubt "seen thousands of them" over the years. But he did quote from one that he especially liked: "And there stood John Ciardi, whom I approached with coffee cup trembling and to whom I said, 'You don't look like I thought you would; I thought you would look like God.'" Surely there were some early warning signs that he missed, but in the face of tributes such as these, Ciardi would have had to be exceptionally prescient to see that his position was slipping.

Particularly gratifying to Ciardi, both professionally and personally, was his triumphant appearance at his mother's hometown of Manocalzati in the summer of 1969. A professor in Italy had discovered Ciardi's 1951 poem about the town (misspelled in *From Time to Time* as "Manocalzata" because of Concetta's mispronunciation) and had translated it into Italian and run it in the local newspapers. The mayor was so moved that he ordered it set in bronze—and then, in the company of a delegation of town fathers, he traveled all the way to Metuchen, New Jersey, to make Ciardi an honorary citizen of the town and to invite him to the unveiling ceremony. Ciardi decided to make it the culmination of a six-week European tour for the entire family, for this particular honor was one he wanted the children to share. They left on 12 June, arriving in Copenhagen, and made stops in London, Paris, Vienna, Venice, and Florence before Manocalzati, which would then be followed by two weeks in Rome. The children, however, were more tolerant than enthusiastic about the trip. Myra was 17 and miniskirted, which caused some embarrassment when she was denied entrance to St. Peter's; and the boys were 16 and 15, too young and self-absorbed to appreciate many of the glories of Western civilization. And all three were more interested in the rapidly developing American counterculture anyway, identifying more with the spirit of the upcoming music festival in Woodstock, New York, in August than their deeper European roots.

They arrived in Avellino, a city of some fifty thousand, in a rented VW microbus that was strained to its limits with Jonnel's six-foot-five-inch frame, four other adult-sized people, and luggage. It seemed the entire town turned out that night for the *passegiata* (the after-dinner walk up and down Main Street), hoping for a glimpse of the American celebrity—and his daughter in the tiny skirt. On the appointed day, Mayor Arturo DeMasi escorted the family into Manocalzati for the official full-scale parade. There were fireworks and welcome posters everywhere, plus dignitaries like Homer Morrison Boyington, the United States consul general in Italy, and local officeholders and bureaucrats. The Seventh Fleet band played and the main street leading to the municipal building was renamed the Avenue of the United States of America. The Ciardi children could barely believe their eyes. "Everybody in the province who had a uniform was lined up, wearing a sash," Ciardi later recalled. And the parade route, strewn with flowers thrown from balconies and windows, was lined with people. The parade stopped long enough for the mayor to point out the house where Concetta had been born, and a twenty-one-gun salute followed, plus photographs and the appearance of previously unknown cousins, who met their American relatives "with great hugging and crying, and everywhere," as Ciardi recorded it, "there was a sense of operatic rejoicing."

After pausing long enough to lay a wreath on the monument to the war dead, the procession wound its way to the municipal building where Judith pulled aside the sheet that had been covering the bronzed translation of the twenty-one-line "Manocalzata (Gloved Hand)," which begins

> Outside my mother's town in Avellino
> There stands a rock with a gloved hand chiseled on it.
> And so it names a place: *Manocalzata.*

That's all I know of it. I've never been
Nearer to it than three thousand miles.
No one knows whose hand or why the glove.

How many times have I thought of it, needing a name
For what will not be named except by chance,
Or for some reason no one can remember?

Refreshments were served by nuns after the official proceedings were concluded. But just when everyone was ready to head home, Italian national television showed up, too late for any footage at all. This was an unacceptable ending to such a fine day, so the paraders re-formed into lines and marched *down* the mountain, reversing the route for television, and thus they all had the pleasure of a double parade and the thrill of watching themselves later on the evening news.

Amid the fanfare of the day, John and Benn, accompanied by cousin Immaculata, found a quiet moment and walked to the ridge-top house where Concetta had been born and where she had lived as a young girl. John was so moved by the sight, despite the presence of his young son—or perhaps because of it—that he wept openly, a rare moment of emotional display, a bonding of the past, present, and future. Moreover, the entire affair at Manocalzati confirmed Ciardi's peculiar sense of being an Italian-American, captured best, perhaps, in a letter he had written some five years earlier, in 1964, to Maria Alessandra Fantoni: "You are especially right in your recognition of the fact that I am not Italian in my moods and sources. Even my command of the language is inadequate. Yet, oddly, I always and instantly have the sense of understanding the feelings of the Italian, especially of the *contadino* [peasant]. Or not oddly, really, they are the feelings, the attitudes, the preconceptions I have always known in my parents and relatives. I have often felt sad, in fact, at the thought that my daughter and my sons can never know those feelings." The events at Manocalzati had raised their consciousness somewhat, but Ciardi was right, for his children never did manage to feel connected to the Old World in the way that he did.

Little more than a year after returning from his emotional triumph at Manocalzati, Ciardi scored another victory of sorts when he was named by the House Internal Security Committee (HISC) as a radical. This new committee was, in fact, nothing more than a renamed version of the old House Un-American Activities Committee. The chairman of HISC was Richard H. Ichord, a Democrat from Missouri, who was prepared to publish a list of "radical revolutionaries" on 14 October 1970. A temporary restraining order had been issued to Ichord and HISC on the thirteenth, however, in an effort to protect the reputations of those being accused, but Ichord gave the list of radicals to the *New York Times* on the same day the order had been filed, and the *Times* obligingly printed the story on the fifteenth. There on the list, in the company of such people as Muhammad Ali, H. Rap Brown, Stokely Carmichael, Dick Gregory, Abbie Hoffman, Le Roi Jones, William Kunstler, Jerry Rubin, and Bobby Seale—all members of the Chicago Seven, black militant groups, leaders of antiwar organizations, or acknowledged communists—was the name of John Ciardi. In all there were sixty-five radicals, each of whom had earned at least one hundred thousand dollars at universities and colleges during the preceding two years. Ichord was reported in the *Times* as saying, "the campus-speaking circuit is certainly the source of disorderly and revolutionary activity among students." Ciardi had earned nearly twice the minimum and had signed a petition in 1963 to abolish the House Un-American Activities Committee. For these reasons, plus a bulging FBI file going back to 1940, he was identified by his government as a "radical revolutionary" and appeared in newspaper and television stories all around the country.

On the eighteenth, Ciardi described himself for his local New Jersey newspaper, which wanted a story on its hometown radical, as "a moderate liberal who is rather entrenched in the establishment." (Jonnel thought that characterizing his father as a radical was the "most ridiculous thing" he'd ever heard: "I mean, he was an arch-conservative. And the idea that someone would say he was a radical was absurd beyond belief.") Mirko Tuma, writing for the *News Tribune* in Woodbridge, New Jersey, wrote a strong defense of his besieged leftist poet. The far right, he said, objected to Ciardi "because he has pointed out certain inadequacies in government. . . . As long as Ciardi hasn't subscribed to 'my country right or wrong,' and has opposed the policing of individual opinion, he apparently cannot be a true patriot." Then, for good measure, he defended Ciardi against criticisms from the radical left which found him suspect "because he doesn't advocate violence, writes fine poems and translates Dante instead of grinding out pseudo-poetic pamphlets about Vietnam, while smoking pot." Of course, the irony in all this was, as Ciardi pointed out to Miller Williams on 26 October, that his speaking engagements had already dropped noticeably by that time. "Choice of speakers has definitely passed from faculty to students and I have practically no bookings because I'm neither an ecologist nor out on bail." Ciardi quipped to Williams on 1 November that "maybe the droopy lecture circuit will pick up now that I'm grouped with the Black Muslims, SDS [Students for a Democratic Society], Black Panthers, bomb throwers, arsonists, snipers, etc."

Quips notwithstanding, however, Ciardi was deeply troubled by this government-made Congressional smear. On 7 November, he wrote a double-length "Manner of Speaking" column, a measured self-defense presented as a civics lesson to Representative Ichord and his committee. He was an ironist by profession, he said, and ordinarily preferred the indirect rather than direct manner of speaking, but for once, here was an occasion that called for "a declaration of clear purposes." The violence erupting on the streets of the country had arisen from "inequities in the system" and was thus "nobly motivated," though it was undeniably "criminal and unbearable" as well. The problems were complex and intractable:

> I know of no easy answers. It is, I believe, a testing time in the American soul, and neither radicalism nor superpatriotism is a good enough answer. I believe that the American system will prove, as it has proved in the past, that it is responsive to its own ideals and that it is capable of adjusting within itself to the strains of changing times. I honor that system, honor its stated ideals without reservation, and dissent from such institutions as HISC because I see them as agencies of distrust that work against the good of the nation.

And for the record Ciardi announced that though he was a dissenter, he was no radical: "I am totally invested in the economy and totally devoted to the founding principles of the American nation." Finally, he said Ichord and the HISC had slandered him—and he demanded a public apology.

On 17 November, Rep. Edward J. Patten of Ciardi's home district in Metuchen read an apology on the floor of the House for inclusion in the *Congressional Record*, which prompted Ciardi to say in a letter to his former student Dan Jaffe three days later that he didn't know of anything he could say in defense of his own character, but "I'm glad for all that reads FUCK HISC." Then, on 10 December, the *New York Times* reported that Ciardi and seven others (including Mark Lane and Linus Pauling) had been deleted from the original list, which would have ended the affair except that Ciardi could not resist one parting shot in *SR* the following May. In order to establish his list of "radical revolutionaries," Ciardi wrote, Ichord had randomly selected 177 colleges and universities to be surveyed out of a pool of some three thousand. Only fifty-two responded fully, twenty-seven more, partially. "The rest either avoided you or told you to go chase your tail through a stinkweed patch. If we give you half credit for the twenty-seven partial answers and add that thirteen-and-a-half to your fifty-two whole points, you score sixty-five-and-a-half out of a possible (plus or minus) 3,000." "Forgive me," Ciardi concluded, "for thinking that a man with 1/46th of the truth isn't exactly qualified to be taken seriously. . . ." The *New York Post* carried this last development of the story in its issue of 11 May under the headline, "De-Smeared, Poet Returns the Mud."

But as juicy as these triumphs were, they were hardly the only ones Ciardi enjoyed, for in literary matters, he not only continued to write well, but also could see his reputation cresting. On 19 March 1969, for example, he received in the mail the first copies of a book edited by Miller Williams called *The Achievement of John Ciardi*, part of the Modern Poets Series put out by Scott, Foresman under the general editorship of William Martz. The book had a history that went back to November 1966, when Ciardi discussed the book in letters back and forth to Martz, who had apparently asked Ciardi to suggest an editor for the project. Bill Sloane, who was happy to give the official Rutgers University Press endorsement to the book, suggested three people for the work. Ciardi, however, rejected all three (whose names have not survived), even though he was friends with each one, he said, and respected their writing. But, he went on, "for honorable personal reasons I don't want any of them to be asked." He suggested Miller Williams instead, whom he had already briefed and who was eager to do it. Within a week, the matter was firmed up between Martz and Williams, and all was in place. Ciardi wrote Williams to offer full cooperation, though he would "not try to persuade your judgment in any way." But he would be happy to provide books if Williams needed them and couldn't find them— and he hoped out loud that *Homeward to America* might be omitted as nothing more than juvenilia. Six months later the typescript for *The Achievement of John Ciardi* was in Martz's hands, and the book took its position on the Scott, Foresman production schedule.

The book itself was a slender, eighty-six-page paperback with fifty-six poems plus a lengthy critical introduction that remains one of the two or three best essays on Ciardi's work. Williams called Ciardi "introspective, iconoclastic, humanistic, and world-affirming," identifying as well, "superlative craftsmanship, a ruthless objectivity, and an unfailing sense of what all men have in common." He observed Ciardi's search for himself and his roots, plus his need for ritual in poetic form and language. And he was pleased to note that Ciardi never exhibited "that pandemic twentieth-century sickness: intellectual pride. His kind of paganism—this humanism which is what we have when all our gods, heavens, hells, and purgatories are nowhere but in every man's moment—is completed with a humility that must surprise, not only the believer, but also the utopian atheist."

When Ciardi first read Williams's introduction in July 1967, shortly after the delegation from Manocalzati had visited Metuchen to make him an honorary citizen of his mother's hometown, he was deeply moved. "I couldn't have foreseen," he wrote to Williams, "how hard it would be to thank you. . . . You've said some powerful fine things about me and if I say how right your portrait seems I'll seem to be saying all those kudos are simply appropriate, and over the corpses of several torn up letters, I don't mean that. For the praises, I don't know of any human possibility but to be grateful and I am." But it was more than that, for Ciardi knew that he had been read "more carefully" by Williams "than any man living." He pondered the deep feelings he had at being read so carefully: "You've said it for me, Miller, and damned well, and generously, but in the psychic profile accurately and even in a way that helps bring it together for me. And how does one say thanks for that?" When the book came out in 1969, he said his thanks again, adding "It's an odd sensation to come on yourself so."

Other literary irons were in the fire as well. A book of children's poems, *Someone Could Win a Polar Bear*, Ciardi's last collaboration with illustrator Edward Gorey, came out in 1970. As usual, children's poems continued to be both soul-soothing and soul-satisfying for Ciardi, but they also, as he put it shortly after he delivered the manuscript to Lippincott, "rest the soul between sweatier engagements." One of the "sweatier engagements" was certainly the finally completed translation of *The Paradiso*, which came out late in the same year and was put on the market by New American Library for $1.25, or all three paperback volumes in a boxed set for $3.75. Ciardi had submitted the manuscript to the scrutiny of two Dante scholars, both former students of Charles Singleton at Johns Hopkins, Marc Musa and John Freccero, both of whom supplied detailed comments, with Freccero supplying as well an introduction to the book. Having worked his way through hell, purgatory, and paradise, in a work that was begun in the late 1940s, Ciardi was finally able to put a long-anticipated closure on the project. With the enormity of all those years of painstaking work behind him, Ciardi wrote to Musa that it had all been built on the simplest of motivations: all he had ever hoped for was "an English experience of Dante for people who can't read the original." Sales figures alone had spoken eloquently of Ciardi's success, as did the permissions requests that regularly came in, like the one from Viking Press in September 1971, which wanted to publish the entire *Inferno* in its world literature anthology. That year, too, Ciardi had to send a series of action-threatening letters to executives at NAL, who had granted hardcover reprint rights to the entire *Divine Comedy* to World Publishers in New York, an NAL subsidiary. Ciardi had no intention of giving up his right to negotiate directly with World for appropriate terms. The issue was not settled at that time, however, with World reorganizing and dropping all trade books, shifting its rights to Ciardi's Dante to Mason/Charter, and Ciardi finally having to buy the rights from them in late 1976, preparatory to signing a contract with W. W. Norton. It was, indeed, a protracted and sweaty business, but Ciardi was pleased when his *Paradiso* was reviewed with Singleton's *Inferno* (*SR*, 6 February 1971) and came out well. Robert J. Clements was respectful to Singleton's prose "monument to American scholarship," but his praise of Ciardi's verse was even greater: "Ciardi's welcome version [of the entire *Divine Comedy*], recognized among Dante scholars as a tour de force, retains the liveliness, simplicity, and directness of the original Tuscan. It is a poet's triumph available to a student's pocketbook."

The sweatiest business of all, however, was that connected with *Lives of X*, Ciardi's long autobiographical sequence. He had been writing it for four years, from 1967 to its publication in 1971, and was totally invested in the project—emotionally, intellectually, and artistically. There were several reasons for this. For one thing, at 51, he had arrived at an age when men regularly look back to reexamine their lives. For another, he was fully aware of recent poetic uses of autobiography that had come from Allen Ginsberg in *Howl* (1956), Robert Lowell in *Life Studies* (1959), and from Anne Sexton, who had achieved meteoric success in the 1960s with her books of confessional poems that used her mental illness and hospitalizations as subject matter. Her first, *To Bedlam and Part Way Back*, had come out in 1960; her second, *All My Pretty Ones*, in 1962; and her third book, *Live or Die* (1966) actually won the Pulitzer Prize in 1967. Ciardi was fully aware, then, that a revealing book of autobiographical self-discovery might be both timely from a literary standpoint and potentially rewarding. His problem was to find an autobiographical format that was not confessional in the manner of Sexton, for hers was a poetry he was deeply suspicious of.

Of course, Ciardi had known Anne Sexton from before her fame. He had awarded her the Robert Frost Fellowship in Poetry at Bread Loaf in 1959, which had provided her with literary opportunities—and the occasion to have two weeks away from her husband and children to spend with her lover of some six months, poet George Starbuck. He'd known her even before that from John Holmes, who had been Sexton's first poetry mentor when she signed up with Maxine Kumin in 1957 for Holmes's workshop at the Boston Center for Adult Education. Holmes may well have reported to Ciardi the talent and instability of Sexton, and perhaps even the awkward moment between them when Sexton had asked for Holmes's advice before publishing *To Bedlam and Part Way Back*—and he let her have it: "I distrust the very source and subject of a great many of your poems," Holmes wrote, "namely, all those that describe and dwell on your time in the hospital. . . . It bothers me that you use poetry this way. It's all a release to you, but what is it for anyone else except a spectacle of someone experiencing release?" (It is perhaps not surprising that another poet largely associated with the 1940s, Karl Shapiro, also spoke disparagingly of confessional poetry as "the psychological vulgarization of poetry as suicide, the Sylvia Plath syndrome. . . .") Holmes's disapproval, of course, was Ciardi's as well. The raw emotionalism of confessional poetry, the exposed nerves, the feverish intensity (akin to the exaggerated and endless importance given to "feelings" in the 1960s), was clearly not to Ciardi's taste. But the impulse to autobiography was.

In one sense, Ciardi had always been autobiographical, as Miller Williams was just then pointing out in his introduction to *The Achievement of John Ciardi:* "Ciardi's poems belong to that literary tradition most clearly exemplified by *The Divine Comedy,* in which the *I* is clearly, literally, the poet." And again: "The self-conscious presence of the poet in John Ciardi's poems is the condition from which all their other qualities arise." But a long autobiographical sequence was different in kind from even the most revealing of the tribal poems that are so prominent in the Ciardi canon. For although he had for many years scratched at psychological scabs to understand some part of what his father's early death had meant to him and his mother and his sisters, Ciardi had never indulged in the sort of extravagant self-absorption that characterized the confessional poets. Ciardi's autobiography would have to be centered elsewhere.

The center he found may have been suggested by his former Rutgers student, Dan Jaffe, whose verse and prose biography, *Dan Freeman,* Ciardi had read and liked in July 1967. He wrote to congratulate Jaffe, then living in Nebraska, for having written the life of a legendary local homesteader by intermingling prose narrative with illustrative poetic interludes. "I just wouldn't have believed a real thing could be made of such material, but you've done it b'God, and as far as I know you've invented a genre":

> It's a compelling book, Dan. And not just in bringing a highly flavored old curmudgeon to life but—and marvelously —to poetry, grand poetry. I'm with you in this way of going. Lyric condensation of the soul's insides is powerfully possible stuff and the world has not run out of need and appetite for

it, but what I think poetry needs at this turning is a way and a form of statement that will allow it to clutch facts to it, and their specification and detail, on the scale the novel is able to. Not in the way of the novel, but on the scale of it.

With these ideas running through the back of his mind, Ciardi wrote *Lives of X* as a sequence of long narrative poems, what he called "autobiographical exorcisms," not a series of confessional lyrics. In November 1968, with the poems for *Lives of X* well under way, Ciardi wrote to Williams: "I need some time now to take stock and see where the book is and if these new ones are right, but I do feel the thing coming together with a good sense that it's right and even true enough to be all new: a way of reclaiming into poetry the kind of detail it could once manage but allowed fiction to usurp."

During the winter of 1969–70, Ciardi "fell ass-first," as he put it in a letter to Williams, into two bad bouts of the flu (which, he imagined with a detectable world weariness, had "something to do with the generation gap"), but by March first he was "about ready" to turn over the final manuscript to Rutgers, though, he said, he had "some feelings of terror." About a month later, on 6 April, after he had "stewed" over the manuscript and "tightened" it, even eliminating an entire chapter, "Innocence, Experience, Innocence" (which has apparently not survived) because it "was the piece that was really fretting me," the manuscript was finally ready. Almost exactly a year later, the book was off the press, and Ciardi wrote to Williams, "Bill Sloane—a really dear gent—made a little ceremony of bringing around first copies of *Lives of X* and it's quite handsome." Moreover, with a large ad in the *New York Times Book Review* plus an advance sale of three thousand copies, Ciardi had high hopes for the book in the spring of 1971.

In mid-May Stanley Burnshaw wrote to Sloane saying that *Lives of X* "is surely the most compelling, the most gripping book of verse that I've read in years." And to Ciardi he wrote to say he'd been "moved, deeply moved." On June first, Ciardi replied that, though he had written thirty books, this one was in a sense his first. "I had to find a way of dealing with this material, and I feel that the material took me into ways recent poetry has turned from but that should be reopened." Six months later, however, in another letter to Burnshaw, Ciardi showed he was feeling the sting of neglect, although he tried to pass it off with a not-too-convincing wave of the hand: "Who doesn't know that echoing silence that follows a book of poems[?]" And in an interview conducted in late 1972, Ciardi lamented that even though the book contained a "breakthrough" in its use of fictional techniques, it had been reviewed in only a few places: "I can't help thinking it deserved a little more critical comment than that." But if there were only about six reviews that he could recall seeing, there were at least a few strong letters of support, like Archie MacLeish's that arrived in September 1971:

> I am not one of those (nor I think, is anyone else) who can receive a volume of verse in one mail and reply in the next or the next after that or after that or after [that]. I have to have time. But when time fills with truth I reply like a duck in a springhole with thanksgiving to God for a live rhythm of English again, begotten by an Italian on the stale roots up in this North-East corner where things still grow and smell and rustle but with no rage in them. You may, my lad, be the antidote for Bill Williams—[what] the dead [grass?] is crying for. Any way you're a delight to me. But I wanta know: how did a writer of your origins come to the Anglo Saxon the way you have? Ah, I delight in that—four bangs of a bronze gong like four sunsets answering each other. You sing, m[a]n, you sing.

MacLeish's high praise was echoed by the *Christian Science Monitor*, which said readers were transported to "Ciardi country . . . , a land rich with local color, folksy anecdote, shrewd observations, and out-of-the-way facts." In Edward Krickel's words, "the real pulse of the book and the subject that has never failed [Ciardi] is his loving depiction of his Italian family and connections, its experiences, and its various meanings." The book itself, at Miller Williams's suggestion, was framed at the beginning and end with two older autobiographical poems that were not properly part of the sequence, "The Evil Eye" and "Talking Myself to Sleep at One More Hilton." Then, between the prologue and epilogue, eleven poems that run to as many as eleven pages each, cover most of the poet's early life. "The Shaft," for example, refers to the stairwell at 25 Sheafe Street where he was born; "The River" is a meditation on the Mystic River's role in the slave trade as he pondered it from his home facing the river at

84 South Street; "A Knothole in Spent Time" tells of his first school-boy experiences; "Feasts" is a warm recollection of bird hunts in cemeteries and hearty Italian Sunday dinners, all framed by the haunting reality of his father's death; "Benefits of an Education" recalls all that he learned during the summer of 1931, when he worked on an excursion boat out of Boston Harbor; "Cal Coolidge and the Co" was about another job, this one in 1933 at the local biscuit company; "A Five-Year Step" recounts some painful incidents from his adolescence—how he grew beyond his mother and the Catholic Church; "The Highest Place in Town" describes his college years at Tufts; "The Graph" is an accounting of his war experiences on Saipan; and "Two Saints" tries to come to terms with the deaths of his boyhood friend, Willie Crosby, and someone named Kiro from the war, who died on Okinawa.

Ciardi had written to Stanley Burnshaw in the letter of 1 June 1971 that he had worried that the new book might not be poetic enough for some readers: "In a real sense, I have been gambling that I wouldn't fall—as some have told me—into prosiness. Believe me, I have sweated over that risk. In the end I had to stake it on my own ear and feeling without ever being anything but desperately (which is to say not entirely) sure." Some fifteen years later, Lewis Turco, in an examination of Ciardi's verse in "A Knothole in Spent Time," wrote what amounts to a carefully reasoned reassurance that this was, indeed, excellent poetry. Turco wrote admiringly that after Ciardi had established the humorous tone of "Knothole," he set "the prosody, normal accentual-syllabics," adding that "Ciardi has always been a formal poet, if one can catch him at it." Describing Ciardi's technique, Turco wrote that "his meter is going to be iambic pentameter blank verse in this poem, but he will allow himself enough freedom to give the impression that he is writing prose: one finds, if one scans a few lines, that there are going to be hexameters among the five-foot lines, and even in the normative lines there will be reversals and substitutions of feet." And Turco identified as well Ciardi's alliteration, internal rhyme, repetitions, consonance, and "consonantal and vocalic echoes." Also speaking of the poetry in *Lives of X*, Judson Jerome praised Ciardi's "shirt-sleeve manner of getting down to business," his ability to incorporate "an immense variety of material without losing control of the relaxed iambic pentameter, keeping the language alive as *poetry*—not just broken prose—a feat that would be impossible in free verse." And X. J. Kennedy said "*Lives of X* is the most readable long contemporary poem I know. Parts of it endure in the mind far more vividly than anything in *Paterson* or the *Maximus Poems* or the *Cantos;* and as those alleged masterworks never have done, Ciardi's immense poem has kept me bolted to my seat, clasping the book, determined to see what happens next."

Although *Lives of X* was nominated for a Pulitzer Prize, it was not among the finalists considered, and it came nowhere near achieving the high hopes Ciardi had had for it. In the end, shortly before his death, he commented, with a sigh of resignation that did not mask his lingering disappointment, "I don't know why it went unnoticed. . . . I have published lesser books that attracted much more attention." The truth was that by 1971 Ciardi himself was beginning to go unnoticed, and even with the advantage of hindsight, he found it difficult to understand just how or why or when the fundamental shifts he had experienced professionally and personally between 1969 and 1972 had taken place.

The End of the Maestro System

Ciardi was not exactly in bad health during these years, but there were a few problems that couldn't be ignored. Earlier, in mid-October 1968, his sore back had needed surgery, a simple procedure that nonetheless took most of the fall to recover from (by late November he was still housebound though working diligently on *Lives of X*)—at the expense of twenty thousand dollars in canceled lecture dates. From about February to June 1971, he had symptoms of a colon disorder. He wrote to Miller Williams on 12 March, "Now the goddamn world closing in. I've just completed the lovely business of a G-I series, complete with castor oil, endless enemas, barium, etc. And now I have to do it all over again. Science has found a shadow on the X-ray plates and doesn't know whether it's a polyp or a stray piece of shit." On 1 May he reported more soberly to

Williams: "I'm going through a lousy time. Next week I have to get set for another G-I series. I suspect the polyp they think they have discovered in the last series is a polyp in fact and not a shit-shadow. Everytime I sit at my desk for a stint of work I begin to feel blah and end up getting next-to-nothing done. I don't guess there's anything fatal in a gut polyp, but if that's what it is, it's time to get on the table and let the night of the long knives in." (Ciardi was evidently unaware of the connection between polyps and colon cancer, else his mood might have been even more somber.) By early June, however, the new X-rays had been completed, and Ciardi heard no more from his doctor. "I told him to let me know if I needed doing to. He has let loose no word. The symptoms seemed to have vanished. I'll let him worry about it."

Ciardi's weight had gone up to 237 in the summer of 1969, then down to 220 in February 1970; but despite periodic diets, by Bread Loaf time 1972, he had ballooned to 255. This was certainly one factor that accounted for his chronic fatigue. On 2 October 1971, he wrote to Doc Klompus: "I just ain't no hombre no more. An hour or two of working up a sweat and I'm bushed. Know a good doctor? I'm too damned heavy, short of breath, the few teeth I have anchoring this goldplated engineering in my mouth are coming loose, and it turns out I have a polyp on my lower colon. I jam the brakes as hard as I can but this thing keeps rolling down hill. Screw it. *Dum spiro spero* [While I breathe I hope] and with bourbon I can even dream." His weight also contributed to his impotence as well, a problem he rarely addressed but in a joke, as in a 9 June 1972 letter to John Stone, the cardiologist-poet who had taken over as Bread Loaf physician when Doc Klompus relocated to San Francisco. Remarking on a recent physical, Ciardi wrote, "There is always a price to be paid. I don't see that a sclerosed, stenotic, deformed pump valve is too much for a firmly licentious, drunken, and deceitful life. As a matter of fact I do pretty well with the drinking and have no trouble being deceitful. It's that firmly licentious life I crave and can't seem to get to. It's what I do really want but I can't pass the physical. Please send the right pills." A week earlier he had written to Miller Williams, "Shit, I'm too busy to be lecherous. Let that be my excuse. . . ." It may have been about this time, too, that he wrote a pair of limericks on the subject of impotence that found their way in 1978 into *Limericks: Too Gross:*

Said a learned old man of Brabant
"The instinct, my dear, is extant:
   The extension's extinct.
   Or to be more succinct:
I would if I could, but I can't."

There was an old geezer who tried
All night long, as a matter of pride.
   By dawn's early light
   He whispered, "Goodnight,"
And went into the bathroom and cried.

Another malaise was what Ciardi called his "busy indolence."
He would get up late during the summer of 1971, glance at his desk,
garden a bit in the backyard, then decide to go to the Metuchen
Country Club for eighteen holes of golf, a shower, and a marathon
gin rummy game that sometimes didn't break up until three in the
morning. He may have been experiencing a form of postpartum
depression over *The Paradiso* and *Lives of X,* or the shadow on his
X-ray may have cast an even longer shadow on his spirits, but the
truth was that he couldn't work with his customary energy. In April,
in the midst of his colon worry, he wrote to Williams, "I am behind
in everything, out of whatever groove there is, and generally spring
fevering, golf[ing], gambling, waiting to garden, [being] glad I'm
alive, getting ready to go to Michigan, doing nothing—well I have
scrubbed some doubtful columns[—]and getting to be too old and
mortal to feel guilty." And in early June, he reported once again to
Williams: "There is, I think I observe, a *force* of indolence. Some
indolence can be static I suppose. Mine is compulsive: I work harder
at it than I do at work." And on 1 August, he wrote to Irv Klompus:
"I have fallen into a fantastic period of indolence. . . . I have done
nothing, period, nothing and not even visited my study. I have gar-
dened some. . . . But basically I have become a bum. I hit a hot
streak at gin rummy (which I have been playing to the point of
idiocy) and bought a color TV (which I have been dawdling in front
of) and playing some golf (which I do with improving badness) and
solving all the puzzles in all the magazines (at which I am mania-
cal) but bills are unpaid, checks undeposited, records unkept,
manuscript[s] unlooked at, and the summer rainy."

Adding to his malaise, in July 1971, *Saturday Review* changed hands, which threatened one of his favorite sources of income. Ironically, Ciardi had just completed fifteen years of service at *SR* and had received a letter of congratulations from Norman Cousins on 5 May:

> Before you came, *SR*'s poetry pages were suggestive of tin-kling teacups, doilies, and lace at the throat. The prevailing tone in our poems was one of ladylike reflection—a gentility so thoroughgoing that even the birds and the bees got into the act. . . . Then came Ciardi! . . . [and] it soon became clear that you were not out just to rattle teacups. What you did, John, was to broaden out *SR*'s horizons, to put your poetry pages in touch with all that is vital, ongoing, and soul-intoxicating in modern letters. You made our readers wince, squirm, then think about it for a bit, and come back for more. You dragged us all, kicking and screaming, into the riptides and cross-currents of modern poetry—and now there isn't a one of us who would go back to the old gingerbread dispensation, even if we could. . . . We thank you, then, for a decade and a half of inspiration, innovation, laughs—yes, and complaints. . . . You are one of *SR*'s prime adornments—and one of its prime gadflies! Accept from all of us our affection, esteem, and gratitude.

When *Saturday Review*, with its 662,000 subscribers, was sold, however, the new owners, John Veronis and Nicholas Charney, had disagreements with Cousins, who left the magazine and soon began a new one, *World*, which he called "a review of ideas, the arts and the human condition." Ciardi's position at *SR* was unclear as late as December, some five months after Veronis and Charney had taken over. He described the new owners as "hard-driving types" who seemed "to flood the office with bearded young men and long-haired girls in velveteen pants." He said the office resembled "an undergraduate invasion of the faculty club." Clearly he was uneasy about the changes, yet he continued to hope for the best. "I am not particularly pessimistic about it," he wrote to Miller Williams on 6 December 1971, "and even think it could be a good thing on bal-ance." He thought Charney "a bit hucksterish," but didn't mind as long as the magazine "remains a congenial place in which to write as I please." The next day, however, he was less hopeful in a letter to Irv Klompus. Reports were that the magazine was moving its headquarters to San Francisco, but he would not be going. If he stayed on the payroll at all, he would be listed as "contributing editor," but, he said, "I begin to see signs that I am not going to." On the seventeenth of the month, he wrote more sharply to Williams, calling the youngsters of the office staff "bell-bottomed" boys and "hot-pantsed" girls—all of them "much turned on and basically illiterate."

By February 1972 decisions had been made at *Saturday Review* and a new format set up for the magazine. As far as poetry was concerned, it would appear once a month in the arts issue. Ciardi had an opportunity to stay on as poetry editor, he wrote in his column on 4 March, but he would have had to commute into New York five days a week, "and I have a large collection of rusty knives with which I would sooner cut my throat than." It was particularly galling for Ciardi that Charney had set up a 1960s-influenced editorial policy "on the democratization of the arts," and for this and other reasons easy to surmise, one can conclude that Ciardi may not have been too troubled about losing the job of poetry editor at *Saturday Review*—it was after all fairly burdensome and repetitious, and required an endless stream of carefully phrased rejection notes to friends. He was, however, on record as wanting to continue writing his column, which he still enjoyed and could do from his home. He remained cautiously hopeful.

Less than two months later, however, Ciardi was out. His last "Manner of Speaking" column appeared on 6 May with no indication that he would not be continuing, but two days later his secretary sent a letter to Lew Turco (returning poems already accepted but not to be published) announcing that Ciardi would be joining Norman Cousins as a contributing editor at *World*. His last submitted "Manner of Speaking" column was returned by *SR*, but Ciardi published it as the last essay ("Goodbye") in *Manner of Speaking*, a collection of his favorite columns, published by Rutgers in 1972. His message in that rejected column was framed as a story about how he had been caught in a storm near the Gulf of Mexico. When the storm had passed, he had the hotel pack him a box lunch and drove a rented car to an island where he saw a "triple row of terns" that wanted him to share his lunch. He gave it all to them, and took special delight giving them the cherry pie he couldn't have brought himself to swallow anyway.

"At the hotel, the bell captain handed me a message to call New York. I was sure I knew who was calling and what the message would be. I was in no hurry to say goodbye to nothing." And he didn't need to reply by phone to Charney and Veronis—he had another plan. "I had already instructed one of my birds—one that would be headed for Labrador—to fly by with my answer." No details have survived explaining why the rug had been pulled out from under Ciardi, but someone at the new *SR* had intelligence enough to realize that the new owners were being smeared with bird turds— and that the column should be returned to its author.

Ciardi was glum when he wrote to Richard Wilbur in June that "the new and even-more-vulgarized *SR* dumped poetry and me." But eventually he was able to quip about the financial loss that accompanied the end of his *Saturday Review* work and the start of his *World* column in July (which he called, "As I Was Saying"): "My magazine income went from over $25,000 to a bit less than $4,000, but my lecture fees were up by enough to keep me in bourbon and Cadillacs, and my boys in prep schools that, properly, threw them out as adolescent delinquents."

In fact, the rebellious Jonnel had been thrown out of Pingry School three years earlier, in 1969, and by 1971 he was actually showing signs of maturity. He could still bait his father into angry explosions over his intention of going to Canada rather than Vietnam, for example, but he also had taken well to public education at Metuchen High School. During the 1970–71 school year, Jonnel had grown up sufficiently to have his hair cut in order to play on the school basketball team that won the county championship. He also had the male lead in the senior class play, sat on the Principal's Senior Advisory Council, and got a report card with four A's and two B's. "Jonnel has bloomed," Ciardi wrote to his old friend Gertrude Kasle in Detroit. Then Jonnel, becoming more like his father than he cared to admit, began his freshman year at Tufts in September 1971.

A year earlier, Myra had begun at Swarthmore, a voice major with hopes of becoming a professional singer. Her first semester had been rough going: four difficult courses, two chorales, and private voice lessons. She was "reeling," according to her father, "but holding on." In March 1971, Ciardi wrote to Milton Hebald, still in Italy, that Myra was "a lovely 19" but that she had become "restive at Swarthmore." She wanted to spend a year in Rome learning the language and taking voice lessons. He said she had "a good musical sense and a good voice but not an operatic one," and she had in mind becoming "an ethno-ballad-collector and singer." He wanted to know if Hebald knew of any voice teachers Myra could study with in Rome, and said he'd be "forever grateful" for the help. Less than a month later, however, Myra came home from Swarthmore with what Ciardi characterized as "a great bearded blond beast," and all talk of Italy stopped forthwith. But seven months later Myra's romance was on the rocks, which prompted Ciardi to say with clear impatience in a letter to Irv Klompus: "Myra came home for the weekend hating Swarthmore, which means her love affair has gone sour, and how the hell long does the world have to be arranged because she is in or out of love[?] She's a lovely child and bless her bubbles, but Shee-it, man!"

When Myra went off to Swarthmore for her sophomore year in September 1971, and Jonnel began at Tufts, John wrote to Miller Williams to say that he and Judith were down to their "last chick" and that they were feeling "a bit lonely about it." But Benn was hardly a last chick to sentimentalize over. He carried himself like the toughened rock guitarist he fancied himself to be, and he was in constant trouble for one thing or another, including two arrests for possession of marijuana. Describing his youthful excesses some years later, Benn took a certain joy in recounting his exploits: he had been one of the first boys in his school to wear an earring, he had gotten himself busted on pot charges, he had cracked up cars, and, he added, he had "screwed girls in the garage." Benn's first arrest had been early in October 1970, his sophomore year in high school, for possessing four and a half ounces of marijuana, a charge that required a court appearance. "Alas," Ciardi wrote to Gertrude Kasle, "the generation abyss, but we'll survive it." The court appearance was on 8 December and went well, as Ciardi explained it to Williams: "The judge told [Benn] to behave himself for 6 months and he would wipe out the whole record. I hope he has learned. All in all it may have been a useful lesson."

It wasn't. Ciardi, fearing that Benn would begin taking hard drugs, was desperate and wound up offering a truce. Originally his rule had been that none of his adolescent children would be allowed to smoke pot at home. He wrote with moral fervor in an autobiographical fragment: "I am not about to be busted for running a pot parlor. The boys and girls understand and have been meticulously honorable in not bringing any stuff to the house. . . . They promised and they have kept their promise." This was no doubt wishful thinking on Ciardi's part, but then, as a result of a "set up" according to Benn, the police raided his music studio, out in the backyard carriage house, for disturbing the peace—and Benn was arrested a second time for possession of marijuana. There was no satisfactory answer to the problem—and Ciardi turned into a parent more angry at the police than at his dope-smoking youngsters. "The lines are fixed," Ciardi wrote. "Yes, the kids smoke pot. They insist on smoking it as a way of life—as they see martinis or scotch or bourbon as their parents' way of life." He concluded, "We are at civil war between the young and the law. The law insists that the young shall not smoke, the young sneer back and insist they will. And on their side of things the police become more criminal in their battle tactics than the outlawed young they harass."

At that point, in a desperate effort to protect Benn from the law and himself, the house rules were changed. Marijuana would be permitted in the house as long as Benn promised not to smoke anywhere but the second floor sun porch facing the backyard. And for his part of the bargain, Benn agreed not to try hard drugs. Ciardi had never made a more naive deal. The house became a haven for pot smoking, and Ciardi, trying to be a pal, became a coconspirator, actually helping to grow and clip the plants. "We had pot plants nine feet tall," Benn said, "and he was having fun showing me how to grow it." Occasionally he smoked a joint, too, although, according to Benn, he did not like it very much. Benn did not keep to the terms of their agreement and soon developed a serious cocaine habit with a group of his high school friends. It wasn't long before he became absolutely uncontrollable and faced his father down. Nothing worked to keep Benn in line, but Ciardi struggled to put the best possible face on the problem, as for example, in a March 1971 letter to Milton Hebald: "Benny is currently in the hinges of adolescence with the door squeezing his psyche. He's basically a good kid. I must suffer patience and forbearance." But when Benn flunked two courses that year and had to go to summer school, Ciardi wrote in anger to Miller Williams that his son was a "fucking pot head idiot," but immediately regretted saying so: "May he find a road. This child worries me."

On 18 March 1972, Ciardi tried to work out his feelings about Benn publicly, in a "Manner of Speaking" column that he called "Of Time and Chances: A Parental Reverie." He called seventeen-year-old Benn "an emotionally confused boy-man full of intellectual uncertainties." He clung to the hope that his younger son would get through his adolescent difficulties, but he worried because he saw Benn as "an emotional machine for going too far." He told himself to "hold the rein lightly" so that it would "be a pleasure for [Benn] to return in his own time":

> The fact is he does drop by now and then. Sometimes, he
> even tries to talk to us and we to him. What failure is it that
> our reaching never reaches? Is it a whole failure? May not
> the act of trying and failing together be itself an inarticulate
> acknowledgment and thereby a communication of its own?
> When he does return as a formed self—and oh, may he!—it
> could be just these fumbling failures of a shared impulse that
> join us again.

Earlier, in 1971, Ciardi had written with regret and frustration that he had an "investment in the younger generation," that he was, after all, "supporting three of it": "Like it or not, I am even committed to loving at least that much of it. And as some part of that love commitment, I do keep trying for a conversation that seems forever to go nowhere."

The fact is that even though everyone realized there was something called a generation gap during the late 1960s and early 1970s, no one could stop its damaging effects. The forces of the GI generation, civic-minded and dedicated to the principle of building America into a post–World War II position of world supremacy, clashed completely with the baby boomer generation that saw in the establishment's new world order a nation bereft of spiritual values and in need of the sort of salvation only it could provide. Each generation saw unbridled arrogance in the other.

By mountain time 1969, Ciardi had been out of teaching for a decade already. He had become by then generally angry with the "school system" and the "measly generation" that had jointly created the crisis in literacy that he also railed at. His term for violent student uprisings on campuses was "brat anarchy." After Bread Loaf 1968, Ciardi parodied a college president's opening-day-of-school remarks in a "Manner of Speaking" column:

> Ladies and gentlemen, welcome—and welcome back—to Diehard University. I shall start the academic year by describing the contract you have entered into by the act of enrolling in this university. That contract is clearly set forth in the university catalogue, but since literacy is no longer prerequisite to admission, let me lip-read the essential points of our agreement. As you emerge from this convocation you will be handed a digest of these remarks in attractively prepared comic-book form with all dialogue limited to basic English and with the drawings carefully designed to help you over any grammatical difficulties. Those of you, moreover, for whom the requirements of Sub-Literacy One have been waived may dial AV for Audio Visual, followed by 0016, and a dramatized explication will appear on your TV sets.

Bread Loaf, however, was not Diehard University. It was, instead, a professional writers' conference, which was a key distinction in Ciardi's mind, for it meant that college administrative types ought to keep hands off—as Middlebury College officials had more or less done since the 1920s. The troubles Ciardi had had with Sandy Martin in 1968 over the average age of the paying customers were solvable, in Ciardi's way of thinking, as were the confrontations with students (who had either not read his columns or were simply unpersuaded as yet that they were the "measly generation"). Because Bread Loaf was not Diehard University—not, that is, part of American higher education—Ciardi felt himself answerable to no such social and political demands as those imposed by the young radicals on college presidents and professors. Bread Loaf was not where the battle was being waged, Ciardi thought, which meant that he was above the fray in a certain sense, and that he could work what he felt to be proper solutions to social problems by dictating respect for elders and respect for tradition, concepts that had lost ground during the Consciousness Revolution. He, for one, would not fall to pieces under the attacks of pushy, arrogant, impolite, disrespectful, and presumptuous youngsters.

Nothing especially untoward occurred at Bread Loaf in 1969. Fresh from his European tour and the ceremonies at Manocalzati,

Ciardi drove up in his Volkswagen squareback with Dippy in the backseat, while Judith and the children followed behind in the family's brand new Cadillac. That year he delivered the conference $455 below its $32,570 budget, which pleased Steve Freeman enough to recommend for the next year a $200 raise for assistant director Sandy Martin, to $3,400—and no increase to Ciardi's salary of $1,750. ("I have assumed that you would prefer that we make no increase in your salary . . . ," he wrote to Ciardi.)

The poetry staff in 1969 included Miller Williams, William Meredith, Maxine Kumin, John Frederick Nims, and Andrew Glaze. When Glaze, on the staff for the first time, received Ciardi's annual three-page, single-spaced July memo outlining the conference's two-week agenda and going over staff duties at lectures and clinics, he made a fatal error. Ciardi had, indeed, recommended that staff members might do well to use the daytime lectures "to discuss specific problems of form . . . and technical management." But he also wrote that his "pronouncements" were not "law," which prompted Glaze to write back that he was more interested in things like "how do you choose what to write" and learning "how to be objective about one's own work": "If I attempted to flog too hard the technical subjects which you propose, I would really feel cramped." After the conference was completed, Glaze wrote Ciardi to say thank you for the invitation, especially because they had had, as he put it, their "divergences." Yet the technical discussions that "cramped" him, must have come in handy, for he added that he didn't think anyone at the conference had learned as much as he had. But Glaze's reluctance to deal with poetry as craft had been registered all too clearly. Ciardi never invited him back.

Week one at Bread Loaf was traditionally given over to staff lectures during the day, hour-long talks on technical matters; in the evenings of both weeks, staff members took turns talking about some personal experiences, perhaps, or a reading from their work, "anything anyone feels passionate about," as Ciardi put it in his annual memo. Week two also featured a series of four, hour-and-a-half clinics in addition to the evening sessions. No two events were ever scheduled at the same time so that theoretically one person could attend every session, although endurance usually gave out before good intentions. The paying customers in 1969 included 133 auditors, who had paid to attend lectures and participate in the discussions on literary art, plus seventy-seven contributors, who had paid as well for detailed criticisms of their manuscripts (submitted with their applications). The exhausting intensity of the two weeks of writing talk was apparent to anyone who had ever attended, but it was especially demanding on the staff members, who had to be protected for their own sanity from auditors who wanted, even demanded, free clinics on their writing. These people Ciardi called the "arm grabbers," and he took it as an important part of his responsibility to discourage them from begging favors that the too-generous but already hard-pressed staff found difficult and sometimes impossible to deny. For years the discouragements had included separate seating in the dining room and staff-only restrictions to Treman Cottage, often called "Delirium Treman," which was by tradition a safe haven where the staff gathered for Bloody Marys before lunch and martinis before dinner, plus late night drinking and talking. This arrangement had worked for decades, but no one in decades had seen anything like the persistence and confrontational manner of the young radicals.

Still, as Ciardi wrote from Bread Loaf to Irv Klompus, who had permanently relocated a continent away in San Francisco, they were enjoying "a quiet conference" in 1969. And when it was finished, he wrote again to say that it had been good, although one of the fellows was still in a local hospital, comatose after a drunk driving accident. The closest thing they had to a "flip," Ciardi reported to Klompus, was "with the least pleasant most mooching goddamn fellow in conf history." Fortunately, however, "Doc. John Stone, your Atlanta understudy, talked him into accepting some sedation, which soon settled him down to being just obnoxious without psychobatics," which, he said, was the term professionals use for "acrobatics of the psyche." As the two letters suggest, Ciardi clearly missed his old pal, who had for years taken up his nightly cribbage or gin rummy position opposite Ciardi at Treman. Even Miller Williams's valiant effort to learn how to play cribbage by reading up on it in the *Encyclopedia Brittanica* couldn't make up for the loss.

There were, nonetheless, some happy additions as well, including Maxine Kumin, who had a special bond with Ciardi due to their common devotion to John Holmes. Kumin, who came back in 1971 as well, recalled Ciardi's "sometimes formidable presence" and their occasional late-afternoon mushroom hunts. She also remembered Ciardi's readings-recitations, especially his tribal poems and the love poems from *I Marry You,* and how she would go away from those readings "in a kind of trance, thinking that poems could say so much in such gorgeously constraining ways." Ciardi was, of course, a seasoned performer, but impressing college audiences was one thing and impressing the likes of Maxine Kumin was something else: "He did not dramatize, he did not embarrass; he simply spoke the lines and they lodged themselves in my head so that I may always have them. . . ."

Another happy addition to the family was John Stone, who was a poet as well as a physician. He had been suggested as Doc Klompus's replacement by Williams and later remembered his duties as being "murky," mostly "to keep access to antacids, to treat hangovers, and to hand out, on occasion, antibiotic prescriptions." Occasionally someone would overdose on something or other, "having been told they were not the next Emily Dickinson." So Stone tended to the sick as well as the sick of soul and attended lectures, too, especially Ciardi's in the Little Theatre. "I heard John hold the rapt attention of us all as he discussed 'Valediction Forbidding Mourning' by John Donne and 'The Eve of St. Agnes' by John Keats. The discussion was all the more remarkable for John's never using notes and quoting huge stretches of the poems from memory. And the readings from his own work were likewise incomparable." In 1970, Doc Klompus was lured back to the mountain for old time's sake, but Stone returned in 1971 and 1972, his soft voice, reassuring professionalism, and devotion to poetry all combining to make him a new Bread Loaf favorite.

Doc Stone felt "privileged," he said, "to sit in on the endless evening and early morning conversations that took place in Treman Cottage" and understood from the outset that Bread Loaf had a hierarchy governed by merit and talent. Ageless rules seemingly beyond challenge remained firmly in place, like the one prohibiting radio playing in Treman. But Ciardi, as the guardian of tradition, could be persuaded to try out some new ideas as well, such as Myra's suggestion that a rock band be allowed to play at a dance in the barn. And, in a more difficult decision, he also allowed for the first time public readings by waiters and scholars as well as impromptu open readings both indoors and out. But all told, the conference ran pretty much as it always had in 1969, well enough certainly to gain the respect of Vietnam veteran David Rabe, who would earn several Broadway honors in the early 1970s. On 5 October the *New Haven Register* published Rabe's account of the conference under the title, "Strenuous Test for Writers." He called Ciardi "the center of Bread Loaf . . . , its strongest voice," and he admired Ciardi's "toughness." At first, he wrote, he had been put off by the emphasis on craft and work, but when the lectures and clinics were finished, he could feel the magic beginning: "It is all put together and something happens. A student, during the long slow walk back to his cottage, begins to see the reality of the errors pointed to in his work. Staff members and fellow students have spoken to him. He begins to hear phrases, bits of rules and notions of craft and they are not so alien as they were at first. They seem nearly his own voice. It is like lifting weights, this acquisition of new skill—the muscle tears, then heals." He grew to appreciate the simple truth he learned from Maxine Kumin, that "drudgery is underrated." And he liked too what he learned from novelist Harry Crews: "All the time I worked at writing," Crews had said, "nobody ever talked about talent. They talked about work. Work you can talk about." These were the lessons Bread Loaf had always taught, always stood for, the lessons John Ciardi was most intent on preserving.

The conference was noticeably worse in 1970. As Bread Loaf historian David Bain put it, it was "as if a hidden thermostat had been turned up several notches until the temperature was on the verge of being uncomfortable." Stolen tableware and blankets were reported, as were bad manners, like noisy partying that interfered with neighbors who were trying to sleep, and noisy entrances and exits during readings at the Little Theatre. There were also several "flips" in 1970, causing more than the usual amount of commotion as "the men in the white coats" had to escort people off the mountain—"to emotionally safer ground," wrote Bain. Even the staff caused Ciardi and the Middlebury College administration both trouble and embarrassment. Dan Wakefield, a semiregular making his fifth appearance since 1959, was constantly drunk by his own admission and carried a half-gallon jug of vodka everywhere he went. And just as Ciardi had had to ban Judson Jerome from the mountain after making a spectacle of his self-described "partying and philandering" in 1968, he had to ban Wakefield as well. The Bread Loaf code of behavior, at least as Ciardi enforced it, was loose, but there were limits—and both men had crossed the line.

The biggest problem for Ciardi in 1970, however, came not from the customers or the drunken staff, but from a poetry staff member with impeccable credentials, Galway Kinnell. At age 43, Kinnell had already achieved the sort of distinction that even Bread Loaf auditors might have heard about. He had published four books of poems plus a novel during the 1960s, and two more books of poetry were due out in 1971. He was not as well known or prolific as Ciardi during the same period, but Kinnell was clearly a man in the midst of making a name for himself.

In terms of generational affiliation, Kinnell was caught in between. He was only fourteen years old when the United States entered World War II, but by the time of the consciousness revolution in the 1960s, he was already well into his thirties. He had, however, decided to support "the young and restless" with whom he had "a particular affinity," as David Bain termed it. Even Kinnell described the differences between himself and Ciardi in 1970 as "generational." He said Ciardi was more conservative than some of the others on the mountain that year because Ciardi objected to political poetry and was very cautious about free verse. As Kinnell saw things, Ciardi was "out of touch" with students, too "defensive" in his contact with them. Maxine Kumin agreed, saying that Ciardi was "running counter to the grain," alienating himself by his "authoritarian ways." And World War II veteran William Meredith, also on the poetry staff in 1970, wrote Ciardi afterward that "the hard line about craft, which most of us take, is not as authoritarian as the tone [in presentation] suggested." But he too had bent to the fashion and wanted "to woo the young writer" and to show more "sensitivity to the insecurity of the young."

All three of them had a staunch ally in boyish-looking Sandy Martin, Ciardi's assistant director, who "continued to press for reforms in the structure and curriculum" at Bread Loaf, according to Bain. To Ciardi, however, Martin was tampering with matters that were none of his business and had a basic misunderstanding of Bread Loaf: it was not a school and it had no curriculum. It was

clear to Ciardi that Martin's real aim was to take over the conference. Moreover, "reform" was a safe word to hide behind in 1970;
it took no courage at all to go along with the anti-GI spirit of the
times. The very idea of traditional values or a hierarchy based on
merit and talent (in poetry as well as most other facets of American
life) was suspect. And to the rigid reformer mindset, anyone who
dared defend any status quo was not merely suspect, but guilty of
what was labeled as the new worst sin, elitism.

Kinnell himself recalled lecturing young poets in the Little
Theatre on "trusting one's instincts," writing in free verse, and not
worrying so much about technical details. But his message, in
Ciardi's view, reinforced a too-loose conception that encouraged
young people to spill out unformed feeling and call it poetry. Kinnell
learned after his lecture that the apparently absent Ciardi had listened in on the performance from a projection booth. Very shortly
afterward, a furious Ciardi carved a space for himself in the busy
Bread Loaf schedule to provide a corrective homily to Kinnell's
heresy. Ciardi's sermon on poetic craft has not survived, but it was
certainly like many he had delivered in the past. He probably
invoked Yeats in "Adam's Curse": "A line will take us hours maybe,
/ Yet if it does not seem a moment's thought / Our stitching and
unstitching has been naught." He might also have tried out some of
the language he would put into a "Manner of Speaking" column
seven months later. There he would address himself to a hypothetical Mr. X, an undergraduate writer of poetry who was supposedly
putting effort into his work, but who had not prepared himself adequately for the task ahead. "Your generation has been told by some
of the names on the spines of books that it must shout social causes,
that meter is reactionary, that rhyme is decadent, that language distinction has Fascist overtones, and that formal structure is an
Establishment sellout." But if Mr. X truly wanted to be a poet,
Ciardi said, he had to learn the tools of his trade, especially if he
wanted to write free verse, which, as a term, can only be understood
as "free of traditional measures because it has invented its own."
There is no hope at all, he wrote, for anyone who misunderstands
free verse to mean "without measure." Poets were, Ciardi may have
gone on by quoting himself, "more like fishermen than fish":

Of Fish and Fishermen

Fish are subtle. Fishermen
are gross and stinking and they lurch
hauling their nets. Which clod of them
could shimmer like a cod or perch
through blue and green and purple spells?
It isn't shimmering grace that tells
in the long run. It's being taught
to track and set and haul and stink.
If stinking's part of it. It's not?
It needn't be? That's what you think.

For the rest of the conference, in Kinnell's no doubt accurate recollection, Ciardi was "frosty" toward him and behaved as though
he'd been "personally affronted."

That craftsmanship in poetry could have divided two such
serious poets as Ciardi and Kinnell is testimony to the wrong-
headedness of the times. Kinnell, though a careful technician himself, had suggested in his lectures and clinics that management of
craft was unimportant. Thinking back twenty years later, long after
the feverish sixties had cooled down, he realized that in an effort "to
light a fire" in the young poets, he had given "a false impression"
of himself. In Ciardi's view the younger generation needed a dose
of reality, not more soothing bromides about self-expression.
Predictably, when Ciardi heard from the projection booth the sort
of thing Kinnell was saying, his blood boiled, for nothing riled
Ciardi more than this sort of unexpected challenge to the Bread
Loaf method. After all, it was this very sort of blind-side attack that
he tried to head off every year with his July memos.

To Ciardi, teaching the importance of technical mastery was
difficult enough, especially to the impatient and rebellious, without
staff members undermining the message. If craft were to be left out
of the equation, only inspiration would be left, and that was a word
Ciardi would sooner "get rid of," as he put it in a February 1970
interview: "It sounds like all you have to do is sit there and get a free
gift from heaven. If you don't study, don't work, the inspiration won't

mean anything." About a month after his face-off with Kinnell, Ciardi was in Cleveland, and his anger had not subsided. "Poetry is no monolithic thing," he told the *Plain Dealer*, "but I guess we could establish two divisions among poets—those who want to be disciplined and those who want to spill out soul. I think of the 'soul' poet as a man with a lot of emotion and no training sitting down at a piano. We'd get lots of noise and no real music."

At Chautauqua a couple of years later, Ciardi was still railing against student resistance to learning craft: "An undergraduate who has written anything whatever receives a deplorable amount of attention on it. The teacher reads it all the way through and tries to make sympathetic comments. There is an hour's personal conference at least over what has been written. It is brought into class and discussed and seriously pondered. *And the poem is not worth that much attention.*" And a couple of years after that, at an appearance in Tulsa, he condemned once again, "the over-encouraged generation who want to decide for themselves what they should learn." The message he delivered right through to the end of his life, sometimes overburdened with bitterness, in fact, was the same:

> I don't like most of the poetry I see. The assumption seems to be loose in the land that the only prerequisite for poetry is the excitation of one's own ignorance. I am told by such poets as Robert Bly and Galway Kinnell, over whose poems I was groaning a couple of days ago, that you should tell it like it is, just spill it out of your psyche. Tell that to your psychiatrist. I think a poem should be *made*. But maybe I am, as Bly has accused me of being, obsolete. I like stanza patterns; I like rhyme. And I have a feeling that one of the reasons these people do not take on rhyme and stanza patterns is that they can't handle it. What is missing from most American poets is that they won't take on the difficulties of form. They have to tell me what they feel—I don't *care* what they feel. I'm interested in what *I* feel when I'm reading the poem. We used to say at Bread Loaf, "Show it, don't tell it." Make it happen.

For John Ciardi, then, the very lifeblood of poetry was at stake when poets like Kinnell jumped on the generational bandwagon to preach feelings rather than discipline in poetry. But it was dangerous standing up for poetic principles at Bread Loaf in 1970, and

Ciardi was branded with the most damaging epithets of the time, like "elitist" and "authoritarian" and "out of touch." Some went so far as to suggest an ethnic explanation (Ciardi was too stubbornly Italian to see the wrongness of his position) rather than crediting Ciardi for taking the high ground, having the courage of his convictions, and refusing to surrender principle.

But though one might have expected him to be, Ciardi was never automatically angry and impatient with young people, whether at Bread Loaf or elsewhere. Nor did he always line up with his own generation in all the conflicts that were emerging everywhere, every day during the time in and around 1970. In fact, he wrote a "Manner of Speaking" column called "Hatred" on 1 August that year based on Myra's high school commencement exercises six weeks earlier, which were disrupted by a confrontation between the graduates and their parents. The demonstration had been occasioned by the class salutatorian's speech, which Ciardi had generally approved of. The unnamed young man

> began by condemning the school system for the endless flow of busy work it had handed out to him in place of a questing education, and he made firm points, though just a bit over-firmly. I found him honorable, refreshing, and relentless. Having just discovered the world, he had yet to discover any doubts about his discovery. Yet he was asking hard questions and asking them well. Some freshman instructor, I found myself thinking, would find in this lad his recompense for the illiterate year. Once softened by a reasonable uncertainty, this would be an intellect. At the moment, however, he had won his honors by what he called "an unthinking docility," and he was in a mood to savor them.
>
> Having categorized the school system, he moved on to the war in Asia, to the race issue, to pollution, to the lack of confidence in the federal government, to the military-industrial complex, to unrest, to the dedication of the socially committed young.

When hecklers among the parents and guests disrupted the speech, it took the superintendent of schools and the president of the board of education to establish the young man's right to continue. When he began speaking again, a few supporters in the audience stood to applaud. Then most of the graduates rose to join them. The angry elders kept their seats. Across the generation gap that was being dramatized in the Metuchen High School gym that night, Ciardi sensed a "flow of hatred" going from the old to the young, and he confessed "that what little is left of my hope rides with the young":

> Think, neighbors; for God's sake think. It may be right-eously self-satisfying to ask—I have heard you ask it—"Why do they hate us?" It will be more useful to ask, "Why do we hate them?" You know why of course. They tell all of us that we have given our lives in tawdry faith to tin gods. They dismiss our sacrifices and our hypocrisies as pointless. They cancel us. And we hate them for it. Even though they are probably right. Especially because they are probably right.

Clearly John Ciardi still had full faith in the young, although three weeks later in another "Manner of Speaking" column he wondered "if parental abuse of authority may not be a shade better for family life than filial abuse of permission." And, he asked, "Is it only in our time that children—like Jacobins, anarchists, and suffragettes—have been so assured of their righteousness as to feel they owe nothing to good manners?" His sympathies were with the young, but how could he engage them in debate or conversation in the face of their confrontational manner? Civility and restraint always seemed to give way to angry shouting on both sides. It was frustrating and infuriating. Ciardi might well have said of his Bread Loaf family what he had said of his own children at home: "I do keep trying for a conversation that seems forever to go nowhere." But it was not in his nature to give up.

During the 1970 conference, just when it was needed most, a humorous incident occurred and relieved some of the mounting tension. Jimmy Orenstein, the teenage son of Ciardi's copilot on Saipan in 1944–45, was visiting the Ciardis that summer, so he went along to Bread Loaf as Ciardi's special guest and the companion of Benn and Jonnel. An accomplished tennis player, Jimmy spent quite a bit of time at the courts, which were situated very close to the Little Theatre, where the lectures were going on. When the Bread Loaf tennis tournament was arranged and the young man easily out-matched Kinnell, who had been proudly and too regularly showing off his tennis skills (instead of his poetic skills, in the view of some), John Frederick Nims was overheard to remark from a window in the Little Theatre: "There, by God, is the triumph of technique over brute soul." The joke was good, and Ciardi never forgot it, but there was no real hope that Kinnell, even if he had actually heard it, might have taken a lesson from the tennis metaphor. Moreover, the threat to Bread Loaf's emphasis on craft was no joke, and Ciardi would never laugh at a lecture, like Kinnell's, that in his eyes diminished and demeaned and dishonored the art of poetry.

Kinnell was not at Bread Loaf in 1971, but the conference was even worse than it had been the year before. Ciardi's problems actually began in January 1971, when Andy Paquette took over for Steve Freeman as director of the language schools at Middlebury College. The conference was under his administrative control, which he took seriously enough to institute some new procedures and forms. When Ciardi got wind of the changes Paquette had in mind, he wrote him brusquely that "they just won't do." Paquette didn't seem to understand what the conference was all about and how it worked: "I think you will find our staff people are easy-going (I have weeded out as much temperament as possible), drunken (there wasn't much sobriety to weed out), loyal, unacademic, a touch iconoclastic, two touches ironic, and very much *inside*—a sort of club of spiney types who respect one another's spines and who come to Bread Loaf, basically, for a tone they exchange there with one another." He was being plain with Paquette, but just in case he hadn't received the full message, Ciardi became blunt:

> We are not a school and the staff is not up for a faculty appointment.
>
> I must veto anything that says "salary" followed by a blank. The implication there is that salaries can vary. It is a fixed principle at the conference—to avoid possible jealousies—that all staff members receive exactly the same pay.
>
> I don't want my people bugged to fill out forms that don't apply to them in the first place. As I say, we have an odd and spiney damn good crew and it just won't sit still for the[se] kinds of forms and systems of brisk administration. It spoils an essential tone of things that I must labor to preserve. We're just not a saluting and form filling crew. I submit it's a good crew and worth keeping. If forms and systems turn out to be the essence, you're going to end up needing a new crew and a new captain.

Given the worsening relationship between Ciardi and the Middlebury management over the previous few years, plus the recent tensions at Bread Loaf, one can imagine the speed with which Paquette shared Ciardi's response with James I. Armstrong, president of the college. They may have decided right then that "a new crew and a new captain" was an idea well worth serious consideration.

If Ciardi was stepping on the toes of his Middlebury College superiors, his own toes were being bruised by his assistant, Sandy Martin. Martin had written early in January to discuss staffing matters for 1971 and to suggest particularly not inviting Miller Williams back—the very same Williams who had been godfather to *Lives of X*, which was dedicated to him as "man, poet, brother." Ciardi, of course, would not hear of it and saw the suggestion as yet another instance where Martin was tampering with matters that were none of his concern. He confided to Williams later in the month: "You probably know I've had problems with [Martin]. Half the time when I think I'm director it turns out that Peggy [his wife] is and that Sandy is her assistant. I wish I could explain to them that Staff, program, and policy is my responsibility and that Bulletin, housing, budget tending etc. is theirs. I don't see how I could have made the point more strongly to Sandy, but that's his deaf ear."

Ciardi must have been deaf himself, and blind, not to have noticed that he was alienating himself from every level of management at Middlebury College. Either that or he felt himself so secure in his position (Hadn't he received not one but four honorary doctorates in 1970–71?), so true to the spirit of his stewardship, so right about what was good for the conference—that he could afford to be blunt, which he no doubt viewed as merely saying what needed to be said. Or perhaps it was his colon condition made him less patient than usual, or his "busy indolence," or his son's drug problem, or his possible postpartum blues after the publication of *Paradiso* and *Lives of X*, or his lingering anger over Galway Kinnell—but for whatever set of reasons, Ciardi was becoming even more blunt than usual. At age 55, he seemed totally unconcerned about the possibility of making enemies.

Then, making matters worse, the 1971 conference was written up—hacked up really—as a feature story in *Audience* magazine by one Rust Hills, the magazine's fiction editor (calling himself "Larry Placebound" in the story), who didn't work very hard to disguise his antipathy toward Ciardi, although it is doubtful that Ciardi would have cared one way or the other, even if he had known in advance what Hills would be saying. In fact, Ciardi might have guessed it because Hills had already been to Bread Loaf in 1962 and written in *Esquire* that it was "Squaresville" and "mediocre," which would have told Ciardi, had he remembered it, that Hills knew what he thought about the conference long before he actually showed up for the two weeks in 1971. Compounding this journalistic deceit, Hills had signed up for the conference under false pretenses as a student, although he was forced to come clean when "he was unable to keep his intentions a secret."

Hills described Ciardi in the *Audience* article as a poet, but added, "he's not one of your ineffective poet-types. . . . He makes the poetry thing work for him." He went on to say in more flatly damaging terms that Ciardi was "an authoritarian man," which he explained with an unabashed ethnic stereotype: "He is a big hulking man . . . of Italian extraction, and he runs Bread Loaf as if he were running an Italian family." Hills then described Ciardi's opening lecture to the conference, which began with Ciardi using the Kinnell fiasco from the year before to get the proceedings off on the right foot. It had been a mistake to invite Galway Kinnell the year before, Ciardi announced formally, because he had run counter to Bread Loaf's traditional emphasis on technique. According to Ciardi, said Hills, "we were not here to discuss the nature of creativity or the emotions of the artist. What could be learned here, [Ciardi] explained, was only what could be taught: craft and technique. 'We believe in the maestro system. . . .'"

This was the nub of the problem in Hills's opinion. The emphasis on technique was a wrong starting point because "in real art, there's no separate technique *to* teach." And even if there were, he went on, the Bread Loaf staff was so full of second-raters that they couldn't do the job. It was "a misassumption that a fairly good writer can teach basic technique to a beginning writer just as well as a really first-rate writer can." If he were in charge, he'd do away with all the mediocre teachers and hire "famous writers." As things stood, according to Hills, Bread Loaf had no maestros, and so it followed there could be no real "maestro system." "The Bread Loaf 'tradition' that's so cherished [by Ciardi] would have to be renounced—maybe even *de*nounced—as having been a fifty-year commitment to mediocrity. . . ."

If Ciardi was the authoritarian dragon at Bread Loaf in 1971, according to Hills, Sandy Martin was its Lancelot, "a good-looking tweeds-and-corduroy young English teacher at Middlebury." Martin was "articulate, realistic, and direct, the soul of common sense, compassionate, energetic, careful in attending to details, hard-working, with a good sense of humor, and thoroughly dismayed by what happens at the conference each year." Presumably Martin bore no responsibility for the fact that the conference was a "nonsensical business" and that "the teaching is virtually worthless" because, after all, he had nothing to do with hiring the staff. But then, apparently changing a big part of his mind, he said that "as teachers, some of them seemed pretty good anyway. . . ." A large chunk of the Hills article was then dedicated to individual comments on the staff. Miller Williams, for example, was "a bearded man with a young wife" who "played a lot of cribbage with John Ciardi." William Meredith was "out of place" because he was so "much more distinguished than the others." Hills found just the right sort of clichés to praise Meredith: he had "extraordinary rapport with the students," a "gentle smile," and "an almost monastic manner." Moreover, he wore love beads and Hills rhapsodized over the possibility that Meredith might "be some kind of modern saint."

Hills pigeonholed all the rest of the staff in the same way, with praise for those who wore love beads (actual or metaphorical) and criticism for those who believed in the maestro system. He dispatched the four fiction staff members by saying that, though he was a fiction editor himself and personally knew "many of the major American writers," he had "never even heard of two of these men and knew the work of the others only faintly." Of the nonfiction staff, Bill Sloane, the man who had done more for Bread Loaf in a quarter century of continuous service than anyone other than Ciardi himself, became Hills's whipping boy. At one point during the conference, Hills had observed in a casual conversation with Judith Ciardi that the nonfiction staff was not very good, which prompted her to answer that "as long as John is alive . . . and as long as Bill Sloane is alive, Bill will teach at Bread Loaf." Hills could not very easily speak out against loyalty, so he turned Ciardi's virtue into a vice. He suggested that Sloane compromised the "integrity" of the teaching at Bread Loaf, which meant that Ciardi was at fault for hiring without regard to qualifications, and that led to his real point, "that it was cronyism that has always made Bread Loaf such a warm and friendly place, and cronyism that's always made it so mediocre an institution." Hills had used the word "mediocre" to describe the conference in 1962, and it kept coming up in his 1971 analysis. Ciardi didn't need to defend Sloane—or himself—but when he wrote the introduction to Sloane's posthumously published *Craft of Writing* (1979), he offered a few words that could actually have been directed at Rust Hills: "I have never known a man who was more learned and more lucid [than Bill Sloane] in discussing the structure of fiction and nonfiction, the management of a scene, or the contract of art and craft that binds reader to author and author to reader in the shared experience of the writing."

The 1971 conference was dogged by a variety of impossible-to-anticipate problems that left it an especially vulnerable target. For several days Ciardi wasn't even available to perform his director's duties because he was so far under the weather with flu symptoms that he was restricted to quarters. On another full day, he had had to work with a large production crew from Vermont educational television, pleasant enough in its own right and with the potential to send out the right message about Bread Loaf, but tiring and distracting as well. Then, topping all, Hurricane Doria delivered five rough days of cold and rain, which, as David Bain pointed out, kept all 250 people indoors for too long: "tempers began to fray," especially when an electrical short-circuit sounded the fire alarms and everyone ran off in every direction. Nothing at that point could have redeemed the 1971 conference. The year could have been written off as an aberration of nature, unfortunate but unavoidable. And it might have worked out that way had it not been for the final clinic of the conference, "a traditionally wide-open session," as Bain described it, where a general discussion plus questions and answers all combined into a sort of evaluation of the two weeks.

The final clinic in 1971 was held on 31 August at the Little Theatre. By then, Ciardi had regained strength enough to stand up under the attacks of the paying customers, holding his ground and answering back volley for volley. He tried hard to avoid testy and impatient answers, regardless of what he thought of the questions and the questioners. And he spoke with conviction and courage, plus his customary forthrightness, which annoyed and frustrated the audience even more, for by 1971 the younger generation had become used to backing down so-called figures of authority. John Ciardi, however, was not an easy man to intimidate.

Change, of course, was what they wanted. And a few changes had already been initiated, like the dining hall, where the staff had been kept slightly apart from the paying customers, both as an expression of respect and a protection against the arm-grabbers. Ciardi had mixed feelings about the change, but in the end allowed faculty tables to be placed throughout the dining room. Students at the final clinic suggested that workshops (clinics) be held in the first week instead of the second, and they wanted a beer bar set up in the barn. Ciardi could hardly have been expected to make changes like these from floor challenges: the schedule had suited the needs of beginning writers since the 1920s, so why shouldn't it be good enough for them? When someone expressed resentment of the Bread Loaf hierarchy, a familiar complaint by 1971, Ciardi passed it off as he always had, as an unworthy topic for serious discussion, for surely there could be no objection to a hierarchy based on talent, merit, and demonstrated achievement. After all, wasn't it true that in democratic societies talent was supposed to rise to the top and be rewarded? When a few auditors objected that they wanted to be treated like contributors, never mind that they hadn't paid for that treatment, Ciardi replied by saying that this was a "swindle" of sorts. Bill Meredith had been wrong if he had agreed to read manuscripts from those who were not entitled to such a reading by virtue of the contract they had agreed to when they accepted the terms that Bread Loaf had to offer.

The dramatic climax of the afternoon, however, was when John Michael Brennan stood up. Brennan, a student in his third year at Tufts, had been nominated for a scholarship by X. J. Kennedy, but had been taken on as a waiter instead. Kennedy characterized Brennan as a "very brilliant young poet" and a "very laid back, hip individual, a most remarkable guy who had a tremendous effect on the life of everyone who was close to him." He was "charismatic" but "unhappy" as a student at Tufts where he strained against the college "Establishment," as Kennedy recalled. He was not only unhappy, but unstable, too, for two years later, still at Tufts, he committed suicide. Hills reported that Brennan, "slightly built" and "with long blond hair," stood up during the final clinic to object to what he called "arrogance" at the conference. "It seems to me that nothing very worthwhile will ever happen here until you recognize that you have just as much to learn from me as I do from you." This particular argument (phrased in just about the same terms) was being addressed to teachers at every level all over the country. Perhaps surprisingly, it was not considered either foolish or self-indulgent at the time; in fact, it was generally accepted as in some vague way true—even encouraged with approving nods by elders like Meredith, whom Hills called a "guru" for his special wisdom. On this occasion, Meredith did, indeed, agree with Brennan, saying that the older generation could learn "generosity of spirit" from the young. Ciardi saw it all as so much nonsense. He gathered himself up and addressed Brennan, Meredith, and anyone else who had taken leave of his senses: "If I haven't more to give you than you have to give me, then you're being cheated here. I have no sense of being arrogant about this. I feel you are part of an over-encouraged generation—encouraged to feel that you are very special. And you're not very good listeners." And then in a few choice sentences he attempted to put the matter in rational focus:

> What we have to teach you and what you have to learn
> from us is technique. I believe in the maestro system. To learn
> to write poetry you must learn to move easily in harness, to
> use Frost's metaphor. You must learn the discipline of the har-
> ness. Before you can fly a plane you need to know how to use
> the controls. Before you can play the piano you must practice
> the scales. This emphasis on learning the craft of writing has
> always been part of the Bread Loaf tradition. This confer-
> ence has been going on for many years. It doesn't chop itself
> down and grow anew every year. Any apparent hierarchy at
> Bread Loaf is to some extent a sense of trusteeship. I feel I am
> trustee for a number of ghosts—Frost, Theodore Morrison,
> Bernard DeVoto, Fletcher Pratt, Joe Green, and there are
> others, but you won't have known them.

There would be no changes unless and until Ciardi was persuaded that they would be in the best interest of the conference. He was willing to listen, and had even shown himself willing to make changes, but he saw himself as responsible to all those whom he had named, plus scores of others. He had a responsibility that stretched considerably beyond the personalities crowded into the Little Theatre that sweaty afternoon in August. And he would not be bullied into abandoning principles. Hills, however, chose to characterize the response to Ciardi by quoting a 1960s flower child at the conference: "That Ciardi gives off ba-a-ad vibes, man." It wasn't a very articulate response, but it served Hills's purpose. As for Brennan, he could not have been pleased with the outcome, but he reported to Kennedy afterward "that Ciardi had treated him decently."

That evening, after Ciardi had read from his own poems in the theater, the staff drifted into Treman Cottage, worn out from two weeks of bad weather, bad colds, and bad karma. Ciardi took his usual window seat and began grousing at once about the disastrous conference. According to Bain, Ciardi "began to dress down Sandy Martin for a number of lapses," after which Martin left Treman and resigned as assistant director. In Hills's account, Ciardi "seemed ready to pick a fight" while Martin "seemed not in the mood to avoid one." Martin, he said, left after about an hour and told Hills the next day that he had resigned. Ciardi left no written account of his version of the scene, but it would no doubt have been in essential agreement with Bain and Hills. Ciardi had taken Martin to task as the enemy in his camp, the traitor who had worked to destroy all the valuable things that Bread Loaf had stood for for so long. It seemed to Ciardi that it was way past time for Martin to be put in his place.

On 13 September Ciardi wrote to Jim Armstrong, who had asked to be "filled in" on the differences between John and Sandy. Ciardi answered by saying that Meredith had written that he wouldn't be back because he felt his loyalties were with, as he put it, "the exec rather than the skipper." This, Ciardi wrote, was a perfect illustration of what had gone wrong at Bread Loaf: Martin had created a situation which made it appear that there were two Bread Loaf policies. Ciardi accepted the blame for allowing such a preposterous situation to have developed, but he was making a correction in course. He had explained to Martin that he should resign if he was unable to implement the policies of the conference, which

Ciardi alone was responsible for formulating. (Apparently on the last night of the conference Martin had resigned to Hills, not Ciardi.) "If he is willing to act as my assistant, implementing my decisions even when they conflict with his view of things, I know him to be a valuable man and I welcome him as my assistant, non-director." He believed, however, that their differences were "fundamental and irreconcilable":

> As best I can say it to myself, Sandy is "undergraduate oriented." That is an honorable condition and I suspect it makes him the more valuable as a teacher at the college. I, on the other hand, think of the conference as a meeting of responsible professionals and would-be professionals and insist that soul talk be held in abeyance for long enough to discuss craft. To indicate how seriously I take the situation, let me say I am pondering (not yet a decision) a recommendation to Andy Paquette that we cut back enrollment to 175, using the 21 deletions to eliminate that many undergraduates. In my experience, Bread Loaf has never been an undergraduate activity and I feel it must not become one, especially at a time when undergraduates tend to be so impatient of precisely those disciplines the conference must put forth as essentials of the craft. I confess I have become a bit testy about the amount of talk about soul and the guru-like infinites that has clouded the last two or three sessions, not because it is irrelevant to the universe but because it is not useful to whatever it is that Bread Loaf can accomplish. Sandy—I think I am saying this fairly—is honorably concerned with the views of the young and wants very much to communicate with them. So am I, and so do I, but I am as honorably convinced that I must insist on my own terms and eliminate the young from the conference if they will not accept those terms.

If Armstrong had had some questions about the differences between Ciardi and Martin, this letter answered them in fair language and a controlled tone.

Although Ciardi did not write or otherwise record his feelings about the events surrounding that disastrous final day of the Bread Loaf conference in 1971, he did allude to it in a letter to Irv Klompus about a month after Bread Loaf, his weariness and anger bleeding through:

Bread Loaf was bad this year. Not only the cold that knocked me out of half of it but Sandy's goddamn (strictly between us) maneuvering to make the conference over in his own undergraduate image. In a way a good thing, though, for it brought matters to a head. He has the word and can stay on with the clear understanding that he does not make policy but implements mine whether he likes it or not. Or he can resign with military honors as a case of conscience. Or he can get his ass fired off the mountain. I hope he chooses military honors, but I'll settle for his becoming ass-director with utterly no co-director nonsense about it.

Then on 13 October, Ciardi wrote to Miller Williams that he had been "absorbed" in "a long series of letters" (none of which has survived) about Bread Loaf and that finally he had had to ask Martin to resign. He had already advised Paquette and Armstrong of his decision. Ciardi knew not only how bad the 1971 conference had been, but how hard it would be to right the course once again.

What comes next is a meticulous business of getting related to a new assistant director and of rebuilding Bread Loaf as the kind of learning excitement it can be. I plan a substantially new staff (half new and half rotated) and I am afraid I am going to be flooding the world with memos. I particularly want to have regular sessions with the staff to discuss how things are going. We can meet an hour early for cocktails, discuss the day's lecture, and try to re-establish a common vocabulary. Well, many more such things. There will be a lot to do.

As it turned out, there was less to do than he had imagined, for the Bread Loaf management, from Armstrong to Freeman to Paquette to Martin—even Ciardi's old friend Paul Cubeta, by then an academic vice president at Middlebury—maneuvered Ciardi into submitting an undated letter of resignation. Ciardi understood that his resignation would not become effective for another three years or more—until after he had put the conference back on it feet. Armstrong dated Ciardi's letter of resignation at once, however, and accepted it effective at the end of the 1972 conference.

The Martin-led palace revolt at Bread Loaf, plus the philosophical differences dramatized by the Ciardi-Kinnell face-off and the generational dynamics in the late 1960s and early 1970s, had all combined to cause Ciardi's downfall. But his position was worsened by two other features of the Bread Loaf status quo during those years, one of which he would have been happy to change and the other which he had no intention of changing. The first was the racial imbalance at Bread Loaf. This was a particularly thorny issue in that applications from contributors and auditors (the paying customers) were beyond Ciardi's control. Blacks simply did not apply in any significant numbers. In 1971, the situation was worse than usual, Ciardi wrote to Meredith, because Middlebury had cut the Bread Loaf budget, which meant there would be fewer fellowships and scholarships to award, the traditional categories for which blacks were recruited.

Certainly, Ciardi's social consciousness did not need raising as he was in full agreement with every measure designed to promote integration. He felt it was among the most important issues facing America in 1970 and wrote in his 19 December "Manner of Speaking" column, "It remains the first order of battle to get out of Vietnam, stop inflation, and see to it that all of us, of whatever color, can get a drink of drinkable water and a breath of breathable air. Let it be understood, moreover, that every issue is part of the race issue." Nor was he new to the subject of race relations. In fact, as early as 1958, Ciardi had been wrestling with one part of the problem in correspondence with black poet Gloria Oden, whom he had invited to Bread Loaf on scholarship. Of course, the full range of social, political, and economic problems facing blacks in America was compelling and complicated, but so were the literary ones facing black poets. The issue, as Ciardi saw it, was that no subject, not even one as honorable and moving as the fight for social justice, would automatically become good poetry, and furthermore that propaganda posing as poetry provided a disservice to both. "I've been there myself," he wrote to Oden, "so dedicated to a conviction that what I wrote turned out to be rhetoric and argumentation rather than poetry." That was the problem black poets in America had always faced, people like Owen Dodson, Langston Hughes, and M. B. Tolson. "The specimen case, I think, is Countee Cullen: He got himself caught in the dilemma of not knowing whether to write white or black and made the mistake of thinking he could answer himself by being more Keats than Keats." In literary terms, Ciardi wrote, it wasn't difficult to state the point: "There can be no

Negro poetry, nor white poetry, nor any but human poetry." The problem, however, as Ciardi understood, was not merely literary: "How you take someone who has had psychic tomatoes thrown at him all his life and ask him to ignore the tomatoes and just sniff the breeze is what I don't know. That calls for a size I don't come in. But I think maybe one can find the size he had to be if he really has to be it and wants to be it." Ciardi was clearly sensitive to racial issues, literary and otherwise, but year in and year out, good intentions notwithstanding, Bread Loaf had very few black students.

If signing up black students for Bread Loaf was essentially beyond Ciardi's control, recruiting black staff members was not. However, with the exception of Ralph Ellison in 1959, the staff had been all white until Ezekiel Mphalele, an African-born novelist who had published mostly in England and was teaching at Denver University, arrived in 1971. In January 1971, Bill Meredith had written to Ciardi to say the conference needed some black staff members, suggesting Clarence Major, Ronald Fair, and James Alan McPherson. Ciardi replied, perhaps with some relief, that Mphalele had already been signed up—but he didn't know the writing of the men Meredith had suggested. And staff selections were by then already complete, so he would keep all three in mind for 1972. Replying to a more accusatory question that he thought was implied by Meredith (or to a direct question in a letter that has not survived), Ciardi bristled a bit: "It would, I submit, be pointless to defend Bread Loaf's policy on race. There is none. I have tried to get good writers for the staff and I have always been especially glad when the good writer was black." He might have added that it was always difficult to get good writers of any color to commit to two weeks in August for very little money, and that he was regularly turned down by Ellison as well as a host of other writers. To any insinuation that he might be too passive in his recruitment of black staff members, Ciardi felt aggrieved. In truth, he might well have been more energetic in searching out good black writers for the staff, but he felt satisfied that any good black writer who was available and could pass muster was genuinely welcome. The writer had to be distinguished by merit, not color: "A poet is a poet not in what he writes about but in his act of language." Ciardi was completely color blind, and especially so when it came to writers. But in

October 1971, shortly after the disastrous Bread Loaf, Ciardi wrote
to Meredith still feeling the sting of the palace revolt and the anger
that had surfaced in the final clinic. He was returning the Clarence
Major books that Meredith had sent him and at the same time
accepting Meredith's decision not to return in 1972 as a good idea.
Moreover, he'd by then had enough criticism, implied or otherwise,
about being a racist:

> I'm sorry I can't find much to admire in the [Clarence
> Major] poems. Nor am I ready to accept a plan for "inte-
> grating" the Conference. It is already open to any black
> writer who will come as an auditor and pay the fees. It is
> available to black fellows and scholars if their writing makes
> it in open competition. I have done my best to recruit black
> staff members whose work I thought worthy. And I have not
> been riled when a group of blacks formed in the corner and
> did nothing but glower at the dumb whiteys. That is as inte-
> grated as I mean to get. If you think skin color can be put
> ahead of writing ability we are at unconquerable odds.

He didn't mention that by then, too, he'd already invited Robert
Hayden to the 1972 conference—and that he'd accepted.

The other aspect of the status quo that weakened Ciardi's
position at Bread Loaf, the one he had no intention of changing,
had to do with socializing. There had been instances of staff members having gone too far in their drinking and partying, and not
being invited back, like Jud Jerome and Dan Wakefield, but by and
large Ciardi gave everyone plenty of latitude in matters of behavior. He was no more willing to reform this part of the Bread Loaf
tradition than the dining room seating or the staff-only policy
at Treman. The students, had they known, would likely have been
as pleased with Ciardi for keeping the wide-open social policies as
they were displeased with him over his enforcement of other traditions. And Ciardi had been under considerable pressure from the
Middlebury administration, especially from Steve Freeman, to do
something about the drinking, the drugs, and the sex. And so, in
order to keep from interfering in the private affairs of the paying
customers, Ciardi actually had to dig himself an even deeper hole
with the same management that was already angry with him for
other reasons.

When Jim Armstrong received Ciardi's September 1971 letter in which he had insisted on replacing Sandy Martin as assistant director of the conference, he called in Paul Cubeta and Robert Pack, a Middlebury poet and professor and the next-to-be-appointed director of Bread Loaf. Armstrong said much later that the decision to replace Ciardi had been made in consultation with them both, although it is doubtful Ciardi ever found out about their roles in his dismissal, for he steadfastly defended them ever after and refused to group them with Sandy Martin. Cubeta was of two minds about firing Ciardi but went along with the decision that Armstrong seemed to have already made as the safe course of action. Afterward, however, he expressed regret that he hadn't spoken up more heartily in Ciardi's defense. Armstrong's stated reasons for replacing Ciardi were that he had become "weary" and that "there were gaps and faults in the two weeks of the conference." Sandy Martin, on the other hand, he characterized as "very determined and tough-minded during this difficult time." Armstrong said he undertook conversations with Ciardi about the conference's problems, but "John didn't hear what I was saying." Then sometime in the fall 1971, they met in New York at the Princeton Club for lunch, and Armstrong again tried to explain the changes that were imminent, but according to Armstrong, "John still did not seem to understand."

It is not known at this point what exactly was said that made the issue murky to Ciardi but clear to Armstrong. Ciardi, however, did submit his undated letter of resignation as a result of his luncheon conversation with Armstrong, with the understanding that Armstrong would hold onto it for as long as it took Ciardi to straighten things out at Bread Loaf, at least three years. He no doubt also thought he would make suggestions, though probably not participate actively, in the search for his successor. Armstrong, meanwhile, agreed to fire Sandy Martin. Probably in the late spring, however, Armstrong managed to convince Ciardi that there was "a college-wide range of problems" that were "invisible" to Ciardi but very real to him, problems that could be solved only by his acceptance of Ciardi's letter of resignation. Unhappy about this turn of events, Ciardi forced himself to accept Armstrong's explanation, and by about the first of June, he began telling people that Pack was going to replace him after the 1972 conference.

Then on 2 August, just before Ciardi's final conference, he saw a news release announcing Sandy Martin's return as assistant director under Pack beginning in 1973. At that point he finally understood that he had been successfully manipulated by Armstrong, fired for all practical purposes. Even worse, Sandy Martin would be returning. Bread Loaf had officially given up its identity as a professional gathering of writers and, in Ciardi's view, was about to take on a new identity, officially sanctioned, as an academic offshoot of Middlebury College. Ciardi wrote to Armstrong on 2 August to say that at last he could see how duplicitous Armstrong had been, and how badly he—and the conference—had been used. He rejected any "ceremonial gestures" at this, his last, conference, and lamented once again a Bread Loaf that was now to be nothing more than "a summer camp for souls." As usual, Judith Ciardi's summation was angrier: "John gave the president an open letter of resignation and about a year later the bastard accepted it. So we went up in '72, all gracious, saying yes, it's time to quit this and move on to some other things. Mad. John wanted to be there."

In May 1972, Bill Meredith wrote to Ciardi to say he'd had dinner with Rust Hills, who had given him a copy of the just published *Audience* article. Meredith was distressed to have been pictured as a guru and sorry that Hills had announced his resignation, which he had foolishly mentioned to Hills in the aftermath of the conference, when he was worn out from the battle and discouraged. Ciardi didn't answer that letter until early in September, after his last Bread Loaf, and by then he felt philosophical: "The universe is a difference of opinion and let it be enough to keep differences genial and open. At Bread Loaf, my disagreement was pressed by the fact that I had, in the end, to come to a decision and to insist upon it. That's all academic now. I am nobody's director of anything, decision is in other hands, and the day I insist my friend must see all things my way, may I have no friend." In fact, Ciardi had managed to project this sense of philosophical acceptance throughout his last Bread Loaf. He had not shrunk from battle over the previous decade, but the Bread Loaf wars were over in 1972, and he allowed himself a healing sense of nostalgia to replace the emotional strains that had already marred too many conferences. He did permit himself a run of angry poems at his final reading, according to Bain, who surmised that Ciardi was thereby saying he had neither forgotten nor forgiven his betrayers. But that aside, Ciardi seemed to enjoy his last hurrah.

His final lecture was held at the Little Theatre on Tuesday night, 29 August. "To me," he said, "this is a haunted place." He named Robert Frost, Fletcher Pratt, Bernard DeVoto, Dick Wilbur, Ted Morrison, Dudley Fitts, and many others. And, just to remind everyone that though he had lost the war, he had not surrendered any part of principle, he said, "There *is* such a thing as the Bread Loaf method. It's here because the staff is never entirely different from year to year. Some of the speakers this year said things that originated years ago before they were here; they didn't know where they came from. They had heard them at Bread Loaf. It's in the atmosphere. That's why there *is* a continuity at Bread Loaf." And then he growled a bit and took small bites out of old enemies, especially enjoying the retelling of his Galway Kinnell story that ended with Nims's comment that Kinnell had been bested at tennis by young Jimmy Orenstein, "the triumph of technique over brute soul."

Then he growled a bit at the ill-effects on poetry of the Beat movement. He said the deterioration of American poetry "starts at City Lights": "I think Ferlinghetti a man with a considerable talent. He lost it by getting the wrong notion of the audience. For him a poem is something to repeat in a guitar joint that has sawdust on the floor. And what works for a sort of nightclub audience, works for poetry. I insist it does not. Poetry addresses a privacy, a silence. It's written to a mortal midnight. And unless it means that, it's nothing." Finally, in an emotionally related continuation, Ciardi noticed in his final lecture that the ladies they used to get at Bread Loaf, the ones with "bluebirds in their hair and a pussywillow behind their ears," were astonishingly similar to the Beat-influenced flower children of the late 1960s, "They were [both] too beautiful to be accurate."

To his replacement, Bob Pack, Ciardi was gracious: "I received this conference from a great man [Ted Morrison], and I know I am passing it on to a great man." That said, he murmured something not completely audible that was no doubt part of the emotion of the moment. It was his goodbye to "the conference, the tradition, and all of its ghosts—one of which I hereby become."

On their way home from Bread Loaf, the Ciardis drove to Cummington, Massachusetts, to visit Dick and Charlee Wilbur, who recalled "how very upset John was." Wilbur said his old friend "was as black and discouraged as I have ever seen him be. He was feeling like an old man. He was feeling rejected by something in which he had done famously." Wilbur never forgot the injustice done to his old friend, and several years after the fact, he tried to set the record straight: "To his great credit, John did not moderate his strong-voiced assertiveness during the late 1960s, a period in which babes and sucklings were thought to know it all, and persons of authority were expected to hang beads around their necks and be concessive. It did him honor to lose the directorship of the Bread Loaf conference through a refusal to muffle his convictions and appease the times."

PART THREE

Felonious Footnotery

TWELVE

"I've gone hermit"

1972 TO 1979

"I seem to be becoming unemployed faster than any man in town."

When Ciardi got back from Bread Loaf in September 1972, one of the first letters he opened was from Smith Kirkpatrick of the English department at the University of Florida. Ciardi had been a featured speaker at UF's Writers' Conference in February and was being offered a position as distinguished poet in residence. Kirkpatrick was writing with details: Ciardi would teach two courses during the winter quarter (from 3 January to 9 March 1973) and give one public reading. The graduate-level poetry writing class, limited to twelve students, was scheduled for three hours on Wednesdays; the other class could be at whatever level Ciardi wanted, on any subject, and at any time. (It turned out to be an undergraduate class for beginning writers that met on Mondays.) His salary was set at ten thousand dollars, with another thousand thrown into the bargain for appearing at the writers' conference late in February. "The bribes," Ciardi recorded in a journal, "were sweet: the season was right, Gainesville is one of the rare places in Florida where it is possible to sit in the sun and talk about something other than seashells, and a half-dozen good friends are on the faculty there." He accepted.

The appointment caused some minor family disruptions, but by then the Ciardi household was already going in different directions anyway, mostly because of college educations. Still, the children all dutifully promised to check in for a couple of weeks with their parents in Florida—probably because they all wanted to check out Gainesville. Jonnel, living with a friend in Somerville, Massachusetts, would visit in January; Myra, living in New York because she had transferred to the Mannes College of Music, planned to take her spring break with her parents. But Benn, who was planning to visit Florida with Myra, figured on living for the rest of the time home alone, a prescription for trouble, so Judith decided she had better spend at least part of the winter with him in Metuchen. It was true that Benn had sworn he was turning over a new leaf after taking a nasty motorcycle spill at Bread Loaf (nearly severing a nerve in his right wrist, which for a time threatened the use of his hand), but it was also true that he had a mid-March court date for his second pot bust. The time did not seem quite right to Judith to leave her younger son (just turned nineteen), and her house, unguarded. Judith decided she would "commute" to Gainesville rather than stay there full time with John.

When it was over, Ciardi found that he had enjoyed the winter quarter more, perhaps, than he thought he would. He said to an interviewer in about May that he had had a "very pleasant schedule" and a "marvelous time." What was more, he had rediscovered a talent: "I remembered what the enthusiasm for teaching was about. I think I broke through and reached some students who began by resisting me." He was, in fact, already planning on a return engagement for the 1974 winter quarter, when he would offer, in addition to his graduate writing seminar, a course on Dante, which despite his expertise, he had never taught before. In fact, he had liked the University of Florida so much that he actually allowed himself the dream of staying on: "If they would make it a permanent arrangement, I would love it. I've even engaged in fantasies of buying some land outside Gainesville and raising some cattle." He was thinking of it as the fixed centerpiece in a sort of semiretirement plan.

And it truly had been pleasant. For one thing, people like Smith Kirkpatrick and department chairman Dick Green and Bread Loafer Harry Crews would stop by in the early evenings to sit on the porch, sip drinks, and talk about language and literature. For another, he was part of a regular foursome at the golf course, where he had a double handicap—twenty-one shots and 257 pounds. Then, too, he also played poker with a few locals, though not for the stakes he was used to. On most evenings, he and Smith played cards or watched television (detective programs or westerns), and, of course, Ciardi sipped his one-hundred-proof J. W. Dant bourbon. There were also plenty of parties. Generally Ciardi would stay in one place most of the evening, entertaining and holding forth, as he had done for so many years from his window seat in Treman.

The Dante course in 1974 was taught in a large auditorium, good for high enrollment, but bad for anything but straight lecture. Even worse, it was offered on Tuesday and Thursday mornings at ten o'clock, well before Ciardi was normally out of bed. With his three-hour poetry writing course on Wednesday afternoons, cotaught with John Nims, plus a two-hour graduate seminar on Thursday nights, he wisecracked to Miller Williams that he was being worked "much harder" than he had the year before. He also wrote to Gertrude Kasle that 1974 had been "much less pleasant" than 1973, although, he added, he wasn't "really complaining & would do it again if asked." Despite what was for him a very early hour, however, Ciardi did put on what one student described as a "spell-binding" performance in his Dante class. Marilyn Moriarty reported that she was "riveted" to Ciardi's lectures, which he delivered in "the sonorous voice of an august preacher reading from the Bible." Throughout the course, she remembered, Ciardi challenged the students to think how Dante could possibly outdo himself in the progression from *The Inferno* to *The Paradiso:* how could his characters "grow more and more insubstantial, more like light?" "That problem became my own," she wrote. "And then, as we approached the end of the *Paradiso,* I remember only that when I received the answer to that question, I left the auditorium with suppressed tears because Dante had in fact transcended himself and it had exceeded my imagination, for even though I had read the text and knew it in advance, Ciardi enabled me to make Dante's problem my own, and when given that solution I was both amazed and dazzled by it." On another level, watching Ciardi twice a week in class (so "exhilarated" that she "could not even entertain, as a possibility, the notion of cutting"), Moriarty thought she saw something else too: "that [Ciardi] had not escaped from his own personal and unknown anguish," that "he did not seem a happy man."

Perhaps as early as mid-March 1974, at about the end of his Dante course, Ciardi knew that he wouldn't be asked back as a regular winter-quarter faculty member of the English department. This was not going to become the "permanent arrangement" he had dreamed about. And yet it came ever so close to becoming one because Harold Hanson, a vice president at the University of Florida, saw hiring Ciardi on a regular basis as a great opportunity, at a modest expense, to enhance the school's national reputation. The possibility of adding Ciardi to the list of poets published by the university press was one attraction; another was the certainty that Ciardi would provide UF's annual writers' conference with instant stature and respectability. Hanson couldn't know what sort of prestige might accrue to the university as a result of having a prominent faculty member publish, perhaps by the university press, a series of scholarly and entertaining books on etymology, but that lingered as a possible additional benefit somewhere down the line. Hanson, with departmental support from Dick Green and Smith Kirkpatrick, had worked out the financial arrangements. Ciardi was to be guaranteed the winter quarter, to coincide with the writers' conference, on a permanent basis for ten thousand dollars per year, then for two other quarters the English department would receive twenty thousand more to attract a nationally known fiction writer and scholar. When Hanson had finally hammered out the funding and gotten the proper approvals, a dinner party was arranged at Kirkpatrick's house. After dinner, to Ciardi's surprise, Hanson made the announcement that the deal had gone through and that Ciardi would, indeed, be returning to Gainesville every winter quarter from then on. Congratulations and toasts followed deep into the night.

But new English department chairman Ward Hellstrom had other thoughts. He had never liked Ciardi personally and was eager to be influenced by a few senior faculty members who, he claimed, had come by his office to complain. Was Ciardi, they wanted to know, really the sort of man they wanted in their department? Hellstrom didn't think so and managed to keep the Ciardi appointment from ever coming to a vote. "I wasn't terribly interested in having Ciardi come," he said. "I didn't know how he'd get on with the rest of the department. He was too self-important." Publicly,

Hellstrom announced that he would rather give young people a chance than to hire "names": "I knew we could have enhanced our reputation nationally, but that wasn't important to me." But privately, Hellstrom blurted out, according to Kirkpatrick, that "no goddamn vice president is going to tell *me* who to hire!" By not taking action on the Hanson initiative, Hellstrom exercised a variety of pocket veto that effectively killed the measure, although Harold Hanson, long after he had left Florida to become vice president at Boston University, continued to maintain that it had been a "sad mistake, a severe loss to the university." In the end, according to Kirkpatrick, Hanson withdrew the entire thirty-thousand-dollar package, leaving Hellstrom to make do with the young people he wanted, but that was of no account to Ciardi, who had to face another rejection. This wasn't exactly a fantasy that turned into a nightmare, but neither would it become the wished-for cornerstone of his retirement plan.

Of course, in 1974, at age fifty-seven, John Ciardi was not quite ready for real retirement. After all, he was still supporting a big family and a big house and expensive habits like the Metuchen Country Club and Lincoln Continental cars, which was why the Florida job with its relative winter warmth and guaranteed ten thousand dollars had been attractive in the first place. That summer passed without a single lecture, as he reported on 12 September to Gertrude Kasle: "For the first time in twenty-plus years no one offered to pay me well to go to some nice place and say my nothing. I don't think I'd have gone, but hate not to be asked." And he needed the money, too, because his *Saturday Review* income had been so dramatically slashed when he followed Norman Cousins to *World* as a contributing editor. In fact, even the four thousand dollars he was getting in his new reduced role would trickle to nothing by 1977. There would be a few soul satisfactions left at *SR*, *World*, *SR/World*, and *SR* (once again), but the end result would be yet another disappointment.

The first of these soul satisfactions came when Charney and Veronis declared bankruptcy in April 1973 and begged Norman Cousins to return to *Saturday Review*. They needed him to rescue their failing financial and literary enterprise, they said, which they planned on publishing more economically by switching to a biweekly schedule. As editor once again, Cousins merged the magazines into *Saturday Review/World* and Ciardi happily resumed his "Manner of Speaking" column, another soul satisfaction. And when Cousins was named by Magazine Publishers Association the publisher of the year for rebuilding *SR/W* in 1973, the old team experienced the sweetness of another victory over Charney and Veronis, whose methods and ideas had fallen flat in the open competition of the public marketplace. But the revival of *Saturday Review* was clearly an uphill fight. Charney and Veronis had changed the highly successful *SR* format into four separate magazines, or so it seemed to a confused readership. In its new two-name format under Cousins, it seemed still to be struggling for an identity. Then, when it went back to being *Saturday Review* in 1975, more confusion followed. The magazine had struggled through what *Adweek* magazine later called "a multiple-personality disorder": it had become so "unfocused" that readers, advertisers, and staff alike were all "bewildered."

The end for Ciardi was actually in sight as early as October 1973, when short paper supplies forced columnists back to 750 words, which turned out to be a special hardship for Ciardi ("it's a lousy length for getting anything said"), as his letters back and forth to managing editor Peter Young testify. When Young wouldn't give Ciardi a little extra space, he went over his head and asked Cousins for a special "dispensation"—and got it. But about a year later, Cousins wrote with more bad news. The paper shortage had been compounded by a 115 percent increase in the cost of paper, which meant the magazine had to be cut back: all columns would be reduced to once a month. Ciardi wrote to John Stone in October 1974 with the news and added, "I seem to be becoming unemployed faster than any man in town. Ah, well. My mind to me a (dwindling) kingdom is." Ciardi continued writing his monthly column for another three years and then noticed in the newspaper that *SR* had been sold again. He wrote to Miller Williams that he didn't know if he would or would not be staying on. The new owner was Carll Tucker, who didn't especially like Ciardi's many columns given over to word histories, an interest Ciardi had by then become passionate about. Three of four such columns were returned to Ciardi in the summer of 1977 as unacceptable, but Ciardi persisted. He wrote back that readers always responded to his columns on word histories with lots of letters: "Let me propose that I do a half dozen columns about language origins as a test-run, and that the reader response be counted." It was all right, he said, if it turned out he was being fired, but he confessed "that it would be a sad divorce to leave *SR* after all these years." Sad or not, on 2 December 1977, Tucker wrote Ciardi that he was adding new columns and features "aimed at broadening out our coverage and appeal" and that he was therefore discontinuing "Manner of Speaking." It had been a "painful decision" and Ciardi had certainly been one of the magazine's "great lights," but he was out—once again. Five months later, Cousins also left. In 1982 *Saturday Review* suspended publication, was revived briefly, then sputtered out for the final time in 1986.

Sometime in 1985, Ciardi wrote about the end of his relationship with *Saturday Review* in an unpublished autobiographical fragment. He characterized Carll Tucker as "a rich semi-literate young man," who "began to tell me what I should write." This, of course, would not do: "I wished him good luck on his road and went my way." Shortly after writing these words, Ciardi commented in an interview on his twenty-one years at *SR*. He said he doubted his poetry editorship had had much of an effect on American poetry: "Does pissing into the ocean raise the sea level?" The magazine, he said, "was always relentlessly middle brow, which is to say, never at the center. Yet it had," Ciardi somewhat reluctantly admitted, "its moments." Certainly he had enjoyed his pulpit, had indulged himself in a wide variety of secular sermons, and had enjoyed the celebrity status that "Manner of Speaking" had helped him achieve. Like Bread Loaf, however, this was another love affair that ended badly.

Key West

While the University of Florida story was being played out and his *Saturday Review* career wound down, Ciardi kept up as much of his customary lecturing as he could get. One stop was at Chautauqua during the first two weeks of July 1973, where he had signed on to run the Writers' Workshop, which he fashioned after the Bread Loaf model. He was billed as Director and Instructor in Poetry (Ted Morrison was "consultant"), with the workshop members allowed to enroll either as participants or auditors. Only participants would be "entitled to an hour's manuscript conference." Auditors, on the other hand, could take part in class discussions but were not allowed to "submit their work for criticism nor take part in conferences." Ciardi had let himself think he could turn the Chautauqua Writers' Workshop into a competitor of Bread Loaf, but he was immediately disappointed with the students and never repeated the experiment. However, his Chautauqua conversations with fiction instructor Bill Decker, novelist and executive editor of the Dial Press, about word origins, cemented his interest in the subject and determined him, in Judith's recollection, to compile a dictionary of interesting words and expressions. When he returned home, Ciardi wrote at once to Miller Williams: "I've begun to jot toward a new very personal book of words, phrases, their origins, and uses." The idea, he said, "came on me at a most-miserable Chautauqua where I filled three large notebooks in two weeks of defensive withdrawal."

Public lectures were scheduled as they could be, clustered whenever possible, but no longer were they confined to six weeks in the fall and six weeks in the spring. They tended to come in spurts, and not always for the same gaudy fees he had commanded through the 1960s. In November 1973, for example, he spoke at York College in Pennsylvania and then the Woman's Club of Richmond, Virginia, for $825 and $750 respectively. But May had been busier, with a trip to the West Coast, plus two weeks in Florida, South Carolina, and Georgia. (In Georgia, Ciardi stopped off to visit cardiologist-poet John Stone, who admitted him to Emory University Hospital for a thorough, three-day checkup. He wrote to Irv Klompus that he was in better health than he had any right to be: "Good circulation, very good on cholesterol, EKG fine, lower gut polyp inconsequential, liver OK, even pulmonary function just a shade below minimal range. No emphysema. A touch of bronchitis. Really not bad for a chain smoker. If I stop eating, drinking, smoking, and breathing I could even pass for healthy.") When he got back home, however, he settled in for another period of busy indolence, as he wrote to Klompus in December: "I have been wasting my time and talent at rather high stakes Gin Rummy in the Grill Room and Sewer of the Metuchen Country Club. I am happy to say that my fellow degenerates have contributed approximately $2,000 in the last three weeks." And six months later, after wintering at the University of Florida and resettling in Metuchen, he wrote to Klompus again to say he had cleared his desk as much as possible in order to play golf, but when rainy weather arrived for a week, he "shifted to gin rummy, which has been more profitable"— fifteen hundred dollars more profitable, to be exact.

After a year or more of surgeries, Bill Sloane died of cancer in October 1974, a sad reminder of common mortality, for Ciardi's health, despite his good test results a year and a half earlier, was also beginning to falter as he suffered from obesity, alcoholism, insomnia, and impotence. He dieted for the last half of 1974 and lost thirty-five pounds, then gained it all back in 1975; he did not see his drinking as the source of any of his health problems; he took an occasional barbiturate to help him sleep if he had to be up before noon; and he dealt with his impotence with smiles that invariably hardened into grimaces. He did not show symptoms of emotional pain or depression stemming from disappointments like Bread Loaf, *Saturday Review*, or the decline of his reputation, but these had all been stresses that certainly added to his developing worries over Benn, who was becoming a preoccupying concern. Ciardi confessed to a Pittsburgh audience in February 1975, that Benn was "troublesome" and that he was "worried about him," most especially because he feared the drugs: "He was mad for rock music, and obviously you can't play rock music without marijuana. . . ." But this was Ciardi's platform voice, which enabled him to continue with a false lightheartedness. Just when he had about given up hope, he said, Benn took a turn for the better: "My worries are over. [Benn] went into business installing lawn sprinklers, became a corporation, and has *steadied*. He's been making money. I never knew how purifying an emotion avarice could be! [Big laugh.] He's not exactly a square in style, but his soul is cubic. He wants the money!" They didn't share much, this father and son, but they did have that much in common.

To encourage Benn, whose poor high school grades and worse attitude put college out of the picture, Ciardi became, as he put it, the "principal creditor" of his son's new corporation, Carnation Enterprises. He wasn't sure exactly how that had come about, he wrote to Irv Klompus, but it was mostly, he thought,

> because [Benn] started with a partner and had to buy him out. Then CPA, legal fees, insurance, etc. Come the end of October the lawn business shuts down. Will our hero make it into and through the winter[?] Will the principal creditor foreclose? Read the next exciting installment of Ty Coon. — Anyhow it is worth it to see Benn change so rapidly from Hippy-in-arms to hard-driving business man. Greed is a pure and uplifting emotion. Once he cleared $1,000 in a day—and it was a revelation unto him: his whole genetic structure surfaced in one holy burst of acquisitiveness. Glory be to greed.

A year later, Carnation Enterprises was out of business, although not before Benn had expanded into trench digging with "a new trenching-boring-mini bulldoze machine" that his father had to buy. "But what the hell," Ciardi wrote, grasping at straws, "he means to make it in business and is working his tail off." Benn, however, was more interested in making it in a rock band, a high-risk business in terms of money and drugs. He ran with a fast crowd and maintained a lifestyle that was hardly conducive to running a business during the sober hours of each day. The fact was that Benn had not steadied all that much in 1975, and he continued to be a deep concern for his father.

Ciardi fell into what he called a "psychic abyss" during the summer of 1975. He had paid the rent earlier in the year with trips to Pennsylvania, Florida, California, and Virginia. Then he had made an appearance at Salem College in North Carolina for twelve hundred dollars, plus a three-stop swing through Texas, and then finished up as commencement speaker at Madison College in Harrisonburg, Virginia. Only after all that and more was completed did he fall into his "psychic abyss," which he also characterized as his summertime "torpor." By September, however, he had sufficiently recovered to serve for eight weeks at Madison College, which had hired him to be its "Distinguished Professor" and "Eminent Scholar," according to President Ronald Carrier's letters of invitation. He collected eight thousand dollars for teaching a three-hour special topics course on *The Divine Comedy,* coaching some advanced creative writing students, and delivering six public lectures. He and Judith were even provided a house off campus, he wrote to Miller Williams, plus "a quite elegant chalet up a mountain for week-ends."

Through the fall of 1975 and all of 1976, Ciardi fell more and more into his word histories, drawn day by available day into the pure passion that he hoped would turn into a marketable book. He began collecting standard and esoteric dictionaries of English and foreign languages, plus reference books, etymological source books, folklore studies, and more, which he gradually squeezed into a side room off his attic study that became known as the dictionary room. His collection grew to such a size that in time, he was able to do almost all his research there, and though he would never have predicted it, he found himself thrilled every day by his discoveries about the roots of language, excited by the surprising freshness that came from his dusty scholarship. He who had once called himself an ironist by profession had to see the irony in his current situation: he had spent a lifetime scornful of academic types, those engaged in "felonious footnotery," as he liked to call it, and suddenly he found himself a professional etymologist—a scholar. It was the one label he had always fought to avoid, even going so far as to insist, though few took him at his word, that he was not a Dante scholar. Perhaps he consoled himself by the fact that he was not attached to any university, that he was, if anyone could possibly conceive of such a thing, a free-lance word historian.

Of course, he turned to his word histories only when he was not otherwise engaged, for lecturing in the provinces was still the way he earned a living. And he was still very good at it, as a February 1976 appearance in Yakima, Washington, testifies. His topic was "Poetry—The Mind Expanding Art," which worried the program organizers because they thought it might not appeal to enough of the eight hundred people in the audience. They were, however, as one enthusiastic listener wrote, "delightfully surprised at the excitement and entertainment that Mr. Ciardi wove so expertly into his intellectually stimulating program." He may not have been writing poetry for the reader of general culture any more, but he was still lecturing that way—much to the relief of general audiences wary of boring talks on versification. Certainly, he needed the money to operate his still-expensive household, and he found himself at age sixty having to accept as many bookings as he could get at a time when he was less popular and competing with many more poets who were crowding the lecture circuit. Cutting back was simply out of the question, although he was tiring more and wasn't feeling as well as he had just a few years earlier. Reducing his schedule was an attractive dream, nothing more. Nor was there a pension looming ahead, for he had left Rutgers before becoming vested in its retirement fund. And despite his many years of service at *Saturday Review* (writing piece work, after all, as an outside contractor), Ciardi worked without any benefits whatsoever. He wasn't hard up, of course, but when he was invited to serve as an honorary board member to the Dante University Cultural Center in mid-February 1976, he accepted but begged off sending a donation: "I feel it only fair to add that I have stumbled into financial straits and have hard work to do to restore my solvency. It is no pleasure to me to report this fact and I hope, in time, to put it behind me for a better reading of things."

Two weeks later, Gov. Brendan Byrne of New Jersey declared the second week of March as John Ciardi Week, "in honor of the poet John Ciardi of Metuchen," according to a tiny notice in the only statewide newspaper. It was surely a welcome recognition, but it is doubtful that it translated into many speaking engagements. Nor did other honors, like the setting to music of *The King Who Saved Himself From Being Saved* and *John J. Plenty and Fiddler Dan* by Philip Hagemann in 1976, or the musical settings of five poems from *Person to Person* prepared by Gerald Kemner, also in 1976. Ciardi was pleased to receive an honorary doctorate from Kean College (New Jersey) in 1977, but upset with the "dull plaque" that passed as a gold medal from the Dante Alighieri Society of Massachusetts in 1978. One honor that did capture Ciardi's imagination was the translation of several of his poems into Russian by Andrei Sergeiev, who had already published one batch of his poems in 1966 in the *Foreign Literature Monthly*. Sergeiev was putting together a new two-volume anthology and had selected half a dozen newer poems. Ciardi wrote back his thanks on 1 April 1977—and took the occasion of the letter to denounce once again "our young poets," who lacked "discipline and a true respect for the art." What they produce, he wrote, "is pap, but many young idiots, rejoicing in one another ('relating' to one another, as they call it) praise such clatter—because, as I suspect, they have never formed an attention capable of responding to the real thing." Then he quoted Yeats once again and signed off.

A different opportunity to spread the word had come on 13 January 1973, when an interviewer had asked Ciardi what significant developments he saw in recent American poetry. Oh sure, there was "a good quantity" being written, Ciardi replied, but "it divided in two ways. I would call them made and unmade poets. I think for the last ten years or so the unmade poets (by analogy to a bed, the rumpled poets) have had it all their way. I have a very strong sense that formalism is about to have a resurgence—simply because it's more satisfying." And in his "Manner of Speaking" column for 9 September 1974 ("The Future of Poetry"), Ciardi wrote that at the moment "the contest is between the poetic and the anti-poetic, between the formally written poetry and the barbaric yawp, between the 'made' and the 'unmade' poets. . . ." Just as he had done at Bread Loaf all those years, Ciardi spoke out for discipline and craft: "For no good poem is an impromptu. The impromptu is what begins to happen at about the twentieth draft." And continuing his Bread Loaf sermon, Ciardi pointed out that free verse wasn't free at all: "William Carlos Williams, our supreme master of *vers libre*, never tired of saying 'Something has to measure.'" In the end, Ciardi wrote, only one measure remained, "and only to that measure will worthwhile poetry be written: *the success of the poem is determined not by how much the poet felt in writing it, but by how much the reader feels in reading it.*"

But though Ciardi would continue to speak out here and there for the rest of his life on the recent American poets who lacked "discipline and a true respect for the art," his day-to-day attentions were with his word histories. He wrote to Miller Williams on 26 September 1976:

> I grub away. A poem or two—too soon to know if any good. Odd jobs. And words, words, words. An obsession. Why is there no verb "to occident" vis-a-vis "to orient"? Because we are descended from Sun-worshippers (Druids) who said their prayers to the sunrise. (Orienting themselves to God.) Because churches still traditionally have their main altars to the east (the worshippers face the rising sun). Because Islam still prays (even its evening prayers) facing east.

Language, goddamn it, has all of mankind's root memories in it. And though I go broke on this [wordbook] (whatever it turns out to be) I have become obsessed by it.

Then, after his signature, he couldn't resist more of the same:

> *Leviration* is the practice of marrying your brother's widow (as commanded by Hebrew law but [from] Latin *levir*, husband's brother). *Sororation* is marriage to one's ex-wife's sister. *To take a powder* (I am sure of this and no dict. seems to know it) is from "powder" in the sense of "medical dosage" (in this case a physic-powder): to take a (laxative) powder and clear (oneself) out. *Cheapskate* is at root "cheap shit" and so to *blatherskite/blatherskate*. [OE *scittan*, to shit. Scotts dialect *skite*, *skyte* a low (shitty) person.] And no dict. seems to know it. I feel like a detective.

Perhaps Ciardi meant he was going "broke" because he was investing in so many dictionaries. In fact, had he not been interested in shopping for obscure etymological reference books at Oxford University, he might have turned down Cunard Line's invitation to make an Atlantic crossing on board the *Queen Elizabeth II* in July 1976. In return for two lectures, he and Judith were given passage to England, but Ciardi was not terribly excited by the prospect of an Atlantic crossing. And once there, he complained that London was "unbearably hot" and "unbelievably expensive." A return-trip fire onboard the *QEII* put the ship in jeopardy, although in the end its only consequence for Ciardi was what he saw as an annoying series of delays getting home. The captain had announced over the ship's public-address system one morning at six o'clock that an overnight fire caused by an explosion in the boiler room had been brought under control and that, although there was no immediate danger, the ship would be limping back to Southampton on half power. When they finally got there, lines formed for airline assignments, immigration, baggage, transportation to Heathrow Airport, and such like matters. By then, however, Ciardi had lost patience. "When the British have a problem," he wrote to Williams, "their reflex is to queue up, the idiots. I did enjoy the cruise but London (hot/ drought/ British) was an oppression. After a week we rented a car and drove to Oxford, Bath, Salisbury (Stonehenge) and Southampton—which was better. But Lord God I was glad to get back. The first thing I did was shower, change and take Judith to the Country Club for dinner.—And it was a pure joy to drive an air-conditioned Lincoln, have the first proper drinks in a month, and eat broiled sea food that hadn't been destroyed by a British cook. 'Cook' is the word—the British have no chefs." Making matters worse, when the invitation was extended again in 1977, Judith took the phone call and accepted before Ciardi had a chance to say no, and so he was off on a repeat performance between 20 August and 13 September. This time, though not especially enjoyable, the trip went by without incident.

Given the fact that he hadn't wanted to go to England at all in 1977 and had had to endure the trip for Judith's sake (plus "a tiresome round of dentistry" a little earlier that left him with what he called "full choppers" and a "mouthful of hardware") Ciardi was very eager to spend his second winter (January 1978) in Key West, which had already seized his imagination as a place where he could restore his health. In December 1975, he and Judith had taken an option to buy a little house Ciardi called a "tiny shack" at 729 Windsor Lane, which they went to see in January 1976, and bought for $18,975. Ciardi then wrote invitations throughout the year to a number of friends saying that "long-distance" repairs were in progress and that he and Judith would be going to Key West for their first season in their new place in January 1977. Repairs amounting to some $8,000 weren't completed by the time they moved in, nor was the house yet fully furnished, but he wrote to Williams in March that despite the great cost of repairs and the tininess of the house, he loved it. He loved it so much, in fact, that in June 1978, he bought a second house in the same compound, this one at 717 Windsor Lane for $26,200, but this one he intended to demolish in order to build a new one. By January 1979, Ciardi was able to sit in his shack at 729 and watch the new house going up: "I spend part of every day watching it happen." He explained his reason for this second house to an old friend from his University of Michigan days: "I don't really need another house, but it sizes up as a fair investment shot, and if I can turn a capital gain every couple of years I can at least deduct vacation expenses. That rings to me like a high poetic concept."

Ciardi had been so pleased with his first two winters in Key West that he wanted to extend his 1979 visit by leaving Metuchen in November 1978. He couldn't quite convince Judith and the kids to spend Christmas in Key West, however, and they didn't approve of his spending Christmas in another state. He reported the situation ruefully to Williams on 13 December from Metuchen: "The clock is ticking and I begin to be restless about getting to Fla. Judith and the kids have a big thing about Xmas. I insist they could learn to adjust their nostalgias to a fat check sent from Key West, which, if they insisted (without being urged) they could use to fly down and carol under the palms. But I was born to lose this one." When he finally got to Key West to watch the erection of his new house "at an over-run on the estimate," Ciardi bought still another property. He wrote triumphantly on 30 March to Williams of his latest real estate speculation: "It adjoins the lot on which I am building and when the idiot who owns it let it be offered for $75,000 I leapt. I'm damned if I can't get $125,000 for it next year—and maybe more. . . . Among other things it makes Key West a business venture and I propose to bill Judith's and my vacations to the IRS at about $70 a day, per diem. How's that for sweet poesy?"

Indeed. The sweet pleasures of poetry and the sweet pleasures of money-making had long been linked inextricably for John Ciardi. He was unique in that his personal fortune had been built on his poetry writing—plus cottage industries like lecturing, column writing, performing on television, and so on—and he'd been remarkably successful at everything. The fact that he was able to pay in cash for all three Key West real estate transactions, some $130,000 plus the cost of the home being built, shows clearly that even with a substantially reduced annual income, Ciardi had sizable cash reserves, the result of shrewd investments as well as his love of taking stock market gambles that left Irv Klompus, who had long served as Ciardi's financial advisor, shaking his head half in disapproval and half in wonder at Ciardi's nerve. He'd been Lucky John when it came to his stock portfolio, just as he had been Lucky John when he left the army in 1945 with approximately $12,000 taken in one wild week of crap shooting.

But if Ciardi had decided to invest in Key West property, it was because he had fallen in love with the beauty and climate of the place (doubly attractive when compared to New Jersey winters), plus the isolation of the fenced-in compound and the core of literary friends living nearby. It rapidly became his haven from the world, a place for retirement. He even enjoyed the tiring eight-day or longer drive from Metuchen to Key West (about 1,500 miles), with stops he would arrange ahead of time with friends in Washington, Charlottesville, Atlanta, Gainesville, or Hollywood (Fla.)—among other stops that were less predictable. And once in Key West, he especially enjoyed his garden, which he described in January 1978: "There [is] a wall of green privacy all around us. The avocado tree that looked sick [last year] had healed and become a canopy. The sickly passion flower vines had become a jungle between us and the signora's [sic] trash cans. One vine had caught her avocado and was dangling passion flowers from ten feet overhead. . . . Glorious." Most of all, however, Ciardi enjoyed the company: Dick and Charlee Wilbur, Jimmy Merrill and David Jackson, John and Barbara Hersey, John Malcolm Brinnin, Peter and Eleanor Taylor, Ralph and Fanny Ellison, and a host of others. Key West was still the winter home of American writers.

"formally dazzling"

It comes as no surprise that Ciardi, even in a state of semiretirement in the 1970s was turning out good books. *The Little That Is All*, his first book of lyric poems to come out since *This Strangest Everything* in 1966, was published in 1974. The next year came *Fast & Slow: Poems for Advanced Children and Beginning Parents* and a second edition of the enormously successful and influential textbook *How Does a Poem Mean?*. After years of wrangling with various publishers over rights, Ciardi was finally able to get two hardcover editions of his translation of the entire *Divine Comedy* published in 1977. Then for a lark he published a book of limericks with Isaac Asimov in 1978, and then yet another book of lyrics, *For Instance*, in 1979. And by 1979, too, Ciardi was nearly ready to publish the first volume of his word histories, *A Browser's Dictionary, and Native's Guide to the Unknown American Language*. Ciardi liked speaking of his "indolence," "torpor," and "psychic abyss" during this period, but as he had regularly done in the past, he vastly understated his industriousness.

The Little That Is All came out in August 1974, only two months before Bill Sloane's death, and was the last of eleven Ciardi books issued by Rutgers University Press over a twenty-year period. It had been a profitable relationship for both sides, with Ciardi electing to stay at the press because of his love for Sloane as well as his satisfaction with the press's production and sale of his poetry. Ciardi advised Miller Williams in about September 1977 to consider a university press for his books, too, because university presses kept books in print longer than commercial houses, a big plus according to Ciardi. And he really had been happy with the sales figures: "I haven't had a book with Rutgers that hasn't sold over 5,000 over the years. Curiouser yet, Rutgers always advance-sells something over 2,000. I wonder if a commercial press could do better—or as well." However, even though his sales were good, he said, he was still only number two at RUP, with the best-selling book on their list being a tome on the artificial insemination of domestic animals. This gave rise to an increasingly characteristic (and painful) quip on his impotence: "I'm not sure how I feel about being runner-up to a quick-frozen fuck, but I guess it's better than no fucking at all. Or maybe I'm being nostalgic."

Struck no doubt by the failure of *Lives of X* to catch the attention of book reviewers and prize-givers, Ciardi abandoned the epic-sized narrative structure of his autobiography and retreated into its exact opposite, *The Little That Is All*. Here he would indulge in a kind of demystified Emersonianism that was filtered through the Ciardi sense of irony into the concept he called the "unimportant poem": the little things in life, everyman's life, may seem slight, but they are, in the end, all there is. Ciardi captured some of his point in "An Apology for Not Invoking the Muse," where he brimmed over with good humor about unpretentious poetry while criticizing by implication the bad poetry that was characterized by the self-conscious high seriousness of poets weighted down by their messages. In the poem, Erato, the muse of lyric and love poetry, had stopped him in the midst of composing a poem to chastise him for not invoking her. They argued about it, a lovers' spat, with Ciardi apologizing, but hoping she would understand that he was just writing an "unimportant poem," one hardly worth her jealous anger. He tried to smooth-talk Erato, calling her "honey," "darling," "angel," and "beloved," all the while sidestepping her accusations that he had permanently abandoned her. He was not, after all, writing the *Aeneid*, he said, and he had not wanted to disturb her over such a small poem. Besides, he had wanted his human qualities to show through, no matter how slight the resulting effort turned out to be: "I thought I could say this little on my own, / the way it happens to us in our smallness." Later, after Erato had gone, he said,

> I read what I had written, and despaired.
> How had I dared imagine I might dare
> be only what I am?
>
> > and yet . . .
>
> > > and yet . . . .

In another poem, "Minus One," Ciardi wrote about the randomness of death, a subject that had troubled him deeply on Saipan and which presented itself this time when a hawk swept down to kill an unsuspecting sparrow sitting on a wire with six other sparrows. He asked in stanza two:

> Is there a kismet
> the size of one of seven
> sparrows? Is it
> written before heaven,
> swami, in the mystic
> billion ungiven
> Names? Is there a loving statistic
> we are motes of?
> Whatever remembers us, finally, is enough.
> If anything remembers, something is love.

This was the poem Edward Krickel had in mind when he wrote in high praise that Ciardi was like Hardy or Frost in that he could "look at something as ordinary as the death of a bird and reach all the way to philosophical meditations without being sentimental or ridiculous." In fact, at age fifty-eight, Ciardi found himself being credited by the few critics who were still bothering to notice as being a wise man: one said he'd earned a "hard-won wisdom" in his new book; another said he had emerged "as a voice of wisdom"; and a third wrote that this was "mellow, vintage Ciardi, a book steeped in his own difficult wisdom." And "Minus One" was also the later poem Richard Wilbur cited to prove that "at any time . . . it was in [Ciardi's] power to be formally dazzling."

The Little That Is All is indeed a strong book, containing many more good poems than weak ones, and adding at least a dozen excellent poems to the Ciardi canon: "Addio," "Minus One," "A Conversation with Leonardo," "Washing Your Feet," "An Apology for Not Invoking the Muse," "On the Orthodoxy and Creed of My Power Mower," "In the Hole," "Requisitioning," "A Poem for Benn's Graduation from High School," "An Emeritus Addresses the School," "Generation Gap," and "Memo: Preliminary Draft of a Prayer to God the Father." Among other things, the poems are about his mother's death and his own aging, about the differences between Leonardo's world and our own, about suburban rituals and the commonplace overlay of religious language on secular life, and about the generation gap as Ciardi saw it large and small—on the national scene and at home.

Buried in almost the exact middle of the book is "In the Hole," which, despite its placement, became one of Ciardi's favorite poems. He called it "an allegory of writing a poem." Audiences loved it too, laughing out loud at the appropriate times, and sensing by the end that more was afoot than they at first had thought. Ostensibly about a man who had some time on his hands and decided to dig a hole in his backyard, the poem becomes an amusing set of surmises as to what the hole is for: "My neighbors / are purposeful about the holes in their lives." In turn, the neighbors learned the hole was for sod, sweat, and fishing worms. Even the pink policeman, Brewster Diffenbach, came by to ask the poet if he had a "building permit," although he could see perfectly well that this was simply a hole, nothing more. In the end, however, the poet came to understand himself better than he had when he had begun digging:

> And there *was* a purpose. This is my last house.
> If all goes well, it's here I mean to die.
> I want to know what's under it. One foot more
> might have hit stone and stopped me, but I doubt it.
> Sand from an old sea bottom is more likely.
>
> Or my fossil father. Or a mud rosary.
> Or the eyes of the dog I buried south of Jerusalem
> to hide its bones from the Romans. Purpose
> is what a man uncovers by digging for it.
> Damn my neighbors. Damn Brewster Diffenbach.

Audiences regularly asked Ciardi if he had actually dug a hole in his backyard, which, of course, he had not, but he *had* written poetry all his life and could see the correspondences, for with poetry as with holes, "Purpose / is what a man uncovers by digging for it."

The last poem in the book is "Memo: Preliminary Draft of a Prayer to God the Father," which contains a weary litany of family problems all contained within a prayer of thanks to a God Ciardi did not believe in. He'd been driving north in the rain from Atlanta, where he'd given a speech, and had stopped at a motel in Towson, Maryland. Addressing God as "Sir," Ciardi thanked him for the "expensive car" that is heavy and safe. And then he thought of his family, stanza by stanza, and thought about their expenses that bound him to the women's clubs he visited along a seemingly endless highway. Judith was in Missouri tending to her aging parents and running up bills for airline tickets, car rentals, and credit card purchases; Benn was busted for pot again and needed a reliable lawyer; Jonnel had wrecked his car and needed a new one; and Myra needed voice lessons and a piano for her musical studies in New York. To pay for all these expenses, Ciardi thanked God for "the road, the bad lunches, and the pleasant ladies"—for "a tour in April" and an invitation to speak "in Claremont in February."

> At times, I confess, it is slightly depressing. The ladies
> who are only slightly brittle and slightly silly, ·
>
> but on any reasonable scale bright and admirable,
> depress me slightly. But so do my own bad habits
> when I am left to them freely. I do not complain:
> I describe. I am grateful but imperfect and, therefore,
> imperfectly grateful. It is all good enough
>
> and I thank you, sir. If you are ever in Towson,
> I can recommend the high level mediocrity
> of the Quality Inn Motel just off the Beltway.
> It is only slightly embalmed. It is clean and quiet.
> With the TV on you do not hear the rain.

Ciardi announced his depression twice, and underscored "slightly" by repeating it five times in the last twelve lines, often enough for a reader to understand his true meaning, that he was much more than slightly depressed. No, he wasn't complaining, and he was grateful, though "imperfectly" so, and yes, his life was "good enough." But in the dreariness of a rainy night in a motel on the Beltway near Towson, his life did, indeed, seem depressing. And just maybe he used the occasion of this poem to describe a weightier and more pervasive soul sadness than he had actually stated. After all, he had gradually come to see that his position in mid-century American poetry had peaked in the 1960s and was thereafter in noticeable (some would say free-fall) decline; moreover, as he faced up to family problems, reduced income, and ill-health, John Ciardi had ample cause for his depression, although it was a condition he was able to hide most of the time even from his closest friends.

Clearly Ciardi was happier writing children's verse, although the title poem of *Fast & Slow* (1975), the first one in the new book, was about the slow "old crow" who knew a lot more that the fast "young crow," a leftover piece of Bread Loaf business that he would never get completely free of. In this fable for children, however, Ciardi was able to make the eminently sensible point that the older generation still had a lot to teach the younger—and children were not likely to protest that he had as much to learn from them as they could learn from him. But even with this more or less unobtrusive social criticism of the times leading the book off, the poems are wonderful excursions into childhood. The first copies of *Fast & Slow* (together with the second half of his three-thousand-dollar advance) reached Ciardi in early March, coinciding roughly with the NCTE announcement that "Mummy Slept Late and Daddy Fixed Breakfast" was the favorite poem of fourth-to-sixth graders surveyed in 1972. It was a dual elation.

By early May, however, Ciardi was complaining to Houghton Mifflin that they weren't doing enough to promote and sell the book. They had, they said, "presented" the book in December to their trade sales force and sent out two hundred review copies "to major review media." And they were placing what they called "single title ads" in *Horn Book, Saturday Review*, and *Top of the News* (a publication of the American Library Association)—plus larger multi-title ads in *Publishers Weekly* and *School Library Journal*. Ciardi, who took to saying about this time that he enjoyed writing for children because they constituted a jury that could not be rigged, was nonetheless earning a living by his pen, which made him ever-critical of publishers whose business decisions cost him actual dollars earned. But Ciardi's complaints in this case yielded little more than a special press release from the publisher that no doubt seemed to him a day late and a dollar short. Furthermore, it was hard to be pleased by lukewarm reviews in the newspapers, like the one in the *New York Times* that said Ciardi was "worth your attention"; or the one in the *Boston Globe* that said the book "makes delightful reading aloud"; or the one in the *San Francisco Chronicle* that called the book "lively, lilting"; or the one by the children's Media Review in the *Puget Sound Council* that said children would like the "predictability of the rhyme patterns" and probably miss the "subtle didacticism" of the title poem. He was surely disappointed as well when Houghton Mifflin returned his follow-up book, which was to have been titled *The Dance on Mud Hole Street*, in August 1977 because "the collection as a whole just doesn't seem strong enough to suggest that we could successfully support a publishing offer." A handful of the poems were published in *Cricket* magazine, but only one found its way (with changes) into Ciardi's next book of children's verse, *Doodle Soup*, which did not appear until 1985—a full decade after *Fast & Slow* and not even a year before his death.

By March 1975, too, Ciardi received the second edition of *How Does a Poem Mean?* from Houghton Mifflin, a book he had almost completely given over to Miller Williams, as co-author, to bring up to date. When it arrived in the mail, Ciardi wrote Williams to say it looked "damn fine" to him, especially seeing their names linked on the title page. The truth was, however, that he was very much relieved to have the book out at all because it, too, had become a problem for him. Houghton Mifflin had written in about May 1972 that if the book was to remain on their textbook list, it would need a major overhaul (despite sales that came to over three thousand in the last half of 1973 alone). But by 25 June 1972, the summer Ciardi was fired from Bread Loaf, he seemed to have run out of ideas and patience with the prospect of remodeling the textbook for a broader market appeal. Ciardi knew, for example, that Vachel Lindsay's "The Congo (A Study of the Negro Race)," regardless of its usefulness as an example of one kind of musical patterning, had to be deleted as socially unacceptable. But it was such a good example and the book seemed to work so well with all its parts intact that

Ciardi found the prospect of tampering with the individual poems almost more than he could bear—and yet he knew it made sense to bring the book up to date both because it was such an excellent text and because it continued to make money for him and the company. And so on 25 June, Ciardi wrote to Williams: "Project. Would you have any interest in joining me on a re-do of *How Does a Poem Mean?* The book has had a good run—over 300,000 copies, but is becoming dated (so saith Houghton Mifflin). They have sent various instructors here and there to report on their feelings about it. Some of the reports make sense. Some don't. I will not, for instance, include 'poems' by Bob Dylan because some asshole instructor thinks that would grab the young." He understood the need to drop "The Congo," but the whole project was maybe beyond what he could do: "What I realize is that I'm out of touch with these college generations. You, on the other hand, are with them."

On 26 November 1973, Ciardi wrote again to Williams, by then on-board as co-author, and confessed his frustration with the work that needed to be done: "I am surprised myself to discover how much I detest revision long after the fact (it's like exhuming bodies). . . . If I said I would try, I know that day by day I would make compulsive excuses to push it aside and let it die on its own." There were a number of insignificant issues to be resolved, like the number and quality of study questions, for example, but the most important and stickiest by far was Houghton Mifflin's request, made through editor David Helmstadter, that the book contain more poetry by black writers. This seemed to Ciardi like another facet of the criticism he had heard at Bread Loaf and to which he was developing a marked sensitivity. "Concerning the minorities question," Helmstadter wrote in November 1973, it was important to include "at least a few selections by black poets and poets of other minority groups as well." This, he said, was driven by the company's sense of "responsibility," not by "crass commercialism." Ciardi, however, was suspicious of such rhetoric and had always been quick to anger whenever a discussion of poetry was redirected from the poetry itself to such nonliterary considerations as gender and race. With respect to this aspect of the revisions needed, Ciardi went on in his 26 November letter to Williams:

> Aside from Langston Hughes' "Early Evening Quarrel,"
> I don't know any black poets that I can read for selfish pleas-

ure. There is some lovely stuff in M. B. Tolson, especially his "Harlem Gallery," but those same bastards [his critics] are going to insist that Tolson is too difficult. As a black man he made the terrible mistake of becoming learned and his allusions are bound to confuse the illiterate. It's possible that something, if only an excerpt, could be culled from Countee Cullen and maybe from James Weldon Johnson's "God's Trombones." (I had thought of substituting something from that book in place of Vachel Lindsay's "Congo.") Whether or not there is any merit in these thoughts, I suspect that Helmstadter could be satisfied by the inclusion of say a dozen or fifteen short poems by the black rhetoricians. Do you think you could dig up that many, along with some ABC questions for discussion? I have tried and pulled a total blank. One possibility might be to go with the relative formlessness of the black yawp and to pair it with more shapely poems for class discussion.

Ciardi made the same suggestion directly to Helmstadter on 14 December, effectively putting the "minorities question" in Miller Williams's hands. Ciardi had never been and was not then a racist and could have proven it by pointing to his thirty-year public and private commitment to fighting racial prejudice, as for example his 1961 essay in *SR*, "Jim Crow is Treason." But for Ciardi poetry in the present case was the overriding issue at hand, not social justice. He believed in 1973 what he had believed in 1958, when he had written to Gloria Oden: "There can be no Negro poetry, nor white poetry, nor any but human poetry."

Ciardi's own art had been praised in a November 1973 article in one of the scholarly journals, which may have salved his year-old Bread Loaf wounds a little. He wrote to thank the author, who could not have known about the setbacks Ciardi had been suffering, asking for "another tearsheet or two": "I am quite set up by it and would love to send copies to a couple of people I care about." And his spirits also improved when the final wrangling over hardcover rights to his translation of *The Divine Comedy* bore fruit in 1977. New American Library had transferred the hardcover rights (which Ciardi insisted they did not own) in 1971 to its subsidiary, World Publishers, which then sent them to Mason & Lipscomb, which sent them to Mason/Charter. Ciardi, of course, was angry over the original transfer to World and the long delay at Mason & Lipscomb, which had acquired the rights without ever telling him. By September 1974 (after Ciardi threatened legal action if the company did not schedule publication), M & L moved the project forward, intending to use the original artwork by Jacob Landau commissioned by World for an initial fee of $2,500. But by the end of the month, Ciardi called the deal off. He next tried to get Houghton Mifflin interested in November, but they declined because, they said, the book would be too expensive at $22.50 to earn a profit. Then in the summer of 1975, he tried to get the University of Pittsburgh Press interested, again without success. Just before Christmas, however, The Franklin Library (part of the Franklin Mint Company) received Ciardi's permission to issue a deluxe limited edition with the Gustave Doré illustrations. The book was published (at $40.00) in August 1977 and sent to subscribers as part of the company's "100 Greatest Books of All Time" series. For Ciardi, who had never wanted his text to be accompanied by the famous nineteenth-century illustrations of Doré, it was nonetheless a satisfying moment to see his long labor in a leather binding with royal blue silk moire end papers, gold leaf pages, and a blue ribbon place marker. It was also satisfying to receive $5,000 as a flat fee for permissions—and then to receive another $3,000 in royalties that he hadn't even known he was getting.

Ciardi had had to buy out the rights held by Mason/Charter for $2,500 in order to give free title to the Franklin Library, which meant that he could also go back to searching for a trade publisher for *The Divine Comedy*. In April 1976, he wrote to Harper and Row granting them permission (for $2,210) to reprint some three thousand lines in a book they were planning on Botticelli's drawings and asked if they might be interested in the trade edition, pointing out that the paperback was in its twenty-seventh or twenty-eighth printing and selling about a quarter million copies a year on college campuses. They were apparently not impressed, for Ciardi pitched the book again on 5 January 1977 to Eric Swenson of W. W. Norton. This time, finally, the answer was yes, and a contract was mailed on 17 February with an advance of $3,000. The book was immediately put on the Norton schedule and came out in the fall, in time for the Christmas trade at $14.95. And there was more good news— Swenson was interested in everything else Ciardi was doing, with the exception of children's books, a line that Norton had discontinued. Swenson was particularly interested in Ciardi's poetry: "We are rather proud of our poetry and the success we have had with it, all things being relative—and would like to number you among the poets all of whose works we publish. . . ." By mid-April, Swenson was showing an interest in Ciardi's word book too, and then, on 2 May, Swenson wrote that he was interested in a book of limericks Ciardi said he had "on hand."

The limerick book turned into a collaboration with Isaac Asimov, each contributing twelve dozen poems, which provided the title, *Limericks: Too Gross*. By March 1978 the poems of both writers were delivered and contracts signed—with a twenty-five-hundred-dollar advance sent to each, a timely check for Ciardi: "It comes like a transfusion at the critical point of an IRSectomy scheduled for April 14." The book was released in the fall, again in time for the Christmas trade, but advance sales of over eighty-five hundred put the book out of stock on 31 October. On 16 April 1979, Ciardi wrote to Lew Turco: "Among this world's jokes would you believe that the limerick book I did with Isaac Asimov . . . sold 12,000 copies by mid-Feb? Crazy—but I love it." And on 17 November 1979, two years after the release of *The Divine Comedy* and a year after *Limericks: Too Gross* had been issued, Ciardi wrote with wry humor to Swenson about the sales figures for both books: "I loved that last royalty statement: *Limericks* $12,000, *The Divine Comedy* $250."

Ciardi did indeed put together a book of poems for Norton in the spring 1978, which they accepted in September over the strenuous objections of their poetry advisor, and published in 1979 as *For Instance*. (For irony's sake, the advance was $250, one-tenth of his share of the advance on the limerick book.) The poetry advisor, who signed her name "Sherry" and had the initials SAH, said she was "wholly unadmiring" of the poems, which seemed to her less like poems than "little prose vignettes" that were "fairly self-evident." There wasn't enough metaphor for her taste, and she didn't like the language, which she called "clumsy." She couldn't follow some of them and thought some of what she could follow was very nearly "grouchy." The poems were "leaden," she wrote, and had "no merit." Then in a grand finale to her twenty-one lines of evaluation, Sherry A. H. wrote: "All I can say is that I see no intrinsic value in these, no life, no interest, no passion, no illumination of the human condition."

There was some merit to Sherry A. H.'s analysis because *For Instance* does have a noticeable number of poems that are little narratives, poetic shorts as it were, that do occasionally fall into prosiness. She did not see, however, that the new book was a continuation of Ciardi's retreat into the "unimportant poems" he had published (to excellent effect) in *The Little That Is All*. Nor could she see that this retreat was a development that had grown from personal and professional setbacks, that they were, in a sense, the way Ciardi found to press on in his life and in his poetry. This was the form and the language Ciardi had developed as he self-consciously and defensively backed away from the national poetry limelight. Moreover, Sherry A. H.'s position and Ciardi's situation were captured perfectly by his October 1979 Toronto book tour for *For Instance*. An arts organization there had arranged a "book launching" and had set him up in a posh hotel and squired him around town for a series of radio, television, and press interviews, but when the actual reading took place, only twenty-six people showed up. He wrote to his friend George Garrett with good-natured disappointment: "My ghost trod a real red carpet up to no throne."

Reviewers like Dana Gioia and Reed Whittemore could see just how out of touch Ciardi had become by 1979, as outdated as his big Cadillacs and Lincolns after the 1973 gas crisis. (In April 1978, he traded in his Lincoln and bought a mid-size Plymouth for Judith and a slightly heavier Chrysler LeBaron for himself.) Ciardi knew how things stood, that his reputation was, as he put it in a July 1978 letter to Garrett, "partly that of a noisy fraud—'a cultural headwaiter.'" But when it came time to say again that he'd been lucky and had no cause to complain, he added a few words that revealed the pain he felt. "I've told myself I have no cause to complain, that I've been egregiously rewarded for doing my own thing. That should be enough for a man, but I confess my [ego]ape doesn't like it. Even *he* hasn't ever meant to be a fraud—except when he was trying to maneuver girls into bed. And by now, having all but achieved the dignity of impotence, that is in the past."

Sherry A. H. had said in her report that "people who ought to know have found [Ciardi] praiseworthy in the past," but she found the new collection so bad that she wondered if "perhaps he has lost the gift." *Publishers Weekly* reported in what they may have taken for praise that the book was "crammed full of suburban wisdom and humor" and that Ciardi was "an old-timer" who was "frank and familiar, fluent and funny." But Dana Gioia, in a review that *Poetry* did not publish until 1982, was no doubt right when he wrote that it was "fashionable to consider John Ciardi a poet long past his prime" and that it was actually dangerous to defend him: "anyone who would venture to defend his recent work in print risks being labeled hopelessly out of touch." Ciardi himself had made it hard on "any would-be defender," wrote Gioia, because "for years he has published no new volume in which the bad poems do not greatly outnumber the good." He then commented on the only two poems in *For Instance* that were "strong, memorable, and unmistakably personal": "Roman Diary: 1951" and "Firsts." Reed Whittemore in his Chicago *Tribune* review in December 1979, wrote more sympathetically: "Ciardi's reputation has declined in recent years, not, I think, because of any marked change in his artistic direction, but because of the change in the direction of poetry itself. Poetry has gone off to make a kind of fin-de-siecle career of mental lapses . . . , and since Ciardi's lapse has not occurred he is slightly passe." Whittemore wrote that the "diminished thing" Ciardi "discovered life to be" was "worth writing poems about" but guessed that Ciardi was nonetheless unfashionable because he was a "lofty generalizer, trying to make sense of the ruck somehow. The sense he makes is usually offbeat—he is a master of anti-platitudes—but it is sense," and making sense was simply out of fashion. The whole thing was becoming clear. Without a broad network of students, without an academic base of operations, without the directorship of the Bread Loaf Writers' Conference, without his weekly *Saturday Review* column, and without doing anything more substantial than entertaining women's clubs and college audiences for fat fees, John Ciardi had cut himself off from the community of poets emerging in the 1970s. And *For Instance* did not win the respect of that community.

Despite the dismissive attitude taken by some reviewers and the apologies and explanations made by some critics, *For Instance* did add a few fine poems to the Ciardi canon, like the ones mentioned by Gioia, plus "Alec," "Birthday," "The Sorrow of Obedience," "Trying to Feel Something," "Bashing the Babies," "No White Bird Sings," and "The Lung Fish." Seven of the new poems were published in *Poetry* (edited by John Frederick Nims, who began his second tenure there on 1 January 1978) in the August 1978 and March

1979 numbers, thus marking the first time Ciardi had been in those pages since Daryl Hine had taken over as editor in April 1969. Hine, Ciardi wrote Nims, had asked him not to submit poems so that younger writers could be stressed, not quite that blatantly, according to Ciardi, but nearly so. "All this has been a sadness unto me. I shrugged as one must and told myself everyone has to take his losses and that I had plenty else to think about. Now . . . I realize I really have felt more strongly than I have admitted about being shut out of *Poetry* and the long happy association I had had with it." In another letter to Nims, Ciardi wrote that when Hine edited the magazine, he felt "shut out of an important house by usurpers. You bring it around to being home again."

Most touching of the poems in *For Instance* may be "Being Called" because it showed Ciardi was finally fully aware of his own dwindling position in the world of modern American poetry. He felt he was like the movie queen, "who lost her looks but kept old reels / for private viewing" trying to remember "as if we still were / what we remember." Then he fell back on the refrain he needed to repeat over and over again in his last years, that he couldn't complain:

> Not that I hurt,
> or only a little, of some imagined
> honesty. I am in Florida,
> a February rose nodding
>
> over my toast and coffee in a soft
> expensive breeze I can afford
> in a sun I buy daily, gladly,
> on a patio under a lime tree.
> There is a pleasantness. With luck
>
> it is a kindly long trip down
> from cramming winter to this basking
> knowledge of nothing. And from Miami
> on the make-do transistor, a cracked
> wrong quaver that began as Mozart.

Always alert to Ciardi's best qualities, Richard Wilbur called this a "boldly sad piece about how hard it is for aging men to admit that they are not what once they were." He added that the poem is "rueful" in its "portrayal of declining powers": "What balances the rue-fulness, of course, is the good metaphor of the southward journey and that brilliant image of the quavering transistor. The fact is that John wrote well to the end."

But more and more toward the end, Ciardi was wrapped up in his word histories. In February 1977, he wrote to Eric Swenson of his new obsession: "I've gone hermit and weary of chasing." To Miller Williams, he wrote on 3 May 1978, "Have been hacking away at the Browser's Dict. Harmless drudgery, Johnson called it. Or felonious footnotery. But the book is coming." By 1979, he was totally captured by it. He wrote to one old friend in May, "I become an increasingly private person and find myself wishing I had made it sooner to this bent hermitage. I never suspected I had a taste for grubbing among dusty old footnotes, but I have; it is what I do with my days, and I am happy at [it]." To another in June, he wrote, "I have become an obsessive wordnapper, lost in felonious footnotery as to secret drinking. I suppose a binge of that sort of thing is all right but this may be on the way to becoming not only a ruling but a blinding passion. . . . It's beautiful stuff, but I keep telling myself I need to moderate—and don't." And in October he wrote to yet another friend, "I have become some sort of immoderate recluse. No matter what else I should be doing, I find myself starting every day with etymologizing, then looking up to find the day is gone. . . . I love the work obsessively and am at the same time afraid it is con-suming me. Sanity says I should ration my hours more wisely, but obsession wins."

What worried Ciardi most, although not enough to stop, was that he was stealing precious moments from his poetry to work on his scholarship. On 13 December 1978, he complained to Williams that he was spending up to ten days at a time working on word his-tories, never even getting out of the house. He was so engrossed in his work, he said, that he had become more compulsive than usual in his unhealthy habits: "I smoke too much, drink too much, and am getting to be plain obese." But most worrisome was that he felt himself getting "stale." "Something about these felonious footnotes chokes Erato." Then, two weeks later, he wrote to Williams again: "I begin to feel a danger in the dictionary. It has become obsessive. And it may be drying me out. . . . One must what one must, I sup-pose. I can no longer *not* etymologize, but I must strike a balance somewhere. The dictionary is much to me, but secondarily." Two months later, in late February 1979, he wrote to George Garrett, "My one sadness is that my absorption on the word-book has choked off all else, and that I have come up with nothing but false starts and dead ends since I got to FLA and chained myself to the typewriter."

Then, on 12 March 1979, he finished typing the entries for volume one of *The Browser's Dictionary*. He and his Windsor Court neighbors, Dick Wilbur and John Hersey, went out to the sun deck and popped a bottle of champagne to celebrate. W. W. Norton had decided in June 1978 not to publish the book, a mistake that Eric Swenson regretted later, and Ciardi had placed it instead with Harper & Row, which had declared itself more "reference minded" than Norton, which wanted something more "chatty" than a straight dictionary. Stressing the word *browser*, Ciardi saw his latest work as "a pick-up and lay-down book . . . , interesting and readable." His aim was simply "to give each word treated its character."

Although Ciardi's success at joining the very small number of book-publishing etymologists is remarkable in its own right, this latest achievement was emblematic of his entire career. Time after time, he had managed to focus and refocus his genius for language in such a way as to be professionally, artistically, and commercially successful. His professionalism was always challenged by some perhaps jealous critics, whether the subject was Dante, children's verse, or word histories, but in fairness, Ciardi never claimed professional status, merely that of the passionate amateur devoted to the art of *The Divine Comedy*, the happy play of rhythmical language for children, and the pursuit of the root histories of English words. What grated on Ciardi's critics was that he was able in every instance to turn his passion into profit. If university professors with Ph.D.'s (specialists whose publications were for earning tenure and academic status rather than cash) considered Ciardi an interloper, he would cope with their backbiting and continue with his work. He would not be turned away by "professionals" who couldn't match his productivity, either in quality or quantity. With *The Browser's Dictionary*, John Ciardi had found yet another way to turn lead into gold—and further torment his critics.

The dictionary, however, wasn't the only way Ciardi found to turn dusty etymological scholarship into spendable income. In

October 1974, he had asked Norman Cousins if he knew of anyone who would be interested in carrying a daily, syndicated paragraph on words (to be called "A Word to the Wise"); but the lead
Cousins provided at the *Los Angeles Times* came to nothing. Of
course, he continued writing occasional word history columns at
Saturday Review, too often apparently for the taste of Carll Tucker,
who factored this into his December 1977 decision to discontinue
"Manner of Speaking." But then in about September 1976, Ciardi
discovered a way to be as chatty as W. W. Norton had wanted him
to be: he proposed a five-minute program on National Public Radio
to be called "A Word in Your Ear." Ken Myers of NPR liked the
idea and pitched it to the assistant director of his department, who
would have to pass it on, if approved, to the department director
and then to a vice president. Then, if all went well, they would have
to get "development" money for a few pilot programs, which would
then be used as the centerpiece of an application to the National
Endowment for the Humanities for funding. Many a good idea gets
strangled in that much red tape, but "A Word in Your Ear" gradually got its approvals, funding, and on-air time slot. The pilot programs were taped in April 1977; more were taped in July; and by
late December Ciardi wrote to Eric Swenson: "I have begun a radio
series with Nat. Pub. Radio, the program to be called A WORD IN
YOUR EAR, a series of talks about words. If the funding comes
through firmly, I will be doing a daily spot on c. 100 NPR outlets
across the country." It did and Ciardi's spot soon became one of the
regular weekly features of *Morning Edition*, which eventually
expanded into 220 markets.

The decade of the 1970s had not been kind to John Ciardi
in many ways, but even as some doors closed, new ones were opening. The movement from a half-hour network television show in
1961–62 to a five-minute weekly radio program in 1978, may have
capsulized Ciardi's decline in one sense, but he hadn't surrendered
his principles or his hard work, and he did manage to continue as
a voice in American letters, albeit a diminished one, into the 1980s.

THIRTEEN

"A man learns how to die."

1980 TO 1986

Stroke

On 3 January 1980, Ciardi attended the White House reception hosted by Jimmy and Rosalynn Carter called "A Salute to Poetry and American Poets." The guest list of more than a hundred poets and their spouses had been prepared in part by John Nims as editor of *Poetry*, and Ciardi, despite his devalued stock (at least as reckoned by many of the younger poets), occupied a prominent position during the celebration. Twenty-one very short readings were scattered throughout seven White House rooms that afternoon; Ciardi, sharing the Blue Room platform with Gwendolyn Brooks and Richard Eberhart, read three new poems from *For Instance*. But notwithstanding his featured position, Ciardi hadn't been looking forward to so many hours of socializing with poets on such a grand scale. In fact, he had always liked relatively small parties where his wit and intelligence were more naturally showcased, and he customarily broke down larger gatherings by sitting off to the side playing cribbage or checkers or gin rummy, sipping a drink, and dominating the conversation. He had little or no taste for the sort of splashy party the Carters were throwing and said he would not have attended at all had it not been for Judith's insistence. At that, he would put up with it only because he and Judith were scheduled to be in Washington anyway (en route to Key West and their newly built house) in order for him to tape some fifty word programs for National Public Radio.

But when January third finally arrived, Ciardi was more than ordinarily grumpy. He complained loudly before, during, and after the reception. For one thing, there was only wine to drink. "My God," X. J. Kennedy (and nearly everyone else) heard Ciardi grousing, "haven't they any *bourbon* here?" When he'd been to the White House fifteen years earlier, he said, when Lyndon Johnson had been president, there had been plenty of bourbon. Why were the Carters serving nothing but a trendy chardonnay? Kennedy recalled that Ciardi took up a position on one side of the Blue Room and held court, as friends and acquaintances who wandered into his room stopped by to pay their respects. His reputation may have slipped, but Ciardi was nonetheless treated deferentially, in Miller Williams's recollection, befitting his position as one of America's senior poets. But Ciardi was not in the mood that afternoon to be flattered by attention, and the lack of bourbon was only one of his problems. Another was the overlong security check. All of the two hundred-odd guests had been detained for over an hour at the southwest gate in a gray, cold January drizzle. Then for another half hour they waited at the door of the White House "while inefficient idiots checked identities." He wrote to Lew Turco, "My identity was tearing mad." Yes, the national celebration of poetry had been "a nice idea," he granted to an interviewer two weeks later, but he was "insulted by the ineptitude of the occasion." "Thank God the [six-inch] snowstorm didn't hit Washington until the next day, or America's community of poets would have come down with pneumonia. But I hate large literary gatherings of any kind," Ciardi said, "they always turn into brawls, with everyone wanting to be seen standing next to someone else. My wife insisted on going, which I will never let her forget." The interviewer dubbed sixty-three-year-old Ciardi America's "curmudgeon emeritus."

It was true that over the years Ciardi had become more and more ill-tempered and blunt, and that there was less and less of the charm he was always capable of and which had made him so attractive to so many people for so long. He still charmed and informed and entertained when he felt like it, and generally when he was being paid for it, but hard edges had begun to appear even in his lectures as well. By 1980, in fact, he had become routinely irascible, especially with family members and close friends. More than anyone,

Judith admitted, she felt the sting of John's abusive language, a trying situation for her that lasted about ten years before John's death—
during the period, she said, "when [his] health began to deteriorate
some." "He was difficult, but I just didn't pay any attention to it.
Other people would have been devastated. But the way you live with
somebody—I just ignored John because if I didn't, I would have
been following around a little heap of dust." Many of their Key West
visitors and neighbors noticed how unhappy their marriage was
becoming, "on both ends," as Nancy Williams put it, but it was left
to old friend John Malcolm Brinnin, who also wintered in Key West,
to attribute the troubled marriage to John's being "too Italian."

Brinnin's stereotyping may have been the explanation of
choice for other observers as well, but Ciardi's behavior, corre-
sponded, as Judith could see better than anyone, to his declining
health and complex family problems. In 1979, trying to regain some
semblance of health, Ciardi tried hard to quit smoking and went
through several difficult withdrawal periods. In January he wrote
to Miller Williams that he'd gone five of six days without smoking
and was "cocked to take heads off at the first slant word." Then,
revealing by slant, as it were, what was really on his mind, what had
become by then a burdensome physical and psychological problem, Ciardi went on: "The average length of the erect male penis
is 6.27 inches. The average depth of the vagina is 6.531 inches.
Problem: compute by states and counties and with allowances for
celibacy due to all causes, the amount of unused vagina at any given
point in time." He then wrote that he wanted a cigarette and connected his sexual longing with his desire to smoke: "Much to my
surprise, I find it quite possible to want one and to be indifferent to
wanting. This may not work but it is instructive. My advice to young
men is don't light up a cigarette: fuck. Now, if only I could practice what I preach." He was trying to make a joke at his own
expense, but there was nothing funny about the pain he felt.

Through the first half of 1979, Ciardi went through agonizing days, weeks, and months without smoking, the longest being
a four-month stretch from February to May. On 23 May he wrote
to George Garrett, "I have about given up cigarettes. Since about
Feb. 20. But when does the ache stop? I have put on an enormous
lot of weight by compensatory nibbling. And I still damn crave and

feel lousy. Ah well." He commented on the double discomfort of cigarette withdrawal and extra weight in several letters, like another to George Garrett in which he announced that he'd grown "grossly obese" or one to Miller Williams in which he wrote, "After [much] back sliding I think I have finally and damn-painfully quit smoking but it cost me: drinking and eating in lieu of puffing has left me obese and I've got to diet." He finished up another accounting of his success by screaming his frustration: "Shit on virtue!"

Then, too, no doubt related to his abstentions, he had begun to feel old. He wrote to Williams about an incident that had occurred in February 1979: "The day I was delayed in Omaha and trying to walk on [glare?] ice while balancing a suitcase, and then collapsing across airport vistas to sit and pant while my knees shook—that day, for the first time unblinkably, I knew I am an old man. Not just a fat slob but an old fat slob." It was not merely a passing feeling, for later that year, on Christmas Eve, he wrote to Osvaldo Ramous: "At 63 my physical energies begin to fade. . . ." Yes, his mind was still "eager," he wrote to Ramous, and he still considered himself "among the lucky ones," but he also feared "a slow lingering death," like the one his mother had suffered. No, he felt no despair about this because he had made up his mind to commit suicide if he developed a terminal cancer. And in the meantime he would continue working: "I am happiest when engaged. Therefore I engage. It need not come to anything—I think I have survived even ambition. It need not come to anything, because it is itself something: not much, but all there is, and therefore everything." Ciardi's new engagements, however, were "not much" only when compared to the high profile engagements that had occupied him from the late 1940s until about 1972. That is, his most recent achievements seemed to him "not much" because they were the fruits of his strategic retreat into solitary, monkish scholarship.

Complicating his psychological condition was what he saw as his estrangement from Jonnel, whose life had centered permanently in the Boston area; his concern for Myra, who had left school on the eve of graduation to pursue a career as a rock singer; and Benn, who was still dabbling in drugs and vacillating between careers in rock music and self-owned businesses. When one figures in the draining Bread Loaf experience in the early seventies and the death of Dippy later in the decade, Ciardi's decline into unpleasantness bordering on bitterness is understandable—if not totally forgivable. (Ciardi wrote despondently in July 1977 to Stanley Burnshaw to say that he had been "distraught" over "family upheavals that have left me low in spirit and with the leaden conviction that I have turned out to be a lousy father [though, Lord, I have tried lovingly]. . . ." He called it a "depression of soul.") A few days after writing so somberly to Ramous about life and death and the salvation of engagement, he and Judith began driving to Washington for the "Salute to Poetry." Ciardi was still smoking, very overweight, impotent, unsteady on his legs, and depressed by family problems—all of which combined to cause an energy-robbing lethargy. Witnesses to Ciardi's White House grumpiness or his rudeness toward Judith and others, could not have known of his physical and psychological slide, although the ones who saw him regularly would all see his behavior worsen over the next five years.

Arriving in Florida on about 7 January and looking "heavy and tired," according to one newspaper account, Ciardi soon settled into the new house at 725 Windsor Lane and immediately began showing signs of improvement—in mind and body. "I love our new house," he wrote to Williams." "The day is a breezy 80. The ceiling fan laves me with breezes. It's the good life." Ciardi did, indeed, seem more content in Key West than in Metuchen during his last six years, especially in 1980. In early March, he wrote to George Garrett about his garden: "Today, despite what is called cold weather (and drizzly) here, [the gardenia bush] opened a bud and produced the loveliest, creamy-whitest, nose-dazzling flower I have ever seen. I have also set out a jasmine, a royal palm, a red passion flower vine, and various spots of color (with more to come)." A day later he wrote to Williams, "In a burst of buried bourgeois symbolism, I bought a park bench. No man ha[s] truly sunk his roots into this earth until he owns a park bench. I had a royal palm set behind it, and a night-blooming jasmine behind the palm, to change the air." He rhapsodized over his "pink tree-hibiscus threaded by a beautiful blue [illegible] vine," plus his orange and key lime trees, "and in time enough our carambola will start to bear those fantastic star-fish shaped citrus apples." It was wonderful: "The world is sun, color, breezes, and nodding green." Three weeks earlier he had written to

Ramous, "I sit in my newly built house and relish it. I like what I feel and see and I have a friend to tell about it. I think I am happy." And, as an added bonus, he wrote to Williams, Key West was good for his health too: "I haven't had my two annual lousy flus since we started hiding in FLA."

Possibly surpassing the joys of climate, new house, and garden was Ciardi's pleasure at joining the Windsor Lane community of writers in the larger literary hideaway Key West was long famous for being. Three or four late afternoons a week John would visit Dick and Charlee Wilbur next door. There were regular anagram games every week as well, with Ciardi, Wilbur, and John Malcolm Brinnin the regular players, joined now and then by Leonard Bernstein, James Merrill, or John Hersey. According to Brinnin, Ciardi and Bernstein were both extremely competitive, with Ciardi expecting to win every game (though he did not) and Bernstein following his own rules that included players hollering out and playing out of turn. In conversation, Ciardi was often as "contentious as a lawyer," as Hersey put it, and seemed to enjoy the role. But "John had no gift," according to Brinnin, "for the kind of gossip we like to exchange." And, of course, the Ciardis invited many writer friends (and others) for overnight visits that sometimes stretched into a week or more. On those occasions, guests had to be squeezed into the tiny study that doubled as a spare room—or sleep on the couch. There were writers virtually everywhere Ciardi happened to glance.

As far as his daily Key West habits were concerned, Ciardi either worked incredibly long hours, as he had in 1979 typing entries for the *Browser's Dictionary*, or fell into long periods of "indolence," like the winter of 1980, when he spent nearly every evening in front of the television. It was also true that he seemed to grow more coarse and insensitive as the years passed—and he seemed less and less able to make himself socially acceptable. Certainly he continued to offend nearly everyone with his constant talk of money. It was exasperating, as Nancy and John Williams recalled, to hear Ciardi go on and on about his wealth, and Nancy many times told him so. "It's *you* I love," Nancy would say to him, "not your money!" But Ciardi himself was fascinated with it, endlessly amazed that, like a ballplayer, he could earn lots of money doing something he loved. But this fascination with money wasn't the whole story. "True," he would say to an interviewer in early 1981, "it has been said that no one but a fool would write for anything but money, and I'm not ready to sneer at money so long as it will buy whiskey[—]but I do not write for money." And commenting on rewards and recognitions in a 1976 article for the *Writer*, Ciardi had commented that good poets do get rewarded, although "any given poet may think his true merit has been slighted. For myself, whatever I have managed to make of my writing (and it has been a love affair, not a sales campaign), I have always felt that my own satisfaction (or at least the flickering hope of it) was a total payment. Whatever else came has always struck me as a marvelous bonus. And there have been bonuses—grants, prizes, even a small, slow rain of checks. How could I fail to rejoice in that overflow of good? I wish it to every writer, and wish him my sense of joy in it." Ciardi's financial successes, however, went far beyond what most other poets ever dream of. As one newspaper writer put it, "John Ciardi long has been the rare American who could walk into a bank, declare his occupation as 'poet,' and emerge with a mortgage." It was a good illustration, but the reporter would no doubt have been even more impressed had he known that John Ciardi had no use for mortgages because he paid for his houses with cash money.

By the mid-1970s, Ciardi had developed his surprising television habit, surprising in that he had never shown much interest in the medium as a viewer. But increasingly he fell into long periods of television watching whenever he wasn't working, and it quickly took over from gin rummy and golf as his indolence of choice. Just about everyone, including family members and visitors, remarked upon it. Myra said her father could watch TV "endlessly" in Metuchen and always at high volume to drown out the rehearsing bands in the basement studio. Judith said he watched "an awful lot of television—on and on and on. And never the kind I liked. So I watched on my SONY [in the kitchen], and he watched on the good set [in the living room]. He'd start watching at 5:00 or so in the afternoon and watch till eleven, twelve, two in the morning." In a typescript essay called "TV, Culture, and Absolute Whim" left among his papers at his death, Ciardi wrote, "I have never turned on a TV set with conscious intent to improve my mind.

TV is merely dull when it sticks to soap opera, quiz shows, and slap-stick. When it tries to be serious, it becomes unbearable. Well, then, what do I watch? . . . Given a choice, and since porno is not available, I'll take a shoot-'em-up." He wrote that he used to watch police and private eye shows but didn't like them anymore because they had begun to mimic one another into a "mushy senility in which the good solid plot-line of cops-and-robbers has succumbed to a mania for showing cops as loving, sincere, cute, psychiatric social workers. Nuts!" He did confess, however, that he loved to watch nature programming, a report confirmed by his family and friends. "I have crossed the Serengeti Plain with the gnus, glided down mountain ranges with the condor, hunted with the leopard, walked the floor of the Gulf with migrating lobsters. These scenes have become part of my imagination, the one thing that fills me as a book can." Occasionally in Key West the temperature would drop into the upper fifties at night, a little lower than Ciardi kept the thermostat in Metuchen, but in the unheated Windsor Lane house, John would sit in front of the TV, according to Judith, with his electric blanket draped around himself and with the compound cats sleeping on the edges of the blanket at his feet.

On about 25 March 1980, John and Judith left Key West for New Jersey, stopping to visit friends in Florida and Georgia along the way. In Atlanta, Ciardi took a plane to Fayetteville to visit Miller Williams and his other friends at the University of Arkansas—as well as to pick up a check for a lecture—while Judith drove the rest of the way by herself. Back in Metuchen on 8 April, Ciardi began reading page proofs for *A Browser's Dictionary*, scheduled for August publication, and he was so pleased that he forgot to complain with his customary fervor: "It feels great," he wrote to John Nims. "Even through the agony of proofreading I feel fine about it. Vol. II is in the notebooks. Vol. III is beginning to accumulate." Then, after what he called a "hodgepodge seminar" on literature and the urban experience at Rutgers-Newark (three days with "more poets than anyone can believe there really are"), John and Judith set off for the West Coast, courtesy of the Woodrow Wilson Foundation. This particular swing included back-to-back weeks in the Los Angeles area at Whittier College and Occidental College, which paid for visits with Bud Orenstein and Norman Cousins. Then after a stopover at UCLA for another check, it was up to Berkeley for a lecture and then "the Italian Cultural Whatever" in San Francisco for yet another, all of which going to pay for their visit to Irv and Ruth Klompus.

By about Ciardi's sixty-fourth birthday on 24 June 1980, a second collaboration with Isaac Asimov was getting started, *A Grossery of Limericks*. W. W. Norton had sent a half-year royalty statement with the good news that their 1978 collaboration, *Limericks: Too Gross*, had sold more than 12,500 copies. It was clear there was plenty of money to be made with those little limericks, and Norton was planning a paperback of volume one at the same time they were planning the hardcover of volume two. But all told, it proved to be a relatively quiet summer for Ciardi, with only a July lecture at Chautauqua and an NPR taping session to interrupt his rest. The taping had taken place in Washington, D.C. and coincided with the meeting of the International Platform Association, which awarded Ciardi a silver bowl (or a reasonable facsimile of one) for being the People's Poet of the Year. It wasn't exactly the kind of recognition Ciardi wanted, especially because it was given "in the great tradition of Carl Sandburg," not a poet upon whom Ciardi's admirations had ever fallen. And then to make matters worse, he learned that the first winner of the award in 1978 had been Rod McKuen. He hinted in letters that the only reason he accepted the award at all was to satisfy Harper & Row, which insisted that it was an opportunity for him to promote *Browser's*—and because he would be in Washington anyway.

A Browser's Dictionary and Native's Guide to the Unknown American Language did indeed come out on schedule in mid-August and Ciardi was immediately pleased with it except for the front cover phrasing that announced the book to be "a compendium of curious expressions and intriguing facts." Prominently displayed on the front flap of the dust jacket was a blurb by Jacques Barzun: "*A Browser's Dictionary* is for word watchers. It will enlighten and amuse, as well as start arguments. . . . John Ciardi has done a piece of work at once scholarly and inspired." In his 1 May letter to Harper's, together with his blurb, Barzun also wrote (more tellingly because not for publication) that he had not browsed the book at all "but *read* through it and enjoyed the experience." Not so the *Times* reviewer on 17 August, as Ciardi reported to Williams: "It got a non-fiction in brief review in yesterday's *Times* and got savaged by a humorless libber who found too many idioms dealing with women as sex objects and too many jokes about marriage. I hope you realize that women are not sex objects. Thank God, men still are. It seems necessary to maintain some sort of tradition." Within a month it didn't matter what the *Times* had said of the book because, as he wrote to Gil Gallagher, it "seems to be doing well." "I get letters every day from all over the country from people who have the book and who want to comment on an entry—sometimes foolishly, sometimes usefully. People seem to be passionate about etymologies. I know I've never had this sort of response to a book before." His royalty check for the period between September and December bore this out: more than nineteen thousand dollars, he reported to Miller Williams, "and that after deducting $7,500 advance. . . . Michener wouldn't be dazzled, but I like it much. There's unexpected gold in them thar roots." But if Michener would not be impressed by such sales figures, university-trained etymologists, linguists, philologists, and lexicographers had to wonder what Ciardi's secret for success was. Ciardi had proved once again that the gifted, hard-working amateur could rise to the top of other people's professions.

In September 1980, Ciardi signed on as visiting professor at the University of Minnesota-Duluth, a position that would last until just before Thanksgiving. At fifteen thousand dollars for the fall quarter to teach a course in Dante and deliver four public lectures, it was a good deal. Before the term began, he went on a Chicago and Detroit swing of book promotions arranged by Harper & Row. Peter Gorner of the Chicago *Tribune* described Ciardi for his readers on 8 September: "The master poet runs a meaty hand through a wild thatch of salt-and-pepper hair. Customarily enveloped by smoky clouds, Ciardi lights one Vantage [cigarette] after another, scavenging flame from the charred ruins of predecessors. Then as he leans back, hands folded over massive tummy, he seems to relax." Ciardi told Gorner he no longer worked the lecture circuit as he once had done: "he doesn't have the energy anymore, he says. Now he's unwillingly presiding over his own physical disintegration. He says at 64 he's old, fat, sick, cranky, and creaky in the joints." All in all, it was a good self-portrait.

From Chicago, Ciardi worked his way to Detroit and the Kasles, where he was to wait for Judith, who was intending to drive up; then the two of them were to head off to Duluth. But Judith was in a car accident in Metuchen and broke her collarbone. On 8 September from Duluth, Ciardi wrote Irv Klompus that Judith was healing well, that he spoke to her every night, that she was up and around, and that she would be joining him in early October. In fact, he flew to Metuchen on 2 October and the two of them drove up to Duluth. "Lord," he wrote to Williams on 27 September, "it will be good to be back together. She is still wearing a neck-piece, but seems comfortable with it. . . ." Moreover, their rented townhouse was near the campus and just around the corner from a hospital—just in case. The Dante class went well as he later reported to John Tagliabue: "It was a joy to unfold a first glimpse of Dante, as a thing the good students would have for the rest of their lives. I even think some of the graduate students were moved to poke into the original." The term passed uneventfully, although he did sell one of his Windsor Lane properties in late October. And when the November *Poetry* arrived with his poem "Thursday Also Happens" next to five of Archie MacLeish's poems, he was very pleased—although he was not happy to hear from John Nims of the precarious financial situation the magazine was in. Ciardi offered a five-day lecture swing in April, with *Poetry* paying for expenses and he donating all fees back to the magazine. Generous as the offer was, no record of a reply has surfaced, and it does not appear that anything more came of it.

Tucked away as John and Judith were up in Duluth, they could not escape from Benn's continuing problems. Ciardi wrote to Doc Stone on 13 October: "Do you know of a good psychiatric center[?] Son Benn is about to blow the business (in which we invested thousands and many of them) because he is in a black mood, the poor undeveloped bastard. Ah, well. I may just have to put him on a weekly allowance for the rest of his (my) life—it would be cheaper." The business was Benn's New York recording studio, which, Ciardi wrote to Stanley Epstein later that fall, "bled me dry" keeping up with rent payments: "So far he has shown a one year profit of about $10,000—all of which he got from me. I could make my peace with supporting him. Do I have to support his business too[?] If you could call it a business." By early February 1981, Ciardi felt able to be more honest with Epstein: "My younger son turns out to have sniffed a business up his nose while I sent him money for bills he didn't pay." By February, too, Benn had gone into analysis, according to various letters, and Ciardi had to pay for that as well. But despite all, as Ciardi went on in his letter to Epstein, he had hope: "There's still a middle-sized angel in that idiot, if the shrink can de-devil him." Hope and love, however, were hard to sustain in this crisis. He wrote to George Garrett on 8 March, "Benn had a flare up and has gone into analysis and I have gone back on the damned lecture trail to earn an extra $15,000 a year to pay the shrink. If only love were really weightless!"

On the drive back home from Duluth, Ciardi came down with a nasty cold that lingered through to the end of the year. He wrote Doc Stone on 13 December that "it hung on for 10 days," and then, when he thought it was finished, he "came down with a real viral lulu. . . . It seems to take all my energies just to manufacture the anti-bodies the infection feeds on. I am a festering exploded diagram of a no-output machine. Thank God for those sleeping pills you pre-scribed. I hadn't used any until this hit. They at least knock me out for a night's sleep, my one source of comfort, if any." Then after a brief pause, he added his real hope: "Mortality aside, I await only time and strength enough to head for Key West and the sun." Two weeks later, he was still under the weather, as he wrote to George Garrett: "Whether this siege has worn me down or I am beginning to fail of my accumulated vices, my physical energy is low, my lungs pump too hard, and my joints howl hatefully."

In March, with $15,000 to raise, Ciardi signed on with a new lecture agent, William Thompson, writing that his son had gone into analysis and that he needed some money—"at least what comes easy. I've been holding out for $2,000 plus expenses or $3,000 with-out. At need I have taken less, but I have 5 $3,000 dates for '81. $1,500 is all right if dates can be grouped. . . ." (He also announced what may have been a new decision, though certainly a firm one: "I won't fly except first class: never again will I risk finding myself in a tourist middle seat. If they insist on reimbursing only for tourist, I will swal-low the difference, but I fly first class or I won't fly.") A late February advance check for $1,250 from Norton for *A Grossery of Limericks* also helped. Weak from more than a month of flu symptoms and disheartened by Benn's condition—plus the expensive remedy that could not promise a cure, Ciardi did not get his usual tonic from the Key West sun in 1981. He flew north for February lectures in Illinois and Ohio, and had another in Arkansas on the eighteenth. Then, at the end of March, he headed to New Jersey via a lecture route that helped pay the shrink. Just a few months shy of his sixty-fifth birthday, Ciardi was very nearly too old for the pace.

The University of Michigan sponsored a fiftieth anniversary of the Hopwood Awards from April 9 to 11. The official conference name was "The Writer's Craft: The 50th Anniversary Hopwood Festival" and it featured thirteen past winners sitting on panels dedicated to poetry, drama, fiction, and essay, plus an audience of scores of other Hopwood winners sprinkled among the many others who were in attendance. The keynote speaker on Thursday night was Arthur Miller, winner of two Hopwoods during his first three years at Michigan, who spoke of his start as a writer and his experiences in the American theater, with a side diatribe on critics and a lingering pause over money. Ciardi had to smile in agreement when Miller said "the main thing about this prize was the money—$1,250." He sounded more like Ciardi than Ciardi himself: "I had already earned more with my first play than I had in three years as a shipping clerk. Needless to say, the contrast was not lost to my mind. And if I seem to linger on the subject of money, it is, I assure you, at the center of the great tradition of playwrighting. As George Bernard Shaw replied to a businessman who had asked to discuss art with him, 'No, I am an artist, not a businessman; businessmen always want to talk about art, but artists only talk about money.'"

X. J. Kennedy, like Ciardi, was one of the earlier Hopwood winners sitting on the Friday afternoon poetry panel. Afterward, Ciardi invited Kennedy to his room for a drink, and with his second "limerick war" (as W. W. Norton was billing it) with Isaac Asimov fresh in his mind, Ciardi began what seemed to Kennedy a two-hour recitation of limericks "as if to prove to me that he was a great limerick writer, and that he had them all down by memory. He recited them by the dozens." After a long while into this performance, Kennedy began to feel trapped, unable to break free to join other friends downstairs, which he finally did by making excuses and backing out the door. Nor was Kennedy pleased when

Ciardi took him and Judith to dinner at "Victor's," which Kennedy thought a pretentious restaurant. It was crowded and they didn't have a reservation, "but John bulldozed us in" declaring to the head waiter that they were "in the Hopwood birthday thing—and you've got to have a table for us." When the drinks arrived, Ciardi calmed down, according to Kennedy, although when a waiter splashed ice water on the table, John ran off "another stream of abuse."

There wasn't anything new in Ciardi's talk at the Friday afternoon poetry panel, but he always managed to breathe life into dull academic conferences with his diatribes against the "measly generation," jabbing always at the Bread Loaf mindset that had unseated him and that he had come to despise. He spoke against a "simplistic soulfulness" and the sort of improvisation that students longed to achieve: "I could even agree with them, with the difference that they believed that the impromptu was what happened when you sat down and let it spill, whereas I find over the years that the impromptu is what begins to happen slowly at the tenth, fifteenth, or twentieth draft." Then came the familiar Yeats quotation: "A line may take us hours maybe. / Yet if it does not seem a moment's thought / Our stitching and unstitching has been naught." And finally came the direct address: "I hope I am speaking to young, socially-activated poets, in many of whom I seem to find the assumption that the one prerequisite for poetry is the excitation of one's own ignorance. Excited ignorance is legal and I mean to be ruled by the constitution. But time's winged chariot hurries, and I have no time to waste sympathy on what bores me." It was more or less the same impolitic message that had made sense and enemies ten years earlier when he attacked Galway Kinnel at Bread Loaf. His speech was received with "mild protests" from the audience, according to Kennedy, plus other "disgruntlements" later on.

Later in April Ciardi was back in Metuchen typing *Browser's* II, a job which continued into May when he got an apologetic letter from John Nims, whose *Harper Anthology of Poetry* had just come out. The prepublication announcement had been a poster of the galaxy with the names of poets appearing as greater or lesser stars (in corresponding type) lighting up the Milky Way. Judging from the size of Ciardi's type, he was to be featured as one of the more important poets in the anthology, yet when it came out, not a single of his poems appeared. Ciardi was upset but too proud to ask his old friend for an explanation. Nims, however, learned of Ciardi's hurt feelings from mutual friends, and on 29 May he wrote to explain what had happened. At the last possible moment, his editor at Harper had announced to him that they had to eliminate "thousands of lines." There were twenty-eight readers and nearly all of them had strong feelings about who and what should be included in the contemporary section of the book. Some, for example, wanted to know why Charles Olson wasn't in—or Robert Bly, Anne Sexton, or Galway Kinnell. Nims reported to Ciardi that he had held his ground about those particular poets but had to include many whose works he didn't like as much as Ciardi's simply because Harper did not want to offend any poetic splinter group. In the end, then, thousands of lines had to be cut from the book, including Ciardi's, Nims said, to make room for lesser poets. It was thus that Allen Ginsberg snuck in to represent the Beat poets, and Robert Creeley to represent the Black Mountain poets, and Margaret Atwood to represent Canadian women, and Ted Hughes to represent contemporary England—and so on. In the end, Ciardi "simply wrote well" without "representing any special school, etc." Nims had bent to "editorial pressures and necessities." The apology was unnecessary, as Ciardi replied on 6 June: "It is generous of you to be concerned but don't be. . . . I am what I appear to be and you are what you appear to be. The po biz scene is shot full of kinks and quirks, but not between us. I believe a poem will get the attention it compels. If it compels none, no literary politics can do more than pancake it."

The day after Nims had written his apology, Ciardi received a more important evaluation of his worth, a more soul-satisfying one at that, when Archie MacLeish wrote to say he had nominated John for membership into the American Academy of Arts and Letters. Ciardi had been in the two-hundred-and-fifty-member National Institute of Arts and Letters for nearly twenty-five years, but this was the first time he had been nominated for membership in the more elite, fifty-member academy. In fact, the distinction between the academy and institute had been dulled but not eliminated when the two clubs had merged into the American Academy and Institute of Arts and Letters in 1976. The merger was designed "to create a clearer public image and to simplify the conduct of regular activities," although the "distinction" between the groups was maintained for "safeguarding" their "special interests." Ciardi's populist image, plus his willfulness, outspokenness, and rough edges, together with the spiny stubbornness and ruthless critical honesty that had earned him many enemies over the years—all combined to explain why he had never been nominated earlier to the elite upper chamber. Nor, he might have admitted with due modesty, had his work been so consistently compelling as to force him upon the attentions of the academy. The nomination, coming from MacLeish, whom Ciardi loved and idolized, was its own kind of gratifying recognition—but nothing came of it. Academy member Richard Wilbur did not recall that the question even came to a vote, and when MacLeish died in April 1982, no new champion emerged to present Ciardi again. In September 1984, soothing Stanley Burnshaw's hurt feelings about not being elected into the institute, Ciardi wrote that he had "never liked the method of selection there. I sense some sort of deadhand inner-clique that works things in its image and I don't like the image. I have ignored the whole thing for years. And by way of confession, let me add that I have been a member for almost 30 years, was nominated once for the Acad (by Archie) and rejected. I confess to not having liked it."

Ciardi had a "long happy summer" in 1981, beginning with a six-week stretch of writing poetry. He and Judith went to Chautauqua for the last two weeks of July, then they were off to western Massachusetts where they visited first with Dick and Charlee Wilbur in Cummington and next with the aging Archie and Ada MacLeish in Conway. From Massachusetts they headed north to Maine for a visit with George and Susan Garrett and then headed back to Boston for a visit with his three sisters. Finally, taking them through Labor Day, they went to Nantucket "for ten days of bad golf," during a visit with John's old roommate from Bates College, Roger Fredland and his wife Dorothy. Shortly before his sixty-fifth birthday that June, Ciardi had received another message from his body, this time his "sacred iliac" which wouldn't let him cut the grass. He wasn't the man he used to be, he said in a letter to George Garrett, "but then I never was. I embark on my senior citizenry as a figment of my former imagination of the man I never was in the first place."

That fall Ciardi lectured in Maine, Illinois, Iowa, Arkansas, Nevada, and elsewhere. William Green, a reporter for the *Arkansas Gazette*, covered Ciardi's three-day, fifteen-hundred-dollar appearance in Little Rock, sponsored by the Poet's Roundtable, on the occasion of its fiftieth anniversary. He described Ciardi as having "shaggy, steel-gray hair" and wearing "thick-rimmed glasses." He reported that Ciardi "slipped on his blue pinstriped suit coat for the interview—for 'appearances'—but it didn't disturb his disheveled look." Ciardi chainsmoked his Vantage 100s throughout the interview and apparently felt comfortable enough to speak on the record and without much indirection of his impotence. "'Habits change,' [Ciardi] said, alluding to his 65th birthday. 'I discovered I don't want to fill all the beds of the world. I used to smoke and drink between acts of sex, now I have more time for smoking and drinking.'"

Determined to get more time in Key West than he had the previous winter, Ciardi decided to drive down in early November 1981, fly home for a week at Christmas, and then fly back to the sun as quickly as possible. Judith would join him in mid-January. He left Metuchen about 1 November and arrived in Key West a week or so later. Having taken the summer off and then lecturing for five weeks in the fall, Ciardi was still typing *Browser's* II and putting off any serious thought about an edition of his selected poems. Claiming to be in "financial straits," he wrote to Harper & Row asking that his two-thousand-dollar advance on *Browser's* II plus royalties on *Browser's* I be mailed as soon as possible after the new year in order for him to make his 15 January quarterly tax payment. He sent a similar request to Norton for money owed him from the limerick books. In December an NPR crew came to Key West to tape thirty-three programs, which meant that he had to have at least that many typescripts ready and proofread. Then it was Christmas and he was "commanded north," as he put it in a letter to Miller Williams on 21 December, which, he added, probably meant "a date with influenza, but loves conquers all. . . ." He estimated the cost of the trip alone to be about fifteen hundred dollars

As his June first 1982 deadline for *Browser's* II got ever closer, Ciardi began working hard on the typescript. He had all but ignored it from April through the first of the year, but by January he was working on it every day and fearing he wouldn't have it finished in time. "I hack away at Browser's Dictionary II," he wrote to George Garrett on the thirtieth. "The word treatments, I feel, are excellent, but page-production is slow. I run just as hard as anyone else but I keep coming in last." In February he wrote to Williams, "My days are a madness. I have been typing, literally 10–12 hours a day, racing toward my deadline . . . , always in fear that I can't make it. I should never have undertaken a second volume in 2 years. In future I shall insist on at least a 4–5 year interval, thus permitting myself the obsession but not at the damned cost of everything else—including, to my great guilt, poetry."

But there were brighter moments for Ciardi during the winter of 1982 as well. In late February he was contacted by a spokesman for the National Council of Teachers of English with the good news that he had been selected to win the NCTE Award for Excellence in Poetry for Children. The announcement would be made on 16 April at the NCTE spring conference in Minneapolis, but the award itself would be presented on 19 November in Washington, D.C. at the annual convention. Then, sweetening the award even more, NCTE invited Ciardi to deliver its keynote banquet speech, which meant that he was to receive not only a plaque that he would be openly proud of for the rest of his life, but also a one-thousand-dollar check (plus all expenses). He also arranged to sign books at the Houghton Mifflin, Harper & Row, and Norton booths. This was good news indeed, as was his two-day stay in April as the Wallace Stevens Fellow at Timothy Dwight College at Yale. Robert Thompson, who had extended the invitation in June 1981, wrote Ciardi on 14 April 1982 to praise his performance and invite him back. Then in early May, John Nims had written accepting four new poems for *Poetry*.

But despite the good things happening, the dark cloud of the deadline loomed in the not-too-distant future. Judith flew back to Metuchen on 1 April, but John remained in Key West through most of May working on the typescript. On the twenty-seventh, he wrote to Stanley Epstein that he had finally mailed it off and driven home, "about 1,600 dreary miles along a front of thunder squalls, arriving 2 nights ago." He also announced that he would be heading down to Atlanta in two days where John Stone was going to give him a thorough physical at the Emory University Hospital "to see what is wrong with my legs, which seem to be failing me. In years gone by I could have propped myself on a perpetual erection but, alas, that too has gone finite." Then after a brief pause, he added his familiar, weary disclaimer: "No complaints. I never expected to live through 1944–45 on Saipan and I have had almost 40 beautiful years since then. There comes a time to pick up the tab." And to make matters worse, he was facing a grueling summer and fall schedule, including Benn's announced wedding on 22 August.

First, however, was his hospitalization. He was admitted on Saturday, 29 May and stayed five days, during which time he had several polyps removed from his colon and underwent a battery of tests that provided a complete picture of his health. The weakness in his legs and the unsteadiness of his gait (both of which he complained of) plus a coordination problem traced to something called "cerebellar dysfuntion" (which he wasn't aware of) were determined to be neurological disorders related to alcohol and possibly to a mild case of diabetes, which he was also diagnosed at this time as having. (He was put on an oral medication, Diabenase, to control his blood sugar.) His constant coughing, frequent colds, and regular flu symptoms were judged to be chronic bronchitis caused by his two- to three-pack-a-day cigarette habit, but fortunately, his lung function was close to normal and he showed no signs of cancer. His diabetes, high alcohol intake, and obesity all had vascular and neurological connections to his impotence, although a serious discussion of prosthetic surgery was postponed, probably until the results of lifestyle changes being recommended by the physicians could be measured. (There is, however, no record that any further discussion about this surgery ever took place.) Doc Stone discharged Ciardi to the care of his Metuchen doctor, Vincent Cannamela, concluding that since so many of Ciardi's problems were related to his drinking, the progression of his symptoms might be "arrested by cessation of alcohol." No clinical problems save the bronchitis were found to be directly attributable to cigarettes, but Stone urged Ciardi to give them up as well.

When he got home, Ciardi wrote to Stone with his thanks. He'd already arranged an appointment with Cannamela to have his blood sugar tested again, he said, and was fully prepared to give up drinking completely. In fact, he'd already just about given it up and didn't even "crave" it: "I *like* the stuff but I am not addicted and have always been able to go dry with[out?] withdrawal systems. Cutting out about 1,500 daily calories of bourbon also amounts to a diet and I should shed a lot of weight, which is all to the good." He was sincere about this, as events would prove, partly because his drinking habits had become so unusual that even he had remarked upon them. Three years earlier he had described himself to Stanley Epstein as an "a-typical toper." "I seldom drink till about 2:00 A.M. as I'm winding down the day. Then I find myself slugging away because the damn stuff trickles into my hollow leg and by the time I get to bed I've finished the book and most of the fifth. So, the worst kind—a solitary non-drunk. I haven't, alas, been tipsy more than twice in twenty years."

Of course, Ciardi did think a lot about the changes in his life without J. W. Dant. He remembered Fletcher Pratt's death more than twenty-five years earlier of cirrhosis of the liver and cancer. Toward the end, under doctor's orders, Pratt had given up his cherished cigars and Scotch whisky and had taken up sucking on sour balls. This had bothered Ciardi, for Fletcher had been one of his great, treasured friends. "He had earned his cirrhosis and his cancer honestly," Ciardi had written. "I have seldom seen him when his cigar was not in his mouth nor his glass of Scotch by his typewriter." He pleaded with Pratt to "go out" in his own style. Wouldn't it be better to die in three weeks with bad habits intact than to die without them in four? "Let my turn come and see what luck they have in turning me from a single one of my chosen evil solaces, damn them all! Once they decide I'm terminal the devil himself won't keep the cigarette out of my mouth and the bourbon out of my guts." But now that the time was closer, though not terminal yet, he compromised with his position of twenty-five years earlier. He wrote a fictional conversation with his "damned doctor" in which he vented accumulated frustrations. In the piece, Ciardi agreed to give up drinking because he didn't want "to start shooting insulin." But he wouldn't stop smoking or watch his diet because of a high uric acid count that might lead to gout. He and the doctor argue, with the doctor telling Ciardi that he should be reasonable. Ciardi replied, "In reason life needs its vices." He would give up drinking, "but I will not cut down on my three packs a day, and I will not diet." And that was final: "Rape, avarice, and ambition have already given me up. What's left but cigarettes, impatience, and an evil mind?" He did, however, agree to riding "your goddamned exercycle" and limit his calories—but only to what he called the "choice ones." This was, in fact, a good description of the compromises Ciardi was willing to make over the last four years of his life.

By early June 1982, Benn's marriage was called off when "the girl got cold feet," as Ciardi explained it to Mac Cordray on the tenth. Myra was doing her "generational thing," living "at half rental" with her boyfriend of seven years in one of Ciardi's investment properties a mile or so from the homestead in Metuchen. "I keep wishing they'd move out and let me sell the thing for a huge profit, but, Hell, I am doing my best to die broke. It's called divesting." Those were the things that seemed to occupy Ciardi's mind during June.

By July he was on the road again: two weeks in Minnesota at a writers' conference, then Chautauqua and Sarasota in August, followed by a taping session in Washington for his NPR program. At the end of August (in an appointment that would stretch to 5 November) Ciardi prepared himself once again to be visiting professor, this time at Northern Kentucky University for fifteen thousand dollars, where he would teach a Dante course that was to be videotaped and televised over public television. By this time he was an old hand at teaching the master in an introductory course that had evolved into "How to Read the *Divine Comedy.*" And he had come to enjoy presenting Dante to young readers, many of whom he knew would cherish the joy of their first exposure for the rest of their lives. Moreover, his classes were bunched in the middle of the week thus allowing him to make a few extra dollars lecturing, as he did in Lincoln, Nebraska ($2,800) and Frankfort, Kentucky.

Sometime during the summer Ciardi developed what he called a "neuralgic nuisance" similar to a problem he had had a couple of years earlier. He reported it to John Stone on 8 September: "It used to come once in a while spoiling a night's sleep for an hour or two and feeling like a hot wire from my upper right gum, past the eye, and into the temple. Now I seem to be able to count on it every damn night, but in becoming a regular boarder, it seems to have become less intense. It also seems to linger on, at a bearable level."

On the nineteenth, he wrote to Stone again: "My nightly head-splitter continues to visit. I can't pretend to be an expert on pain. When this is most intense it comes close to being unbearable. I guess I can manage to live with it if it comes to no more than a bad half hour to an hour nightly, with an occasional abeyance. But if anything can be done, I am prepared to go to considerable lengths to get it done." Stone consulted a neurologist at Emory and they agreed on a diagnosis of cluster headaches; they also arranged for John to see a specialist at the University of Cincinnati Hospital, only about ten miles away from the NKU campus across the Ohio River. Ciardi made the appointment for Monday, 4 October, and in the meantime was taking Emperin #3 (with codeine), prescribed by Stone, as needed for pain. The pills did relieve the sharp pains at night, but the side effects left Ciardi "listless and blah," he wrote to Stone on 2 October. Privately (in an undated essay fragment on pain left among his papers), Ciardi revealed how grave the situation had become and the lengths he had contemplated to resolve it: "[The headaches] passed in an hour or two, after I had sat and held my head and raged . . . , but in the third week I decided that if the medicine did not work I would put my affairs in reasonable order and take fifty Seconal with a bottle of bourbon."

Ciardi saw the Cincinnati specialist on Monday, 4 October, and he confirmed the diagnosis of cluster headaches, putting Ciardi on new medication that did not leave him so worn out and weary all day. Two weeks later, however, on Tuesday, 19 October, Ciardi woke with numbness along his left side. At about 10:00 A.M. Judith called Dr. Peter Welt, husband of John's friend at NKU, novelist Elly Welt. Peter was himself ill at the time, but he was nonetheless very concerned by John's symptoms and the possibility that the medication for the cluster headaches might have been the immediate cause of a stroke. Moreover, he was aware of the danger of a second stroke and wanted John hospitalized as quickly as possible. He and Elly drove over to the Ciardi rental house about a mile from campus, and they drove to the hospital in two cars. John, however, was alert and bright, so it was difficult for Judith or Elly to think this sudden affliction could be either permanent or debilitating. Their amateur evaluation was right. The stroke or TIA (transient ischemic attack), which the doctors seemed to prefer as a diagnosis, hardly slowed

Ciardi down at all. By the next day not only was he writing impatient letters from his hospital bed, but he was also holding court in his normal fashion and smoking in the corridor waiting for his doctor to stop in on rounds. He was already making plans to make up the two classes he'd missed, and, as Judith wrote to Gertrude Kasle on the twenty-seventh, he was "determined to keep up his schedule for November."

The Joy Conference

Ciardi did, indeed, keep up his fall 1982 schedule and was apparently well enough to head alone to Key West right after Thanksgiving. He wrote to Gil Gallagher that he expected to be there about 10 December and to spend Christmas there. "Judith will join me in January. It will be my first Xmas away from the kids—unless one counts last year when I flew home for sweet sentiment's sake (Judith's) and managed to get at least six words in between hello and goodbye." Shortly after arriving in Key West, he did have a boil on his back treated, which John Stone reminded him, "is nothing to fool around with, especially in diabetes." After having his boil lanced, Ciardi seems to have gone directly to an Oldsmobile dealership to buy himself a Christmas present, what he called "a scandalously expensive new 98 with tape deck and a great sound system." The stroke of a mere two months earlier had not forced itself on Ciardi's attention for long, and he had gone on with his life almost as if nothing had happened.

Compared to the hard work Ciardi had done the previous winter and spring in Key West getting *Browser's* II ready for Harper & Row, the winter of 1983 was much easier, with plenty of time for gardening, anagrams, and afternoon visits with Dick and Charlee Wilbur. He spent a week as distinguished visiting professor at Miami Dade Community College in January, but otherwise his winter indolence seems to have been uninterrupted—save perhaps by the happy mid-April arrival of *A Second Browser's Dictionary and Native's Guide to the Unknown American Language.* He was, however, gearing up for a difficult month ahead. On 20 April he flew to Colorado for a lecture in Boulder (parlayed into a short visit with John and Nancy Williams in Denver), and then it was back to Key West and preparations for a rushed, two-and-a-half-day return to New Jersey. He had barely enough time to unpack before he was chauffeured by Benn up to the Rhode Island School of Design for a lecture; then it was back to New Jersey just long enough to repack for the thirty-eighth reunion of the 73rd Bomb Wing in Lexington, Kentucky. Visiting with Mac and Mary Cordray and Bud and Floss Orenstein, John and Judith had a good time, "beautiful days," as John put it in a letter to Floss. But his legs had started bothering him again in Florida, which his local doctor had treated by putting him on Lasix (because he was retaining water), which left him worn out. He wrote to Floss, "I apologize for being so pooped and early to bed. I just saw my M.D. [Cannemela in Metuchen] who says my bedraggledness may be due to potassium deficiency induced by medication I have been on. May he be right! He put me on potassium tablets." On 25 May, he wrote to Doc Stone that the pills seemed to be working and his legs were "beginning to behave better." (A month later he wrote to Stone that he felt "spryer": "It would be too ridiculously easy to defend myself against charges of multiple aggravated rape, alas, but I am prepared to be mentally abusive.") What was more, he was still on the wagon, he reported: "nary a drink since last October"—which meant that though he claimed at the time to have given up drinking after his May 1982 physical, he did not truly give it up until after his October stroke. But, he added, "I took a sip of Judith's dry manhattan last night—a tsp. full—and damned if I haven't lost my taste for the stuff." And oh yes, and he'd also had "some Amaretto on ice cream about 3 months ago." But that was it, he muttered, like a forgetful ten-year-old at Saturday afternoon confession, waiting to be scolded by the priest.

Ciardi returned home from Kentucky by way of Washington, D.C., where he signed five hundred copies of *Browser's* II for Constance Erskine, the "beloved Aunt Connie" the book was dedicated to. He and Judith were in Metuchen for only a couple of days, however, before they headed up to Medford for John's forty-fifth reunion at Tufts and a visit with Jonnel who introduced them to Valerie Mauro, the girl he would eventually marry. But when Ciardi finally settled back into 359 Middlesex Avenue about 1 June, he had no choice but to give some serious thought to an edition of his selected poems he had agreed to publish at the University of Arkansas Press. Miller Williams, as director of the press, had asked for the manuscript by 1 September 1983, and Ciardi couldn't put it off any longer.

Ciardi's first mention in surviving letters to a selected poems came on 1 October 1979, when he mentioned to George Garrett that it was a book he ought to get around to sometime "soon." Then two weeks later he wrote to Garrett that he would be leaving all word histories behind when he got to Florida in order "to concentrate on a rigidly culled *Selected Poems.*" But in another letter to Garrett seven months later, on 16 April 1980, Ciardi revealed that he had not done much with the project and was beginning to feel a little uneasy about it: "I have had too many chances to publish and consequently published too much. I'd like time to prune and to see what emerges. If anything." That summer Ciardi asked Eric Swenson if Norton would be interested in publishing his selected poems, but nothing came of the inquiry and he repeated it some fifteen months later, in November 1981. He was thinking of a three-hundred-page book; "a sort of retrospective show." This time Swenson answered that the size of the book was a problem and asked if it could be reduced. With nothing more hopeful to go on than that, Ciardi may well have wondered if there was a future for him at W. W. Norton, a reasonable question considering that a month later Swenson wrote to say that *For Instance* was being remaindered after being in print a mere two years. On 21 December, Ciardi wrote Williams to say that Swenson was "wary as hell" of publishing his selected poems "as a commercial venture and asked if I could get a U Press to do it. You, I know, are more or less bound to Arkies, of which I am other than. Do you know of a U Press that might go for it, possibly on a joint imprint and distribution?" Almost at once, Williams offered Ciardi a contract to publish *Selected Poems,* and by 8 February 1982, papers were signed and Ciardi was ready to begin working with his last publisher of adult poems.

But from February 1982 to June 1983, Ciardi procrastinated. With his September 1983 deadline fast approaching, Ciardi wrote to Stuart Wright in May that he had to get "seriously to work" on the project: "I've told myself to get at it for 3 years and keep running into a block about going over old stuff, but I must delay no longer." Some six weeks later he wrote to Saipan buddy Ed Lawson, "I find I hate going back [over the poems]. As a generalization, dead's dead." As the summer wore on, Ciardi became more and more depressed about selecting his poems; it was so disagreeable a job, in fact, that he fell into another period of indolence rather than face it. On 23 June he wrote to John Nims: "Beethoven festered in his locked room working on the *[Sinfonia pastorale]* with trays of food mouldering untouched, his clothes filthy, his chamber pot unemptied, the score looking like the mud of a chicken run, snarling when the woman knocked. I'm not quite that messy. And would that I had such a score at the center of my wallow. But I have sunk into a doodlesome and compulsive rhythm of nothing and a table piled like a dumpster." A week later he wrote to Nims again, this time to apologize "if I gave off a general sound of lamentation." He explained that he was working on his *Selected Poems:* "I could not have imagined how hateful the task is (it is probably at the root of any bitching I did). I have invented every way of dodging the task. Now I am out of dodges and time and must do it. Having done too much, I end up dismally aware that I have done nothing, and hate replowing my acre of stone. Thank God for the blindness that permits an engagement with work-in-process. To look back is to sight through the wrong (right?) end of the telescope. Dwindledom."

Ciardi's depression was also caused by his sixty-seventh birthday on 24 June. Judith wrote to Nancy Williams that she had served up a birthday dinner of mussels and quiche, which she hoped had "boosted his morale." Ciardi wrote to Gil Gallagher, trying to mask his feelings behind self-deprecating humor, "I have, alas, birthdayed! I, dashing dancer, dandy man, golden boy gunner, promising young poet, and Mother's darling cuddle woke to find myself trapped in this crapped out old man's body! What am I doing here? Help!" But by early July Ciardi had somehow managed to get past his birthday and most of the work for *Selected Poems.* He wrote to George Garrett that he'd be sending the manuscript to Arkansas by the end of the month and was much relieved to have it nearly behind him: "Never will I have taken greater pleasure in being rid of a weight of dead paper. At least I have learned in trying to put this stuff into a book that there is no order to my life. The style of it is whimsical random."

On about 19 July, Ciardi did indeed mail off the manuscript for *Selected Poems*, which he and Williams agreed should contain the entire *Lives of X*. However, he had failed at providing an introductory note, coming up, as he wrote to Williams, "with nothing to which silence was not to be preferred." Perhaps, he added, "the jacket copy might say that the poems are not strictly chronological and that *Lives of X* is reproduced entire for some reason I am not able to phrase." Once he mailed *Selected Poems*, his spirits rose and his energy for "work-in-process" returned. He wrote with relief to his sister Ella that *Selected* had been delivered to the publisher and that other things were afoot too: "Have also finished a new book of dirty limericks. Am pounding away at the manuscript of some children's poems. And have a good bulge on *Browser's* III." When galleys of *Selected Poems* reached him a year later about 20 August 1984, Ciardi wrote to fellow etymologist Walter Newman that he was tempted to subtitle it "43 Blathering Years." He and Judith spent the next two weeks with the Fredlands on Nantucket where he rested, looked over the galleys (which he was very pleased with), and kept up with a little correspondence. One letter was to Jeff Lovill, a young man from Arizona State University who was writing a Ph.D. dissertation on Ciardi and had written on 23 August with a variety of questions. Lovill was particularly curious about Ciardi's religious beliefs, which John tried to explain: "I think of [religion] as an adolescent imbalance I survived. . . . The simple fact is that I do nothing with reference to God or an after life. I am a member of this species. I am interested in it. God and language seem to be its principal inventions, and I am interested in the inventions as clues to the inventor. Dante and the *Browser's Dictionaries* are part of one absorption in the same curiosity." In place of this reply, Ciardi could have sent Lovill "Diary Entry," an author's proof of which reached him about 1 September for publication in a festschrift in honor of James Tate and which was later published in *The Birds of Pompeii* (1985), the last of his books that Ciardi saw through production and into print.

> I was in a mood for disaster
> but couldn't afford much.
> At the God store I counted out
> my last three worn *perversos*
> and ordered an ounce of avalanche.

His thumb on the scale,
it came to one grain of sand
which He blew in my eye,
perhaps to teach me something.

Which He did. A rule of thumb:
all else being equal,
I'll not be caught, not soon again,
trying to do business on His scale. .

On 9 September 1983, Ciardi wrote to John Stone and reported on the galleys of *Selected Poems*. "I'm a bit surprised," he wrote, "at how heavily Italo-American it is. If anyone gets around to reviewing it, I'll hear about that. And it will miss the point that the Italian background was my first pasture, not where I went. So I'll be typed. So be it." Many of his early poems, of course, plus many of the reminiscences in *Lives of X*, and a smattering of poems that had appeared through the years—displayed a strong pull toward his Italian-American childhood and what is generally called a "cultural heritage." But to Ciardi, nationality was secondary to the process of looking inward for self-discovery, which he always believed was a universal experience that everyman could share. The outer trappings were particular to the man, but the process of searching into oneself opened the poems to all men—that is, if one could look deeply enough and write compellingly enough. On 9 September 1983, when he wrote to his friend Vince Clemente about the galleys of *Selected*, Ciardi repeated his concern over "how Italian it is" but remembered again a story he liked to tell about Robert Lowell. In the final analysis, he wrote to Clemente, anyone who noted "how Italian" his new book was would miss the point: "Lowell missed it once. I published in *The Atlantic* 'SPQR, A Letter from Rome,' and he wrote to say it was the best Italian-American poem he had read. As if he wrote Am and I wrote It-Am. Well, yes and no. About the way Archie MacLeish, bless great memory, wore a tam with a Scottish clan emblem. Mine was a pick and shovel rampant, gold on a dinner pail ebon. Later it was two martinis on an expense account lunch tab."

Clemente had, in fact, drawn Ciardi out about his Italian-Americanism five years earlier, in November 1978. Clemente at that time was thinking about putting together a book of poems and commentary by Italian-American poets who were to describe how their common backgrounds helped to form their poetic consciousness. Ciardi wanted to help his friend and had agreed to provide an introduction to the book, but he had reservations.

> I like the sense of the project you suggest. I find myself, however, oddly blocked by "the Am-It esthetic." Can another word be found? I am not sure there is such a thing; and if there is I doubt I have it. It isn't that I am *l'Italiano dirazzato* [denationalized Italian], though I guess I am. Though I also know I am not. I have poured out endless poems about the Italian "roots." Yet Jefferson, Tom Paine, and even—God save the mark, Emerson—are as much at the roots of my mind and feeling as the It. of my Am.

Five days later, still troubled with the idea of an Italian-American aesthetic, Ciardi wrote again to Clemente with a stronger version of the Lowell story he had told in September: "I don't know of anyone who thinks in terms of Italo-Am poets. I had a longish poem about Italy in the *Atlantic* some years back, and when Robert Lowell wrote to praise its Italo-Am voice, I took offense. Did the s.o.b. suppose I had used an Am. Eng. inferior to his or that . . . mine [was] less Am. Eng. than his? Well, even the good ones can be fools." At Christmas 1978, Ciardi wrote to Lew Turco that although he was still wary of Clemente's project, he would do what he could "short of cash—not with one son in law school (Jonnel) and Benn and Myra successfully (and permanently, I suspect) unemployed."

He couldn't shake entirely free of the Italian-American question whenever he wrote to Turco or Clemente, and there are references to it on and off over the next couple of years. He wrote to Turco on 28 February 1979, "I really don't know what to make of so much Italo-Am. I've never thought in terms of I-Am poetry. I don't know any I-Am poets, as such. Lew Turco is an Am. poet who happened to have It. parents. T. Roethke is a ditto with Ger. parents." Still toying with the idea two weeks later, in the afterglow of having just finished typing the entries to *Browser's* I in Key West, Ciardi repeated himself once again to Turco, but added a reflective afterthought on his own work as a poet: "Increasingly, I have the feeling that I write only for the dead, and that the mind and idiom of those I write for and to, once the last few have died, will not be duplicated. I have the feeling that we are coming to an age that lacks memory. For whom, then, are poets to do their remembering? Scratch it on the inside of the skull wall—maybe the last church mouse will find it to puzzle at. No one else gives a damn. Maybe it all died the day Kenneth Rexroth decided to list Bob Dylan as a leading poet." No, he wrote, "I'm just not sure there is anyone out there . . . there certainly is no one out there along It-Am lines. Tend your garden."

The entire question seemed to fluster Ciardi. He liked Turco and Clemente, but he didn't feel the same connections to an Italian-American poetry that they seemed to feel. He had commented to an interviewer in 1978 that he often did not like Italian-American gatherings because they tended to become "jingoistic," as though Italian culture was "infinitely better than some other culture." He couldn't agree with that point of view. "I think Italy has bequeathed magnificent things to Europe and Europe has bequeathed some magnificent things back to Italy, but I'd like to be known as a person of European culture." And so it was with genuine surprise that Ciardi noticed "how heavily Italo-American" *Selected Poems* had turned out to be, although it may be argued from one point of view that this was more optical illusion than reality. What made the book look more Italian-American than it was was its arrangement. There were 136 poems in all, broken down into seven parts or chapters. Ciardi opened with a twenty-three-poem section that he called "Tribal Poems," taking him autobiographically from his baptism in "The Evil Eye" to the death of his mother in "Addio." Then, by way of additional ethnic emphasis, Ciardi ended with his entire *Lives of X*, about half of which included long sections on his Italian background and family memories, plus his experiences as an Italian-American boy in a German-Irish neighborhood. Exactly half of the book's 222 pages (but only 36 poems) were given over to these two chapters, and sandwiched in between them were five additional chapters ("I Marry You," "Thickets," "On the Patio," "Bang Bang" [World War II poems], and "Conversations"), 105 poems in all. Italian-American or not, the book had an attractive quirkiness to it, with poems grouped in such a way as to make them appear fresh in their new surroundings.

A key to Ciardi's mindset when he put *Selected* together was his inability to think long about poems from the 1940s, '50s, and '60s and his decision to reprint great amounts from the 1970s: all of *Lives of X*, twenty-two poems from *The Little That Is All*, and twenty-seven from *For Instance*. The real imbalance in *Selected* was not the inclusion of too many Italian poems but the omission of too many excellent early poems: there is nothing from *Homeward to America*, only four from *Other Skies*, two from *Live Another Day*, six from *From Time to Time*, and so on, with the best representation among early books coming from *As If* (nine), *39 Poems* (nine), *In the Stoneworks* (eleven) and *Person to Person* (thirteen). With respect to subject matter, Ciardi chose more of the things that were interesting him in the 1970s over earlier sub-jects, as for instance, he included nearly twice as many suburban poems in "On the Patio" as there are World War II poems in "Bang Bang." During the forty years that had elapsed between the dra-matically important and life-threatening events of World War II and *Selected Poems*, Ciardi had been transformed from a reluctant warrior into a successful member of "po biz," with a suburban home in Metuchen and a winter residence in Key West, all of which accounts for his heavy interest in observations made from the patio—and the unfortunate imbalance in *Selected*. Moreover, by selecting a mere 13 percent of his poems for *Selected*, Ciardi chose a way of representing himself that was far too narrow, for Ciardi reads best when one spans the decades with him, reading at length among the poems that were important to him moment by moment and year by year. Only then do his love of family and art, his religious skepticism, his search for identity, his fascination with everyday events, his passion for the unimportant poem—emerge as an impressive catalogue of concerns, themes deliberately developed over a lifetime. And only then does his voice, described so well by Edward Krickel as "slangy yet learned," emerge as warmly human in its sympathies and mercies.

Almost lost in the 1983 summertime attention given to *Selected* was the disappointment over the sales figures for *Browser's* II. Ciardi complained to Williams in late August that he was "unhappy" with Harper & Row. The book had been out four months and sold ten thousand copies, but Ciardi felt that it would never match the fifty thousand sold of volume one because Harper & Row had given it "no promotion." "I'm not eager to go crawling around TV shows, but it seems to help sales. It did for B. I. But no plans are on for B. II." In a letter to Gil Gallagher on 9 September, Ciardi went so far as to say that sales were "dragging—largely for lack of promotion, alas, but I can't seem to reach my editor. Well. It's only money. I'm tempted to hold back on *Browser's* III till this tired old gal retires and some sort of energy takes up residence." Judith wrote to Nancy Williams in late June to say the new book "has met with a stunning silence," and yet the publishers "seem to be happy with their part."

The sales record of *Browser's* II notwithstanding, Ciardi had to begin gearing up for more travel by late September. On the twenty-fourth, he and Judith were in Medford for his fiftieth high school reunion, where they had "an astonishingly good time," as he reported to Nancy Williams. Then followed "a needed lucrative month" to make up in part for some large stock market losses. He earned seven thousand dollars, he told Nancy, "cash I am beginning to need." His first stop was Washington University in St. Louis, followed by three days at the University of Missouri-Kansas City (his old University of Kansas City), where on 18 October Ciardi was awarded his eighth honorary doctorate for being "a major force in American poetry for four decades." After a round of radio, television, and newspaper interviews set up finally by Harper & Row for Ciardi to promote *Browser's* II, among other things, John and Judith were off to Detroit on the twenty-second for rest and relaxation with the Kasles and their other Detroit friends. Ciardi made a quick side-trip one day to Chicago to pick up an easy lecture check, but for the rest of the time he stayed in Detroit, visiting and tending to a new round of publicity interviews. The *Detroit Free Press*, for example, reported that Ciardi was a "literary whiz": "a no-nonsense sort who used to aspire to a fifth of bourbon a day—until he got diabetic symptoms and quit drinking instantly. He is a chesty man of about six feet, with the clear bass voice and nonstop delivery of the classroom veteran."

Partly because the New York State Reading Association canceled Ciardi's two-thousand-dollar talk, scheduled for 11 November 1983, the month passed quietly. Ciardi wanted to head down to Key West before the holidays—again, but he could not talk Judith into it and did not want to go down alone—again. So he stayed home and groused. He wrote to Irv Klompus on 1 November playfully but unhappily: "I wish we could go to Key West, but Judith insists on staying for Xmas so I can have my annual flu. I could go down by myself, but I am miserable when I don't have her around to abuse." He complained to Miller Williams on New Year's Day that Christmas expenses that year were way out of hand because "Judith just won't be held back." Christmas had, in fact, developed into a family bone of contention during all of Ciardi's last years. It had never had any religious significance for him, and more and more he needed the healing sun of Key West instead of the frozen darkness of New Jersey Decembers. Nor could he see the season as a time for family bonding—or perhaps healing. And to make matters worse, he wasn't even able to drown his indifference with Christmas spirits. "I confess," he continued to Williams, that "I grow a bit weary of watching $100 bills stream away like autumn leaves in a blow." But then again, as Judith kept reminding him, "what would we be saving them for? Damned if I know. And I got a sweater, shirt, and moccasins, none of which fit, along with a set of amplifiers that distort everything. It's the spirit that counts." Ciardi's grumpiness was eased a bit when Jeff Lovill arrived to spend a few days visiting and interviewing for his dissertation. But then a family crisis arose when Myra broke up with her longtime boyfriend, thus delaying the needed sun for yet another month. All in all, the 1983 holidays had been a prolonged disaster, as Ciardi revealed with equal measures of impatience and barely contained anger, in a letter of 6 February to Walter Newman: "We finally solved various problems of house sitters and demented offspring, sacrificing January to genetic malfunction, and made it to FLA for Feb. 1."

Making the late arrival in Key West worse was the need for an early departure. After only six weeks, John and Judith drove to New Jersey just long enough to pack for UM-KC where Ciardi had been named the first distinguished visiting professor for the Carolyn Benton Cockefair Chair in Continuing Education. The five-week appointment extended from 26 March to 29 April 1984 and paid fifteen thousand dollars, plus lodging in a very comfortable two-room suite at the Raphael Hotel. It was to be, as Ciardi had written on the first to Miller Williams, "a sort of festive month of public lectures." There were, in fact, only two such occasions, one on

29 March when his topic was "Poetry: A Closer Look," and one on 19 April, "An Evening with John Ciardi," which was a poetry reading. The rest of the time he led seminars, did radio interviews (one recorded with David Ray for "*New Letters* On the Air"), gave a five-lecture series on Dante at the Plaza Library auditorium, visited a few classrooms, and attended an ongoing series of luncheons and receptions. His days were thus fully accounted for—busy perhaps, but not terribly demanding. In fact, Ciardi wrote to Williams on 14 April, he was being pampered and he liked it: "I couldn't have been treated more royally than UMKC is doing. I'm getting the native-son-plus-big-shot treatment. Good for the ego." What was more, the checks were also rolling in: one he called "not bad" for *How Does a Poem Mean?*; "a fine fat" one for his Dante translation; and "an astonishing tax refund" of sixteen thousand dollars because he had overpaid his quarterly estimated taxes. Plus, as soon as his Kansas City stint was completed, he was in line to pick up "nice fat checks" in Mississippi and Oklahoma. For the moment, at least, things were looking up.

From Kansas City Ciardi flew to Greenwood, Mississippi, for an arts festival and two days later took a series of connecting flights to Oklahoma City where he met Judith, who had gone there from Kansas City to visit a cousin. From there they went to Tulsa where one newspaper reporter called him "enchanting" and a "versatile writer [who] mesmerized his audiences with his deep, resonant voice and his mastery of language." From Tulsa they drove to Fayetteville for a quick visit with Miller and Jordan Williams and then up to Chicago for a lecture on 12 May. After that they stopped in Detroit to visit the Kasles and then home to New Jersey by 18 May. After a few days home, Ciardi went to Florence, South Carolina, and then Long Island, New York, on 3 June, where Vince Clemente had made arrangements for John to speak at the Walt Whitman Birthplace and receive an award, a joint celebration of Walt Whitman's birthday and John Ciardi's contribution to American letters. Vince was trying to raise at least one thousand dollars for his friend's minimum lecture fee, but Ciardi, who rarely gave away lectures, was uncharacteristically generous about this one because of his fondness for Vince. "Don't worry about the check. I have almost $25M of fat lecture fees in April and May, and

$1,000 for a pleasant visit to Setauket is a gilded lily." Then on 14 June, Ciardi was off to Shangri-La (Oklahoma) where he spoke at the Hallmark cards "Creative Conference"—and collected three thousand dollars plus expenses. He reported to Walter Newman that "Hallmark was fun. . . . I had nothing to say about greeting cards—I talked about poetry and about language and they took it straight."

During what time he could pry loose from his travel schedule that spring, Ciardi was also putting together a book of new poems for the University of Arkansas Press and a ten-thousand-word, one-thousand-dollar autobiographical article for the Gale Research Company, which was published in 1985 as "About Being Born, and Surviving It." On 24 June 1984, his sixty-eighth birthday, Ciardi wrote to Jeff Lovill about the autobiographical project: "I have been agonizing at it and I think it has assumed something like its final shapelessness in the last two weeks or so. I'll see that you get [a copy], if I don't turn sane and decide to burn all those damned pages. Make read: Nothing is harder than to write about yourself without making up two other guys." As to the book of poems, Ciardi wrote to Williams on 14 April that though he had plenty of poems to choose from, he was concerned about finding the right title. "If I can find the right theme, the rest will fall into place. As a sign of old age I incline more and more to stanza forms, rhyme, off-rhyme, and even sonnets. I really don't need to prove that I am obsolete, but grow insistent about it—another symptom of senility. I still do some things in looser form, but I find myself happier as the form gets tighter. Insecurity. Since I have nothing to say, the fun has to be in making it pass through measures."

Measures were on Ciardi's mind partly because he was thinking of a new book of children's poetry that he was discussing in sporadic correspondence with Elizabeth Gordon, who was vice president and associate publisher of Harper & Row's Junior Books Group (which had bought out J. B. Lippincott). Regular rhythms and rhymes and stanzas were especially important for children's poetry, which reminded Ciardi of their abandonment by most modernists and their descendants right into the 1980s—which brought him back to feeling obsolete. It was a subject that always troubled Ciardi even though he regularly hid his feelings behind a self-deprecating humor. Occasionally, however, bitterness crept into his voice. He wrote to Walter Newman on 23 May that he had been reading the poems of Robert Francis, whom he characterized as "a marvelous nature poet with an eye to make God glad," but a man who had been "generally ignored" for fifty years. He, too, had been ignored, Ciardi was really saying: "If I went in for chainsaw murders, people would start reading me and maybe discover I wrote a few pretty good things. But I'd rather not turn bloody. . . ." In the final analysis, as the Francis example illustrated, poetic fame was dependent on "extraneous things rather than poetic merit." But no sooner had he made his point, than he realized it was self-pitying, so he added his familiar denial that he'd been treated badly. He'd been "egregiously lucky" in that he had been paid well enough to do things his own way: "You can't make any money by selling poetry, but you can make them pay through the nose for explaining it, especially on the lecture circuit, on which I turn out to be an affable gasbag. Who's complaining?"

For nearly a year he'd been waiting to hear from Liz Gordon about a new book of children's poems. When she finally wrote on 2 February with a contract offer, Ciardi agreed but raised a few questions that were still unanswered on 8 March. "Today," he wrote to Jeff Lovill, "I wrote to break off the engagement. I haven't time to go steady with a gal that is so slow. Over a year wasted, dammit!" But he hadn't actually broken off the engagement yet because on 12 April he made the official announcement—and in the most unambiguous language. He wrote to Gordon that her correspondence had revealed a pattern that he was not prepared "to live with": "If I were huffy I would say you have been insultingly slow in reply. It isn't a question of ego but of time: I don't think I can live long enough to do what I want to get done—not with you as my editor." And then, just in case she did not get the message, he spelled it out for her: "I don't want to work with you. I have, in fact, concluded that there is no way I *can* work with you." He wanted all his manuscripts back so that he could "set about peddling [the book] somewhere else."

The somewhere else turned out to be Houghton Mifflin, the company that had rejected his manuscript called *The Dance on Mud Hole Street* in August 1977. Walter Lorraine, director of children's trade books wrote on 5 June 1984, that he wanted to publish Ciardi's new book; after all, *I Met a Man* was still one of their "more successful" titles and "one of the few collections of poetry" that was "truly appealing to children." Ciardi was elated and wrote back immediately to make plans.

> Time matters to me. In about two weeks I shall be 68. That's not dead yet, but it leaves me no time to waste. I project at least five books plus a book of limericks for children, plus another notion or two that I may not get to. At this moment I have on hand enough or almost enough poems for five children's books. If I am not mocking the gods by projecting 10 more good working years, I should like to get those into print, if only as a terminal self-indulgence. It will, I suggest, take some expedition to get them out at the rate of one every two years. If need be, I should like to get them edited and ready for posthumous publication. My wife, a major in Pollyanics, calls those morbid thoughts, but I explain them by saying "Shut up and let's get going."

During the summer, Ciardi worked with senior editor Matilda Welter, who had been warned to move matters speedily along, and by mid-August, when John and Judith went out to Nantucket to visit with the Fredlands for two weeks, *Doodle Soup* was ready to be put on the production schedule, even though the contract numbers had to be hammered out. The original offer had been for 6 percent, with the remaining 4 percent of royalties going to the illustrator. But Ciardi objected strenuously to this division because he had always received the full 10 percent, with the companies making separate arrangements with the illustrators. He was annoyed that *he* had to pay the illustrator under the new arrangement, and he wanted this book especially to earn as much as possible because the copyright and all proceeds were to go to Myra, who desperately needed the money. They settled on 8 percent, but not before the first of November, at which point Ciardi wrote almost nervously to Welter that he might not be able to survive any more delays. "At the rate at which my dearest friends are dying, I confess to feeling urgent about time."

The urgency had been underscored during the summer of 1984. Dan Jaffe's father, Herb, who had worked to clear Ciardi's name from the radicals list in 1970, had undergone serious surgery in June, and John wrote to Dan on the thirtieth: "I feel more than an abstract sympathy for him. First because I have always liked him. Second because I can feel myself faltering. . . ." Then on 21 July, Ciardi consoled Jeff Lovill over the death of his father: "To bury a father is a numbing experience but at least in the life-order. . . ." And Ciardi confessed in the same letter to his own deep loss over the recent death of Bud Orenstein: "I am drained by the news that my old buddy, former co-pilot, and much loved friend, Bud Orenstein went to a party and died of a heart attack. Life is a bubble." Six days later, Ciardi wrote consolingly to Vince Clemente about death, a subject that had threaded its way into their correspondence since February, when Vince had told John that he was taking his father for cancer cobalt treatments—and how much he loved his father. Ciardi answered in kind: "I watched my mother start to die at 80 and take five years to do it. It is a horror to watch a great personality fade out of itself. With every loving sympathy, I hope your father will be spared that long last unraveling to nothing. A man learns how to die. I think what he hopes for is to remain a man to the end."

Ciardi was also feeling poorly again by late summer—and limping—which gave his thoughts about death an even greater immediacy. On 12 September he wrote to Gil Gallagher that his medications had induced "a sub-human state of blank no energy." At least that was what he hoped was the cause because by changing the medication he hoped to improve. On the other hand, he said, "if it is terminal debilitude, it sure as hell feels terminal." On the twenty-sixth, he wrote to Doc Klompus that he was just back from a lecture jaunt to North Carolina but "dragging all the way" because he had "picked up a cold that won't quit." Besides that, he said, he was suffering from "general debility," as witness the fact that "crossing an airport has become an adventure." Then to Gil Gallagher, also on the twenty-sixth, Ciardi sounded even more disheartened: that "persistent cold" had made him feel "like a damp dishrag." If the medication change did not work, he said he would be checking into the hospital in November for "a real battery of tests." "I hate this," he confessed. "I can't walk more than $\frac{1}{4}$ mile before my legs turn into wet noodles. Well." Ciardi's symptoms of "terminal debilitude" could not have come at a worse time with lectures scheduled and several books in various stages of completion: *Doodle Soup*, the new book of adult poems that would be called *The Birds of Pompeii*, *Browser's* III, plus his just finished autobiographical essay and soon-to-be-released *Selected Poems*, which was to be launched at a party hosted by Elly Welt at Northern Kentucky University in late October. This was not a time that Ciardi could afford to feel like a "damp dishrag."

Over and above all these health considerations and depressions of spirit, serious financial problems kept Ciardi planning for more work and more money. For one thing he had "lost heavily in the market," according to his letter to Gil Gallagher of 12 September. For another, he had become irritated that at age sixty-eight he had no pension checks coming in. He had left Rutgers two years shy of qualifying for a pension, and even Social Security was denied him because he was earning too much money. Even more irritating, he had to continue paying Social Security at the rate of about three thousand dollars a year until age 70, when he had hopes of receiving about a thousand dollars a month. What created all this pension interest and general financial crisis was Benn's latest business venture, a carpet outlet, that Ciardi was being asked to finance. And this time, the stakes were high.

On 7 May, Ciardi had written a check for $17,550 to a realty company for the rental of a store plus a security deposit. On 5 June, he wrote another check, this time to Benn, for $20,000 to pay contractors. On 3 July, he wrote Benn another check for $12,450, followed by one for $20,000 on 13 August. Months later he claimed that he was promised promissory notes at 12 percent interest for his investment, but that Benn and his partner had never produced them. He knew it had been foolish, but in the end he had "yielded unwisely" to Benn's "importunities (as I would have done for no one else)." With an additional $5,000 figured in for Benn's car lease, Ciardi's investment in Benn's carpet business came to $75,000 during the summer of 1984. From that point on, Ciardi's correspondence is peppered with references to his son's business and his own investment. He generally joked half-heartedly about how he was going broke supporting Benn's latest business venture, but he seemed pleased at the same time with Benn's initiative and his own ability to be the chief financial backer. Moreover, Ciardi had always liked the thrill of gambling, and he was now rolling the dice for a good reason—to prepare a career for his nonacademically minded younger son. If Benn was not to become a professional like his brother, Ciardi was hoping that perhaps he could launch Benn in a lucrative retail concern. And secretly, Ciardi loved Benn's wild enthusiasms and grand business plans; he wanted to be a part of his son's big moneymaking scheme. On 30 June, Ciardi wrote to his sister Cora with his usual cautionary but hopeful patter:

> Please look around your kitchen to see if you have an old tin cup. I may have to rattle it on Main Street. Benn, the demon salesman[,] and a partner, have just invested in a big carpet outlet not far from here, and all is wild activity. Except in my bank account. But Benn is so happy to invest my money that it doesn't seem friendly to complain. He promises to make us all rich. I'll settle for just staying out of the poor house. But I must say, it looks good. Had I known this was going to happen, I would have insisted that you become a nun so that your prayers would be sure to count. Anyhow wish him enough luck to keep us out of the poorhouse.

Optimism ran high when Tops Carpet City opened on the Labor Day weekend with what Ciardi called in a letter to Floss Orenstein on the fourth, "a spectacular blast-off." Benn was working from seven in the morning until nine thirty at night, he wrote, "seven days a week and loving it, at least as long as the money rolls in. Avarice is an adamantine character base. And the store looks good. In reasonable expectation I can even look forward to having a rich son. . . ." To Miller Williams Ciardi wrote on the seventh that Benn was "furiously in the carpet business—really a quite imposing and handsome outlet—and with good prospects of making a heap of money. He thinks he can average a gross of $10,000 a day!—and damned if he hasn't been doing that, at least so far. The mind-boggling goal is $3 million a year, which should leave about $1 m[illion] to divide with his partner! (55%–45%) I think he might just carry it off. . . . It is a sleazy hard-sell business, but I never realized what money there was to be grabbed in it. And they are already talking of one store begetting another—and another and another, so that in 10 years they can sit in their plush offices as executives, and execute the peasants." Ciardi was so hopeful that

Benn had finally found his own way in life that he was able to reveal his greatest fear in the midst of his standard banter in a letter to Jeff Lovill on the sixteenth: "I have already messed up this family because I had no experience of how to be a rich father, but they took care of that by making sure I should go broke."

While all the arrangements for Tops Carpet City were being worked out during the summer and fall of 1984, Ciardi was also keeping up with his own schedule of writing and lecturing, which included about a two-week October loop in Kentucky. The centerpiece was at Northern Kentucky University, where Elly Welt had arranged for Ciardi to be writer in residence from the fifteenth to the seventeenth. The event was, in fact, planned as a launching party for *Selected Poems*. Ciardi flew in from a speaking engagement in Jackson, Wyoming, and Judith drove out and met him there. Miller Williams, John Stone, and George Garrett all flew in especially for the party. And the book itself was already back to the press for a second printing. "It wasn't, to be sure, a huge printing," Ciardi wrote to Jeff Lovill on the twenty-ninth, "but it's good to see a second one so soon." Ciardi, of course, was able to read from *Selected* at his 8:00 P.M. poetry reading in the ballroom of the University Center on the fifteenth. It was a festive occasion, and joyous. Everyone got along so famously and enjoyed himself so thoroughly that there was wild talk of gathering everyone together again, maybe in a year, maybe for an old-fashioned writers' conference, with John presiding as director, just like Bread Loaf. They'd call it, at least among themselves, the Joy Conference. At the end of the month, Ciardi wrote with some surprise to Stone that according to Elly Welt, plans for the Joy Conference were actually proceeding, even though it all seemed so very far-fetched. Still, he wrote, "I'll hope the administration finds lots of money for us to have fun on." Even if nothing came of it, he said, "it's a sweet dream."

By the beginning of November, the long, tiring year was wearing on Ciardi and he resolved to head to Key West on the fourteenth. There was a great deal to do on *Browser's* III, but the real reason was that Ciardi desperately needed the restorative warmth and quiet of his Windsor Lane retreat. His new diabetes medication seemed to be working out better because he felt more energy, Ciardi wrote to Stanley Burnshaw on the twenty-ninth—although at Bellarmine

College in Louisville (where he had squeezed in a two-day, fifteen-hundred-dollar stopover on October 22–23), he'd had to deliver his talk seated because he didn't have strength enough to stand. He planned to spend the first two weeks in November taking care of accumulated errands (including a date with a Metuchen doctor to remove what Ciardi called a "carbuncle" that had grown again on his back) and then he would be heading to Virginia to visit with George and Susan Garrett, followed by a stopover in Atlanta to visit with John and Lu Stone. Once in Florida, he visited old friends in Gainesville, had a lecture at the University of South Florida in Tampa on 27 November, and managed to get to Key West on the twenty-eighth because Jonnel and Myra were waiting for him with bad news about Benn. On 1 December, Ciardi wrote to Walter Newman: "I look forward to some quiet time for I have been spinning since early Oct. First on a lecture tour to Wyo. and (mostly) Kentucky Colleges. Then home to some bleak family problems with a junkie son. . . . I think I have at last buried the lost son in my mind and will make my peace with that delayed funeral. —I won't mention this again." And on the same day, he wrote to Gertrude Kasle that he had sold some twenty-five thousand dollars worth of prints and posters by Chagall, Lautrec, Miro, and Matisse at a Christie's auction (not mentioning how much money he'd lost that summer) before giving her his heartbreaking news: "Bad problems with Benn. He turns out, alas, to be a goddamn junkie. I'll hope for a miracle but I have had to shut him off and out. A funeral in my heart."

December was a difficult month of mourning in Key West for Ciardi, made some easier by his friends and neighbors, plus visitors like Elly and Peter Welt and Gil Gallagher. But he was irritable and difficult most of the time as he hammered away at *Browser's* III in the middle of most nights and conferred during part of most days with Elly about her nearly completed novel *Berlin Wild*. They played Scrabble and gin rummy in the afternoons and early evenings, but at night Elly and Peter went to the master bedroom that John had given up for them, Gil retired to the spare room, and John worked at the dining room table until the wee hours of the morning, after which he would sleep on the couch. They all tried to get John to try some modest exercise, but he could not even get to the mailbox, maybe twenty-five yards away, without his legs turning into noodles, he said. When they would all go to the beach, John would usually sit in one place and smoke while the others walked, and once when they had begun to walk to a restaurant for dinner, John had to return for the car. Through it all, Ciardi was irritable and, in Elly Welt's view, feeling guilty about not being in New Jersey. He knew, however, that his presence back home would not alter unfolding events, that open hostilities between him and the rest of the family would not help anything, and that he needed Key West's warmth as a partial fix to all that was ailing him spiritually and physically. Still, it was not easy being so far from his loved ones at such a critical juncture.

Then, on Christmas day, Benn's thirtieth birthday, matters at home came to a head. Suicidally stoned on drugs, Benn had to be talked down from the roof by Jonnel and a friend; it was a close call, but once safely on the ground, having survived his brush with death, Benn was able to admit to his addiction and seek the help he needed. That very day he signed himself into a drug detoxification and rehabilitation program in Princeton, the Carrier Clinic, and began his ascent from Hell. When Judith phoned with the news (including the fact that their health insurance did not cover this hospitalization, that she had to raise about thirteen thousand dollars in cash, and that she would be delayed), Ciardi poured out tears of happy gratitude. Three years later, and free of drugs, Benn understood his Christmas Day decision to enter the clinic as a kind of gift to his father, "one of the greatest things that I ever did for him." It was a thirty-day program, so John and Judith did not know exactly how Benn was doing during the month of January 1985, but there was reason, finally, for hope. When the month was over and Benn was released, Ciardi was no longer the man with a funeral in his heart. He wrote to Miller Williams in early February: "Benn is out of rehab and calls nightly. He sounds great. I hope & glow! Ah, may it work." He closed in newfound high spirits, "Love to Jordan. Love to you. Hell, love to everyone!"

But Ciardi, whose social skills had grown unpredictable, with charm and rude outbursts equally possible in daily intercourse, showed more strain than love. John Malcolm Brinnin saw Ciardi as a trial during this time, a "social problem" whom his friends had difficulty tolerating. He agreed with Dick and Charlee Wilbur, who noted that John had an "attention span" problem, possibly due to all those years of heavy drinking, they thought. "He became very bluntly inattentive," according to Wilbur, who was "distressed" to see his old friend nearly unable "to have an interchange with anybody," often redirecting conversation to himself or repeating long etymologies in place of conversation. He interrupted everyone, especially Judith, who was rarely able to finish a sentence, according to Charlee. They agreed that John was becoming "more difficult to know, more trouble." In fact, they said, "a lot of people found him too much trouble."

However, David Jackson, one of Ciardi's Key West neighbors and the long-time companion of James Merrill, recalled an incident during the winter of 1985 when Ciardi's deteriorating social skills had come in handy. An artist named Ilse Getz, whom Jackson termed "an egomaniac who spoke constantly of herself," had alienated herself from the inner circle of Key West literary society. One evening after a cocktail party at John Malcolm Brinnin's, the group retired to "Claire's," a chic restaurant very popular that season, for dinner. According to John Malcolm, they deliberately sat Getz next to Ciardi fully expecting the "fur to fly"—and it did. According to Dick Wilbur, no such conspiracy was at work, and Ciardi was several seats away, which made his outburst even more embarrassingly noticeable. No one afterward could recall exactly what Ciardi had said as he put the annoying artist in her place, but all agreed that it was long and loud and was followed by silence. Wilbur said that Ciardi had been "stentorian" and that his face was "frozen with anger." According to Jackson, Ciardi's scene not only drove Getz out of their social group, but off the island altogether—just what some of them had apparently been hoping for. What they hadn't counted on was Judith, who was so mortified by her husband's behavior that she stormed out of the restaurant. Back in the privacy of their home, John and Judith had one of the fiercest fights of their married life with Ciardi taking the position that his wife had not backed him up when he needed her support.

This incident aside, and with Benn recovering nicely, the month of February actually passed rather well for Ciardi, the more so because from the twelfth to the sixteenth a film crew from CBS television arrived in Key West, with producer Jim Houtrides and interviewer Haywood Hale Broun, to shoot a segment on Ciardi for *Sunday Morning*, the long-running network program then hosted by Charles Kuralt. Ciardi wrote to Stan Epstein on the twenty-seventh that Broun was "an impressive fine gent" and that "running around with [him] was fun." By the eighteenth, Ciardi was in Atlanta to speak to the Atlanta Bar Association (twenty-seven hundred dollars plus accommodations and meals) and to visit with the Stones. His thoughts turned toward death again in a letter to Jeff Lovill on the twenty-sixth, when he advised this newest and last of his sons, "Don't be sad about the fact that I am old enough to drop dead. The sadness would be if you did first." And Ciardi wrote on 1 March to Dan Jaffe, consoling him on the death of his father: "Your father would have wanted no deep grief. As one now waiting in line I attest to that sentiment." Then from Northern Kentucky University, Elly Welt wrote with good news, as Ciardi reported to Miller Williams: "believe it or not NKU has funded a trial JOY CONFERENCE. I'm due there in April to talk about it. Prob. for sometime in Oct."

March, too, was a good month. On the tenth, the *Sunday Morning* segment was aired. It opened with a beautiful shot of sunset in Key West, with gulls lazily dancing over the water, then gave way to the Windsor Lane compound, the house itself, and finally the small guest room-study where the camera found Ciardi banging away on his typewriter with two fingers. Ciardi read a poem, Broun narrated a little bit of Ciardi's biography, (accompanied by photographs of his army days and Bread Loaf, plus thirty seconds of an *Accent* program that had aired on CBS some twenty-three years earlier), and then they sat by the compound pool to talk about poetry. Broun asked Ciardi about his autobiographical poems while the screen flashed one photograph of John with his mother and another one of his father. But Ciardi walked carefully around the question, insisting that his poems were not confessional but "sounding chambers of old echoes." And when the subject turned to inspiration, again Ciardi spoke carefully, this time of "distrusting" the word because while one might "write hot," he had to "revise cold." When Broun asked what "separated" Ciardi from the "younger poets," Ciardi replied, "The same thing that separates me from my children." They didn't speak the same language, Ciardi said, and he hadn't been able to teach any of them about the function of memory. Then with his normal shrug of the shoulders that tried to hide the deep feelings he had, Ciardi gave one of his standard remarks: "So I grow used to being obsolete and I become stubbornly obsolete about it." Broun characterized Ciardi as "a man separated from a changing world," and Ciardi countered, with apparent contentment, that "a man *is* what he does with his attention." In the end, Ciardi told Broun what he kept telling himself (and anyone else who happened to be within earshot) over his last years: he had nothing to complain about: "Language summoned my attention, and I have found no reason to regret it. It's been a lovely life. There've been problems in it, but in the long run, I've been given a pretty fair living for doing almost exactly as I pleased. That's a wealth."

Meanwhile, Benn was in the middle of his successful recovery, and Ciardi's elation could barely be contained in correspondence. On 29 April, he wrote to Walter Newman that his son had been "reborn": "I know on medical evidence that he has been clean since Christmas. I am ready to believe he is truly cured and that I have this son again." The next day he wrote to Jeff Lovill: "My joy is that I have my son Benn again. . . . He has done me out of heavy money—I'd guess $150,000—on his junk trip and back, but he *is* back, and damn all else!" Then on 8 May, Ciardi wrote to Bob Snyder, one of his friends in Jupiter, Florida: "I am ready to believe [Benn] is gutsy enough to see it through. Above all, he is not too ebullient. He is facing it hard and clear. I went to an AA meeting with him—I have my role to learn—and heard a guy say, 'I am Joe Blow. I am an alcoholic. I have built a twenty-nine and a half year sobriety. That doesn't lick the problem, but I'm learning to manage it, I think.' Somehow I find that impressive, and have a great feeling that Benn has the will and guts to face it out in just that way. Goddamnbless life!" On 25 May, again to Newman, Ciardi wrote, "It's a new kid. A guy has to compensate, He doesn't even drink beer or smoke pot these days. He has become a health freak, exercises, works hard, and goes to meetings. I've gone with him and will keep going, and tawdry as the AA and NA rituals are, they seem to work. It's astonishing to see inarticulate people reach into themselves and grope for their lives. Those meetings do what good art reaches for, and even if they have the style of bad art, there is something very moving under the boredom. At least I have been moved by it."

While Ciardi attended with increasing hope to his son's recovery, a different sort of pain was developing. Yes, he was looking forward to the Joy Conference in October, Ciardi wrote to Miller Williams on 21 April, but that had put him in mind of a sadness. Bread Loaf was celebrating its sixtieth anniversary in August, and by way of celebration, Robert Pack (who had had to fire Sandy Martin as his assistant in 1978 for taking too much of the director's responsibility and authority—just as Ciardi had predicted) extended an olive branch to Bread Loaf's ousted leader during the turbulent sixties. But it wasn't much of a branch, as Ciardi put it in his letter to Williams. "Pack asked me to drive up Aug. 14–16 to *listen* to some of the lectures and to bask in the splendor of his achievement. He even offered to provide room and board for 3 nights. I'm awed. I bear him no ill will—even like him in a way—but he's a complacent ass. I told him I would be on a cruise. I won't be, but I'd be all asea at B.L." Pack, of course, was being forced into nostalgia by the occasion but no doubt saw the anniversary also as a welcome opportunity to reintroduce Ciardi, as one of the conference's great past presences, to the annual mountain gathering. He did not count, however, on Ciardi's pride, for having been dismissed by Bread Loaf's management in the early 1970s and increasingly by the community of poets since then, Ciardi had retired into his own world of word histories, lectures, and poems. He had grown "stubbornly obsolete" and would not accept window dressing status at Bread Loaf.

But having been left behind and even ridiculed by many, Ciardi was nonetheless still eager to recoup his lost reputation. Unfairly or not, he had lost ground throughout the 1970s. He'd been most pained by the failure of *Lives of X* (1971) to catch on critically and/or popularly, but the losses kept mounting with *The Little That Is All* (1974) and *For Instance* (1979). Neither did his book of children's verse, *Fast & Slow* (1975) nor his hardcover Dante (1977) halt the slide. But Ciardi still had hopes that *Selected Poems*, never mind the difficulties he had had putting it together, would vault him once again into the first rank of contemporary American poets, a position his friends would rarely admit he had lost. He even had unspoken hopes, he confessed to Elly Welt, that he might win the Pulitzer for it. But by April 1985, it was clear that no such thing was about to happen, for *Selected* had been out about six months and received almost no attention from reviewers, big or small. On the twenty-first, Ciardi wrote to Miller Williams that he was "already too obsolete to be noticeable": "You're clearly stupid to be publishing obsolete poets, but after the total silence with which *Lives of X* was greeted, I expect no notice. I'd be a liar if I said I am pleased by it, but I have learned to shrug it off. Because we all hoard our failures, I tell myself it's my own fault for thinking sanity may yet speak."

On 29 May 1985, in the midst of his depression over dashed hopes for *Selected*, Ciardi heard even darker news from John Nims, who had gone into his favorite bookstore in Chicago and bought the June *Poetry*, which had not yet been mailed to subscribers. In it was a group review that covered Ciardi's book and one by Karl Shapiro, and as Nims put it in a letter to Ciardi, "it's quite hard on both of you." Nims kept the letter for a couple of days, then added to it on 1 June, when he wrote "that dumb review has been like a black cloud in my mind." He was most unhappy with the reviewer, David Wojahn, who was "a young man . . . on the make—and what better can he do than deride his elders. And his betters." Nims apologized (presumably because he had been a two-time editor of the magazine himself) on behalf of *Poetry*. Ciardi tried to be clever in his disappointment when he wrote back to Nims on the fifth: "I have stopped complaining about the world I never made. I grow inured to my status as an obsolete X. If Wojahn (whose name I never had heard before) is perceptive enough to think I'm as bad or worse than Karl Shapiro, I can at least go to Hell in admired company."

But quips aside, Wojahn had been brutal. If Shapiro "had trouble finding a style," Wojahn wrote, then Ciardi "had the more difficult problem of finding a voice." (This particular charge perplexed and riled Ciardi supporters more than anything else in the review.) Then he backtracked by saying that Ciardi had indeed found a voice in the late 1950s, but wasted it on poems of "trivial social satire." He called Ciardi "smug and self-important" and "mostly just a crank." To Wojahn, Ciardi was so "nasty" that he couldn't even be playful enough for light verse. Yes, he admitted, "Ciardi is a personal poet, but he is not a personable one." Wojahn did allow that some of Ciardi's poems had "interesting stories" plus "some fine detail about growing up in an Italian immigrant family," including some "affectionate portraits of [his] father," but in the end Wojahn didn't like Ciardi's characteristic irony, which, he thought, too often "turn[s] into ridicule of his subjects or into preposterousness." All this he offered without entering so much as a quoted line or an examined poem in evidence. And then suddenly he quoted two stanzas from "Elegy Just in Case" to illustrate what he called "howlers"—although the example he cited may fairly call into question his own ear as much as Ciardi's voice. Still Wojahn continued: when Ciardi left off being "curmudgeonly," he was "apt to become saccharin," and his love poems in *I Marry You* "[came] close to being greeting card verse." While it was certainly reasonable to be suspicious of love poetry in general, and even to dislike Ciardi's for stated reasons, Wojahn dismissed many fine poems with the merest wave of a cliché.

Although he closed with a few words of unexpected and begrudging praise for *Lives of X* (which had some "notable poems" written with "a charm and generosity of spirit"), Wojahn and many of his contemporaries seemed to feel that Ciardi didn't even belong to the community of poets any more, having sold out to large lecture fees, a television program, a *Saturday Review* column, money-making word histories, and so on. Ciardi had helped carry the banner of modern poetry into the late 1960s and beyond, but he was out—out of the picture and out of touch. The Wojahn review in *Poetry*, with its narrowness and intolerance, not to mention its errors, was the official, public entombment of Ciardi's reputation.

On 24 February 1985, in the Sunday *Chicago Tribune*, George Garrett had already published the case for the opposition. He had called Ciardi and Shapiro "major American poets" who had "suffered a serious eclipse beginning in the late 1960s." They had both become "unfashionable" because "where achievement is too deeply rooted, something can be gained by ignoring what cannot be openly denied." There was plenty to like in *Selected*, said Garrett, but most particularly he singled out Ciardi's voice, which was different from Shapiro's: "tougher, harder-edged, more various in both subject and treatment." Both Shapiro and Ciardi were "much closer to the hard facts of our lives and times than most of the younger poets," Garrett concluded. This defensive review had reacted to the well-known and commonly accepted criticisms of the younger generation toward a couple of members of the older, but because it was published in February, Garrett wasn't able to address the specifics contained in Wojahn's review, which wasn't published until June. Miller Williams, however, wrote to Ciardi on 14 June what he thought of the Wojahn review: "The fact is that it will be seen as garbage. All of us here [at the University of Arkansas Press] are sorry for the review only because we hate to think of you reading this crap. Wojahn's tirade is so obviously motivated by shameful impulses that no one who ought to be reading poetry can take it seriously."

Ciardi's best public defense came from Judson Jerome in the October 1985 issue of *Writer's Digest*. Ciardi, wrote Jerome, was "one of the best-known, most prolific, and least appreciated of modern American poets." Although Ciardi was rarely anthologized, Jerome went on, his "power and artistry" were "much greater" than such "better known" poets as John Ashberry, James Dickey, Stanley Kunitz, Denise Levertov, W. S. Merwin, David Wagoner, "to name a few." Yes, Ciardi had been on *Sunday Morning* a few months back, but he was nonetheless suffering a "lack of recognition"; the reason he'd been on television at all was because he was a "public personality, known for his pungent language and sharp wit." The reason Ciardi had been overlooked by anthologists and critics, wrote Jerome, had "something to do with his prominence in the public eye. Robert Frost had a similar problem. He was treated with condescension by critics because of his popularity with the general public. The literary establishment is governed by snobs."

But, Jerome went on, there were other reasons Ciardi was neglected, like being "lucid and formally controlled," as in the exquisite miniature "Gulls Land and Cease to Be," which "deliberately *uses* the formal elements to dramatize and to reinforce the imagery. It's artistic. And, in poetry, art is out of fashion." So were families, Jerome continued, and *Selected Poems* was "rife with family, especially Ciardi's memories of his Italian parents." Jerome delighted in Ciardi's poems, which he said were "varied and rich, ranging in speculation and sharp observation, always in language charged with vigor, wit and passion, beating and breaking against tight forms." Next Jerome spent the best part of a page discussing one of the narratives in *Lives of X*, "Cal Coolidge and the Co (Poem for $98.41 plus, hopefully, bonuses)." And then he finished with high praise:

> Especially notice those longer poems in which Ciardi has developed a shirt-sleeve manner of getting down to business, on with the story, chewing and incorporating an immense variety of material without losing control of the relaxed iambic pentameter, keeping the language alive as *poetry*—not just broken prose—a feat that would be impossible in free

verse. Anecdotes, digressions, speculations, lyrical flights and comic teetery perchings all became part of the fabric. Few poets today know how to do that as well as Ciardi does (and Robert Frost did before him). And few poets know as well how to keep you reading, poem after poem, balancing the satisfaction of each as a work of art with that of the whole book as a tapestry of experience.

Jerome had come forward in a public forum with a wide readership to champion the lifetime achievements of John Ciardi.

As usual, however, Ciardi had to take his feelings on the road. After a Memorial Day gathering of the Ciardi clan in Boston, which John himself had requested with a sense, perhaps, that this would be his last, and at which he saw Jonnel and Valerie's new house in Medford (with a wedding planned for the following May), Ciardi had June dates in Washington, D.C. and Ann Arbor; July dates in Detroit, Chautauqua, and Miami (including a three-day cruise); and August dates in Sarasota, Gainesville, and someplace in North Carolina. Then it was off to visit the Fredlands for the weeks before and after Labor Day. Check-chasing and visiting old friends were good cures for depression, but there was another development during the summer that boosted Ciardi's sagging ego: Vince Clemente was actively working on a festschrift in his honor. It had begun as an offhand remark by Vince in a 10 June letter to Ciardi: "I'd love to see, for your 70th Birthday, a *John Ciardi Retrospective*—all the ways of looking at Ciardi the poet-critic-man-of-letters-browser. If there are thirteen ways of looking at a blackbird—think of all the ways of looking at/into Ciardi?" Ciardi replied two days later that he had indeed been thinking about an "extended autobiography" but had decided against it because it sounded "pretentious": "In ego I tell myself that I uphold the good old fashioned religion, which seems to mean God loves me and I'm saved. But what good is the sermon if no one shows up for Sunday services? A retrospective or festschrift for my 70th birthday would be flattering but. . . . I am no major exhibition and I have no significant complaints. I have written as an alcoholic drinks, compulsively for its own sake, and why should I claim rewards for being in Writers Anonymous?"

Ciardi had not on 12 June taken Clemente's intention seriously, but by the middle of July, sensing how serious Vince was, Ciardi wrote gently to discourage the project: "I am touched by your thought of a 70th birthday Festschrift, but I suspect you over-rate my critical reception in these United States. I have tried to think of as many as twelve people who might be moved to write for it, and I doubt they exist. . . . I am trying to point out to you that I am not exactly a critically widely acclaimed specimen. Of course it would be ego-gratifying to see myself puffed up in a Festschrift, but it might be even more critically embarrassing to find no one much has anything much he/she/it is moved to say about the less-than-dazzling figure J. Ciardi has cut in American letters. . . . I am not even sure it would get off the ground. I am out of fashion, as befits my stubborn obsolescence." But Clemente would not be dis-couraged. By the end of the summer he wrote on letterhead that proclaimed "A John Ciardi Festschrift": "I'm pressing ahead." His one "hope and prayer" was that he would be able "to get down the full measure of the man in all his loving complexity, and in a book worthy of its subject."

Clemente worked tirelessly on *Measure of the Man*, which came out in spring 1987, as a memorial tribute rather than a seventieth birthday testimonial. But Ciardi wrote several times in the fall 1985 how "astonished" he was at the number of people Clemente had lined up for the festschrift, thirty-seven in all, including reprinted pieces from John Holmes and Roy Cowden. The book would begin and end with Ciardi speaking, first in a generous excerpt from his Gale autobiography, "About Being Born, and Surviving It" and then at the end with a long interview. In between were contributions by X. J. Kennedy, Donald Hall, Richard Elman, John Nims, John Williams, Maxine Kumin, Judson Jerome, Miller Williams, Richard Wilbur, Elly Welt, Isaac Asimov, George Garrett, Norman Cousins, and many others. It turned out to be a warm and loving book, with a balance struck between reminiscences and critical essays on Ciardi's many and diversified accomplishments. Although he did not live to see the book published, Ciardi was kept abreast of its development and was deeply grateful to Clemente for doing it—and heartened, too, that so many friends and admirers were contributing.

With respect to his health, Ciardi was still having trouble with his legs. He was able to play nine holes of bad golf with a cart, he told Cordray on 5 September, but he had to sit down between shots, and he could not walk two holes without "collapsing on wet-noodle stems." He was aware always of his mortality, especially when friends died, as one did in August. Chris Norton had been one of Ciardi's Chautauqua friends, and it was there they saw each other for the last time on about 10 July. When Ciardi wrote to Bob and Bea Snyder, also friends of Chris Norton, he took on the foreboding tone of impending death that had crept into his conversation and corre-spondence: "I am in that season and you two are approaching it. The death of a good man is no rare and shocking news. He died in his sleep in a place he loved. There is no particular place I love, but I'll call it a good death if it's not too painful, escapes the needles-and-tubes squad, and especially if it manages not to distract my attention." Then, by way of a tension-easing quip, he added, "When you get word of mine—sometime certainly before A.D. 2185, have a drink to the old bastard and say he had it coming."

But there was still life left in September 1985, and Ciardi turned eagerly to it: two days at Luther College in Iowa in mid-September, then October lectures in Arkansas and Michigan, build-ing to the long-anticipated Joy Conference at Northern Kentucky University during the week of 21 October, the details of which had been worked out in exhausting detail by Elly Welt. In Chicago, how-ever, on the way home from Luther College, Ciardi's legs simply col-lapsed at the airport while he was trying to get from one terminal to another, and he had to call for a wheelchair. He told Mac Cordray about it on 21 September: "I confess to having felt the need many times in the past, but always insisted on toughing it out. On that sad day I was finally forced to succumb, and that weighs upon me." The trip to Fayetteville was for the launching of Ciardi's newest book of poems, *The Birds of Pompeii*, plus a poetry reading, an autograph party, and a talk to the students in the University of Arkansas's trans-lation program.

Except for his second volume of limericks with Isaac Asimov in 1981, *The Birds of Pompeii* was Ciardi's first book of new poems since the 1979 *For Instance*. Of course, *Selected Poems* had come out of the University of Arkansas Press a year earlier, October 1984, but to relative critical silence—that is, until the Wojahn review appeared in the June 1985 *Poetry*. But Ciardi had Judson Jerome's *Writer's Digest* rave review to cheer him up by October, so the publication celebra-tion was not appreciably darkened. And there was much to cel-ebrate, for *The Birds of Pompeii* proved that Ciardi was still, regardless of family problems, poor health, and failing reputation, writing well.

There were several poems about his own mortality, quite a few about poetry, and a group that dismissed pie-in-the-sky spiritualism in favor of the human race's common, and glorious, humanism. In all, the new book represented a late-in-life reaffirmation of Ciardi's faith, not in God or religion of course, but in art. In "The Glory" (which bears an epigraph that wonders in part if "Heaven is a broken appointment"), Ciardi wrote of an angel who had come calling too early one morning, while he was still wearing his "frayed robe." He instructed his wife to say that he was not at home, but if the angel could come back at ten,

> "I shall make it an homage to rearrange my day
> to the convenience of Heaven."

> Since then
> I have shaved, showered, dressed, and waited till the sky
> clotted the trees. I have sat here needled numb
> by congested hope, my shoes shined holy, my tie
> precise as a Credo. Let the Glory come

> if I am fit to receive it in the dress
> and form that is its due. My wife and son
> wait with me in their observant best. Unless
> the Glory is met in ritual, there is none.

Ritual, as it had been all along, was the key, for poetry had long ago taken the place of religion for Ciardi, who clung more and more to tight poetic forms—and his own colloquial language—as he got older. Not only was the satisfaction greater when one solved a poem's structural demands (including rhyme), but the resulting order provided the sort of precision and security that religion might have provided him in an earlier age. Free verse, however one defined it, did not provide ritual enough as a substitute for religion, which accounts for one part of the quarrel Ciardi had with it. Life and poetry provided the real glory.

In "Happiness" Ciardi ritualized again, in a tightly written poem with stanza and rhyme, about his own happy existence as an "animal, / in glandular reprieve." He woke one morning to find himself feeling at one with the fish and birds and slugs—indeed, all life forms—himself transported to boyhood again, from the "wheezy" old man he had grown to be. But soon he came back to reality, the present moment, which he actually preferred:

> Inanely happy, humanly out of place,
> I sip black coffee and the morning news,
> the collected daily rages of the race,
> till everything is as bad as it always was.
> And I grow serene. I have not lost my mind.
> I recognize our disastrous humankind
>
> and am in control of my own wits again
> to live and die in accurately. Amen.

Ciardi ended his prayer with his feet firmly planted on the ground and looking unflinchingly at what he called "our disastrous humankind." Always he had the courage to be fully and exclusively human, not the mysterious repository of a soul that had something better to look forward to.

Poetry was humbling as well as glorious —a principle that was never far from Ciardi's conscious mind. In our mere mortality, we ache always to get to the bottom of things, as in "True or False," which he thought enough of to reprint on the dust jacket of the book:

> Real emeralds are worth more than synthetics
> but the only way to tell one from the other
> is to heat them to a stated temperature,
> then tap. When it's done properly
> the real one shatters.
>
>   I have no emeralds.
> I was told this about them by a woman
> who said someone had told her. True or false,
> I have held my own palmful of bright breakage
> from a truth too late. I know the principle.

The test, if it was one, had been in Ciardi's mind for nearly twenty-five years. He had related the story originally in a "Manner of Speaking" column (21 July 1962) under the subtitle "Testing," but it had been put aside, either as an interesting idea for a poem or as a half-finished one, for all those years. According to Richard Wilbur,

Ciardi knew this was the best poem in the book. Wilbur observed that the poem was "metrically limber" with just "a reminiscence of the pentameter": "It has the natural movement of developing thought or unfolding talk. Its language is about how the most precious truths cannot be proven; how we miss out on them if we ask for proof, since such truths call only for belief." When he had finished quoting the poem in its entirety, Wilbur said simply, "That is beauty."

After *The Birds of Pompeii* had been properly launched, Ciardi left Fayetteville for Ann Arbor, where another Hopwood celebration had been planned for 10 October. This time John Knott, chairman of the English department, was raising money for the Hopwood Visiting Writers Fund, an endowment set up some six months earlier in New York to support readings and workshops by visiting authors. The goal was to raise $250,000, $50,000 of which had already been donated in March by Arthur Miller, still the best known and most successful of all the Hopwood winners. On the fourteenth, after Ciardi had gone back to Metuchen, he wrote John Knott thanking him for hospitality, but begging off a contribution: "If my son staves off bankruptcy and eventually pays back my blown nest egg, I hope to contribute at least a token check to the cause, for as I said the Hopwood Award has meant a great deal to me both in sentiment and in the enormously useful practical opportunities that flowed from it. At the moment I am trying to keep afloat till next June when social security is supposed to begin its, uh, largesse."

A year earlier, at the dinner party in Ciardi's honor to mark the publication of *Selected Poems*, a small group of writers and administrators from Northern Kentucky University had gathered at the Fort Mitchell Country Club. Standing up to toast the group after dinner, Ciardi had said, "If I were a rich man, I would have a large estate with little cottages, and I would invite all of you for the summer for a joy conference." That had been the seed that NKU president Leon Booth immediately planted, and with support from the Kentucky Arts Council and the National Endowment for the Humanities, plus the year-long, day-to-day nurturing provided by Project Director Elly Welt, the Joy Conference took place during the week of 21 October 1985. Thirty-six local participants (plus eight advanced students called "Fellows") had signed up for what was officially called the Ohio Valley Writers' Conference, with John Ciardi (for a fee of three thousand dollars, including all expenses) once again reprising his Bread Loaf role as director. That the conference went off on time, as planned, and without a hitch, was a testimony to Elly Welt's love of Ciardi, who had been both her good friend and mentor, a literary godfather.

Ciardi seemed to enjoy his role as director, especially as it was so largely honorary, with Elly and associate directors Miller Williams and Margery Rouse doing most of the work. (He had been forthright about his own participation from the outset, although it perhaps had the sound of false modesty when he announced in the conference bulletin that once he had chosen the staff he had nothing to direct.) Most of the conference days had readings, workshops, and talks, with occasional panels or lunch and dinner speakers. At 8:00 P.M. on Monday the twenty-first, Ciardi gave a reading that was followed by a reception. The next afternoon he and John Stone conducted a poetry workshop. On Wednesday, for twenty-five dollars a ticket (plus a cash bar), was "Dinner with John Ciardi and Friends" at the Fort Mitchell Country Club. On Thursday and Friday, Ciardi seems to have had no formal duties at all. If the conference was to be measured as a well-deserved tribute to Ciardi in the twilight of his career, it was indeed joyous; but if one takes into account Ciardi's performance at his one workshop, according to one of the participants, Michael Shapiro (Elly Welt's son), it was not at all a joy. Shapiro reported, and the story was corroborated by others in attendance, that Ciardi was "needlessly brutal." In Shapiro's words, Ciardi did make good points about bad writing, "but he *was* an asshole at that conference. There's no other way to say it." Moreover, just as he had taken to dominating so many conversations in his last year or two, he took over just about every panel he attended at the Joy Conference, either as a scheduled speaker or as a member of the audience. Even though the quality of the student writing was low, according to Shapiro, Ciardi showed little sensitivity to the tender feelings of those learning the craft.

Yet Shapiro was there for the good moments too, like the after-hours sessions at Ciardi's suite, when John was in "high form," according to Shapiro, holding forth in what sounds like his old Bread Loaf fashion, pontificating and entertaining in equal measure. On one evening, Ciardi and Williams engaged in a limerick contest that kept getting more involved until they were making them up in Italian. Shapiro recalled too that Ciardi spent the entire week in either a bright green sport coat or a magenta one, thus dominating the conference in more ways than one. And by way of excusing Ciardi's behavior with students, Shapiro pointed out that Ciardi may have been "crotchety" because he wasn't feeling well and was planning to see his doctor as soon as he got back to Metuchen.

Margery Rouse recalled that Ciardi had intended to sit down through a good part of the conference, but that he had been too intense to sit, pacing the floor as often as not. She also reported a story that Ciardi had been drinking one night and wound up skinny dipping at 1:00 A.M. in the motel pool. But Rouse, too, recalled how hard Ciardi was on the participants: he was "more irascible than ever," she said, using words like "devastating" and "cruel" to describe his performance: "He was not even as tolerant as he had been in earlier years." Ciardi's conduct was generally seen to have been indefensibly harsh and personally antagonistic, yet it isn't clear how much more abusive he had become over the years—or if it simply seemed that way because frank criticism had become more and more taboo in a permissive age. Both points were no doubt true, but either way, it became increasingly clear all week that the Ohio Valley Writers' Conference had not worked out as expected. As Elly Welt put it, they were all "reliving something embarrassingly dead."

Ciardi himself, however, seems to have been unaware of his own failings or anything like an embarrassing attempt to relive the past. He reported on the conference to John Frederick Nims, who had been unable to join the staff, on 1 November: "I'm back to running a Wrotter's [sic] Conf. For Northern Kentucky University. This last was a trial balloon, but I think it flies and that we'll be going on with it. . . . I want you to join us. It's privately known as the Joy Conference. I pick the staff and the test is simply that I have to love everyone I invite. That's the joy of it." Then on the thirteenth, Ciardi wrote to Miller Williams that he was still "aglow" about the conference:

> It bodes well for continuance. It will have to be tinkered
> with and I'm not for rushing into anything, but I think it
> could *evolve* into a good thing. I am insisting for starters that

[executive assistant] Becky Williams and her husband Ron are dangerously ambitious (beyond their qualification), and that they be removed at once. I'd like to try some other locale, ideally some resort where staff and conf. members could be together (perhaps with students bussed in), and in the summer. Reichert (head of Eng.) told Elly the Dept. would be interested in cooperating if it could appoint two of the staff, and the answer to that is NO WAY. The first principle I will insist on is that the director *alone* appoints staff, and that he has to love you as a writer and as a person. It's a beautiful and beautifully simple premise—and see how well it worked. I think we staged the first zero-backbiting conf. in history.

Ciardi may have heard about student criticisms of his performance, but there is no way to tell it from his upbeat excitement about repeating the conference. He imagined a new Bread Loaf built on the old model, with himself exclusively in charge of staff, and an assistant who took orders better than either Sandy Martin or Becky Williams.

When the Joy Conference ended, Ciardi drove to Lexington to visit the Cordrays, then headed to New Jersey, so pumped up by the swirl of recent events that he got a thirty-dollar speeding ticket along the way. At home, of course, there was a great deal to be done before he could leave for Key West. On November 15–17, Ciardi was in Boston, for a reading at the Boston Public Library arranged by Houghton Mifflin for the launching of *Doodle Soup*, an advance copy of which had arrived in Metuchen on the first. (The *New York Times Book Review* mentioned it as one of the "additional titles of interest" in its 5 January page on children's books. After a careful reading, all an unidentified reviewer could manage to say was that it was "a collection of good-natured poems.") In the meantime, Matilda Welter at Houghton Mifflin was interested in more poems and a word book for children, and Ciardi replied that he was very interested, but the word book could not be ready for 1987 publication, which led him to suggest a book of children's limericks first. "Does this make sense to you? (PLEASE do not file and forget. Time matters to me. I'll hit 70 in 1986. Let's say I have 10 working years left (??). It will take me that long to publish what I have on hand. I can't afford to skip a year. And I really see no way to get the word book *done right* in time for 1986 publication. . . . I'll look forward to hearing from you: will be here until Turkeygiving. Then off to Fla. with stops en route, arriving about Dec. 10."

On 29 November, the day after Thanksgiving, Ciardi left for Key West, once again leaving Judith to tend to Christmas with the children before joining him in January. He visited with the Garretts in Charlottesville for five days, then visited with the Stones in Atlanta before arriving in Key West, where Benn, who had flown down, met him. It was a time of healing and loving between father and son, which meant a great deal to both of them.

Ciardi kept busy in the winter of 1986, probably too busy. From January 7 to 11 he was in Miami for a meeting of the National Foundation for Advancement in the Arts, then he was in Jupiter, Florida, for two free lectures at the Lighthouse Gallery as a memorial for his old Chautauqua friend Chris Norton, then a stopover in Sarasota before heading to Young Harris College in Georgia for a talk that netted twenty-one hundred dollars. On the twenty-fourth, Ciardi wrote to Jeff Lovill of his January travel and travail: "I hate hitting the lecture trail so early but Benn went bankrupt—at my expense of course—and I'm out $100,000 and feeling poor." He was still picking away at the proofreading of his typescript of *Browser's* III, a job he'd been putting off since the previous April. He wrote to Vince Clemente on 9 February that he was having "unforeseen difficulties with my Intr. to *Browser's* III. At the going rate I may never finish it and just throw the typescript in the fireplace. It's safe to do so here in FLA." On the eighteenth, however, Ciardi reported to Stuart Wright that he had mailed off the typescript of *Browser's* III *and* his book of limericks. But all the work and travel had left him weak. Elly Welt and Peter joined John Williams for dinner with John and Judith on the twelfth. Elly was very impressed with the meal Judith had prepared: black fin tuna, tortellini with pesto, chicken aspic, broccoli, and orange juice pie—according to her journal entry for that day. But Elly continued her entry: "John is not well. He is irritable, short of breath, and always, always, a cigarette in his hand. I must begin those interviews [for a biography]—but John is slated for a few lectures in February and will actually leave in March."

"Jeff, where is death's sting?"

Ciardi was much more heavily booked in March than February, with six speaking dates scheduled, and the rest of the month was a constant rush of travel. On the first he flew from Key West to Washington, D.C., where the next day he delivered a Dante talk at the Hirshhorn Auditorium. On the third, he took a Metroliner to Philadelphia in time for a six-thirty reception and a lecture at the American Poetry Center (five hundred dollars) on children's litera- ture at eight. The next day he took a commuter flight to Pittsburgh for another talk on Dante at the Carnegie Lecture Hall for Sam Hazo's International Poetry Forum. For the Washington and Pitts- burgh lectures, Ciardi earned twenty-three hundred dollars, plus most expenses—all, in fact, except for the difference between the first class airplane ticket that he insisted on and the coach fare that Hazo could afford. An appearance at Birmingham Southern College on March 7 and 8 for seventeen hundred dollars was postponed at the last minute by the school. From Pittsburgh, Ciardi flew to New Jersey, and on the eighth he spoke at Rockeville Center, a lecture arranged by his agent at Program Corporation of America, for three thousand dollars. Finally, on the tenth, Ciardi flew back to Key West, where he packed up and gathered some strength for a week before beginning the long drive back to New Jersey.

And he needed strength to fight off the flu symptoms that had gripped him, "a gift of the uninhabitable North," as he put it in a letter to Sam Hazo on the twelfth. The next day, Ciardi wrote to John Nims, thanking him for writing "John Ciardi: The Many Lives of Poetry," a copy of which Nims had sent along a few days earlier. The paper was written for delivery as the Cockefair Chair lecture at the University of Missouri-Kansas City on 19 March (and later published in the August *Poetry* and included in Vince Clemente's 1987 festschrift). The long essay was an appreciation of Ciardi as poet. It began, "It is not easy to know, when about to explore the poetry of John Ciardi, where to enter so diverse a region and how to proceed when once there. It is hardly too much to say that here— as Dryden said of Chaucer—here is God's plenty." Ciardi replied that he was "immensely grateful": "You have done me the honor of paying the closest attention to my work, and you have been generous to its weaknesses; you have praised most the things that are most important to me. How shall I not be grateful? I assure you, I am." But the letter had been written in the middle of a night when fever had caused him to toss and turn and finally get up. He told Nims that he had come down with "a dizzy-making cold" that had him "feeling like mildewed laundry." The next day, the fourteenth, Ciardi wrote to Bob Snyder: "I'm packing the car for an early pound north to N. J. It will be a pound. I flew North for a short lecture trip and came back with a horrible cold that has me down for too long. Must get to N. J. fast so I can take off on another lecture trip. Madness."

John and Judith left Key West on the fifteenth, with John feeling so poorly that Judith drove the entire way home, with only two stopovers, one in Altamonte Springs, Florida, and one in Dunn, North Carolina. They pulled into their driveway late on the seventeenth, which left Ciardi barely three days to see Dr. Cannamela for something to get him feeling better—and to rest up for his four-day stint at the University of Southern Indiana in Evansville. It wasn't nearly enough time, especially in light of the fact that he planned to go from Evansville to Kansas City to visit Nims, then fly to Topeka and a five-thousand-dollar talk to the Ecumenical Librarians of Kansas, then to Denver for a Celebration of John Williams, which he was doing for love rather than money. He had put aside the month of April to rest up for Jonnel's wedding on 10 May.

First, however, the weakened Ciardi had to get through his Indiana commitment. It had been arranged through the Program Corporation of America for four thousand dollars minus commission. The university had been waiting and planning for Ciardi's visit with more than ordinary anticipation, for he was to be the school's first Enlow Distinguished Humanities Scholar. The Enlow family's gift to the school was fifty thousand dollars, donated as a way of celebrating the school's having achieved full university status, but administrators had had to wait a full year before the gift earned enough dividends to pay for their first distinguished scholar. At that, they needed another thousand dollars from the Indiana Committee for the Humanities to meet all their expenses, so they were very conscious of what they viewed as an obligation to squeeze as much value as possible from their multitalented guest. The idea to name Ciardi had come from composer Philip Hagemann, who suggested to his friend James Blevins, chairman of the Division of the Humanities, that they might stage some musical adaptations of Ciardi poems at the university's newest division, the restored utopian village known as Historic New Harmony, some ten miles from Evansville.

Ciardi's late Saturday afternoon flight to USI had been routed through Pittsburgh, where he needed a wheel chair to get through the airport to make his connecting flight. At the Evansville airport, he was met by Hagemann and Blevins at nine-thirty and taken to the Red Geranium Inn at New Harmony where he sat down to a steak and potato dinner at ten, a huge meal for such a late hour they thought. Afterward, Blevins drove Ciardi to the special quarters that had been arranged for him at New Harmony, the Mother Superior House at the corner of Main and Granary. The house was privately owned and the local arrangements committee led by painter Katie Waters and poet Matthew Graham, had secured permission for Ciardi to stay there. It was a lovely house with wide floorboards, a fireplace, an antique four-poster with curtains, and various religious paintings and carvings, like the *Nuestra Senora de Caysaysay* done by an unidentified Oriental sculptor in the Philippines in the eighteenth century. There was also a large bay window looking out over an enormous, fenced-in backyard, which was not at all visible in New Harmony's pitch black night.

Late Sunday morning, Hagemann drove Ciardi around New Harmony to see the sights. He had already noticed the night before how badly Ciardi was hobbling around, but he nonetheless laughed politely when Ciardi joked that his body would be going to the Rutgers medical school and that he wanted to get a tatoo on his arm inviting surgical students to cut away—"but damn you if you flunk!" At three-thirty and seven-thirty there were performances of Hagemann adaptations of Ciardi works at the Thrall Opera House with a reception at the New Harmony Gallery of Contemporary Art following the 3:30 performance. The event was presented by the Division of Humanities and billed as a "musical potpouri": "The poems of John Ciardi with music composed by Philip Hagemann." The program was in three parts. The first had seven choral pieces performed by the University of Evansville Children's Choir. The second was a ballet based on *Fiddler Dan* and performed by the Evansville Dance Theatre. The third was a one-act opera based on

The King Who Saved Himself from Being Saved, performed by members of the local opera company. The Thrall Opera House was a brick, two-story building with seating for two hundred in the main auditorium plus fifty more in the balcony. They had a full house and an enthusiastic audience at both performances. According to Sherry Durrell, another member of the local arrangements committee, during the intermissions Ciardi went outside to smoke and immediately became the center of attention as the paying customers swarmed around him for conversation and autographs. During the reception between shows, Ciardi was interviewed for the *Evansville Courier* and said a few of the things that had long ago become part of his message: "I think there are some lovely poets in the United States today, but there are a lot more of them that are noisy." He went on as usual: "There seems to be loose in the land an assumption that all you need to write poetry is the excitation of your own ignorance. And it produces terrible poetry." And the interviewer paraphrased still another familiar Ciardi comment: "He said many poets need to write more closely to the spoken voice, and adhere more to mnemonic elements, including form, pattern, rhythm, and rhyme, which make a poem memorable." According to reports by Hagemann, Blevins, and Tom Wilhelmus, a professor of English, Ciardi "loved" the Opera House program, was "charmed" by the performance, and was "very pleased" by it.

By Monday Ciardi had grown weary of his New Harmony isolation and asked to be moved to Evansville, "to be nearer the university," he said. At nine-thirty he was brought to campus by an assigned student driver and met at ten with English and language classes to discuss translation. At eleven he was interviewed for later broadcast on local television. He had lunch with students in the President's Suite off the main cafeteria, an arrangement that was repeated on Tuesday and Wednesday with different students each time. In the afternoon, he was taken to West Terrace, a local elementary school, where he read for the Horizons classes. Then at six-thirty, he attended a dinner in his honor at the home of President and Mrs. David Rice. Some of the college's honors students were also guests, and Matthew Graham remembers being invited too—to tend bar. By nine the party was over and Ciardi was delivered to his new quarters, the Executive Inn on Walnut Street.

On Tuesday Ciardi was picked up at nine o'clock, and at ten he discussed poetry, particularly children's poetry, to university students in education and creative writing classes. He had to deliver the lecture seated and sounded at times defensive, perhaps even angry, with students, teachers, and the "school system" at large. Perhaps his lingering flu symptoms and weak legs combined with the subject matter of the talk to make him a little irritable. At the end he asked for questions, got none, and finished abruptly. Following his lunch with students, Ciardi had a few hours to collect himself for an evening lecture, "Why Read?", which he changed at the last minute to a lecture on word histories. That was followed by a reception and then a party at Katie Waters's house. Matthew Graham recalled that Ciardi spied a bottle of J. W. Dant from across the room, and some of the guests recalled that Ciardi was drinking that night. His party conversation, fueled by bourbon perhaps, was designed to shock his young friends that evening, ranging from the fact that he felt no remorse about killing Japanese civilians during World War II to reminiscing about Bread Loaf, which then turned into his running down various poets of the past twenty-five years, people like Robert Bly, Galway Kinnell, the Beats, and the collective bunch known as the confessionals, but which he called the Couch Poets in honor of their psychiatric common ground. And for good measure, he went over Benn's long torment and expensive rehabilitation.

On Wednesday Ciardi was picked up in time for an on-campus book signing at eleven o'clock, an hour-long affair with a constant line, followed by lunch with writing and communication students, and a one o'clock meeting with classes to discuss "Arts and the Media." Again he sat but seemed confused by the topic, which had apparently caught him by surprise. The speech began well enough but ended badly because he had at least half an hour to kill and wandered about grasping for ideas. Jim Blevins recalled that Ciardi didn't look well that day and that they had spoken briefly about his health, perhaps after his afternoon talk, but Ciardi passed it off by saying that he had fallen off the wagon the night before and was actually hung over. At two he was interviewed for a story to appear in the *Mount Vernon Democrat,* and then he was interviewed by Matthew Graham for WNIN-FM radio. By then, however, he had already phoned Jeff Lovill in Denver to say that he had had to cancel all his stops after USI because he felt so terrible. Jeff remembered that Ciardi had sounded terrible too, both for what he said and how he said it: "Jeff, where is death's sting? Alas, death would be a welcome sight for me."

Graham drove Ciardi to the airport for his 5:35 flight, but it was delayed, so with his car double-parked at the curb, Graham stayed distractedly with Ciardi, and it suddenly came to him that Ciardi "just seemed worn out." And with that came another realization: "We had worked him too hard." (A regretful Jim Blevins seconded the opinion afterward, adding, "We didn't know how frail he was.") When the plane was ready to leave, Graham slipped a copy of his recently published first book of poems into Ciardi's hand and said goodbye. The delay, however, caused a mixed connection in Pittsburgh and a very late arrival into Newark, where Judith had finally left without knowing if or when John would be arriving. He took a cab and finally got home, exhausted and sick, well into the evening.

In a letter written to Vince Clemente probably the next day, though dated 26 March, Ciardi told his friend about how he had had to cancel the rest of his western swing, even the five-thousand-dollar talk in Topeka: "What good is it to a dead man?" He went on, "I have made up my mind irrevocably that *nothing* will tempt me north hereafter before April 15 (earliest date). I just don't have Sgt. Ciardi's resilience these days—nor the bastard's legs." He was, however, thrilled to open a letter from a Fedora Giordano with a photocopy of what Ciardi told Clemente was "a richly laudatory article": "An Archetypal World: Images of Italy in the Poetry of John Ciardi." Also on the twenty-seventh, he saw Dr. Cannamela and began taking medications to help him feel better. On the next two days, Good Friday and Holy Saturday, Ciardi took care of isolated correspondence—thank you notes to people like Graham, Blevins, and others in Indiana; apologies to friends in Denver; and even a difficult letter to a lawyer in which he threatened legal action if he was not supplied with proof for tax purposes that he had lost money in an "investment" in Tops Carpet City rather than in a "gift" to his son. But for the most part, Ciardi was resting up, hoping, as he wrote to Jim Clark in Denver on Friday, that he would soon "become human again."

On Easter Sunday, Judith cooked a little turkey, and late in the afternoon, she went to Myra's house to feed the cats. When she returned about six-thirty, the television was on in the living room, as she recalled it later, and John was in his usual seat. "I thought, well, I'll just finish dinner and call him, but when I did, he didn't come. I finished something else and went in there—and he was sitting there dead of a heart attack. Sunday, about 7:30 I guess." The emergency medical technicians were unable to revive Ciardi but rushed him anyway to the John F. Kennedy Medical Center in Edison, where he was declared dead on arrival.

In an undated typescript called "Reflections at Rex Davis's Funeral," found in a folder among Ciardi's assorted attic papers, he had commented on his own death: "I have heard too many preachers speak about too many of my friends the last words that have become the ritual of the last lie. Every funeral service I have ever heard has been a barefaced effort to say that the dead man is not really dead. When my turn comes, I refuse to authorize any such wheedlesome primitive word-magic, however resonant the poetry in which it is chanted." He said he wanted this to be his final exit line: "Goodbye in love. I'm off to chemistry."

Abbreviations

ABB. John Ciardi, "About Being Born, and Surviving It." In *Contemporary Authors Autobiography Series*, edited by Adele Sarkissian, Vol. 2. 79–96. Detroit: Gale Research, 1985: Good on the years to 1948. [Ciardi also wrote frequently about aspects of his life in M/S articles and poems. In addition to these autobiographical sources, see also "Fruit Salad." *Atlantic Monthly* (November 1948): 122–24; "The Middle Muddle (Notes of a 'Confused Progressive')." *Harvard Advocate* (28 February 1949): 10–11, 13; "WLB Autobiography: John Ciardi." *Wilson Library Bulletin* (February 1964): 480–82; and "The Bombers and the Bombed." In *"The Good War": An Oral History of World War II*, edited by Studs Terkel. 198–203. New York: Pantheon Books, 1984.]

ABB, PS. Unpublished postscript to ABB, covering JC's years at *Saturday Review:* 13 manuscript pages in Papers, LC.

AF, I to XLV. Autobiographical fragments. These have been collected and numbered in Papers, LC. Several are drafts of essays that appeared in M/S columns, but most are unpublished and undated mss.

      I. "When I was forty-five. . . ."
     II. "In Vermont, behind the house. . . ."
    III. "*Truth in Advertising.* . . ."
    IV. "I no longer go to the world. . . ."
     V. "I had my first teaching job. . . ."
    VI. "My godfather. . . ."
   VII. "Long drives. . . ." 11 January 1978. Key West.
  VIII. "In 1950. . . ."
    IX. "*A Visit.*"
     X. "I was on Saipan. . . ."
    XI. "I read galleys. . . ." 20 September 1961.
   XII. "My father-in-law. . . ."

AT. Autobiographical Typescript. Untitled and unpublished: "It was cold in Rome in the Spring of fifty-one." 58 pages. Papers, LC.

Broughton. "John Ciardi." In The *Writer's Mind: Interviews with American Authors,* Edited by Irv Broughton. Vol. 1. 363–86. Fayetteville: University of Arkansas Press, 1989.

Cifelli. Edward M. Cifelli. Interview with JC, May 1973.

Clemente.   Vince Clemente. "'A Man Is What He Does with His Attention': A Conversation with John Ciardi." *Poesis: A Journal of Criticism*, 7 no. 2 (1986): 1–17. Reprinted in *MM*.

Cora.   Cora (Ciardi) Fennessey. Interview on 12 January 1988.

"Difference."   John Ciardi. "The Difference Was Love." In *Growing Up Italian*," Edited by Linda Brandi Catenra. 141–46. New York: William Morrow, 1987.

Edith.   Edith (Ciardi) Rosi. Interview on 13 January 1988.

Ella.   Ella (Ciardi) Rubero. Interview on 13 January 1988. Later interviews are identified by date in the notes.

FBI.   File # 100–17136. 160 of 169 pages released. The file contains information from the FBI, the Department of State, and the U. S. Army. It was requested by William Barrett pursuant to the Freedom of Information Act and given to Judith Ciardi after JC's death. In addition to the nine missing pages, a great many passages are blacked out to protect FBI sources.

Judith.   Judith Ciardi. Interview on 19 August 1987. Until her death on 16 July 1992, Judith Ciardi graciously made herself available to what must have seemed to her an endless string of questions and conversations about her husband and their lives together.

Krickel.   Edward Krickel. *John Ciardi*. Boston: Twayne Publishers, 1980.

Letters.   *The Selected Letters of John Ciardi*. Edited by Edward M. Cifelli. Fayetteville: University of Arkansas Press, 1991.

MM.   *John Ciardi: Measure of the Man*. Edited by Vince Clemente. Fayetteville: University of Arkansas Press, 1987. Contains 44 chapters, including a partial reprint of ABB, poems by and about Ciardi, letters, biographical reminiscences, and critical observations.

M/S.   "Manner of Speaking" column written by JC for the *Saturday Review*.

Papers, LC, and Papers, WSU.   Ciardi Papers. Wayne State University (Detroit) has a large archive of Ciardi papers from the 1960s. ("A Guide to the Ciardi Papers" is available from the special collections department of the library upon request.) The Library of Congress has a 1970 collection of Ciardi papers, some 260 items, and is currently (1997) being given the remainder of Ciardi's papers. The LC also has "The Charles E. Feinberg Collection of John Ciardi Manuscripts" (see William White below for a description of the collection). In addition, LC has miscellaneous Ciardi letters in other collections, like the Merrill Moore Papers, for example. See also *Letters* for libraries around the country with large Ciardi holdings.

Saipan. *Saipan: The War Diary of John Ciardi.* Fayetteville: University of Arkansas Press, 1988.

SR. *Saturday Review.*

White. William White. *John Ciardi: A Bibliography.* Detroit: Wayne State University Press, 1959.

Notes

The notes have been put into a necessary shorthand. Many are keyed to the abbreviations listed above; others are simplified references to the selected bibliography. Only sources not listed in either place will be identified fully. For the occasions when I have used photocopies of Ciardi letters supplied by individuals, organizations, or businesses, the originals are in the hands of the persons written to, and their ownership is indicated after the note by the word "Recipient." When a letter is owned by a university library, the library and school name follow the note. Ciardi's own carbons of his letters are identified by "File Copy." Bold face type indicates the beginning of a new paragraph in the text; notes for each paragraph follow the bold face and are organized according to a key word or phrase.

ONE

Little Italy and the Irish Trinity, 1916 to 1936

25 Sheafe Street
(pages 3–10)

On the evening/ The preferred pronunciation of the family name was CHAR-dee, although many of the extended family used the Anglicized See-YARD-i. The abbreviated story of Antonio's death is told by JC in ABB, 85; additional details supplied by Ella, who was ten or eleven at Antonio's death. **Had the young/** birthdate: On a passport application, JC gave his father's birth date as 8/18/82 and his mother's as 5/8/81 (FBI, 9/7/61). The dates are useful but suspect because the family frequently claimed not to know the exact ages of either parent. San Potito Ultra: JC claimed in AF XL (1969) that there were no Ciardis left in his father's hometown, but that some two hundred had migrated from there to Dover, New Jersey. laborer/tailoring/agent: ABB, 84; "Difference," 151. president: "Difference," 152. "big and talkative": AF XLV. At home: Ella. **Reports of the**/ Descriptions of the accident are from Ella and ABB, 85. "It took four. . . .": *In the Stoneworks.* only real memory: ABB, 82 and Edith. ABB, 83: "I have no memory of him as a person, not of his face, not of his voice, not of the fact that he must have picked me up and kissed and cuddled me and romped a bit. . . . Of the man I remember nothing." **However, Concetta Ciardi**/ Lorenzo: AF XL (1969). five children: Phyllis, Anne, Cristina, Pasquale, and Concetta. Both versions: Ella and Edith. "Letter to Mother": *Homeward to America.* **Concetta Di Benedictis**/ Description of household is from Ella (including follow-up int. 8/21/89) and ABB. **The bride and**/ "Bridal Photo, 1906": *39 Poems.* seamstress: Ella. **With the birth**/ Details of the birth supplied by Ella. **A short time**/ poem, "The Evil Eye": *From Time to Time.* **Rejoicing over the**/ Industrial Board: See ABB, 85; AF XL; and AF XLV. **But a macabre**/ "He was 'there'": AF XL. Poem: *Person to Person.* **Whatever psychological groping**/ two jobs/public assistance: Ella.

84 South Street
(pages 11–29)

The first major/ purchased: ABB, 85. "leafy, elmy": Cifelli. "clean enough": Broughton, 369–70. old barges: "WLB Autobiography," 481. **The short six**/ "country": AF VI. North End cousins: "Difference," 143. On being an outsider in Italian communities, JC commented, "I myself have never really lived amidst Italians and have been to the communities only as a privileged visitor. I got to know the North End by visiting my cousins and relatives there, but I always lived *outside*" ("Difference," 150). authoritative manner/matriarch: "Difference," 147. **Of course, in**/ St. Leonard's: ABB 84, 87. shopping: AF VI. Memorial Day: story and quotation: ABB, 83. **In Medford Concetta**/ vegetable garden: ABB, 85; "Difference," 143. "One of my jobs": Broughton, 369. castration: "I do recall some recurrent dreams, such as falling when I was small, or flying. . . . And then I suppose there's that insecurity of all boys when they dream that their genitals have fallen off" (Broughton, 372). He even put this dream into a poem ("A Five-Year Step," *Lives of X*):

[I] fell asleep
falling off roofs and clouds to wake up screaming,
holding my genitals that had fallen off

because they belonged to the Devil and he'd come for them
and changed me into a girl for punishment.

There were cultural/ "a generalized intolerance": ABB, 86. "a little alienated": Broughton, 366. "some alienation": "Difference," 151. **Even within
the/** "ritual pagan": ABB, 86. "Whatever the case": AF XLV. Concetta,
quotation: AF XLV. faith: ABB, 86. **Medford's Irish population/** rarely
attended: AF XLV. "Irish Trinity": ABB, 87. "she concluded": ABB, 86. first
communion: Edith and Ella. "If I have blanked": ABB, 86. "I never met":
"Difference," 145. **Whether Italian or/** "heavy dosage" and "I found
myself": lecture, Pittsburgh Forum, 2/5/75. single prayer too soon: ABB,
85. "At Mother's prompting": AF XLV. infused with guilt: ABB, 85. "guilt-
twisted": Clemente, 16. **Making matters worse/** "roughneck": "John
Ciardi Memorial" (radio broadcast) *"New Letters* on the Air," 5/86. "until
[John] was twelve": Holmes, *MM,* 43. killing Cavalcante: letter to Holmes,
12/30/55, Papers, LC. "wild bunch": Broughton, 368; see also "Difference,"
145. **Evil or not/** cat-o'-nine-tails: ABB, 87. "drove herself": AF XLV.
"hagiological rally": poem, "A Five-Year Step": *Lives of X;* see also ABB, 88.
her worst fears: "[Mother] had firmly decided that I was 'a good boy,' as even
God must plainly see" (AF XLV). **Few details of/** pheasant poaching:
Most of the information in this paragraph is from the poem "Feasts" *(Lives
of X)* supplemented by AF XVI. **John's sister Edith/** poem, "The
Lamb": *From Time to Time.* **Probably in 1928/** built a house: Ella. "I felt
that": Broughton, 366. **Uncle Alec, whose/** "pagan Greek": AF XXVII.
Young John did not: "Difference," 147. Poem, "Alec": *For Instance.* Puppy:
"Difference," 147. to read Italian: "Difference," 142. **For the most/** "five
women": AF XLV. Poem, "Bedlam Revisited" *In the Stoneworks.* "I grew mental flaps": AF XLV. "Half-deep in books"/"guilty of happiness": poem,
"The Shaft": *Lives of X.* **How much guilt/** "insufferable brat"/"trained to
be": "Difference," 144. "We did not argue": Ella. "I simply acquired" and
remaining quotations: ABB, 81. **Ciardi seems to/** "linking object":
"Sometimes the mothering person passes on her own fantasies to her child,
perhaps even 'depositing' in her child's self-system the concept that he is the
dead person's representative; then the child becomes the mother's 'living
linking object.'" (Vanik Volkan, *Linking Objects* . . . , (New York; 1980), 321.
"Day by day": letter to John Holmes, 10/30/55, Papers, LC. "avid and indiscriminate": ABB, 84. "first oppression": ABB, 85. **From 1923 to/** skipped
fifth grade/"pretty good"/"double promotion": "Difference," 152. "father's
doing": ABB, 84. Rover poem: news clipping supplied by UM-KC, 2/12/40.
For grades seven/ respectable but undistinguished grades: official tran-
scripts from the Medford School District. "I had stacks": ABB, 84. He also
read: "Difference," 152. THE BOOK: ABB, 84. The writing was:

Broughton, 367–68. **Ciardi recalled many**/ "fever": "WLB Autobiography," 481. looking for father figures: ABB, 86. "unacknowledged kin": "Difference," 147. Uncle Pat: Edith. John Follo: AF XVI. **Knowing that Troop**/ story of JC's introduction to Boy Scouts: ABB, 88. By the time he was sixteen/"makeshift bridge": Broughton, 367. **Although his inability**/ "must have sensed": AF XLV. fully equipped workshop: AF XLV. lopsided birdhouse: ABB. 88. **The crisis came**/ Sunday School: ABB, 88. "flatly told": this quotation and all the others in this paragraph, except for the last one are from AF XLV. "If my Perfect": ABB, 88. **Unfortunately, Ciardi's declaration**/ wasn't achieved that easily: ABB, 88. "It was at least": AF XLV. "The act of ripping": AF XLV. **Working his way**/ his family tried: "Difference," 149. fourteen-dollar-a-week: Much of this paragraph is from "Cal Coolidge and the Co" *(Lives of X)*. His routine: "Sincerity": ms. fragment in Papers, LC. for a florist: Bates College Application for Admission. **During his teenage**/ caddy camp: AF VI. "the grandma duffers": "Summer in Winchester," in Arthur Griffin, *New England: The Four Seasons* (Boston, 1980): 40. smoking: ABB, 95. **At age sixteen**/ All quotations in this paragraph except the last one are from AF XLV.

Bates College
(pages 29–32)

Perhaps because of/ Bates College: application for admission. hitchhiked: Ella. patched pants/new clothes: Ella; John L. washed dishes: Judith. Name of Matthew Frangedakis supplied by his grandson, Jonathan B. Conant, in a letter to me, 3/8/88. **Ciardi's record at**/ Grades: Bates College transcript. "bored" himself: "WLB Autobiography," 482. "his seriousness": Clemente, 5. Louis Untermeyer lecture and quotation: Roger Fredland, "Promising Poet," *Bates Alumnus* (June 1940): 7. **On 25 May**/ "hizzoner": *Letters.* "so if you come up"/"green of the dollar": *Letters.* **But work was**/ Information for this paragraph came from copies of letters supplied by Kenseth. **Although Ciardi did**/ financial crisis: Ella. Grades: Bates College transcript. Heelers' Club and Spofford Club: 1935–36 Bates yearbook, *Mirror.* **Twenty years later**/ "cheerfully threw away": Holmes, 21. "heavily Baptist"/"relentlessly concerned": ABB, 80. "I ran into": Roy Newquist, 114. **Fifty years after**/ "I didn't find": Pease, 12.

TWO
Holmes and Cowden, 1936 to 1940

The Holmes Years
(pages 33–44)

Even though Holmes/neither glib nor oratorical: quotations and paraphrase in this paragraph are from Hayford, int. **No student, however**/ "master teacher"/"ideal father figure": ABB, 89. "I lived on": M/S 7/8/61. **Ciardi later wrote**/ "junior member": ABB, 89. "It was as if": Pease, 12–13. "almost at once": ABB, 89. **For his part**/ "lanky undergraduate": Maxine Kumin, *MM*, 131. "would bring": Holmes, *MM*, 43. poet's "great pleasure": Holmes, "The Great Rich Vine," *Atlantic Monthly* (Apr. 1935): 480, 482. "Time after time": Clemente, *MM*, 218. "watching shark fins": Broughton, 373. **The fact that**/ on the couch: Stephenson, int. "over beer": Harrison Hayford [untitled paragraphs about Ciardi, with photograph], *The Tuftonian* (fall 1937): 36. "*I* pay half": Hayford, int. "assertive, alert": letter to me from Richard Carpenter, 4/12/89. **Collectively, this is**/ "He happened to": Holmes, *MM*, 42. GPA: Tufts transcript. competition for grades: Hayford, int. "not happy that": Holmes, *MM*, 43. **To dramatize the**/ National Youth Administration: AF XV. Harry Hayford, too: Hayford, int. rich boy's tennis: letter to me from Richard Carpenter, 4/12/89. **Sweating over jackhammers**/ "the 'gentleman'": AF XV. biology/philosophy/geology: AF XV. **The English courses**/ "born in the Middle Ages": JC at the Pittsburgh Poetry Forum, 2/5/75. "I wish I might have time": Hayford, *Tuftonian*, 36. **At Tufts, too**/ play production: Tufts transcript. *Winterset:* playbill supplied by Harrison Hayford. "Shadow was"/"never able to act again": Broughton, 376. **Certainly in the**/ Josephine Bosworth Wishart: The story of the Ciardi-Wishart courtship is from the Harrison Hayford and Josephine Wishart Hayford int. "house mother"/Packard Ave. Tufts Catalogue, 1937–38. **If there were**/ "My boy, what": Eyges, int. **Ciardi was only**/ "Hey, this guy's": Lovill, diss., 354. "had great energy": *MM*, 32. **Nor did it**/ inter-office memo: *Letters,* 10/27/37. **What "stuff" Ciardi**/ "they are wise": *Letters.* **In early October**/ "My interest"/"This year": Cowden, *MM*, 49. Holmes knew some: ABB, 89. "Since I had": Tufts Class of 1938, twenty-fifth reunion booklet, 6–8 June 1963.

The Hopwood Award
(pages 44–58)

The road to/ tuition scholarship/cash: *Current Biography* (Oct. 1967): 10; ABB, 90. NYA student-aide jobs/rats in a maze: "The Rat Race," ms., no date, Papers, LC; bussing tables: from JC's coworkers at the Michigan Wolverine, Stanley Epstein and Ted Mandel. grading papers: *Current Biography*, 10. took a bus: from Jeff Lovill in unpublished pages of his interview with JC. **On 26 October**/ "I get letters": Recipient. "When I first": Cowden, *MM*, 50. **Ciardi completed his**/ His program included [and grades]: University of Michigan transcript. In "WLB Autobiography," JC wrote that he had written an M.A. thesis: "Donne and Bradstreet (John and Anne, that is)." "The other members": Cowden, *MM*, 50. The story of Cowden's lectures and conferences is from "A Praise of Good Teachers," *SR* (7/8/61): 64, and ABB, 89. **For John Ciardi**/ "radical": Cornella, 7. **Of course, most**/ John Malcolm Brinnin: int. "I fired off": ABB, 90. "important convictions": *Ciardi Himself*, 58. "Style and form": *MM*, 51. **If Ciardi actually**/ "To a Young American . . . ," "To One 'Investigated' . . . ," and "Reply to S. K." in the next paragraph are all from *Homeward to America*. **President Roosevelt could**/ be faulted: typescript, "My Poetic Generation," no date, Papers, LC. **Theoretical frameworks, however**/ "In Boston": autobiographical note attached to a letter to M. Paul Bordry, 10/24/46, File Copy. "the bloody battles"/"All these things": *Ciardi Himself*, 58. **Ciardi also fell**/ "Special Work": Ciardi explained this course in a letter to Clarence Decker, 2/10/39: "By way of supplementing the work of the Proseminar [with Cowden] I shall spend the remainder of the year in work on the physiological and psychological aspects of aesthetics. . . . ," UM-KC. apparently smitten: The story of JC's relationship with Virginia Johnson is pieced together from interviews with Judith Ciardi, John Malcolm Brinnin, Richard Beal, and Dion Johnson, Virginia's younger son. According to Dion Johnson, letters from JC to Virginia were not to be made public under terms of Virginia Johnson's will until after the death of Judith Ciardi. However, after Judith's death in 1992, the letters, according to Mr. Johnson, were lost. **Virginia Johnson, whom**/ "I've had my focus": *Letters*. **The spring term**/ Avery Hopwood: "Michigan Student Writing," *New York Times*, 6/3/39, Clipping, Papers, LC. Thomas Aquinas: ABB, 90. Horace Gregory, Louise Bogan, and David McCord: *New York Times*, 6/3/39. "There I sat": ABB, 89. "May Easter bless": Holmes, *MM*, 42. 1931 Model-A/"endless blue fog": "Difference," 149, and M/S 8/22/64. JC rarely felt discriminated against because of his Italian descent, but he told the following story of his return to Medford in the Model-A: "As a kid, I occasionally ran into people who had anti-Italian feelings. And my reaction was basically: 'There's something wrong with him.' At one time I had a job with a local gent. It was a night job during my postgraduate year [1933–34] in high school. . . . Well, I hadn't seen this gent for a while, and on coming back from Michigan, I had a broken-down model-A car. Passing him on the street one day, I stopped and gave him a ride. And he gave me a lot of stuff like, 'You goddamned Italians coming over here and getting all the cars, while native Americans like myself don't have one.' What could I say? There's something wrong with this guy." "Difference," 149. **Before they could/** departmental assistant: ms. fragment on teaching, teacher incompetence, and teacher training, no date, Papers, LC. "with ill-concealed": 8/12/39, Recipient. "three courses": *Letters* 8/4/39. "snowed under": *Letters* 7/20/39. **Ciardi's short trip/** the trade manager: ABB, 90. "As a matter": Sloane to Ciardi 6/8/39, Papers, LC. "Thanks for": *Letters*. "I finished": *Letters* 7/20/39. "Letter for Those.": letter to George Dillon, *Letters* 7/27/39. See also Lovill, 363 and ABB, 90. "fairly optimistic": 8/12/39 Recipient. **Ciardi's five-week/** Wyoming, California, and Utah: postcards sent to Arnold Kenseth; copies in Papers, LC. cash advance: ABB, 90. galley sheets: *Letters* 10/24/39. "I'm really almost": *Letters* 12/26/39. "The point is": *Letters* 6/4/42. "That winning manuscript": ABB, 89. "I was actually": AF XX. **Homeward to America/** "A perusal of": FBI, 12/17/42, Papers, LC. Bogan called him: *New Yorker,* 1/27/40, 54. Untermeyer said: "Look Homeward America," *Yale Review* (spring 1940): 603. Frajam Taylor: "A New Adventure," *Poetry* (Sept. 1940): 337. Of course, Holmes/most comprehensive: "Ciardi Uses Letter Form to Bring His Thoughts Nearer Hearts and Minds of Readers of Verse," *Boston Evening Transcript,* 1/17/40. Book Section, Clipping. **Homeward to America/** Krickle: *John Ciardi,* 40. **Ciardi drifted back/** window display: AF XX. looking for a job: ABB, 90. "blow in tonight": This and several other letters from Virginia to her parents were sent to me by her son Dion. The letter of 3 February 1940 captures more of their relationship: "One thing happened in regard to John that I was glad of while he was here. He has liked me from the beginning, I know, partly because I cannot remember that he is a 'lion' and I stand between him and a lot of things that nag at him and drain him. Some I manage to help by letters, but much I can't. He is so large and vivacious that people, even his family[,] cannot grasp the fact that he gets utterly fagged out, both mentally and physically. I put him to bed a little while after he came and kept him there most of the time for a week. Also I blandly refused invitations for him that I knew were the wrong kind. Also I feed him the theory that as yet he really is not so much of a 'lion' and still has himself to prove. Also that what talent he does possess is a trust and not a toy and also that, while what he does may be pretty, it won't be any bigger than John himself. He knows it well, without being told, but loves getting it from someone who likes him and does not want to use him. But I had wondered if he could ever do any good work where I was and had been afraid that he could not. So had he[,] it appears. Anyway, some time ago, we were sitting in front of the fire. He got some paper and went to work. When he got through he tore around like a puppy, 'Ginny I've written a really good poem, right here with you.' He wrote two more while he was here and took them to Cowden, who said that they were the three best poems he had ever written. I think there are two more as good written at home, but those three are good. . . . We were both delighted. We all enjoy him and want him here. It certainly does his health and his point of view good to come and stay. But neither he nor I should be happy about it if it meant that he could not get anything written. We were both uneasy about it until he wrote those. At the rate he's going he should have another book ready to print, that means all put together, by next June and it will be much better than his first book. One that he did here is a beautiful flaming thing, not somber as his frequently are. Its idea is not as important, I suppose, as some of the others but it blazes off the page and is lovely. I have pushed him to do as many types of things as he can, and was glad to see this one that is not as he [has] often written. All three he wrote here are unlike each other which is good. Anyway, he is coming back in the spring to paint my kitchen for me and we shall see what he has done by then." **Meanwhile Untermeyer, who**/ could recommend: Clemente, 4. application for employment: UKC, now UM-KC, 1/12/40.

THREE
Teacher, Gunner, Poet, 1940 to 1945

The UKC and FBI (pages 59–70)

Clarence R. Decker/ Information on Decker and university history is from UKC *Bulletin,* 1940–41. "a way with things": AF V; also ABB, 90. $800: Western Union telegram to Wallace Brown, Chairman of English, UKC, 1/30/40, Papers, LC. $850: contract letter from Decker to JC, 9/1/40, Papers, LC. "five dollars would buy": Cifelli. Richardson family/"quiet individual": FBI, 9/25/43. "My needs were simple": ABB, 90. **With respect to**/ "In Kansas City": AF XLI. **Earlier, in 1940**/ "in and out of love"/faculty parties: AF XXIV and AF V. wasn't enough time: AF V. "I had a number": *Ciardi Himself,* 11. **When he wasn't/** "The skyscrapers are nice"/"I got my picture": *Letters* 2/23/40. The UKC *University News* (no date) ran a picture and story ("Ciardi, Modern Poet, Excels in Verse") when JC joined the faculty: "If you think a poet is necessarily a fellow with long wavy hair, effeminate manners, and a flare of temperament, just take a look at John Ciardi. The twenty-five year old poet is a great upset to the popular conception of an esthete." radio broadcast: UKC, *University News,* 5/3/40, 1. **In Kansas City/** attending flight classes: October ? [1941], Recipient. "On a clear": Broughton, 376. **On the literary/** Louis Adamic wrote: Papers, LC. three new Ciardi poems: None of the new *Common Ground* poems was collected in a future book. Tom Boggs had written: See Boggs letters in Papers, LC. flirted openly: Boggs letters, Papers, LC. **Ciardi did not/** summer session: index to *Kansas City Star & Times* 6/9/40. home with Ginny Johnson: *Letters* 7/29/40. Bill Sloane: ABB, 90. **Bread Loaf had/** Robert Frost/Archibald MacLeish: Scott Donaldson, *Archibald MacLeish: An American Life* (Boston, Mass.: Houghton Mifflin, 1992), 274–75. See also Wallace Stegner, *The Uneasy Chair: A Biography of Bernard DeVoto* (Garden City, N.Y.: Doubleday, 1974), 206–7. **The clashing of/** "demonic concentration": Stegner, 118. "wonderful year"/"major over-haul": Form letter sent by JC to Bread Loaf staffers, no date, but during his directorship, 1955–72. **Meanwhile, after Bread/** "not very satisfying": *Letters* 12/10/40. "very Communistic": FBI report is unclear as to date of complaint, although the file date is 3/27/41; however, as JC was not at UKC that semester, it probably refers to fall 1940. "I regret that": FBI 1/23/42. "a stocky fellow": FBI 1/23/42. He was described: FBI 5/26/41. **Added to Ciardi's/** cancel gift-giving: *Letters* 12/10/40. **Ciardi returned home/** "a second volume": UKC news clipping, 1/1/41, UM-KC. 84 South Street: FBI 5/26/41. traveled widely: AF XX. "I didn't have": Cifelli. **During their April/** reprinted from *Homeward:* "Boy or Girl" and "I Warn You, Father Smith"; from *YR,* "Museum." second book of poems: on 1/9/41 Sloane referred to the book as *Atlantic Crossing,* Papers, LC. **There may have/** record his poems: *Letters* 11/14/41. spent the Christmas: letter from Virginia Johnson to her parents, 1/4/42, Recipient's estate. **The Kansas City/** informants: FBI 9/25/43. **Perhaps the most/** Alexander Cappon: int. "by all means": October ? [1941], Recipient. "I'm definitely washed up with it": In fact JC published four more poems in the spring 1942 *Review* and two more in the summer. **The "virile connection"/** "average American thinks": news clipping, UKC, 2/14/40. UM-KC. Twenty-one years: "Ciardi on Tape," 20. Whether Ciardi's feelings: Richard Wilbur has commented that JC's "literary taste" was "seriously limited in that he couldn't give women writers a fair shake. He was incapable of that." Wilbur also commented on what he thought might be the reasons for this limitation: "If one looks through *Lives of X* and other evidence about John's early life, I think it's pretty clear that here was this bright, bookish kid who grew up in a family where books were not excessively prized. He also grew up in a family where he was the only male. He had to resist the feminine a great deal—and to be both bookish and surrounded by women is likely to turn you into a resister of the overly delicate, the overly refined in literature." int. **Ciardi may have/** The early twentieth century: See Frank Lentricchia, *Ariel and the Police* (Madison: University. of Wisconsin Press, 1988): 153–54. "positively lady-like": Lentricchia, 138. "A lot of them were ladies": Robert Frost, 9/6/30. *The Letters of Robert Frost to Louis Untermeyer* (New York: Holt, Rinehart and Winston, 1963). **Paradoxically, however, given/** "explorer of the female psyche": Giordano, 306–7.

The United States Army Air Corps (pages 70–86)

Rather than be/ leave of absence: news clipping, UKC, 2/5/42, UM–KC. "final round": *Letters* 3/4/41. *Elegy for the First America:* letter to John Malcolm Brinnin, *Letters* 3/25/41. "Duell Sloan & Pearce": October 1941, Recipient. man-of-the-house: letter from Virginia Johnson to her parents, 3/31/42, Recipient's estate. **On 19 May/** "excellent character": 3/18/42, UM-KC. in Boston to enlist: FBI 10/22/43. "dreams of being a pilot": Terkel, 198. almost didn't make it: letter from Virginia Johnson to her parents, 5/15/42. Ciardi was on call: JC waited from 5/19/42 (or slightly earlier) to 10/28/42, when he was called to Nashville. On 1/16/43, he reported to navigation school in Louisiana. moved in with the Ciardis: Dion Johnson, int., 8/28/89. Additional information from DJ came in interviews on 8/17/92 and 8/10/93. **The relationship between/** legal separation: Dion Johnson, int., 8/10/93. **The call from/** "delivered by slow": M/S 3/13/65. "slogged through the mud": ABB, 91. "excellent"/"satisfactory"/"delinquency charges": FBI 10/22/43. **Considering that Ciardi/** "darkest Louisiana": letter to John Malcolm Brinnin, *Letters.* "I finally qualified": ABB, 91. "Premature Anti-Fascist": AF XXV. "obviously phony charges": unpublished passage from Lovill dissertation, int. **According to army/** "disaffection investigation": FBI 9/6/43. not an "eager cadet"/"irresponsible": FBI 9/3/43. "character and conduct charges"/"seventy-seven demerits"/"know-it-all type'": FBI 5/7/56. **Making the 3/** "unauthorized absence"/"confinement"/"disrespect": FBI 9/7/43. As part of Maj. William Fritz's "disaffection investigation," JC's mail in Medford was being routinely examined. The FBI report of 9/20/43 says that an unidentified person had written JC on 9/11 to say that he had spoken to John's mother, who was concerned that John had been AWOL three times. "I told her AWOL in a cadet simply meant running into town. . . ." "I was disturbed": letter from JC to E. Farrar Bateson Jr. (JC's Flight Commander in navigation class), 3/16/60, Papers, LC. **On Friday, 4/** Capt. Charles Coble: FBI 9/21/43. "unsatisfactory": FBI 9/6/43. "very troubled": FBI 9/21/43. **Perhaps Ginny Johnson's/** "Monroe, April 17": photocopy supplied by Dion Johnson, Papers, LC. something else as well: Letter testifying to the incident written to me by Burton L. Appleton, who had the story from an eyewitness in 1947. **In the end/** "Subject is a Communist": FBI 9/23/43. **On the day/** first salutes: FBI 9/21/43. **No documents have/** "bucked for duty": AF XL. By 27 September: FBI 10/22/43. "Adverse Information": FBI 10/22/43. central fire control: ABB, 91. **The Boeing B-29/** Information on B-29s comes chiefly from Anderton, Birdsall, and Lloyd. **But the Superfortress/** Charles Hawkes: Anderton, 22. George Gray: Anderton, 23–24. Wrong engines/"nothing but trouble": Anderton, no page. "I always thought": letter JC to Ed Lawson (known as Levin in *Saipan*) 6/19/63, Recipient. **In early April/** "looked at John": int. "the one unit": AF I. "You belonged to": Terkel, 199. **Probably during the/** Fredland reported: ABB, 91. **From 5 November/** "We had a good steak": *Saipan*. Most of the information on Ciardi's Saipan experience is taken from this book; unless otherwise noted, all quotations are from it. **On 11 November/** eight cases of whiskey: M/S 11/9/63. **Saipan, part of/** American war strategists: The story of invading and securing Saipan is told in Anderton and Birdsall. 73rd Bomb Wing: Birdsall, 101–2, 105. two hundred B-29s: Mac Cordray, int. **There is a/** "a forest of B-29s": AT, 12. **The first bombing/** one hundred planes: Most of the information on the first attack is from Birdsall, 107–8; 120–21; 326. As Ciardi put it: ABB, 91. **On December third/** third big daylight attack: Birdsall, 125–26. "The miracle system": ABB, 91. **Ciardi and the/** 40 percent chance: Terkel, 199. "diving head first" and remaining quotations in this paragraph: JC to Ed Lawson (Levin in *Saipan*) 11/13/84, Recipient.

War Poetry and Desk Duty
(pages 86–96)

The **"flood of/** John Malcolm Brinnin: *Letters.* "certain sort of lethargy": news clipping, UKC, 1/24/46, UM-KC. **However, all during/** managed to publish: See White for details. **For someone who/** "Most of our nightly": Robert M. Cordray, foreword to *Saipan*, xxiii. **From a military/** Accuracy ratings: Anderton, 80. **The by-then sporadic/**

"Able Baker Charlie": ms. fragment, no date, Papers, LC. **Many years later/** "damn his iron pants": unpublished ms. on poetry, no date, Papers, LC. five full-scale: Birdsall, 192–94. more air time: Birdsall, 198. **Although the odds/** "I refuse to tell lies": AT, 19. "This might be": AT, 17. **Ciardi had written/** The excuse came: story from Nick Brown, int. **And so, when/** It was even better: ms. fragment, "Burning the Files," no date, Papers, LC. Also ABB, 92. **For his last/** "I did the best": Gorner, 2. his former plane: ABB, 92; Terkel, 200. **Letters of condolence/** "full chicken colonels": ABB, 92. "many a Colonel": "Fruit Salad": (Nov. 1948): 122–24. **On 15 August/** rotation points: ABB, 92. nearly four thousand dollars: ABB, 93. "almost $12,000": AF XIX.

FOUR

The Harvard Years, 1946 to 49

Myra Judith Hostetter
(pages 97–102)

Already by 1946/ Morrison had begun: int. "twice renewable": letter TM to JC, 3/20/46, Papers, LC. more than three times/"By the time": AF XIX. **But in October/** "It took me": ABB, 93. silk parachute: Judith. "live food and dead food": ABB, 93. Ginny Johnson in Pittsfield: Dion Johnson, int, 8/10/93. **Despite his plan/** "ponderous balancing": JC to Decker, *Letters* 12/1/45. (spring 1946) in Kansas City: ABB, 93. **The student newspaper/** "a great deal of interest": "Ciardi Returns to KCU Campus," *University News,* 2/8/46: 1. "well-known poet": "John Ciardi Will Read Poetry at Reading Hour," *University News,* 2/13/46, no page. advisor/Easy Chair: "Interest Revived in 'Easy Chair,'" *University News,* 3/18/46, 1. "a tall, very dark": letter to me from Ciardi student Shera H. Roberson, 1/27/89. **The 1946 Kangaroo/** "as a returning hero"/ "Miss Hostetter dutifully": ABB, 93. "I guess I just": Judith. "bent down": JC to Dudley Fitts 12/30/55, copy in Papers, LC. **Myra Judith Hostetter/** "over-home" in Pike County: AF IX and XII. straight-A work: most details in this paragraph are from Judith, int. "most gorgeous thing": Judith. "John Ciardi appeared—WOW!": Judith left a record of her courtship in a diary covering 1/21/46, before she met Ciardi, to 6/20/46, shortly before he proposed. The diary is currently in the possession of her daughter, Myra. **That semester Ciardi/** Epperson House/Judith lived: Judith. Unless otherwise noted courtship details in this paragraph are taken from Judith's diary. at once proposed: Judith. "a personal apocalypse descends": *Letters*. **After the couple/** "John is being married": Virginia Johnson to her parents, 7/21/46, Recipient's estate. two o'clock ceremony: details supplied by a news clipping, 8/4/46, Papers, LC. "wasn't truly a golfing date": ABB, 93. "I scratched": Judith. **After their honeymoon/** Edith was delighted: Edith. "Mother fell in love": "Difference," 147. bedroom off the kitchen: Judith. "Cora was": Judith. **For his part/** "From the start": "Difference," 148. "America's Most Married Poet": JC to JMB, *Letters* 12/1/46.

Writing and Teaching at Harvard (pages 102–12)

Richard Wilbur, age/ Ciardi "was already": Wilbur, *Proceedings*, 58. obsessed with anagrams: int. "John was esteemed": *Proceedings*, 59. **Harvard after the/** Details for this paragraph are from Hall, int. **Those were, in/** "poetic ferment"/Ciardi's "difference": Wilbur, *Proceedings*, 58–59. **Those same qualities/** "forceful, brilliant": Holmes, *MM*, 44. "I never meant to be": Cifelli. **Student testimonials confirm/** "quite by accident"/"brilliant and inspiring": Rinehart, int. "superb teacher"/"give us a bad time": Hall, "English C, 1947": 53. "wonderful teacher"/"thrusting masculine walk": Hall, int. "insured the black lock": Hall, "English C, 1947": 52. "it was very thrilling": Hall, int. **Early in December/** "some unimaginable": Hall, "English C, 1947": 53. black Mercury: Judith. crap-shooting/under-the-table: Judith. *New Yorker* poems/$315: check stubs, Papers, LC. **As successful as/** "refreshing"/ "unpreacherly": Levin, int. "scathing yet accurate comments": letter to me from Ciardi student Frederick J. Davis, 6/2/89. **In October 1946/** "I'm teaching English A": JC to JMB, *Letters* 10/31/46. His 1947 production: see White. **Scarcely two weeks/** "I don't completely understand": JC to JMB, *Letters* 12/1/46. (All told, in 1946: see White. See also *New Yorker* check stub for "A Christmas Carol," Papers, LC. **Perhaps the best/** "advisable to publish"/"drastic alterations": Spencer's report is dated 6/12/46; in Papers, LC. **Weeks did not/** "I'll bite my": JC to Jeanette Cloud, File Copy. "my mother-instinct": JC to Weeks, *Letters*. revised manuscript "makes sense": JC to Weeks, *Letters*. **Other Skies featured/** the verse "jingly": "The Problem of the Second Volume" (May 1948): 101. Donald Hall: "The New Poetry . . ." in *New World Writing* (NY: Mentor, 1955): 239. "slangy yet learned": Krickle, 45–46. "wry quirk of history": ABB, 93. **The poems in/** "the difference between": Nims, 106. the sergeant does not: handwritten by JC in the margin of an essay by Steven Goldstein, 6/18/65, Papers, LC.

The UKC Review and Bread Loaf
(pages 112–21)

Therefore, when Ciardi/ "I know you'll see": *Letters* 8/5/46. "dump the responsibility": UM-KC. "advisory editor"/"power to act": Decker to JC, 8/19/46, UM-KC. **Ciardi accepted Decker's/** "esteemed colleagues": UM-KC. "As per my minor acidities": *Letters* 10/12/46. **When Decker replied/** "Infallibility we leave": UM-KC. "Notes from the end of a limb." *Letters* 10/12/46. **The controversy subsided/** review-essay: see Scott. **In the remaining/** "The Mayo article": UM-KC. **The other literary/** The history of Bread Loaf has been until recently a scattered affair with many magazine articles, chapters in books, and anecdotes written but uncollected. Morrison's pamphlet *The First Thirty Years* has been the only careful effort to tell the Bread Loaf story until David Haward Bain's *Whose Woods These Are* came out in 1993. I have drawn from both accounts, relying heavily on Bain's chronology and raw data, less heavily on his interpretations. **The 1947 conference/** "Instruction will have": Morrison, 40. Chapter 4, "Teaching at Bread Loaf," reveals Morrison's internal struggle over this question. John Farrar's 1926: Morrison, 9, 40. Robert Gay: Morrison, 41. "It is impossible really," he wrote, to teach anyone": Morrison, 41. "no course can provide talent": Morrison, 42. **This exclusionary attitude/** President Paul Moody: Morrison, 42. **In 1947, the/** "a new locus of energy": Bain, 61. "will swear": unpublished ms. on writer's conferences, no date, Papers, LC. "I haven't an appetite left", 8/28/47, Papers, LC. **As was the/** "one of my steadies"/"one of my best": Morrison int. "We used to exaggerate": Wilbur, int.

Presidential Politics—
and Controversy
(pages 121–28)

The 1946–47 academic/ "a much better reading schedule": postcard to Ed Levin: no date, but February or March 1947, Recipient. executive secretary: autobiographical note attached to a letter to M. Paul Bordry, 10/24/46, File Copy. Progressive Citizens of America: FBI 5/27/48. Most of the remaining information in this paragraph and the next is from the same FBI file. **But Ciardi's involvement/** "golden-tongued boy": Hall, int. **As Donald Hall/** rang doorbells in South Boston: Hall, "English C, 1947," 53. "I became a firebrand": This and most of the

remainder of the paragraph is from AF XVIII. "I spouted": ABB, 94.
Election year events/ five thousand dollars in pledges: W. E. Mullins,
"Convention Attendance Dispels Impression Wallace Followers All Reds,
Crackpots," *Boston Herald* 7/26/48. **Ciardi, however, was/** "I became
absolutely": Cornella, 7. "not even writing"/"malignant decency" ABB,
94, 93. in a 1983 interview: Lovill, diss., 337. **Although he made/** Holmes,
in a four-page letter: Papers, LC. "Some time ago": *Letters* 10/22/62. **In
April 1949/** "so-called 'Progressive' rally": copy in Papers, LC. **By
admitting that/** President Conant replied: See *Letters*, 57–63.

FIVE
The Harvard Years,
1949 to 1953

Poetry Editor: Twayne Publishers
(pages 129–43)

The Harvard Law/ "Is there any chance": Moore
Papers, LC. **Some months earlier/** seven-thousand-dollar start-up:
Steinberg, int. **The young publishing/** *Dream of the Red Chamber:*
Steinberg, int. On the eleventh: Papers, LC. Ciardi kept a careful record
of correspondence to and from Steinberg, all of which is at the LC. The
remainder of this paragraph and the next two are from this collection.
Twayne Publishers announced/ "is basically a plan": JC to Charles
Abbott, 9/26/49. Cited with the permission of the Poetry/Rare Books
Collection, University Libraries, State University of New York at Buffalo.
"In essence Steinberg": 11/21/49, File Copy. "taking their rewards": File
Copy. **Editorially, Ciardi had/** "building up a business": letter to
Edward Nappon, 1/2/52, File Copy. **Ciardi's first book/** "to get things
started": JC to Charles Abbott, 9/26/49. Quoted by permission; see two
paragraphs above. "I shoulda stood": 7/26/49, copy in Papers, LC. "one
of America's": advertising brochure, Papers, LC. **After the long/** "be
delighted": 2/24/49, File Copy. "I *like* your new book": Papers, LC. "I shall
have my son": letter to John Holmes that was forwarded to Ciardi, Papers,
LC. ***Live Another Day/*** Maurice Irvine: "Two Poets in Progress,"
10/23/49, 47. *Sacramento Bee:* 9/10/49. *Long Beach (Calif.) Press-Telegram:*
12/3/49. *Oklahoma City Oklahoman:* 2/19/50. *Youngstown (Ohio) Vindicator:*
1/8/50. *Newark (N. J.) Evening News:* 3/3/50. **The more self-conscious/**
David Daiches: "Rich, Controlled Imagery," 1/1/50, 6. **I. L. Salomon/**
"several egregious": 2/11/50, 30. "John Ciardi, beloved": "New Verse"

(winter 1950): 68–69. **The most important/** John Holmes: "'Live Another Day' Lifts John Ciardi to New Poetic Rank," 12/4/49, no page. *Live Another Day/* "Letter to Virginia Johnson" is bold: *Poetry* (June 1947): 146. The poem itself appeared in the same issue. In the words: Krickle, 50. **Not linked by/** "the poet owes": "WLB Autobiography," 482. Later still: Clemente, 15. **Simple or not/** "I have written honestly": 8/2/49, Recipient. **On 15 April/** "slugging"/"Shit on": JC to Dudley Fitts, 12/30/55, File Copy. "to put my notions": this and the remainder of this paragraph is from JC to Richard Wilbur, 4/16/49, Recipient. **For the next/** "My special concern": *Letters* 4/29/49. **The poets were/** "Works of art": *Mid-Century American Poets*, 1. **Shapiro, however, claimed/** "without a physical revulsion": KS to JC, 7/2/49, Shapiro Papers, LC. "new phase": DS to JC, 10/2/49, Schwartz Papers, LC. "it all depends": *Mid-Century American Poets*, 267. **In his introduction/** "recruiting literature": *Proceedings*, 59. **Ciardi began the/** "it must be evident": *Mid-Century American Poets*, ix. This paragraph and the next are drawn from the foreword, ix–xxx. **Some of John/** "remains one of the": quoted from the *Dictionary of Literary Biography Yearbook 1986*, 223. "seminal anthology": "Ciardi Remembered," 135. "high risk/high gain": *MM*, 69–70.

Expanding the Center
(pages 144–51)

Ciardi had been/ course in versification/"psychic resources": JC to BJW, 12/13/48, File Copy. **Perhaps the most/** "large photographs of the poet": *Proceedings*, 59. "eager to go anywhere": ABB, 93. **As Ciardi's speaking/** American Committee: FBI 2/28/49. **Still another center/** building a china cabinet: JC to John Holmes, 7/28/49, Papers, LC. to peel wallpaper: Judith. **Another of John/** "very bad prose-literal translations": Lovill, 357–58. "there was something fascinating"/ "'excrement'": "Difference," 153–54. **In the spring/** "I'm translating the *Inferno*.": *Letters* 3/20/49. half a million dollars: Judith. **To support the/** Guggenheim fellowship/"project sheet": *Letters*, 7/14/49. Gordon Bowles: Copy of letter from GB to Clarence Decker, 1/4/50, Papers, LC. Clarence Decker recommended: 1/5/50. UM-KC. **Hillyer's position was/** "Among those not applauding": 2/26/50. "stalked out of the room": H. Russell Austin in the Milwaukee, Wisconsin *Journal*, 3/12/50. New York literary agent: letter from John Schaffner to JC, 2/3/50, Papers, LC. **Ciardi had announced/** Holmes read the manuscript: JH to JC, 4/26/50, Papers, LC. "It won't conflict": 5/20/50 File Copy. "This is wonderful":

June Harding to Howard Moss, 6/4/50 Papers, LC. **Of course, Ciardi/** "sure critical touch": Steinberg, int. "rankest sort of check-chasing": 5/5/50, File Copy. **During a brief/** "Frank was funny": Hall, int. "Only today": *Letters* 8/2/50.

Europe
(pages 151–58)

Ciardi's essay, "Edna/ Ciardi's essay: See *Dialogue with an Audience* (16–17 and 61–73) for the essay plus the controversy. **The problem was/** "late one Friday": *Dialogue with an Audience*, 16–17. **Unfortunately, the quotations/** Norma Millay: Reprinted in *Dialogue with an Audience*, 72–73. **The perfect weather/** "met and talked"/"powerful and vivid": Clemente, "Writing *Treat It Gentle*," 82. **Ciardi, however, insisted/** 'vaguely scented": Clemente, "Writing *Treat It Gentle*," 82. "her own dreadful prose": JC to Jason Berry, Amistad Research Center, Tulane University, 2/16/76, File Copy. some 310 pages: See the Ciardi-Steinberg letters of this period in Papers, LC. "to recover what she claimed": Clemente, "Writing *Treat It Gentle*," 83. Papers, LC contains a three-page letter from Joan Williams to Ciardi (10/9/51) and a two-page reply from him to her (10/13/51). Ciardi asked about Williams's "stake in the book" and whether or not she could work out a dollar figure with Bechet for her work—and would her name have to appear on the contract. "The NY office would insist on dropping this like a hot potato if there was any question of disputed rights." Hill and Wang: The 1978 Da Capo reprint says that the original 1960 publication was by Cassell & Company, Ltd. in England, but the copyright was shared with Twayne. "I could have sued": Clemente, "Writing *Treat It Gentle*," 83. **Who was responsible/** "Sidney Bechet's musicianship": Elman, *MM*, 80–81. **During December, January/** "hit a snag": The Harry Ransom Humanities Research Center, University of Texas at Austin. **For the Christmas/** "in Germany that Christmas": AF VIII. **The honeymooners stayed/** *pensione*/Cavaletto: AF XLII and XIX. make love before calling for coffee: AF XIX. "I hardly spoke their language": AT, 9. "rapturously incoherent": AF XIX. **Then, after a/** Via Montepertica: AF XVII. "had grown up a miser": AF XIX. Dana Gioia/"the unique tone of Ciardi's best work": Review of *For Instance, Poetry* (May 1982): 113. **Even though Judith/** "I drudged night after night": AF XLII. "I wore two sweaters": AT, 1. **The return home/** "I did want children": AF, an unnumbered notebook, Papers, LC. "the smartest thing in the world": Judith.

Plotting the Future
(pages 158–65)

Ciardi spent the/ "craggy face": Asimov, "John Ciardi and the White Line Under the Snow," in *MM*, 185. **From Time to/** "particularity and immediacy": *Times* 5/25/52, 11. "as urbane and precise": *Antioch Review* 12 (Dec. 1952): 489–91. **The Twayne announcement/** Wallace Stevens influence: Cf. Krickle, 59: "A few phrases, an idea or two that would be more at home in the work of the older poet—it amounts to not much more than that." "Elegy III": It is not known if Ciardi actually attended Cavalcante's wake or imagined it. **"Another Comedy" had/** The Ciardi-Strobel exchange is in the Ciardi Papers, LC. **In early October/** "with all imaginable reluctance": Papers, LC. monthly check: letter from Jack Steinberg to JC, 10/17/51, and JC's agreement to the arrangement 10/19/51, Papers, LC. **Through the end/** Dollar figures and editorial royalties are from Statement of Account for Twayne, dated 12/31/52 and 12/31/53, in Papers, LC. an anxious letter: JC to Jack and Joel Steinberg, 9/7/52, File Copy. **In the meantime/** "I know I can trust you": MM to JC, 9/11/51, Moore Papers, LC. "One of these days": JC to MM, *Letters,* 10/7/51. "About the rewriting": MM to JC, 2/5/52, Moore Papers, LC. **Moore had been/** "But never again": copy in Papers, LC. **The plans most/** "For the next several months": File Copy. **In the fall/** "This is *top secret*": File Copy.

SIX
The Rutgers Years, 1953 to 1955

From "The Hypnoglyph" to The Inferno
(pages 169–75)

On 22 January/ "homebound": *Letters* 1/22/53. Twayne Triplets: Much of this paragraph is taken from file copies of documents found in Papers, LC: "Triplets Lineup as of 27 March 1953"; "Publisher's Note: What Is a New Idea in Science Fiction"; and "If You think the Critics Raved." The Ballantine-Ciardi copublishing venture is found in letters between them and Fletcher Pratt from 9 February to 22 March 1953, Papers, LC. Ciardi seems to have been most pleased with his editorial collaboration with Fletcher Pratt in the first Triplet, *Witches Three* (1952): "Conjure Wife" by Fritz Lieber, "There Shall Be No Darkness" by James Bush, and "The Blue Star" by Pratt. Ciardi wrote the introduction. **But something else/** "Let's face it": Welt, 180–81. Story of "The Hypnoglyph" wager is told in Broughton, 377–80 and Welt, 180–84. "a rich yarn": Ed Mayo to JC 7/12/53, Papers, LC: "By the way, I suspect you of writing "Hypnoglyph" in *Fantasy and Science Fiction* for July. Whether you did it or not, it's the sort of story you would write, if you did write one. Confess? If you didn't write it, read it. It's a rich yarn with as many levels as a skyscraper." "s f double-talk": Anthony Boucher to JC 1/6/53, Papers, LC. **Ciardi had every/** "the pseudonym": JC to editors of *F&SF, Letters* 12/8/52. "hiding from myself": JC to editors of *F&SF, Letters* 1/8/53. **In later life/** "I am tired": *Letters.* **Just when Ciardi/** *"nom de plume,"* Papers, LC. Humphries' "real peeve'": File Copy. **Later, when *New*/** "clerkly tick-tock verses": It is unclear if this review was published; it is quoted here from Ciardi's copy-edited ms., but there is no record of publication in White, nor has it sur-faced, to my knowledge, as an item missed by White. **Ciardi was doing/** "delighted by its appearance": *Letters* 1/8/53. "worked many lines": *Letters* 1/23/53. "My starting premise": File Copy. JC once commented on his rhyme innovation, "Finally I found myself doing a dummy *terza rima*, a ham sandwich in which the bread rhymes, but the ham doesn't. So it would be A blank A, B blank B, C blank C, D blank D; and my sins upon my own head, my ear told me that was as much rhyme as you needed in English and that it would convey a sense of the original. It did sound something like the original to me." (Broughton, 371). **But while Ciardi/** working hard to revise it: For example, the first canto was largely the same between the *Review* publication and the book publication, but four tercets (numbers three to six) were totally overhauled and some sixteen additional, smaller changes were made. *Inferno* publication information is from NAL letters to JC dated 3/3, 3/13, and 3/18/53, Papers, LC. **Between March and/** "The excellence of your translation": AM to JC, 3/24/53, Papers, LC. "struck at once": "The Literature of Italy," 158–59. **As Ciardi was/** "Wife Judith is flour-ishing": *Letters* 5/19/53.

Rutgers
(pages 175–84)

Leaving Harvard was/ Archie MacLeish's effort: Most of this paragraph is from the unpublished section of the Lovill int. "John didn't want": Judith. **In December 1952/** one-semester appointment at UKC: file copy of letter, Papers, LC. making inquiries: MF to JC, 1/23/53,

Papers, LC. "Have a job offer": *Letters* 1/30/53. **Some of those/** "Eventually, I hope": JC to HH, 1/31/53, File Copy. "a new sort of 'resident-writer' post": HH to JC, 2/7/53, Papers, LC. Less than a week later: HH to JC, 2/12/53, Papers, LC. **In February, French/** "writer-in-residence": JC to MF, 3/12/53, File Copy. **Owen had played/** According to Remigio Pane: Much of this paragraph is from Pane interviews, plus his letter to me of 3/4/92. **All this special/** Fred Main: Much of this paragraph is from Main, int. Paul Fussell, who joined the department in 1955, described the English faculty at Rutgers as being "as little energetic as the students" and wrote that "few" of the senior members "had minds interesting in any way." But he liked Ciardi: "A shining exception to such dolts was John Ciardi, recently of Harvard, whose coarse satiric presence was what the department desperately needed, but he was around only a few days a week and resigned finally to deal in real estate." *Doing Battle* (Boston: Little Brown, 1996), 225-26. **The house hunting/** "My notion": File Copy. "slightly superior"/ "umbrageous surroundings": Papers, LC. **For about the/** "novel"/ "controversial": Beirne, int. "the best—wonderful": Musa, int. "During my four years": letter from WJ to Richard Ichord, 10/19/70, copy in Papers, LC. Ciardi was very impressive: Bauer, int. "amazing": Rutgers *Targum*, 10/20/53. **But Ciardi was/** "Although one has": This paragraph is from "On Writers and Writing," *Forum* (1962): 3-4. [An interview conducted at Ball State University in June 1961.] **Dan Jaffe, who/** "terribly discouraging"/"complained bitterly": Review of Ciardi's *Selected Poems. New Letters* [formerly the UKC *Review*] (spring 1989): clipping. infuriating: This and the remainder of the paragraph is from Jaffe, "Ciardi Imprint," 12. **There was another/** "richest poet in America": Cheuse, int. "The current POETRY": *Letters* 4/8/53. **Meanwhile, in 1952–53/** Maxine Kumin/"surely a classic": *MM*, 131. Diane Wakoski/Ciardi "at his most brilliant": "Stalking the Barbaric Yawp," 811.

The Nation *and* The Inferno
(pages 184–93)

For reasons having/ Ciardi took them all to task: The review was titled, "Two Nuns and a Strolling Player." **Frances Frost's book/** "rather sweepingly harsh": 1/21/55, Papers, LC. "You publish a book": *Letters* 1/25/55. **In June and/** Dudley Fitts/Marianne Moore: "Strictness and Faithfulness," *The Nation* (6/19/54): 525. Louis MacNeice: "Something Like a Poem," *The Nation* (6/19/54): 525. **The subject of/** "Translation is the wrong word": The essay appears under the column title, "Speaking of Books." **In the spring/** "an odd coincidence":

Newquist, 115. **The Rutgers edition/** Even John Crowe Ransom: Ransom's comment was quoted in at least one newspaper, the San Francisco *Argonaut* (7/9/54), but may have appeared elsewhere as well. **Some, however, were/** Hugh Kenner/Howard Nemerov: Hugh Kenner, "Problems in Faithfulness and Fashion," *Poetry*, 85 (Jan. 1955): 225–31. Howard Nemerov, "A Few Bricks from Babel," *Sewanee Review*, 62 (Oct. 1954): 655–63. **But from nearly/** "So at last it is here": Papers, LC. "I have been reading slowly": 12/12/79, Papers, LC. Published by permission of the estate of Archibald MacLeish. **If MacLeish was/** "John's translation simplified": *Proceedings*, 64. **Perhaps so. At/** Sales figures taken from extant royalty statements and Judith Ciardi's estimate of overall sales. Ciardi reported to Eric Swenson: 1/5/77, Papers, LC.

As If
(pages 193–97)

From Time to/ "I ask my questions": AF XLV. "I feel very strongly": *Letters.* **Holmes, however, had/** "It feels too strained": Papers, LC. "the other possible gambit": 1/19/55, Papers, LC. "And you're right": *Letters* 1/22/55. **There were dissenting/** "spoiled by a slavish cleverness": Brodsky, 90. "crude power": Randall Jarrell, "Graves and the White Goddess," *Yale Review* (1956): 479. "holds everything together": Krickle, 65. **Some of that/** "As for the neutrality": *Letters* 4/9/53. **John Holmes had/** "I have reread AS IF": letter from IAS to JC 10/5/55, Papers, LC. "nothing I'd like better": 12/30/55, File Copy. "Too many of the poems": *Letters* 10/26/55.

SEVEN
The Rutgers Years,
1955 to 1957

Director of the Bread Loaf Writers' Conference and Poetry Editor of Saturday Review
(pages 199–212)

By August 1954/ "stale": Bain, 67. For the Ciardi years, see especially the following chapters in Bain: "Morrison's Twilight," "Ciardi

Rampant," and "Roller Coaster." "connections to the conference": Bain, 70. **At the time**/ "much more apprehensive": This paragraph is from Morrison, int. **When first approached**/ "When I say": File Copy. "For six weeks": *Letters.* "One more chain": Michigan Historical Collections, Bentley Historical Library, University of Michigan. **The formal announcement**/ letter of acceptance: 9/6/55, File Copy. **The "soul talks"**/ "backbreaker": Recipient. **Surviving letters, many**/ "they had to be marvelous": Judith. "immensely successful": Morrison, int. **And it was**/ "pure spec": 6/24/54, File Copy. 31 Graham Avenue: See also letter to J. F. Nims, *Letters* 8/13/55. Sales figures are from tax records, 1957. "wrenched sacroiliac": Ciardi used the term on his 1955 tax return. In a letter to A. B. Guthrie, Jr. of 11/7/55 (File Copy), Ciardi said he'd been in bed "several days" and was just then getting up a little. X-rays were taken and his doctor told him to be on "limited service" until Christmas. **When Cousins first**/ "I had, I told him frankly": ABB, PS. [were so annoying]: ABB, PS is a handwritten first draft of Ciardi's *SR* years, and in this sentence he left out the verb. I have supplied one of several that seem to fit Ciardi's intended meaning. "uneasy"/"relentlessly middle brow": ABB, PS. **On 29 December**/ "I see nothing to do": *Letters.* he regretted "any disappointment": Form letter in Papers, LC. "I take a personal pride": *Letters* 12/29/55. **If Ciardi had**/ "This in haste": *Letters* 12/29/55. "Amy Loveman": ABB, PS. "Am ass deep": File Copy. **Ciardi would prove**/ "Bill Benét sometimes allowed"/Amy Loveman was another: "Ciardi at *The Saturday Review,*" in *MM*, 114. "poesy": Pease, 12. **Meanwhile, looking for**/ "crisp, articulate, provocative": *Present Tense,* 52. "unambiguous, unequivocal, uncompromising": "Ciardi at *The Saturday Review*" in *MM*, 114. "combination of a Hemingway": *Present Tense,* 52. **Then, with his**/ "The American Academy": *Letters* 4/8/56. **Ciardi may have**/ Bill Sloane would/"via airmail": JC to PC, *Letters* 7/20/56. "I obviously have": 1/5/56, copy in Papers, LC. "Captain John runs": Middlebury College archives. **The 1957 conference**/ The Frost letter remains in the hands of the Ciardi family, but copies of the exchange are in Papers, LC. Reprinted by permission of the estate of Robert L. Frost, copyright 1997. Frost signed it, "Robert": Cifelli, "Ciardi on Frost," 479. **Despite his commitment**/ a number of changes: See Bain, 74–75. **On 14 April**/ "Everyone Writes (Bad) Poetry," *SR* 5/5/56. **The *Saturday Review***/ "a couple of well-selected": File Copy. "sincerity" but no "pleasure": 11/10/56, File Copy. "captions to cartoons": *Letters.* **In the midst**/ "clearing some of the": *Letters* 2/7/57.

Anne Morrow Lindbergh
(pages 212–21)

Ciardi's Lindbergh review/ "the least temporizing man": *Present Tense,* 53. **According to Dorothy**/ "Anne was deeply wounded"/"in the main correct": *Anne Morrow Lindbergh: A Gift for Life* (New York: Ticknor & Fields, 1992), 293–97. "thousands": *Present Tense,* 54. "a baseball bat": *SR* 2/16/57. "one may chide": *SR* 2/9/57. "I suggest you": *SR* 2/9/57. **After the first**/ "Please telephone": Copy of cable in Papers, LC. "a fairly substantial"/"lower the temperature": *Present Tense,* 55. **Ciardi received the**/ "serious question": *Letters* 2/13/57. **The next day**/ "why I am so powerfully distressed": This and the remainder of this paragraph and the next is from *Letters* 2/16/57. **Cousins replied on**/ "manner"/"shocked"/"ambush": NC to JC, 2/21/57, Papers, LC. "I was going to say": *Letters.* "Well, peace.": *Letters* 2/25/57. **To Lask's long**/ "successive attacks": Papers, LC. "Let me add": File Copy.

"whispered assignations"
(pages 221–25)

In some ways/ "marble tomb": JC to NC, *Letters* 11/21/56. "Semi-Eureka!": no date, but context places it in early March, copy in Papers, LC. "Instead of doing": letter from JC to an unidentified "Joe," ca. October 1957. From the College Information Services, Rutgers Univ. **In addition to**/ Cavaletto: AF XIX. two weeks in Greece: JC to M. L. Rosenthal, 3/17/57, Recipient. some sixty stopovers: Gertrude Kastle's estimate, int. **Probably during April**/ "placebos of good will"/"medical talismans": AF XLIV. "dashed out and returned": Irma Cavat (Kachadoorian), int. **In "Victor Emanuel**/ "been catching merry hell": 4/22/57, Papers, LC. "this horrible Norse blooper": JC to NC, Recipient. "I can only speculate": 5/4/57, File Copy. "slipped by without ruckus": 5/8/57, Recipient. three-page, single-spaced: 5/17/57, File Copy. "CONFIDENTIAL: NC ONLY": File Copy. Fernando Tambroni: File Copy. **Although he was**/ "what was involved": 6/15/57, Papers, LC.

EIGHT
The Rutgers Years, 1957 to 1961

A Changed Literary Landscape (pages 227–33)

When the Ciardis/ forged a letter/"out of there in no time": JC to Irma and Zubel Kachadoorian. *Letters* 11/10/57. stocked the refrigerator: Judith to the Kachadoorians, 8/18/57, Recipient. "This lovely spot": Judith to the Kachadoorians, 8/18/57, Recipient. Ciardi took Irv: Klompus, int. Originally, according to Klompus, he had invited himself, and JC so liked the idea that he made arrangements for him to become a regular. **Ciardi was fortunate**/ "attacked by a local character": 8/18/57, copy in Papers, LC. **As to fellows**/ "one of the best times": "Confessions of a Summer Camper (Lit'ry Division)," 1966, quoted by Bain, 235. "deficient": WS to JC, 5/27/55, quoted by Bain, 76. "The focus of everything": Bain, 233. **Trudy Drucker, a**/ "worshipped the ground": Drucker, int. He had quit: This and the remainder of the paragraph is from a letter to me from EK, 7/9/89. **The winds of**/ "The first part of 'Howl'": quoted from a front-page story of the San Francisco *Examiner*, 10/4/57. **With so much**/ "beatniks": Strauss and Howe, 288. "who are as competent": Paul Riley and Ed Blake, "An Interview with John Holmes," *Scribe. The Literary Quarterly of Emerson College* (fall 1959): 46. **Ciardi's response to**/ "Thanks for the nice letter.": 11/30/57, Papers, LC. "Ciardi did not sneer": *SR* 4/20/68, 26. "an impressive catalogue": Lovill, diss., 353. "Well, I'm not his psychiatrist": Owen, 23. "The whole beat generation": Owen, 22. **Perhaps the Beat**/ "I know of no good poet": foreword, *Mid-Century American Poets*, xi. "West Coast Renaissance"/"gone stale": "Ciardi Remembered" in *MM*, 137.

"dedicated to the profit motive" (pages 233–44)

When the Ciardis/ "I have an acre": Papers, LC. "descended"/"still eating us bare": Recipient. "I've done more looking": 4/29/58, Papers, LC. **Too bad, perhaps**,/ "Do you need any": *Letters* 6/5/58. "The carpenters have redescended": 6/24/58, Recipient. "dedi-

cated to the profit motive": 5/6/58, File Copy. "I'm averaging about 18%":
to John Westcott, 9/25/58, File Copy. "I'm doing too damn much": Papers,
LC. **On 13 November**/ "My sympathies are with you": *Letters* 9/22/62.
A List: FBI 6/14/61. Hanover College/honorary doctorate: 2/12/60,
Papers, LC. Tufts/honorary doctor of literature: 2/16/60, Papers, LC. **All
through the**/ "My last three days": no date, but November 1957. Ciardi
vehemently objected/"least relevant": JC to Amram Novack, 6/10/58,
File Copy. **In late April**/ "dashing like a migratory bird": 4/29/58,
Recipient. "Ciardi literally took": Owen, 21. **Meanwhile, if he**/ "onerous": Judith to the Kachadoorians, 4/29/58, Recipient. "no indication
whatever": *Dialogue with an Audience*, 220. **And Ciardi found**/ "The horizontal audience consists": *Dialogue with an Audience*, 35–6. **The Frost
essay**/ "a phrase I should never have used": Cifelli, "Ciardi on Frost,"
483. Some years later, Frost was quoted as saying that he had read a different article about him by Ciardi: "It's one of the few about me that I've
read." He called it "uncannily accurate." (Burnshaw, *Robert Frost Himself*,
109). Ciardi was right: See John Evangelist Walsh: *Into My Own: The English
Years of Robert Frost* (New York: Grove Weidenfeld, 1988), 130 and note, 251.
Although the contretemps/ "It mattered a great deal": Wilbur, int.
"was full of ideas": *Robert Frost Himself*, 109. **At Bread Loaf**/ In 1958 alone:
Bain, 78 and 82. three hundred dollars in 1959: Judith. **Ciardi arrived
at**/ "push-button windows": *Letters* 7/30/59. **Alan Cheuse, who**/ wanted
to take a course: Cheuse, int. "'Old Black Joe'": Most of the information
for the rest of this paragraph is from Bain, 81. **X. J. Kennedy**/ "hobnob":
This and the remainder of the paragraph are from Kennedy, int. **Ciardi
argued as**/ "endless details"/"staggering correspondence": File Copy.
"to carry the burden": File Copy. **But if Ciardi**/ "I think it would be":
Letters 5/18/61. two hundred dollars of his own money: Williams, int.

Books upon Books
(pages 244–53)

    Edward Krickel, however/ "a relative failure": *John
Ciardi*, 73. "truly original"/"heavy, unfunctional imagery": *TLS*, 3/6/59,
Clipping. "at his worst"/"vulgar and tasteless": *MAQR*, 5/23/59, 275–76.
"particularity": *YR* (winter 1959): 302. "tone it down": *HR*, 11 (1958): 445–46.
Love poems are/ "mastery of convoluted clarity": *Times*, 6/5/58. "truly
refreshing": *NYTBR* 63 (8/3/58): 6. "direct emotion": *Tribune*, 12/14/58,
Clipping. "tenderness and roughness"/"beautiful and alive": *Poetry* 93 (Oct.
1958): 46–47. 550 copies: letter, W. Sloane to JC, Papers, LC. more than

5,000: "Ciardi on Tape," 24. **"Most Like an**/ "I ponder this objection": This exchange between Rosenthal and Ciardi is on page 22 of *I Marry You* worksheets, Papers, LC. **Years later, Ciardi**/ "The shimmering word": ca. December 1981, Lilly Library, Indiana University. **On the dust**/ *In the Year of the Longest Cadillac:* JC to Richard Wilbur, 12/12/59, Recipient. Josephine Jacobsen: "Comment: Whittemore, Engle, Scott, Ciardi," 96 (July 1960): 235–37. **Once again the**/ "pull no punches": *Letters* 3/14/59. "I have had to hold out": *Letters.* "I am reasonably pleased": *Letters.* **Perhaps it was**/ "the *Times* either doesn't recognize it": 3/6/60, Recipient. "German-Jewish equivalent": letter to a Professor Pommer, 2/4/80, File Copy. Ciardi once commented on "The Gift": "'Hell,' I was once moved to observe, 'is the denial of the ordinary.' I had been reading a book about concentration camps, wherein depraved men have certainly done their best to stage a production of hell on earth. The essence of that hell, I found myself thinking was in the fact that the trivial had been swept away by a nightmare in which everything—a remark, a crust of bread, the mood of a jailer, the irritations of a fellow sufferer—become portentous and deadly." (M/S, "The Trivial History of Our Time," 1/19/62). **The manuscript of**/ "Ciardi poleaxes": Gorner, 4. "better than well": *Letters* 7/18/61. 300,000 copies/3,000 copies: *Letters* 6/25/72 and 4/21/85. **Less than two**/ "I'm not a very": White, 6. "poor at keeping files": White, 10. **In September 1959**/ "I'd never gotten": "Ciardi on Tape," 26. "I've got a book of children's poems": 11/8/51. The University of Washington Libraries. "the yellowed folder": "Ciardi on Tape," 26. "Myra is dancing": 6/16/59, Recipient.

Leaving the Academic Life
(pages 253–58)

From the outset/ "Another School Year—Why?" *Rutgers Alumni Monthly* (Nov. 1954): 2–3. **But there was**/ radio and television: Pane, int. Pane also wrote to me (3/4/92) that JC appeared with him on WNYC radio in New York to discuss *The Inferno.* "yelping patriotism": Reported in the Rutgers *Targum,* 3/16/54. "notions that have been forming": File Copy. "The Rutgers Plan": Papers, LC. **Ciardi took the**/ "day by day goes by": *Letters* 2/6/59. "when a fat check": copy in Papers, LC. "true devotion": File Copy. **Privately, Ciardi was**/ "standards are trampled": unpublished, ca. 1958, Papers, LC. "I was once employed": M/S, "Mailbag (Outgoing)," 4/11/64. "Reasons: first": *Letters* 8/7/59. "most academics begin": M/S, "To the Damnation of Deans (A Prejudice),"

3/24/62. **By September 1959**/ poet in residence: *Letters* 11/4/59. "camouflages in catalogue": "September ? 1960." Recipient. **Six months later**/ "regretfully": 3/18/61, File Copy. "I hesitated": AF I.

NINE
"The Capitalist of Po Biz," 1961 to 1968

Scrambling for Dollars
(pages 259–67)

Back in 1958/ "You're kidding": File Copy. "How does being": "Ciardi on Tape," 17. millionaire: Williams, int. **Ciardi's first opportunity**/ "as an autonomous": Cousins, *Present Tense*, 67; Circulation figures, 69. **In general, Ciardi**/ "I confess": Early version of M/S, "Goodbye and Hello," 3/4/72. **Ciardi understood his**/ "rapport"/ "excellent offers": 11/28/62, File Copy. "a hobby job": Wilson, 116. **Stretching from October**/ five hundred dollars/twelve hundred dollars: check stubs, Papers, WSU. "I won't try": File Copy. *Accent* **had been**/ "with slightly mixed emotions": Recipient's estate. **In mid-May, as**/ "crazy and all over the country": *Letters* ca. 5/12/62. **By 1961, however**/ "Not since the days": Program note for Rutgers award that JC won that year. "deservedly popular figure": "Memorial to John Ciardi," *Solares Hill* [newspaper/magazine], Key West, Fla. (May 1986): 32. "As notions occurred to him": Wilbur, int. "electrifying": Stryk, 117. "basic pontification": Garrett, int. "real pro": Kennedy, int. **Ciardi thought, spoke**/ "a quarter of my life": An essay fragment on success, Papers, LC. "There's no other reason": "Ciardi on Tape," 17. **Ciardi was perfectly**/ "Back through the Looking Glass": *This Strangest Everything.*

Home Life
(pages 267–76)

John Ciardi's period/ a celebrity: John L., int. "Come spring": M/S, "The Lecture Circuit (Airborne Division)," 6/6/64. "We were *very*": John L., int. "Jonnel is huge": 6/16/59, Recipient. "the eternal discipline problem": 3/23/60, Recipient. **Yet Jonnel was**/ spanked:

Details for this paragraph are from John L., int. **In a lighter/** "I came out of it": AF I. **As the 1960s/** "fuckin' pighead": Benn, int. "fairly contentious": John L., int. "Loud is only the rustle": M/S, "The Monster Den," 2/22/64. **In the summer/** "I wanted our monsters": Unidentifiable ms. fragment, Papers, LC. **None of the/** "thought we should have": Myra, int. "Our local Presbyterian Church": M/S, "Religion and Citizenship," 9/22/62. "It is possible": Papers, LC. **By her own/** pleasant, unrebellious: Myra, int. "grades, attitude, and citizenship": Letter, 4/25/66 from Charles B. Atwater, headmaster of the Pingry School to the Ciardis. "goody-goody boys": This and the remainder of the paragraph are from John L., int. **Young Benn was/** "I happen to have": M/S, "When Do They Know Too Much?" 5/11/62. "I am moved to hope": M/S, "Parents and Proverbs," 5/26/62. **Beginning with the/** "youth-centered"/"dreary, pampered": M/S, "Prejudices and Damnations," 9/15/62. **The troubling direction/** "in discomfort these days": 7/16/61, Papers, LC. lingering respiratory/pains in his hip: Doris (Holmes) Eyges, int. "for new strategy": 4/2/62. **Meanwhile, Concetta Ciardi's/** "Would it help": Recipient's family. John wrote as though: Recipient's family. **Soon, however, the/** little doll/Johnny: Cora, int. "She rambled": ABB, 82. **The fact that/** "My mother remained": Radio broadcast, "John Ciardi I," *New Letters on the Air* (Dec. 1983). Tape available from UM-KC.

Principles, Positions, and Personality; Honors, Hobbies, and Health
(pages 277–86)

A minor controversy/ "Jim Crow Is Treason": This paragraph is from newspaper clippings from the *Perth Amboy (N.J.) News* and the *Birmingham (Ala.) News*, Papers, LC and Papers, WSU. "I hope you collect": 3/8/61, Papers, LC. **In a related/** "How much can the peace marchers take": M/S, "Black Man in America," 7/6/63. **Ciardi spent a/** Gil Gallagher interceded: Letter from GG to me, 3/23/89. **As another measure/** "Mr. Ciardi's is a voice": John C. Vorrath, 6/8/64, Papers, LC. **During the 1964–65/** John Holmes Visiting Professor: contract, Papers, LC. "loved and idolized": Kennedy, int. "rumblings": 3/5/66. **Tufts students may/** "Ciardi Report"/"The Tufts Plan": M/S, "Student Publications and the Tufts Plan," 9/11/65. **In addition to/** fall 1962 tour: M/S, "The Air Age," 12/8/62. one West Coast week: JC to Bud Orenstein, 4/19/63. Recipient's family. spring 1964 tour: JC to

Leonard and Gertrude Kasle, 3/2/64, Recipient. "rousing, two hour speech": letter from FS to me, 7/14/93. **Ciardi was at/** "in such lounging duds": M/S, "The Slush Pile," 11/5/66. **The sequence shot/** "'I read just'"/ "the badness of bad poetry": M/S, "The Slush Pile," 11/5/66. "I read just the first line. . . ." is quoted in the essay from the "Creative Person" television program. "Physically, what I do": Newquist, 116. **In September 1966/** "what it most of all": 9/16/66, Recipient. paying it off: M/S, "Burning the Files," 2/1/64. "He earns his living": Essay draft, Papers, LC. **Politically, Ciardi identified/** "hold your nose": Tufts Reunion Booklet (1963): 8. "take the position": 4/15/68. Papers, WSU. **Ciardi claimed in/** "I used to have character": "WLB Autobiography," 482. "listed as sponsor": FBI, 7/31/64. communist front group: FBI, 4/9/65. golf and gardening: *Current Biography*, 12. "played cards like an enlisted man": Description of game and quote are from Klompus, int. high stakes gin rummy: Myra, int. "He played the stock market": Klompus, int. $6,500/$16,500: Papers, WSU. **With hindsight it/** "Doctuh! I need": Stone, 145. "I hereby announce": M/S, "Kathy, the Bad Man, and Charlie McCarthy," 4/16/66. "As with all men": M/S, "Eve: An Expert View," 7/23/66. "Grant me at least": 6/17/68. Lilly Library, Indiana University.

"Daddy was charming . . . and Mom was First Lady." (pages 286–94)

Every August in/ "The real pleasant": John L., int. "Daddy was charming": Myra, int. **The turbulent 1960s/** "one of the luckiest people": "Ciardi on Tape," 22. "The Establishment"/ Lyndon Johnson: Strauss and Howe, 274. he dutifully obeyed/"who really runs": "WLB Autobiography," 482. **It was not/** "Among the diehards": M/S, "Whose Usage Counts?" 10/27/62. "not long ago"/"may be good salesmen": Newquist, 119, 121. "what the presence": Newquist, 120. **Ciardi went on/** "disciplined containment": Kahl, 18–19. "the pleasure of taking pains"/"we demand difficulty": M/S, "Is Everybody Happy?" 3/14/64. "A poem's reader": JC to David Shapiro, 9/17/63, File Copy. **But none of/** "modern poet": "Ciardi, Modern Poet, Excels in Verse," UKC *University News*, 2/16/40, UM-KC. "the only prerequisite": Lovill, diss., 338. "get excited enough": Huisking, 16. "Students, as I watch them": Newquist, 119. "With their generation": essay fragment on his children's generation, Papers, LC. **Despite the high/** Ciardi had slipped: Cubeta, int. "enjoyed and admired": Freeman, int. Freeman, a teetotaler: Bain, 98. **Meanwhile,**

unaware of the/ twelve thousand dollars in endowments: JC to Samuel Stratton, President of Middlebury College, 8/29/62, File Copy. four thousand dollars/ten thousand dollars: letter from RR to JC, 6/23/65. Papers, WSU. three thousand dollars: JC to RR, 6/5/65, File Copy. turned back his four-hundred-dollar fee: Judith; also Klompus, int. See also BL budget for 1963, Papers, LC. new porch: As director, JC offered the money, "following high example," he said in a letter to new president James Armstrong on 9/14/65. Copy in Papers, WSU. **Moreover, social changes/** "clinic"/"a disease": Bain, 94. **But even in/** "ask Mr. Ciardi": Turco, int. Ciardi suggested: Martin, int. the much fairer appraisal: Rabe, 18–21.

TEN
Binge Worker,
Books of the Sixties

Children's Verse
(pages 295–303)

An interviewer in/ "no good at strict": Cargas, 20. **For John Ciardi/** "I love to scold": Diane Allen [Announcement that JC had won the NCTE award for excellence in poetry for children], *Language Arts* (May 1982): 431–32. **Binge work or/** "has made few additions": Smith, 154. "Practically singlehandedly": *Dictionary of Literary Biography, Yearbook, 1986*, 223. national survey: See Ann Terry, *Children's Poetry Preferences* (Urbana, IL: NCTE, 1974. **Yet controversy hounded/** too violent: Cf. Groff, 158: "Ciardi seems to want to add to the circle of violence and mistrust that now surrounds the modern child." "intensities and losses": This and the rest of the quotations in this paragraph are from "WLB Autobiography," 481. **On another occasion/** "Children are savages": Kahle, 17–18. **A number of/** "Let the Healthy Be Tended, Too": JC told the same story a second time, three years later, "Angel Fluffs, Savages, and Dispensable Adults," *Woman's Day* (Oct. 1965), 44, 126–29. "John Ciardi's verse": *Poetry* 101 (Dec. 1962): 208. **Ciardi was surely/** "What man can fail": from "Let the Healthy Be Tended, Too." **The second story/** Adding to her delight: Myra, int. "to set up an interview": JC told this story regularly on the lecture circuit, never exactly the same way twice. It was published posthumously as "'Juvenile Poetry' and Poetry for Children" in *Ciardi Himself,* but this paragraph quotes taped lectures as well as the printed version. This he thought: *Ciardi Himself*, 81–82. "I love that little poem": *Ciardi Himself*, 82. "a pure exercise": *Ciardi Himself*, 83. **The uncontested truth**/ "He made me feel"/reassuring presence: Arrigon, 158, 159. **Moreover, even though**/ "slightly disreputable": Kennedy, afterword, 61.

Dante "by itch and twitch" (pages 303–8)

Ciardi was not/ "Having been this slow": 2/10/60, Papers, WSU. **Within two weeks**/ "very much pleased": Papers, WSU. **Ciardi also observed**/ Roy P. Basler: letter to JC, 4/20/64, Papers, LC. **The 1965 celebrations**/ "*Paradiso* moves along": Recipient. "then nothing till I finish": Recipient. "I did the last line": Papers, LC. "sweating at the final typescript": 9/7/68, Recipient. "Toward celebrations": Recipient.

"the poet's necessary love for the living language" (pages 309–21)

Rutgers University Press/ "irritating"/"a quieter sensitivity": Rosenthal, "An Unfair Question," 50 and 51. "No matter how simply": Krickle, 104. **Ciardi said of**/ "an experiment in writing the poem quickly": Lovill, diss., 331. "some note of stay": "Poetry Chronicle," *Poetry* 102 (July 1963): 253. "trivial, the weakest": Krickle, 104. **"The Size of**/ "I like to watch birds": Lovill, diss., 321. **But *Person to***/ "this damn straightness"/"What am I trying to say?": DF to JC, no date, but early January 1964, Papers, WSU. "For better or worse": Papers, WSU. **Four days later**/ "generally raised Hell": *Letters* 1/25/64. **Following his instincts**/ "God, how I admire": JMB to JC, 12/5/64, Papers, LC. "best and most significant": Harmon, 504. "cheerful scepticism": Ernest Sandeen, "A More Comic Spirit," *Poetry* 106 (June 1965): 233. "they seem to achieve": Krickle, 107. John Ciardi and Robert Frost: See also Sandeen (above) and Krickle, 108. **But among the**/ "rendered unique": Gallagher, item 28. **Ciardi's fourth and**/ "[Poets] are, I submit": 4/15/67.

ELEVEN

"The goddamn world closing in," 1969 to 1972

Riding High
(pages 323–37)

In 1969, for/ judge/National Book Awards: Wilson, 115. "charming and dynamic"/"letter of adulation": Papers, LC. **Particularly gratifying to**/ A professor in Italy: Prof. Americo Tirone. AF XL. They left on 12 June: Parts of this story are from interviews with Judith and John L., but Ciardi himself provided most details in "Difference," 155–56 and AF XL. **Amid the fanfare**/ he wept openly: Benn, int., 4/15/91. "You are especially right": 9/16/64, File Copy. **Little more than**/ *Times* obligingly printed: David E. Rosenbaum, "Congressman Lists 65 'Radicals' Despite Injunction," *New York Times* (15 Oct. 1970),: 24. See also Sanford J. Ungar, "'Radical Revolutionary' List Delayed by Court," *Washington Post* (14 Oct. 1970): A3. "the campus-speaking circuit": Rosenbaum, 24. **On the eighteenth**/ "a moderate liberal": *Home News* (18 Oct. 1970), clipping. "most ridiculous thing": John L., int. "because he has pointed out": "Ciardi's a Target of the Right and Left" (27 Oct. 1970): 5. "Choice of speakers": *Letters* 10/26/70. "maybe the droopy": Recipient. **On 17 November**/ "FUCK HISC": *Letters* 11/20/70. "The rest either avoided you": M/S, "An Open Letter to the Honorable Richard Ichord," 5/15/71. **But as juicy**/ "for honorable personal reasons": File Copy. "not try to persuade": Recipient. **The book itself**/ "introspective, iconoclastic": This and other quotations in this paragraph are from Williams, "John Ciardi—'Nothing Is Really Hard But to Be Real.'" **When Ciardi first**/ "I couldn't have foreseen": *Letters* 7/29/67. "It's an odd sensation": *Letters* 3/19/69. **Other literary irons**/ "rest the soul": JC to Miller Williams, 1/30/70, Recipient. "an English experience of Dante": 4/14/69, File Copy. Viking/action-threatening: copies of this correspondence is in Papers, LC. **Of course, Ciardi**/ her lover of some six months: With respect to AS's affair with GS at Bread Loaf in 1959, Diane Wood Middlebrook wrote: "Among poets they were not particularly discreet about their liaison." *Anne Sexton: A Biography* (Boston, Mass.: Houghton Mifflin, 1991), 118. "I distrust": Middlebrook, 98. "the psychological vulgarization": foreword to *The Letters of Delmore Schwartz*, ed. Robert Phillips (Princeton, N.J.: Ontario Review Press, 1984), xii. **In one sense**/ "Ciardi's poems belong": "John Ciardi—'Nothing Is Really Hard But to

Be Real,'" 1. **The center he**/ "I just wouldn't have believed"/"It's a compelling book": *Letters* 7/15/67. "autobiographical exorcisms": JC to Doris Holmes, 9/2/67, File Copy. "I need some time now": *Letters* 11/15/68. **During the winter**/ "generation gap"/"about ready"/"some feelings": *Letters* 3/1/70. "stewed"/"tightened": *Letters* 4/7/70. "Bill Sloane—a really dear": 4/11/71, Recipient. advance sale of three thousand: JC to Miller Williams, *Letters* 5/1/71. **In mid-May Stanley**/ "is surely the most compelling": copy in Papers, LC. "I had to find"/"Who doesn't know": File Copies. "I am not one of those": 9/13/71, Papers, LC. Published by permission of the estate of Archibald MacLeish. **MacLeish's high praise**/ "Ciardi country": quoted on the dust jacket of fourth printing of *Person to Person*. "The real pulse": Krickle, 130. **Ciardi had written**/ "In a real sense": *Letters* 6/1/71. "the prosody, normal accentual-syllabics": Turco, 34. "shirt-sleeve manner": Jerome, "Ciardi's Art," 20. "the most readable": Kennedy, "John Ciardi's Early Lives," 31. **Although *Lives of***/ "I don't know why": Clemente, 13.

The End of the Maestro System (pages 337–73)

Ciardi was not/ twenty thousand dollars in canceled: JC to Miller Williams, 1/30/70, Recipient. "Now the goddamn world closing in": *Letters* 3/12/71. "I'm going through": *Letters* 5/1/71. "I told him": JC to Miller Williams, *Letters* ca. 6/7/71. **Ciardi's weight had**/ "I just ain't": *Letters*. "Shit, I'm too busy": Recipient. limericks: reprinted by permission of W. W. Norton & Co. **Another malaise was**/ "busy indolence": JC to Miller Williams, *Letters* 7/28/70. "I am behind in everything": 4/11/71, Recipient. "There is, I think": *Letters* ca. 6/7/71. "I have fallen": *Letters* 8/1/71. **Adding to his**/ "Before you came": Papers, LC. **When *Saturday Review***/ "hard-driving types": M/S, "Goodbye and Hello," 3/4/72. "I am not particularly pessimistic": *Letters*. "bell-bottomed"/"hotpantsed": *Letters*. **By February 1972**/ "I have a large collection": M/S, "Goodbye and Hello," 3/4/72. **Ciardi was glum**/ "the new and even-more-vulgarized": 6/22/72, Recipient. "My magazine income": ABB, PS. **In fact the**/ Canada rather than Vietnam: John L., int. hair cut/male lead/"Jonnel has bloomed": JC to Gertrude Kasle, 11/20/70, Recipient. **A year earlier**/ Her first semester: JC to Miller Williams, *Letters* 12/11/70. "a lovely 19": 3/24/71, Recipient. "great bearded blond beast": JC to Robert Cordray, 4/22/71, Recipient. "Myra came home": *Letters* 11/12/71. **When Myra went**/ "last chick": 9/22/71, copy in Papers, LC. Benn took a certain joy: Benn, int. "the generation abyss": 10/7/70, Recipient. "The judge told [Benn]": 12/11/70, Recipient. **It wasn't. Ciardi**/ "I am not about": AF XXII. "set up": Benn, int. "The lines are fixed": AF XXII. **At that point**/ The house became a haven: Benn, int. "We had pot plants": Benn, int. "Benny is currently": 3/24/71, Recipient. "fucking pot head": ca. 6/7/71, Recipient. **On 18 March**/ "investment in the younger generation": AF XXXIX. **By mountain time**/ "brat anarchy": unpublished ms., no date, on student uprisings, the taking of buildings, and duties of college presidents, Papers, LC. "Ladies and gentlemen": "Unsolicited Opening Day Address," 9/28/68. **Nothing especially untoward**/ Volkswagen squareback: JC to Milton Hebald, 9/4/69, Recipient. $455 below: This and all budget figures in this paragraph are from Stephen Freeman to JC, 11/25/69, Papers, LC. **The poetry staff**/ "to discuss specific problems": from the 1969 Memo to Staff Members, Papers, LC. "how do you choose": AG to JC, 7/10/69, Papers, LC. "divergences": AG to JC, 9/8/69, Papers, LC. **Still as Ciardi**/ "a quiet conference": *Letters* 8/18/69. "least pleasant most mooching": *Letters* 9/4/69. **There were, nonetheless**/ "sometimes formidable presence"/"a kind of trance": "John Ciardi and the 'Witch of Fungi,'" 132. **Another happy addition**/ "murky"/"antacids": Stone, int. "I heard John": "John Ciardi: His Wit and Witness," 142. **Doc Stone felt**/ "privileged": Stone, "John Ciardi: His Wit and Witness," 142. Ageless rules: Stone, int. Myra's suggestion: Bain, 100. public readings by waiters: Bain, 101. "Strenuous Test for Writers": (5 Oct. 1969): 18–21. **The conference was**/ "as if a hidden thermostat": Bain, 101. constantly drunk by his own admission: Wakefield, int. "partying and philandering": "Ciardi Remembered," 138. **In terms of**/ "a particular affinity": Bain, 102. "generational"/"out of touch"/ "defensive": Kinnell, int. "running counter to the grain": Kumin, int. "the hard line about craft"/"sensitivity to the insecurity": 9/22/70, Papers, LC. **All three of**/ "continued to press": Bain, 104. **Kinnell himself recalled**/ "trusting one's instincts": Kinnell, int. "Your generation": "On Leaving the Bench," 3/13/71. "frosty"/"personally affronted": Kinnell, int. **That craftsmanship in**/ "to light a fire"/"a false impression": Kinnell, int. **To Ciardi, teaching**/ inspiration/"get rid of": "John Ciardi's Poetry," *Morristown (N.J.) Daily Record* (13 Feb. 1970): 7. "Poetry is no monolithic thing": 9/20/70. **At Chautauqua a**/ "An undergraduate who": from a taped Chautauqua lecture, no date, but early to mid-1970s. "the over-encouraged generation": Cathy Traugott, *Tulsa World* (19 Feb. 1978): no page. "I don't like": taped lecture "On Poetry," Bellarmine College, Louisville, Ky., 10/22/84. too stubbornly Italian: see for example Bain, 102, "It would have been a hard time for any figure of authority, teacher or administrator, but especially for someone like John Ciardi who had come to consider Bread Loaf as an extension of his family—an Italian family it must be added, modern but still old world, with Ciardi as the increasingly firm *patrone*." **Clearly John Ciardi/** "parental abuse of authority": "Fantasy," 8/22/70. **During the 1970/** "There, by God": Ciardi repeated this story often; the quote here is from his final Bread Loaf lecture, 8/29/72, taped by John Stone. **Kinnell was not/** "they just won't do": *Letters* 1/7/71. **If Ciardi was/** "You probably know": *Letters* 1/26/71. **Then making matters/** feature story: "'We Believe in the Maestro System': The Bread Loaf Process," *Audience* 2 (May-June 1972): 90–108. "he was unable": Hills, 91. **Hills described Ciardi/** "he's not one of your"/"an Italian family": Hills, 94. "we were not here to discuss": Hills, 95. **This was the/** "in real art": Hills, 108. It was "a misassumption": Hills, 108. "The Bread Loaf 'tradition'": Hills, 106. **If Ciardi was/** "a good-looking tweeds-and-corduroy": Hills, 96. "nonsensical business"/"the teaching is virtually worthless": Hills, 97. Miller Williams/"a bearded man": Hills, 97. William Meredith was "out of place": Hills, 98. "extraordinary rapport"/"a modern saint": Hills, 98. **Hills pigeonholed all/** "many of the major"/"never even heard of": Hills, 100. "integrity"/ "that it was cronyism": Hills, 104. "I have never known a man": *The Craft of Writing*, ed. Julia H. Sloane (New York: W. W. Norton, 1979), 11. **The 1971 Conference/** "tempers began to fray": Bain, 105. "traditionally wide-open": Bain, 105. **Change, of course/** dining hall/Students at the final clinic: See Bain, 105. "swindle": Hills, 104; Bain, 105. **The dramatic climax/** "very brilliant young poet": The characterizations here of Brennan are from Kennedy, int. "slightly built": Hills, 105. Hills did not know the name of the waiter who stood up; X. J. Kennedy has supplied it. "arrogance": Brennan's short speech is recorded in Hills, 105 and Bain, 105. "generosity of spirit": Hills, 105. Cf. Strauss and Howe, p. 308: "Reform-minded educators began insisting that adults had as much to learn from youths as vice versa. The curriculum stressed learning skills over subject matter, social relevance over timeless facts. New student 'rights' were litigated. . . ." "If I haven't": Hills, 105. **There would be/** "ba-a-ad vibes": Hills, 106. "Ciardi had treated him decently": Kennedy, int. **That evening, after/** "began to dress down": Bain, 106. Ciardi "seemed ready"/Martin "seemed not": Hills, 106. **On 13 September/** "filled in": All quotations in this paragraph are from this letter, Papers, LC. **Although Ciardi did/** "Bread Loaf was bad": *Letters* 10/2/71. **Then on 13/** "absorbed"/"What comes next": *Letters* 10/13/71. **The Martin-led/** In 1971, the situation: JC to WM, 1/21/71, Recipient. **Certainly Ciardi's social/** "I've been there myself": *Letters* 9/6/58. **If signing up/** Bill Meredith had written: 1/19/71, Papers, LC. Ciardi replied: JC to WM, 1/21/71, File Copy. "A poet is a poet": M/S, "Dear N," 1/11/69. "I'm sorry

I can't find": *Letters* ca. 10/17/71. **When Jim Armstrong**/ he expressed regret: Cubeta, int. "weary"/"gaps and faults": This and the remaining quotations in this paragraph are from Armstrong, int. **It is not**/ "college-wide range of problems": *Letters* 8/2/72. **Then on 2**/ how duplicitous Armstrong had been: JC to JA, *Letters* 8/2/72. Judith Ciardi's summation: Judith, int. **In May 1972**/ Meredith was distressed: 5/11/72, Papers, LC. "The universe is a difference": JC to WM, 9/6/72, Recipient. a run of angry poems: Bain, 108. **His final lecture**/ "this is a haunted place": Ciardi's final lecture was tape-recorded by John Stone. All quotes from this and the next two paragraphs are from the Stone tape. **On their way**/ "how very upset John was": Wilbur, int. "To his great credit": "Memorial to John Ciardi," 32.

TWELVE
"I've gone hermit,"
1972 to 1979

"I seem to be becoming unemployed faster than any man in town." (pages 377–83)

When Ciardi got/ was being offered: SK to JC, 9/8/72, Papers, LC. "The bribes": AF III. **The appointment caused**/ Jonnel, living with a friend: Information for this paragraph is from JC to his sister Ella, 9/11/72, Recipient's family. **When it was**/ "a very pleasant schedule": This and the following quotations in this paragraph are from Cifelli, int. **And it truly**/ sit on the porch and talk: Information for this paragraph is from Kirkpatrick, int. **The Dante course**/ Tuesday and Thursday mornings/being worked "much harder": 2/16/74, Recipient. "much less pleasant": 3/9/74, Recipient. "spell-binding" performance/ Marilyn Moriarty: Letter to me from MM, 5/31/89. Remaining quotations in this paragraph are from this letter. **Perhaps as early**/ Hanson, with departmental support: The story of JC at UF is from interviews with Harold Hanson, Smith Kirkpatrick, Ward Hellstrom, Harry Crews, John Frederick Nims, and Raymond Beirne. ten thousand dollars per year: Figure is from Kirkpatrick, confirmed by Hanson. dinner party: Kirkpatrick, int. **But new English**/ "I wasn't terribly interested": Hellstrom, int. "no goddamn vice president": Kirkpatrick, int. "sad mis-

take, a severe loss": Hanson, int. **Of course, in/** "For the first time":
Recipient. **The first of/** "multiple-personality disorder": "Casualties of
'82: Five Magazine Post Mortems." *Adweek* (March 1983): 74–76. **The end
for/** "it's a lousy length": Letter to Harriet [?] at *SR,* 10/18/73, File Copy.
"I seem to be becoming": Stone, "John Ciardi: His Wit and Witness," 143.
if he would or would not be staying: 3/12/77, Recipient. Three of four
such columns: Information taken from a notebook draft of a letter to
Norman Cousins, ca. August-September 1977, Papers, LC. "aimed at
broadening": 12/2/77, Papers, LC. **Sometime in 1985/** "a rich semi-
literate young man": ABB, PS. "Does pissing into the ocean": Clemente, 9.

Key West
(pages 383–93)

While the University/ competitor of Bread Loaf:
Kirkpatrick, int. was immediately disappointed: Alfreda Irwin, Chautauqua staff member, int. "I've begun to jot": *Letters* 7/20/73. **Public lectures were/** "Good circulation": 6/5/73, Recipient. "I have been
wasting": 12/22/73, Recipient. "shifted to gin rummy": no date, but late
June 1974, Recipient. **After a year/** Benn was "troublesome": Tape-
recorded lecture at the Poetry Forum, 2/5/75. **To encourage Benn/**
"principal creditor": This and longer quote are from JC to Irv Klompus,
no date but late June 1974, Recipient. "bulldoze machine": JC to Irv
Klompus, 6/10/75, Recipient. **Ciardi fell into/** "psychic abyss": JC to
Miller Williams, 6/30/75, Recipient. "torpor": JC to Miller Williams, ca.
8/1/75, Recipient. "Distinguished Professor": RC to JC, 4/19/75, Papers,
LC. "Eminent Scholar": RC to JC, 8/4/75, Papers, LC. "a quite elegant
chalet": ca. 8/1/75, Recipient. **Of course, he/** "delightfully surprised":
Jane T. Fritz to the Harry Walker Agency (Ciardi's lecture agent most of
the time), 2/12/76, copy forwarded to Ciardi, Papers, LC. "I feel it only
fair": JC to Adolph Caso, 2/19/76, File Copy. **Two weeks later/** a tiny
notice: *Star-Ledger,* 3/11/76. "our young poets": *Letters* 4/1/77. **A different
opportunity/** "a good quantity"/"made and unmade poets": Cargas,
18–20. **But though Ciardi/** "I grub away.": 9/26/76, Recipient.
Perhaps Ciardi meant/ had he not been interested: Judith. "unbearably
hot"/"unbelievably expensive": postcard to Gil Gallagher, 7/22?/76,
Papers, LC. fire onboard the *QEII:* The story of the fire follows JC's
account to Miller Williams, "August ? 1976." Judith took the phone call: JC
to Stanley Burnshaw, 7/25/77, File Copy. **Given the fact/** "full choppers"/"mouthful of hardware": JC to Dan Jaffe, no date, but early 1977,

Recipient. "tiny shack": JC to Irv Klompus, early January 1976, Recipient. "long distance" repairs: JC to John Stone, ca. June 1976. "I spend part"/"I don't really need": JC to Stan Epstein, 3/25/79, Recipient. **Ciardi had been**/ "The clock is ticking": *Letters* 12/13/78. "at an over-run"/"It adjoins the lot": JC to Miller Williams, 3/30/79, Recipient. **But if Ciardi**/ "There [is] a wall": AF VII. Ciardi enjoyed the company: John and Nancy Williams recalled these as the friends and neighbors who were Ciardi regulars between 1979 and 1983.

"formally dazzling"
(pages 393–409)

The Little That/ "I haven't had a book"/"quick-frozen fuck": "August ? 1976." **In another poem**/ "look at something as ordinary": Krickle, 145. "hard-won wisdom": Harmon. "voice of wisdom": Haynes. "difficult wisdom": Krickle, 144. "formally dazzling": Wilbur, 62. **Buried in almost**/ one of Ciardi's favorite/"an allegory": Taped lecture at Bellarmine College (Ky.), 10/22/84. **By early May**/ "presented": Joyce Copland of Houghton Mifflin to JC, 5/7/75, Papers, LC. "worth your attention": Nancy Willard, 5/4/75. "makes delightful reading": Elizabeth Coolidge, 5/22/75. "lively, lilting": Charlotte Jackson, 5/4/75. "predictability of the rhyme patterns": May 1975. "the collection as a whole": Melanie Kroupa, editor of children's books, Houghton Mifflin, 8/2/77, Papers, LC. **By March 1975**/ "damn fine": 3/7/75, Recipient. "Project. Would you have": *Letters.* **On 26 November**/ "I am surprised myself": Recipient. "concerning the minorities question": DH to JC, 11/30/73, Papers, LC. **Ciardi's own art**/ November 1973 article: Edward M. Cifelli, "The Size of John Ciardi's Song," *CEA Critic,* 36 (Nov. 1973): 21–27. "I am quite set up": *Letters* 12/14/73. $5000/$3000: JC to Miller Williams, no date, but 1978, Recipient. **Ciardi had had**/ (for $2,210): JC to Frances Lindley, Harper & Row, 4/8/76, File Copy. the answer was yes/"We are rather proud": ES to JC, 1/5/77, Recipient. This and all further editorial comment is used by permission of W. W. Norton & Co. **The limerick book**/ twenty-five-hundred-dollar advance/"an IRSectomy": *Letters* 3/20/78. "Among this world's jokes": *Letters.* "I loved that last royalty": 11/17/79, Recipient. **Ciardi did indeed**/ "wholly unadmiring": Copy of reader's report supplied by Eric Swenson and quoted by permission. **There was some**/ "My ghost trod": *Letters* 11/1/79. **Reviewers like Dana**/ he traded in his Lincoln: JC to Miller Williams, 4/24/78, Recipient. "'a cultural headwaiter'": *Letters* 7/1/78. **Sherry A. H.**/ "people who ought to know": Sherry A. H., reader's report, see above. "crammed full of suburban wisdom": undated photocopy mailed to JC on 9/13/79, Papers, LC. "fashionable to consider": (May): 112–13. "Ciardi's reputation": 12/16/79. **Despite the dismissive/** "All this has been a sadness": *Letters* 11/18/77. "shut out of an important house": *Letters* 2/9(?)/77. **Most touching of/** "boldly sad piece": Wilbur, *Proceedings*, 63. **But more and/** "I've gone hermit": 2/10/77, Recipient. "Have been hacking away": Recipient. "I become an increasingly private person": to Stanley Epstein, *Letters* 5/14/79. "an obsessive wordnapper": to John Frederick Nims, *Letters* 6/24/79. "I have become some sort": to Miller Williams, *Letters* 10/?/79. **What worried Ciardi/** "I smoke too much": *Letters*. "I begin to feel a danger": 12/26/78, Recipient. "My one sadness": 2/28/79, Recipient. **Then on 12/** more "reference minded": JC to Eric Swenson, 6/21/78, File Copy. "a pick-up and lay-down book": JC to Eric Swenson, 12/29/77, Recipient. **The dictionary, however/** Ken Myers of NPR: KM to JC, 10/14/76, Papers, LC. "I have begun a radio series": 12/29/77, Recipient.

THIRTEEN
"A man learns how to die."
1980 to 1986

Stroke
(pages 411–33)

But when January/ "My God": Kennedy, int. "while inefficient idiots": JC to Lew Turco, no date, but early February 1980, Recipient. "a nice idea"/"Thank God"/"curmudgeon emeritus": Huisking, 16. **It was true/** "when [his] health began": Judith. "on both ends": John and Nancy Williams, int. "too Italian": Brinnin, int. **Brinnin's stereotyping may/** "cocked to take heads off": *Letters* 1/15/79. **Through the first/** "I have about given up": *Letters*. "grossly obese": *Letters* April 17/18 1979. "After [much] back sliding": 4/18/79, Recipient. "Shit on virtue": JC to MW, ca. April/May 1979, Recipient. **Then, too, no/** "The day I was delayed": *Letters* 2/27/79. "At 63 my physical": *Letters* 12/24/79. **Complicating his psychological/** "family upheavals": *Letters* 7/25/77. **Arriving in Florida/** "heavy and tired": Charles Benbow, 1/10/80, in the *St. Pete Times*, Clipping, No title. "I love our new house": 1/?/80, Recipient. "Today, despite what": 3/5/80, Recipient. "In a burst": 3/2/80, Recipient. "I sit in my newly": *Letters* 2/13/80. "I haven't had my two annual": 3/2/80.

Recipient. **Possibly surpassing the/** Three or four late afternoons: Wilbur, int. According to Brinnin: int. "contentious": Hersey, int. "John had no gift": Brinnin, int. **As far as/** "It's *you* I love": Nancy Williams, int. "True," he would say: Wilson, 118. "any given poet": partly quoted in Wilson, 117. "John Ciardi long has": Gorner, 1. **By the mid-1970s/** "endlessly": Myra, int. "an awful lot": Judith. "I have never turned on": no date, Papers, LC. the compound cats sleeping: Judith. **On about 25/** "It feels great": Lilly Library, Indiana University "more poets than anyone can believe": JC to George Garrett, 4/16/80, Recipient. **By about Ciardi's/** People's Poet: JC to John Stone, *Letters* 7/14/80. *A Browser's Dictionary/* "but *read* through it": JB to Frances Lindley at Harper & Row, 5/1/80, copy in Papers, LC. "It got a non-fiction": 8/18/80, Recipient. "seems to be doing well": 9/16/80, Papers, LC. "Michener wouldn't be dazzled": 4/1/81, Recipient. **In September 1980/** At fifteen thousand dollars: Salary given in a letter to George Garrett, *Letters* 8/14/80. "The master poet runs": Gorner, 1. **From Chicago, Ciardi/** "Lord," he wrote: Recipient. "It was a joy": 3/8/81, Recipient. Ciardi offered: JC to John Frederick Nims, 11/14/80. Lilly Library, Indiana University **Tucked away as/** "Do you know of a good": *Letters* 10/13/80. "bled me dry": 11/4/80, Recipient. "My younger son": 2/6/81, Recipient. "Benn had a flare up": Recipient. **On the drive/** "it hung on for 10 days": *Letters* 12/13/80. "Whether this siege": *Letters* 12/30/80. **In March, with/** "at least what comes easy": 3/13/81, File Copy. **The University of/** "the main thing about the prize": Arthur Miller, "The American Writer: The American Theatre," *Michigan Quarterly Review*, 21 (winter 1982): 8–9. **X. J. Kennedy/** "as if to prove": This and remaining quotations in this paragraph are from Kennedy, int. **There wasn't anything/** "simplistic soulfulness": Ciardi's speech was published as "On the Importance of Unimportant Poems" in the *Michigan Quarterly Review*, 21 (winter 1982): 34–42. "mild protests"/"disgruntlements": Kennedy, int. **Later in April/** "simply wrote well": JFN to JC, 5/29/81, Papers, LC. "It is generous of you": Lilly Library, Indiana University. **The day after/** "to create a clearer": As announced in legal papers mailed to JC announcing the merger, Papers, LC. "never liked the method": *Letters* 9/29/84. **Ciardi had a/** "long happy summer"/"ten days of bad golf": JC to Vince Clemente, *Letters* 9/2/81. "sacred iliac"/"never was in the first place": JC to GG, 7/18/81, Recipient. **That fall Ciardi/** "shaggy, steel-gray hair": This and remaining quotations in this paragraph are from Green, B1 and B6. **Determined to get/** "financial straits"/similar request to Norton: To Frances Lindley of Harper & Row, 2/8/82, and Eric Swenson of Norton, 12/21/81. File Copies. "commanded north": Recipient. **As his June/** "I hack away": Recipient. "My days are": *Letters* 2/8/82. **But there**

were/ the NCTE Award: Letter from Glenna Sloane for NCTE, 3/3/82, Papers, LC. **But despite the/** "about 1,600 dreary miles"/"to see what is wrong": Recipient. See also JC to John F. Nims, *Letters* 5/27/82. **First, however, was/** hospitalization/complete picture: Information for this paragraph is from interviews with Dr. John Stone plus JC's copies of test results and a copy of the report mailed to his local physician in Metuchen. **When he got/** "I *like* the stuff": *Letters* 6/4/82. "a-typical toper": 11/2/78, Recipient. **Of course, Ciardi/** "He had earned": Manuscript essay on Fletcher Pratt, no date, Papers, LC. "damned doctor": AF XXXIV. **By early June/** "the girl got cold feet"/"generational thing": JC to Mac Cordray, 6/10/82, Recipient. **Sometime during the/** "neuralgic nuisance"/"It used to come": *Letters.* "My nightly head-splitter": *Letters.* "listless and blah": Recipient. "[The headaches] passed in an hour": One sheet of paper by JC on pain, no date, Papers, LC. **Ciardi saw the/** At about 10:00 A.M.: The story of Peter's concern and the trip to the hospital is from Elly Welt, int. "determined to keep up": Recipient.

The Joy Conference
(pages 433–70)

Ciardi did, indeed/ "Judith will join me": 10/16/82, Papers, LC. "nothing to fool around with": 12/13/82, Papers, LC. "a scandalously expensive": JC to Stuart Wright, Recipient. **Compared to the/** "beautiful days"/"I apologize": *Letters* 5/20/83. "beginning to behave": Recipient. "spryer": *Letters* 6/20/83. "nary a drink": 5/25/83, Recipient. **Ciardi's first mention/** sometime "soon": Recipient. "to concentrate on a rigidly culled": 10/15/79, Recipient. "I have had too many chances": 4/16/80, Recipient. That summer/fifteen months later: 8/11/80 and 11/13/81, File Copies. "wary as hell": Recipient. **But from February/** "seriously to work": *Letters* 5/3/83. "I find I hate": 6/19/83, Recipient. "Beethoven festered": *Letters* 6/23/83. "if I gave off"/"I could not have imagined": 6/30/83. Lilly Library, Indiana University. **Ciardi's depression was/** birthday dinner: 6/28/83, Recipient. "I have, alas": *Letters* 6/27/83. "Never will I have taken": 7/?/83, Recipient. **On about 19/** "with nothing to which"; *Letters* ca. 7/19/83. "Have also finished": *Letters* 7/22/83. "43 Blathering Years": 8/22/83, Recipient. "I think of [religion]": *Letters* 8/27/83. **On 9 September/** "I'm a bit surprised": Recipient. "how Italian"/"Lowell missed it once": Recipient. JC apparently got the poem or magazine wrong here, for "SPQR, A Letter from Rome" was published in *Poetry* (Feb. 1958). He may have had another poem in mind that had appeared in *Atlantic,* which published twelve Ciardi poems beginning in February 1942. One possible "tribal" poem that Lowell could have praised was "A Visit to Aunt Francesca" (Sept. 1947). The best study of JC's literary connections to Italy is Fedora Giordano, "An Archetypal World: Images of Italy in the Poetry of John Ciardi," *Rivista di Studi Anglo-Americani,* 3 (1984–85): 305–13. **Clemente had, in/** "I like the sense": *Letters* 11/10/78. "I don't know of anyone": *Letters* 11/15/78. "short of cash": Recipient. **He couldn't shake/** "I really don't know": *Letters.* "Increasingly, I have": 3/13/79, Recipient. **The entire question/** "jingoistic": Cornella, 5. **A key to/** "slangy yet learned": Krickel, 45. **Almost lost in/** "unhappy": 8/25/83, Recipient. "dragging—largely for": Papers, LC. "has met with a stunning silence": Recipient. **The sales record/** "an astonishingly good time"/"a needed lucrative month": 9/27/83, Recipient. "a major force": From the official UM-KC citation, dated 5/10/83. "literary whiz": Lawrence DeVine, "Linguist Derives Pleasure from Delving into Derivations," *Detroit Free Press,* 31 (Oct. 1983): 3E. **Partly because the/** "I wish we": *Letters* 11/1/83. "Judith won't be held": *Letters* 1/1/84. "We finally solved": Recipient. **Making the late/** "a sort of festive month": Recipient. "I couldn't have been treated": Recipient. **From Kansas City/** "enchanting": Teresa McUsic, "Ciardi: He Loves Kids and Especially Words," *Eastern Oklahoma Catholic* (27 May 1984): 20. "Don't worry": 3/6/84, Recipient. "Hallmark was fun": 7/23/84, Recipient. **During what time/** "I have been agonizing": 6/24/84, Recipient. "If I can find": 4/14/84, Recipient. **Measures were on/** "a marvelous nature poet": *Letters.* **For nearly a year/** "I wrote to break off": Recipient. "If I were huffy": File Copy. **The somewhere else/** "Time matters to me.": File Copy. "At the rate": File Copy. **The urgency had/** "I feel more than": *Letters.* "To bury a father": *Letters.* "I watched my mother": Recipient. **Ciardi was also/** "sub-human state": Papers, LC. "dragging all the way": Recipient. "persistent cold"/"damp dishrag": Papers, LC. **On 7 May/** check for $17,500: Figures for this paragraph are from JC's file copy of a letter to attorney Warren Wilentz, 3/28/86. The page is titled "Investment in Tops Carpet City." "Please look around": Recipient. **Optimism ran high/** "spectacular blast-off": Recipient. "furiously in the carpet business": Recipient. "I have already messed up": *Letters.* **While all the/** "It wasn't, to be sure": *Letters* 10/29/84. "I'll hope the administration": 10/30/84, File Copy. **By the beginning/** "I look forward": Recipient. "Bad problems with Benn": Recipient. **December was a/** difficult month of mourning: Information for this paragraph is from Gil Gallagher and Elly Welt interviews. **Then on Christmas/** "one of the greatest things": Benn, int. "Benn is out of rehab": no date, but early February 1985, Recipient. **But Ciardi, whose/** "social problem": Brinnin, int. "attention span"/"bluntly inattentive": This and remaining quotations in this paragraph are from Wilbur, int. **However, David Jackson/** "an egomaniac": Jackson, int. "fur to fly": Brinnin, int. no such conspiracy: Wilbur, int., 9/15/95. **This incident aside/** "an impressive fine gent": Recipient. "Don't be sad": Recipient. "Your father would have": *Letters*. "believe it or not": *Letters* 2/27/85. **Meanwhile, Benn was/** "I know on medical evidence": Recipient. "My joy is": Recipient. "I am ready to believe": Recipient. "It's a new kid ": Recipient. **While Ciardi attended/** had to fire Sandy Martin: Pack, int. "Pack asked me": *Letters*. **But having been/** unspoken hopes: Welt, int. "already too obsolete": *Letters*. **On 29 May/** "a young man . . . on the make": Papers, LC. "I have stopped": Lilly Library, Indiana University. **But quips aside/** "finding a style"/"finding a voice": Wojahn, 169. All quotations in this and the next paragraph are from Wojahn, 169–70. riled Ciardi supporters: Cf. X. J. Kennedy in "John Ciardi's Early Lives": "In a recent issue of *Poetry* appeared a wide-of-the-mark attack on Ciardi's *Selected Poems*, charging that Ciardi in his poems never developed any distinctive voice. If a critic wanted to go for Ciardi with a vengeance, I suppose he could find some ways to do it, but I can't imagine any wilder, less effective way than that. If any poet of our time has firmed himself a voice, it is John Ciardi. The voice is so distinctive that it is like the 'sound of sense' Frost cultivated, whose tone could be understood through a closed door. It is a vigorous, gutsy, no-nonsense voice of authority: a voice of passion unfeigned and absolutely devoid of sentiment" (p. 30). **On 24 February/** "major American poets": "Small Presses Come to Rescue of Two Elder Statesmen," 40. "The fact is": Papers, LC. **Ciardi's best public/** "one of the best-known": "Ciardi's Art," 16. Quotations from the Jerome essay are scattered through this and the next paragraph. **As usual, however/** "I'd love to see": Papers, LC. "extended autobiography": *Letters* 6/12/85. **Ciardi had not/** "I am touched by": 7/16/85, Recipient. "I'm pressing ahead": Papers, LC. **Clemente worked tirelessly/** "astonished": JC to VC, *Letters* 9/24/85. **With respect to/** "collapsing on wet-noodle stems": Recipient. "I am in that season": *Letters* 8/19/85. **But there was/** "I confess to having felt": *Letters*. JC "confessed" to needing a wheel-chair at airports at least twice on different occasions to different correspondents. Cf. JC to Walter Newman, *Letters* 12/1/84: "In the Denver airport in October I finally gave up and got a skycap to wheelchair me 42 miles to my connecting gate. Time does not march on: it totters off." **Poetry was humbling/** "metrically limber": "Memorial to John Ciardi," 33. **After *The Birds*/** "If my son": File Copy. **A year earlier/** "If I were a rich man": Quoted from an unidentified news clipping, no date, but probably 10/20/85, "A Poet's Toast Spawned Northern's Writing Conference." **Ciardi seemed to/** "needlessly brutal": This and quotations in the next paragraph are from Shapiro, int. **Margery Rouse recalled/** had intended to sit: Rouse, int. "reliving something":

Welt, int. **Ciardi himself, however/** "I'm back to running": Lilly Library, Indiana University. "It bodes well for continuance": Recipient. **When the Joy/** "a collection of good-natured poems": 1/5/86. "Does this make sense": 11/19/85, Recipient. **Ciardi kept busy/** "I hate hitting": 1/24/86, Recipient. "unforeseen difficulties": Recipient. book of limericks: The book of limericks referred to here is *Phonethics*.

"Jeff, where is death's sting." (pages 471–77)

And he needed/ "a gift of the uninhabitable North": Recipient. "It is not easy to know": *MM*, 91. "immensely grateful": *Letters* 3/13/86. "I'm packing the car": Recipient. **First, however, the/** the university had been waiting and planning: Information on JC's trip comes from my visit to the university, from his expense book, records from the PCA, and from interviews with most of the people named in the next seven paragraphs. **In a letter/** "What good is it": *Letters.* "become human again": *Letters* 3/28/86. **On Easter Sunday/** "I thought, well": Judith. **In an undated/** "I have heard too many": 4 ms. pages, no date.

Books by John Ciardi

Homeward to America. New York: Henry Holt and Company, 1940. Poems.

New Poets. Anthology edited by Tom Boggs. Prairie City, Ill.: The Press of James A. Decker, 1941. Includes 13 Ciardi poems.

Other Skies. Boston: Little, Brown and Company, 1947. (An Atlantic Monthly Press book.) Poems.

Live Another Day. New York: Twayne Publishers, 1949. Poems.

Mid-Century American Poets. Anthology edited by JC. New York: Twayne Publishers, 1950. Includes 11 Ciardi poems.

From Time to Time. New York: Twayne Publishers, 1951. Poems.

The Inferno. Translation of Dante. New Brunswick, N.J.: Rutgers University Press, 1954. Hardcover edition.

The Inferno. Translation of Dante. New York: A Mentor Book from New American Library, 1954. Paperback edition.

As If: Poems New and Selected. New Brunswick, N.J.: Rutgers University Press, 1955.

I Marry You: A Sheaf of Love Poems. New Brunswick, N.J.: Rutgers University Press, 1958.

39 Poems. New Brunswick, N.J.: Rutgers University Press, 1959.

The Reason for the Pelican. Philadelphia: J. B. Lippincott, 1959. Illustrated by Madeleine Gekiere. Reprint, Wordsong, 1994, with new illustrations by Dominic Catalano. Children's poems.

How Does a Poem Mean? Boston: Houghton Mifflin, 1959. Revised edition with Miller Williams as coauthor, 1975. Textbook.

Scrappy the Pup. Philadelphia: J. B. Lippincott, 1960. Illustrated by Jane Miller. Children's verse.

Treat It Gentle: An Autobiography [of jazz musician Sidney Bechet] New York: Hill & Wang (by agreement with Twayne Publishers), 1960.

Reprint, Da Capo, 1978. JC was largely responsible for the writing and revising and shaping of Bechet's taped words into book form.

In the Stoneworks. New Brunswick, N.J.: Rutgers University Press, 1961. Poems.

The Purgatorio. Translation of Dante. New York: A Mentor Book from New American Library, 1961. Paperback edition.

I Met a Man. Boston: Houghton Mifflin, 1961. Illustrated by Robert Osborn. Children's verse.

The Man Who Sang the Sillies. Philadelphia: J. B. Lippincott, 1961. Illustrated by Edward Gorey. Children's poems.

In Fact. New Brunswick, N.J.: Rutgers University Press, 1962. Poems.

The Wish-Tree. New York: The Crowell-Collier Press, 1962. Illustrated by Louis S. Glanzman. Children's story.

You Read to Me, I'll Read to You. Philadelphia: J. B. Lippincott, 1962. Illustrated by Edward Gorey. Children's poems.

Dialogue with an Audience. Philadelphia: J.B. Lippincott, 1963. *SR* controversies reprinted, plus selected essays.

John J. Plenty and Fiddler Dan: A New Fable of the Grasshopper and the Ant. Philadelphia: J. B. Lippincott, 1963. Illustrated by Madeleine Gekiere. Children's poems.

Poetry: A Closer Look. With James M. Reid and Laurence Perrine. New York: Harcourt, Brace & World, 1963. Textbook.

Person to Person. New Brunswick, N.J.: Rutgers University Press, 1964. Poems.

You Know Who. Philadelphia: J. B. Lippincott, 1964. Illustrated by Edward Gorey. Reprint, Wordsong, 1991. Children's poems.

The King Who Saved Himself from Being Saved. Philadelphia: J. B. Lippincott, 1966. Illustrated by Edward Gorey. Children's story in verse.

This Strangest Everything. New Brunswick, N.J.: Rutgers University Press, 1966. Poems.

The Monster Den or Look What Happened at My House—and To It. Philadelphia: J. B. Lippincott, 1966. Illustrated by Edward Gorey. Reprint, Wordsong, 1991. Children's poems.

An Alphabestiary. Philadelphia: J. B. Lippincott, 1967. Poems. Illustrated by Milton Hebald. Also issued as a portfolio book. New York: Touchstone Publishers, 1967. Limited Edition.

A Genesis. A portfolio book of 15 poems by JC and 15 original etchings by
   Gabor Peterdi. New York: Touchstone Publishers, 1967. Limited
   Edition.

The Achievement of John Ciardi. A collection of 56 Ciardi poems, plus a
   critical introduction by Miller Williams. Glenview, Ill.: Scott,
   Foresman and Co., 1969.

The Paradiso. Translation of Dante. New York: A Mentor Book from New
   American Library, 1970. Paperback edition.

Someone Could Win a Polar Bear. Philadelphia: J. B. Lippincott, 1970.
   Illustrated by Edward Gorey. Reprint, Wordsong, 1993. Children's
   poems.

Lives of X. New Brunswick, N.J.: Rutgers University Press, 1971. Verse
   autobiography.

Manner of Speaking. New Brunswick, N.J.: Rutgers University Press, 1972.
   A collection of 104 columns.

The Little That Is All. New Brunswick, N.J.: Rutgers University Press,
   1974. Poems.

Fast & Slow: Poems for Advanced Children and Beginning Parents. Boston:
   Houghton Mifflin, 1975. Illustrated by Becky Gaver. Children's
   poems.

The Divine Comedy. Complete translation. New York: W. W. Norton, 1977.
   Hardcover edition.

Limericks: Too Gross. With Isaac Asimov. New York: W. W. Norton 1978.

For Instance. New York: W. W. Norton, 1979. Poems.

A Browser's Dictionary and Native's Guide to the Unknown American Language.
   New York: Harper & Row, 1980. Etymology.

A Grossery of Limericks. With Isaac Asimov. New York: W. W. Norton, 1981.

*A Second Browser's Dictionary and Native's Guide to the Unknown American
   Language*. New York: Harper & Row, 1983. Etymology.

Selected Poems. Fayetteville: University of Arkansas Press, 1984.

The Birds of Pompeii. Fayetteville: University of Arkansas Press, 1985.
   Poems.

Phonethics: Twenty-two Limericks for the Telephone. North Carolina: Palaemon
   Press, 1985. Limited Christmas edition.

Doodle Soup. Boston: Houghton Mifflin, 1985. Illustrated by Merle Nacht.
   Children's poems.

Good Words to You: An All-New Dictionary and Native's Guide to the Unknown American Language. New York: Harper & Row, 1987. Etymology. (Posthumously published.)

Poems of Love and Marriage. Fayetteville: University of Arkansas Press, 1988. (Posthumously published.)

Saipan: The War Diary of John Ciardi. Fayetteville: University of Arkansas Press, 1988. (Posthumously published.)

Blabberhead, Bobble-Bud & Spade: Selected Poems of John Ciardi. Edited by Anna M. Aschkenes. North Brunswick, N.J.: Middlesex County Cultural and Heritage Commission, 1988. Illustrated by Robert J. Byrd, Edward S. Gazsi, Lonni Sue Johnson, and Charles Waterhouse. Children's poems. (Posthumously published.)

Ciardi Himself: Fifteen Essays in the Reading, Writing, and Teaching of Poetry. Fayetteville: University of Arkansas Press, 1989. (Posthumously published.)

Echoes: Poems Left Behind. Fayetteville: University of Arkansas Press, 1989. (Posthumously published.)

The Hopeful Trout and Other Limericks. Boston: Houghton Mifflin, 1989. Illustrated by Susan Meddaugh. Children's limericks. (Posthumously published.)

Mummy Took Lessons and Other Poems. Boston: Houghton Mifflin, 1990. Illustrated by Merle Nacht. Children's poems. (Posthumously published.)

Stations of the Air. Kansas City: BkMk Press of the University of Missouri-Kansas City, 1993. Poems. (Posthumously published.)

The Collected Poems of John Ciardi. Compiled and edited by Edward M. Cifelli. Fayetteville: University of Arkansas Press, 1997.

Selected Bibliography

Interviews

I conducted some 150 interviews in the preparation of this book. Following is a partial list with dates: James Armstrong 7/12/88; Isaac Asimov 2/3/88; David Bain 7/7/88 (plus follow-up conversations and letters); John Bauer 12/21/93; Richard Beal 1/14/88; Raymond Beirne 4/6/91; James Blevins 10/6/89; John Malcolm Brinnin 1/22/89 (plus follow-up letters); Nicholas Brown 3/26/91 (plus follow-up letters); Alexander Cappon 6/19/89; Irma Cavat (formerly Kachadoorian) and daughter Nika 4/26/89; Alan Cheuse 12/15/93; Alfonso Ciardi 2/3/89; Benn Ciardi 8/19/87 (plus regular conversations thereafter); Ella Ciardi 1/13/88 (plus several follow-up conversations); John Lyle and Valerie Ciardi 1/11/88 (plus regular conversations thereafter); Judith Ciardi 8/25/87 (plus ongoing conversations thereafter); Myra Ciardi 8/20/87 (plus regular conversations thereafter); Phil Cioffari 6/12/90; Robert Cordray 10/3/87; Norman Cousins 4/19/88; Harry Crews 7/6/95; Paul Cubeta 7/6/88; Richard Eberhart 2/14/88; Seymour Epstein 9/6/89; Stanley Epstein (interview and taped recollections) 7/15/89; Constance Erskine 8/9/89; Doris (Holmes) Eyges 5/7/89 (plus several follow-up conversations and letters); Cora (Ciardi) Fennessey 1/12/88 (plus several follow-up conversations); John Freccero 2/27/92; Stephen Freeman 12/28/88; Gil Gallagher ca. 3/20/89 (plus follow-up conversations and letters); George Garrett 2/22/91; Andrew Glaze 4/1/92; Matthew Graham and Katie Waters 10/8/89; Donald Hall 6/15/88; Harold Hanson 3/15/91; Richard Harteis (for William Meredith) 9/6/89; Harrison and Josephine

Hayford 10/21/90 (plus several follow-up conversations and letters); Ward Hellstrom 2/27/91; John Hersey 1/23/89; David Jackson 1/23/89; Dion Johnson 8/28/89, 8/17/92, and 8/10/93; Zubel Kachadoorian (taped comments) 4/21/89; Gertrude Kasle 7/21/89 and 3/2/96; X. J. Kennedy 1/12/88 (plus several follow-up conversations); Edward Kessler 12/21/93; Galway Kinnell 7/21/89; Smith Kirkpatrick 2/14/88 and 2/23/96; Irv and Ruth Klompus 1/12/91 (plus follow-up conversations); Maxine Kumin 10/3/90; David Levin 5/27/89; Richard Ludwig 4/23/92; Fred Main 12/21/93; Joseph Maiolo 8/9/89; Edward Martin 7/8/88; James Merrill 1/17/89; Theodore Morrison 6/16/89; Mark Musa 2/3/92; John Frederick Nims 2/13/88 (plus several follow-up conversations); Gloria Oden 1/6/89; Robert Pack 8/26/88; Remigio Pane 2/28/92 and 3/11/92; Laurence Perrine 2/27/94; George Rinehart 3/29/89; Edith (Ciardi) Rosi 1/13/88; Norman Rosten 2/13/91; Margery Rouse 1/22/92; May Sarton 3/25/91; Donald Sears 3/23/88; Michael Shapiro 3/16/91; Jack Steinberg 9/20/89; Richard Stephenson 10/3/90; John Stone 4/30/88 (plus many follow-up conversations); John Tagliabue 1/27/91; Lewis Turco 6/16/88 (plus several follow-up conversations and letters); Dan Wakefield 10/7/92; Theodore Weiss 1/24/92; Elinore Welt 7/29/89 (plus several follow-up conversations); James Whitehead 3/14/88; Richard and Charlee Wilbur 6/13/88 and 1/18/89 (plus several follow-up conversations and letters); Thomas Wilhelmus, 10/6/89; John and Nancy Williams 11/16/88; and Miller Williams 1986–1996 (ongoing conversations).

Primary Sources

In addition to books by John Ciardi (above), one should consult White, Krickel, and *MM* to form a fairly complete bibliographical record of JC's work. White is very dependable, though not absolutely complete, up to 1959. One can also piece together part of Ciardi's verse publication record in the 1970s and 1980s by consulting *The Index of American Periodical Verse* compiled by Sander Zulauf and others. There is a big gap in the record for the years 1960 to 1970, however, because Ciardi kept no records at all of his magazine publications. As for anthology inclusions, the eighth edition of *Granger's Index to Poetry* (1986) identifies 103 Ciardi poems appearing in forty-one books. JC's essays are virtually impossible to tally up: M/S ran from 4/15/61 to 5/6/72, 305 columns in all, but Ciardi's *World* column ("As I Was Saying") and his resumed M/S column in *SR/World* and *SR* have not been collected. In addition, JC wrote many features for *SR* as poetry editor, mostly before 1961, and he published articles in a wide variety of professional and popular magazines all through his life. Most of this material is irretrievable, except as there are fragmentary hints as to its whereabouts.

Secondary Sources

The following is a partial list and does not include the hundreds upon hundreds of book reviews written on JC's books, although many of them are quoted in the text and identified in the notes.

Anderton, David A. *B-29 Superfortress at War.* New York: Charles Scribner's Sons, 1978.

Arrigon, Terri. "Ciardi's Dialogue with Children." In *MM:* 157–61.

Bain, David Haward. *Whose Woods These Are: A History of the Bread Loaf Writers' Conference 1926–1992.* Hopewell, N.J.: Ecco Press, 1993.

Bergin, Thomas G. "Dante Translations." *The Yale Review* 60 (1971): 614–17.

Bezanson, Walter E. "John Ciardi." Program note for Rutgers Award to JC "for a distinguished contribution to literature for children and young people." 16 November 1966. [Copy in Papers LC.]

Birdsall, Steve. *Saga of the Superfortress.* Garden City, N.Y.: Doubleday, 1980.

Bogan, Louise. "Verse: Ciardi's *Homeward to America.*" *New Yorker* 15 (27 January 1940): 52–54.

Boorstin, Robert O. "John Ciardi, Poet, Essayist and Translator, 69." *New York Times* 2 April 1986: B6. [Obituary]

Booth, Philip. "The *Mid-Century* Fifteen, a Memoir." In *MM*, 68–70.

Brodsky, Bernard. "Definition of a Wit." *Chicago Review* 10 (autumn-winter 1956): 87–90.

Burnshaw, Stanley. *Robert Frost Himself.* New York: George Braziller, 1986.

———. "Seeing Ciardi Plain." In *MM,* 119–22.

Cargas, Harry J. "Poetry and the Poet: An Interview with John Ciardi." *America* 13 (13 January 1973): 18–20.

Caruba, Alan. "Bread Loaf 1970: Boot Camp for Writers." *Publisher's Weekly.* 21 September 1970.

"Ciardi, John (Anthony)." *Current Biography* 28 (October 1967): 9–12.

"Ciardi on Tape." *The Tuftonian* 17 no. 2 (February 1961): 16–27. [Interview]

Cifelli, Edward M. "The Size of John Ciardi's Song." *CEA Critic* 36 (November 1973): 21–23, 26–27.

———. "Ciardi on Frost: An Interview." In *Frost: Centennial Essays,* edited by Jac L. Tharpe. Vol. 1. 471–95. Jackson: University Press of Mississippi, 1974.

Clemente, Vince. "Remembering John Ciardi." *VIA* 5 no. 2 (1994): 15–24.

———. "Writing *Treat It Gentle.*" In *MM,* 82–83.

Cornella, Alex. "In Search of the Golden Contract: An Interview with John Ciardi." *Vector Magazine* 1 no. 1 (September 1978): 4–8.

Cousins, Norman. *Present Tense: An American Editor's Odyssey.* New York: McGraw Hill, 1967.

———. "Ciardi at *The Saturday Review.*" In *MM,* 114–16.

Cowden, Roy W. "A Note on John Ciardi at Michigan." *The Tuftonian* 4 (1944): 118–19. Reprint, *MM,* 49–51.

"Critic Under Fire." *Time* 69 (18 February 1957): 44–46.

Di Piero, W. S. "Ciardi's Dante." In *MM,* 71–73.

Elman, Richard. "John Ciardi and *Treat It Gentle.*" In *MM,* 79–81.

Fitts, Dudley. "Translated into American." *New York Times Book Review* (4 July 1954): 4.

Freccero, John. "Introduction" to JC's translation of *The Paradiso.* New York: New American Library, 1970.

Fuller, Edmund. "A Modern Bard Views Himself." Review of *Lives of X. Wall Street Journal* (June 1971).

Gallagher, Edward J. "Tenzone." *Explicator* 27 (December 1968): item 28.

Garrett, George. "Small Presses Come to Rescue of Two Elder States-men of Poetry." *Chicago Tribune* 24 February 1985: section 14: 40.

———. "The Good Influence of John Ciardi." In *MM,* 199–210.

Giordano, Fedora. "An Archetypal World: Images of Italy in the Poetry of John Ciardi." *Rivista de Studi Anglo-Americani* 3 (1984–85): 305–13.

Gorner, Peter. "Historian of Words, Poet Ciardi Nurtures the Seeds of Language." Review of *A Browser's Dictionary*. *Chicago Tribune* 8 September 1980: section 2: 1+.

Green William. "John Ciardi Is Still Ticking As the Words Keep Clicking." *Arkansas Gazette* 20 October 1981: B1+.

Groff, Patrick J. "The Transformation of a Poet: John Ciardi." *Horn Book* 40 (April 1964): 153–58.

Guenther, Charles. "Form and Style in Ciardi's Dante." In *MM*, 74–78.

Hall, Donald. "English C, 1947." In *MM*, 52–54.

Harmon, Maryhelen C. "John Ciardi." *In Critical Survey of Poetry*, edited by Frank N. Magill. Vol. 2. Englewood Cliffs, N.J.: Salem Press, 1982.

Haynes, Alice Smith. "John Ciardi." *Dictionary of Literary Biography*, edited by Donald J. Greiner. vol. 5 part 1. Detroit: Gale Research, 1980.

Hills, Rust. "'We Believe in the Maestro System': The Bread Loaf Process." *Audience* 2 (May-June 1972): 90–108.

Holmes, John. "John Ciardi: Tufts Poet." *The Tuftonian* 12 no. 1 (fall 1955): 21–24. Reprint, *MM*, 42–48.

———. "A Note on John Ciardi at Tufts." *The Tuftonian* 4 (1944): 122.

Hughes, John W. "Humanism and the Orphic Voice." *Saturday Review* 54 (22 May 1971): 31–33.

Huisking, Charlie. "Poet John Ciardi Just an Ode-Fashioned Fella." *Florida West* section in *Sarasota Herald-Tribune* 20 January 1980: 16.

Humphries, Rolfe. "Verse Chronicle." *Nation* 171 (12 August 1950): 152–53.

Jaffe, Dan. "Ciardi Imprint." *UMKC Magazine* 14 no. 2 (1984): 11–12.

———. "Tribute to John Ciardi." *New Letters* 52 (winter-spring 1986): 40–42.

Jerome, Judson. "Among the Nightingales." *Antioch Review* 16 (spring 1956): 115–25.

———. "Ciardi's Art." *Writer's Digest* (October 1985): 16–18, 20.

———. "The Major Leagues." *Writer's Digest* (November 1985): 14–17.

———. "Ciardi Remembered." In *MM*, 135–40.

Kahle, Roger. "John Ciardi, Dante's Twentieth-Century Voice." *This Day* (February 1969): 16–19, 39, 48.

Kennedy, X. J. "John Ciardi's Early Lives." In *MM*, 24–31.

———. Afterword: "John Ciardi's 'Big Rain That Rattles and Roars.'" Written for a new edition of Ciardi's *The Reason for the Pelican*, 61–64 (Honesdale, Pa.: Wordsong, 1994).

Kenner, Hugh. "Problems in Faithfulness and Fashions." *Poetry* 85 (January 1955): 225–31.

Krickel, Edward. "Ciardi's Winter Words: Some Oblique Notes on a Southern Education." In *MM*, 192–98.

Krieg, Joann P. "Light Years Near: Ciardi's Poems for Children." In *MM*, 150–52.

Kumin, Maxine. "John Ciardi and the 'Witch of Fungi.'" In *MM*, 131–32.

Lattimore, Richmond. "The *Inferno* as an English Poem." *Nation* 179 (28 August 1954): 175.

Lloyd, Alwyn T. *B-29 Superfortress* Part I. Blue Ridge Summit, Pa.: Tab Books, Inc., 1983.

Lovill, Jeffry. "The Poetry of John Ciardi: How Does It Mean?" Ph.D. diss., Arizona State University, 1985. [Includes a 52-page interview. A portion of the interview was published as "At Home with Words," *New Letters* (fall 1987): 47–63.]

MacAllister, Archibald T. Introduction to JC's translation of *The Inferno*. New Brunswick, N.J.: Rutgers University Press, 1954. Also appeared in the NAL paperback edition.

———. Introduction to JC's translation of *The Purgatorio*. New York: New American Library, 1961.

———. "The Literature of Italy." *The Yale Review* n.s., 44 (September 1954): 155–59.

MacBride, Doris. "John Ciardi: Poet, Literary Critic, Oral Interpreter. His Literary Concepts and Their Significance for the Field of Oral Interpretation." Ph.D. diss., UCLA, 1970.

Martin, Edward. "Frost Heaves and Other Signs and Images of the Bread Loaf Writers' Conference." *Middlebury News Letter* (spring 1969): 6–13.

"Memorial to John Ciardi." *Key West (Fla.) Solares Hill* 14.5 May 1986: 30–34; 36; 39–40. [Newspaper record of the memorial service at the Monroe County Library held shortly after Ciardi's death. Participants: David Jackson, Elly Welt, Richard Wilbur, Philip Burton, John Hersey, Arnold Sundgaard, and Tom Sanchez.]

Meredith, William. "The Problem of the Second Volume." Review of *Other Skies. Poetry* (May 1948): 99–102.

Mickelberry, William. "An Interview with John Ciardi." *Florida Quarterly* 5 (1973): 69–84.

Morrison, Theodore. *The Bread Loaf Writers' Conference: The First Thirty Years (1926–1955)*. Middlebury, Vt.: Middlebury College Press, 1976.

Nemerov, Howard. "A Few Bricks from Babel." *Sewanee Review* 62 (October 1954): 655–63.

Newquist, Roy, "John Ciardi: An Interview." In *Counter Point*. New York: Rand McNally, 1964: 113–26.

Nims, John Frederick. "John Ciardi: The Many Lives of Poetry." *Poetry* 148 (August 1986): 283–99. Originally presented as the Cockefair Chair Lecture at the University of Missouri-Kansas City, 19 March 1986. Reprinted in *MM*, 91–113.

Notini, Sylvia. "John Ciardi's Translation of *The Divine Comedy*." *Rivista di Studi Anglo-Americani* 3 (1984–85): 329–41.

"On Writers and Writing." *Ball State Teachers College Forum* 3 (spring 1962): 3–12. [Interview]

Owen, Guy. "Ciardi on Campus." *Trace* 38 (July-August 1960): 21–26. [Interview]

Parisi, Joseph. "Personae, Personalities, Ciardi's *The Little That Is All*." *Poetry* 126 (July 1975): 220–22.

Pease, Theresa. "John Ciardi: The Poet at 70." *Tufts Criterion* 19 no. 2 (1986): 12–13.

Peragallo, Olga. *Italian-American Authors and Their Contribution to American Literature*. New York: S. F. Vanni, 1949.

Perrine, Laurence. "Ciardi's 'Tenzone.'" *Explicator* 28 (May 1970): item 82.

"Poets, Society, and Religion." *The Lutheran Witness* (November 1968): 20–22. [Interview]

Ponsot, Marie. "Poems for Children." *Poetry* 101 (December 1962): 208–09.

Rabe, David. "Strenuous Test for Writers." *New Haven Register* (5 October 1969): 18–21.

Rexroth, Kenneth. *American Poets in the Twentieth Century.* New York, 1971.

———. "Animals, Stars, and People." *New York Times Book Review* 63 (3 August 1958): 6.

Rosenbaum, David E. "Congressman Lists 65 'Radicals' Despite Injunction." *New York Times* 15 October 1970: 24.

Rosenthal, M. L. "An Unfair Question." Review of *In the Stoneworks. The Reporter* (15 February 1962): 48–51.

Roth, Philip. "Mrs. Lindbergh, Mr. Ciardi, and the Teeth and Claws of the Civilized World." *Chicago Review* 11 (summer 1957): 72–76.

Salomon. I. L. "Revelation in Rhyme." *Saturday Review* 38 (28 January 1956): 24.

Saul, George Brandon. "From Aridity to Affirmation." *Western Review* 15 (autumn 1950): 68–73.

Scott, Winfield Townley. "Three Books by John Ciardi." [The University of Kansas City] *Review* 16 (winter 1949): 119–25.

Smith, William Jay. "Energy and Gusto: A Note on John Ciardi." In *MM,* 153–54.

Southwork, James G. "The Poetry of John Ciardi." *English Journal* 50 (December 1961): 583–89.

Spender, Stephen. "Poetry vs. Language Engineering." *New Republic* 143 (15 August 1960): 17–18.

Stanislaw, Rebecca Wetzel. "The Poetic Voice of John Ciardi." Ph.D. diss., Ball State University, 1992.

Steinberg, Gail. "An Interview with John Ciardi." *Writing!* (September 1985): 12–14.

Stone, John. "John Ciardi: His Wit and Witness." In *MM,* 141–47.

Strauss, William and Neil Howe. *Generations.* New York: William Morrow and Company, 1991.

Stryk, Lucien. "John Ciardi: National Treasure." In *MM,* 117–18.

Thompson, John. "Just a Bit of This and That." *Hudson Review* 11 (1958): 445–46.

Tumo, Mirko. "Ciardi's a Target of the Right and Left." *Woodbridge (N.J.) News Tribune* (27 October 1970): 5.

Turco, Lewis. "Ciardi the Taler." In *MM,* 34–39.

Untermeyer, Louis. "Look Homeward America." Review of *Homeward to America. Yale Review* (spring 1940): 599–603.

Volkan, Vamik D. *Linking Objects and Linking Phenomena: A Study of the Forms, Symptoms, Metapsychology, and Therapy of Complicated Mourning.* New York: International Universities Press, 1981.

Wakoski, Diane. "Stalking the Barbaric Yawp." Review of five books, including JC's *Echoes. The Georgia Review* 43 (winter 1989): 804–15.

———. "Dionysian Memories." In *MM*, 133–34.

Walsh, Jeffrey. *American War Literature: 1914 to Vietnam.* New York: St. Martin's Press, 1982.

Welt, Elly. "John Ciardi, Science Fiction Writer." In *MM*, 180–84.

White, Gertrude M. "Six Poems by John Ciardi." *Odyssey: A Journal of the Humanities* 4 (1979): 12–19.

White, Lawrence Grant. "Dante for Americans." *Saturday Review* 37 (18 September 1954), 13, 27.

Whittemore, Reed. "Cynical Prayer, Astonishing Power." Review of *For Instance. Chicago Tribune* (16 December 1979): section 7:2.

Wilbur, Richard. "John Ciardi 1916–1986." *Proceedings of the American Academy and Institute of Arts and Letters.* 2nd ser., 37. New York: American Academy and Institute of Arts and Letters, 1986: 58–63.

Williams, John. "Looking for John Ciardi at Bread Loaf." In *MM*, 126–30.

Williams, Miller. "John Ciardi—'Nothing Is Really Hard But to Be Real.'" Introduction to *The Achievement of John Ciardi*, 1–19. Glenview, Ill.: Scott, Foresman, 1969: Reprinted in *MM*, 162–77.

———. "John Ciardi." *Dictionary of Literary Biography, Yearbook 1986:* 219–24.

Williams, William Carlos. "Voices in Verse." *New York Times Book Review* (16 April 1950): 6, 28. Review of *Mid-Century American Poets.*

Wilson, Michaela Swart. "Ciardi, John (Anthony)." *Contemporary Authors,* new rev. ser., vol. 5 (also vol. 33). Edited by Ann Evory. Detroit: Gale Research, 1982. Includes an interview conducted by Jean W. Ross on 12 February 1981.

Wojahn, David. Review of *Selected Poems. Poetry* (June 1985): 169–70.

Wright, James. "Four New Volumes." *Poetry* (October 1958): 46–50.

Index

Works:

Harrington, Evans, 324

Hayden, Robert, 369

Hayford, Harrison, 33–40, 43, 47, 48, 125, 222

Haynes, Alice Smith, 195

Hazo, Sam, 471–72

Hebald, Cecille, 281

Hebald, Milton, 222, 233, 236, 281, 283, 308, 309, 342–43, 344, 345; collaborated with JC on *An Alphabestiary*, 309

Heffner, Hubert, 252

Hellstrom, Ward, 380–81

Helmstadter, David, 400–401

Herrmann, Dorothy, 214

Hersey, John, 393, 408, 416

Hills, Rust, 359–61, 364, 365, 371

Hillyer, Robert, 126, 147–48, 203

Hine, Daryl, 406

Hobart, Rev. Alfred W., 277

Holmes, Doris, 273, 515

Holmes, John, 33–36, 40, 41, 42, 43, 44, 45, 48, 52, 53, 55, 56, 57, 61, 63, 72, 88, 101, 104, 125–26, 132, 133, 134, 138–39, 149, 171, 172, 176, 186, 193–94, 197, 204, 231, 235, 241, 249, 252, 273–74, 278, 279, 292, 320, 332–33, 348, 462

Hopwood Award, 44–45, 51–53, 54, 423–24, 466

Horn, Clayton, 230

Hostetter, Lulu, 100–101

Houtrides, Jim, 454

Howard, Richard, 313

Hubbell, Lindley Williams, 113–15

Hughes, Langston, 66, 367, 401

Hughes, Ted, 425

Humphrey, Hubert, 284

Humphries, Rolfe, 171–73

Hutchens, John K., 148

Ichord, Richard H., 327, 329

Irvine, Maurice, 133, 194

Jackson, David, 393, 454

Jacobsen, Josephine, 248–49

Jaffe, Dan, 180–81, 201, 240, 257, 308, 329, 333–34, 447–48, 455

Jaffe, Herb, 447–48

Jarrell, Randall, 41, 139–40, 191, 195, 303

Jerome, Judson, 143, 194, 231, 233, 313, 336–37, 350, 369, 460–61, 462, 463

Johnson, Dion, 51, 72

Johnson, James Weldon, 401

Johnson, Lyndon, 283, 287, 307, 412

Johnson, Ralph, 51, 57, 72, 101

Johnson, Samuel, 407

Johnson, Virginia, 51–52, 54, 57, 60, 62, 68, 71–72, 73, 75, 87, 88, 98, 101, 155, 320, 489–90

Jones, Howard Mumford, 147, 176

Jones, Le Roi (Amiri Baraka), 327

Jones, Lewis Webster, 176, 255

Joy Conference (Ohio Valley Writers' Conference), 451, 455, 457, 463, 466–69

Joyce, Walter, 179